To Andrew Wodzinski

A modest tribute to all
the good work we have
produced in Global Analysis .

RISK MANAGEMENT

MICHEL CROUHY
DAN GALAI
ROBERT MARK

McGraw-Hill
New York   San Francisco   Washington, D.C.   Auckland   Bogotá
Caracas   Lisbon   London   Madrid   Mexico City   Milan
Montreal   New Delhi   San Juan   Singapore
Sydney   Tokyo   Toronto

Library of Congress Cataloging-in-Publication Data

Crouhy, Michel
    Risk management / by Michel Crouhy, Dan Galai, Robert Mark.
      p. cm.
    Includes bibliographical references.
    ISBN 0-07-135731-9.
    1. Risk management. I. Galai, Dan. II. Mark, Robert. III. Title.
HD61.C774 2000
658.15'5—dc21

                                                        99-048928

McGraw-Hill

A Division of The McGraw·Hill Companies

1 2 3 4 5 6 7 8 9 0   DOC/DOC   0 9 8 7 6 5 4 3 2 1 0

ISBN 0-07-135731-9

This book was set in Palatino by ATLIS Graphics.

Printed and bound by R.R. Donnelley & Sons Company.

This publication is designed to provide accurate and authoritative information in regard to the subject matter covered. It is sold with the understanding that the publisher is not engaged in rendering legal, accounting, or other professional service. If legal advice or other expert assistance is required, the services of a competent professional person should be sought.
    —From a declaration of principles jointly adopted by a committee of the American Bar Association and a committee of publishers.

♳ This book is printed on recycled, acid-free paper containing a minimum of 50% recycled de-inked fiber.

McGraw-Hill books are available at special quantity discounts to use as premiums and sales promotions, or for use in corporate training programs. For more information, please write to the Director of Special Sales, Professional Publishing, McGraw-Hill, Two Penn Plaza, New York, NY 10121. Or contact your local bookstore.

This book is dedicated to those in the past who have provided the solid foundation for us to build on

CONTENTS

Chapter 7

Credit Rating Systems   259

Chapter 8

Credit Migration Approach to Measuring Credit Risk   315

Chapter 9

The Contingent Claim Approach to Measuring Credit Risk   357

Chapter 10

Other Approaches: The Actuarial and Reduced-Form Approaches to Measuring Credit Risk   403

Chapter 14

Capital Allocation and Performance Measurement   529

Chapter 15

Model Risk   579

Chapter 16

Risk Management in Nonbank Corporations   615

FOREWORD

Risk is the fundamental element that influences financial behavior. In its absence, the financial system necessary for efficient allocations of resources would be vastly simplified. In that world, only a few institutions and financial instruments would be needed, and the practice of finance would require relatively elementary analytical tools. But, of course, in the real world, risk is ubiquitous. Much of the structure of the financial system we see serves the function of the efficient distribution of risk. Much of the financial decision making by households, business firms, governments, and especially financial institutions is focused on the management of risk. Measuring the influence of risk, and analyzing ways of controlling and allocating it, require a wide range of sophisticated mathematical and computational tools. Indeed, mathematical models of modern finance practice contain some of the most complex applications of probability, optimization, and estimation theories. Those applications challenge the most powerful of computational technologies.

Risk Management provides a comprehensive introduction to the subject. Presented within the framework of a financial institution, it covers the design and operation of a risk-management system, the technical modeling within that system, and the interplay between the internal oversight and the external regulatory components of the system. That its authors, Michel Crouhy, Dan Galai, and Robert Mark, are significant contributors to the science of finance, active practitioners of finance, and experienced teachers of finance is apparent from both its substance and form. The range of topics is broad but evidently carefully chosen for its applicability to practice. The mathematical models and methodology of risk management are presented rigorously, and they are seamlessly integrated with the empirical and clinical evidence on their applications. The book also patiently provides readers without an advanced mathematical background the essential analytical foundations of risk management.

The opening four chapters provide a fine introduction to the function of the risk management system within the institution and on the management of the system itself. Recent regulatory trends are presented to illustrate the expanded role that the internal system plays in informing and meeting the requirements of the external overseers of the institution.

With this as background, the book turns to the core substance of a risk management system with the analysis and modeling of risk measurement and control. Market risk is the first topic explored, including the ubiquitous VaR models and stress testing for identifying and measuring risk exposures to stock market, interest rate, currency, and commodity prices. The analysis shows how to incorporate option, derivative and other "nonlinear" security exposures into those models.

Nearly a third of the book is devoted to the management of credit risk, and for good reason. Banks are in the business of making loans and they also issue guarantees of financial performance for their customers. They enter into bilateral contractual agreements such as swaps, forward contracts, and options on enormous scales that expose them to the risk that their counterparts to those contracts will not fulfill their obligations. Similarly, insurance companies hold corporate bonds that may default and some guarantee the performance of bonds issued by municipal governments. The credit derivatives business is one of the fastest growing areas for financial products. However, credit risk analysis has even greater importance to risk management in its application to the soundness of the institution itself. Indeed, for financial institutions with principal businesses, which involve issuing contingent-payment contracts such as deposits, annuities, and insurance to their customers, creditworthiness is the central financial issue. The mere prospect of a future default by an institution on its customer obligations can effectively destroy those businesses. Unlike investors in an institution, its customers do not want to bear its credit risk, even for a price. The book presents the major competing models for measuring and valuing credit risk and evaluates them, both theoretically and empirically.

In addition to market and credit risk exposures, a comprehensive approach to risk measurement and risk management must also include operational risks, which is the subject of Chapter 13. Furthermore, no risk management system can be effective without well-designed performance measurement and testing. This is needed both to estimate the risk exposures ex ante and to provide an ex post assessment of those estimates relative to predictions, as a feedback on the performance of the system. As laid out in Chapter 14, the system's risk estimates provide the basis for capital attribution among the activities and the accuracy of those estimates determine the amount of equity capital "cushion" needed as a whole.

Mathematical models of valuation and risk assessment are at the core of modern risk management systems. Every major financial institution in the world, including sovereign central banks, depends on these models and none could function without them. Although mainstream and indispensable, these models are by necessity abstractions of the complex real world. Although there is continuing improvement in those models, their accuracy as useful approximations to that world varies significantly across time and situation. Thus, a dimension of risk management that by definition is outside the formal risk management model is *model risk*. Chapter 15 explores that issue. It drives home the point that there is no "safe harbor" in model error, whether complex mathematical models or traditional measures with rules of thumb. For example, in the case of financial institutions, the traditional accounting leverage ratio measured by total assets/equity can be cut in half by using a "borrow-versus-pledge" method to finance security inventory versus using a "repo-reverse repo" method even though the economic risk of the two methods is identical. Furthermore, the institution can use derivative securities to greatly alter its measured leverage ratio without changing its economic risk. The risk-measurement approaches emphasized in the book are ones that give consistent readings among these different institutional ways of taking on the same risk exposure.

The pace of financial innovation has been extraordinary over the past quarter century and there is no sign of abatement in either product and service innovation or changes in the institutional structures of the providers. As discussed in Chapter 16, a major growth area will be in providing integrated risk management to nonfinancial firms. More generally, from individual households to government users, the trend in financial services lies with integrated products that are smarter, more comprehensive, simpler to understand, and more reliable for those users. The future of risk management, as articulated in Chapter 17, rests in helping the pro-

ducer handle the greater complexity of creating and maintaining those products. The prescriptions contained herein will age well.
    To the reader: Learn and enjoy.

Robert C. Merton

Harvard Business School

INTRODUCTION

The traditional role of the risk manager as corporate steward is evolving as organizations face an increasingly complex and uncertain future. The mandate to clearly identify, measure, manage, and control risk has been expanded and integrated into best practice management of a bank. Today's risk manager is a key member of the senior executive team who helps define business opportunities from a risk-return perspective, presents unique ways of looking at them, has direct input into the configuration of products and services, and ensures the transparency of all the risks. Innovation necessitates new yardsticks for measuring and monitoring the resulting activities. The savvy corporate leader uses risk management as both a sword and a shield.

At the end of the last millennium, financial institutions and investors experienced increased volatility in the major financial and commodity markets, with many financial crises. At the start of the new millennium, we are in the midst of a technological revolution resulting in changes in the operation of markets, increased access to information, changes in the types of services available to investors, as well as major changes in the production and distribution of financial services.

If there is concern about an institution's ability to manage risk, then its share price will be penalized. Risk is a cost of doing business for a financial institution and consequently best practice risk management is a benefit to our shareholders. To manage the risks facing an institution we must have a clearly defined set of risk policies and the ability to measure risk. But what do we measure? And how do we measure such risks? We must also have a best practice infrastructure. The starting point is that we need a framework.

This book provides such a framework. The content of the book is consistent with our own risk management strategy and experience. Our risk management strategy is designed to ensure that our senior management operates together in partnership to control risk while ensuring the independence of the risk management function. Improvements in analytic models and systems technology have greatly facilitated our ability to measure and manage risk. However, the new millennium brings new challenges. There are risks that we can identify and measure and there is the uncertainty of the unknown. The challenge facing risk managers is to minimize the consequences of the unknown. This book should help all risk and business managers address the issues arising from risk and uncertainty.

John Hunkin
Chairman & Chief Executive Officer
Canadian Imperial Bank of Commerce

Risk Management introduces, illustrates, and analyzes the many aspects of modern risk management in both financial institutions and nonbank corporations. It consolidates the entire field of risk management from policies to methodologies as well as data and technological infrastructure. It also covers investment, hedging, and management strategies.

The shift to flexible exchange rates in the late 1960s has led to more volatility in exchange rates. As volatility increased, financial markets began to offer a new breed of securities, that is, derivatives such as futures and options, to allow institutions to hedge their exposures to currency fluctuations. The increase in inflation in the early 1970s and the advent of floating exchange rates soon began to generate interest rate instability. Again, the market responded by offering new derivative products to hedge and manage these new risks. Banks found themselves increasingly engaged in risk intermediation and less in traditional maturity intermediation. Banks also started to innovate and offer new customized derivative instruments, known as over-the-counter (OTC) products, that both compete with and complement traded derivatives.

In 1988 the Bank for International Settlements (BIS) set the capital adequacy requirements for banking worldwide to account for credit risk. This was the first international effort to deal with the growing exposure of financial institutions to risk and volatilities, and especially to risk of off-balance sheet claims such as derivative instruments. The 1988 BIS Accord was followed by the 1998 BIS Accord, accounting for market risks in the trading book, as well as by many documents of the BIS discussing the many facets of risk management. The SEC implemented its risk exposure disclosure requirements in 1998 for all exchange traded companies in the United States.

Risk management is not an American phenomenon. Today it covers all continents and all countries. What we observe today is a convergence of regulation and disclosure requirements across the globe. More than in any other field, the tools and reporting requirements of risk management are universal.

This book is based on our academic as well as practical work in the field of risk management. We try to cover both institutional aspects and organizational issues, while not forgetting that risk management is based on statistical and financial models.

The book is a comprehensive treatment of all aspects of risk management. It starts by discussing the new regulatory framework that is shaping best practice risk management in the banking industry worldwide. The risk management techniques that have been developed by and for banks are now migrating to the corporate sector. There is mounting pressure from regulators, such as the SEC in the United States, financial analysts, and investors for more and better disclosures of financial risks and the techniques and instruments being adopted to control these risks.

The book provides a consistent and comprehensive coverage of all aspects of risk management—organizational structure, methodologies, policies, and infrastructure—for both financial and nonfinancial institutions. It offers an up-to-date exposition of risk measurement techniques for market, credit risk, and operational risk. The risk measurement techniques discussed in the book are based on the latest research. They are presented, however, with considerations based on practical experience with the daily application of these new risk measurement tools. The book also elaborates on the issues that the next generation of risk measurement models will have to address, such as the full integration in a consistent multiperiod framework of liquidity, market, and credit risk; the measurement of risk for illiquid positions, as for example the merchant banking book; the risk assessment over a long-term horizon of structural positions, such as the "gap" of the corporate treasury in a financial institution; and stress testing to assess risk in periods of financial crises.

The book relies heavily on the experience of the authors in developing the risk management function in a bank from the ground up. It goes beyond the technical aspects of risk measurement. It proposes an integrated framework for managing risks and an organizational structure that has proven successful in practice.

We have incorporated the latest evolution of the regulatory framework and the current BIS proposal to reform the capital

Accord. The book offers a unique presentation of the latest credit risk management techniques. It provides clear guidance to implement a risk management group in a financial institution. It also discusses how to adapt to a nonfinancial corporation the risk management techniques that have been originally developed and implemented in banks. The book provides one-stop shopping for knowledge in risk management ranging from current regulatory issues, data, technological infrastructure, hedging techniques, and organizational structure.

STRUCTURE OF THE BOOK

The book is arranged according to the major subjects of modern risk management. Chapter 1 discusses the need for risk management systems. Chapter 2 presents the new regulatory framework that is shaping modern risk management in financial institutions and nonbank corporations. Chapter 3 provides an integrated framework for best-practice risk management. We explain how financial institutions should establish appropriate firm-wide policies, methodologies, and infrastructure in order to measure, price, and control risks in a comprehensive manner. Chapter 4 reviews the new BIS capital requirements for market risks and compares the "standardized approach" and the "internal models approach" that banks can use to report regulatory capital.

The topic of Chapters 5 and 6 is market risk measurement. We present the standard value-at-risk (VaR) approach. We also discuss some extensions of the VaR method: "incremental-VaR" and "delta-VaR" to isolate the component risks that contribute most to the total risk, "dynamic-VaR" to assess market and liquidity risks over a long time horizon, say a quarter, and "E-VaR," the expected loss in the tail, as an alternative risk measure to VaR. We also look at stress testing and scenario analysis to analyze extreme events that lie outside normal market conditions assumed by the standard VaR model. Finally, we discuss measurement errors and backtesting issues.

Chapters 7 to 12 cover credit risk. These six chapters constitute a unique and comprehensive coverage of topical credit risk-related issues: credit risk rating, credit risk measurement with a detailed presentation of the four industry-sponsored approaches (credit migration, contingent claim, actuarial, and reduced form approaches), and credit mitigation techniques. Credit risk is currently the major risk to which banks are exposed, and yet techniques to model and mitigate credit risk are still in their infancy. Regulators with the new BIS Capital Adequacy Framework currently under discussion are setting new standards that will give a definitive competitive advantage to the banks that can achieve sophistication in credit risk assessment and credit risk management.

Chapter 13 proposes a framework for operational risk control. We describe four key steps in implementing bank operational risk, and highlight some means of risk reduction. Finally, we look at how a bank can extract value from enhanced operational risk management by improving its capital attribution methodologies.

Chapter 14 is devoted to capital allocation and performance measurement. This chapter presents the Risk Adjusted Return on Capital (RAROC) analysis to measure performance and allocate economic capital. It provides managers with the information they need to make the trade-off between risk and reward more efficient.

Chapter 15 elaborates on "model risk," that is, the special risk that arises when an institution uses mathematical models to value and hedge securities. We discuss some classic examples of what can go wrong when trading strategies are built on theoretical valuation models.

Chapter 16 is on risk management for nonfinancial corporations. In this chapter we discuss in detail the pros and cons of modern risk management techniques as applied to nonbank corporations. The relevant question is not whether corporations should engage in risk management but, rather, how they can manage risk in a rational way. We also discuss some new accounting standards that have been introduced to deal with the derivative and hedging activities of corporations.

Chapter 17 presents our views on risk management in the future. In this chapter we look at how risk management will be induced—and facilitated—by advances in technology, the introduction of more sophisticated regulatory measures, rapidly accelerating market forces, and an increasingly complex legal environment.

ACKNOWLEDGMENTS

Our appreciation goes to many friends and colleagues at CIBC, the Hebrew University, and other institutions for their generous help. Particular thanks go to the members of the Senior Executive Team (SET) at CIBC, whose insights toward building best practice as well as practical risk management tools have been invaluable. Parts of the book were presented in conferences, seminars, regulatory bodies, and internal CIBC round tables around the world and we have greatly benefited from the comments of numerous participants. Most of all our appreciation goes to our extended families.

We would like to extend our debt of gratitude to our outstanding editor Robert Jameson for the many valuable suggestions that substantially shaped the book, and to Catherine Schwent, acquisitions editor at McGraw-Hill, for her devotion and patience. Our special thanks go to all those that provided administrative and typing assistance. They have done a wonderful job considering the tough clients they had to serve. Parts of the book appeared previously in the working paper series of the Global Analytics group at CIBC and in a variety of journals, books, and specialized risk publications over the past many years.

Michel Crouhy

Dan Galai

Robert Mark

CHAPTER 1

The Need for Risk Management Systems

1. INTRODUCTION

The international banking system has experienced many significant structural changes over the last 25 years. Major banks have merged,[1] many institutions have become global,[2] and banks seem increasingly likely to pursue mergers and other alliances with insurance companies.[3] Although institutions have grown in size, competition has substantially increased. This is because, over the same period, regulators have relaxed their rules and have allowed banks to offer new products and to enter new markets and new business activities.

The Financial Services Act of 1999 will lead to further far-reaching changes in the U.S. financial system. It will repeal key provisions of the Glass–Steagall Act, passed during the Great Depression, which prohibits commercial banks from underwriting insurance and most kinds of securities. Most significantly, brokerage firms, banks, and insurers will be able to merge with each other; this sort of alliance was prohibited by the Bank Holdings Act of 1956. The proposed reform is intended to allow bank holding companies to expand their range of financial services and to take advantage of new financial technologies such as web-based e-commerce.

The new legislation will also put brokerage firms and insurers on a par with banks by allowing them to enter into the full range of financial activities and compete globally.

The expansion of the activities of bank holding companies will incur new market, credit and operational risks. The consolidations will also precipitate a thorough revision of capital adequacy requirements, which are currently tailored to the needs of traditional bank holding companies.

This trend toward consolidation complements longer-term changes in industry structure. Over the past 20 years, many corporations have found it less costly to raise money from the public (by issuing bonds) than to borrow directly from banks. Banks have found themselves competing more and more fiercely, reducing their profit margins, and lending in larger sizes, longer maturities, and to customers of lower credit quality.

Customers, on their part, are demanding more sophisticated and complicated ways to finance their activities, to hedge their financial risks, and to invest their liquid assets. In some cases, they are simply looking for ways to reduce their risk exposure. In other instances, they are willing to assume additional risk, if they are properly compensated for it, in order to enhance the yield of their portfolio.

Banks are, therefore, increasingly engaged in what might be called "risk shifting" activities. These activities demand better and better expertise and know-how in controlling and pricing the risks that banks manage in the market.

As the banking industry has evolved, the managerial emphasis has shifted away from considerations of profit and maturity intermediation (usually measured in terms of the spread between the interest paid on loans and the cost of funding) toward risk intermediation. Risk intermediation implies a consideration of both the profits and the risks associated with banking activities. It is no longer sufficient to charge a high interest rate on a loan; the relevant question is whether the interest charged compensates the bank appropriately for the risk that it has assumed.

The change in emphasis from simplistic "profit-oriented" management to risk/return management can also be seen in non-bank corporations. Many major corporations are now engaged in active risk management. Of course, "risk" was always a major consideration in deciding whether to take advantage of investment opportunities. However, rejecting projects because they seem to be risky can lead companies to reject investment opportunities that in fact offer an excellent return. The real problem is how to *quantify* risk and thus *price* it appropriately.

In the banking industry, the classic risk is credit risk. Through history, banks have sought to manage this risk as a key part of their business. However, it was not until 1988 that a formalized universal approach to credit risk in banks was first set out. Based on the 1988 Bank for International Settlements (BIS) Accord (Chapter 2), banks were required by their regulators to set aside a flat fixed percentage of their risk-weighted assets (e.g., 8 percent for corporate loans, 4 percent for uninsured residential mortgages) as regulatory capital against default. Since 1998, banks have also been required to hold additional regulatory capital against market risk in their trading books.[4]

At some point in the future, banks may incur regulatory capital charges for funding liquidity risk, regulatory risk, human factor risk, legal risk, and many other sources of risk.[5] These diverse risks, often grouped together under the term "operational risk," are monitored increasingly closely by banks. They were the cause of various well-publicized financial disasters during the 1990s, such as the collapse of Barings Bank in 1995 (the bank lacked adequate operational controls). They have also provoked many expensive court cases, such as the dispute in 1994 between investment bank Bankers Trust and corporate giant Procter & Gamble—a case that came to typify the risk that derivatives contracts might not be legally enforceable or might lead to reputational damage.[6]

Many risks arise from the fact that today's banks are engaged in a range of activities. They trade all types of cash instruments, as well as derivatives such as swaps, forward contracts, and options—either for their own account or to facilitate customer transactions. The Federal Reserve Bank estimates that in 1996, U.S. banks possessed over $37 trillion of off-balance-sheet assets and liabilities, compared to approximately $1 trillion dollars only 10 years earlier. The multitude and magnitude of the instruments, and their complexities, make it essential to measure, manage, and control the risk of banks.

In this chapter, the process leading to the introduction of risk management systems is described. A major impetus behind the implementation of risk management systems has been the Basle Committee on Banking Supervision,[7] which is an international extension of the regulatory bodies of the major developed countries.

Banks are also beginning to realize that sophisticated risk control tools make for sounder economic management. This chapter therefore also explores the trend to make risk management an integral part of the management and control process of financial institutions, rather than simply a tool to satisfy regulators. We conclude with a discussion of the recent adoption of formal risk management systems by nonfinancial corporations.

2. HISTORICAL EVOLUTION

Regulation strongly affects the attitude of financial institutions to risk taking, and often dictates how they accommodate risk. Around the world, the banking industry is regulated in a variety of ways, and through a multitude of governing bodies, laws, and bylaws. Two related observations can be made: nowadays there is a worldwide recognition of the need to measure and control risks in global and local banking activities, and regulation is converging and becoming more consistent across countries. But before we look at how this is happening, we need to understand some of the historical foundations of the banking industry.

The crash of 1929 and the economic crisis that followed led to major changes in bank regulation in the United States. The regulators focused on what is termed today "systemic risk," i.e., the risk of a collapse of the banking industry at a regional, national, or international level. In particular, regulators were concerned to prevent the "domino effect": the chance that a failure by one bank might lead to failure in another, and then another. In a series of acts and laws, the government tried to increase the stability of the banking system in order to avoid this and other types of economic crisis. At the same time, the safety of bank deposits was enhanced by the establishment in 1933 of the Federal Deposit Insurance Corporation (FDIC). A third set of legislation defined the playing field for commercial banks: crucially, they were barred from dealing in equity and from underwriting securities. The famous Glass–Steagall Act of 1933 effectively separated commercial banking and investment banking activities.

The regulation of the banking industry in the United States in the early 1930s reduced the risk in banking operations but also acted to reduce competition. For example, in 1933 Regulation Q put a ceiling on the interest rate that could be paid on savings accounts. Reserve requirements encouraged banks to offer current (checking) accounts that did not pay interest.

Furthermore, a combination of the McFadden Act (1927), which prohibited banks from establishing branches in multiple states ("interstate branching"), and state regulations led to the establishment of many small banks that specialized in a particular local market. In effect, the regulations helped to support "natural" regional monopolies in the supply of banking services.[8]

The 1956 Bank Holding Company Act, and the amendments to this act from 1970, limited the nonbanking activities of commercial banks. Again, the motivation was to reduce the risks to which banks might be exposed. It was felt that if banks expanded their activities into new and risky areas, they might introduce idiosyncratic risk, or specific risk, that would affect the soundness of the whole banking system.

Meanwhile, the environment in which banks operated had begun to change. During the period from World War II to 1951, interest rates had been pegged and were not used as a tool in the monetary policy of the Federal Reserve. As a result, bank interest rates were stable over an extended period of time, with only small changes occurring from time to time. From 1951, however, interest rates became more volatile. The volatility intensified in the 1970s and 1980s as shown in Figure 1.1.

In effect, the governments of developed economies had begun their slow but consistent withdrawal from their role as insurers, or managers, of certain risks. The prime example of this change is the foreign currency market. From 1944, with the signing of the Bretton Woods Agreement, international foreign exchange rates were artificially fixed. Central banks intervened in their foreign currency markets whenever necessary to maintain stability. Exchange rates were changed only infrequently, with the permission of the World Bank and the International Monetary Fund (IMF). These bodies usually required a country that devalued its currency to adopt tough economic measures in order to ensure the stability of the currency in the future.

The regime of fixed exchange rates broke down from the late 1960s due to global economic forces. These included a vast expansion of international trading and inflationary pressure in the

FIGURE 1.1

Short-Term Interest Rates, Business Borrowing Prime Rate (Effective Date of Change), Commercial Paper (Quarterly Averages)

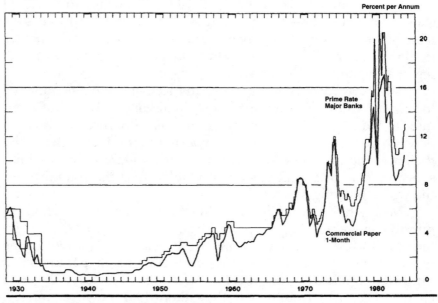

Source: Board of Governors of the Federal Reserve System

major economies. The shift to flexible foreign exchange rates introduced daily (and intraday) volatility to exchange rates. As the hitherto obscured volatility surfaced in traded foreign currencies, the financial market began to offer currency traders special tools for insuring against these "new" risks.

Figure 1.2 depicts the percentage change in the value of the German deutsche mark with regard to the U.S. dollar. The shift in the levels of volatility is very noticeable in the early 1970s, as the currency market moved to floating exchange rates. As indicated in the figure, the shift precipitated a string of novel financial contracts based on the exchange rates of leading currencies.

The first contracts tended to be various kinds of futures and forwards, though these were soon followed by foreign currency options. In 1972 the Mercantile Exchange in Chicago (CME) created the International Monetary Market (IMM), which specialized in

FIGURE 1.2

Month-End German Deutsche Mark/U.S. Dollar Exchange Rates

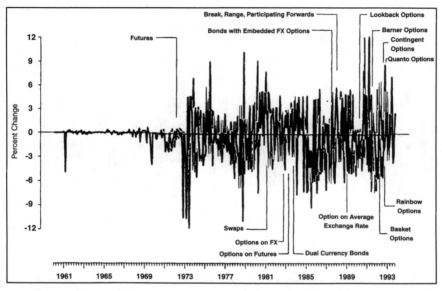

Source: Smithson et al. (1995)

foreign currency futures and options on futures on the major currencies. In 1982 the Chicago Board Options Exchange (CBOE) and the Philadelphia Stock Exchange introduced options on spot exchange rates. Banks joined the trend by offering over-the-counter (OTC) forward contracts and options on exchange rates to their customers.

The increase in inflation and the advent of floating exchange rates soon began to affect interest rates. From the early 1970s, interest rates and bond prices became increasingly volatile. This volatility grew substantially from the early 1980s onwards, after the Federal Reserve Bank under chairman Paul Volcker decided to use money supply (rather than interest rates) as a major policy tool. From that point on, interest rates were able to react to changes in the money supply without prompting interference from the Federal Reserve.

Figure 1.3 charts the volatility of interest rates as measured by percentage changes in the yield of U.S. Treasury bonds with five

FIGURE   1.3

Percentage Change in Yields on Five-Year U.S. Treasury
Bonds

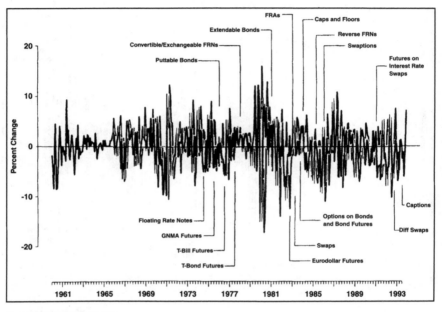

Source: Smithson et al. (1995)

years to maturity. The figure notes the various financial contracts
on interest rates or bond prices that have been introduced since
1975.

As the figure suggests, the market response to the increased
interest rate volatility was to create a wide range of new instruments to trade these risks. New options on Treasury bills, Treasury
notes, and long-term government bonds, as well as futures on synthetic government bonds, were offered by the exchanges; a multitude of over-the-counter (OTC) interest-sensitive instruments were
marketed by banks and other financial intermediaries.

Futures were the first type of instrument to be introduced. The
first traded futures on the long-term bonds issued by the U.S.
Government National Mortgage Association (GNMA)—the bonds
are backed by mortgage portfolios—appeared in October 1975 on
the Chicago Board of Trade (CBOT). The CME added futures on
Treasury bills in early 1976, and on Eurodollars in 1981. The CBOT

introduced futures on Treasury bonds in August 1977, and on Treasury notes in May 1982.

In the second wave of instruments, options on fixed-income securities were introduced. In October 1982, the CBOT started trading options on Treasury bond futures. The Chicago Board Options Exchange (CBOE) introduced options on Treasury bonds in the same month. The CME introduced options on Eurodollar futures in March 1985, and on Treasury bill futures in April 1986.

Banks came up with their own form of OTC interest rate derivative—the interest rate swap—in 1982. In early 1983 they added to their arsenal forward rate agreements (FRAs). Since then commercial banks and investment banks have introduced a huge number of different types of derivative; the OTC instruments both compete with exchange-traded derivatives and, in a sense, complement them.

Figure 1.4 depicts the evolution of risk management instruments over a period of 20 years, starting in 1972. Some of the products are exchange-traded, but most are OTC or interbank products.

The huge expansion in derivative product trading around the world spurred the creation of new specialized exchanges in many countries. In turn, the existence of publicly traded and liquid derivative contracts helped banks to promote new, more complex, OTC products—and encouraged additional financial institutions to participate in the new markets.

In April 1995 the Bank for International Settlements, based in Basle, Switzerland, coordinated the first major survey of derivative markets among 26 central banks of the most developed countries. The survey, which came to be repeated every quarter, gathered data on the notional amounts of derivative contracts that were outstanding in each of the participating countries, turnover data, and market values. Table 1.1 shows the notional amounts and market values of outstanding OTC derivative contracts, globally and for the United States, at the end of December 1998, compared to the values at the end of March 1995.

The global market for OTC derivatives amounted in 1995 to over $47 trillion, of which $12 trillion was booked in the United States.[9] The global market had increased by almost 80 percent and had reached over $80 trillion by the end of 1998. Interest rate derivatives reached $26 trillion in March 1995, and almost 70 percent

FIGURE 1.4

The Evolution of Risk Management Products

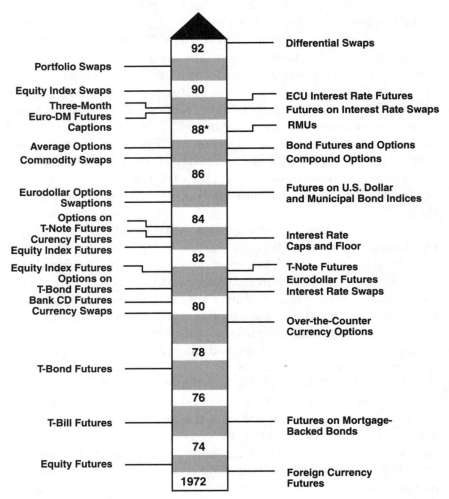

Source: *The Economist*, April 10, 1993

of this sum took the form of swaps. Volumes almost doubled to $50 trillion by the end of 1998. Foreign exchange derivatives reached over $13 trillion in 1995, and $18 trillion in 1998, mainly in forward contracts. (Note that the OTC market for equity derivatives remained relatively small, especially in the United States.)

TABLE 1.1

The Global Over-the-Counter (OTC) Derivative Markets[1]
Positions at End-December 1998 in Billions of U.S. Dollars

	End-December 1998		Memorandum Items: Positions at End-March 1995[2]	
	Notional Amounts	Gross Market Values	Notional Amounts[3]	Gross Market Values[3]
A. Foreign exchange contracts	18,011	786	13,095	1,048
Outright forwards and forex swaps	12,063	491	8,699	622
Currency swaps	2,253	200	1,957	346
Options	3,695	96	2,379	71
B. Interest rate contracts[4]	50,015	1,675	26,645	647
FRAs	5,756	15	4,597	18
Swaps	36,262	1,509	18,283	562
Options	7,997	152	3,548	60
C. Equity-linked contracts	1,488	236	579	50
Forwards and swaps	146	44	52	7
Options	1,342	192	527	43
D. Commodity contracts[5]	415	43	318	28
Gold	182	13	147	10
Other	233	30	171	18
Forwards and swaps	137	—	120	13
Options	97	—	51	5
E. Estimated gaps in reporting	10,371	490	6,893	432
Grand total	80,300	3,230	47,530	2,205
Gross credit exposure[6]		1,329		
Memorandum items:				
Exchange-traded contracts[7]	13,549		10,310	

[1]All figures are adjusted for double-counting. Notional amounts outstanding have been adjusted by halving positions vis-à-vis other reporting dealers. Gross market values have been calculated as the sum of the total gross positive market value of contracts and the absolute value of the gross negative market value of contracts with nonreporting counterparties.

[2]In addition to changes in reporting months, differences in the reporting basis (locational reporting in 1995; worldwide consolidated reporting in 1998) and in the number of participating countries (26 in 1995; Group of Ten countries in 1998) mean that the two surveys are not really comparable.

[3]Data for outright forwards and forex swaps are incomplete because they do not include outstanding positions of reporting dealers in the United Kingdom. Data for total foreign exchange and interest rate contracts include "other" products that are not shown separately.

[4]Single-currency contracts only.

[5]Adjustments for double-counting at end-June 1998 have been estimated using the results of the 1995 Triennial Central Bank Survey of Foreign Exchange and Derivatives Market Activity.

[6]Gross market values after taking into account legally enforceable bilateral netting agreements.

[7]Sources: Futures Industry Association and various futures and options exchanges.

Source: BIS

Here we should introduce a note of caution. The "notional value" of a derivative contract is a term that is used to describe the amount of the underlying price reference (e.g., foreign currency) stipulated in the derivative contract. This means that the notional value is not always related very strongly to the economic value of the derivative contract. For example, a deep-out-of-the-money option might have a high notional value, but a very small or negligible market price (or economic value). Thus, aggregating derivative notional values—e.g., those for options that are deep out and deep in the money—can generate some very misleading statistics.

The second and fourth columns of Table 1.1 attempt to get around this problem by offering estimates of the market value of OTC derivatives. The total global market value of OTC products was, for March 1995, $2.2 trillion, and $3.23 trillion at the end of 1998. Exchange-traded contracts possessed a gross market value of $1.33 trillion on December 1998.

In Table 1.2, Part A and Part B show, respectively, the breakdown of the global OTC foreign exchange and interest rate derivatives market. The survey results for the end of December 1998 are compared to the survey results six months earlier, but the main point of interest for our purposes is the different kinds of products that can be seen in each market. In the foreign currency OTC market, more than 80 percent of the contracts are for terms of shorter than one year. The dominant currency is the U.S. dollar.

For interest rate products, the majority of the contracts are for terms of between one and five years, and approximately 20 percent are for terms longer than five years. The dollar is the most prominent currency, but it accounts for only about one-quarter of the interest rate contracts.

The outstanding notional amount of derivatives is not necessarily correlated with the intensity of trading. Table 1.3 provides data on the average daily turnover in notional amounts for foreign currency and interest rate derivatives, comparing the positions on April 1995 to the positions recorded for April 1998.

Of the $961 billion of daily OTC turnover in foreign currency derivatives in April 1998, $699 billion was in the form of foreign currency swaps and $106 billion was in the form of forward contracts. Almost 90 percent of the foreign currency contracts are in U.S. dollars (i.e., U.S. dollars versus other currencies).

TABLE 1.2: Part A

The Global OTC Foreign Exchange Derivatives Markets[1]
Amounts Outstanding in Billions of U.S. Dollars

	End-June 1998		End-December 1998	
	Notional Amounts	Gross Market Values	Notional Amounts	Gross Market Values
Total contracts	18,719	799	18,011	786
with other reporting dealers	7,406	314	7,284	336
with other financial institutions	7,048	299	7,440	297
with nonfinancial customers	4,264	186	3,288	153
up to one year[2]	16,292	—	15,795	—
between one and five years[2]	1,832	—	1,624	—
over five years[2]	595	—	592	—
U.S. dollar	16,167	747	15,810	698
Deutsche mark	4,685	109	4,505	115
Japanese yen	5,579	351	5,319	370
Pound sterling	2,391	55	2,612	62
French franc	1,418	36	1,241	40
Swiss franc	1,104	35	937	30
Italian lira	1,051	24	822	35
Other	5,043	241	4,777	222
Memorandum item:				
Exchange-traded contracts	103	—	57	—

[1]See footnote 1 to Table 1.1. Counting both currency sides of every foreign exchange transaction means that the currency breakdown sums to 200 percent of the aggregate.
[2]See footnote 6 to Table 1.1.

The breakdown of daily turnover of interest rate derivatives between exchange-traded and OTC-traded shows that $1361 billion were traded on exchanges in April 1998 and only $275 billion in the OTC markets. The situation is completely different in the case of foreign currency contracts: here most of the daily trading is in OTC instruments.

It is interesting to note that in this period nonfinancial firms engaged in a daily volume of $168 billion in foreign currency products, but traded only a volume of $27 billion in interest rate

TABLE 1.2: Part B

The Global OTC Interest Rate Derivatives Markets[1]
Amounts Outstanding in Billions of U.S. Dollars

	End-June 1998		End-December 1998	
	Notional Amounts	Gross Market Values	Notional Amounts	Gross Market Values
Total contracts	42,368	1,160	50,015	1,675
with other reporting dealers	18,244	4,63	24,442	748
with other financial institutions	18,694	515	19,790	683
with nonfinancial customers	5,430	182	5,783	244
up to one year[2]	17,423	—	18,185	—
between one and five years[2]	16,805	—	21,410	—
over five years[2]	8,141	—	10,420	—
U.S. dollar	13,214	311	13,762	370
Deutsche mark	6,483	191	9,222	362
Japanese yen	7,164	194	9,763	212
Pound sterling	3,288	58	3,911	130
French franc	3,196	106	3,576	177
Swiss franc	1,055	19	1,320	31
Italian lira	2,082	116	2,130	169
Other	5,887	164	6,331	224
Memorandum item:				
Exchange-traded contracts[3]	13,107	—	12,305	—

[1]See footnote 1 to Table 1.1.
[2]Residual maturity.
[3]See footnote 6 to Table 1.1.
Source: BIS "Central Bank Survey of Foreign Exchange and Derivatives Market Activity, 1998". Basle, May 1999.

products. Undoubtedly, the exposure to foreign currency risk is the key risk factor for many nonbank corporations.

The various needs of the multinationals explain some of the changes in the banking industry in the 1970s and 1980s. The rapid changes in global markets and the creation of large multinational corporations, on the one hand, and technological change in the form of computerized information systems on the other, offered incentives to merge banks. It was argued that merged banks would

TABLE 1.3

Global Turnover in OTC Derivatives Markets
Daily Averages in Billions of U.S. Dollars

	Total		Foreign Exchange[1]		Interest Rates[2]	
	April 1995	April 1998	April 1995	April 1998	April 1995	April 1998
Total reported gross turnover	1,368	1,990	1,114	1,576	254	415
Adjusting for local double-counting[3]	−206	−306	−161	−235	−45	−71
Total reported turnover net of local double-counting ("net-gross")	1,162	1,684	953	1,341	209	344
Adjustment for cross-border double-counting[3]	−323	−457	−265	−380	−58	−78
Total reported "net-net" turnover	839	1,226	688	961	151	265
with reporting dealers	529	764	427	615	102	150
local	207	306	162	235	45	71
cross-border	322	457	265	380	57	78
with other financial institutions	181	267	149	178	32	89
local	90	125	74	80	16	46
cross-border	91	142	75	99	16	44
with nonfinancial customers	129	195	111	168	17	27
local	88	127	76	110	12	16
cross-boarder	41	68	35	58	5	10
Estimated gaps in reporting[4]	41	39	32	29	9	10
Estimated global turnover	889	1,265	720	990	160	275
Memorandum item:						
Exchange-traded products[5]	1,222	1,373	17	12	1,205	1,361

[1]Including outright forwards and foreign exchange swaps.

[2]Single-currency contracts only.

[3]Made by halving positions vis-à-vis other local reporting dealers and other reporting dealers abroad respectively.

[4]Estimates have been prepared for less than full coverage of derivatives market activity in the reporting countries.

[5]Sources: Futures Industry Association and various futures and options exchanges.

Source: BIS, "Central Bank Survey of Foreign Exchange and Derivatives Market Activity – 1998," Basle, May 1999.

be able to exploit economies of scale, and be better placed to serve the changing needs of their global clients.

Regulatory bodies also became more willing to allow competition on a global scale: foreign banks were allowed to operate in local markets, both directly and by acquiring local banks.[10]

The trend of mergers and globalization continued through the 1990s among nonbank corporations. The August 1998 merger of Chrysler of the United States with Daimler-Benz of Germany, and Ford's expansion into Europe and Japan through the purchase of local manufacturers, illustrates this continuing trend. Major technological leaders such as Microsoft and IBM are naturally becoming global giants, but smaller technological companies are also becoming international. This quickening process of globalization exposes banks and other corporations to ever-greater foreign currency and interest rate risks.

Currently, banks remain the major players in derivatives trading. Table 1.4 shows the revenues generated by the top eight commercial banks in the United States, and totals for the other 496 commercial banks dealing in derivatives for the first quarter of 1997. The first column of the table shows the notional value of derivatives activity, which amounted to over $20 trillion.

It is interesting to note that Chase Manhattan Bank, for example, had income from derivatives of $121 million in 1992 and $201 million in 1993, compared to $375 million for the first quarter of 1997. For JP Morgan, the numbers for 1992 and 1993 were, respectively, $333 and $797 million, compared to $590 million for the first quarter of 1997. In notional amounts, JP Morgan expanded its activity from $1654 billion on December 31, 1993, to $5217 billion on March 31, 1997.

Table 1.5 provides information about the annual growth of derivative products, in terms of notional and gross replacement value (GRV), for four leading U.S. banks from 1992 to 1996. (Gross replacement value is simply the sum of the positive replacement values of the instruments that a bank holds: in other words, the gross market value.)

The numbers emphasize the growing importance of derivatives in banking activities, as well as in the financial markets. It is interesting to note that the notional amount of derivatives has increased steadily, while the GRV is not fully correlated to the growth

TABLE 1.4

Trading Revenues from Cash Instruments and Off-Balance-Sheet Derivatives, March 31, 1997

	Notional Value of Derivatives Activity	Trading Revenues ($ million)				
		Interest Rate Positions	Foreign Exchange Positions	Equity Positions	Commodities and Other Positions	Total Cash and Off-Balance-Sheet Revenue
Chase Manhattan	6,357,063	168	155	12	41	375
JP Morgan	5,216,959	552	−33	67	3	590
Citibank	2,540,614	219	224	114	0	557
Bankers Trust	1,951,705	149	43	36	25	253
Bank of America	1,672,667	100	48	0	−5	143
NationsBank	1,370,518	37	18	13	13	21
First National Bank of Chicago	1,091,173	−9	14	6	1	72
Republic Nat. Bank of New York	331,346	15	27	−9	10	43
Top eight commercial banks with derivatives	20,532,045	1,231	495	239	88	2,054
Other 496 commercial banks with derivatives	1,335,619	118	195	7	9	329
Total amounts for all 584 banks with derivatives	21,867,664	1,350	690	246	97	2,383

Data are preliminary; revenue figures are for first quarter (not year-to-date).

Currently the report does not include trading revenues from credit derivatives. Credit derivatives have been excluded from the sum of total derivatives here. Trading revenue is defined here as "trading revenue from cash instruments and off-balance-sheet derivative instruments."

Before first-quarter 1995, total derivatives included spot foreign exchange. Beginning in first-quarter 1995, spot foreign exchange was reported separately.

Numbers may not add up due to rounding. Source: Office of the Comptroller of the Currency.

Source: *Risk*, August 1997.

TABLE 1.5

Notional Amounts of Derivatives of Leading Banks and Their Gross Replacement Value (GRV), 1992–1996, in Billions of U.S. Dollars

Banks	1992[1]		1993[1]		1994[2]		1995[3]		1996[3]	
	Notional	GRV[4]	Notional	GRV	Notional	GRV	Notional	GRV	Notional	GRV
Chase Manhattan	841	18.0	925	14.5	1293	14.5	4834	ng[5]	5712	ng
Chemical	1621	23.0	2479	24.2	3182	18.0				
CitiCorp	1539	29.5	1975	23.5	2665	27.5	2376	16.1	2522	17.5
JP Morgan	1278	22.0	1654	30.7	2972	31.1	3447	16.1	4716	62.4

[1] Risk 7 (9) Sept. 94, p.93.

[2] Risk 8 (10) Oct. 95, p.26.

[3] Risk 10 (9) Sept. 97, p.39.

[4] GRV = Gross replacement value is the sum of positive replacement value or gross market value.

[5] ng = not given.

of the notional amount, due mainly to the hedging strategy used by each bank. For example, the notional amount and the GRV of the JP Morgan derivative book increased by a ratio of 3.69 and 2.82, respectively, over the five-year period.

3. THE REGULATORY ENVIRONMENT

So far in this chapter, we have explained how the global environment became riskier as the financial markets were liberalized, and we have charted the consequent growth in risk management products in terms of the types of instrument and the volumes traded. Now it is time to turn our attention back to the regulatory environment.

In 1980 the Depository Institutions Deregulation and Monetary Control Act (DIDMCA) marked a major change in regulatory philosophy in the United States. This act was an important step in the deregulation of the banking system, and the liberalization of the economic environment in which banks operate. The act initiated a six-year phase-out period for Regulation Q, which had placed a ceiling on the interest rates that banks could offer deposit accounts with check facilities and savings deposits. The act allowed commercial banks to pay interest on accounts with withdrawal rights (the so-called "NOW" accounts).

This trend continued with the 1982 Garn–St. Germain Depository Institution Act (DIA), which allowed banks to offer money market deposit accounts, and the so-called "super-NOW" accounts (i.e., accounts that paid interest but offered limited check-writing privileges).

These regulatory moves opened up the banking industry to further competition from federally chartered thrift institutions, but they also allowed commercial banks to expand by buying failed savings banks. By the late 1970s and early 1980s, the numbers of such failed institutions had increased substantially. The main reason was an economic squeeze on banks that held sizable fixed-rate loan portfolios and which had financed these portfolios by means of short-term instruments. The inflationary environment of the 1970s left such institutions exposed to rising interest rates.

Regulation Q, before it was changed, also helped to drive small depositors away from such banks. They turned instead to market-traded instruments that offered a better return, such as Treasury bills, certificates of deposit (CDs are short-term debt instruments issued by banks), and, later, to money market deposit accounts and NOW accounts.

Many of the banks exposed to the mismatch between short- and long-term funds failed to hedge this exposure. In part, they were simply not familiar with the risk-shifting mechanism provided by derivatives, though often their charter acted to prevent them from using such instruments.

Interestingly, the push to implement risk management systems in banks came, primarily, from the regulators (rather than from inside banking institutions). In the mid-1980s, the Bank of England and the Federal Reserve Board became concerned about the growing exposure of banks to off-balance-sheet claims, coupled with problem loans to third-world countries. At the same time, regulators in the United Kingdom and the United States came under pressure from international banks with headquarters in the two countries. The banks complained of unfair competition from foreign banks, especially from Japan and the Far East, that were subject to much more lenient regulations and, especially, that were not subject to formal capital requirements.

The response of the Bank of England and the Federal Reserve Bank was, first of all, to strengthen the equity base of commercial banks by requiring that they set aside more capital against risky assets. As far as capital requirements were concerned, the approach was to demand more capital than before: at least 8 percent against risk-weighted assets. In addition, the regulators proposed translating each off-balance-sheet claim into an equivalent on-balance-sheet item, so that capital could be assessed against derivative positions.

Secondly, the regulators attempted to create a "level playing field." They proposed that all international banks should adopt the same capital standard and the same procedures. The Federal Reserve Board and the Bank of England assigned to the BIS the job of studying the positions of banks worldwide, planning out the details of the proposition, and proposing a set of common procedures to the regulating bodies.

The BIS continued the process initiated by the Federal Reserve Bank and the Bank of England by sending drafts of the proposals to the banks and asking for their comments and suggestions. It was clear at the outset that the task was very complicated and would require a high level of both investment and commitment from all the banks.

It was the explicit intention of the BIS that their interim proposals should be adopted, tested, and later amended according to any accumulated experience. Thus, the story of bank regulation since the 1980s has been one of an ongoing dialogue between the BIS and commercial banks all over the world, with the active involvement of local central banks and local controllers of banks.

The first results of this process, the 1988 BIS Accord and its subsequent amendments, are introduced in Chapter 2 and described in detail in Chapter 4. As Chapter 2 recounts, while the regulatory bodies initiated the process and drew up the first set of rules, they have accepted that sophisticated banks should have a growing role in the setting up of their own internal risk management models. With the principles set and the course defined, the role of the regulators has begun to shift to that of monitoring sophisticated banks' internal risk management systems.

Few professionals in the banking industry believe that the systems proposed (or imposed) by the BIS are, in any sense, perfect. Nevertheless, the role of the BIS in forcing the banks to quantify risks, evaluate risks, price risks, and monitor risks has proved invaluable. Further, regulators seem increasingly open to the idea of a two-tier approach. This allows the more sophisticated financial institutions to make use of their own internal models, while applying a simpler standardized approach to the majority of institutions.

There have also been important industry initiatives over the last 10 years. The Group of Thirty (G-30) study published in July 1993 was the first industry-led and comprehensive effort to broaden awareness of advanced approaches to risk management. The G-30 study provides practical guidance in the form of 20 recommendations, addressed to dealers and end-users alike, in terms of managing derivatives activities. We discuss these recommendations in more detail in Chapter 2.

4. THE ACADEMIC BACKGROUND AND TECHNOLOGICAL CHANGES

Risk management cannot be understood independently of the body of academic research published on risk management techniques and derivative valuation that has evolved since the early 1950s. A common deficiency in risk management systems and policy proposals is the lack of a firm theoretical foundation (and therefore consistency).

In this section we review some of the key theories and models, and show how they relate to the development of approaches to risk management in banking. However, it is worth making clear at the outset that the theoretical work on risk management is based on many simplifying assumptions, and that the implementation of theoretical work is not always straightforward. Real life is complicated and is composed of many details that models cannot, and maybe should not, accommodate. Instead, the role of models is often to simplify complicated structures and to highlight the most important factors. A "good" financial model is one that helps the analyst separate out the major explanatory variables from a noisy background.

Milton Friedman, in his seminal article "The Methodology of Positive Economics" (1953), emphasizes that a model can be only evaluated in terms of its predictive power. It cannot be evaluated in terms of the assumptions employed, or in terms of whether the model seems to be sufficiently complicated to capture all the relevant details from "real life." In other words, a model can be simple, and yet be judged successful if it helps in predicting the future and in improving the efficiency of the decision-making process.

The word "risk" has many meanings and connotations. It is widely used by professional traders, risk managers, and the public. Many articles in newspapers and magazines talk about risky and choppy markets. They warn their readers from investing "too much" in "risky assets," and they wonder whether financial markets have become "too risky" and volatile. A proliferation of names has emerged to describe the various risks: business risk, financial risk, market risk, liquidity risk, default risk, systematic risk, specific risk, residual risk, credit risk, counterparty risk, operations risk, settlement risk, country risk, portfolio risk, systemic risk, legal risk, reputational risk, and more.

The foundations of modern risk analysis are contained in Markowitz's (1952) paper concerning the principles of portfolio selection. Markowitz showed that a rational investor, i.e., an investor who behaves in a way that is consistent with Von Neuman–Morgenstern's expected utility maximization, should analyze alternative portfolios based on their mean and on the variance of their rates of return. Markowitz makes two additional assumptions: first, that capital markets are perfect,[11] and second that the rates of return are normally distributed.

Since the utility choices of a consumer can be expressed in terms of two parameters only—mean and variance—*portfolios* of investments can also be presented for selection according to these two parameters.

Note that the two-parameter presentation, while valid for well-diversified portfolios, does not apply to individual securities. A security should be evaluated only in the context of the portfolio of investments to which it belongs, through its contribution to the mean and variance of the portfolio. More specifically, the risk of a single investment should be measured in terms of the covariability[12] of its rate of return with the rate of return of the portfolio.[13]

Markowitz's portfolio analysis suggests that the specific or idiosyncratic risk of a single security (i.e., the elements of its risk profile that it does *not* share with other investments) should not be measured in terms of its volatility as measured by the variance of the rates of return. The variance measures the potential dispersion of future rates of return, but this is not a relevant risk measure for a single security. This is because most of the specific risk due to volatile returns can easily be diversified away and eliminated at virtually no cost. It follows that the specific risk, or idiosyncratic risk, of a security, should not be priced in the marketplace if it can easily be offset against the returns of other securities.

Sharpe (1964) and Lintner (1965) take the portfolio approach one step further by adding the assumption that a risk-free asset exists. They show that financial markets are in equilibrium when all investors hold a combination of a riskless asset and the market portfolio of all risky assets in the economy. Therefore, prices of risky assets are determined in such a way that they are included in the market portfolio. They show that in order to be "in" the market portfolio, a risky asset must be priced according to its relative contribution to the total risk of the market portfolio, as measured by the variance of its rate of return distribution, σ_M^2:

$$\beta_i \equiv \frac{\mathrm{cov}(R_i, R_M)}{\sigma_M^2} = \frac{\sigma_i}{\sigma_M} \rho_{i,M} \qquad (1)$$

where R_i and R_M are the rates of return on asset i and the market portfolio, respectively, σ_i and σ_M are the standard deviations of the rates of return on asset i and the market portfolio, respectively, and $\rho_{i,M}$ is the correlation coefficient between i and M.

This ratio is called the "beta" of asset i (β_i). It measures the systematic risk of the asset, i.e., the risk that cannot be diversified away.[14]

The relative contribution is measured by the ratio between the covariance of the rate of return of the asset, and the rate of return of the market portfolio, and the variance of the market portfolio. It should be noted that the weighted sum of all the covariances is equal to σ_M^2, the total risk of the market portfolio:

$$\sum_{i=1}^{N} x_i \, \text{cov} \, (R_i, R_M) = \sigma_M^2$$

Here, x_i denotes the relative weight of security i in the market portfolio, N is the number of assets in the market portfolio, and $\sum_{i=1}^{N} x_i = 1$. The previous expression can be rewritten as:

$$\sum_{i=1}^{N} x_i \, \beta_i = 1$$

The beta risk measures the relative comovements of security i for which investors should be compensated.

Sharpe (1964) and Lintner (1965) proved that the expected rate of return on security i under the above assumptions, is given by the following equation:

$$E(R_i) = R + \beta_i \, [E(R_M) - R] \tag{2}$$

where $E(\cdot)$ is the expected value operator, and R denotes the rate of return on the riskless bond over same holding period as the asset. The term in brackets measures the risk premium in the market for a unit of beta risk. The product of β_i and $[E(R_M) - R]$ is the expected compensation that holders of asset i require above the risk-free rate R in order to hold the asset.

If we rewrite the equation above in terms of σ_i, σ_M, and $\rho_{i,M}$, then $E(R_i) = R + \sigma_i \, \rho_{i,M} \, [E(R_M) - R]/\sigma_M$. Accordingly, the excess expected return above the risk-free rate is a function of the systematic component of risk $\sigma_i \, \rho_{i,M}$ times the unit price of risk $[E(R_M) - R]/\sigma_M$.

Concurrently, most investment banks and brokerage firms calculate the beta of individual securities as well as their volatility, or total risk as measured by σ_i. The beta is estimated from the regression equation,

$$R_{it} = a_i + b_i (R_{Mt} - R) + \epsilon_{it} \tag{3}$$

where R_{it} and R_{Mt} are the rates of return measured between time t and $t-1$ for security i and an index representing the "market portfolio of risky assets," respectively. R is the short-term riskless interest rate, ϵ_{it} is the residual value, and a_i and b_i are the two regression parameters, with b_i being the statistical estimate of β_i.

The original model, known as the "Capital Asset Pricing Model" (CAPM), was proved and tested in discrete time, for example, over a one-year or one-month horizon. Merton (1972) has shown that the CAPM can also be derived in a continuous time framework, under the assumptions that trades can be executed at any time and that the return-generating process for stock prices is smooth, with no jumps in prices (i.e., it behaves like a diffusion process).

The next important development in the analysis of risk occurred in 1973, with the publication of two seminal papers by Fischer Black and Myron Scholes, and Robert Merton, on the pricing of options. The papers make use of a framework similar to that used by Markowitz, Sharpe, and Lintner; namely, they assume the existence of perfect capital markets and assume that security prices are lognormally distributed or equivalently, that log-returns are normally distributed. To these, they add the new assumptions that trading in all securities is continuous and that the distribution of the rates of return is stationary. The Black–Scholes (BS) option pricing model (OPM) for European call options on stocks (without dividends) is given by:

$$C = S\,N\,(d_1) - Ke^{-r\tau}\,N\,(d_2) \tag{4}$$

where C is the premium of a European call option, S is the price of the underlying security, K is the exercise or strike price, r is the riskless instantaneous interest rate,[15] τ is the time period to the maturity of the option, $N(\cdot)$ is the cumulative standard normal distribution, and where

$$d_1 = \frac{\ln(S/K) + (r + \frac{1}{2}\sigma^2)\,\tau}{\sigma\sqrt{\tau}}$$

$$d_2 = d_1 - \sigma\sqrt{\tau} \tag{5}$$

Here, σ is the standard deviation of the rate of return distribution of the underlying security, ln is the natural logarithm operator, and e is the exponent operation ($e = 2.714\ldots$).

For example, a one-year ($\tau = 1$) at-the-money ($K = S$) call on a stock with current price of \$100 ($S = \$100$) and standard deviation of 20 percent ($\sigma = 0.20$), when the annual interest rate is 10 percent, is valued at \$13 according to the Black–Scholes model.

The pricing model for a European put option can easily be derived from the call value by using what has become known as the "put-call parity relationship":[16]

$$C - P = S - Ke^{-r\tau}$$

where P is the premium on a European put. The BS model for a European put is therefore:

$$P = -SN(-d_1) + Ke^{-r\tau} N(-d_2) \tag{6}$$

Continuing our numerical example, the price of an at-the-money put should be \$3.90.

The risk of the underlying security, which determines the premium on the option and its risk, is measured by its volatility σ. An increase in the volatility of the underlying stock, with all other parameters unchanged, causes an increase in the option's premium. It can be shown that the instantaneous volatility of the option is given by:

$$\sigma_c = \eta_{c,s}\,\sigma$$
$$\sigma_p = |\eta_{p,s}|\,\sigma$$

where σ_i and $\eta_{i,s}$ are, respectively, the instantaneous standard deviation of derivative i and the elasticity of the derivative i with respect to the underlying asset, S, and subscript c stands for a call and p for a put. For a call option, the elasticity is

$$\eta_{c,s} \equiv \frac{\partial C}{\partial S} \cdot \frac{S}{C} = N(d_1) \cdot \frac{S}{C} \geq 1 \tag{7}$$

and for a put

$$\eta_{p,s} \equiv \frac{\partial P}{\partial S} \cdot \frac{S}{P} = -N(-d_1) \cdot \frac{S}{P} \leq 0 \tag{8}$$

Continuing with our example, since $N(d_1) = 0.72$ and $-N(-d_1) = -0.28$, therefore $\eta_{c,s} = 5.53$ and $\eta_{p,s} = -7.23$. Accordingly, $\tau_c = 5.53 \cdot 0.20 = 1.11$ (or 110 percent) and $\sigma_p = 7.23 \cdot 0.20 = 1.45$ (or 145 percent).

In a similar way the systematic risk of a call (β_c) and a put (β_p) is given by:

$$\beta_c = \beta\eta_{c,s}$$
$$\beta_p = \beta\eta_{p,s} \qquad\qquad (9)$$

where β is the systematic risk of the underlying asset.

If we assume that the underlying asset has a beta of 1, then the instantaneous beta of the call is 5.53, and -7.23 for the put. By adding the put to the portfolio of securities with positive beta risk, the systematic risk of the portfolio is reduced; conversely, adding calls increases the beta of the portfolio.

Note that $N(d_1)$ and $-N(-d_1)$ are the hedge ratios, known also as the "delta" of the option, of a call and of a put, respectively. The hedge ratio measures the change in the value of an option resulting from a small change, say a dollar, in the price of the underlying security. The hedge ratio shows how the risk of the underlying security over a very short time interval can be hedged dynamically with derivatives assets. A fully hedged position over an arbitrarily small interval of time is often called a "delta-neutral" position.

In order to complete this brief introduction to the theoretical basis of modern risk management, we must turn to the work Franco Modigliani and Merton Miller published in 1958.[17] These academics showed that in a perfect capital market, with no corporate and income taxes, the capital structure of a firm has no effect on the value of the firm. A corporation cannot increase its value by issuing more debt, despite the fact that the expected cost of debt is lower than the expected cost of equity. Instead, the greater leverage in the capital structure in the firm, brought about by the increased level of indebtedness, means that the equity holders immediately face a greater level of financial risk. Naturally, they will demand compensation for this in the form of higher rates of return.

This implies that management should concentrate on identifying and implementing investments that will increase the economic value of the firm, rather than reengineering the capital structure of the firm. The cost of capital of the firm, which is equal to the weighted cost of equity and debts, is important mainly in the sense that it offers a marginal "hurdle rate" for management in their evaluation of new investments.

Many of the contributors to the intellectual framework that we have just sketched out were eventually awarded the Nobel Prize. Their fundamental results will accompany us throughout this book, providing an essential framework for risk analysis and evaluation. In Chapter 9 we present an integrated approach that combines the Black–Scholes option pricing model with the CAPM in the Modigliani–Miller framework, in order to evaluate credit risk and default risk.

Furthermore, in order to understand the BIS recommendations concerning capital adequacy in the banking industry, one has to understand Markowitz's approach to risk and reward; the importance of measuring the correlation coefficients among different bank assets and liabilities is directly linked to the portfolio diversification effects of the fundamental model.

Readers unfamiliar with the work of Markowitz, Sharpe, Lintner, Modigliani and Miller, or indeed Black and Scholes, may wish to study one of the standard text books devoted to these theoretical advances as they read further into this present book.[18]

Of course, developing fundamental theories on risk management and implementing those theories within a business are two very different challenges. There are two prerequisites for any risk management system: first, reliable, broad, and up-to-date databases concerning both the bank's transactional positions and the financial rates available in the wider marketplace; and second, statistical tools and procedures that allow the bank to analyze the data.

Global banks and corporations are engaged in many transactions each day, and may carry millions of open positions in their books. All these positions have to be evaluated periodically, usually on a daily basis for international banks, to assess the net risk exposure of the bank. This often means a bank must bring together data from a multiplicity of legacy systems with different data structures, from all of its branches and businesses worldwide—as we discuss in later chapters. The data collected must be as accurate as possible, while minimizing omissions. In addition, market data history for interest rates, foreign exchange rates, commodities, equities, and other associated derivatives must be collected and analyzed in order to estimate volatilities and correlations of major risk factors. The results of these analyses form key inputs into the pricing models used to assess the risks inherent in the various financial claims. Measuring risk is thus based on statistical procedures.

The major tools used by financial analysts in this regard are often based on research by academics seeking to improve statistical estimation procedures. For example, in the last decade, in reaction to evidence that volatility in financial markets may be nonstationary, researchers have begun to make use of increasingly sophisticated procedures such as ARCH, GARCH, and other extensions.[19]

5. ACCOUNTING SYSTEMS VERSUS RISK MANAGEMENT SYSTEMS

So far in this chapter we have looked at risk as it has developed in the financial markets, and at how banks have sought to analyze this risk. In this section, we take a look at how risk affects financial reporting.

The traditional accounting approach is, in essence, backward looking. Past profits (or losses) are calculated and analyzed, but future uncertainties are not measured at all. This was not entirely satisfactory even when banks derived their profits primarily from two major sources: providing loans and providing intermediation services.

As we recounted above, however, since the 1980s the growing importance of OTC products has added a third source of profitability. As the Generally Accepted Accounting Principles (GAAP) could not easily accommodate derivatives, the instruments have largely appeared in the footnotes to the bank balance sheet; i.e., they have largely remained an off-balance-sheet activity.

In the major banks, however, this has meant that the size of off-balance-sheet claims, as measured in notional amounts, have grown to be larger than those that are recorded on-the-balance sheet. The same sort of accounting problems affect nonbank corporations that engage in derivatives trading.

The end result is that a major component of bank profitability over the last decade does not appear in any consistent way in the financial reports of banks. Shareholders and financial analysts find it difficult to assess bank performance, while regulators and rating agencies face problems when they try to determine the riskiness of bank activities. Likewise, the true risk profile of some nonbank corporations may also be unclear from their financial reports.[20]

A thought-provoking illustration of this problem in bank accounting is provided in Table 1.6, which appeared in *The Wall Street Journal* (19–20 June 1998). The table shows the problem loans of Japanese banks as of March 31, 1998, under conventional accounting practices in Japan, as compared to the new proposed measurement standard. For the largest nine banks in Japan, the average difference between the reported figures and the figures that would be produced by the proposed standard is 42 percent (ranging between 29 and 62 percent).

Ideally, the financial world would create a new reporting system based on what might be called "Generally Accepted Risk Principles" (GARP). The system would be forward looking, and

TABLE 1.6

Measuring Problem Loans for Japanese Banks Under The Old and New System of Reporting, March 31, 1998, in Billions of Yen

Bank	Old	New	% Change
Dai-Ichi Kangyo Bank	1,185	1,471	24
Sumitomo Bank	1,005	1,469	46
Fuji Bank	1,218	1,629	39
Sakura Bank	1,140	1,475	29
Sanwa Bank	873	1,288	47
Bank of Tokyo Mitsubishi	1,389	2,250	62
Daiwa Bank	673	958	42
Tokai Bank	866	1,222	41
Asahi Bank	704	995	41
Total	9,053	12,757	41

Source: Goldman Sachs

designed to help managers and regulators analyze and understand the operations of financial institutions. The system would also be two-dimensional: the added dimension would be risk, or uncertainty, concerning future profitability (i.e., potential losses) from different banking activities.

Any such risk-sensitive accounting system would have to compromise between accuracy and sophistication, on the one hand, and applicability and aggregation on the other. Major problems arise in any aggregating system when it is applied to factors that are nonlinear, and therefore "nonadditive."

For example, systematic risk (or beta risk) is additive over securities for any given portfolio, but specific risk, measured by the standard derivation of the residual return, is nonadditive. In other words, the standard deviation of a portfolio is *not* the sum of the standard deviations of the securities in the portfolio. This is why a careful aggregation of risk demands the estimation of many parameters, and especially the degree of correlation between all the possible pairs of securities in a portfolio.

This has not proved an easy lesson to learn in the banking industry. In 1986, when the Federal Reserve in the United States and the Bank of England started to create a new system for banks in Western economies in order to assess capital required to cover the banks' risks, the starting point for the study was the existing accounting system. The idea was simply to translate off-balance-sheet claims into their on-balance-sheet equivalents. After the investment of considerable effort, this simplistic approach was abandoned in favor of the much more comprehensive solution that we outlined above. It was realized that simply translating each off-balance-sheet claim to its on-balance-sheet equivalent, and then adding up these individual claims, would hugely overstate the real position and impose a significant cost on banks. (Chapter 2 introduces the initial minimum required regulatory capital procedures suggested by the BIS, and Chapter 4 provides details of the procedures of BIS 1998.)

6. LESSONS FROM RECENT FINANCIAL DISASTERS

Since modern banks began to evolve in the seventeenth century, most bank failures have been due to exposure to bad debts.

However, some spectacular bank failures over the last 25 years have been due in part to market exposures generated by derivative positions—and politicians and the media have suggested that this is because the banking system as a whole is failing to control these new forms of risk.

It is true that for many years, banks concentrated their efforts on assessing credit risk. Rating agencies, such as Moody's and Standard and Poor's, were employed to evaluate (or confirm) the credit quality of large firms that applied for a loan (see Chapter 7). Internal procedures were also developed in major banks, though they were often lacking, or inadequate, in smaller institutions. The key weakness in this traditional risk analysis, however, was that credit risk was evaluated on a case-by-case basis. Correlation risk, i.e., the risk associated with cross-dependencies among loans, such as the concentration of loans in a certain geographical location or in a given industry, was often ignored. As a result, American commercial banks suffered large losses to Latin American counterparties in the 1980s as a result of the economic crisis in that continent—losses that eventually led to the collapse of Continental Bank in Chicago. Concentration by business sector can also be catastrophic: Crédit Lyonnais suffered huge losses from clients engaged in the real estate business in France when this sector entered into a slowdown in 1992.

Credit correlations are one source of risk, but it has become increasingly clear that concentrations among different kinds of risks are also crucial. Perhaps the most striking case of correlation risk across market risk and credit risk is the crisis of the savings and loan industry in the United States in the 1980s. We have already mentioned in this chapter how these institutions, locked into long-term fixed-interest loans, were surprised by rising interest rates on short-term deposits; a crucial additional factor was that many of the loans they had extended were used to purchase real estate. Unfortunately, but predictably, the value of this real estate was negatively correlated to the level of interest rates.

It is only in the late 1990s that the banking industry has begun to appreciate the risks of correlations between credit and market risk, on the one hand, and liquidity risk on the other. The near-collapse of Long-Term Capital Management (LTCM) in 1998 highlighted the risks of high leverage to an individual institution. But it also showed how problems in one institution might spill over into the entire financial system when, simultaneously, market prices fall and market liquidity dries up—making it almost impossible for wounded institutions to unwind their positions in order to satisfy margin calls.[21]

LTCM discovered too late how negatively correlated its returns were with liquidity risk (see Chapter 15 for a more detailed discussion of liquidity risk and the LTCM case). The industry as a whole is now looking at how the relationship between liquidity risk, leverage risk, and market and credit risk can be incorporated in risk measurement and stress testing models.

It remains uncertain as to whether risk management can prevent all kinds of major crises. Will the risk management system really send advance warning signals? Will capital requirements really reduce the risk of bankruptcy? If not, will they at least diminish the spillover risk or the "domino effect" risk?[22] As Chapters 5 and 8 describe, innovations by the banking industry, such as the development and publication by JP Morgan of its RiskMetrics and CreditMetrics systems to address market risk and credit risk, are significant advances in risk management methodology. Yet they do not offer a panacea to the problem of substantial changes in default rates, interest rates, exchange rates, and other key indexes over a short time period, say, a day, a week or a month. Increasingly, banks recognize they must subject their positions to "stress analysis" to measure their vulnerability to unlikely (but possible) market scenarios (see Chapters 6 and 11).

If "correlation risk" can be identified as one principal source of hidden bank risk, then operational risks are surely the second major source. The downfall of Barings in February 1995 is often depicted as the result of the actions of a single trader, Nicholas Leeson, who exposed the bank to huge futures positions (betting mainly on an increase in the value of the Nikkei 225 index). As the investigation into the disaster revealed, the bank's collapse also bore witness to the failings of senior managers. Put simply, they lacked the ability to monitor effectively Leeson's trading activities.

This was partly due to a lack of proper risk management systems, but it was also due to a disregard for risk management procedures. In particular, Leeson had been placed in charge of trading at the Singapore branch of Barings Bank while at the same time taking charge of the back-office operation. Yet it is a first principle of risk control that the assessment of risk, and control over tracking transactions, must be independent of the trading function.

One additional lesson of the Barings debacle is that bank management must scrutinize success stories in order to evaluate the risks incurred. This is also the lesson from the crisis in Orange County, California, in 1994. The treasurer of the County borrowed heavily and invested in mortgage-backed securities, only to incur losses of over $1.6 billion when the cost of borrowing rose. In both the Orange County and Barings Bank cases, the man in charge showed excellent results at first, and was therefore allowed to continue to transact without proper surveillance or controls. Managers must remember the cardinal rule of all investments: reward does not come without risk. (The management of operational risk is discussed in more detail in Chapter 13.)

7. TYPOLOGY OF RISK EXPOSURES

In Section 4 we summarized the theoretical framework of risk under the assumption that all assets are traded in perfect capital markets. In this section, we present a typology of risk exposures from the point of view of the bank's management, taking into consideration practical issues including the limitations of models and theories, human factors, existence of "frictions" such as taxes and transaction cost, and limitations on the quality and quantity of information, as well as the cost of acquiring this information, and more.

Financial risks can be divided into market risk, credit risk, liquidity risk, operational risk, legal and regulatory risk, and human factor risk (Figure 1.5).

Market risk is the risk that changes in financial market prices and rates will reduce the value of the bank's positions. Market risk for a fund is often measured relative to a benchmark index or portfolio, and is referred to as the "risk of tracking error." Market risk also includes "basis risk," a term used in the risk management industry to describe the chance of a breakdown in the relationship between the price of a product, on the one hand, and the price of the instrument used to hedge that price exposure on the other. The

FIGURE 1.5

Typology of Risks Faced by a Financial Institution

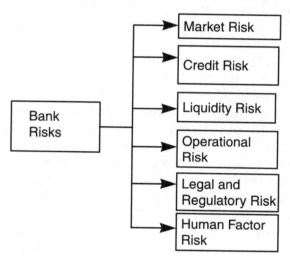

market-VaR methodology, discussed in Chapter 5, attempts to capture multiple components of market risk such as directional risk, convexity risk, volatility risk, basis risk, etc.

Credit risk is the risk that a change in the credit quality of a counterparty will affect the value of a bank's position. Default, whereby a counterparty is unwilling or unable to fulfill its contractual obligations, is the extreme case; however, banks are also exposed to the risk that the counterparty might be downgraded by a rating agency.

Credit risk is only an issue when the position is an asset, i.e., when it exhibits a positive replacement value. In that instance, if the counterparty defaults, the bank either loses all of the market value of the position or, more commonly, the part of the value that it cannot recover following the credit event. (The value it is likely to recover is called the "recovery value"; the amount it is expected to lose is called the "loss given default.")

Unlike coupon bonds or loans, the potential loss given default on derivative positions is usually much lower than the nominal amount of the deal, and in many cases is only a fraction of this amount. This is because the economic value of a derivative instrument is related to its replacement or market value rather than its nominal or face value. However, the credit exposures induced by the replacement values of derivative instruments are dynamic: they can be negative at one point in time, and yet become positive at a later point in time after market conditions have changed. Therefore, banks must examine not only the current exposure, measured by the current replacement value, but also the profile of future exposures up to the termination of the deal.

Chapter 7 discusses the traditional external and internal systems that banks adopt to measure and manage credit ratings. Chapters 8, 9, 10, and 11 review the new models that have recently become available to measure credit risk. Chapter 12 reviews the different approaches that banks can employ to mitigate credit risk.

Liquidity risk comprises both "funding liquidity risk" and "trading-related liquidity risk," though these two dimensions of liquidity risk are closely related. Funding liquidity risk relates to a financial institution's ability to raise the necessary cash to roll over its debt, to meet the cash, margin, and collateral requirements of counterparties, and (in the case of funds) to satisfy capital withdrawals. Trading-related liquidity risk, often simply called liquidity risk, is the risk that an institution will not be able to execute a transaction at the prevailing market price because there is, temporarily, no appetite for the deal on the "other side" of the market. If the transaction cannot be postponed, its execution may lead to substantial loss on the position. This risk is generally very hard to quantify. (In current implementations of the market-VaR approach, liquidity risk is included only in the sense that one of the parameters of a VaR model is the period of time, or "holding period," thought necessary to liquidate the relevant positions.) Trading-related liquidity risk may reduce an institution's ability to manage and hedge market risk as well as its capacity to satisfy any shortfall on the funding side through asset liquidation.

Funding liquidity risk is affected by various factors such as the maturity of liabilities, the extent of reliance on secured sources of funding, the terms of financing, and the breadth of funding sources, including the ability to access public markets such as the commercial paper market. It is also influenced by counterparty arrangements, including collateral trigger clauses, the existence of capital withdrawal rights, and the existence of lines of credit that the bank cannot cancel.

Funding can be achieved through cash and cash equivalents, "buying power," and available credit lines. (Buying power refers to the amount a trading counterparty can borrow against assets under stressed market conditions.) In Chapter 15 we discuss in detail the liquidity aspects of the LTCM crisis mentioned above; in Chapter 6 we present a multiperiod model to incorporate liquidity risk in scenario analysis and in the VaR framework.

Operational risk refers to potential losses resulting from inadequate systems, management failure, faulty controls, fraud, and human errors. As we discussed above, many of the recent large losses related to derivatives are the direct consequence of operational failures. Derivatives trading is more prone to operational risk than cash transactions because derivatives are, by their nature, leveraged transactions. This means that a trader can make very large commitments on behalf of the bank, and generate huge exposures into the future (even up to 30 years ahead), using only a small amount of cash (at the time that the transaction is executed). Very tight controls are an absolute necessity if a bank is to avoid large losses.

Operational risk includes "fraud," for example when a trader or other employee intentionally falsifies and misrepresents the risks incurred in a transaction. Technology risk, and principally computer systems risk, also falls into the operational risk category. In Chapter 13, we explore some new approaches to the management of operational risk.

The valuation of complex derivatives also creates considerable operational risk. This risk, generally referred to as "model risk," is discussed in detail in Chapter 15.

Legal risk arises for a whole variety of reasons. For example, a counterparty might lack the legal or regulatory authority to engage in a transaction. Legal risks usually only become apparent when a counterparty, or an investor, loses money on a transaction and decides to sue the bank to avoid meeting its obligations.[23] Another aspect of regulatory risk is the potential impact of a change in tax law on the market value of a position. For example, when the British Government changed the tax code to remove a particular tax benefit during the summer of 1997, one major investment bank suffered huge losses.

Human factor risk is really a special form of operational risk. It relates to the losses that may result from human errors such as

FIGURE 1.6

The Dimensions of Market Risk

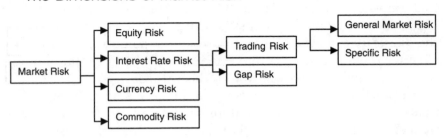

pushing the wrong button on a computer, inadvertently destroy-ing a file, or entering the wrong value for the parameter input of a model.

These financial risks can be further decomposed into more specific categories. For example, market risk could be subdivided into equity risk, interest rate risk, currency risk, and commodity risk (Figure 1.6). Interest rate risk might be further divided into trading risk and gap risk: the latter relates to the different risk char-acteristics of bonds based on their maturities. As we discussed ear-lier, liquidity risk can be decomposed into two interrelated di-mensions: funding liquidity risk and trading-related liquidity risk (Figure 1.7).

We can slice and dice each risk type down to the most detailed level (Figure 1.8). The more detailed the decomposition, the more

FIGURE 1.7

The Dimensions of Liquidity Risk

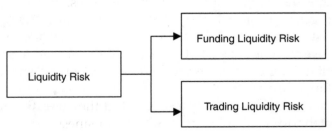

FIGURE 1.8

Schematic Presentation, by Categories, of the Risk Exposure of a Bank

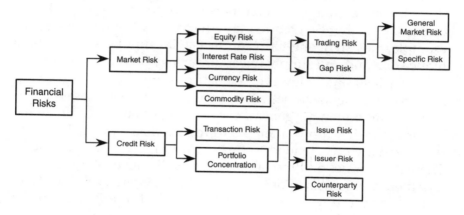

closely the bank's risk will be captured. In practice, this process is limited by the level of model complexity that can be handled by the available technology and by the cost and availability of internal and market data.

8. EXTENDING RISK MANAGEMENT SYSTEMS TO NONFINANCIAL CORPORATIONS

Risk management techniques first developed by, and for, banks are now being adopted by firms such as insurance companies, hedge funds, and industrial corporations. Indeed, there is mounting pressure from regulators such as the SEC (Securities and Exchange Commission) in the United States, and from shareholders, for more and better disclosure of financial risk exposures.

The main purpose of risk management systems for nonfinancial institutions is to identify the market risk factors that affect the volatility of their earnings, and to measure the combined effect of these factors. The risk issues faced by corporations are different from those faced by financial institutions. They generally need to look at risk over a longer time, and they must look at how to combine the effects of their underlying business exposures with those of any financial hedges that they have put in place. The effects of risk on planning and budgeting must be considered, as opposed to the trader's need to consider profit and loss.

Of course, in a sense nonfinancial corporations have always engaged in activities intended to reduce or control their risks. For example, they sign long-term contracts with suppliers or clients to reduce demand and supply uncertainty; they hold inventories and purchase insurance. However, while firms are already engaged in such risk management activities, they often do not possess a formal system to monitor general corporate risks and to evaluate the impact of their various attempts to reduce risks. Meanwhile, academic research has tended to treat each of these areas separately. There are theories and models to optimize the level of inventories, and there are models to optimize financial hedging activities (e.g., against exposure to foreign currency risks). There is little in the way of a unified approach to corporate risk management.

Corporations are often exposed to interest rate risk. For example, they might borrow money from their bank or provide credit to their customers. They may also be exposed to foreign currency risk if they export their products or services, or if they depend on supplies from abroad. Most firms have to account for potential losses that might arise from any default by their clients on receivables, and they may also incur credit risk if they purchase corporate bonds, or if they engage in OTC derivative trading. Nevertheless, the risk exposures of nonbank corporations are generally not regulated with the intensity seen in the risk-related regulation of banks and other financial institutions.

Essentially, this is because the main risk of nonfinancial institutions is business risk, while market risks and credit risks are secondary in importance. The "domino effect" that is the major worry of bank regulators is not a major concern in the nonfinancial sector. Nonfinancial corporations are also not as heavily leveraged as financial corporations. The ratio of debt to total assets in the United States for nonfinancial corporations is around 30 percent, and in Japan it is approximately 50 percent. For banks, the ratio is 82 to 92 percent. Finally, the leverage of nonfinancial institutions is primarily of concern to the firm's creditors, which are usually banks and financial institutions, and not to the general public and smaller savers.

There is one reason, however, why it is now important for nonfinancial corporations to reexamine their attitudes to risk management. Ironically, this is the huge expansion in derivatives trading itself. In Table 1.3, we can see that nonfinancial firms have increased their daily average turnover in OTC derivatives (foreign currency and interest rate contracts) from $129 billion in April 1995 to $195 billion in April 1999. While nonfinancial corporations have increased their use of derivatives mainly with the aim of reducing their financial risk, their involvement in the market means that they must adopt some of the risk control measures devised by the banking community.

Since current accounting procedures are inadequate for controlling and managing risks, new procedures must be devised. SEC requirements in effect since 1998 have set new rules for the disclosure of the market risk exposures of traded companies. In addition, a quantifiable measure of the exposure to market risk and how it may affect the firm's value or profitability must be supplied.

The trend in many countries is to demand greater transparency with regard to risk management policies and strategies. Boards of directors will be required to take a more active role in managing risks, and they will be expected to evaluate returns within the context of the risk. We discuss many of these themes in more detail in Chapter 16, which is devoted to risk management by nonbank corporations. Nevertheless, the reader should keep in mind that many of the concepts introduced in other chapters of this book are also applicable to the risk management efforts of nonfinancial corporations.

NOTES

1. For example, in 1993 the old Chase Manhattan Bank and Chemical Bank merged into the new Chase Manhattan Bank.
2. For example, HongKong and Shanghai Banking Corporation (HSBC).
3. For example, Citicorp, correctly anticipating the new law (Financial Services Act of 1999), has already merged with insurer Travelers to form the giant one-stop financial conglomerate Citigroup. This built on an earlier merger (1997), when Travelers, a major insurance and consumer finance concern, and the U.S. brokerage firm Smith-Barney, merged with the U.S. investment bank Salomon Brothers.

4. Chapters 2 and 4 discuss in great detail regulatory capital under both the 1988 and 1998 Accords, as well as the new BIS proposal for reform of the 1988 Accord.

5. Chapter 13 deals with the management of operational risk, and Chapter 15 discusses different facets of model risk.

6. Procter & Gamble lost $157 million on two interest swaps that it had entered into with Bankers Trust, and then sued Bankers Trust for misrepresentation of the risks involved in the transactions. For details of these financial disasters, see, e.g., Steinherr (1998). Over a nine-day period in April 1994, Procter & Gamble, Gibson Greetings, and Mead Corporation announced hefty losses from leveraged swap agreements with Bankers Trust. All three companies filed suits against Bankers Trust.

7. The Basle Committee meets at the Bank for International Settlements (BIS), located in Basle, Switzerland.

8. In the mid-1980s, there were over 14,000 commercial banks in the United States and 5000 savings and loan and mutual savings banks.

9. For comparison, the outstanding worldwide securities market debt was $24.4 trillion at the end of 1994 (BIS, 65th Annual Report, 1995) and the outstanding U.S. credit market debt was $17.3 trillion at the end of March 1995 (Federal Reserve Bulletin, Oct. 1995).

10. HongKong and Shanghai Bank, for example, was allowed to purchase Marine Midland Bank in the United States and Midland Bank in the United Kingdom.

11. By perfect capital markets, we mean markets with no transaction costs or taxes, where all traders have free and costless access to all available information and are perfect competitors.

12. The weighted sum of all the covariances is equal to the variance of the portfolio, where the weights are the same as those used in constructing the portfolio.

13. To illustrate, let us assume that the firm expects to receive an income stream of $15, −$15, and $15 at the end of years 1, 2, and 3 respectively. The average net income over the three years is $5. Assume that, as managers of the firm, we have the chance to invest in a project with zero average value, with net income of −$5 at the end of the year and $5 the year after. If we add this project to the firm, the expected average profit will remain unchanged at $5. However, the income stream will be $10, −$10, $15, which is less risky compared to the initial stream $15, −$15, $15.

14. Technically, the total risk of asset i, σ_i^2, can be decomposed into the systematic risk component $\sigma_i^2 \rho_{i,M}^2$ and the specific risk $\sigma_i^2 (1 - \rho_{i,M}^2)$.

Observe that as $\rho_{i,M}$ approaches 1, total risk becomes composed of pure systemic risk.

15. r denotes the continuously compounded rate of interest. It can be derived from the annualized discrete interest rate R by the relation $r = \ln(1 + R)$.

16. See Stoll (1969). See also Galai (1977) for a characterization of options.

17. Their major paper was published in 1958 and an important correction appeared in 1963. The best presentation and explanation of their model is found in Fama and Miller (1974). See also Miller (1977).

18. See, e.g., Brealey and Myers (2000).

19. ARCH stands for Auto Regressive Conditional Heteroskedasticity. The G in GARCH stands for General. See a summary of these procedures in Engle (1982) and Bollerslev (1986).

20. From 1998, the SEC required listed companies to report their exposures to market risk factors related to their derivative positions, and to positions in other financial instruments. (See Chapter 16 for a brief description of the SEC requirements.)

21. In Chapter 15 we discuss the issue of liquidity risk and how it interplays with market and credit risk.

22. See Chapter 2. The G-12 recommendations are intended to reduce the likelihood of another crisis similar to that of LTCM and, perhaps more important, to reduce the impact of such an event on market stability.

23. See, e.g., Procter & Gamble example (footnote 6).

The New Regulatory and Corporate Environment

1. INTRODUCTION

In Chapter 1 we discussed the importance of the regulatory environment to the development of risk management in financial institutions. In this chapter, we take the story one step further by explaining how sophisticated methodologies in risk management are starting to become part of the new regulatory and corporate risk environment.

First, though, we need to ask a fundamental question. Regulators impose a unique set of minimum required regulatory capital rules on commercial banks. Why do they do so?

Banks collect deposits and play a key role in the payment system. While the deposits are often insured by specialized institutions (such as the Federal Deposit Insurance Corporation or FDIC[1] in the United States, the Canadian Deposit Insurance Corporation or CDIC in Canada, etc.), in effect national governments act as a guarantor for commercial banks; some also act as a lender of last resort. National governments therefore have a very direct interest in ensuring that banks remain capable of meeting their obligations: they wish to limit the cost of the "safety net" in the case of a bank failure.[2] This is one reason why the amount of capital retained by a bank is regulated. By acting as a buffer against unanticipated losses, regulatory capital helps to privatize a burden that would otherwise be borne by national governments.

Moreover, in banking it seems that capital structure matters more than in other industries because of the importance of confidence to banks, and to the financial services industry in general. Regulators try to make sure that banks are well enough capitalized to avoid any "systemic effect," whereby an individual bank failure would propagate to the rest of the financial system. Such a "domino effect" would disrupt world economies and incur heavy social costs. The problem here is that banks often act as the transmission belt on which setbacks in the financial sector are transmitted to the wider economy.

However, fixed-rate deposit insurance itself creates the need for capital regulation because of the moral hazard and adverse selection problems that it generates. Under current regulations, insured banks have an incentive to assume relatively more risk than if they were uninsured. This is because fixed-rate (non-risk-based) deposit insurance is akin to a put option sold by the government to banks at a fixed premium, independent of the riskiness of their assets. As the rate is fixed, this option increases in value as the bank's assets become riskier.[3] Moreover, as deposits are insured, there is no incentive for depositors to select their bank cautiously. Instead, depositors may be tempted to look for the highest deposit rates, without paying enough attention to a bank's creditworthiness.

Prior to the implementation in 1992 of the 1988 Basle Accord, bank capital was regulated by imposing uniform minimum capital standards. These were applied to banks regardless of their individual risk profiles, and the off-balance-sheet positions and commitments of each bank were simply ignored. The increased international competition among banks during the 1980s emphasized how inconsistently banks were regulated with regard to capital. Japanese bank regulations contained no formal capital adequacy requirements, while in the United States and the United Kingdom banks were required to finance more than 5 percent of their risky assets by means of equity.

The major increase in off-balance-sheet activity by banks that took place in the 1980s altered the risk profile of banks, while the regulatory requirements concerning equity ratios remained the same. The 1988 Basle Accord (known also as the 1988 BIS Accord, or the "Accord") established international minimum capital guidelines that linked banks' capital requirements to their credit exposures. The Accord was intended to raise capital ratios, which were generally perceived as too low. It was also intended to harmonize minimum capital ratios. However, the regulators focused primarily on credit risk, and ignored market risk and other risks.

More recently, the "1996 Amendment" extended the initial Accord to include risk-based capital requirements for the market risks that banks incur in their trading accounts.[4]

Under the Accord and its Amendment, banks are currently required to satisfy three capital adequacy standards: first, a maximum assets to capital multiple of 20; second, an 8 percent minimum ratio of eligible capital to risk-weighted assets;[5] and third, a minimum capital charge to compensate for market risk of traded instruments on and off the balance sheet.

In addition to these capital adequacy requirements, the Bank for International Settlements (BIS) has set limits on concentration risks. Risks that exceed 10 percent of the bank's capital must be reported, and banks are forbidden to take positions that are greater than 25 percent of the bank's capital without explicit approval by their local regulator.[6] In addition to incorporating market risk, the 1996 Amendment officially consecrates the use of internal models based on the value-at-risk (VaR) methodology to assess market risk exposure. (VaR modelling is discussed in detail in Chapter 5.)

The international regulators clearly intend to encourage banks to develop their own proprietary risk measurement models to assess regulatory, as well as economic, capital. The advantage for the banks should be a substantial reduction in regulatory capital, and a more accurate allocation of capital that reflects the actual risk embedded in their positions, compared to the capital charge arising from the standardized approach proposed by BIS. However, to benefit from this capital relief, the 1996 Amendment made it clear that banks must implement a risk management infrastructure that is fully integrated with their daily risk management—in particular, with their setting of trading limits and their risk monitoring of operations. It is not enough for banks to develop sophisticated analytical approaches to measure and report regulatory capital. The bank's risk managers and traders should themselves use these analytical approaches to monitor their positions and their risk limits.

This more qualitative concern with the infrastructure and application of risk measurement and management techniques can be traced back to recommendations of a seminal report published by the Group of Thirty (G-30) in 1993. Section 2 of this chapter discusses these Group of Thirty recommendations, and prepares the ground for the more detailed discussion of how to structure the price risk management functions of a bank provided in Chapter 3.

Section 3 of this present chapter discusses the original 1988 BIS Accord. Section 4 introduces the 1996 Amendment which became mandatory in January 1998 and which is therefore now known as "BIS 98"; again, this section prepares the reader for the more detailed comparison of the BIS 98 standardized approach versus the internal models approach provided in Chapter 4. As that chapter demonstrates, the difference in capital charges between the two approaches is so considerable that banks subject to the standardized approach may face a severe competitive disadvantage.

Finally, in Section 5 we discuss a consultative paper, released in June 1999 by the Basle Committee on Banking Supervision. This paper proposes a New Capital Adequacy Framework to replace the 1988 Accord. This consultative paper will probably go through many amendments before it becomes the new BIS 2000+ Accord. We also review the Group of 12 recommendations for the improvement of counterparty risk management practices in the light of the severe market disruptions of August 1998—and the near-collapse of the hedge fund Long-Term Capital Management (LTCM).

2. GROUP OF THIRTY (G-30) POLICY RECOMMENDATIONS

In 1993 the Group of Thirty (G-30) published a report that described 20 best-practice price risk management recommendations for dealers and end-users of derivatives, and four recommendations for legislators, regulators, and supervisors. The report was put together by a G-30 working group composed of a diverse cross-section of end-users, dealers, academics, accountants, and lawyers involved in derivatives. Their work was based in part on a detailed survey of industry practice among 80 dealers and 72 end-users worldwide, involving both questionnaires and in-depth interviews.

The policy recommendations in the G-30 report were the first comprehensive industry-led effort to take stock of what the industry had learned, and to broaden awareness of the more successful approaches to price risk management. The G-30 focussed on providing practical guidance in terms of managing derivatives businesses. The recommendations also offered a benchmark against which participants could measure their own price risk management practices.

2.1 Recommendations

The G-30 recommendations for dealers and end-users can be categorized into general policies, market risk policies, credit risk policies, enforceability policies, infrastructure policies, and accounting and disclosure policies (Table 2.1). Note that the terms "dealer" and "end-user" in the report do not refer to particular types of institutions, but rather to the nature of their derivatives activity. A bank, for instance, may participate both as a dealer and as an end-user. Likewise, some corporate end-users of derivatives may also be involved as dealers.

2.2 General Policies

The first G-30 recommendation relates to the role of senior management. Senior management plays a key role in ensuring that risk is controlled in a manner consistent with the overall risk management and capital policies approved by their Board of Directors. Clearly, these policies should be reviewed as business and market circumstances change.

Specifically, the G-30 recommended that "policies governing derivatives use should be clearly defined, including the purposes for which these transactions are to be undertaken. Senior management should approve procedures and controls to implement these policies, and management at all levels should enforce them."

2.3 Market Risk Policies

The G-30 felt strongly that entities should have an independent market risk management function (Recommendation 8). Specifically, the G-30 stated, that "dealers should have a market risk management function with clear independence from the position management function." Further, they stated that "dealers should have

TABLE 2.1

Taxonomy of G-30 Recommendations

General policies	1. The role of senior management
Market risk (valuation, measurement, and management)	2. Marking-to-market
	3. Market valuation methods
	4. Identifying revenue sources
	5. Measuring market risk
	6. Stress simulations
	7. Investing and funding forecasts
	8. Independent market risk management
	9. Practices by end-users
	10. Measuring credit exposure
Credit risk (measurement and management)	11. Aggregating credit exposures
	12. Independent credit risk management
	13. Master agreements
	14. Credit enhancement
Enforceability	15. Promoting enforceability
Infrastructure (systems, operations, and controls)	16. Professional expertise
	17. Systems
	18. Authority
Accounting and disclosure	19. Accounting practices
	20. Disclosures
Recommendations for legislators, regulators, and supervisors	21. Recognizing netting
	22. Legal and regulatory uncertainties
	23. Tax treatment
	24. Accounting standards

a market risk management function with clear independence and authority."

The G-30 also stressed the importance of measuring market risk in terms of a VaR measure (Recommendation 5), as well as the importance of stress testing (Recommendation 6). Specifically, the G-30 pointed out that "dealers should use a consistent measure to calculate daily the market risk." The G-30 also stressed that the VaR should be compared to market risk limits. The G-30 encouraged stress testing by pointing out that "dealers should regularly perform simulations to determine how their portfolios would perform under stress conditions."

The G-30 further recommended that institutions should ensure that the mark-to-market process (Recommendation 2), is rigorously conducted. Specifically, the G-30 pointed out that dealers "should mark their derivatives positions to market at least on a daily basis for risk management purposes." The G-30 did not provide specific guidance on how to mark a portfolio to market, but they did provide broad market valuation guidelines (Recommendation 3). For example, they pointed out that "derivatives portfolios should be valued at mid-market levels less specific adjustment. Mid-market valuation adjustment should allow for expected future costs such as unearned credit spread, close-out costs, investing and funding costs, and administrative costs."

The G-30 stressed the importance of identifying revenue sources (Recommendation 4) in terms of managing market risk. For example, the G-30 stated that "dealers should measure the components of revenue regularly and in sufficient detail to understand the sources of risk."

The G-30 also emphasized that "dealers should periodically forecast the cash investing and funding requirements arising from their derivatives portfolios" (Recommendation 7).

2.4 Credit Risk Policies

The G-30 stated that dealers and end-users "should have a credit risk management function with clear independence and authority, and with analytical capabilities in derivatives" (Recommendation 12).

The G-30 also stated credit exposure should be measured for each derivative transaction, based on both current and potential credit exposure (Recommendation 10). The G-30 did not provide any specific guidance about how this calculation should be performed. Nevertheless, the G-30 pointed out the importance of aggregating credit exposures (Recommendation 11). For example, the G-30 pointed out that "credit exposures on derivatives, and all other credit exposures to a counterparty, should be aggregated, taking into consideration enforceable netting arrangements. Credit exposures should be calculated regularly and compared to credit limits."

The G-30 also provided recommendations on credit enhancement (Recommendation 14). They recommended that dealers and end-users "should assess both the benefits and the costs of credit enhancement and related risk-reduction arrangements."[7] The G-30 also pointed out that if credit downgrades trigger early termination or collateral requirements, then participants should carefully consider their own capacities, and those of their counterparties, to meet the potentially substantial funding needs that might result.

Trigger provisions based on downgrade or other adverse changes have the potential to create sudden and sizeable liquidity requirements. An alternative procedure that limits this risk of unexpected liquidity crises is the periodic cash settlement of the underlying exposure (see Chapter 12).

2.5 Operational Risk Policies

The G-30 emphasized the control of operational risk. For example, the G-30 emphasized the importance of hiring skilled professionals. Specifically, the G-30 pointed out (Recommendation 16) that one should "ensure that derivatives activities are undertaken by professionals in sufficient number and with the appropriate experience, skill levels, and degrees of specialization."

The G-30 stressed the importance of building best-practice systems (Recommendation 17). They pointed out that one should "ensure that adequate systems for data capture, processing, settlement, and management reporting are in place so that derivatives transactions are conducted in an orderly and efficient manner in compliance with management policies." For example, the G-30 pointed out that dealers and end-users "should have risk management systems that measure the risks incurred in their derivatives activities based upon their nature, size, and complexity."

The G-30 (Recommendation 19) emphasized that accounting practices should highlight the risks being taken. For example, the G-30 pointed out that dealers and end-users "should account for derivatives transactions used to manage risks so as to achieve a consistency of income recognition treatment between those instruments and the risks being managed."

These 20 recommendations constitute the backbone of the qualitative requirements of the 1996 BIS Amendment, as we discuss in Chapter 4.

3. THE 1988 BIS ACCORD: THE "ACCORD"

International risk-based capital adequacy standards rely on principles that are laid out in the "International Convergence of Capital Measurement and Capital Standards" document, published in July 1988 (cf. Basle 1988), or the "Accord." This Accord was initially developed by the Basle Committee on Banking Supervision, and later endorsed by the central bank governors of the Group of Ten (G-10) countries.[8] The approach is quite simple and somewhat arbitrary, and it has been the subject of much criticism. In fact, it is really only a first step in establishing a level playing field across member countries for internationally active banks.

It defined two minimum standards for meeting acceptable capital adequacy requirements: an assets-to-capital multiple and a risk-based capital ratio. The first standard is an overall measure of the bank's capital adequacy. The second measure focuses on the credit risk associated with specific on- and off-balance-sheet asset categories. It takes the form of a solvency ratio, known as the Cooke ratio, and is defined as the ratio of capital to risk-weighted on-balance-sheet assets plus off-balance-sheet exposures, where the weights are assigned on the basis of counterparty credit risk.

The scope of the Accord is limited since it does not address various complex issues related to capital adequacy, such as portfolio effects and netting. "Portfolio effects" is the term used to describe various benefits that arise when a portfolio is well diversified across issuers, industries, and geographical locations; naturally, a well-diversified portfolio is much less likely to suffer from massive credit losses than is a portfolio of deals concentrated with one party, one industry, and/or one geographical area.[9]

Netting is a legally enforceable agreement by means of which counterparties can offset their claims against each other on a replacement cost basis, recognizing only the net amount.[10] When there are netting agreements in place, the net exposure of the portfolio to a particular counterparty may be quite small.

The Accord also completely ignored the problem of setting aside capital adequacy for the tradable securities in the trading book. For example, government holdings were excluded from the capital calculations. In recognition of these drawbacks, the Basle Committee amended the Accord in 1996, as we discuss in Section 4. Interest risk in the banking book and other risks, such as liquidity and operational risks, were also disregarded.[11]

Below, we review the main features of the Accord on credit risk, as it stands today after several modifications.

3.1 The Assets-to-Capital Multiple

A simple test for determining the overall adequacy of a financial institution's capital is the assets-to-capital multiple. This is calculated by dividing the bank's total assets, including specified off-balance-sheet items, by its total capital. The off-balance-sheet items included in this test are direct credit substitutes (including letters of credit and guarantees), transaction-related contingencies, trade-related contingencies, and sale and repurchase agreements. All of these items are included at their notional principal amount.

At present, the maximum multiple allowed is 20. It is conceivable that a bank with large off-balance-sheet activities might trigger this multiple as the minimum capital requirement, but in general the assets-to-capital multiple is not the binding constraint on a bank's activities.

3.2 The Risk-Weighted Amount Used to Compute the Cooke Ratio

In determining the Cooke ratio, it is necessary to consider both the on-balance-sheet as well as specific off-balance-sheet items. On-balance-sheet items have risk weightings from zero percent for cash and OECD government securities to 100 percent for corporate bonds and others. Off-balance-sheet items are first expressed as a credit equivalent (see Section 3.3), and then are appropriately risk-weighted by counterparty. The risk-weighted amount is then the sum of the two components: the risk-weighted assets for on-balance-sheet instruments and the risk-weighted credit equivalent for off-balance-sheet items. Table 2.2 gives the risk capital weights

TABLE 2.2

Risk Capital Weights by Broad On-Balance-Sheet Asset
Category (WA)

Risk Weights (%)	Asset Category
0	Cash and gold bullion, claims on OECD governments such as Treasury bonds or insured residential mortgages.
20	Claims on OECD banks and OECD public sector entities such as securities issued by U.S. government agencies or claims on municipalities.
50	Uninsured residential mortgages.
100	All other claims such as corporate bonds and less-developed country debt, claims on non-OECD banks, equity, real estate, premises, plant and equipment.

(WA) by asset categories, and Table 2.3 shows the weights that apply to credit equivalents by type of counterparty (WCE).

Risk-weighted amount

$$= \sum \text{Assets} * \text{WA} + \sum \text{Credit equivalent} * \text{WCE}$$

There is an apparent inconsistency between Table 2.2 and Table 2.3, since the risk weight for corporate assets as they relate to off-balance instruments is half that required for on-balance-sheet assets. BIS's rationale for this asymmetry is the better quality of the corporations that participate in the market for off-balance-sheet products. It is true that there was a time when only the most

TABLE 2.3

Risk Capital Weights for Off-Balance-Sheet
Credit Equivalents by Type of Counterparty
(WCE)

Risk Weights (%)	Type of Counterparty
0	OECD governments
20	OECD banks and public sector entities
50	Corporations and other counterparties

financially sophisticated corporations entered the world of derivatives, but this is no longer the case.

3.3 Calculation of the Credit Equivalent for Off-Balance-Sheet Exposures

3.3.1 The Case of Nonderivative Exposures
A conversion factor applies, as the notional amount of these instruments is not always representative of the true credit risk that is being assumed; the value of the conversion factor is set by the regulators at somewhere between zero and 1, depending on the nature of the instrument (Table 2.4). The resulting credit equivalents are then treated exactly as if they were on-balance-sheet instruments.

3.3.2 The Case of Derivative Positions Such as Forwards, Swaps, and Options
The Accord recognizes that the credit risk exposure of long-dated financial derivatives fluctuates in value. The Accord methodology estimates this exposure by supplementing the current marked-to-market value with a simple measure of the projected future risk exposure.

TABLE 2.4

Credit Conversion Factors for Nonderivative Off-Balance-Sheet Exposures

Conversion Factor (%)	Off-Balance-Sheet Exposure Factor
100	Direct credit substitutes, bankers' acceptances, standby letters of credit, sale and repurchase agreements, forward purchase of assets.
50	Transaction-related contingencies such as performance bonds, revolving underwriting facilities (RUFs), and note issuance facilities (NIFs).
20	Short-term self-liquidating trade-related contingencies such as letters of credit.
0	Commitments with an original maturity of one year or less.

FIGURE 2.1

Calculation of the BIS Risk-Weighted Amount for Derivatives

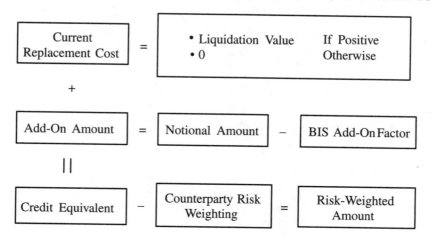

Calculation of the BIS risk-weighted amount for derivatives proceeds in two steps, as shown in Figure 2.1. The first step involves computing a credit equivalent amount, which is the sum of the current replacement cost when it is positive (and zero otherwise), and an add-on amount that approximates future replacement costs.

The current replacement value of a derivative is its marked-to-market or liquidation value, when that value is positive. (When the value is negative, the institution is not exposed to default risk as the replacement cost of the contract is zero.)

The add-on amount is computed by multiplying the notional amount of the transaction by the BIS required add-on factor, as shown in Figure 2.1. In Table 2.5, five categories of underlying are considered, i.e., interest rate, exchange rate and gold, equity, precious metals except gold, and other commodities. The add-on factor differs quite substantially from one category to another, although the rationale for such differences is not always clear.

Interest rate contracts include single-currency interest rate swaps, basis swaps, forward rate agreements and products with similar characteristics, interest rate futures, and purchased interest rate options. Exchange rate contracts include gold contracts (which

TABLE 2.5

Add-on Factors by Type of Underlying and Maturity

Residual Maturity	Interest Rate (%)	Exchange Rate and Gold (%)	Equity (%)	Precious Metals Except Gold (%)	Other Commodities (%)
One year or less	0.0	1.0	6.0	7.0	10.0
Over one year to five years	0.5	5.0	8.0	7.0	12.0
Over five years	1.5	7.5	10.0	8.0	15.0

are treated in the same way as exchange rate contracts), cross-currency swaps, cross-currency interest rate swaps, outright forward foreign exchange contracts, and purchased currency options.

Equity contracts include those based on individual stocks as well as those based on equity indices. Table 2.5 also lists the add-on factors for precious metals contracts (except for gold), and contracts on other commodities, such as energy products, agricultural commodities, and base metals (aluminum, copper, and zinc). For equities and commodities the add-ons apply to forwards, swaps, and purchased options.

For example, a $100 million five-year interest rate swap would have an add-on amount of $0.5 million, i.e., 0.5 percent × $100 million, where 0.5 percent is the add-on factor given in Table 2.5 for this instrument.

The credit equivalent amount can be interpreted as an on-balance-sheet amount for regulatory purposes. Unfortunately, the BIS approach fails to distinguish between the credit risk of plain vanilla swaps and that of more volatile structures, such as highly leveraged swaps. The difficulties that can arise with respect to the latter have led to some highly public disputes, e.g., the $200 million five-year leveraged interest rate swap that Bankers Trust entered into with Procter & Gamble.[12]

The second step in the BIS calculation consists of calculating the amount of regulatory capital that is related to credit risk exposure. It is derived by simply multiplying the credit equivalent amount by the counterparty risk-weighting factor given in Table 2.3. The result of this calculation is the final risk-weighted amount.

3.4 Netting of Derivatives Positions

In 1995 the initial BIS agreement was modified to allow banks to reduce their "credit equivalent" totals provided that bilateral netting agreements are in place. According to some surveys, netting reduces the gross replacement value of a bank's credit exposure by, on average, half.

The BIS formula for add-on amounts became:

Add-on amount = notional * add-on factor * (40% + 60% * NPR)

The add-on factors are the same as in Table 2.5. NPR denotes the net replacement ratio, which is the net replacement cost when positive, or zero otherwise, divided by the gross replacement cost calculated as before, without taking into account netting, i.e., the sum of the positive replacement cost for the transactions covered by the netting agreement.

Note that the new BIS formula does not allow for *complete* offsetting even if netting agreements are in place. It is tempting to believe that the rationale favoring a minimum add-on amount stems from the legal risk that courts might find netting agreements unenforceable in certain jurisdictions or, if the netting agreements are upheld, that delays in reaching a settlement might negate the benefits of netting. However, this reasoning is not valid. Leading global financial institutions negotiated with the BIS, arguing that mature portfolios exhibit stable ratios of net to gross mark-to-market values. It was argued that 100 percent of this ratio should be allowed. The BIS did not agree that the ratio is stable in the long run and therefore imposed the 40 percent minimum add-on. In effect, the formula discounts the probable benefits of netting.

These calculations are performed by the counterparty, and then the counterparty risk weight is used to derive the risk-weighted amount. Table 2.6 illustrates the calculations using a simple example.

3.5 Capital and the Cooke Ratio

Banks are required to maintain a capital amount equal to at least 8 percent of their total risk-weighted assets (as calculated in the previous section). Capital, as defined by the Cooke ratio, is broader than equity capital. It has three components:

1. Tier 1, or core capital, which includes common stockholder's equity, noncumulative perpetual preferred stock, and minority equity interests in consolidated subsidiaries, less goodwill and other deductions.

2. Tier 2, or supplementary capital, which includes hybrid capital instruments, such as cumulative perpetual preferred shares and qualifying 99-year debentures. These instruments are essentially permanent in nature and have some of the characteristics of both equity and debt. Tier 2 capital also includes instruments with more limited lives, such as subordinated debt with an original average maturity of at least five years.

TABLE 2.6

Illustration of the Calculation of the Add-on and Risk-Weighted Amounts Including Netting

Risk Capital Weight	Add-on Factor	Counterparty A 20%			Counterparty B 50%		
		Notional Amount	Marked-to-Market Value	Add-on Amount 1988	Notional Amount	Marked-to-Market Value	Add-on Amount 1988
Transaction 1	0.5%	1,000	400	5	700	−100	3.5
Transaction 2	1.5%	500	−200	7.5	1,000	200	15
Transaction 3	5%	1,000	−100	50	500	−200	25
Add-on amount 1988 (A1988)				62.5			43.5
Gross replacement cost (GR)			400			200	
Net replacement cost (NR)			100			0*	
NPR (=NR/GR)			0.25			0	
Add-on amount 1995 (A1995)			34.375			17.4	
Credit equivalent			134.375			17.4	
Risk-weighted amount with netting			26.875			8.7	
Risk-weighted amount without netting			(400+62.5)×.2=92.5			(200+43.5)×.5=121.75	

A1995 = A1988 (0.4+0.6 NPR).

Credit equivalent=NR+A1995.

*Note that "negative" replacement cost for counterparty B cannot be used to offset positive replacement costs of counterparty A. This is why it is set to zero.

3. Following the 1996 Amendment to the original BIS Accord, banks can use a third tier of capital to cover market risk in the trading book (but not credit risk in the banking book). Tier 3, or sub-supplementary capital, consists of short-term subordinated debt with an original maturity of at least two years. It must be unsecured and fully paid up. It is also subject to lock-in clauses that prevent the issuer from repaying the debt before maturity, or even at maturity should the issuer's capital ratio become less than 8 percent after repayment. In Chapter 4 we review in some depth how tier 3 capital can be allocated against market risk for the trading book.[13]

According to the original Accord, tier 1 and tier 2 capital should represent at least 8 percent of the risk-weighted assets, to protect the bank against credit risk. At least 50 percent of this amount must take the form of tier 1 capital.

In practice, capital levels of regulated banks tend to exceed these minimum requirements. In 1997 the risk-based capital ratios for six large banks all exceeded the minimum 8 percent total requirement, as shown in Table 2.7. In addition, at all of these banks the ratios for tier 1 capital exceeded the 4 percent minimum requirement. According to regulatory officials, the risk-based capital ratios of almost all U.S. banks exceed the minimum required level. Interestingly, on average the top 50 insured commercial banks in the United States already finance in excess of 2 percent their risk-weighted assets by means of subordinated debt.[14]

4. THE "1996 AMENDMENT" OR "BIS 98"

In April 1995 the Basle Committee issued a consultative proposal to amend the Accord which became known as the "1996 Amendment" or, after it was implemented, "BIS 98." This proposal was adopted by the U.S. regulatory agencies in July 1995, and became mandatory for all U.S. financial institutions with significant trading activities as of January 1, 1998.[15] It requires financial institutions to measure and hold capital to cover their exposure to the "market risk" associated with debt and equity positions in their trading books, and foreign exchange and commodity positions in both the trading and banking books.[16] These positions include all financial instruments that are marked-to-market, whether they are

TABLE 2.7

Risk-Based Capital Ratios for Six Large Holding
Companies, as of December 31, 1997

	Dollars in Billions			
	Total Risk-Based Capital		Tier 1 Risk-Based Capital	
Bank Holding Company	**Dollar Amount**	**Percentage of Total Risk-Weighted Assets**	**Dollar Amount**	**Percentage of Total Risk-Weighted Assets**
BankAmerica Corporation	$26.6	11.6%	$17.3	7.5%
Bankers Trust New York Corp.	11.0	14.1	6.4	8.3
Canadian Imperial Bank of Commerce*	14.5	9.8	10.2	7.0
The Chase Manhattan Corp.	33.3	11.6	22.6	7.9
Citicorp	31.1	12.3	21.1	8.3
First Chicago NBD Corp.	12.7	11.7	8.5	7.9

Note: All figures rounded.

*The fiscal year for the Canadian Imperial Bank of Commerce ended on October 31, 1997. The capital ratios in the table above for the Canadian Imperial Bank of Commerce were calculated using regulatory guidelines for Canadian banks. Under U.S. rules, its ratios would have been 8.8 percent for total capital and 6.4 percent for tier 1 capital.

Source: GAO (1998) and 1997 Annual Reports.

plain vanilla products such as bonds or stocks, or complex derivative instruments such as options, swaps, or credit derivatives. Marking financial instruments to market must be performed for both accounting and management purposes.

The most significant risk arising from the nontrading activities of financial institutions is the credit risk associated with default. The Accord treated all instruments equivalently, whether they reside in the trading or banking book. The 1996 Amendment introduced the requirement of measuring market risk, in addition to credit risk, in the trading book. The initial Accord continues to apply to the nontraded items both on-balance-sheet and off-balance-sheet, as well as to off-balance-sheet over-the-counter (OTC) derivatives. Market risk must be measured for both on- and off-balance-sheet traded instruments. However, on-balance-sheet assets are subject to the market risk capital charge only, while off-balance-sheet derivatives, such as swaps and options, are subject to both the market risk charge, and to the credit risk capital charges stipulated in the original 1988 Accord.

To summarize, a bank's overall capital requirement is now the sum of the following:

- Credit risk capital charge, as proposed in the initial 1988 Accord, which applies to all positions in the trading and banking books, as well as OTC derivatives and off-balance-sheet commitments, but which excludes debt and equity traded securities in the trading book, and all positions in commodities and foreign exchange.

- Market risk capital charge for the instruments of the trading book, on as well as off the balance sheet.[17]

In BIS 98 the authorities recognized the complexity of correctly assessing market risk exposure, especially for derivative products. Flexibility in the modeling of the many components of market risk is thus allowed. The most sophisticated institutions—i.e., those that already have an independent risk management function in place, with sound risk management practices—are permitted to choose between their own "internal VaR model," referred to as the "internal models approach," and the "standard model" proposed by BIS, referred to as the "standardized approach," to determine the regulatory capital that they need to set aside to cover market risk.

The new capital requirement related to market risk is largely offset by the fact that the capital charge calculated under the 1988 Accord to cover credit risk no longer needs to be held for on-balance-sheet securities in the trading portfolio. The capital charge for general market risk and specific risk should, on aggregate, be much smaller than the credit risk capital charge for large trading books. Also, banks adopting the internal models approach should realize substantial capital savings, in the order of 20 to 50 percent, depending on the size of their trading operations and the type of instruments they trade. This is because internal models can be designed to capture diversification effects by realistically modeling the correlations between positions. The standardized model designated in BIS 98 does not attempt to model correlations accurately in this way.[18]

The internal models approach provides for greater disclosure of trading market risks than the BIS 98 standardized model. For example, internal models make use of the fact that market risk is made up of both "systematic risk" and "specific risk," and distinguish between these risk components. Systematic risk, which is sometimes called "general market risk," refers to changes in market value resulting from broad market movements. Specific risk, on the other hand, refers mainly to idiosyncratic or credit risk. It is the risk of an adverse price movement due to idiosyncratic factors related to the individual issuer of the security.

Highly concentrated portfolios, which have a great deal of specific risk, as shown on the left-hand side of Figure 2.2, contain products that are highly correlated with one another. The more diversified a portfolio, the greater the ratio of systematic to specific risk and vice versa.

The regulatory capital charge for banks using internal models for both general market risk and specific (credit) risk is set according to the following:

[3 * (10 *day Market Risk VaR*)

$$+ \; 4 * (10 \; day \; Specific \; Risk \; VaR)]* \; \frac{trigger}{8}$$

FIGURE 2.2

Systemic Risk, Specific Risk, and the Level of Diversification

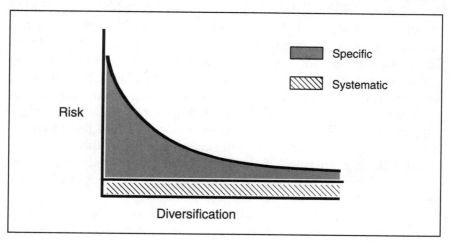

A two-tier multiplier system applies:

- The multipliers of 3 and 4, which apply to market risk and credit risk, respectively, reward the quality of the models. In fact these values of 3 and 4 are the minimum values that banks can currently expect. The regulators may decide to set the multipliers anywhere between 3 and 4, and 4 and 5, depending on how well the models capture the various aspects of market and credit risk, respectively.
- The trigger is related to the quality of the control process in the bank. This trigger is set to 8 for all banks in North America, while it currently varies between 8 and in the neighborhood of 25 in the United Kingdom.[19]

4.1 BIS 98 Qualitative Requirements

Before an institution can become eligible to use its own internal VaR model to assess the regulatory capital related to market risk, it must put sound risk management practices in place. This "best practice" risk management satisfies the standards set out in the G-30 recommendations discussed in Section 2. The institution should have a strong risk management group which is independent from the business units that it monitors, and which reports directly to the senior executive management of the institution. The main features of a prototype risk management organization are discussed in Section 4.2.

The internal model should not be used only for calculating regulatory capital, but should be fully integrated into the daily risk management of the institution. Models should also be used to set limits, allocate economic capital to business units, and measure performance via risk-adjusted return on capital (RAROC) calculations (as explained in Chapter 14). In addition the regulators require that systematic backtesting and stress testing be conducted on a regular basis, in order to test the robustness of the internal model to various extreme market conditions and crises. Improvements should be implemented if the model fails to pass the tests, e.g., when backtesting reveals that trading losses are happening more frequently than the VaR calculation would suggest.

Implementing a VaR model is a significant endeavor. The aim, ultimately, is to build a truly integrated, global, real-time system that records all positions centrally in a data warehouse, and which maps these positions in terms of their "risk factors;" as we explain in more detail in Chapter 5, risk factors are a vital component of the VaR calculation. Part of the challenge of implementing such a system is ensuring that the model inputs, and therefore the risk measures, are reliable and accurate:

- A formal vetting system is needed to approve the models and their modifications, assumptions, and calibration.
- Model parameters should be estimated independently of the trading desks to avoid the temptation by the traders to "fudge" volatility numbers and other key parameters to make their positions smaller.
- The financial rates and prices which feed the risk management system should come from sources independent of the front office, and be located in a financial database independently controlled by risk management.

4.2. Best-Practice Risk Management

The Board and the bank's senior management have the primary responsibility to ensure that the bank implements a best-practice risk management system. "Best practice" can be usefully discussed in relation to the G-30 recommendations listed earlier in this chapter.

Senior managers play a critical role in establishing a corporate culture in which best-practice risk management can flourish. They need to encourage the implementation of best-practice risk management in order to control risk and provide the appropriate risk oversight for their dealing rooms. Dealers and risk management personnel will ultimately behave in a way that is related to the rewards offered to them by senior management. A challenge for senior management is to harmonize the behavior patterns of dealers and risk managers, and to create an environment in which both sides cooperate.

The trade-off between maximizing short-term revenue and the incremental expense required to control risk requires delicate balancing. To achieve best-practice risk management banks will often have to invest in longer-term risk management projects whose benefits will not accrue for several years. Significant pressure to build revenue in lean years often serves to discourage this kind of long-term investment. Instead, the risk manager in low-corporate governance banks is typically asked to install necessary risk controls for the "least possible" cost. Unfortunately, short-term revenue maximization is often diametrically opposite to the behavior required to encourage first-class risk management.

Senior management in banks must make sure that risk managers are skilled so that compensation systems between dealers and risk managers can be harmonized. Risk managers themselves need to be adequately rewarded if the bank is to attract the best talents to its risk management function. Otherwise, talent will simply flow from the risk management function to the business functions.

Many organizations dealing in financial instruments have not invested in establishing appropriate policies or in developing appropriate risk methodologies. Chapter 3 offers an overview of the kind of organizational environment that facilitates best-practice risk management. Specifically, Chapter 3 presents the framework for risk management in terms of "three pillars": best-practice policies, best-practice methodologies, and best-practice infrastructure.

Senior managers need to encourage the development of integrated systems that aggregate the various risks (market risk, credit risk, liquidity risk, operational risk, etc.) generated by their businesses in a consistent framework across the institution. This may be a necessary condition to obtain regulatory approval of internal models. An environment where each business unit calculates their risk separately with different rules will not provide a meaningful oversight of firm-wide risk. The increasing complexity of products, the linkages between markets, and the potential benefits offered by portfolio effects are pushing risk-literate organizations toward standardizing and integrating their risk management. Dealers and risk managers need an integrated price risk management capability to ensure that their returns (net profits) outweigh the risks that they take.

5. THE BIS 2000$^+$ ACCORD

The BIS 1988 rules are generally acknowledged to be flawed. First, as we noted earlier, the Accord does not address complex issues such as portfolio effects, even though credit risk in any large portfolio is bound to be partially offset by diversification across issuers, industries, and geographical locations. For example, a bank is required to set aside the same amount of regulatory capital for a single $100 million corporate loan as for a portfolio of 100 different and unrelated $1 million corporate loans.

Second, the current rules assume that a loan to a corporate counterparty generates five times the amount of risk as does a loan to an OECD bank, regardless of their respective creditworthiness. For example, a loan to General Electric Corporation, an AAA-rated entity, has to be supported by five times as much regulatory capital as a similar loan to a Mexican (BB) or Turkish bank (B). General Electric is also considered to be infinitely more risky than the sovereign debt of Turkey or Mexico. Clearly, this is the opposite of what one might think appropriate.

Third, regulatory rules assume that all corporate borrowers pose an equal credit risk. For example, a loan to an AA-rated corporation requires the same amount of capital as a loan to a B-rated credit. This is also clearly inappropriate.

Fourth, revolving credit agreements[20] with a term of less than one year do not require any regulatory capital, while a short-term facility with 366 days to maturity bears the same capital charge as any long-term facility. The bank is clearly at risk from offering short-term facilities, yet so long as the term is less than one year no regulatory capital is required. This has led to the creation of the "364-day facility," by means of which some banks commit to lend for 364 days only, although the facility is then continuously rolled over. Such a facility attracts no capital charge, even if the terms of the facility are such that if the commitment is cancelled, the obligor has the right to pay back the drawn amount over a number of years.

Finally, as we previously discussed, the Accord does not allow sufficiently for netting and does not provide any incentive for credit risk mitigation techniques such as the use of credit derivatives.

These shortcomings have produced a distorted assessment of actual risks and have led to a misallocation of capital. In some instances, they have even led financial institutions to take on too much risk. The problem is that as the definition of regulatory capital drifts further away from the bank's understanding of the economic capital needed to support a position, the bank faces a strong incentive to play the game of "regulatory arbitrage." Banks are tempted to incur lower capital charges while still incurring the same amount of risk by using financial engineering tricks such as securitization (through various types of collateralized debt obligations, or CDOs, and the use of credit derivatives). In the process, banks transfer high-grade exposures from their banking book to their trading book, or place them outside the banking system. This means that the quality of the assets remaining on the books of a bank deteriorates, defeating the purpose of the Accord.

These problems have led the banking industry to suggest that banks should be allowed to develop their own internal credit VaR models, in lieu of the 1988 BIS Accord. They would use these regulator-approved models to calculate the minimum required regulatory credit risk capital associated with traditional loan products located in the banking book. This would be the credit risk equivalent of the BIS 98 Accord we discussed earlier, which allowed banks to use approved internal models for determining the minimum required regulatory capital for market risk.

Over the last five years, a series of industry-sponsored credit VaR methodologies have been devised, including CreditMetrics (developed by investment bank JP Morgan) and CreditRisk+ (developed by Credit Suisse Financial Products, now Credit Suisse First Boston or CSFB). Credit VaR models have also been developed by various software and consultancy firms: The KMV approach to model expected default frequencies is now in use at many U.S. financial institutions, and has added much value in terms of advancing the practical utility of using a model-based approach to credit risk. All these models are reviewed in much more detail in Chapters 8, 9, and 10. Here, it is worth noting that a major challenge facing every model developer is to ensure that proprietary credit VaR formulas are comprehensible and practical enough to be accepted by the regulatory community.

With the advent of products such as credit derivatives, the financial community is moving towards valuing loans and loan-type products on a mark-to-model basis. Moreover, there is a trend toward applying quantification techniques similar to those used to measure market risk to the measurement of credit VaR—especially in the case of products whose value is mostly driven by changes in credit quality.

A related but separate challenge is to develop an integrated approach to calculating market VaR and credit VaR. For example, typically most financial institutions use one set of rules to value trading products and another set of rules to value loan products. The integration of market VaR and credit VaR is at the leading edge of a new wave of risk management. One model for an integrated risk measurement approach builds on the Black–Scholes theoretical framework and related work by Robert Merton. (Merton and Scholes won the Nobel Prize in Economics in 1997 for their work on the "valuation of contingent claims."[21]) Merton's model (1974) is becoming the industry-standard approach for the estimation of credit VaR; in fact, the CreditMetrics and KMV models we mentioned above both use Merton's model as the theoretical foundation for their credit VaR models.

Developing an integrated model will have important implications from both a risk transparency and a regulatory capital perspective as the banking industry moves into the twenty-first century. This is because simply adding market VaR to credit VaR to obtain total VaR, rather than developing an integrated model, greatly overstates the amount of risk. Summing the values ignores the interaction or correlation between market VaR and credit VaR. We expect that, over time, regulators will move to allow banks to use their own internal credit VaR model, in lieu of the standardized BIS 1988 rules. Eventually, they will also move toward an integrated risk model that encompasses both market VaR and credit VaR. From this point, it will be possible to envisage a truly integrated price risk framework that risk managers will be able to use to generate both regulatory capital and economic capital (Figure 2.3).

5.1 A New Capital Adequacy and Credit Risk Modeling Framework: The 1999 Consultative Papers

Global competition is now affecting banks in emerging market countries. Regulators need to make sure that the regulatory framework does not inadvertently drive a competitive wedge between G-10 and non-G-10 competing banks. Over, the last 10 years the risk profile of banks has changed dramatically. Its composition and complexity, and the methodologies used to describe risks, now make strong supervision and enhanced market discipline important complements to capital regulation.[22] Finally, the banks' regulators realize that there is an urgent need to revise the 1988

FIGURE 2.3

Integrated Risk Models

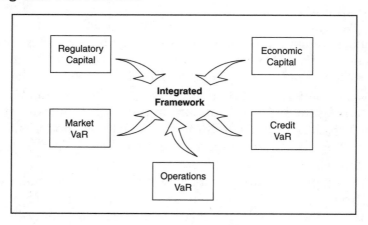

Accord to eliminate the kind of regulatory arbitrage we mentioned earlier. This can only be achieved by a better alignment of regulatory and economic capital.

Banks' regulators also recognize that the biggest risk facing commercial banks is the oldest risk of all, i.e., credit risk, rather than the risk of rogue traders losing fortunes in the capital markets. Recent high-profile trading losses, even including the significant losses to Barings Bank at the hands of Nick Leeson, amount to a few billion dollars. The damage caused by reckless lending at Credit Lyonnais in the 1980s amounted to more than $20 billion. The credit losses incurred by banks in Japan and East Asia will reach hundreds of billions of dollars.

In June 1999 the Basle Committee on Banking Supervision (BIS) issued a proposal for a new capital adequacy framework to replace the 1988 Accord. The consultation process with banks and various industry groups will continue until March 2000.

The objectives of the New Accord are to:

- Promote safety and soundness in the financial system by maintaining at least the same level of capital as banks maintain in today's system.[23]
- Enhance competitive equality. The new rules should not offer incentives for regulators in some countries to make

their rules more attractive to banks to attract investment in the industry in their country. Two banks with the same portfolios should hold the same capital wherever they are located.

- Constitute a more comprehensive approach to risks, to eliminate the criticisms of the 1988 Accord, and to cover more risk types such as interest rate risk in the banking book and operational risk.

- Focus on internationally active banks. However, the principles governing the approach should be suitable for application to banks of varying levels of complexity and sophistication.[24]

To achieve these objectives, the Basle Committee proposes a framework that rests on three pillars (Figure 2.4):

- Minimum capital requirements. The objective is to propose a new standardized approach: the default approach basing risk weights on available external credit ratings. The most sophisticated banks will be allowed to use alternative

FIGURE 2.4

The Three Pillars of the New Approach

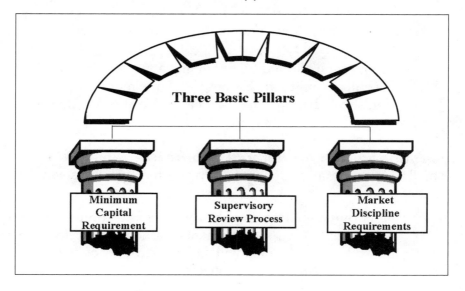

Three Basic Pillars

Minimum Capital Requirement

Supervisory Review Process

Market Discipline Requirements

models based on the use of their own internal credit ratings. Critical issues, however, include how to validate a bank's internal risk ratings and how to link risk weights to these internal ratings so as to ensure economically meaningful and reasonably consistent capital treatment of similar risks across banks. The most sophisticated banks may also be allowed to use portfolio credit models when data limitation and validation issues have been satisfactorily addressed.

- Supervisory review process to ensure that banks follow rigorous processes, measure their risk exposures correctly, and have enough capital to cover their risks. Regulatory arbitrage will be scrutinized.
- Market discipline as a lever to strengthen the safety and soundness of the banking system through better disclosure of capital levels and risk exposures, to help market participants to better assess the bank's ability to remain solvent.

5.1.1 The First Pillar: Minimum Capital Requirements

The new approach to minimum capital requirements can be thought of as a ladder with three rungs (Figure 2.5):

- An improved standardized approach.
- A kind of simplified modeling approach, based on the bank's internal ratings.
- A more sophisticated full modeling approach. In effect, this will extend to the banking book the more sophisticated approaches that banks are already allowed to use for their trading accounts.[25]

A. Standardized (or default) approach

The Basle Committee proposes to improve the 1988 BIS standardized approach by:

- Better differentiating among various credits through the use of external credit assessments, particularly for loans in the banking book; there will still be no provision to allow banks to capture portfolio effects.

FIGURE 2.5

Minimum Capital Requirements

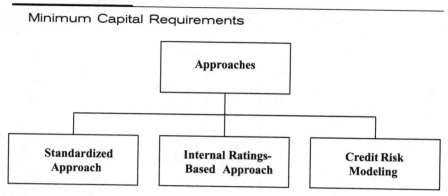

- Incorporating new risk categories, such as interest risk in the banking book and operational risk.
- Adding a capital charge for other risks such as liquidity, legal, and reputational risks.
- Better recognizing and factoring in credit mitigation techniques.

For credit risk, the new weighting scheme proposed for claims on sovereigns, banks, and corporations is summarized in Table 2.8, where the Standard & Poor's methodology has been chosen for the sake of illustration.

Claims on sovereigns

Claims on sovereign credits and central banks determined to be of the highest credit quality might be eligible for a zero-risk weight (AAA to AA, according to Standard & Poor's rating system). There are, however, some reservations about the performance of rating agencies in assessing the rating of borrowers that are less than ultra-prime credits. Export insurance agencies in the G-10 countries may be used as a dual source of credit assessment for sovereigns. Note that sovereigns, banks, and corporations rated below B+ receive a risk weight of 150 percent.[26]

Claims on banks

Two options are proposed for claims on banks. The first option attributes to claims on banks a risk weight that is based on the

TABLE 2.8

Risk Weights for Claims on Sovereigns, Banks, and Corporations, Based on Standard & Poor's Rating Methodology

Claim		AAA to AA−	A+ to A−	BBB+ to BBB−	BB+ to B−	Below B−	Unrated
				Assessment			
Sovereigns		0%	20%	50%	100%	150%	100%
Banks	Option 1[1]	20%	50%	100%	100%	150%	100%
	Option 2[2]	20%	50%[3]	50%[3]	100%[3]	150%	50%[3]
Corporations		20%	100%	100%	100%	150%	100%

[1]Risk weighting based on risk weighting of sovereign in which the bank is incorporated.

[2]Risk weighting based on the assessment of the individual bank.

[3]Claims on banks of a short original maturity, for example less than six months, would receive a weighting that is one category more favorable than the usual risk weight on the bank's claims.

weighting of the sovereign country in which the bank is incorporated. The weight is one notch less favorable than that applied to the sovereign, with a cap at 100 percent, except for claims on the lowest-rated banks (below B− in Standard & Poor's methodology), where the risk weight is set at 150 percent. For example, a claim on an AA bank would receive a risk weight of 20 percent, which corresponds to the risk weight of a sovereign of the credit category just below (i.e., A+ to A−).

The second option would be to use a rating assigned directly to the bank by an external rating agency. In this case, a maturity element is added to the framework. Claims on banks of a short original maturity, e.g., less than six months, would receive a risk weight that is one category more favorable than the usual risk weight on the bank's claim. For example, if a claim on a bank is normally weighted at 50 percent, a short-term claim on that bank would receive a risk weight of 20 percent. The floor on all banks' claims is 20 percent, and no claim on a bank could receive a risk weight less than that applied to its sovereign.

Claims on non-central-government public sector entities and securities firms would be weighted in the same way as claims on banks.

Claims on corporations

For claims on corporations, the new Accord proposes to retain a risk weight of 100 percent except for highly rated companies, i.e., those rated AAA to AA−. Highly rated companies would benefit from a lower risk weight of 20 percent. Short-term revolvers with a term of less than a year would be subject to a capital charge of 20 percent, instead of zero percent under the 1988 Accord. The new proposal would put highly rated corporate claims on the same footing as the obligations of bank- and government-sponsored enterprises.

What is not clear at this stage is whether the risk weights apply to the issuer rating or the facility rating. Naturally, the banking industry was hoping that there would be more granularity in the differentiation between corporate credits. In the proposed framework, an investment-grade firm rated A+ and a speculative firm rated BB+ would receive the same risk weight of 100 percent. Unfortunately, this proposal will not eliminate the current incentives for regulatory arbitrage. Figure 2.6 compares capital weights

Capital Weights According to the New Proposed Capital Accord Versus CIBC's Internal CreditVaR Model

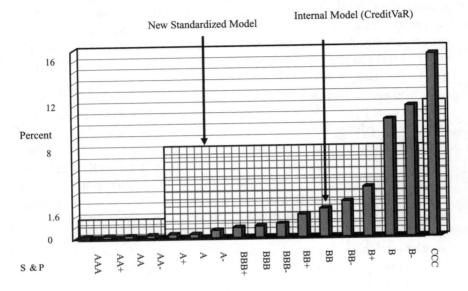

according to the new proposal to those generated by CIBC's internal credit value-at-risk model,[27] for a well-diversified portfolio of corporate loans. There is a huge discrepancy between the figures for economic capital produced by CIBC's internal model and the capital charges arising from the new BIS proposal.

Companies rated below B− would receive a risk weight of 150 percent, according to the proposals, while unrated companies would receive a 100 percent risk weight. This does not make much sense since there is no incentive for companies rated B− and below to obtain a rating. Clearly, the highest risk weight should apply to any firms that elect to remain unrated.

Loans secured by property

For loans secured by property the new Accord proposes a different treatment for residential mortgages, which would continue to be weighted at 50 percent, while mortgages on commercial real estate would, in principle, be attributed a 100 percent weighting of the loans secured.

Asset securitization

The new Accord addresses the issue of the credit quality of obligations secured on a pool of assets, and issued through the medium of special purpose vehicles (SPVs), provided these obligations have a credit rating. The Basle Committee proposes to use an external ratings-based approach to measure the relative exposure to credit risk and determine the associated risk weights. Those rated B+ or below, and the first loss positions, would be deducted from capital, or equivalently would be applied a risk weight of 1250 percent so that the capital charge is 100 percent, i.e., 12.5 *8 percent (Figure 2.7).

The tranches of the obligations that are rated below investment grade (BB+ and BB−) would receive a higher risk weight (i.e., 150 percent) than regular bond holdings with the same rating. This does not address the issue of regulatory arbitrage. The elimination of regulatory arbitrage will follow naturally from the convergence of economic and regulatory capital. Taxing the CLO tranches below investment grade may eliminate the use of securitization for regulatory arbitrage purposes, but will also discourage banks from using asset securitization to manage and mitigate credit risk.

Off-balance-sheet items

No changes are contemplated to the current treatment of off-balance-sheet items, except in the case of the credit conversion factors that apply to loan commitments (Table 2.9). Under the current

FIGURE 2.7

Asset Securitization

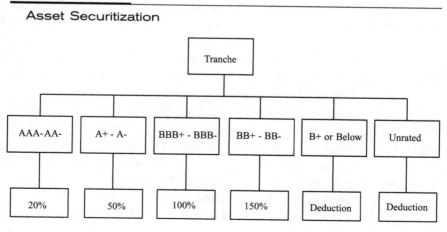

Table 2.9

Credit Conversion Factors for Loan Commitments

Current Treatment	Proposal
0% for original maturity of up to one year	20% for business commitments
0% for commitments that are unconditionally cancellable	0% for unconditionally cancellable commitments
50% for original maturity one year and over	

Accord banks can avoid any capital charge on loan commitments by structuring these commitments so that they run for a term of less than 365 days. The new proposals remove this loophole.

The Basle Committee is proposing to increase the short-term commitment risk weight to 20 percent unless the instrument is unconditionally cancellable or can be cancelled automatically by the bank without prior notice due to deterioration in the borrower's creditworthiness.

High-risk categories and other claims
There is a 150 percent risk weight for instruments rated below B−, whether these are issued by sovereigns, banks, or corporations, and securitization tranches that are rated BB+ and BB−.

For all other assets the 100 percent risk weighting would continue to apply.

Issues with external credit ratings
Moody's, Standard & Poor's, and most of the other rating agencies in the United States have a long and good track record for accurately rating investment-grade obligors. The industry track record is much shorter, and not as convincing, for the rating of sovereigns and corporations with sub-prime ratings. The Basle Committee has set out a list of criteria for eligible credit assessment institutions such as: objectivity, independence, transparency, credibility, resources, and recognition by the national supervisor.

The question also arises as to whether credit assessments might be produced using market data, such as credit spreads. Such an approach might rely on option pricing methodologies such as Merton (1974), Duffie and Singleton (1994), or Jarrow and Turnbull (1995).

B. Internal ratings-based approach

As of late 1999, the proposals for an internal ratings-based approach are still very sketchy. Before the proposals are refined, banks' internal rating systems will need to be examined more thoroughly, and the industry will need to evaluate various methodologies for linking capital requirements to internal ratings. For example, banks could map their internal rating categories to Moody's and Standard & Poor's rating systems and then to the standardized risk weights given in Table 2.8. This is not satisfactory as it would dilute all the proprietary information on individual obligors accumulated by banks. The Basle Committee could also design a capital charge that explicitly reflects banks' estimates of possible credit losses. A better approach would combine a bank's internal rating system and credit portfolio models to attribute capital to each facility on the basis of its risk contribution to the overall risk of the portfolio. The capital weights could be based on the average of the risk contributions for several well-diversified representative portfolios and the use of various well-established credit models. This would present the advantage of setting "standard" capital weights that capture some portfolio effects.[28]

While it makes a lot of sense to factor in the internal information that banks have on their counterparties, especially for small- to medium-sized companies, a way would have to be found of ensuring consistency in internal credit rating across different banks.

For example, the following issues would have to be addressed:

- What is the meaning of placing an entity in category xyz?
- Does it mean that the obligors in this category exhibit an expected default probability (EDF) within a prespecified range?
- Or, is the rating associated with an expected loss given default?
- What is the horizon over which these estimations are derived? For example, for the rating system to be consistent with the credit migration approach to modeling credit risk (as described in Chapter 8), each rating class

should correspond to a range of default probabilities over a one-year period.

The internal risk ratings-based approach has many practical implications for supervisors. Some key considerations will have to be addressed when assessing a bank's rating system:

- Are the number of gradations appropriate to the range of risks incurred by the bank?
- What is the role of the internal rating system in the management process? Credit ratings are a basis for regular risk reports to senior management and boards of directors. They are also the basis for continuous loan review processes, under which large credits are reviewed and regraded at least annually in order to focus attention on deteriorating credits well before they become problems.
- Is the rating process independent of credit approval and pricing functions? How often should the ratings be updated?
- How can regulators provide a linkage to the concept of "measurable loss," and how can they translate a rating into a capital charge? Should internal ratings be mapped into the regulatory bucketing scale (0 percent, 20 pecent, 50 percent, 100 percent, 150 percent) or into an expanded version of it?
- Are all appropriate risk factors incorporated?
- How can regulators compare different internal rating systems? For the new proposal to be applicable, and to maintain a level playing field, it will be necessary to ensure that internal rating systems across banks and countries are consistent with one another.
- How can regulators backtest an internal rating system? Do the losses behave as expected?

Notwithstanding these issues, the use of the internal ratings-based approach would pave the way to the adoption of full credit risk modeling for the banking book. It is a promising signal of the regulators' willingness to bring regulatory capital closer to economic capital.

C. Credit risk modeling
The Basle Committee issued a companion paper on April 21, 1999, analyzing current practices in credit risk modeling. This report as-

sesses the potential uses of credit risk models for supervisory and regulatory capital purposes.

Before any model can be approved to report regulatory capital for any asset class, the Committee would have to be confident that the model is being used to actively manage the risks, set limits, and allocate economic capital to the various business units. Unlike market risk, for which the measurement models are all essentially very similar, the underlying conceptual frameworks for models that measure credit risk are quite different. This raises some challenging issues:

- Are these models conceptually sound and do they capture accurately all the dimensions of credit risk?
- Do these models produce similar results for the same portfolios?[29]
- Are the data available to run these models, e.g., spread curves for different rating categories, recovery rates, usage given default, default probabilities and migration frequencies, and asset return correlations? In addition, credit data such as default probabilities are not stationary and vary with the credit cycle. The scarcity of data and their lack of accuracy in some instances underscores the need to better understand the models' sensitivity to structural assumptions and key parameters.
- How can credit VaR models be validated when the horizon is one year, and default data are so relatively scarce?[30] As a practical matter, empirically validating models might not be feasible. Instead, it might be more realistic and meaningful to validate input parameters and assumptions such as loss given default and default rates.[31]
- Can we feel comfortable with capital charges calculated by a model even when they differ substantially from those generated by the standardized approach?

While these issues constitute significant hurdles, regulators are strongly encouraging banks to start working on credit risk modeling for the banking book. Regulators recognize that only the credit risk modeling approach will allow banks to manage concentration risk in a portfolio context. Models offer the natural framework to assess the hedging efficiency of various credit risk mitigation techniques, such as the use of credit risk derivatives, in a portfolio context.[32]

Furthermore, only credit risk modeling can bring regulatory capital into closer alignment with the true riskiness of the underlying portfolio, and therefore with economic capital. Some regulators, such as the FSA (Financial Services Authority) in the United Kingdom, are committed to rewarding banks that use credit risk models for allocating economic capital to their loan book by reducing the trigger ratio which currently applies to the banking as well as the trading books.

D. Credit risk mitigation techniques

State-of-the-art credit risk management relies on credit mitigation techniques such as the use of collateral, guarantees, credit derivatives, and on-balance-sheet netting (Figure 2.8). The current Accord only partially recognizes collateral, guarantees, credit derivatives, and on-balance-sheet netting agreements (when they are legally enforceable).

The new proposal acknowledges the benefits that can be derived from the use of credit mitigation techniques and the key role they can play in active credit risk management. Just as foreign exchange derivatives allow corporations to transfer part of their foreign exchange risk exposure to third parties in the global markets, credit derivatives allow banks to achieve the same objective with regard to credit risk exposures. The end result should

FIGURE 2.8

Credit Mitigation Techniques

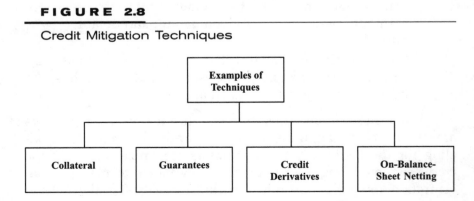

be a reduction in the concentrations of credit risk in the banking industry.

The issue of how to treat imperfect hedges needs to be addressed. Residual risks deriving from imperfect hedges take different forms, such as:

- Maturity mismatch when the hedging instrument expires before the underlying asset. Should regulators allow for recognition if there is a mismatch in maturities? In the case of credit derivatives, how should regulators account for the forward risk beyond the maturity of the derivative? Should regulators charge capital to cover this risk, or ignore it?

- Basis risk, e.g., when the exposure and the hedging instrument are subject to market risks that have different sensitivities, which could create a shortfall in the value of the hedge. For example, if the bank is using collateral, how should regulators account for liquidity risk? What level of "hair cut," or adjustment, should regulators apply?

- Asset mismatches can occur when an asset is hedged by means of a credit derivative that is referenced to an asset with different risk characteristics. How should regulators factor in correlation risk?

E. Treatment of other risks in the banking book: Interest rate risk and operational risk

The current BIS 88 Accord only explicitly recognizes *credit risk* in the banking book. The new Accord intends to expand risk coverage to incorporate other major sources of risks, namely interest risk in the banking book and operational risk. Other risks may be considered such as settlement risk, legal risk, reputational risk, and macroeconomic risks.

Simply adding together any capital charges related to these individual risks leads to an overestimation of the capital that is needed. The key question here is how banks can validate the level and nature of the portfolio effects that occur between risk classes.

Interest risk capital charges would only apply to banks where interest rate risks in the banking book are significantly above average ("outliers"). This raises the question of quantifying the duration of core deposits. The problem of how to define what we mean by outliers also needs to be worked out.

F. Consistency between the methodologies developed for the banking and trading books

The regulators will review the treatment of the trading account to ensure consistency with the methodologies developed for the banking book (in order to reduce the incentive for regulatory arbitrage). One interesting issue is how to incorporate liquidity risk into the risk measurement frameworks, so as to allow for a differing treatment of the various instruments in both the trading account and the banking book.

5.1.2 The Second Pillar: The Supervisory Review Process

The supervisory review process of capital adequacy should ensure that a bank's capital position and strategy are consistent with its overall risk profile. Early supervisory intervention will be encouraged if the capital is thought not to provide a sufficient buffer against risk.[33] The following principles are relevant to the supervisory review of a bank's capital adequacy.

Capital above regulatory minimum

Supervisors should have the ability to require banks to hold capital in excess of minimum regulatory ratios depending on a variety of factors such as the experience and quality of its management and control process, its track record in managing risks, the nature of markets in which the bank operates, and the volatility of its earnings. In assessing capital adequacy the regulators will have to consider the effects of business cycles and the overall macroeconomic environment, as well as the systemic impact on the banking system should the bank fail.[34]

One could envisage a system similar to that which the FSA has put in place, which makes use of an additional multiplier, the "trigger," which applies on the top of the minimum regulatory capital.

Before such a process could be implemented, regulators need to define a sound conceptual framework for the determination of banks' capital adequacy. The key questions here are: How can "soundness" be defined and quantified? What is the minimum acceptable soundness level, and how can regulators be sure that a bank operates above this minimum soundness level?

To be consistent with the RAROC methodology (as described in Chapter 14), soundness should be defined as the probability of insolvency over a one-year horizon. Minimum soundness then becomes the insolvency probability consistent with an investment-grade rating for the bank, i.e., BBB or better. Most banks currently target an insolvency probability of four to five basis points, which is consistent with an AA rating.

The danger of the proposed approach is that determinations of capital adequacy on a bank-by-bank basis will prove to be arbitrary and inconsistent.

Banks' internal assessment of capital adequacy

Under the new Accord, all internationally active banks will be expected to develop internal processes and techniques to carry out a self-assessment of their capital adequacy in relation to objective and quantifiable measures of risks. Banks should perform comprehensive and rigorous stress tests to identify possible events or changes in market conditions that could have an adverse effect on the bank.

The supervisory process

The new Accord will impose a close partnership between banks and their supervisors. Supervisors are expected to become familiar with the increasingly sophisticated techniques developed by the banks to assess and control their risks. They also should be involved in the development of those techniques.

It is clear that the position of banks' supervisor will become more challenging under the new proposal. Regulatory agencies should therefore engage in an active program of recruiting and educating their new generation of supervisors.

The supervisory intervention

The need for early intervention reflects the relatively illiquid nature of most bank assets and the limited options that banks have when they try to raise capital quickly.

5.1.3 The Third Pillar: Market Discipline

The Basle Committee intends to foster market transparency so that market participants can better assess bank capital adequacy. New requirements will be set regarding disclosures of capital levels, including details of capital structure and reserves for credit and other potential losses, risk exposures, and capital adequacy (Figure 2.9).

These recommendations are likely to follow the guidelines published in September 1998 by the Basle Committee on "Enhancing Bank Transparency." The Committee recommended that banks provide timely information across six broad areas: financial performance; financial position (including capital, solvency, and liquidity); risk management strategies and practices; risk exposures (including credit risk, market risk, liquidity risk, operational risk, legal risk, and other risks); accounting policies; and basic business, management, and corporate governance information. These disclosures should be made at least annually, and more frequently if necessary. These recommendations have also been adopted by the G-12.

Certain issues related to disclosure need to be addressed:

• Should the banks report risks using market-value accounting or risk-value accounting? These two methods may produce divergent figures. For example, a written option or a swap may have a zero marked-to-market value, while the potential future exposure of these instruments may be substantial.

• Effective disclosure cannot be achieved unless banks document internally their risk measurement and management procedures, such as internal credit rating process, measurement of loss distributions, and internal economic capital attribution. It is

FIGURE 2.9

Market Discipline

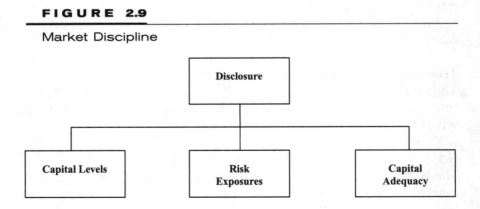

expected that these requirements will be enforced in the new regulatory review process.

• Shareholders and debt holders have divergent objectives, the interests of the debt holders being more aligned with the goals of the regulators. In this context, the Federal Reserve is contemplating obliging large banks to issue subordinated debt, a form of debt that is particularly effective in increasing market discipline. First of all, subordinated debt is the most junior of all bank liabilities. Therefore, these bondholders are the least likely to be bailed out in the event of bank failure, and the most likely to demand disclosures of a bank's condition. Second, subordinated debt holders do not participate in the upside gains associated with risk taking. Hence, the primary and secondary market spreads on subordinated debt should directly reflect the bank's expected default probability. The issues of who will buy these subordinated bonds and whether the market for these bonds be liquid enough for the spreads to be informative about the bank's actual probability of default still need to be addressed.

5.2 G-12 Recommendations for the Improvement of Counterparty Risk Management Practices

In January 1999 a group of 12 internationally active financial institutions, together with a number of other market participants including insurance companies, hedge funds, investment management companies, industry associations, and law firms, formed the "Counterparty Risk Management Policy Group" or what is now known as the "G-12."

The formation of the group was inspired by the near-collapse of the hedge fund Long-Term Capital Management (LTCM) during August 1998. In August 1998, after the Russian government had defaulted on its debt, liquidity suddenly evaporated from many financial markets, causing asset prices to plunge and producing large losses for many financial institutions. By September 1998 LTCM, which had built up huge market exposure by borrowing from major financial institutions, was on the brink of collapse. It was rescued only by means of a $3.6 billion cash injection. The cash came from 14 financial institutions coordinated by the Federal Reserve

Bank of New York.[35] The rescue was motivated by the fear that the collapse of LTCM would not only leave these institutions with heavy losses but would also threaten financial stability (Chapter 15 offers a more detailed discussion of the collapse of LTCM).

The objective of the G-12 was to make a comprehensive set of recommendations to reduce the likelihood of such events in the future and, perhaps more importantly, to reduce the impact of such events by improving the management of such failures. Some of the recommendations were intended to make it easier to liquidate a failed institution; this sent the message to the world that no financial institution is "too big to fail" anymore.

The recommendations published by the G-12 comprise a framework of six major building blocks:[36]

- Enhanced information sharing between counterparties, both prior to engaging in dealings likely to generate significant credit exposure, and on an ongoing basis. If banks are to improve information sharing they must address the issue of confidentiality, e.g., the net asset value of a fund, its liquidity position, detailed portfolio composition, and collateral margin calls.[37]

- Integrated analytical framework for evaluating the effects of leverage on market risk, funding arrangements and collateral requirements, asset liquidity risk, and credit risk. This framework should consider the interplay between these factors not only under normal market conditions but also under stressful conditions when the impact of leverage is magnified.

- Liquidation-based measures of potential counterparty credit exposures that integrate market, liquidity, and credit risk factors. The framework for stress testing should encompass liquidity, market, and credit risks in an integrated model. Mark-to-market replacement values should be supplemented by different measures of liquidation-based replacement values, which incorporate the potential for adverse price movements during the liquidation period. Limits should be set against these various exposure measures.

  Stress testing should assess concentration risk to both a single counterparty and to groups of counterparties, correlation risk among both market risk factors and credit risk factors, and the risk that by liquidating its positions the bank might move the market.

- Strengthen internal credit practices by factoring potential liquidation costs into limit-setting and collateral standards.
- Enhancements in the quality of information provided to senior management and Board of Directors. Senior management should convey clearly information on its overall tolerance for risks, including loss potential in adverse markets. This information should be approved by the Board of Directors.
- Voluntary disclosure of statistical information to the regulatory authorities as well as the market participants.[38]
- Improvements to, and harmonization of, standard industry documents, as well as better internal controls around documentation.

This report constitutes a tacit recognition that, in the past, standards have been inadequate. The LTCM crisis would have been unlikely to have reached such extreme proportions had all these safeguards and recommendations been in place at the time.

NOTES

1. The creation of the Federal Deposit Insurance Corporation (FDIC) in 1933 provided unconditional government guarantees for most bank creditors. The fixed-rate (non-risk-based) deposit insurance lowered market capital requirements by guaranteeing depositors repayment even if their bank failed. The original explicit deposit-insurance premium was fixed by law at one-twelfth of 1 percent of domestic deposits. Among other regulatory changes of the time, restrictions were placed on the interest rates that banks could pay on deposits. This provided an additional subsidy to banks that also made uninsured bank deposits safer, reducing further market capital requirements (see Berger et al. 1995).

2. The "safety net" refers to all government actions designed to enhance the safety and soundness of the banking system other than regulatory and enforcement of capital regulation, such as deposit insurance.

3. See Merton (1977) and Crouhy and Galai (1986, 1991).

4. It should be noted that both the Bank of England and SFA (now, the FSA) in the United Kingdom have had model-based market risk capital charges for many years under the Amsterdam Accord.

5. The precise definition of these capital ratios under the 1988 Accord and the new 1996 Amendment is discussed in Sections 3.1–3.5.

6. Ironically, had these rules been effective in 1994, Barings could not have built these huge futures positions on the SIMEX and OSE, and its failure could have been avoided. Indeed, when Barings collapsed in February 1995, Barings' exposures on the SIMEX and OSE were 40 percent and 73 percent of its capital, respectively (cf. Rawnsley 1995).

7. Chapter 12 offers a detailed presentation of credit risk enhancement techniques and the credit derivatives that are available to mitigate credit risk.

8. The G-10 is composed of Belgium, Canada, France, Germany, Italy, Japan, the Netherlands, Sweden, the United Kingdom, and the United States. On the Basle Committee sit senior officials of the central banks and supervisory authorities from the G-10 as well as officials from Switzerland and Luxembourg. The Accord was fully implemented in 1993 in the 12 ratifying countries. This Accord is also known as "the BIS requirements" since the Basle Committee meets four times a year, usually in Basle, Switzerland, under the patronage of the Bank for International Settlements (BIS). BIS is used in the text as a generic term to represent indifferently the Basle Committee and the regulatory authorities that supervise the banks in the member countries.

9. Default correlation increases with concentration. To make a simple analogy, when one house is burning, the house next door is more likely to be set on fire than a house situated further away.

10. Netting is, de facto, in effect in many derivatives transactions, such as interest rate swaps where only interest payments are exchanged and not the principal amounts.

11. According to the banks' regulators, however, the Accord takes account of these risks by setting a minimum capital ratio that acts as a buffer to cover not only credit risk but also all other risks. This argument is far from convincing.

12. See, e.g., Chew (1996).

13. Tier 3 capital, however, cannot support capital requirements for the banking book.

14. See also Section 5.1.3.

15. Cf. Basle (1996). In 1993, the European Commission adopted the Capital Adequacy Directive (CAD), imposing uniform capital

requirements for securities trading books of banks and securities houses chartered within the European Community. In many ways, the CAD follows the new BIS guidelines (cf. Elderfield 1995). It has been effective since January 1996, two years before the BIS market risk proposal was applied, giving banks in the rest of the G-10 countries a comparative advantage over their European counterparts. It should be noted that in North America, large securities houses such as Goldman Sachs, Salomon Brothers, and Merrill Lynch, which are not regulated by the Office of the Controller of the Currency (OCC), the Federal Reserve System, or the Federal Deposit Insurance Company (FDIC), in the United States, or the Office of the Superintendent of the Financial Institutions (OSFI) in Canada, will not have to satisfy any such minimum capital adequacy requirements. Instead, they are subject to the rules imposed by the Securities and Exchange Commission (SEC) in the United States, which are less stringent. However, trading opportunities and the profitability of those securities houses depend heavily on their credit ratings. It is probable that rating agencies such as Moody's and Standard and Poor's will play an active role in promoting similar standards among securities houses, and will condition their attribution of top ratings to the implementation of best-practice risk management.

16. Cf. Basle (1995).
17. By "trading book" we mean the bank's proprietary positions in financial instruments, whether on or off the balance sheet, which are intentionally held for short-term trading, and/or which are taken on by the bank with the intention of making profit from short-term changes in prices, rates, and volatilities. All trading book positions must be marked-to-market or marked-to-model every day. For market risk capital purposes, an institution may include in its measure of general market risk certain non-trading-book instruments that it deliberately uses to hedge trading positions.
18. In fact, the real issue at stake here is not whether to lower the amount of capital that is required, but how to allocate the right amount of capital. The current regime charges too much capital to investment-grade facilities and not enough to the most risky facilities. It has encouraged massive regulatory arbitrage (see Section 5 of this chapter).
19. The new BIS proposal contemplates generalizing the system adopted by the FSA in the United Kingdom to all the G-10 countries. See Section 5.1.2 on the supervisory review process.
20. A revolver is a facility that allows a bank customer to borrow and repay a loan at will within a certain period of time.

21. Robert Merton and Myron Scholes received the award. Fischer Black died in 1996; the Nobel Prize is not awarded posthumously.

22. See McDonough (1998).

23. There is an obvious contradiction between maintaining the current level of capital and reducing the divergence between regulatory and economic capital. The objective should be rather to make sure that banks carry the right amount of capital for the risks they incur. If banks reduce the amount of risk they undertake, we would expect a lower regulatory capital to apply to them. If banks increase their overall risk level, regulatory capital should also be set at a higher level.

24. According to the Basle Committee the proposal only applies to internationally active banks on a fully consolidated basis, including holding companies that are parents of banking groups. This proposal could be costly to Japanese banks which, unlike U.S. banks, are not accustomed to having capital rules that apply at the holding company as well as at the bank level. However, in some instances some banking groups are registered not as banks but as entities such as insurance companies or investment houses. Firms such as Merrill Lynch, Morgan Stanley, AIG, or Prudential might decide, for example, to engage more fully in banking activities.

    Smaller banks that do not fall under the "internationally active" designation to which Basle rules apply may seek an exemption from the new framework. There is obviously the risk that a two-tier system will develop over time.

25. See Chapters 8, 9, and 10.

26. In order to be eligible for lower than 100 percent weighting, a sovereign would have to subscribe to the IMF's Special Data Dissemination Standard (SDDS).

27. Chapter 8 describes the methodology of CreditVaR, the internal credit value-at-risk model implemented at CIBC.

28. See, e.g., ISDA (2000, p. 26)'s "Index Approach." ISDA, 2000, "A New Capital Adequacy Framework: Comments on a Consultative Paper Issued by the Basle Committee on Banking Supervision in June 1999," February.

29. ISDA (the International Swaps and Derivatives Association) and IIF (the Institute of International Finance) formed a joint working group in 1998 to explore how the various industry-sponsored credit VaR models (CreditMetrics, KMV, CreditRisk+, and various proprietary models) perform for different portfolios: corporate bonds and loans,

middle markets, emerging market bonds, mortgages, and retail credits. Results from this study are reported in Chapter 11.

30. Market VaR models are backtested by comparing the daily profit and loss (P&L) of the trading account to the daily VaR (see Chapter 5). Each year 250 observations are produced to assess the validity of the model. Since most credit risk statistics are produced on an annual basis and credit risk models typically employ a one-year horizon, credit VaR produced on one day needs to be compared with the P&L over the next 365 days.

31. The analogy with fixed-income derivative models for OTC products is especially relevant here. No secondary market for exotic customized structures exists. While the positions are marked-to-model every day using complex analytic algorithms, there is no easy way to backtest these models. The first step in the model approval process consists of making sure that the model is theoretically sound and consistent with finance theory. For example, a simple Black–Scholes type of model to value a two-year option on a three-year bond would immediately be rejected. Deciding between, say, a one-factor or a multifactor interest rate model is an act of faith since both models may be perfectly sound. The final choice should be based on the judgement and experience of the trader and the financial engineer. However, once the model has been chosen, it is essential to validate its calibration and the key input parameters.

32. See the next subsection on credit risk mitigation techniques, as well as Chapter 11.

33. The proposed framework is similar to the "prompt corrective action" in the Federal Deposit Insurance Corporation Improvement Act of 1991 under which supervisors would intervene as a bank's capital position slipped. See Jones and King (1995).

34. As we noted earlier, most banks already hold capital beyond the minimum risk-based capital ratios (see Table 2.7). However, regulators may impose more regulatory capital than the minimum requirement for large banks given the large systemic effect that may result from their failure.

35. Most of these institutions participated in the G-12 recommendations.

36. The G-12 recommendations elaborate greatly on the guidelines released by BIS in January 1999 to enhance banks' risk management practices in respect of highly leveraged institutions. See the two documents: "Banks' Interactions with Highly leveraged Institutions" and "Sound Practices for Banks' Interactions with

Highly leveraged Institutions." See also the "Report of The President's Working Group on Financial Markets: Hedge Funds, Leverage, and the Lessons of Long Term Capital Management."

37. It is interesting to note that the general theme of enhanced transparency and better disclosure is common to the proposals issued by BIS and industry-sponsored groups.

38. See also Gibson (1999) who proposes a comprehensive framework for the disclosure of market and credit risks to all market participants (rather than just to supervisory authorities). Such a policy should benefit firms by reducing their cost of capital, since it reduces moral hazard and adverse selection problems.

CHAPTER 3

Structuring and Managing the Risk Management Function in a Bank

1. INTRODUCTION

If they are to measure, price, and control risk in a comprehensive manner, financial institutions must establish appropriate firm-wide policies, and develop relevant firm-wide risk methodologies that are coupled to a firm-wide risk management infrastructure. This chapter provides an integrated framework for just such an approach to risk management, in the context of best-practice risk management.

An important component of integrated risk management is the measurement and management of all the firm's risk in terms of a common measurement unit and strategy. The risks that need to be covered include trading market risk, corporate treasury gap market risk, liquidity risk, credit risk in the trading book, credit risk in the banking book, and operational risk. (Section 5 of this chapter offers a treatment of gap market risk and liquidity risk; other chapters of this book offer in-depth discussions of credit, market, and operational risk.)

Risk integration offers all sorts of benefits. For example, financial institutions can combine the measurement of trading market risk and gap market risk to ensure that market risk is covered completely and consistently. It also allows institutions to rationalize their approach to market and credit risk measurement. For example, trading market risk and credit risk can be assessed from the

FIGURE 3.1

Steps Toward Integrated Risk Management

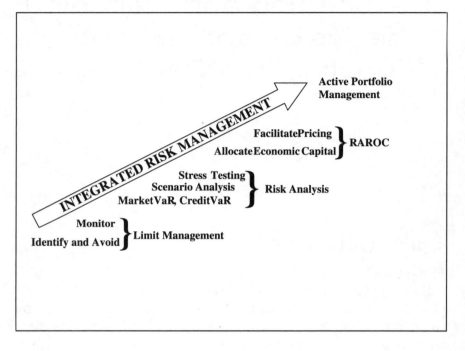

same market value distribution, taken at selected points in time over the life of a transaction.

What do we mean by best-practice risk management? Best-practice risk management philosophy can be envisioned along the arrow of Figure 3.1. The ultimate objective is to manage risks actively in a portfolio context. First, a limit management process is needed to help identify and select those risks that the firm is willing to take. A process to monitor closely the risks that are retained in the books is also required.

Financial institutions need to implement best-practice risk analysis and risk measurement to capture accurately their risk exposures. This is the purpose of the market and credit value-at-risk (VaR) models we discuss in later chapters, which should be implemented for all trading businesses. Risk analysis should be complemented by stress testing and scenario analysis to assess the extent of potential losses during exceptional market crises.

Best practice is also about the management of day-to-day risk communication. For example, risk managers should discuss their risk analysis with senior trading management in a daily trading-room risk conference; the discussion should be prior to the opening of trading and might take around 30 minutes. Automated daily exception reports should be distributed at the meeting. Risk management should also conduct a weekly (say, two-hour) risk meeting with their internal business partners in order to review major risk-related business issues.

The measurement of risk-adjusted return on capital (RAROC) is a particularly important part of an integrated risk management framework, and is the foundation of performance measurement. This measurement allows a bank to manage all its businesses in terms of their risk-adjusted return through the assignment of reserves and economic capital, as we discuss in more detail in Chapter 14. Each time a new transaction is considered, the bank can assess its marginal impact on economic capital, and make sure that the pricing is consistent with its target adjusted return on capital, also known as the hurdle rate.

Then, all the pieces are in place to ensure optimal risk pricing and active portfolio management.

2. ORGANIZING THE RISK MANAGEMENT FUNCTION: THREE-PILLAR FRAMEWORK

Today, it is relatively unusual to find sophisticated risk literate organizations with a decentralized risk management structure, where risk is managed to a minimum standard and risk assessment remains under the direct control of risk takers.

Firms understand that they need to establish a risk management function that is independent of direct risk takers. But at many firms senior managers need to encourage risk takers and risk managers to accelerate their efforts toward establishing a more uniform and sophisticated risk management framework.

Such a framework can be benchmarked in terms of policies, methodologies, and infrastructure (Figure 3.2). The bank needs to develop best-practice policies (e.g., price risk authorities for the trading book, credit risk authorities for the loan book), best-practice methodologies (e.g., market and credit value-at-risk, stress

FIGURE 3.2

Risk Management Framework

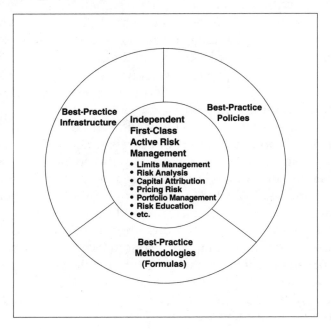

testing) that protect against losses while supporting a profitable business, and also a best-practice infrastructure.

The independent first-class active management of risk, as shown in the center of Figure 3.2, includes the capability to attribute capital, to appropriately price risk, and to actively manage the portfolio of residual risks.

2.1 Best-Practice Policies

Risk tolerance must be expressed in terms that are consistent with the bank's business strategy (Figure 3.3). The business strategy should express the objectives of the financial institution in terms of risk/return targets. This should lead to setting risk limits, or tolerances, for the organization as a whole, and for its major activities.

2.1.1 Market Risk Policy

Business and risk managers should establish a policy that explicitly states their risk policy in terms of a statistically defined potential or "worst case" loss: dealers and loan officers require a

FIGURE 3.3

Best-Practice Policies

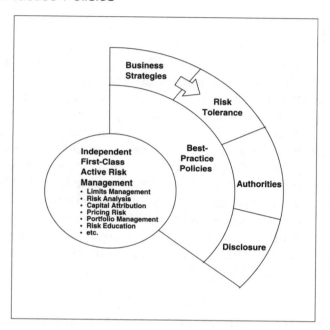

policy that states how much money can be put at risk. To this end, most major financial institutions are moving toward a value-at-risk (VaR) framework, which calculates risk in terms of a probabilistic worst-case loss.

A best-practice market risk policy should state the statistically defined worst-case loss in a way that considers the probability of both parallel and nonparallel shifts in the yield curve (see Chapter 5). The policy should also define the worst-case loss in terms of a sufficiently low level of probability, say, 1 percent.

Management should decide how to allocate capital and risk units across activities and divisions in the institution in order to achieve their goals, while controlling exposure to market risk. The greater the market risk, the higher the expected rate of return that the bank can expect. The question is, how much risk exposure can the bank afford? Management should also set the authorities for assuming market risks, and specify the nature of the market risks to which the institution should be exposed. For example, a local or regional bank might decide to limit its exposure mainly to interest rate and local credit risks, while minimizing its exposure to currency risks.

2.1.2 Credit Risk Policy

Every bank must determine a credit risk policy: how much credit to supply, for what duration, for which type of clients, and so on. Apparent profitability is only one consideration, the second being the risk of the loan. Therefore, bank policy should specify the extent of diversification, limits on size, and more. Banks need to tie their tolerance for risk and associated economic capital into their desired credit rating. For example, a desired AAA rating would require that more economic capital be charged to business units than for a AA rating.

Some of the credit risks can be diversified away, and others should be priced. Management should specify its tolerance to credit risk, and limit the loan losses (in probability terms). Authorities for approving credit by size and by risk exposure should be set. A reporting system to track exposures to credit risk is required, coupled with a routine for updating information about creditors.

2.1.3 Operational Risk Policy

Operational risks are inherent in all banking and business activities (see also Chapter 13). These are the risks stemming from human errors, computer failures, employing large amounts of data for estimation purposes, and implementing pricing and valuation models. Management should decide which operational risks it should insure, and which it should manage. Assigning responsibilities is of utmost importance, but it cannot be effective without first-class control procedures.

All trading authorities should include a full review of operational risks. It is particularly important to set policies that establish how to

- Review the introduction of all new products.
- Evaluate (or "vet") all the pricing models that are used to value positions—a duty that must be undertaken by an independent risk management function.

Operational risk management is not only about "model risk," but also about the administrative management of the trading process (Chapters 13 and 15). It was the ability of a trader at Barings to act without authority and detection that resulted in such large losses. The Bank of England report on Barings revealed some general operational risk lessons.

First, management teams have the duty to understand fully the businesses they manage. Second, responsibility for each business activity has to be clearly established and communicated. Third, relevant internal controls, including independent risk management, must be established for all business activities. Fourth, top management and the audit committee must ensure that significant weaknesses are resolved quickly.

2.2 Best-Practice Methodologies

Going forward, banks with sophisticated risk measurement systems will be able to use their own internal risk methodology to calculate the required amount of market risk regulatory capital in lieu of the more onerous standardized regulatory approach.

For example, as we mentioned above, a bank might develop a policy that conservatively defines a statistically "worst case" loss in "normal markets" as an amount such that there is less than, say, a 1 percent probability of losing more than the worst case amount in one day. In other words, the bank might expect to exceed the statistically defined worst case loss in one out of every 100 business days.

The best-practice methodologies illustrated in Figure 3.4 refer to the application of "appropriate" analytic models to measure market risk, credit risk, operational risk, and so on. The objective is not solely to measure risk, but also to ensure that the pricing and valuation methodologies are appropriate.

As pointed out in Chapter 2, the Group of Thirty (G-30) recommends that dealers should value derivatives at market prices. Further, it recommends that risk managers should quantify market and credit risk using a VaR framework. Specifically, the G-30 recommends that credit risk exposure should take account of both current and potential exposure.

Finally, measurement tools should be developed to ensure that the bank's positions are on the efficient frontier of the trade-off between risk and reward. To this end, implementing a RAROC approach is particularly important. Simply put, what you can't measure well, you can't manage or price well (see also Chapter 14).

FIGURE 3.4

Best-Practice Methodologies

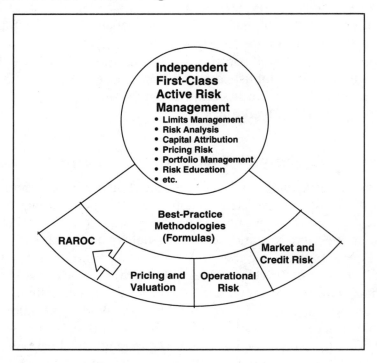

2.2.1 Risk Measurement Methodology

A simple example will serve to illustrate what we mean by a statistically defined worst case market risk policy for a bond, e.g., a short position in a five-year Treasury note. Typical old-style risk methodologies (i.e., duration calculations) posit a simple parallel shift in the yield curve. One might calculate the amount at risk by assuming that every point along the yield curve shifts downwards in a parallel fashion by some arbitrary amount (say, one basis point, two basis points, or 25 bp[1]).

For example, assume the five-year yield to maturity is 6.75 percent. One might arbitrarily assume that the five-year yield to maturity declines overnight by 25 bp from 6.75 percent to 6.50 percent, and also that every point on the yield curve declines in parallel by the same amount, i.e., 25 bp. This is clearly a simplistic approach since the yield curve rarely shifts in a parallel fashion.

A more realistic approach is to calculate a statistically defined worst case risk by taking into account the more complicated non-parallel shifts in the yield curve, i.e, the yield curve might flatten, steepen, or invert.

If interest rates were to rise, then the portfolio would gain in value. The value of the portfolio at the current yield of 6.75 percent is $43.764 million. Assume further that if interest rates fall by one basis point from 6.75 percent to 6.74 percent, then the value of the short position falls to $43.744 million. Accordingly, the sensitivity of the portfolio is the difference between the value at 6.75 percent and 6.74 percent, which represents a loss of $20,000 for the short position.

However, more sophisticated systems would capture the effects of level and shape changes in the curve. A full VaR measurement methodology encompasses more intricate types of risk, e.g., credit spreads or vega-related option risk. This approach permits a consistent measurement of market risk across all business units.[2]

Senior management should adopt a credit risk measurement policy which calls for measuring credit risk for the loan book and off-balance-sheet derivative products according to an analytic approach that is consistent with the approach implemented for market risk.

2.2.2 Pricing and Valuation Methodologies

It is particularly vital that banks develop appropriate techniques to differentiate between transactions where prices are transparent, and those where price discovery is more limited. For example, price discovery can be limited in the case of long tenor or highly structured derivative transactions (e.g., a 10-year option on a 20-year swap). These instruments can only be valued using assumption-driven methodologies, and thus require the use of mark-to-model risk control techniques.

The G-30 recommends that one should take the mid-market price of the trade, less the sum of the expected credit loss and the future administrative costs, when valuing a perfectly matched derivative transaction. Banks need to ask themselves whether their approach to estimating the expected credit loss is "reasonable." The G-30 also suggests additional adjustments for close-out costs—i.e., the cost of eliminating market risk at any given point—as well as for investing and funding costs.

2.2.3 Accounting for Portfolio Effects

Pricing risk at the transaction level, without considering portfolio effects across an entire organization, tends to "price in" too much risk because it does not take into account portfolio effects. On the other hand, pricing in risk at the portfolio level is complicated.

If portfolio effects are taken into account, then one can calculate the required economic capital for the entire organization. Economic capital is attributed as a function of risk, and is sometimes referred to as risk capital. The economic capital required at higher organization levels is less than the sum of the economic capital across organizational units required at lower levels. Economic capital should be compared across organizational levels and within each level (e.g., across products). A portfolio-based risk measurement system that incorporates correlations between positions can assist an organization in understanding its risk profile not only by counterparty, but for the organization as a whole.

A well-designed portfolio risk measurement approach enables one "to slice and dice" risk vertically and horizontally across an organization to facilitate the pricing of risk.

2.3 Best-Practice Infrastructure

How important is risk infrastructure? Well, imagine a situation in which policies and methodology have been developed but where there is no infrastructure to make them work.

The first and most important component of infrastructure in a financial services company is people (Figure 3.5). Given the right environment and support, it is people who make everything else happen. Best-practice risk measurement cannot be derived solely from complex analytical approaches: judgment will always be a significant input.

Likewise, ensuring the integrity of data provides an important competitive advantage, as data are translated into risk management information for both transaction makers and policy makers. Finally, a key goal, critical to the successful management of risk, is to integrate risk management operations and technology.

Increasingly, financial institutions are using sophisticated computer technology to accelerate their efforts to establish best-practice risk management. The most important effects of this ac-

FIGURE 3.5

Best-Practice Infrastructure

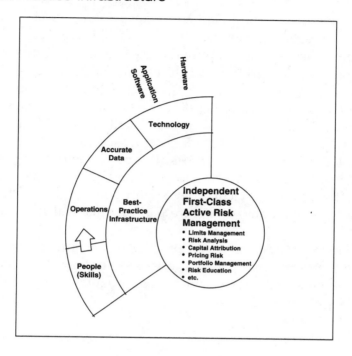

celeration are increasing competition, shortened time horizons for the development and distribution of financial products, and the need to maintain a rational and consistent risk management approach.

Typically, firms are faced with the problem of fragmentation in their existing systems. The systems cannot easily communicate with each other—the "islands of automation" problem.

Many risk management systems are developed to perform unique functions, but in some cases the functions overlap. This causes redundancy, expensive processing, and increased costs, as each system must be supported separately. However, new technologies facilitate the development of firm-wide risk management support applications. The implementation of an integrated risk management system should enable a firm to maintain a competitive advantage by allowing the firm to monitor and manage all of its risk on a global basis.

2.4 Integrated Goal-Congruent Risk Management Process

An integrated goal-congruent risk management process that puts all the elements together, as illustrated in Figure 3.2, is the key that opens the door to an optimal firm-wide management of risk. "Integrated" refers to the need to avoid a fragmented approach to risk management. Risk management is only as strong as the weakest link. "Goal-congruent" refers to the need to ensure that policies and methodologies are consistent with each other. One goal is to have an apple-to-apple risk measurement scheme so that the bank can compare risk across all products and aggregate risk at any level. Advanced analytical techniques combined with sophisticated computer technology open up new value-added possibilities, as illustrated in Figure 3.6, for financial risk management.

The end product is a best-practice management of risk with actions that are consistent with business strategy. This is a "one firm, one view" approach, which also recognizes the specific risk dynamics of each business.

FIGURE 3.6

Opening up New Value-Added Possibilities

3. DATA AND TECHNOLOGICAL INFRASTRUCTURE

3.1 Introduction

The key features of an effective risk management system are shown in Figure 3.7. An effective risk management system needs to be able to generate the necessary risk management information on all risks, perform specific analytical functions, and permit multitasking. Clearly, the bank also needs well-designed back-up/ retrieval capabilities. The system should allow for easy integration of new applications and platforms, but balance this flexibility with the need for management control.

The panels in Figure 3.8, which build on the features introduced in Figure 3.7, imply that having a first-class risk management system is a necessary condition for an optimal return-versus-risk profile.

FIGURE 3.7

Key Features of a Best-Practice Risk Management System

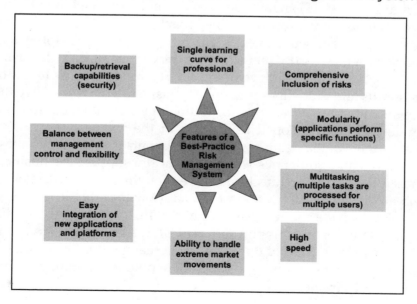

FIGURE 3.8

Enhancing Return Versus Risk

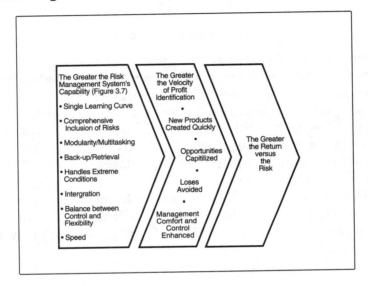

3.2 Information Technology Architecture

The risk management system needs to be supported by an information technology (IT) architecture that is employed in all of the company's information processing. The IT architecture is essentially a set of standards and guidelines (input from business principles) that should be adhered to by staff when they make technological decisions.

The logic behind developing an IT architecture in terms of standards and guidelines is simple. If business principles drive the organizational requirements for technology (and if standards and guidelines are developed in support of the business principles), then it follows that technological investments that adhere to these standards and guidelines will automatically support the business principles. The IT architecture can be thought of as a collection of sub-architectures that support each entity within the firm.

Banks have many business units, which are engaged in different activities and support different products. The design of the IT infrastructure should optimize the exchange of information between each entity within the firm. All should be operating within a unified IT framework.

An "application architecture" establishes the technical, functional, and operational characteristics of application systems (their construction and use). A "data architecture" (e.g., object-oriented) deals with the establishment of an environment in which all information can be accessed and understood by any associate of the firm. The "organization architecture" deals with the responsibilities and interrelationships necessary to ensure the comprehensive information interchange between parties.

A complete risk management system approach is not simply an aggregate of applications, data, and organization; instead, it is born out of an IT vision. The IT design (Figure 3.9) clearly needs to take into account the means by which key risk management information is gathered from the various internal and external systems into a risk data warehouse. A key task is to organize the nec-

FIGURE 3.9

Risk Data Warehousing

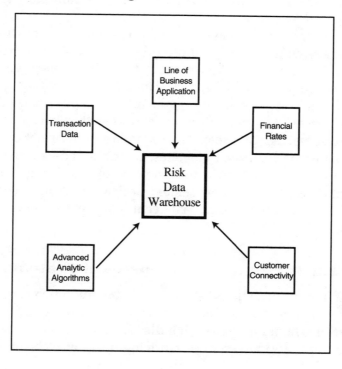

essary risk management data (transmitted to the risk management system from multiple legacy systems) into a common format (data dictionary).

Furthermore, IT planning needs to take account of how key risk management information might change over time. The information might be static (e.g., contractual details of a transaction such as the coupon of a corporate bond) or dynamic (e.g., market information such as daily closing prices). The IT platform and operating system should be designed such that they do not place constraints on managers trying to obtain risk management data.

Attempting to calculate and manage risk on a global basis requires the centralized control of algorithms and immediate access to large amounts of data. Risk management data include both historical statistics and current risk characteristics, for each transaction in every portfolio.

Bank trading units are typically dispersed among markets in multiple time zones. To centralize the risk calculation, and provide immediate access to data, an organization must develop its IT architecture from best-in-class database and communication technologies.

A distributed database approach is often used to distribute risk management data. Distributed databases promote the distribution of data and decision making to regional sites (e.g., New York, Toronto, London, Singapore, Hong Kong, and Tokyo). A distributed database enables an organization to store data on the network wherever it is most economical, rather than on each remote database server. An overseas office can request information on any financial instrument from other sites. Distributed data technologies offer a low-cost solution to the problem of providing risk management data for global risk-related decision making. Figure 3.10 illustrates a distributed database technology with interconnected servers.

3.3 Tiered Risk Management Systems

Trading institutions should select a suitable three-tiered risk management system to integrate their front office, middle office, and back office. The middle office handles functions such as risk management, monitoring key trades, pricing deals, etc. The back office

FIGURE 3.10

Distributed Database Technology with Interconnected Servers

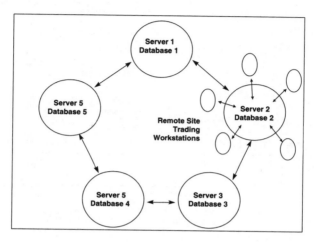

performs routine functions such as recording the amount of interest paid, maintaining tax accounting information, performing regulatory reporting, etc. New trading platform technologies are being engineered and constructed to integrate the front and back offices with the middle office.

Managers in major institutions need to ensure that their enterprise-wide risk management computing is capable of running on centrally located hardware (Figure 3.11a). The risk management database (e.g., a UNIX-based database) must be able to store extracted data and to allow for interactive unscheduled access or "interrupt functionality" (Figure 3.11b).

Also, the institution needs to establish an effective and integrated workgroup computing environment (Figure 3.11c). The workgroup computing environment supports risk management end-users, policy makers, and application developers.

Finally, the bank needs to ensure that the corporate networks connect all three risk management tiers (Figure 3.12), so that risk management data can be exchanged. The corporate network connects all the tiers by allowing software and data to be easily transferred through the network. Multiple users at different organizational levels should have easy access to risk software applications,

FIGURE 3.11a

Enterprise-Wide Centralized Risk Management

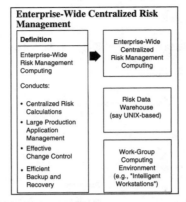

FIGURE 3.11b

Risk Data Warehouse

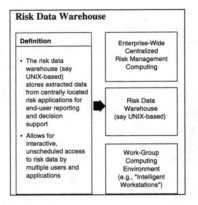

FIGURE 3.11c

Work Group Computing Environment

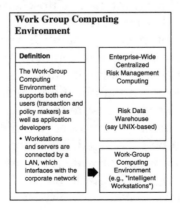

FIGURE 3.12

Three Tiers to an Integrated Risk Management System

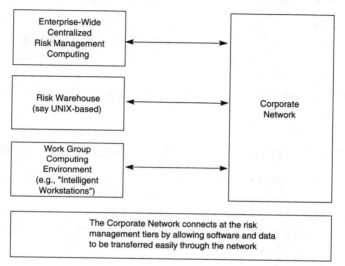

data, and reports. Advanced risk management software—e.g., object-oriented programming languages (such as C++)—facilitates ambitious integration projects.

The risk management system should be designed to support the transport and integration of risk information from a variety of technology platforms, as well as from multiple internal and external legacy systems around the world. The risk management infrastructure is similar to a highway system in that it enables these legacy systems to transport information without the bank having to continuously build new roads for its data.

The bank's risk data warehouse should be populated daily with transaction and market information. The transaction information should also be reconciled daily to ensure that market risk is reported accurately. The risk data warehouse should also store a time series of market data in its financial database.

Risk reports should be generated daily by an analytic engine that has been designed by the bank's risk management function. The analytic engine should be built with a flexible architecture to accommodate advanced risk measures. As a whole the system should be able to: (1) develop and distribute financial instruments quickly; (2) aggregate risks across the institution; and (3) supply transaction personnel with information on limits, as well as RAROC expectations.

A major challenge is to integrate existing risk management systems with new platform technologies. Financial institutions will likely have to make substantial and significant investments in their computer technology in order to provide their clients, risk takers, and risk managers with the speed and analytics necessary to monitor and perform risk management.

4. RISK AUTHORITIES AND RISK CONTROL

We begin this section with the issue of risk management roles and responsibilities. Second, we describe standards for risk authorities and how these risk authorities should be monitored. Third, we provide standards for limit design. Fourth, we provide standards for risk monitoring. Finally, we briefly discuss the role of a bank's audit function.

4.1 Roles and Responsibilities

Market risk roles and responsibilities should be understood at all levels of the bank. An independent market risk management function should develop risk policy, and monitor adherence to such policy. A knowledgeable internal audit function should provide an in-depth assessment of internal risk management controls, including controls over the risk management function.

Best-practice corporate governance demands that a subcommittee of the board of directors (say, a risk management and conduct review committee) reviews and approves risk management policies at least once a year. A senior operating policy committee (say, an asset/liability management committee) should be responsible for determining the extent of financial risk to be accepted by the bank as a whole.

The asset/liability management committee (ALCO) is typically responsible for establishing, documenting, and enforcing all polices that involve market risk, such as liquidity, interest rate, and foreign exchange risk. ALCO is also responsible for the delegation of market risk limits to the president and chief risk officer (CRO) of the bank. ALCO should also ensure that the bank's infrastructure can support the bank's market risk management objectives.

The chief risk officer is responsible for risk management strategy, policies, methodologies, and overall governance. ALCO delegates to the chief risk officer the authority to make day-to-day decisions on its behalf, including the authority to extend business unit mandates beyond their annual renewal date until it is convenient for ALCO to review them, and to approve excesses of limits provided that these do not breach overall risk limits approved by the board (i.e., the risk management and conduct review committee of the board).

A business-level risk committee should be responsible for ensuring that the desired risk/reward trade-offs are successfully managed. The committee should manage design issues that set out how risk will be managed, reflecting the agreed relationship between the business and the bank's risk management function. The committee should also approve policies applicable to the appropriate measurement and management of risk, and provide a detailed review of risk limits for trading and credit authorities.

Managers are necessarily dependent upon each other when they try to manage risk in a bank (Figure 3.13). Senior management approves business plans and targets, sets risk tolerances, establishes policy, and ensures that performance targets are met. Trading-room managers establish and manage risk exposures. Trading-room managers also ensure timely, accurate, and complete deal capture and sign off on the official profit and loss (P&L) statement.

The bank's operations function independently books trades, settles trades, and reconciles front- and back-office positions. Operations staff also prepare the daily P&L report. Operations staff are also responsible for providing an independent mark-to-market of the bank's positions, and support the operational needs of the various businesses.

The finance function develops valuation and finance policy, and ensures the integrity of P&L—including reviews of any independent valuation processes. Finance also manages the business planning process, and supports the financial needs of the various businesses.

Meanwhile, the risk management function develops risk policies, monitors compliance to limits, manages the ALCO process, vets models and spreadsheets, and provides an independent view

FIGURE 3.13

Interdependence for Managing Risk

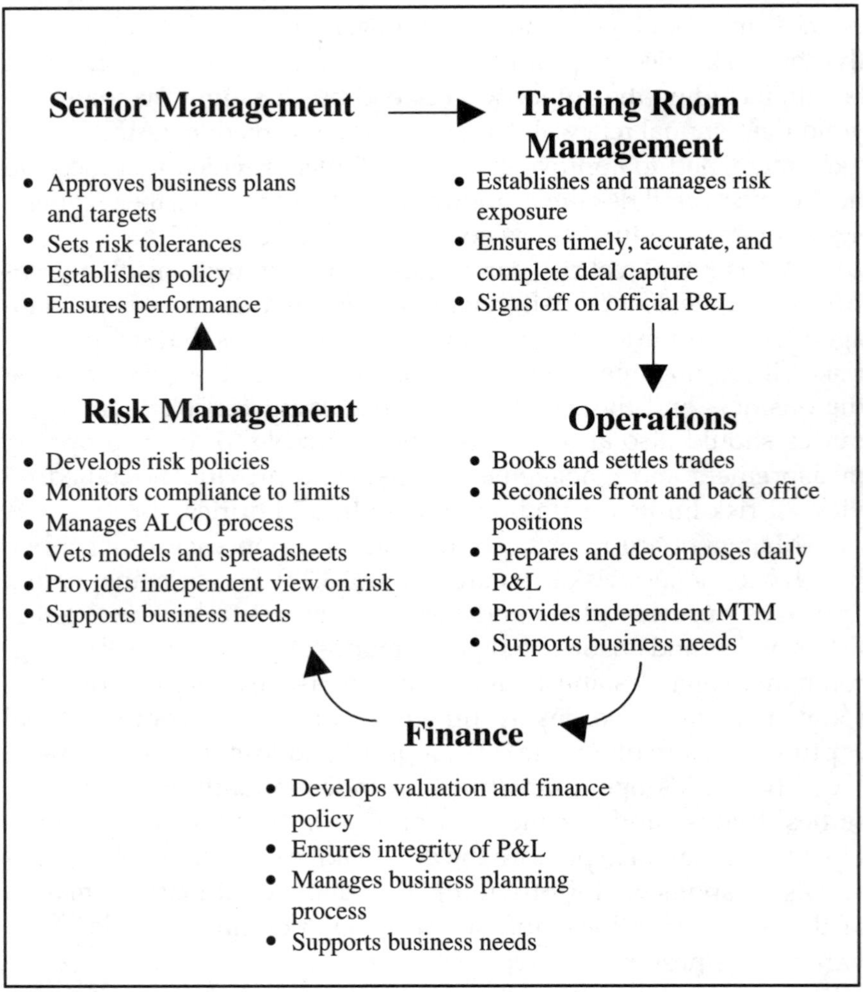

Senior Management ⟶ **Trading Room Management**

- Approves business plans and targets
- Sets risk tolerances
- Establishes policy
- Ensures performance

- Establishes and manages risk exposure
- Ensures timely, accurate, and complete deal capture
- Signs off on official P&L

Risk Management

- Develops risk policies
- Monitors compliance to limits
- Manages ALCO process
- Vets models and spreadsheets
- Provides independent view on risk
- Supports business needs

Operations

- Books and settles trades
- Reconciles front and back office positions
- Prepares and decomposes daily P&L
- Provides independent MTM
- Supports business needs

Finance

- Develops valuation and finance policy
- Ensures integrity of P&L
- Manages business planning process
- Supports business needs

---

on risk. The function also supports the risk management needs of the various businesses.

4.2 Standards for Risk Authorities

It is best practice for institutions to write down the policies and procedures that govern their trading activities. These policies include how a bank approves new products as well as how it establishes market risk limits. The standards should cover the nature of any formal reviews of market risk exposures, as well as the analytic methodology used to calculate the bank's market risk exposures. The standards should also establish procedures for approving limit exceptions.

4.2.1 Business Unit Mandate

The process for developing and renewing authorities should be explicit. For example, business unit mandates should expire one year after they are approved by ALCO. The senior risk officer may approve an extension of an authority beyond one year, to accommodate ALCO's schedule.

A balance must be struck between ensuring that a business has the limits set high enough to allow it to meet its business goals, and the maintenance of overall risk standards (including ensuring that limits can be properly monitored). Key infrastructure and corporate governance groups must be consulted when preparing a business unit's mandate.

The format for obtaining approval of a business unit mandate should be standardized. First, the manager seeking approval should provide an overview and restate the key decisions that need to be taken (as requested by the senior policy committee).

Second, the manager should bring everyone up to date about the business, e.g., key achievements, risk profile, and a description of any new products (or activities) that may affect the risk profile.

Third, the manager should outline future initiatives.

Fourth, proposed risk limits should be put forward. The report should note the historical degree of use of any current limits, as well as current and proposed limits. It should analyze the impact of any full use of limits on liquidity and capital.

Fifth, the report should describe the operational risks that the business unit is exposed to. This would include the impact of any finance, legal, compliance, and tax issues.

4.2.2 Delegation Process for Risk Authorities

The risk management and conduct review committee of the board should approve the bank's risk appetite each year and delegate authority to the chief executive officer of the bank as chair of ALCO. ALCO should approve each business unit mandate (say, annually).

ALCO also approves the impact of each mandate in terms of the market risk appetite of the bank and, in turn, delegates market risk authority to a business-driven risk committee.

The risk committee provides a detailed review and approval (say, annually) of each business unit mandate. The committee also approves the impact of each mandate in terms of the respective risk limits, and delegates these limits to a chief risk officer. The chief risk officer is responsible for independently monitoring the limits—and may well order that positions be reduced, or closed out because of concerns about market, credit, or operational risks. The chief risk officer also delegates some responsibilities to the head of global trading.

The head of global trading is responsible for risk and performance of all trading activities, and in turn delegates the management of limits to the business manager. The business manager is responsible for the risk management and performance of the business and, in turn, delegates limits to the bank's traders. This delegation process is summarized in Figure 3.14.

FIGURE 3.14

Delegation Process for Market Risk Authorities

4.3 Standards for Limit Design

What is the best way of designing the various risk limits? Market risk should be measured using a VaR-style risk measure that is based on a common confidence interval and on an appropriate time horizon. Market risk limits should control the risk that arises from changes in the absolute price (or rate), as well as changes in delta, gamma, volatility (vega), time decay (theta), basis, correlation, discount rate (rho), and so on. Policies should also be set out regarding exposure to liquidity risk, especially in the case of illiquid products. Banks should also include limits related to stress events and scenario analyses, to make sure the bank can survive extreme volatility in the markets.

Institutions should employ both tier I and tier II limits. Tier I limits should include a single overall VaR limit for each asset class (e.g., a single limit for foreign exchange products), as well as a single overall stress test limit and a cumulative loss from peak limits.

Tier II limits should include authorized markets/currencies/instruments, and concentration limits (e.g., by maturity, region, etc.). All risk limits should be consistent with the standards for risk limits proposed by the risk management function, and approved by the risk committee. Limits should balance the needs of the business to meet its financial targets with a realistic assessment of the use of past limits. The tier I limits should generally be set at a level such that the business, in the normal course of its activities, has exposures of about 40 percent to 60 percent of its limit (in normal markets). Peak usage of limits, in normal markets, should generate exposures of perhaps 85 percent of the limit.

The actual and proposed limits should be based on an evaluation of the bank's tolerance for risk, as well as the risk management function's ability to provide timely and accurate reporting on relevant risks, and the historical usage of risk limits.

A consistent limit structure helps a bank to consolidate risk across its various trading floors. With a common language of risk, tier II limits become fungible across business lines. Nevertheless, such transfers would require the joint approval of the head of trading and the chief risk officer.

4.4 Standards for Monitoring Risk

How should a bank monitor its market risk limits? Firstly, all positions should be marked-to-market daily. All the assumptions used in models to price transactions and to value positions should be independently verified. Daily profit and loss statements should be prepared by units that are independent of traders, and provided to (nontrading) senior management.

There should be timely and meaningful reports to measure compliance to policy and to trading limits. There should be a timely escalation procedure for any limit exceptions or transgressions; i.e., it should be clear what a manager must do if his or her subordinates breach limits.

The variance between the actual volatility of the value of a portfolio, and that predicted by means of the bank's market risk methodology, should be evaluated. Stress simulations should be executed to determine the impact of market changes on P&L.

Data used in limit monitoring must conform to a set of standards. First, the source of data must be independent of the front office. Second, the data need to be reconciled to the official books of the bank in order to ensure its integrity. Third, data feeds must be consolidated. Fourth, the data format must allow risk to be properly measured; e.g., it might employ the VaR methodology.

The bank must distinguish between data used for monitoring tier I limits—where data must be independent of traders—and data used to supply other kinds of management information. For other types of analysis, where timeliness is the key requirement, risk managers may be forced to use front-office systems as the most appropriate sources. Real-time risk measurement, such as that used to monitor intraday exposures, may simply have to be derived from front-office systems.

Business units should advise the risk management function before an excess occurs. For example, there might be an alert when an exposure is at, say, 85 percent of the tier I or tier II limit. The chief risk officer, jointly with the head of business, might petition ALCO for a tier I excess, in which case the business risk committee should be notified. If risk management is advised of a planned excess, then it should be more likely that an excess will be approved.

FIGURE 3.15

Limited Excess Escalation Procedure

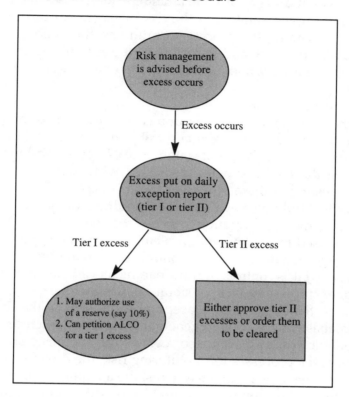

What happens if the limit is breached? Risk management, as illustrated in Figure 3.15, should immediately put any excess on a daily tier I or tier II exception report, with an appropriate explanation and a plan of action to cope with the tier I excess. The chief risk officer may authorize the use of a reserve.

Tier I excesses must be cleared or corrected immediately. Tier II excesses should be cleared or approved within a relatively short time frame of, say, a week.

Risk management should report all limit excesses on an exception report, which might be tabled at a daily trading-room meeting and which should distinguish between tier I and tier II limits. No manager should have the power to exclude excesses from the daily excess report.

4.5 Role of Audit

A key role of audit is to provide an independent assessment of the design and implementation of the risk management process. This includes examining the process surrounding the building of risk models, the adequacy and reliability of the risk management systems, and, especially, compliance with regulatory guidelines.

4.5.1 Scope of Work

Audit should provide overall assurance on the adequacy of the risk management processes. A key audit objective should be to evaluate the design and conceptual soundness of both the VaR measures (including the methodologies associated with stress testing) and the back-testing of these VaR measures.

Audit should also evaluate the soundness of elements of the risk management information system—the risk MIS—such as the processes used for coding and implementation of internal models. This should include examining controls over market position data capture, as well as controls over the parameter estimation processes.

For example, audit responsibilities often include providing assurance on the design and conceptual soundness of the financial rates database that is used to generate parameters entered into the VaR analytic engine. Audit also reviews the adequacy and effectiveness of the processes for monitoring risk, the progress in plans to upgrade risk management systems, the adequacy and effectiveness of application controls within the risk MIS, and the reliability of the vetting processes.

Audit should also examine the documentation relating to compliance with the qualitative/quantitative criteria outlined in regulatory guidelines. Audit should comment on the reliability of the value-at-risk reporting framework.

4.5.2 Regulatory Expectations

Regulatory guidelines typically call for internal audit groups to review the overall risk management process. This means addressing the adequacy of documentation, the effectiveness of the process, the integrity of the risk management system, the integration of risk measures into daily risk management, and so on.

Regulatory guidelines typically also call for auditors to address the approval process for vetting risk pricing models and valuation systems used by front- and back-office personnel, the validation of any significant change in the risk measurement process, and the scope of risks captured by the risk measurement models. Regulators also require that internal auditors examine the integrity of the management information system and the accuracy and completeness of position data.

Audit should verify the consistency, timeliness, and reliability of data sources used to run internal models, including the independence of such data sources. One important duty is to examine the accuracy and appropriateness of volatility and correlation assumptions, as well as the accuracy of the valuation and risk transformation calculations. Internal auditors should verify the accuracy of models through an examination of the back-testing process. Finally, audit should avoid providing measures of risk (e.g., operational risk), as their role of auditing the key precesses would be compromised.

4.5.3 Statement of Audit Findings

If all is well from a risk management perspective, then audit should state that adequate processes exist for providing reliable risk control and to ensure compliance with local regulatory criteria (e.g., the 1998 BIS Capital Accord).

For example, the audit group's conclusion might be that (1) the risk control unit is independent of the business units; (2) the internal risk models are utilized by business management; and (3) the bank's risk measurement model captures all material risks.

Further, if all is well then the audit group should state that adequate and effective processes exist (4) for risk pricing models and valuation systems used by front- and back-office personnel; (5) for documenting the risk management systems and processes; (6) for validation of any significant change in the risk measurement process; (7) for ensuring the integrity of the risk management information system; (8) for the position data capture (and that any positions that are not captured do not materially affect risk reporting); (9) for the verification of the consistency, timeliness, and reliability of data sources used to run internal models, and that the data sources are independent; (10) for ensuring the accuracy and appropriateness of volatility and correlation assumptions; (11) for ensuring the accuracy of the valuation and risk transformation calculations; and (12) for the verification of the model's accuracy through frequent back-testing.

5. ESTABLISHING RISK LIMITS FOR GAP AND LIQUIDITY MANAGEMENT

Asset/liability management (ALM) can be defined as a structured decision-making process for matching and mismatching the mix of assets and liabilities in a bank. The aim of the process is to maximize the net worth of the bank's portfolio while assuming reasonable amounts of gap and liquidity risk.

Simply stated, the key objectives are:

- To stabilize net interest income (accounting earnings)
- To maximize shareholder wealth (economic earnings)
- To manage liquidity

Gap market risk arises from directional risk (mismatch risk of the interest rate sensitivity of a bank's assets and liabilities), spread risk, and any options risk embedded in the gap.

The amount of gap market risk relates to the extent to which net interest income and price changes are a function of a change in rates. Liquidity risk refers to the risk that the bank might not be able to generate sufficient cash flow to meet its financial obligations.

Asset/liability management involves the deliberate mismatching of a bank's assets and liabilities in terms of their maturity and repricing characteristics. For example, instead of waiting for new deposits, it is standard practice for banks to make long-term corporate loans by borrowing short-term wholesale money. The idea is to add to the bank's profits while assuming a reasonable amount of risk.

A principal source of gap market risk arises from "riding the yield curve." For example, gap "carry profits" can be created by carrying a bank asset "further out" on a positively sloped yield curve than the associated bank liability. Positive gaps are created when a bank possesses more assets in a specific maturity bucket than it possesses liabilities. A negative gap in a short-maturity bucket will benefit from a fall in rates, while a positive gap in a short-maturity bucket will benefit from rising rates. Gap carry profits are locked in until the first liability repricing date.

5.1 Gap Market Risk

Gap market risk can be viewed from two distinct perspectives: accounting and economic. The former focuses on the impact of changing interest rates on reported net interest income. Specifically, earnings risk in the near term can be observed through the income statement and through the quality of the balance sheet.

The economic perspective looks at the impact of changing interest rates on the market value of a portfolio. In other words, the focus is on the risk to the net worth of the bank that arises from all the bank's interest-sensitive positions. Generally, the economic risk cannot be observed by monitoring accounting flows.

In a stable interest rate environment, the accounting (or book value) perspective of a bank's position is similar to the economic (or market value) perspective. This is because there is little movement in the market value of the bank's positions, or its net interest income. The situation is quite different in a volatile interest rate environment. Net interest income is at risk due to the interest rate mismatch embedded in any gap in the bank's portfolio of positions. From an economic perspective, the capital (i.e., market value) of the bank changes substantially as interest rates fall or rise, reflecting the present value of expected future cashflows.

5.2 Measuring Gap Market Risk

The techniques used to measure gap market risk range from relatively simple and static gap analysis, through duration analysis, to sophisticated VaR-type approaches.

A static gap analysis examines the nominal amount of the tactical and strategic gaps in the bank's overall position, and determines if these are appropriate in terms of perceived reward/risk. The "tactical gap" typically represents the combined gap position within one year. The "strategic gap" represents the combined gap position beyond one year. The "contractual gap" refers to the net gap position for assets and liabilities that have defined maturity dates. It is often difficult to determine maturity for noncontractual balances. For example, "core balances" typically refer to the stable portion of nonmaturity balances that are projected to remain on the balance sheet of the bank for an extended period of time.

One can calculate gap risk management units (RMUs) in a similar way to the RMU calculation for a trading book. For example, assume that the bank's balance-sheet position consists of a three-month eurodollar-based liability and a six-month eurodollar-based asset (a liability-sensitive balance sheet).

Here, the risk manager can think of the gap market risk as having the equivalent market risk to that of any hedging portfolio that might be used to hedge away the gap. For example, one might hedge the unmatched portion of a three-month asset starting three months from the present, by buying a 3 × 6 forward rate agreement. Accordingly, the gap RMU of this position can be viewed as the worst case change in value for this forward rate agreement.

5.3 Transfer Pricing Rules for Match-Funding a Unit

Banks need to develop a best-practice transfer pricing system (TPS) in order to properly characterize the gap market risk. A TPS allows the risk to be managed by, say, the corporate treasury function. There is no single right answer for building a best-practice TPS. Nevertheless, certain properties of a TPS are more optimal than others.

Specifically, the bank will need to establish transfer pricing rates (TPRs) for a variety of complex products: indeterminate maturities (e.g., demand deposits), options features (e.g., consumer loans with caps), basis risk (e.g., prime-based loans), etc.

A TPS should have a clear statement of purpose, e.g., "to decentralize decision making." Business units should not, on the whole, concern themselves with funding issues. The TPS can be used to measure the net interest contribution of a business, based on factors that are within its control and against a single standard.

The TPS should be consistent with a financial institution's business objectives and risk management practices. It must be credible, comprehensible, practical—and fully embraced by senior management.

Neither regulators nor practitioner working groups have provided any position papers that serve to define a best-practice TPS. Figure 3.16 attempts to fill this gap: It is a schematic representation of the ten commandments of transfer pricing. The commandments are also tabulated in Box 3.1.

FIGURE 3.16

Schematic Representation of the Ten Commandments

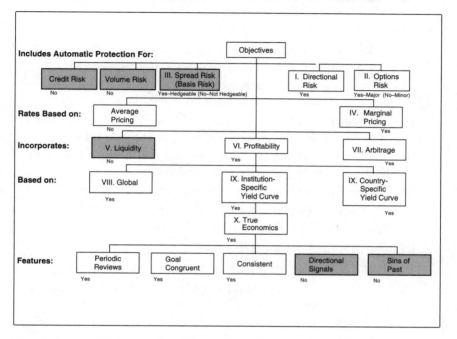

Starting with the upper right-hand corner of the figure, observe that a best-practice TPS provides business units with automatic protection from both directional risk (commandment I) and major options risk (commandment II), but does not provide protection against credit risk or volume risk. The TPS does not automatically provide protection against spread risk (commandment III), unless that risk is hedgeable. TPS best practice is based on marginal pricing (commandment IV) as opposed to average pricing.

Further, a TPS should not confuse liquidity pricing issues with transfer pricing issues. In other words, liquidity credit/charges are kept outside of the TPS (commandment V). A best-practice TPS is designed to reflect the profitability that can be achieved by the institution (commandment VI) and is impervious to arbitrage (commandment VII). A well-designed TPS is global in scope (commandment VIII), and is based on the institution's specific—i.e., inclusive of country-specific dynamics—yield curve (commandment IX).

B O X   3.1

THE TEN COMMANDMENTS OF TRANSFER PRICING

    I. Units shall be protected from directional risk.

   II. Units shall be protected from significant options risk.

 III. Units shall not be protected from basis (spread) risk, unless the risk is hedgeable and the units pay for the hedge based on current market rates and for an agreed volume.

 IV. The transfer pricing rate (TPR) will be based on minimizing spread volatility, while striving to price at the margin.

  V. The transfer pricing (TP) rules for match-funding a unit shall be determined by interest rate sensitivity.

 VI. The transfer pricing system (TPS) shall reflect the profitability that can be achieved by the institution.

 VII. The TPS shall be impervious to arbitrage.

VIII. The TPS shall be global in scope.

 IX. The TPS shall be institution and country specific.

  X. The TPR shall be determined solely by the true economics of the transaction and the TPS shall be explicit, consistent, and goal-congruent.

Most importantly, a well-designed TPS reflects true economic values (commandment X).

The TPS should be reviewed periodically, and be consistent with other measurement systems (e.g., liquidity pricing system). Finally, a best-practice TPS is internally consistent and should not be used to send directional signals; neither should the rules be changed in an attempt to mitigate the sins of the past.

5.4 Liquidity Risk Measurement

One should not confuse interest rate sensitivity with liquidity risk. Interest rate sensitivity is determined by the frequency of the repricing of an instrument. In contrast, it is the contractual maturity of an item that determines whether it contributes to a liquidity gap.

For example, a three-year fixed-rate loan has an interest rate sensitivity of three years, and a liquidity maturity of three years.

A variable-rate, three-year loan priced off six-month Libor has an interest rate sensitivity of six months, and a liquidity maturity of three years.

A business unit's impact on institutional liquidity can be characterized by means of a liquidity measurement system. This must be "directionally correct"; a liability-gathering unit should be credited for supplying liquidity, and an asset-generating unit should be charged for using liquidity.

For example, Table 3.1 illustrates a spectrum of funding sources and indicates that a bank might assign a higher liquidity credit for "stable funds" than for "hot funds." "Hot funds" are funds that are supplied by depositors (e.g., dealers) and could be quickly removed from the bank in the event of a crisis. Table 3.1 ranks the sources of funds in terms of their liquidity.

One can illustrate the key features of a best-practice liquidity quantification scheme through a simplified version of a liquidity ranking process. The liquidity ranking process should enable the bank to quantify credits and charges, depending on the degree to which a business unit is a net supplier or net user of liquidity.

Liquidity can be quantified using a symmetrical scale. Such scales help managers to compute a business unit's liquidity score more objectively, through a ranking and weighting process.

TABLE 3.1

Funds Source Spectrum

Open Market	Direct	Unconventional	Core Funds	Capital Market Funds

HOT ◄──────────────────────────────────► STABLE

Brokers/Dealers (e.g., Negotiable CDs)	Wholesale Placements (e.g., Large CDs, BAs, Repos, Fed Funds)	Customized Term Placements (e.g., Special 5-Yr CDs)	• DDAs • MMAs • Savings • CDs	• Common Equity • Preferred Equity • Term Notes/ Bonds

A quantification scheme such as this also helps the bank to determine the amount of liquidity in the system, and to set targets in terms of a desirable and quantifiable level of liquidity.

The liquidity rank (LR) attributed to a product is determined by multiplying the dollar amount of the product by its rank. For example, if business unit XYZ is both a supplier and a user of liquidity, then a net liquidity calculation needs to be made. Looking at Table 3.2, if we assume that business unit XYZ supplied $10 million of the most stable liquidity, $3 million of the next most stable, and so on, then a total credit of 94 ($10 \times 5 + 4 \times 3 + 3 \times 6 + 2 \times 5 + 1 \times 4 = 94$) would be assigned.

Similarly, if we assume in our example that business unit XYZ used $10 million of the most expensive liquidity, $3 million of the next most expensive, and so on, then a total charge of -100 ($4 \times 1 + 8 \times 2 + 6 \times 3 + 3 \times 4 + 10 \times 5 = 100$) would be assigned. The net result of the two calculations is a liquidity rank of minus $6 million.

The LR approach is simply a heuristic tool that helps managers to control the liquidity profile of their financial institution.

TABLE 3.2

Liquidity Rank Measurement Units

Business Unit XYZ's Net Liquidity Rank Measurement Units			
Liquidity Suppliers		**Liquidity Users**	
Rank Score	**Amount ($MM)**	**Rank Score**	**Amount ($MM)**
+5	$10	−1	$4
+4	$3	−2	$8
+3	$6	−3	$6
+2	$5	−4	$3
+1	$4	−5	$10
Total	94	Total	−100
Net		−6 (= 94 − 100)	

The next step is to charge each business unit for the liquidity risk that it generates.

6. CONCLUSION: STEPS TO SUCCESS

In the past, financial institutions have treated each type of risk separately. This approach has been undermined by the increasing complexity of products, linkages between markets, and the growing importance of portfolio effects. Today, the profitability of a financial institution depends on its ability to price risk and to hedge its global exposure.

How can the ideas that we have introduced in this chapter be turned into reality? One of the first steps is to tailor the vision by identifying user and business needs, and by defining objectives, deliverables, and benefits. One must also obtain the commitment of top management, and gain sponsorship at the board level.

Second, the bank needs to agree on its risk management policy. For example, senior management must approve a clear notion of how the institution defines a "worst case risk."

Third, the bank needs to agree on the risk measurement methodologies, for example, how to define risk in terms of VaR. A best-practice VaR system can be applied to gain both a defensive advantage and an offensive advantage. Defensive advantages include providing risk control for shareholders and senior management. Offensive advantages include utilizing VaR as a basis for capital attribution as well as improving the bank's return-to-risk ratio. The bank can use its VaR methodology to mine the risk management database for trade opportunities.

Next, the managers of the bank need to agree on their organizational infrastructure. How should the risk management function be organized to best manage the bank's risks?

A key to designing an efficient organization is to ensure that the roles and responsibilities of each risk unit are carefully spelled out and remain complementary to one another. A detailed breakout of typical responsibilities within trading market risk, trading credit risk, and risk analytics is shown in Figure 3.17.

Trading-Room market risk (TRMR) management and trading-room credit risk (TRCR) units have a responsibility to work with risk analytics and risk MIS in rolling out price risk reporting systems. The

FIGURE 3.17

MRM Organization

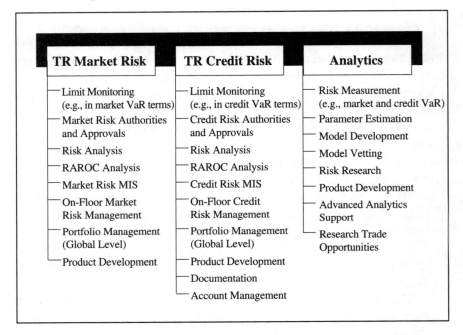

TR Market Risk	TR Credit Risk	Analytics
Limit Monitoring (e.g., in market VaR terms)	Limit Monitoring (e.g., in credit VaR terms)	Risk Measurement (e.g., market and credit VaR)
Market Risk Authorities and Approvals	Credit Risk Authorities and Approvals	Parameter Estimation
Risk Analysis	Risk Analysis	Model Development
RAROC Analysis	RAROC Analysis	Model Vetting
Market Risk MIS	Credit Risk MIS	Risk Research
On-Floor Market Risk Management	On-Floor Credit Risk Management	Product Development
Portfolio Management (Global Level)	Portfolio Management (Global Level)	Advanced Analytics Support
Product Development	Product Development	Research Trade Opportunities
	Documentation	
	Account Management	

TRMR and TRCR units approve deals and monitor risks. The risk analytics unit typically develops the mathematics required in the implementation of market VaR and credit VaR methodologies. The analytics function also vets all the models that are developed by dealers; develops robust, accurate, and computationally efficient models to price and hedge complex securities; and conducts research.

Each of the units gears its infrastructure to satisfy specific objectives. For example, each morning the head of TRMR might chair a meeting of senior managers and global dealers in order to review and debate (in light of, say, current market conditions) the previous end-of-day market risk exposures.

For the rest of the trading day, the head of TRMR would keep abreast of ongoing developments and changes in market risk exposures—following markets and talking to traders. The head of TRMR is likely to sit on the trading floor alongside the chief dealers.

The TRMR unit itself might well be divided into distinct, but related, groups, for example, a policy group responsible for developing risk management methods and standards, an operating group charged with continuously monitoring the firm's market risk exposures, and a third group of market risk mangers who cover specific regions (e.g., Asia, Europe, North America, South America) or products (e.g., commodity derivatives, high-yield securities). Product specialists within TRMR might provide direct risk management support to each product manager.

Similarly, the TRCR unit infrastructure must be geared to its aims. One of these might be to shrink to a minimum the time between an idea occurring in a trader's head to the credit approval of the trade.

Fifth, as discussed earlier in this chapter, banks need to build a first class risk MIS system.

Sixth, the bank should encourage businesses to use the risk infrastructure as both a tactical management and strategic planning tool. Risk information is a critical component of a globally integrated bank.

Seventh, set clear short-term and regular deliverables. For example, every three months the risk management function might aim to roll out upgrades to the risk management system—to include another product or another location or to encompass another legacy system. One should build one small subset of the risk management system at a time, and enhance the system over time. (For example, it makes no sense to attempt to build a risk management data warehouse all at once.)

Next, one needs to clearly define the ultimate aims of the risk management process. For example, one objective might be to allocate economic capital based on risk. A key deliverable would be to continually refine capabilities and reports.

Finally, one needs to establish a clear philosophy for the group. For example, a philosophy might call for the risk management function to deliver solutions, be application-driven, and remain conscious of user needs.

NOTES

1. The term basis point (bp) denotes 1/100 of 1 percent, or 0.0001.
2. At CIBC we refer to Risk Management Unit, or RMU, the common unit of risk measurement across business.

The New BIS Capital Requirements for Financial Risks

1. INTRODUCTION

In this chapter we compare the two alternative ways to assess market risk set out in the Bank for International Settlements (BIS) 1998 regulatory reform described in Chapter 2. The differences between the two methodologies strike to the heart of the modern regulation of risk management. Furthermore, choosing between the two methodologies is a significant issue in the business strategy of banks. As we will demonstrate, the difference in capital charges between the two approaches is so considerable that banks subject to the "standardized approach" may find themselves facing a severe competitive disadvantage. Ideally, this competitive disadvantage should encourage banks to invest in more sophisticated methodologies in order to reap the benefits of lower regulatory capital. The "carrot and stick" approach associated with BIS 98 is one of its most powerful features.

The standardized approach, which employs constant factors determined by the BIS for various instruments, is detailed in Section 2. The alternative approach, the "internal model approach," is based on the proprietary models of individual banks and the probability distributions for changes in the values of claims. Before a bank can adopt this second approach, it must gain the approval of its regulator. The BIS sets rules and guidelines for regulators that guide the process by which regulators award this approval. These guidelines are detailed in Section 3. (Readers unfamiliar with the basic tenets of value-at-risk modeling may wish to read Chapter 5 before reading this section.)

In Section 4 the pros and cons of the two approaches are discussed and a new approach, the "precommitment approach," is proposed. Finally, in Section 5, a numerical example is presented to illustrate the savings in capital requirements that can arise if internal models are employed rather than the standardized approach.

2. THE STANDARDIZED APPROACH

The standardized model uses a "building block" methodology. The capital charge for each risk category, i.e., interest rates, equities, foreign exchange, and commodities, is first determined separately. Then, the four measures are simply added together to obtain the global capital charge that arises from the bank's market risk. In this section we present, and illustrate with simple examples, the main thrust of the method for the four risk categories.

2.1 Interest Rate Risk

The model encompasses all fixed-rate and floating-rate debt securities, zero-coupon instruments, interest rate derivatives, and hybrid products such as convertible bonds. The latter are treated like debt securities when they trade like debt securities (i.e., when their price is below par), and are otherwise treated like equities. Simple interest rate derivatives such as futures, forward contracts, including forward rate agreements (FRAs), and swaps are treated as if they were a combination of short and long positions in debt contracts. (Options are treated separately and will be covered later in this section.)

The interest risk capital charge is the sum of two components of market risk, each of which is separately calculated. The first component, "specific risk," applies to the net holdings for each particular instrument. The second component is related to "general market risk," and in this case the long and short positions in different securities or derivatives can be partially offset.

2.1.1 Specific Risk
The capital charge for specific risk is designed to protect the bank against an adverse price movement in the price of a security that

TABLE 4.1

Specific Risk Charge Factor for Net Debt Positions

Debt Category	Remaining Maturity	Capital Charge (%)
Government	Any	0.00
Qualifying	Six months or less	0.25
	Six to 24 months[1]	1.00
	Over two years	1.60
Other	Any	8.00

[1]For Canada, OSFI has set the horizon of the second bucket to 12 months instead of 24.

is due to idiosyncratic factors related to the individual issuer of the security. For this reason, offsetting is restricted to matched positions in the same issue, including derivatives. The capital charge applies whether the bank has a net long or net short position. Even where the issuer of two securities is the same, but there are differences in maturity, coupon rates, call features, etc., no offsetting is allowed. This is because a change in the credit quality of the issuer may have a different effect on the market value of each instrument.

Table 4.1 shows the specific risk charge for various types of debt positions. The weighting factors apply to the market value of the debt instruments, and not to their notional amount.

The "government" category in the table includes all forms of debt instrument issued by OECD central governments, as well as non-OECD central governments provided certain conditions are satisfied. The "qualifying" category includes debt securities issued by OECD public sector entities, regulated securities firms of the G-10 countries plus Switzerland and Luxembourg, and other rated investment-grade bonds. The "other" category receives the same specific risk capital charge as would a private sector borrower under the credit risk requirements of the 1988 Accord, i.e., 8 percent.

A specific risk charge also applies to derivative contracts in the trading book, but only when the underlying reference of the derivative contract is subject to specific risk. For example, an interest rate swap based on LIBOR is not subject to a specific risk charge, while an option on a corporate bond is subject to the charge. (Note that all over-the-counter derivative contracts are subject to a counterparty credit risk charge arising from the direct counterparty to the contract. The capital charge is derived according to the guidelines of the 1988 Accord, even where a specific risk charge is required.)

2.1.2 General Market Risk

Capital requirements for general market risk are designed to capture the risk of loss arising from changes in market interest rates. Banks can choose between two methods, the "maturity" method and the "duration" method. The duration method is simply a variant of the maturity method, and in this chapter we will describe only the former.[1]

The maturity method uses a "maturity ladder," i.e., a series of "maturity bands" that are divided into "maturity zones" according to the rule given in Table 4.2. These maturity bands and zones are chosen to take into account differences in price sensitivities and

TABLE 4.2

Maturity Bands and Risk Weights

Zone	Coupon 3% or More	Coupon Less Than 3%	Assumed Changes in Yield (in Percentage Points)	Risk Weights (Sensitivities)
1	1 month or less	1 month or less	1.00	0.00%
	1 to 3 months	1 to 3 months	1.00	0.20%
	3 to 6 months	3 to 6 months	1.00	0.40%
	6 to 12 months	6 to 12 months	1.00	0.70%
2	1 to 2 years	to 1.9 years	0.90	1.25%
	2 to 3 years	to 2.8 years	0.80	1.75%
	3 to 4 years	2.8 to 3.6 years	0.75	2.25%
3	4 to 5 years	to 4.3 years	0.75	2.75%
	5 to 7 years	to 5.7 years	0.70	3.25%
	7 to 10 years	5.7 to 7.3 years	0.65	3.75%
	10 to 15 years	7.3 to 9.3 years	0.60	4.50%
	15 to 20 years	9.3 to 10.6 years	0.60	5.25%
	over 20 years	10.6 to 12 years	0.60	6.00%
		12 to 20 years	0.60	8.00%
		over 20 years	0.60	12.50%

interest rate volatilities across different maturities. A separate maturity ladder must be constructed for each currency in which the bank has a significant trading position. No offsetting is allowed among maturity ladders of different currencies. This has a considerable impact upon financial institutions that trade in one currency and hedge in another currency (due to the high correlation between the two currencies). For instance, an institution that entered into a swap in U.S. dollars and then performed an exactly offsetting swap in Canadian dollars would be only exposed to some residual foreign exchange risk and cross-currency basis risk in economic terms. The BIS methodology, however, imposes an onerous amount of capital for this trade and its hedge.

The first step in the maturity method consists of allocating the marked-to-market value of the positions to each maturity band. Fixed-rate instruments are allocated according to the residual term to maturity, and floating-rate instruments according to the residual term that applies to the next repricing date.

Derivatives, such as forwards, futures, and swaps, are converted into long and short positions in the underlying positions. Options are treated separately (see below). For example, a long one-year forward contract on a two-year bond is equivalent to a short position in the six- to 12-month maturity band for an amount equal to the discounted value of the forward price of the bond, and a long position in the one- to two-year maturity band for the same market value. In the case of swaps, the paying side is treated as a short position and the receiving side as a long position on the relevant underlying instruments. Offsetting is only allowed for matched positions in identical instruments that have exactly the same issuer.

In the second step the positions in each maturity band are risk-weighted according to the sensitivities given in Table 4.2.

The third step consists of calculating capital requirements for general market risk according to the following principles:

1. Vertical disallowance to account for basis risk. In each maturity band, the matched weighted position is awarded a capital charge of 10 percent. The unmatched positions in each maturity band are considered in the calculation, related to the horizontal disallowance and a parallel shift in the yield curve (principles 2 and 3).

2. Horizontal disallowance to account for the risks caused by possible twists in the yield curve. The matched weighted positions in each zone (zones 1, 2, and 3, respectively), between adjacent zones (between zones 1 and 2, then between zones 2 and 3), and between the two extreme zones (between zones 1 and 3) are allocated a capital charge given in Table 4.3. Again, only the unmatched positions at each step are considered in the remaining calculations, related to a parallel shift in the yield curve (principle 3).
3. To account for the risk associated with a parallel shift in the yield curve, the residual unmatched weighted positions are given a capital charge of 100 percent.

The example presented in Table 4.4 illustrates the allocation process to each maturity band, and the calculation of the capital charge for general market risk.

TABLE 4.3

Horizontal Disallowances for the Risk Related to Twists in the Yield Curve

Zones	Time Band	Within the Zone	Between Adjacent Zones	Between Zones 1 and 3
Zone 1	0–1 month			
	1–3 months	40%		
	3–6 months			
	6–12 months		40%	
Zone 2	1–3 years			
	2–3 years	30%		100%
	3–4 years			
Zone 3	4–5 years		40%	
	5–7 years			
	7–10 years			
	10–15 years	30%		
	15–20 years			
	over 20 years			

Note that there is vertical disallowance only in zone 3 for the seven- to 10-year maturity band. There is no horizontal disallowance within zones 2 and 3, since there are no offsetting positions between time bands within each of these two zones. However, there is horizontal disallowance within zone 1, and between zones 1 and 3. The short risk-weighted position in the three- to six-month time band partially offsets the long positions in the adjacent time bands in zone 1. Then, after vertical disallowance in the seven- to 10-year time band for $0.5 million, the net unmatched position in zone 3 becomes a net short position of $5.125 million.

Given the net long position for $1.125 million in zone 2, there is partial offsetting for this amount between zones 2 and 3, which leaves a net unmatched position of 0 in zone 2 and a net short position of $4 million in zone 3. After horizontal disallowance in zone 1, the net unmatched position becomes a net long position of $1 million in this zone.

Finally, there is partial offsetting for $1 million between zones 1 and 3, which leaves an overall net unmatched position of $3 million.

The total capital charge is (in $ million):

- For the vertical disallowance (basis risk) $ 0.050
- For the horizontal disallowance in zone 1 (curve risk) $ 0.080
- For the horizontal disallowance between adjacent zones (curve risk) $ 0.450
- For the horizontal disallowance between zone 1 and 3
  (steepening of the curve risk) $ 1.000
- For the overall net open position (parallel shift risk) $ 3.000

                 Total $ 4.580

2.1.3 Treatment of Options

There are three different approaches. The "simplified approach" applies to banks that buy options but do not write them, while the "delta-plus method" and the "scenario approach" should be used by banks that both buy and write options.

(i) Simplified approach

Table 4.5 shows the capital charge according to the simplified approach. As an example, suppose the bank is long 100 shares

TABLE 4.4

Illustration of the Calculation of the Capital Charge to Cover General Market Risk for Interest Rate Instruments (Except Options)

Portfolio:

A. Qualifying bond with a $13.33 million market value, a residual maturity of eight years, and a coupon of 8%.

B. Government bond with a market value of $75 million, a residual maturity of two months, and a coupon of 7%.

C. Interest rate swap at par value, i.e., with a zero net market value, with a notional amount of $150 million, where the bank receives floating and pays fixed, with the next fixing in nine months, and a residual life of eight years.

D. Long position in interest rate futures contract with six-month delivery date, for which the underlying instrument is a government bond with a three-and-a-half-year maturity and a market value of $50 million.

Time band	Zone 1 (months)			Zone 2 (years)					Zone 3 (years)					
	0–1	1–3	3–6	6–12	1–2	2–3	3–4	4–5	5–7	7–10	10–15	15–20	>20
Coupon >3%	0–1	1–3	3–6	6–12	1–1.9	1.9–2.8	2.8–3.6	3.6–4.3	4.3–5.7	5.7–7.3	7.3–9.3	9.3–10.6	10.6–12	12–20	>20
Coupon <3%	0–1	1–3	3–6	6–12	1–1.9	1.9–2.8	2.8–3.6	3.6–4.3	4.3–5.7	5.7–7.3	7.3–9.3	9.3–10.6	10.6–12	12–20	>20

144

Positions	0.00	0.20	0.40	0.70	1.25	1.75	2.25	2.75	3.25	3.75	4.50	5.25	6.00	8.00	12.5
A															
B		+75 Gov.													+13.33 Qual.
C				+150 Swap											
D			−50 Fut.				+50 Fut.			−150 Swap					
Weight (%)	0.00	0.20	0.40	0.70	1.25	1.75	2.25	2.75	3.25	3.75	4.50	5.25	6.00	8.00	12.5
Postion x Weight		+0.15	−0.20	+1.05			+1.125			+0.5					
Vertical Disallowance										−5.625 0.5 × 10% = 0.05					
Horizontal Disallowance 1			0.20 × 40% = 0.08												
Horizontal Disallowance 2										1.125 × 40% = 0.45					
Horizontal Disallowance 3								1.0 × 100% = 1.0							

T a b l e   4.5

Capital Charge for Options According to the Simplified
Approach

Position	Treatment
Long cash and long put Or Short cash and long call	The capital charge is the market value of the underlying security multiplied by the sum of specific and general market risk charges for underlying, less the amount the option is in the money (if any), bounded at zero.
The capital charge will be the lesser of:	
Long call Or Long put	• The market value of the underlying security multiplied by the sum of specific and general market risk charges for the underlying. • The market value of the option.

currently valued at $10, and has a put option on these shares with
a strike price of $11. The capital charge would be:

+ $1,000 * 16%   = $160
  (8% for specific risk plus 8% for general market risk)
  − the amount the option is in the money, i.e.
  ($11 − $10) * 100   = $100

                                                                Total: $60

(ii) Delta-plus approach

For the purpose of calculating the capital charges related to general market risk, the option is first considered as its "delta equivalent" in the underlying instrument. The delta equivalent is then
allocated into the time band corresponding to the maturity of the
option (see example in Table 4.4).[2]

Then, two additional capital charges are added. The first one
adjusts the capital charge for gamma risk or convexity risk,[3] i.e.,

$$\text{Gamma capital charge} = \tfrac{1}{2} \text{ gamma} * \Delta V^2$$

This is simply the second-order term in the Taylor expansion[4]
of the option price formula, where ΔV denotes the change in the

value of the underlying. For interest rate products, the calculation of the charge is based upon the assumed changes in yield in the maturity band, as given in Table 4.2. For equities and foreign exchange and gold the price change in the calculation is taken as a fixed change of 8 percent, while for commodities it is taken as 15 percent (the approach is illustrated in Table 4.6).

The second capital charge compensates for vega risk, i.e.,

$$\text{Vega capital charge} = \text{vega} * 25\% \, \sigma$$

where vega is the sensitivity of the option price to a change of one unit of volatility, σ.

This vega charge represents the impact that a 25 percent increase or decrease in volatility would have on the value of the position.

(iii) Scenario matrix approach

The scenario matrix approach adopts as a capital charge the worst loss that might arise from the positions in a series of scenarios. The scenarios are generated by a grid that allows for a combination of possible values of the underlying price, the volatility, and the cost of carry. The range of values that is considered in the calculation is the same as for the delta-plus approach.

Table 4.6

Delta-plus Approach for an Equity Option

Consider a short position in a European one-year call option on a stock with a striking price of $490. The underlying spot price is $500, the risk-free rate is 8% per annum, and the annualized volatility is 20%. The option value is $65.48, with a negative delta and gamma of -0.721 and -0.0034, respectively, corresponding to a $1 change in the underlying price; its vega is 1.68 associated with a change in volatility of one percentage point.

The three components of the capital charge are:

Delta equivalent: $500 * 0.721 * 8%	=	$28.84
Gamma adjustment: 1/2 * 0.0034 * ($500 * 8%)^2	=	$ 2.72
Vega adjustment: 1.68 * (25% * 20)	=	$ 8.40
	Total	$39.96

2.2 Equity Risk

The charge for the general market risk incurred by equity positions is 8 percent of each net position. The capital charge for any specific risk is 8 percent, unless the portfolio is both liquid and well diversified, in which case the charge is 4 percent.

Equity derivatives are treated in the same way as interest rate derivatives. While there is no specific charge when the underlying is a government security or a market rate such as LIBOR, for diversified broad market indices there is a specific risk charge of 2 percent of the underlying market value.

The example given in Table 4.6 illustrates the delta-plus approach as it applies to equity option positions. Note that the gamma adjustment is based on an 8 percent move in the stock price. If the underlying were a commodity, the adjustment would be based on a 15 percent move in the underlying price, and the delta-equivalent would have been allocated to the time band corresponding to the maturity of the option (see Table 4.8).

2.3 Foreign Exchange Risk, Including Gold Price Risk

There are two steps in the calculation of the capital charge. First, the exposure in each currency is measured and, second, the net long and net short exposures in all currencies are translated into an overall capital charge according to a rule called the "shorthand method."

The measurement of the exposures is straightforward. It consists of the net spot position, the net forward position,[5] the delta-equivalent for options as discussed in Section 2.1.3, accrued interest and expenses, and other future income and expenses which are already fully hedged.

The capital charge is the absolute value of 8 percent of the greater of the net open long positions and the net open short positions in all currencies, plus 8 percent of the absolute value of the net open position in gold plus the gamma and vega adjustments for options. The example in Table 4.7 illustrates the application of the rule.

Table 4.7

Shorthand Approach to Capital Charge for Foreign Exchange and Gold Risk

Assume the net positions in each currency, expressed in the reporting currency, i.e., dollars, are as follows:

Long			Short		
Yen	DM	GB	FFR	US$	Gold
+50	+100	+150	−20	−180	−35

Aggregate positions: +300   −200   −35

Capital charge = 8% * 300 + 8% * 35 = $26.80

2.4 Commodities Risk

Commodities are broadly defined as physical products that can be traded on an organized market, such as agricultural products, oil, gas, electricity, and precious metals (except gold, which is treated as a foreign currency). The risk of commodities is often more complex to measure than that of other financial instruments as the markets are less liquid, prices are affected by seasonal patterns in supply and demand, and inventories play a critical role in the determination of the equilibrium price.

The main components of market risk are:

- Outright price risk, i.e., the risk of price movements in the spot prices.
- Basis risk, i.e., the risk of a movement in the price differential between different but related commodity prices. This risk is inherent for energy products whose prices are quoted as a spread over a benchmark index.
- Interest rate risk, i.e., the risk of a change in the cost of financing any investment in the commodity (a key component in the "cost of carry").
- Time spread risk, or forward gap risk, i.e., the risk of movements in forward commodity prices for reasons other than a change in interest rates; the shape of the forward

curve is a function of supply and demand in the short run, and fundamental factors in the longer run.
- Options risk, i.e., delta, gamma, and vega risk as already discussed for other classes of products.

The standardized model for commodities is somewhat similar to the maturity ladder approach for interest rate products. In effect, it attempts by means of a simple framework to capture directional risk, curve risk, and time spread risk.

First, positions are converted at current spot rates into the reporting currency, and placed in the relevant time band. Forwards, futures, and swaps are decomposed into a combination of long and short positions (as for interest rate products). The delta equivalent of options is placed in the time band corresponding to the maturity of the option.

To capture spread risk and some of the forward gap risk, the matched position in a time band is allocated a capital charge of 3 percent. The unmatched position is carried forward into the nearest available time band at a cost of 0.6 percent per maturity band. For example, if it is moved forward by two maturity bands, it is charged 2 * 0.6% = 1.2%. At the end of the process, the net unmatched position is given a capital charge of 15 percent.

The example in Table 4.8 illustrates the principle of the maturity ladder for commodities.

3. THE INTERNAL MODELS APPROACH

Nowadays, those institutions that trade in financial products rely on their proprietary expertise in modeling as much as they rely on traditional trading skills. The risk that these models will be wrong or wrongly implemented—what is known in the derivatives industry as "model risk"—is likely to remain an issue since it is inherent in the trading of derivatives. Indeed, the ability of a trading institution to remain profitable relies in part on the skill of its financial engineers and traders to build and continually renew the appropriate pricing and hedging models. State-of-the-art modeling provides many institutions with a unique competitive edge.

Pricing models are kept relatively secret, although most of them are based on published papers in academic journals. However,

Table 4.8

Maturity Ladder Approach for Commodities

Time Band	Spread Capital Charge	Position	Capital Charge		
0–1 m	1.5%	—			
1–3 m	1.5%	—			
3–6 m	1.5%	Long $600	Matched position:		
		Short $1,000	$600 × 3%	=	$18
			$400 carried forward 2 time bands:		
			$400 × 2 × 0.6	=	$4.8
6–12 m	1.5%	—			
1–2 y	1.5%	Long $500	Matched position:		
			$400 × 3%	=	$12
			$100 carried forward 1 time band:		
			$100 × 0.6	=	$0.6
2–3 y	1.5%	Short $300	Matched position:		
			$100 × 3%	=	$3
Over 3 y	1.5%	—			
			Net unmatched position:		
			$200 × 15%	=	$30
			Total		$68.4

the implementation and calibration of these models requires ingenuity, strong numerical and computer skills, and a good understanding of the products and the markets. Very few professionals are able to produce this elaborate cocktail.

The proprietary models that are used in pricing market positions are also used for position risk management. This is how banks derive risk exposures such as deltas, gammas, vegas, and other "greeks" (see Chapter 5). However, as regularly reported in the financial press, using the wrong model not only leads to large trading losses, but can also lead to a poor assessment of market risk exposure.

The regulators accept that it is in the nature of the modern banking world that institutions will use different assumptions and modeling techniques. The regulators take account of this for their own purposes by requiring institutions to scale up the value-at-risk number derived from their internal model by a factor of 3, referred to in the following as the "multiplier." This multiplier can be viewed as insurance against model risk, imperfect assessment of specific risks, and other operational risks. Alternatively, it might be regarded as a safety factor that guards against "nonnormal" market moves. However, as we discuss later on, the use of multipliers in this way is open to criticism.

3.1 Quantitative and Modeling Requirements

The "internal model" approach is intended to capture all the material market risks of the bank's trading positions. The technique most widely recognized by the financial industry and regulators for the assessment of market risk in a portfolio context is the value-at-risk methodology described in Chapter 5.

Although each institution has some discretion in the choice of the risk factors used in the VaR model, these risk factors should be selected with great care so as to guarantee the robustness of the model. Oversimplification and a failure to select the risk factors that are inherent in the trading positions may have serious consequences, as the VaR model would be likely to miss the financial exposures generated by risks such as basis risk, curve risk, or spread risk.

These shortcomings are likely to be revealed when back-testing the model, and may lead to penalties in the form of the imposition by the regulators of a multiplier greater than the usual multiplier of 3.

Market risk can be broken down into four categories: interest rate risk, equity risk, exchange rate risk, and commodity price risk:

- Interest rate risk modeling applies only to the trading book. The base yield curve in each currency (government curve or swap curve) should be modeled with a minimum of six risk points, i.e., six yields with different maturities such as one month, six months, one year, etc. The other relevant yield curves, e.g., the yield curves of corporate debt and provincial yield curves for Canada,[6] are defined with regard to the base curve by the addition of a spread (positive or negative). The model should also incorporate separate risk factors to capture spread risk.

- Equity price risk modeling should incorporate risk factors corresponding to each of the equity markets in which the trading book holds significant positions. At a minimum, there should be a risk factor designed to capture market-wide movements in equity prices, e.g., the broad market index in each national equity market. This could be used to assess both market risk and idiosyncratic risk, according to the capital asset pricing model (CAPM). The most extensive approach would be to assign risk factors that correspond to each asset in the portfolio.
- Exchange rate risk modeling should include risk factors corresponding to the individual currencies in which the trading and banking books have positions.
- Commodity price risk should incorporate risk factors that correspond to each of the commodity markets in which the trading and banking books have significant positions. The model should account for variations in the convenience yield.[7] It should also encompass *directional risk* to capture exposure from changes in spot prices, *forward gap* and *interest rate risk* to capture exposure to changes in forward prices arising from maturity mismatches, and *basis risk* to capture the exposure to changes in price relationship between similar commodities (e.g., energy products that are defined relative to a price for a benchmark crude oil such as WTI).

As we explain in Chapter 5, the confidence level and holding period of any VaR calculation are critical to the validity of the risk assessment. The 1996 Amendment requires VaR to be derived at the 99 percent (one-tailed)[8] confidence level, using a 10-day holding period. In effect, this means the regulators are asking banks to take into account in their VaR figure the risk that they might not be able to liquidate their positions for a period of 10 days. However, in the initial phase of implementation of the internal model, the BIS allows the 10-day VaR to be proxied by multiplying the one-day VaR by the square root of 10, i.e., 3.16.[9]

Table 4.9

Multiplier Based on the Number
of Exceptions in Back-Testing

Number of Exceptions	Multiplier
4 or fewer	3.00
5	3.40
6	3.50
7	3.65
8	3.75
9	3.85
10 or more	4.00

The daily regulatory capital requirement corresponds to the maximum of previous day's VaR (VaR$_{t-1}$) and the average of daily VaR experienced over the preceding 60 business days ($\overline{VaR} = 1/60$ $\sum_{i=t-1}^{t-60} VaR_i$) scaled up by the multiplier k, which normally should be equal to 3:

$$\text{Market risk capital charge (t)} = \text{Max}\{\text{VaR}_{t-1}, k\ \overline{\text{VaR}}\} \qquad (1)$$

As we discussed in Section 2.1, this arbitrary multiplier is intended to compensate for model errors, and the imperfect assessment of specific risks and operational risks. The regulators can increase it, up to 4, if the models do not meet back-testing requirements (Table 4.9).

Institutions are allowed to take into account correlations among risk categories. Volatilities and correlations should be estimated using historical data, with a minimum history of 250 days,[10] i.e., approximately one year of business days. Market parameters should be updated at least once every three months, or more frequently if market conditions warrant. If empirical correlations between risk categories are unavailable, then the aggregate VaR is calculated as the simple arithmetic sum of the VaR for each block, i.e., equity, interest rate, foreign exchange, and commodities. In that case, the aggregate VaR does not benefit from the risk reduction that results from any diversification across risk classes.

The internal model should capture not only linear risks, known as delta risks, but also nonlinear risks, such as the convexity risk (gamma) and volatility risk (vega) inherent in options positions. One important point is that the choice of the VaR methodology is otherwise left to the institution. As Chapter 5 describes, it can choose to implement historical simulation, full Monte Carlo simulation, or other pseudo-analytic methods based on the Greeks (variance-covariance approach).

Banks that cannot meet all the requirements for internal models are allowed to use a combination of standard models and internal models, but are expected to move towards the full internal models framework. Each risk category, however, must be measured by means of a single approach. If a combination of approaches is used, then the total capital charge is determined by a simple arithmetic sum. This, of course, cannot take into account the possible correlation effects between the risk categories.

3.2 Specific Risk

As we explained at the beginning of this chapter, according to the 1996 Amendment banks are required to hold capital in support of the "specific risk" associated with any debt and equity positions in their trading books. In return, no further capital charges are allocated to these positions in respect of credit risk. In other words, specific risk is simply a substitute for credit risk for traded on-balance-sheet products.

Derivative instruments incur a specific risk capital charge when the underlying is subject to specific risk. Thus, when they are traded on an exchange, there is no specific risk charge for interest rate and currency swaps, FRAs, forward foreign exchange contracts, interest rate futures, and futures on an interest rate index. However, when the instruments are traded over-the-counter (OTC), and thus do not benefit from the credit guarantees extended by an exchange environment, the instruments generate counterparty risk and are charged a capital amount to cover their credit risk exposure (according to rules of the 1988 Accord).

The capital charge for specific risk can be determined either by using internal models, scaled up by a multiplier of 4, or the standardized approach.

So how should such a charge be determined using internal models?[11]

The new 1998 regulatory framework views specific risk, and consequently credit risk, as an outgrowth of market risk. As such it should be modeled using assumptions that are consistent with the market risk model. This is a significant improvement with respect to the 1988 Accord, where the credit risk capital charge was calculated according to somewhat arbitrary ratios that did not correctly account for the specificity of the instruments.[12]

At CIBC, the internal model for bonds captures both spread risk and credit risk. Credit risk arises out of default events, but also from credit migration, i.e, when a company's credit rating is upgraded or downgraded. An approach such as CreditMetrics, proposed by JP Morgan (1997), provides a good practical framework for building an internal model that relates to the specific risk of bonds (see Chapter 8).

For equities, the approach is different since market risk, measured by the volatility of stock returns, already captures both general market risk and specific risk. In other words, both the market risk and the default risk of stocks are already fully accounted for by the current spot price. So how can we break the total risk for a stock into its general market risk and specific risk components? To do this, we turn to the statistical properties of a "single-index model," known also as the market model.[13] The fundamental idea is that the rate of return on any stock i is related to some common index I by a linear equation of the form:

$$R_i = \alpha_i + \beta_i I + u_i \tag{2}$$

where

R_i is the rate of return on stock i
α_i is the constant component of the return of stock i
I is the value of the index
β_i is a measure of the average change in R_i as a result of a given change in the index I
u_i is a deviation of the actual observed return from the regression line $\alpha_i + \beta_i R_m$, i.e., the error term, which is assumed to be normally distributed, $N(0, \sigma_{u_i})$

The index generally used for this model is the rate of return on the market portfolio (approximated in the United States by the S&P500 Index or by the NYSE Index), which we denote R_m. The crucial assumption is that for every pair of stocks (i,j) the error terms are uncorrelated; i.e., $\text{Cov}(u_i, u_j) = 0$. The error term is also assumed to be uncorrelated with the market portfolio; i.e., $\text{Cov}(u_i, R_m) = 0$. The parameters of Equation (2) are estimated in practice by using the ex-post historical rates of return, and by running a time series regression. It follows that:

$$\beta_i = \frac{\text{Cov}(R_i, R_m)}{\text{Var}(R_m)}$$

Taking the variance of both sides of Equation (2) we obtain:

$$\sigma_i^2 = \beta_i^2 \sigma_m^2 + \sigma_{u_i}^2$$

The total risk of a security, as measured by its variance, can be divided into two components:

(i) $\beta_i^2 \sigma_m^2$ — systematic risk, or general market risk, which is nondiversifiable and associated with market fluctuations, where σ_m denotes the variance of the market return

(ii) $\sigma_{u_i}^2$ — idiosyncratic risk, or specific risk, which can be eliminated through diversification

Given a stock, or a portfolio, whose price is denoted S_i, the general market risk (GMR) of the position is, according to the market model:

$$\text{GMR}_i = S_i \times \beta_i \times \sigma_m$$

and its specific risk (SR) is:

$$\text{SR}_i = S_i \sigma_u = S_i \sqrt{\sigma_i^2 - \beta_i^2 \sigma_m^2}$$

These risks can be easily aggregated. For a portfolio with a total value of P composed of n securities S_i, $i = 1, \ldots, n$, the general market risk for the portfolio is:

$$\text{GMR}_P = \sum_{i=1}^{n} S_i \beta_i \sigma_m = P \sum_{i=1}^{m} \frac{S_i}{P} \beta_i \sigma_m$$

$$= P \beta_P \sigma_m$$

where $\beta_P = \sum_{i=1}^{m} [S_i/P]\beta_i$ represents the beta of the portfolio P, which is the weighted average of the betas of the individual stocks, with the individual weight, $x_i = S_i/P$, being the proportion of stock i in the portfolio.

Under the assumption that the error terms are uncorrelated, the specific risk for the portfolio is simply:

$$SR_P = P \sqrt{\sum_{i=1}^{n} x_i^2 \sigma_{ui}^2}$$

3.3 New Capital Requirements

Banks are allowed, under the 1996 Amendment, to employ a new category of capital known as tier 3 capital. This consists mainly of short-term subordinated debt, subject to certain conditions. However, banks can use tier 3 capital only to meet their daily market risk capital requirement as defined in Equation (1). Banks should first allocate tier 1 and tier 2 capital to meet credit risk capital requirements according to the 1988 Accord, so that together they represent 8 percent of the risk-weighted assets. The risk-weighted assets should be adjusted for the positions that are no longer subject to the 1988 credit risk rules, i.e., the traded instruments on the balance sheet such as bonds, and equities that are already subject to the capital charges for specific risk.

Then, the bank should satisfy a second ratio that compares the eligible capital to the risk-weighted asset equivalent. The risk-weighted asset equivalent is simply the sum of the risk-weighted on-balance-sheet assets, the risk-weighted off-balance-sheet items, and 12.5 times the market risk capital charge, where 12.5 is the reciprocal of the minimum capital ratio of 8 percent.

Eligible capital is the sum of, first, the whole bank's tier 1 capital; second, all of its tier 2 capital under the limit imposed by the 1988 Accord (i.e., tier 2 capital may not exceed 50 percent of tier 1 capital); and, third, some of its tier 3 capital. Banks will be entitled to use tier 3 capital solely to satisfy the market risk capital charge, under some limiting conditions. The market risk capital charge should be met with tier 3 capital, and by means of the additional tier 1 and tier 2 capital not allocated to credit risk. Tier 1 capital should constitute the most substantial portion of the bank's capital, with the final rule stating that:

- At least 50 percent of a bank's qualifying capital must be tier 1 capital, with term subordinated debt not exceeding 50 percent of tier 1 capital.
- The sum of tier 2 and tier 3 capital allocated for market risk must not exceed 250 percent of tier 1 capital allocated for market risk; i.e., 28.57 percent of market risk capital charge should be met with tier 1 capital.[14]

Suppose that a bank has:

- Risk-weighted assets that amount to 7500
- A market risk capital charge of 350

The bank capital is assumed to be constituted of tier 1 capital for 700, tier 2 capital for 100, and tier 3 capital for 600. Does this bank meet the BIS capital ratio requirements? The example in Table 4.10 illustrates the calculation of the capital ratio and one possible allocation of capital.

From the table we can see that, after allocating tier 1 and tier 2 capital to credit risk, there is 200 of unused tier 1 capital left available to support market risk. This means that the maximum eligible tier 3 capital is only 500, according to the 250 percent rule. After the full allocation for credit risk, 250 of tier 3 capital is left unused, but eligible; there is also 100 unused tier 3 capital that is not eligible.

In this example, the capital ratio is greater than the minimum of 8 percent, since the numerator of the capital ratio is the sum of the minimum capital requirement (8 percent) and the unused portion of tier 1 capital.

3.4 Back-testing

Back-testing a bank's internal models provides a key test of how accurate and robust the models are. In effect, back-testing compares the bank's internally generated VaR figures with the actual performance of the bank's portfolio over an extended period of time. It is a vital part of the regulatory oversight of the use of internal models.

Table 4.10

Calculation of the Capital Ratio Under the 1996 Amendment

Risk-Weighted Assets	Minimum Capital Charge (8%)	Available Capital		Minimum Capital for Meeting Requirement		Eligible Capital (Excluding Unused Tier 3)		Unused but Eligible Tier 3		Unused but Not Eligible Tier 3
Credit risk 7,500	600	Tier 1	700	Tier 1	500	Tier 1	700			
		Tier 2	100	Tier 2	100	Tier 2	100			
Market risk 4,375	350	Tier 3	600	Tier 1	100	Tier 3	250	Tier 3	250	Tier 3 100
(i.e., 350 × 12.5)				Tier 3	250					
						Total 1050		250		
						Capital ratio: 1,050/11,875 = 8.8%		Excess tier 3 capital ratio: 250/11,875 = 2.1%		

When they are being employed in relation to regulatory capital requirements, back-tests must compare daily VaR measures calibrated to a one-day movement in rates and prices and a 99 percent (one-tailed) confidence level, against two measures of the profit & loss (P&L):

- The actual net trading P&L for the next day
- The theoretical P&L, also called "static P&L," that would have occurred if the position at the close of the previous day had been carried forward to the next day[15]

Assuming that the risk factors are correctly modeled and that markets behave accordingly, then we would expect the absolute value of actual P&L over the last 250 days to be greater than the calculated VaR figure on only two and a half days on average (i.e., in practice, three days).[16]

Regulators stipulate that back-testing should be performed daily.[17] In addition, an institution must identify the number of times that its net trading losses, if any, for a particular day exceeded the corresponding daily VaR. If the number of exceptions during the previous 250 days is greater than 5, the multiplier we described earlier in this chapter may be increased, and can rise up to 4 if the number of exceptions reaches 10 or more during the period (Table 4.9).

However, there is some doubt as to how seriously this rule will be enforced. Exceptions to the rule are already envisaged by the regulators when abnormal situations occur, such as a market crash, a major political event, or a natural disaster. In addition, the regulators seem likely to acknowledge the fact that all financial institutions, including the regulatory bodies, are "learning by doing." It may thus not be appropriate to penalize an institution by applying a higher multiplier, providing that the institution reacts quickly to improve its VaR model.

The ISDA/LIBA Joint Models Task Force (ISDA 1996) criticized the scaling factor of 3, suggesting that the rule should simply be repealed. It considered that a multiplier of any size is an unfair penalty on banks that are already sophisticated in the design of their risk management system, and in the modeling of general as well as specific risks. Back-testing is a powerful process with which to validate the predictive power of a VaR model. It is, in effect, a self-assessment mechanism that offers a framework for continuously improving and refining risk modeling techniques.

The Task Force argued that regulators should use this framework to develop the incentives for banks to implement best practices: only banks that failed to take appropriate action should suffer a scaling factor greater than 1. An arbitrarily high scaling factor may even provide perverse incentives to abandon initiatives to implement prudent modifications of the internal model.

3.5 Stress Testing

When developing a VaR model, many assumptions have to be made for practical reasons. In particular, most market parameters are set to match "normal" market conditions. This leaves risk managers and regulators with a number of practical considerations. How robust is the VaR model? How sensitive are the VaR numbers to key assumptions?

Value-at-risk models, which calculate the maximum that an institution could lose in a normal day's trading, work well in normal market conditions, but not in extremes. This is the reason why regulators require that a bank complement its VaR analysis with a series of stress testings of their portfolios. Stress scenarios calculate the losses that might arise as the result of imagined crises—crises relevant to the bank given the nature of its portfolios. (See Chapters 5 and 11 for a detailed discussion of stress testing for market risk and credit risk models, respectively.)

Regulators require that banks set limits not only for their VaR exposures, but also for their stress losses.

4. PROS AND CONS OF THE STANDARDIZED AND INTERNAL MODELS APPROACHES: A NEW PROPOSAL–THE "PRECOMMITMENT APPROACH"

The standardized approach has been much criticized. It applies the same capital charge to vastly different financial instruments, e.g., to plain vanilla swaps and highly levered transactions, and it fails to account for any portfolio effects on the true levels of risk (for both credit and market risk).

The internal models approach remedies many of these criticisms, and can be seen as an attempt to improve the accuracy of the standardized approach. However, some regulators question the ability of banks to capture properly the key risks embedded in their portfolios, i.e., directional, spread, curve, volatility, and liquidity risks.[18] They argue that even if banks are now able to develop analytical approaches to cope with these problems, they do not have the resources to implement the right infrastructure—especially in terms of their transactions databases and their financial rates databases.

However, the conservative multipliers used in the present approaches are not a panacea. They may discourage the most sophisticated banks from improving their internal models, at least for regulatory capital purposes. Worse, they may also induce a distorted allocation of capital.

Rating institutions such as Standard & Poor's have expressed their concern that the new 1998 regulatory framework may substantially reduce the amount of regulatory capital. For on-balance-sheet traded products such as bonds and stocks, the expensive credit risk capital charge according to the initial 1988 Accord will be replaced by the less onerous capital charge associated with specific risk. The net effect, as we discussed earlier, should be an average net capital savings of 20 to 50 percent for the largest trading banks.

Standard & Poor's (1996) argues that market risks in a trading operation are largely overshadowed by other risks which are difficult to quantify such as operating risks related to employee fraud and systems failure, legal risk related to the potential for lawsuits from frustrated clients, reputation risk, liquidity risk, and operating leverage.

In recognition of the weaknesses inherent in both the standardized approach and the internal models approach, two senior economists at the Board of Governors of the Federal Reserve Board, P. Kupiec and J. O'Brien (1995b, 1995c, 1995d, 1996) have proposed an alternative approach, the so-called "precommitment approach" (PCA). The PCA would require a bank to precommit to a maximum loss exposure for its trading account positions over a fixed period.

This maximum loss precommitment would, in effect, form the bank's market risk capital charge. Should the bank incur trading losses that exceed its capital commitment, it would be subject to penalties. Violation of the limit would also bring public scrutiny to the bank—a further feedback mechanism for sound management.

Under the PCA, the bank's maximum loss precommitment would reflect the bank's internal assessment of risks, including formal model estimates as well as management's subjective judgments. The PCA approach is an interesting initiative since it aims at replacing regulatory capital requirements that are based on ex ante estimates of the bank's risks, with a capital charge that is set endogenously, through the optimal resolution of an incentive contract between the bank and its regulators.

Indeed, it can be shown that the PCA takes the form of a put option written on the bank's assets and issued to the regulators. The value of this liability for the bank increases with the penalty rate, set by the regulator, and the riskiness of the bank's assets, while it decreases with the strike price of the put, i.e., the precommitment level. When the bank increases the risk of its assets, it increases the value of its precommitment liability, which is more or less than offset by the increase in the value of the fixed-rate deposit insurance (see Chapter 2).

Each bank would have to discover the optimal trade-off between the riskiness of its trading book and the level of precommitted capital. Its objective in doing so would be to maximize the shareholder value and to minimize the exposure of the deposit insurance institution.[19]

The PCA has been criticized by Gumerlock (1996). Gumerlock compares the PCA to speed limits and fines for reckless driving, while he compares the internal models approach to inspections that guarantee that vehicles are roadworthy at all speeds and on all types of roads and weather conditions.

One key point to remember here is that risk management consists of much more than internal models. They are only one important element in risk measurement. In practice, risk managers should rely on their experience, judgment, and controls, and not simply on formulas that translate model results into capital charges. The PCA is interesting in that it attempts to take the multiple facets of risk management into account.

5. COMPARISONS OF THE CAPITAL CHARGES FOR VARIOUS PORTFOLIOS ACCORDING TO THE STANDARDIZED AND THE INTERNAL MODELS APPROACHES

In general, the standardized approach produces a much larger capital charge than any reasonable VaR-based model. At CIBC we have compared the capital charges attributed to general market risk using actual market positions over a six-month period. The capital savings, i.e., the reductions in the capital charge realized by adopting our internal model instead of the standardized approach, vary between a low of 60 percent to a high of 85 percent. The capital saving is higher when the portfolio is highly diversified across maturities and across countries, and when the portfolio is relatively well hedged in a VaR sense, i.e., its VaR exposure is small. The multiplier of 3 makes the capital charge generated by the internal model quite sensitive to market risk exposure.

To gain a better understanding of the extent of the differences in capital charges generated by the standardized method and CIBC's internal method, we investigated four basic portfolios and a relatively well-diversified cross-currency portfolio. The portfolio contents are given in Table 4.11. The cross-currency portfolio has products in both Canadian and U.S. dollars covering a wide range of maturities. These portfolios are limited to linear interest rate products. All bonds are considered to be government issue to avoid the calculation of a specific risk capital charge. All of the following examples focus only on general market risk.

To illustrate the differences between the two methods in capturing the portfolio effects, we consider portfolios with short and long positions, first in a single currency, and then in two different currencies, namely the U.S. and the Canadian dollar. The interest rate curves that we used to perform the computations are given in Table 4.12 and correspond to market data as of April 5, 1997.

The first portfolio is simply a plain vanilla swap with a corporation, with the bank receiving the fixed rate. The internal model is a simple VaR model where the risk factors are the zero-coupon rates for the maturities shown in Table 4.12. The changes in those rates are supposed to follow a multivariate-normal distribution; Table 4.13 provides the volatilities for the U.S. swap curve.[20]

Table 4.11

Portfolios of Fixed-Income Instruments

	Portfolios
1	USD 100 million 10-year swap, receive fixed against three-month LIBOR; counterparty is a corporation
	Portfolio 1
2	+ 100 million USD 5-year swap, pay fixed against three-month LIBOR; counterparty is a corporation
	• long a 100 million USD 10-year government bond with a 6.50% semi-annual coupon
3	• 100 million USD 10-year swap, pay fixed against 3-month LIBOR; counterparty is a corporation
	• 100 million USD 10-year swap, pay fixed against 3-month LIBOR; counterparty is a corporation
4	• 140 million CAD 10-year swap, receive fixed against 3-month LIBOR; counterparty is a corporation
5	CAD
	• long 100 million 3-month T-bill
	• long 75 million 8% government bond maturing in 20 years
	• long 25 million 8% government bond maturing in 3 years
	• short 25 million 8% government bond maturing in 12 years
	• 100 million 5-year swap, receive fixed against 3-month LIBOR
	• 100 million 20-year swap, pay fixed against 3-month LIBOR
	USD
	• short 300 million 3-month T-bill
	• long 100 million 6-month T-bill
	• short 200 million 9-month T-bill
	• long 100 million 6.5% government bond maturing in 4 years
	• long 200 million 6.7% government bond maturing in 5 years
	• long 100 million 7% government bond maturing in 12 years
	• 100 million 2-year swap, pay fixed against 3-month LIBOR
	• 100 million 10-year swap, pay fixed against 3-month LIBOR
	• 100 million 20-year swap, pay fixed against 3-month LIBOR

The VaR for this swap is $US927,000, while the sum of the VaR for each risk point on the curve is $US962,549.[21] As the changes in the rates are highly correlated, the risk reduction due to the portfolio effect is relatively modest, i.e., 3.7 percent in this example. The application of the standardized approach for general market risk,

Table 4.12

Interest Rate Curves Zero-Coupon Curves with
Continuously Compounded Rates (April 5, 1997)

| Term | U.S. (USD) | | Canada (CAD) | |
	Treasuries	Swaps	Treasuries	Swaps
On	5.31%	3.04%	3.00%	3.00%
1m	5.32%	5.50%	2.92%	3.10%
2m	5.31%	5.55%	3.05%	3.18%
3m	5.39%	5.56%	3.15%	3.25%
6m	5.44%	5.62%	3.46%	4.70%
9m	5.45%	5.70%	3.75%	5.09%
1y	5.46%	5.79%	3.89%	5.34%
1.25y	5.73%	5.88%	4.28%	5.50%
1.5y	5.94%	5.96%	4.57%	5.64%
1.75y	6.12%	6.03%	4.92%	5.75%
2y	6.24%	6.10%	5.17%	5.85%
3y	6.41%	6.41%	5.72%	6.59%
4y	6.47%	6.56%	6.06%	6.62%
5y	6.54%	6.66%	6.27%	6.58%
7y	6.56%	6.66%	6.55%	7.13%
10y	6.61%	6.66%	6.96%	7.73%

as presented in Section 2.1.2, is shown in Table 4.14. It produces a capital charge of $US3,750,000.

The capital charges calculated according to the standardized and the internal model approaches are shown in Table 4.15. For this 10-year swap, the adoption of the internal model does not realize any capital saving, but on the contrary generates a capital surcharge of 132 percent.

There is also a capital surcharge of 103 percent for the second portfolio, which consists of long and short positions in two plain vanilla swaps of different maturities, but in the same currency, the U.S. dollar. The bank receives a fixed rate on the 10-year swap, and pays fixed on the five-year swap. Since there is partial offsetting of cash flows up to five years, the portfolio effect is expected to be more substantial than for the first portfolio.

Table 4.13 shows the details of the derivation of the VaR number. The standardized approach for general market risk is detailed

Table 4.13

Internal Model for Portfolios 1 and 2

	DV01 (USD)		Volatility (bp)	VaR/Risk Point (USD)	
Term	Portfolio 1	Portfolio 2	σ	Portfolio 1	Portfolio 2
3m	(2,459)		3.59	20,588	
6m	28		3.35	215	
9m	123		3.46	988	
1y	162		3.58	1,350	
1.25y	195		3.95	1,794	
1.5y	230		4.33	2,319	
1.75y	264		4.70	2,894	
2y	746	2	5.08	8,824	27
3y	1,681	5	5.29	20,742	63
4y	2,092	6	5.50	26,808	81
5y	3,579	(34,320)	5.50	45,897	440,110
7y	7,308	7,308	5.63	95,878	95,878
10y	58,138	58,128	5.42	734,252	734,252

Notes:

DV01, denotes the sensitivity of the position to a fall of 1 bp in the corresponding zero-coupon rate, and is expressed in currency units.

σ denotes the daily volatility of the zero-coupon rate and is expressed in bp.

VaR/risk point denotes the VaR for the corresponding zero-coupon rate, at the 99% confidence level (one-tailed) and for a one-day horizon, i.e., 2.33 σ |DV01|, assuming that interest rate changes are normally distributed.

	Portfolio 1	Portfolio 2
(1)Sum of the VaR/risk point	= 962,549 USD	= 1,270,411 USD
(2) VaR	= 927,000 USD	= 407,532 USD
Portfolio effect: (1) − (2)	= 35,549 USD	= 862,879 USD

in Table 4.14, and shows a capital charge of $US1,845,000, with $US1 million related to the risk of a parallel shift in the yield curve, and $US845,000 to compensate for curve risk. In this case the cash flows are not well distributed among the various buckets. As a consequence, there is only a small capital charge for basis risk and curve risk among the different zones of the interest rate curve.

The third portfolio consists of a long government bond position that is hedged by means of a swap of the same tenor (10 years, in our example), and in the same currency. The capital saving is 62 percent as shown in Table 4.16. In this case, the position is relatively well hedged in a VaR sense, since its VaR exposure is only $US19,068. The internal model, with its multiplier of 3, greatly benefits from this situation with respect to the standardized approach.

The fourth portfolio is constituted of two 10-year swaps, a long and a short position, this time in two different currencies, the U.S. dollar and the Canadian dollar. In this instance the capital saving is 11.5 percent. The calculations are detailed in Tables 4.16 and 4.17. For this portfolio the internal model benefits from the diversification of the portfolio across two different currencies. The standardized approach treats each currency independently, adding the capital charges without any of the benefits from diversification and hedging across two currencies.

Finally, the fifth portfolio reveals the full benefit of the internal model when the bank's position is well diversified across maturities and countries. Here, we obtain capital savings of 51 percent (Table 4.18).

6. CONCLUSIONS

The BIS 1998 framework for capital requirement represented a big leap forward in the risk management of financial institutions. The fact that banks were required to hold capital to cover market risk associated with their trading book, and foreign exchange and commodity positions in both the trading and the banking books, helped to change their business model. All of a sudden, there were considerable incentives for banks to develop their own internal VaR model for both regulatory capital purposes, but also to closely monitor their risks, and actively manage the risk/return trade-off and the pricing of new deals.

Since January 1998, leading banks have put in place internal models for the measurement of market risk. The next challenge is for those banks to develop appropriate internal models for credit risk, and then to implement an integrated framework for market risk and credit risk to fully account for portfolio effects within, and across, all types of risk.

Table 4.14

Standardized Approach for General Market Risk: Portfolios 1 and 2

Portfolio 1	Zone 1 (months)				Zone 2 (years)						Zone 3 (years)				
Time band															
Coupon >3%	0–1	1–3	3–6	6–12	1–2	2–3	3–4	4–5	5–7	7–10	10–15	15–20	>20		
Coupon <3%	0–1	1–3	3–6	6–12	1–1.9	1.9–2.8	2.8–3.6	3.6–4.3	4.3–5.7	5.7–7.3	7.3–9.3	9.3–10.6	10.6–12	12–20	>20
USD		(100)													
10-yr swap fixed receiver										100					
Weight (%)	0.00	0.20	0.40	0.70	1.25	1.75	2.25	2.75	3.25	3.75	4.50	5.25	6.00	8.00	12.5
Position × weight long										3.75					
Position × weight short		(0.20)													
Vertical disallowance															
Horizontal disallowance 1	0 × 40% = 0				0 × 30% = 0						0 × 30% = 0				
Horizontal disallowance 2					0 × 40% = 0						0 × 40% = 0				
Horizontal disallowance 3								0.2 × 100% = 0.20							
Overall net position								3.55 × 100% = 3.55							

Total capital charge for general market risk = 3.75

Portfolio 2

	Zone 1 (months)				Zone 2 (years)			Zone 3 (years)							
Time band															
Coupon >3%	0–1	1–3	3–6	6–12	1–2	2–3	3–4	4–5	5–7	7–10	10–15	15–20	>20		
Coupon <3%	0–1	1–3	3–6	6–12	1–1.9	1.9–2.8	2.8–3.6	3.6–4.3	4.3–5.7	5.7–7.3	7.3–9.3	9.3–10.6	10.6–12	12–20	>20
Positions															
A		(100)						(100)							
B		100								100					
Weight (%)	0.00	0.20	0.40	0.70	1.25	1.75	2.25	2.75	3.25	3.75	4.50	5.25	6.00	8.00	12.5
Postion × weight															
long		.20								3.75					
short		(.20)						(2.75)							
Vertical disallowance		0.20 × 10% = 0.02													
Horizontal disallowance 1			0 × 40% = 0			0 × 30% = 0						2.75 × 30% = 0.825			
Horizontal disallowance 2					0 × 40% = 0				0 × 40% = 0						
Horizontal disallowance 3								0 × 100% = 0							
Overall net position								1 × 100% = 1							

Total capital charge for general market risk = 1.845

Table 4.15

Standardized versus Internal Models: Capital Charge for Portfolios 1 and 2

		Portfolio 1 (in USD)	Portfolio 2 (in USD)
Internal model			
(1) VaR	=	927,000	407,532
(2) General market risk: $3 \times \text{VaR} \times \sqrt{10}$	=	8,794,294	3,866,188
(3) Counterparty risk* (1988 Accord)	=	60,000	120,000
Capital charge: (2) + (3)	=	8,854,294	3,986,188
Standardized approach			
(4) General market risk (cf. Table 4.14)	=	3,750,000	1,845,000
(5) Counterparty risk* (1988 Accord)	=	60,000	120,000
Capital charge: (4) + (5)	=	3,810,000	1,965,000
Capital addition**	=	132%	103%

*Details for the calculation of the capital charge for counterparty risk:
- Replacement cost = 0 (at-the-money swap)
- Add-on (cf. Table 4.4) = $ 100m × 1.5% = $1,500,000
- Risk-weighted amount (cf. Table 4.2) = $1,500,000- × 50% = $750,000-
- Capital charge = $750,000 × 8% = $60,000

**Capital addition (saving) is the addition (saving) of capital realized by the bank by adopting the internal models instead of the standardized approach.

Table 4.16

Standardized versus Internal Models: Capital Charge for Portfolios 3 and 4

		Portfolio 3 (in USD)	Portfolio 4 (in USD)
Internal model			
(1) VaR	=	19,068	970,330
(2) General market risk: $3 \times \text{VaR} \times \sqrt{10}$	=	180,898	9,205,390
(3) Counterparty risk (swap) (1988 Accord)	=	60,000	166,800***
Capital charge: (2) + (3)	=	240,898	9,372,190
Standardized approach			
(4) General market risk*	=	575,000*	10,425,000**
(5) Counterparty risk (1988 Accord)	=	60,000	166,800
Capital charge: (4) + (5)	=	635,000	10,591,800
Capital saving	=	62%	11.5%

*The derivation is left to the reader. The capital charge is made of 375,000 USD for basis risk and 200,000 USD for the overall net outright position. Obviously, for this portfolio the standardized approach appears to be excessively onerous, while the VaR is small as the portfolio is relatively hedged.

**According to the standardized approach the CAD swap has a capital charge of 5,250,000 CAD while it is 3,750,000 USD for the U.S. swap, i.e., 5,175,500 CAD.

***The capital charge for the U.S. swap is 60,000 USD, i.e., 82,800 CAD assuming an exchange rate of 1 USD = 1.38 CAD. The capital charge for the CAD swap is 84,000 CAD.

Table 4.17

Internal Model for Portfolio 4

	CAD SWAP			USD SWAP		
Term	DV01 (CAD)	Volatility (bp) (σ)	VaR (CAD)	DV01 (USD)	Volatility (bp) (σ)	VaR (USD)
On	0	10.40	0	0	30.23	0
1m	0	4.63	0	0	6.30	0
2m	(161)	4.07	1,523	0	3.91	0
3m	(3,300)	5.09	39,150	2,459	3.59	20,588
6m	131	6.67	2,042	(28)	3.35	215
9m	196	7.16	3,264	(123)	3.46	988
1y	250	7.64	4,446	(162)	3.58	1,350
1.25y	307	8.11	5,796	(195)	3.95	1,794
1.5y	362	8.58	7,230	(230)	4.33	2,319
1.75y	433	9.05	9,124	(264)	4.70	2,894
2y	1,152	9.51	25,541	(746)	5.08	8,824
3y	2,614	9.13	55,584	(1,681)	5.29	20,742
4y	3,253	8.63	65,407	(2,092)	5.50	26,808
5y	5,551	8.14	105,280	(3,579)	5.50	45,897
7y	11,049	7.55	194,397	(7,308)	5.63	95,878
10y	73,161	7.00	1,193,291	(58,138)	5.42	734,252
15y	0	6.39	0	0	5.44	0
20y	0	6.07	0	0	5.07	0
30y	0	5.79	0	0	5.18	0

Exchange rate 1 USD = 1.38 CAD
VaR USD-Swap = 1,279,000 CAD
VaR USD-Swap = 1,626,000 CAD
VaR of Portfolio 4 = 970,330 CAD

With this capital attribution infrastructure and those risk measurement tools in place, the focus is gradually shifting toward performance measurement. The board and top management of financial institutions are moving towards compensation systems that are based on adjusted return on economic capital—an approach also known as RAROC (risk adjusted return on capital). This new paradigm will spark further research in the integration of market risk, credit risk, and other types of risks such as operational risk.

Table 4.18

Standardized versus Internal Models for
Portfolio 5 Capital Charges for General
Market Risk

Internal model		
VaR for the CAD position	=	408,350 CAD
VaR for the USD position	=	425,660 CAD
VaR for Portfolio 5	=	662,610 CAD
Capital charge $3 \times \text{VaR} \times \sqrt{10}$ =		6,286,078 CAD
Standardized approach		
CAD position		3,570,000 CAD
USD position		9,239,100 CAD
Total	=	12,809,100 CAD
Capital savings	=	51%

We can also expect the regulatory environment to evolve in the future toward a generalized use of internal models across all types of risks, provided data are available to support the models.

NOTES

1. In Canada, only the maturity method is allowed by the regulator, OSFI. The duration approach differs only by its more accurate method of calculating the sensitivities, or risk weights (see Table 4.2).
2. See Chapter 5. Delta represents the first-order approximation of the sensitivity of an option value to a change in the underlying price.
3. See Chapter 5. Gamma denotes the second-order adjustment of the sensitivity of an option value to a change in the underlying price. It is also the sensitivity of delta to a change in the underlying price.
4. A Taylor expansion of a function designates its polynomial approximation, which agrees with the value of the function and some of its derivatives at a given point, say the price of the underlying instrument (see Apostol 1967.)
5. It is valued at current spot exchange rates, since we are interested in the present value of the forward exposures.
6. Each of the seven provinces in Canada issues its own debt, which is not guaranteed by the government of Canada. As a consequence

provincial debts trade at a spread above the government debt of Canada, and the spread varies from one province to another.

7. The convenience yield for commodities, like energy products, reflects the benefits from direct ownership of the physical commodity, e.g., when there is a risk of shortage. It is affected by market conditions as well as specific conditions such as the level of inventory and storage costs. Accordingly, the convenience yield may be positive or negative. When inventory is high, demand is low, and marginal storage costs are high, the convenience yield is likely to be negative.

8. When assessing the risk of a position, we are only focussing on the "downside" risk, i.e., the risk of a loss that is contained in the left tail of the distribution.

9. The square root of 10 rule is only valid when the changes in the portfolio values are not correlated and are identically distributed.

10. If historical data are weighted to estimate volatilities and correlations, the weighted average time lag of the individual observations should be at least half a year, which is what would be obtained if the observations were equally weighted.

11. From the previous section we know that under the standardized approach, specific risk charges vary across debt and equity instruments, with individual equities receiving 8 percent charges, while those held in well-diversified and liquid portfolios are charged at 4 percent. Major stock indices are subject to 2 percent charges and certain arbitrage positions receive lower requirements. For bonds, specific risk charges vary between 0 percent and 8 percent depending on the issuer and the maturity of the instrument, but no diversification is recognized.

12. See ISDA (1996) and IIF (1996). ISDA (1996) sets out the conclusions of a joint task force of members of the International Swaps and Derivatives Association (ISDA) and the London Investment Banking Association (LIBA) on aspects of the Basle Committee's standards for the use of the internal models to calculate market risk capital charge. IIF (1996) reports the conclusions on the specific risk issue of a task force composed of the representatives of 15 banks that were members of the Institute of International Finance (IIF).

13. See Sharpe and Alexander (1990), Chapter 8.

14. The limits on the capital used vary slightly from one country to the other. For example, OSFI in Canada limits the use of tier 2 and tier 3 capital to meet market risk requirements to 200 percent of tier 1

capital used to meet these requirements. In addition, tier 1 and tier 2 capital cannot, in total, exceed 100 percent of tier 1 capital.

15. VaR is an assessment of the potential loss for a given, static portfolio, i.e., the closing position at the end of the day. Obviously, the portfolio is traded all the time, so its composition continues to change during the trading day. Risk management is also active, and decisions to alter the risk exposure of the bank's position may be taken during the course of the day. This is why VaR should be compared ex-post to these two measures of P&L.

16. Indeed, a 99 percent one-tail confidence level means that we expect losses, but also profits, to be greater than VaR in absolute value 2.5 days per year.

17. The obligation to back-test was effective only after a year, i.e., in 1999, after institutions had accumulated one year of historical market data to be used in back-testing. Initially, during 1998, the regulators required only a comparison of VaR against actual P&L.

    From our point of view, a better approach to back-testing would be "historical simulation" where, each day, the position would be re-evaluated based on the last 250 days closing market data. Then, the "historical distribution" of the changes in the position value would be compared with the "theoretical distribution" derived from the internal VaR model. This approach would permit one, over time, to revisit the key assumptions made in the VaR model which, through historical simulation, are revealed to be inconsistent with market data—and which might produce a very biased picture of the bank's exposure.

18. See Kupiec and O'Brien (1995c, 1995d, and 1996).

19. See Kupiec and O'Brien (1997).

20. For reasons of space, we do not present the relevant correlation matrix.

21. The VaR methodology for market risk is presented in Chapter 5.

Measuring Market Risk: The VaR Approach

1. INTRODUCTION

As discussed in Chapter 2, the original purpose of the 1988 BIS Accord was to impose minimum capital requirements for credit risk. More recently, the 1996 Amendment (BIS 1998) extended the Accord to incorporate market risk arising from the trading book of financial institutions. This chapter discusses what is meant by the term market risk, and then describes the most widely accepted methodology for modeling this risk: the value-at-risk (VaR) approach.

Put simply, "market risk" is the risk that changes in financial market prices and rates will reduce the value of a security or a portfolio. In trading activities, risk arises both from open (unhedged) positions and from imperfect correlations between market positions that are intended to offset one another.

Market risk is given many different names in different contexts. For example, in the case of a fund, the market risk is often measured relative to a benchmark index or a portfolio, and is therefore referred to as "risk of tracking error."

As discussed in Chapter 1, there are four major types of market risk:

Interest rate risk—The simplest form of interest rate risk is the risk that the value of a fixed-income security will fall as a result of a change in market interest rates. Open positions arise most often from differences in the maturities, nominal values, and reset dates of instruments and cash flows that are assetlike (i.e., "longs") and those that are liabilitylike (i.e., "shorts").

The exposure that such differences, or "mismatches," generates depends not only on the amount held and each position's sensitivity to interest rate changes, but also on the degree to which these sensitivities are correlated within portfolios and, more broadly, across trading desks and business lines.

Imperfect correlation between offsetting instruments, both across the yield curve and within the same maturity for different issuers, can generate significant interest rate exposures. Although they may be intended to produce a hedged portfolio, offsetting positions that have different maturities may leave the portfolio holder exposed to imperfect correlations in the underlying reference rates. Such "curve" risk can arise in portfolios in which long and short positions of different maturities are effectively hedged against a *parallel shift* in yields but not against a change in the *shape of the yield curve*.

Parallel shifts occur when a shock in the market has an equal effect on yields with different maturity dates; the yield curve is said to change shape when a shock in the market has a stronger effect on, say, the returns of shorter-dated instruments than it has on the returns of longer-dated instruments.

Alternatively, even where offsetting positions have the same maturity, "basis" risk can arise if the rates of the positions are imperfectly correlated. For example, three-month Eurodollar instruments and three-month Treasury bills both naturally pay three-month interest rates. However, these rates are not perfectly correlated with each other, and spreads between their yields may vary over time. As a result, a three-month Treasury bill funded by three-month Eurodollar deposits represents an imperfect offset or hedged position.

Price risk for fixed-income products can be decomposed into a "general market" risk component and a "specific" risk component. Specific risk is the idiosyncratic component of the financial transaction, and in this sense it is akin to the credit risk that is analyzed in Chapters 8 to 10.

Equity price risk—The price risk associated with equities also has two components. "General market risk" refers to the sensitivity of an instrument or portfolio value to a change in the level of broad stock market indices. "Specific" or "idiosyncratic" risk refers to that portion of a stock's price volatility that is determined by characteristics specific to the firm, such as its line of business, the quality of its management, or a breakdown in its production process. A well-known result of portfolio theory is that general market risk cannot be eliminated through portfolio diversification, while specific risk can be diversified away.

Foreign exchange risk—The major sources of foreign exchange risk are imperfect correlations in the movement of currency prices and fluctuations in international interest rates. As with all other market risks, foreign exchange risk arises from open or imperfectly hedged positions. Although it is important to acknowledge exchange rates as a distinct market risk factor, the valuation of foreign exchange transactions requires knowledge of the behavior of domestic and foreign interest rates,[1] as well as of spot exchange rates. Foreign exchange risk is one of the major risks faced by large multinational corporations. Foreign exchange volatility can sweep away the return from expensive investments, and at the same time place a firm at a competitive disadvantage vis-à-vis its foreign competitors.[2] It may also generate huge operating losses and inhibit investment.[3]

Commodity price risk—The price risk of commodities differs considerably from interest rate and foreign exchange risk, since most commodities are traded in markets in which the concentration of supply can magnify price volatility. Moreover, fluctuations in the depth of trading in the market (i.e., market liquidity) often accompany and exacerbate high levels of price volatility. Therefore, commodity prices generally have higher volatilities and larger price discontinuities—i.e., moments when prices leap from one level to another—than most traded financial securities.

2. MEASURING RISK: A HISTORICAL PERSPECTIVE

The measurement of risk has changed over time. It has evolved from simple indicators, such as the face value or "notional" amount for an individual security, through more complex measures of price sensitivities such as the duration and convexity of a bond, to the latest methodologies for computing VaR numbers (Figure 5.1). Each measure has tended at first to be applied to individual securities,

FIGURE 5.1

Traditional Measures of Market Risk

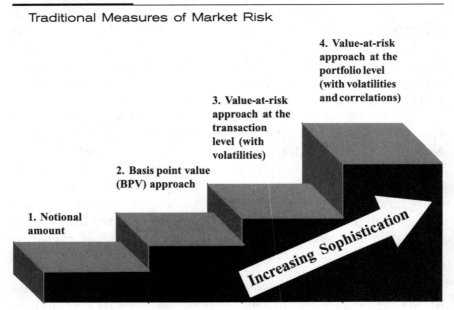

and then to be adapted to measure the risk of complex portfolios such as those that contain derivatives.

The quest for better and more accurate measures of market risk is ongoing; each new market turmoil reveals the limitations of even the most sophisticated measures of market risk. This said, VaR is proving to be a very powerful way of assessing the overall risk of trading positions over a short horizon, such as a 10-day period, and under "normal" market conditions. In effect, the methodology allows us to capture in a single number the multiple components of market risk we introduced in the previous section (curve risk, basis risk, volatility risk, etc.). For example, bond prices fall when interest rates rise according to a nonlinear relationship. Given a measure of the volatility of market yields, and their correlations, the market risk of a bond portfolio can be represented as a VaR number.

VaR is less reliable as a measure over longer time periods. The danger posed by exceptional market shocks,[4] which are often accompanied by a drying up of market liquidity, can only be captured by means of supplemental methodologies such as stress testing and scenario analysis.

2.1 The Notional Amount Approach

Until recently, trading desks in major banks were allocated economic capital by reference to notional amounts. The notional approach measures risk as the notional, or nominal, amount of a security, or the sum of the notional values of the holdings for a portfolio, as illustrated in Figure 5.2.

This method is flawed since it does not:

- Differentiate between short and long positions
- Reflect price volatility and correlation between prices

Moreover, in the case of derivative positions in the over-the-counter market, there are often very large discrepancies between the true amount of market exposure, which is often small, and the notional amount, which may be huge. For example, two call options on the same underlying instrument with the same notional value, and the same maturity, with one option being in-the-money and the other one out-of-the-money, have very different market values and risk exposures.

As another example, imagine a situation in which interest rate swaps are written with many different counterparties, and where

FIGURE 5.2

The Notional Amount Approach

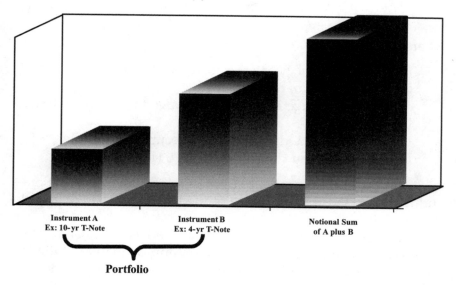

some of these swaps are being used to hedge the market risk exposure created by the others. In this instance, simply adding up the notional amounts of the deals gives a misleading picture of the portfolio market risk—though it provides some indication of the overall credit risk exposure.

2.2 Factor Sensitivity Measures

Measures of factor sensitivity capture the sensitivity of an instrument or portfolio to changes in the value of primary risk factors such as interest rates, yield to maturity, volatility, stock price, stock index, etc. Risk factors are said to be primary when their dynamics, or behavior, are specified externally to the measurement model.[5]

For fixed-income products, a popular risk measure among traders is "DV01," also known as "value of an 01."[6] This describes the sensitivity of security prices to a one-basis-point (bp) parallel shift in the yield curve, or to a 1-bp change in a specific rate. This measure is consistent with the conventional "duration" analysis of a bond, as described in Appendix 1. For small parallel shifts of the yield curve, the price sensitivity of a fixed-income product can be approximated by a linear function of the change in yield (see relation A9 in Appendix 1):

$$\frac{dP}{dy} = -P\,\frac{D}{1+y} = -PD^* \tag{1}$$

where:

P denotes the price of the security
y is the yield to maturity
dP/dy is the change in the security price for a change in the yield to maturity
D is the Macaulay duration of the security[7]
D^* is the modified duration ($D^* = D/(1+y)$)

The longer the maturity of the bond, the higher its duration—and the more sensitive the price of the bond to a change in yield (Figure 5.3).

The price-yield relationship for a bond is nonlinear, which means that duration is only a first-order approximation of the impact of a change in yield on the price. As shown in Appendix 1, a

FIGURE 5.3

Interest Rate Sensitivity Measures: Value of an "01"

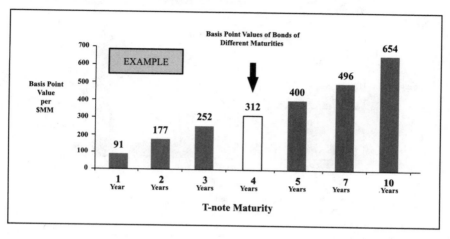

more accurate approximation is provided by the second-order expansion of the bond price formula (see relation A13):

$$\frac{dP}{P} = -D^*dy + \frac{1}{2} CX \, dy^2 \tag{2}$$

where CX denotes the convexity of the bond.

- For a portfolio of instruments priced from the same yield curve, price sensitivities can be easily aggregated by calculating the weighted average duration of the instruments held in the portfolio.
- Alternatively, price sensitivities can be expressed in terms of one representative instrument, e.g., the four-year Treasury note (T-note) in Figure 5.3. In this case, each position is converted into the duration equivalent of the reference instrument, i.e., the four-year T-note. For instance, the 10-year T-note has a duration that is 2.1 times greater than the duration of a four-year T-note, so a $1 million 10-year T-note is said to be equivalent to $2.1 million dollar of the reference four-year T-note (Figure 5.4). The risk of the portfolio is then evaluated as if it were a single position in the reference asset.

FIGURE 5.4

Interest Rate Sensitivity Measures: Relative Value of an "01"

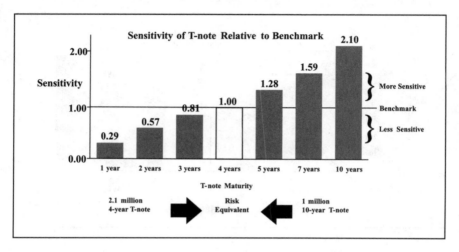

2.3 Other Price Sensitivity Measures

Practitioners in the derivative markets have developed their own specialized risk measures. They refer to the sensitivities of derivative instruments to various risk factors using a set of measures named after letters in the Greek alphabet, and therefore known collectively as the "Greeks." How do these measures relate to the risk measures we have just discussed?

First, let us look again at the Black-Scholes (1973) formula (3), which represents the value, C, of a European call option on an individual stock that does not pay any dividend:[8]

$$C = SN(d_1) - Ke^{-rT}N(d_2) \tag{3}$$

where

S = the stock price which is assumed to follow a log-normal distribution

K = the strike price

$N(.)$ = the cumulative standard normal distribution

r = the continuously compounded risk-free rate of interest which is assumed to be a constant

σ^2 = the instantaneous variance of the stock return, assumed to be a constant

T = the time to maturity of the option

$d_1 = [\ln(S/K) + (r + 1/2\ \sigma^2)T]/\sigma\sqrt{T}$

$d_2 = d_1 - \sigma\sqrt{T}$

The stock price, S, in the option price equation (3), plays the same role as the yield, y, in the bond price equation (A4) shown in Appendix 1. The sensitivities of the call option price with respect to the price of the underlying instrument, S, are known as the delta and gamma. The delta and gamma price risks of a derivative are analogous to the duration and convexity of a bond, respectively. Table 5.1 describes the relationships between the Greeks in more detail, and presents their mathematical representations.

The list of sensitivities for derivatives in Table 5.1 is longer than a similar list for a standard bond. This is because the value of a derivative is affected by other risk factors such as volatility, σ, the discount rate, r, the passage of time, t, and, when several risk factors are involved, the correlation between the risk factors, ρ.

In the Greek formula, above, the expression

$$N'(x) = \frac{1}{\sqrt{2\pi}}\ e^{-x^2/2}$$

denotes the density function of the univariate standard normal distribution.

2.4 Weaknesses of the Greek Measures

Each of the sensitivities measured by the Greeks provides only a partial measure of financial risk. The measurements of delta, gamma, and vega complement each other, but they cannot be aggregated to produce an overall measure of the risk generated by a position or a portfolio. In particular:

- Sensitivities are not additive across risk types; e.g., the delta and gamma risk of the same position cannot be summed.

- Sensitivities are not additive across markets; e.g., one cannot sum the delta of a Euro/$US call and the delta of a call on a stock index.

TABLE 5.1

The Greek Alphabet for a European Equity Call Option[1]

Delta, or price risk $= \delta = \dfrac{\partial C}{\partial S} = N(d_1)$	Delta measures the degree to which an option's value is affected by a small change in the price of the underlying instrument.
Gamma, or convexity risk $= \gamma = \dfrac{\partial^2 C}{\partial S^2} = \dfrac{N'(d_1)}{S\sigma\sqrt{T}}$	Gamma measures the degree to which the option's delta changes as the reference price underlying the option changes. The higher the gamma, the more valuable the option is to its holder. For a high gamma option, when the underlying price increases, the delta also increases, so that the option appreciates more in value than for a gamma neutral position. Conversely, when the underlying price declines, the delta also falls, and the option loses less in value than if the position was gamma-neutral. The reverse is true for short positions in options: high gamma positions expose their holders to more risk than gamma-neutral positions.
Vega, or volatility risk $= \nu = \dfrac{\partial C}{\partial \sigma} = S\sqrt{T}\, N'(d_1)$	Vega measures the sensitivity of the option value to changes in the volatility of the underlying instrument. A higher vega typically increases the value of the option to its holder.
Theta, or time decay risk $= \theta = -\dfrac{\partial C}{\partial T} = -\dfrac{SN'(d_1)\sigma}{2\sqrt{T}}$ $- rKe^{-rT} N(d_2)$	Theta measures the time decay of an option. That is, it reflects how much the value of the option changes as the option moves closer to its expiration date. Positive gamma is usually associated with negative time decay, i.e., a natural price attrition of the option as its maturity declines.
Rho, or discount rate risk $= \bar{\rho} = \dfrac{\partial C}{\partial r} = KTe^{-rT} N(d_2)$	Rho measures the change in value of an option in response to a change in interest rate, more specifically a change in the zero-coupon rate of the same maturity as the option. Typically, the higher the value of rho, the lower the value of the option to its holder.

[1]For a detailed analysis of the Greeks for various types of options see Hull (2000).

Since the sensitivities cannot be aggregated, they cannot be used to assess the magnitude of the overall loss that might arise from a change in the risk factors. As a consequence:

- Sensitivities cannot be used directly to measure capital at risk.
- Sensitivities do not facilitate risk control. Position limits expressed in terms of delta, gamma, and vega are often ineffective since they do not translate easily into a "maximum loss acceptable" for the position.

This explains the desire for a comprehensive measure of risk for individual securities and for portfolios. Value-at-risk (VaR) is one answer to this quest for a consistent measure of risk.

3. DEFINING VALUE AT RISK

Value at risk[9] can be defined as the worst loss that might be expected from holding a security or portfolio over a given period of time (say a single day, or 10 days for the purpose of regulatory capital reporting), given a specified level of probability (known as the "confidence level").

For example, if we say that a position has a daily VaR of $10 million at the 99 percent confidence level, we mean that the realized daily losses from the position will, on average, be higher than $10 million on only one day every 100 trading days (i.e., two to three days each year).

VaR is not the answer to the simple question:

How much can I lose on my portfolio over a given period of time?

The answer to this question is "everything," or almost the entire value of the portfolio! This answer is not very helpful in practice. It is the correct answer to the wrong question. If all markets collapse at the same time, then naturally prices may plunge and, at least in theory, the value of the portfolio may drop near to zero.

Instead, VaR offers a probability statement about the potential change in the value of a portfolio resulting from a change in market factors, over a specified period of time. VaR is the answer to the following question (Figure 5.5):

What is the maximum loss over a given time period such that there is a low probability, say a 1 percent probability, that the actual loss over the given period will be larger?

FIGURE 5.5

Defining Value at Risk

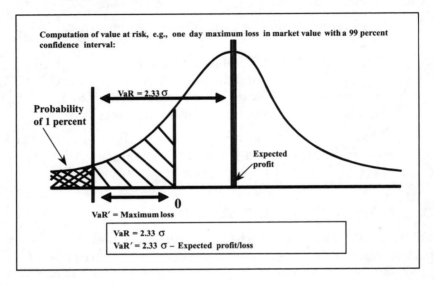

Computation of value at risk, e.g., one day maximum loss in market value with a 99 percent confidence interval:

VaR = 2.33 σ

Probability of 1 percent

Expected profit

0

VaR′ = Maximum loss

VaR = 2.33 σ
VaR′ = 2.33 σ − Expected profit/loss

Note that the VaR measure does not state by how much actual losses will exceed the VaR figure; it simply states how likely (or unlikely) it is that the VaR figure will be exceeded.

Most VaR models are designed to measure risk over a short period of time, such as one day or, in the case of the risk measurements required by the regulators to report regulatory capital, 10 days. BIS 1998 imposes a confidence level, c, of 99 percent.[10] However, for the purposes of allocating internal capital, VaR may be derived at a higher confidence level, say c = 99.96 percent, which is consistent with an AA rating.[11]

As illustrated in Figure 5.5, calculating VaR involves the following steps: First, derive the forward distribution of the portfolio, or alternatively the returns on the portfolio, at the chosen horizon, H (of, say, one day or 10 days). As we describe below, the distribution can be derived directly from historical price distributions (nonparametric VaR) or the distributions may be assumed to be analytic; e.g., it is common practice to assume that prices are log-normally distributed, or equivalently that returns follow a normal distribution (parametric VaR). Second, assuming that the confidence level, c, is 99 percent, calculate the first percentile of this distribution; if the confidence level is 99.96 percent, then calculate the 4-bp quantile.

The VaR is the maximum loss at the 99 percent confidence level, measured relative to the expected value of the portfolio at the target horizon, i.e., VaR is the distance of the first percentile from the mean of the distribution.[12]

$$\text{VaR} = \text{Expected profit/loss}$$
$$- \text{worst case loss at the 99 percent confidence level} \quad (4)$$

An alternative definition of VaR is that it represents the worst case loss at the 99 percent confidence level:

$$\text{VaR}' = \text{Worst case loss at the 99 percent confidence level} \quad (5)$$

VaR' is also known as "absolute VaR." Only the first definition (4) of VaR is consistent with economic capital attribution and RAROC calculations (see Chapter 14). Indeed, in VaR the expected profit/loss is already priced in, and accounted for, in the return calculation. Capital is provided only as a cushion against unexpected losses.

Note that VaR relates to the economic capital that shareholders should invest in the firm to limit the probability of default to a given predetermined level, $1-c$, while regulatory capital is the minimum amount of capital imposed by the regulator (Chapter 2). Economic capital differs from regulatory capital because the confidence level and the time horizon chosen are different. Most of the time, banks choose a higher confidence level than the 99 percent set by the regulator to determine their economic capital. However, the time horizon in economic capital calculations may vary from one day for very liquid positions, such as a government bond desk, to several weeks for illiquid positions, such as a long-dated OTC equity derivatives portfolios. By contrast, the regulator arbitrarily sets the time horizon to 10 days for any position in the trading book.

More formally, if V denotes the current marked-to-market value of the position, R is the return over the horizon H, μ is the expected return [$\mu = E(R)$], and R^* denotes the return corresponding to the worst case loss at the c, e.g., 99 percent, confidence level, so that if $V^* = V(1 + R^*)$, then:

$$\text{VaR } (H; c) = E(V) - V^* = V(1 + \mu)$$
$$- V(1 + R^*) = V(\mu - R^*) \quad (6)$$

and

$$\text{VaR}' (H; c) = -VR^{*13} \quad (7)$$

Example:

$V = 100$, $\mu = 5$ percent and $R^* = -20$ percent, then VaR = 100 $(0.05 - (-0.20)) = 25$ and VaR' = 20.

Note that R^* is negative so that VaR is the sum of the absolute value of the worst case loss and of the expected return. If the expected return happens to be an expected loss, then VaR is the difference between the absolute values of the worst case loss and the expected loss. For example, if $\mu = -5$ percent, then VaR = $100(-0.05 - (-.20)) = 15$ and VaR' = 20.

3.1 Nonparametric VaR

Nonparametric VaR is derived from a distribution that is constructed using historical data. It is called nonparametric VaR because, unlike the parametric approach described below, the calculation does not involve estimating the parameters of a theoretical distribution. In the illustrative example in Figure 5.6, the average daily pure net trading related revenue (e.g., net of fees) for CIBC during 1998 was C\$0.451 million. The first percentile of the distribution, i.e., the cutoff point on this distribution, such that only 1 percent of the daily revenues lie on its left-hand side, is C\$-25.919 million.[14]

This means that VaR = $0.451 - (-25.919) = $ C\$26.370M, and VaR' = C\$25.919M.

3.2 Parametric VaR

In the previous example, VaR was derived from the empirical distribution (histogram) of the daily revenues generated by the position over a one-year period. No assumption was made about the distribution of the returns of the position.

FIGURE 5.6a

CIBC Net Daily Trading Revenues During 1998 versus One-Day VaR at the 99 Percent Confidence Level

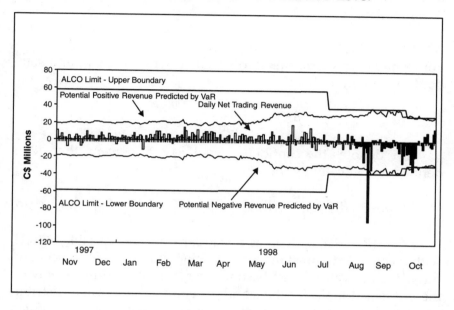

FIGURE 5.6b

CIBC Net Daily Trading Revenues for 1998 (CAD Millions)

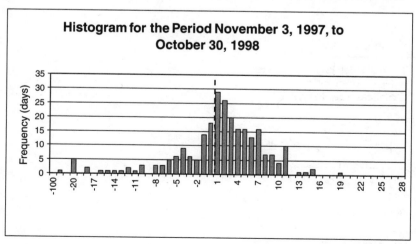

To simplify the derivation of VaR we may choose to assume that the returns have an analytic density function, $f(R)$. Historical data are used to estimate the parameters of the assumed distribution function.

3.2.1 Normal Return Distribution

For example, if R is normally distributed with mean, μ, and standard deviation, σ, then:

$$f(R) = \frac{1}{\sqrt{2\pi}\sigma} \, e^{-\frac{1}{2}\frac{(R-\mu)^2}{\sigma^2}}$$

If c denotes the confidence level, say 99 percent, then R^* is defined analytically by the following expression:

$$\text{Prob}(R < R^*) = \int_{-\infty}^{R^*} f(R)dR = \text{Prob}\left(Z < \frac{R^* - \mu}{\sigma}\right) = 1 - c \quad (8)$$

$Z = (R - \mu)/\sigma$ denotes a standard normal variable, $N(0,1)$, with mean 0 and unit standard deviation. In the case of normal returns, the derivation of R^* becomes very simple and relies only on the published tables of the standard cumulative normal distribution. The threshold limits, α, for various confidence levels are given in Table 5.2.

The cut-off return R^* can be expressed as:

$$R^* = \mu + \alpha\,\sigma \qquad (9)$$

TABLE 5.2

Threshold Limits, α, as a Function of the Confidence Level

c	$\alpha = \dfrac{R^* - \mu}{\sigma}$
99.97%	-3.43
99.87%	-3.00
99%	-2.33
95%	-1.65

From the definition (6) of VaR and (7) of absolute VaR', it follows that:

$$\text{VaR } (H; c) = -\alpha \sigma V \tag{10}$$

$$\text{VaR' } (H; c) = -(\alpha \sigma + \mu) V \tag{11}$$

3.2.2 Student-t Return Distribution

There is a large amount of evidence that many individual return distributions are not normally distributed, and exhibit what are known as "fat tails." The term "fat tails" arises out of the shape of certain distributions when plotted on a graph. In these distributions, there are more observations far away from the mean than is the case in a normal or bell-shaped distribution. So whereas a normal distribution tails off quickly to reflect the rarity of unlikely events, the tail of a fat-tailed distribution remains relatively thick (e.g., Campbell, Lo, and MacKinlay, 1997).

Fat tails in distributions are particularly worrying to risk managers because they imply that extraordinary losses occur more frequently than a normal distribution would lead us to believe.

Luckily, even if the returns of an individual factor do not follow a normal distribution, the returns of a well-diversified portfolio across many different risk factors might still exhibit a normal distribution. This effect is explained by the central limit theorem, which tells us that the independent random variables of well-behaved distribution will possess a mean that converges, in large samples, to a normal distribution.

In practice, this result implies that a risk manager can assume that a portfolio has a normal returns distribution, provided that the portfolio is fairly well diversified and the risk *factor* returns are sufficiently independent from each other (even when they are not themselves normally distributed).

If it is felt that the normal distribution is inadequate for describing the portfolio returns,[15] one can use as an alternative the class of Student-t distributions. As illustrated Figure 5.7, these distributions allow for fat tails and, at the same time, produce derivations as tractable as those produced by the normal distribution.

The Student-t distribution is fully characterized by the mean, μ, and the variance, σ^2, of the portfolio return, and by an additional

FIGURE 5.7

Comparison of the Unit Normal and Student-t Distributions

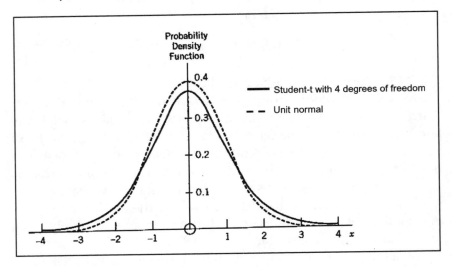

parameter called the "degree of freedom," v, that controls the fat-ness of the tail, i.e., the degree of leptokurtosis.[16] The smaller v, the fatter the tails of the Student-t distribution. As v gets larger, the dis-tribution converges to the normal distribution with mean, μ, and variance, σ^2. According to Jorion (1995), v varies in the range 4 to 8 for most financial time series.

We would expect the VaR derived from a Student-t distribu-tion to be higher than that derived from a normal distribution. To find VaR when the portfolio return is distributed according to a Student-t distribution, simply replace $f(R)$ in equation (8) with the appropriate Student-t distribution. For example, when v is equal to 5, VaR at the 99 percent confidence level is 3.365 standard devia-tions, instead of 2.33 when the distribution is normal.

3.3 From 1-Day VaR to 10-Day VaR

When VaR is used to manage risk on a daily basis, then one-day VaR is needed. One-day VaR must be derived from the daily dis-tribution of the portfolio values. However, 10 days is the time hori-zon set by the regulators for the purpose of reporting regulatory capital. Ideally, the 10-day VaR should be derived from the corresponding distribution over a 10-day horizon. However, can one also derive the 10-day VaR, or the VaR over any other time horizon, from the daily VaR?

If we assume that markets are efficient and daily returns, R_t, are independent and identically distributed (i.i.d.), then the 10-day return, $R(10) = \sum_{t=1}^{10} R_t$, is also normally distributed with mean μ_{10} = 10μ, and variance $\sigma_{10}^2 = 10\sigma^2$, since it is the sum of 10 i.i.d. normal variables. It follows that:

$$\text{VaR } (10; c) = \sqrt{10} \text{ VaR } (1; c) \qquad (12)$$

This means that the 10-day VaR can be approximated by multiplying the daily VaR by the square root of time (here, 10 days). This result would not hold if the stock returns exhibit mean reversion, are serially correlated, or more generally are not i.i.d.[17]

3.4 VaR Is for Managing, As Well As Measuring, Risk

To implement the VaR methodology, analysts must make simplifying assumptions. We discuss the problems and limitations inherent in those assumptions below. But first, let us stress that VaR is a powerful approach and has far-reaching uses:

• VaR provides a common, consistent, and integrated measure of risk across risk factors, instruments, and asset classes, leading to greater risk transparency and a consistent treatment of risks across the firm. For example, it allows managers to measure the risk of a fixed-income position in a way that is comparable and consistent with their risk assessment of an equity derivative position. VaR also takes account of the correlations between the various risk factors. If two risks offset each other, VaR allows for this offset and tells us that the overall risk is relatively small. If, on the contrary, one risk increases another risk, then VaR takes this into account and produces a higher risk estimate. In other words, VaR measures risk in a portfolio framework somewhat in the spirit of portfolio theory.

• VaR provides an aggregate measure of risk: a single number that is related to the maximum loss that might be incurred on a position, at a given confidence level. This single number can then be easily translated into a capital requirement. VaR can also be used to reward employees on the basis of the risk-adjusted return on capital generated by their activities. In other words, it can be used to measure risk-adjusted performance (see Chapter 14). VaR can therefore be used to discourage risk taking that does not add value from the shareholder's perspective.

• The risks taken by the business line can be monitored using limits set in terms of VaR. These limits can be used to ensure that individuals do not take more risk than they are allowed to take. Risk limits expressed in VaR units can easily be aggregated up through the firm: from the business line, at trading desk level, to the very top of the corporation. The drill-down capability of a VaR system allows risk managers to detect which unit is taking the most risk, and also to identify the type of risk to which the whole bank is most exposed, e.g., equity, interest rate, currency, credit spread, equity vega, etc.[18]

• VaR provides senior management, the board of directors, and regulators with a risk measure that they can understand. Managers and shareholders, as well as regulators, can decide whether they feel comfortable with the level of risk taken on by the bank in terms of VaR units. VaR also provides a framework to assess, ex ante, investments and projects on the basis of their expected risk-adjusted return on capital.

• A VaR system allows a firm to assess the benefits from portfolio diversification within a line of activity, but also across businesses (such as the equity and fixed-income businesses). It allows managers to assess the daily revenue volatility they might expect from any given trading area.

• VaR has become an internal and external reporting tool. VaR reports are produced daily for managers of business lines, and are then aggregated for senior management. VaR is also communicated to the regulators, and has become the basis for calculating regulatory capital. The rating agencies take VaR calculations into account in establishing their rating of banks. Increasingly, VaR is also published in banks' annual reports as a key indicator of risk (Figure 5.6).

4. CALCULATING VALUE AT RISK

As we discussed, to calculate VaR we first need to generate the forward distribution of the portfolio values at the risk horizon or, equivalently, the distribution of the changes in the value of the portfolio. Only after this can we calculate the mean and the quantiles of this distribution (Figure 5.5).

There are three approaches to deriving this distribution:

- The analytic variance-covariance approach
- The Monte Carlo approach
- The historical simulation approach

These all share the following two preliminary steps.

(i) Selection of the risk factors

The change in the value of the portfolio is driven by changes in the market factors that influence the price of each instrument. The relevant risk factors depend on the composition of the portfolio. The selection of risk factors is straightforward for a simple security, but it requires judgement for more complex products.

In the case of a simple security, such as a $US/Euro forward, the value of the position is affected only by the $US/Euro forward rate. In the case of a $US/Euro call option, the value of the position depends not only on the $US/Euro exchange rate, but also on the dollar and the Euro interest rates over the maturity of the option, as well as the $US/Euro volatility (Table 5.3).

The market factors that affect prices vary by instruments. In the case of a stock portfolio, the risk factors are the prices of the individual stocks that compose the portfolio. For a bond portfolio, the choice of the risk factors depends on the degree of "granularity" that one needs to achieve. For example, the risk factor for each bond might simply be its yield to maturity.

TABLE 5.3

Example of a Selection of Risk Factors

USD/Euro forward	USD/Euro option
• USD/Euro forward rate	• USD/Euro exchange rate
	• USD interest rates
	• Euro interest rates
	• USD/Euro volatility

Alternatively, it could be a selection of zero-coupon rates on the risk-free term structure of interest rates for each currency. For example, the selection might comprise the overnight, the 1-month, 3-month, 6-month, 1-year, 3-year, 5-year, 10-year, and 30-year zero-coupon rates, as well as the spread in prices between different issuers for the same terms (so that the calculation captures issuer risk).

(ii) Choice of a methodology for modeling changes in market risk factors

The analytic variance-covariance approach assumes that the risk factors are log-normally distributed or, equivalently, that their log-returns are normally distributed.

The historical simulation approach does not oblige the user to make any analytic assumptions about the distributions. VaR is derived from the empirical distribution generated by the historical realizations of the risk factors over a specified period of time. However, at least two or three years of data are necessary to produce meaningful results.

The Monte Carlo methodology can be implemented by choosing any analytic multivariate distribution for the risk factors. The only limitation is the ability to estimate the parameters of the distribution, such as the means, the variances, and the covariances. The Monte Carlo methodology is flexible and allows the analyst to choose distributions that exhibit fat tails and skewness (e.g., Student-t distributions). Processes with mean reversion can also be simulated. Complex distributions, such as mixtures of normal distributions or the mixture of a normal and a jump process (alternative ways to capture fat tails), can also be dealt with easily.

4.1 Analytic Variance-Covariance, or "Delta-Normal," Approach: Case of a Portfolio Linear in Risks[19]

The analytic variance-covariance approach assumes that the distribution of the changes in the portfolio value is normal.[20] Since the normal distribution is completely characterized by its first two moments, the analyst must simply derive the mean and the variance of this normal distribution from:

- The multivariate distribution of the risk factors; and
- The composition of the portfolio.

The analytic approach is an extension of the portfolio model as pioneered by Markowitz (1952, 1959), and is illustrated in the following example.

Example 1: Stock Portfolio

Consider a portfolio composed of two stocks, say Microsoft and Exxon, with n_1 shares of Microsoft valued at S_1 per share, and n_2 shares of Exxon valued at S_2 per share.[21] Then, the value of the portfolio is:

$$V = n_1 S_1 + n_2 S_2 \tag{13}$$

1. Selection of the risk factors

The risk factors are the stock prices, S_1, and S_2, respectively. It follows that:

$$R_V = \frac{\Delta V}{V} = \frac{n_1 S_1}{V} \frac{\Delta S_1}{S_1} + \frac{n_2 S_2}{V} \frac{\Delta S_2}{S_2} = \omega_1 R_1 + \omega_2 R_2$$

$$= \sum_{i=1}^{2} \omega_i R_i \tag{14}$$

where

R_V = the rate of return on the portfolio
R_i = the rate of return on stock i, $R_i \equiv \Delta S_i / S_i$
ω_i = the percentage of the portfolio invested in stock i,
$\quad i = 1,2$, with $\sum w_i = 1$

2. Distribution of the risk factors

Prices are assumed to be log-normally distributed, so that log-returns during the *period* $(t - 1, t)$, i.e.,

$$R_t = \ln\left(\frac{S_t}{S_{t-1}}\right) = \ln\left(1 - \frac{S_t - S_{t-1}}{S_{t-1}}\right) \sim \frac{\Delta S_t}{S_{t-1}},$$

are normally distributed, where S_t (S_{t-1}) denotes the price of the stock at time t ($t - 1$), and ΔS is the price change during the period, $\Delta S = S_t - S_{t-1}$.[22]

More specifically, we assume that R_i = the rate of return on stock i, $i = 1,2$, follows a multivariate normal distribution with mean, μ_i, and standard deviation, σ_i, and correlation coefficient ρ between the rates of return on the two stocks.

3. One-day and 10-day VaR calculation for an individual stock

The marginal distribution for each stock return is univariate normal:

$$R_i = \frac{\Delta S_i}{S_i} \sim N(\mu_i, \sigma_i) \text{ for i} = 1,2$$

so that, according to (10) and (11), the one-day and 10-day VaRs at the 99 percent confidence level are, respectively:

$$VaR_i(1;99) = 2.33 \cdot \sigma_i \cdot S_i \tag{15}$$
$$VaR_i(10;99) = \sqrt{10} \cdot VaR_i(1;99) = 2.33\sqrt{10}\sigma_i \cdot S_i$$

4. One-day and 10-day VaR calculation for the stock portfolio

The return on the portfolio, as defined in (14), being a linear combination of normal distributions, is also normally distributed:

$$R_V \sim N(\mu_V, \sigma_V)$$

with

$$\mu_V = \sum_{i=1}^{2} \omega_i \mu_i$$

$$\sigma_V^2 = \omega_1^2 \sigma_1^2 + \omega_2^2 \sigma_2^2 + 2\omega_1\omega_2 \text{ cov}(R_1, R_2)$$

$$= \omega_1^2 \sigma_1^2 + \omega_2^2 \sigma_2^2 + 2\omega_1\omega_2\rho\sigma_1\sigma_2$$

$$= (\omega_1 \quad \omega_2) \begin{pmatrix} \sigma_1^2 & \rho\sigma_1\sigma_2 \\ \rho\sigma_1\sigma_2 & \sigma_2^2 \end{pmatrix} \begin{pmatrix} \omega_1 \\ \omega_2 \end{pmatrix} \tag{16}$$

$$= (\omega_1 \quad \omega_2) \begin{pmatrix} \sigma_1 & 0 \\ 0 & \sigma_2 \end{pmatrix} \begin{pmatrix} 1 & \rho \\ \rho & 1 \end{pmatrix} \begin{pmatrix} \sigma_1 & 0 \\ 0 & \sigma_2 \end{pmatrix} \begin{pmatrix} \omega_1 \\ \omega_2 \end{pmatrix}$$

$$= w\Omega w^T = w\sigma C\sigma w^T$$

where $w = (\omega_1 \quad \omega_2)$ denotes the 1×2 weight vector, Ω is the variance-covariance matrix, σ is the 2×2 diagonal standard deviation matrix, C is the 2×2 correlation matrix and w^T denotes the transpose of w.

Formula (16) is general, and applies to a portfolio that is linear in risks[23] with N risk factors, while the dimensions of the vectors and matrices are adjusted accordingly. However, to reduce the dimensionality of the correlation matrix, one can rely on the market model, also known as the "beta" model, as shown in Appendix 3.

Then, according to (10) and (11), the one and 10-day VaRs for the portfolio at the 99 percent confidence level are, respectively:

$$VaR_V(1;99) = 2.33 \cdot \sigma_V V$$
$$VaR_V(10;99) = \sqrt{10}VaR_V(1;99) = 2.33 \cdot \sqrt{10} \cdot \sigma_V V \qquad (17)$$

The expression (17) for VaR, using (16), can also be rewritten as:

$$VaR_V(1;99) = 2.33[w\sigma C\sigma w^T]^{1/2}V = [VaR \cdot C \cdot VaR^T]^{1/2} \qquad (18)$$

where VaR denotes the 1×2 vector of individual $VaRs$ for each stock position, i.e., $VaR = [VaR_1 \quad VaR_2]$ as specified in (15), adjusted for the number of shares.[24]

Expression (18) offers a convenient way of showing the impact of correlations on the overall VaR of a portfolio. If stock returns are perfectly correlated, with the correlations equal to one, then VaR_V is simply the sum of the $VaRs$ of the individual stocks that compose the portfolio. In that instance, there is no diversification effect. When correlations are less than one, then VaR_V is less than the sum of the individual $VaRs$. The following numerical application illustrates the portfolio effect for different values of the correlation coefficient.

Numerical application

From historical data we estimate the simple historical mean and standard deviation of the daily returns over a one-year period for two stocks, e.g., Microsoft and Exxon, denoted by S_1 and S_2, respectively. We can also estimate the correlation coefficient, ρ, between their rates of return. As of November 26, 1999, we obtain the one-day means and standard deviations based on the last 260 trading days:

$$\mu_1 = 0.155\% \qquad \mu_2 = 0.0338\%$$
$$\sigma_1 = 2.42\% \qquad \sigma_2 = 1.68\% \qquad \rho = 0.14 \qquad (19)$$

Assume that the portfolio is composed of 100 shares of Microsoft and 120 shares of Exxon valued at $91.7 and $79.1, respectively. Then, the value of the portfolio is:

$$V = n_1 S_1 + n_2 S_2 = \$18,662$$

and the relative investments in both stocks are, respectively:

$$\omega_1 = \frac{n_1 S_1}{V} = 0.49 \qquad \omega_2 = \frac{n_2 S_s}{V} = 0.51$$

so that the one-day mean and standard deviation of the rate of return on the portfolio are:

$$\mu_V = \omega_1 \mu_1 + \omega_2 \mu_2 = 0.093\%$$
$$\sigma_V^2 = \omega_1^2 \sigma_1^2 + \omega_2^2 \sigma_2^2 + 2\rho\omega_1\omega_2\sigma_1\sigma_2 = 0.00024$$
$$\sigma_V = 1.55\%$$

The one-day VaRs at the 99 percent confidence level are:

$$VaR_1(1; 99) = 2.33 \, \sigma_1 \, n_1 \, S_1 = \$517$$
$$VaR_2(1; 99) = 2.33 \, \sigma_2 \, n_2 \, S_2 = \$370$$
$$VaR_V (1; 99) = 2.33 \, \sigma_V \, V = \$677$$

where VaR_1, VaR_2, and VaR_V denote the one-day value at risk at the 99 percent confidence level for Microsoft, Exxon, and the portfolio, respectively. Note that $VaR_V (1; 99) = \$677$ is less than the sum of $VaR_1(1; 99)$ and $VaR_2(1; 99)$, i.e., \$887.

The difference, \$210, represents the portfolio effect that results from the imperfect correlation between the equity returns. VaR is in fact quite sensitive to the correlation structure of the risk factors. Table 5.4 shows the sensitivity of VaR to the correlation coefficient for the previous equity portfolio.

We can also derive the absolute VaR', i.e.:

$$VaR_1'(1; 99) = (2.33 \, \sigma_{1-\mu_1}) \, n_1 \, S_1 = \$503$$
$$VaR_2'(1; 99) = (2.33 \, \sigma_{2-\mu_2}) \, n_2 \, S_2 = \$367$$
$$VaR_V' (1; 99) = (2.33 \, \sigma_{V-\mu_V}) \, V = \$657$$

Example 2: A Zero-Coupon Bond

1. Consider a hypothetical position in a 10-year French zero-coupon "OAT" bond with a nominal value of 100 million French francs (FRF).

The risk factor is the 10-year yield, y, whose current value is supposed to be $y = 7.96$ percent. It is also assumed to be normally distributed with a daily volatility $\sigma (y) = 9.63bp$ (or 0.0963 percent). It follows that the price of the bond is $B = 100/1.0796^{10} = 46.491$ million FRF.

TABLE 5.4

VaR of a Stock Portfolio for
Different Correlation Coefficients

ρ	VaR (1;99)	Portfolio Effect
−1.0	$887	$0
0.5	$772	$115
0	$636	$251
−0.5	$461	$426
−1.0	$146	$741

If we now assume that the change in the bond price is governed by the duration-based relation (1) (Section 2.2), we have:[25]

$$dB = -B \frac{D}{1+y} dy = -46.491 \frac{10}{1.0796} dy = 430.63 dy$$

so that, dB is normally distributed with a daily volatility:

$$\sigma(B) = -B \frac{D}{1+y} \sigma(y) = 430.631 \cdot 0.000963 = 0.415 \text{ million FRF}$$

and:

$$VaR(1;99) = 2.33 \cdot \sigma(B) = 2.33 \cdot 0.415 = 0.967 \text{ million FRF}$$
$$VaR(10;99) = \sqrt{10} \cdot VaR(1;99) = \sqrt{10} \cdot 0.967 = 3.06 \text{ million FRF}$$

2. Now, suppose that the French bond is held by a U.S. investor, for whom the risks should be denominated in $US. Assume also that the exchange rate, e, is 5.402 FFR per $US, the daily volatility of its log-return is $\sigma(de/e) = 0.58$ percent, and the correlation between the French yield and the exchange rate is $\rho(dy, de/e) = -0.0726$. Then,

$$B_\$ = B_{FFR} \frac{1}{e} = \frac{46.491}{5.402} = \$8.606 \text{ million}$$

and

$$\frac{dB_\$}{B_\$} = \frac{dB_{FFR}}{B_{FFR}} - \frac{de}{e} = -\frac{D}{1+y} dy - \frac{de}{e} \tag{20}$$

Thus,

$$\sigma^2 \left(\frac{dB_\$}{B_\$} \right) = \frac{D^2}{(1 + y)^2} \sigma^2(dy) + \sigma^2 \left(\frac{de}{e} \right) - 2\rho \frac{D}{1 + y} \sigma(dy)\sigma \left(\frac{de}{e} \right)$$

and

$$\sigma(dB_\$) = B_\$ \sigma \left(\frac{dB_\$}{B_\$} \right)$$

$$\sigma(dB_\$) = 8.606 \sqrt{ \frac{100}{1.0796^2} 0.0963^2 \cdot 10^{-4} + 0.58^2 \cdot 10^{-4} - 2 - 0.0726 \frac{10}{1.0726} 0.0963 \cdot 0.58 \cdot 10^{-4} }$$

$$= \$88,479$$

Note, from (20), that the change in the value of the bond expressed in \$US is normally distributed, as it is the weighted sum of two normal distributions. Then:

$$VaR(1;99)_\$ = 2.33 \cdot \sigma(dB_\$) = 2.33 \, \$88,479 = \$206,156$$

The risk of this position is reduced by a negative correlation between the yield of the French bond and the exchange rate. If the correlation was +1 instead of $-.0726$, then the one-day VaR would be \$295,173. The portfolio effect associated with the imperfect correlation is:

$$\text{Portfolio effect} = \$295,173 - \$206,156 = \$89,017.$$

4.2 Delta-Normal VaR for Other Instruments

The previous analysis can be easily generalized to any type of financial instruments for which the equilibrium value, V, can be expressed as a function of n risk factors, f_i, $i = 1, \ldots, n$. The change in value, dV, can be approximated by a first-order Taylor expansion of the pricing equation, i.e.:

$$dV = \sum_{i=1}^{n} \frac{\partial V}{\partial f_i} df_i = \sum_{i=1}^{n} \Delta_i df_i \tag{21}$$

where Δ_i denotes the "delta" of the position in the instrument, i.e., the small change in V in response to a small change in factor i. From (20) it follows that:

$$\sigma(dV) = \sqrt{\sum_{i=1}^{n} \Delta_i^2 \sigma^2 \, (dfi) + \sum_{i=1}^{n} \sum_{\substack{j=1 \\ j\neq i}}^{n} \Delta i \Delta j \, \mathrm{cov}(df_i, df_j)} \qquad (22)$$

If we assume that the changes in the risk factors are normally distributed, the change in the asset value, dV, is also normally distributed, so that:

$$VaR(1:99) = 2.33 \cdot \sigma(dV) \qquad (23)$$

In the following we illustrate the calculation of equation (21) for two simple derivatives: a forward contract and an option. Once (21) has been derived, the calculation of VaR according to (22) becomes straightforward. It only requires the variance and covariance statistics for the risk factors.

(i) Forward Contract[26]

This is the simplest type of derivative contract. Under a forward agreement, the buyer is obliged to take delivery of a given quantity of financial asset or commodity, at a prearranged date and price (the forward price). The seller of the forward contract is also obligated to deliver under the same terms. The forward price is set so that the value of the contract is zero at inception, and the value at time t of the forward contract for the buyer is F_t:

$$F_t = S_t e^{-y(T-t)} - F_T e^{-r(T-t)} \qquad (24)$$

such that:

S_t = current price of the security or commodity to be delivered

F_T = forward price, i.e., delivery price

t, T = current time and delivery time (time when the forward contract matures), respectively

r = risk-free rate of interest with continuous compounding, for an investment maturing at time T

y = continuous dividend yield paid out by the security, and assumed to be continuously reinvested in the security[27]

Equation (24) is derived from the no-arbitrage argument.[28] The investment in the underlying security over the period (T, t) can be replicated by buying the existing forward contract at its current price, F_t, and setting aside the present value of the contractual purchase price, F_T. Then, the change in value of the forward value expressed in terms of the changes in the risk factors S_t, r, and y, is:

$$dF_t = \frac{\partial F_t}{\partial S_t} dS_t + \frac{\partial F_t}{\partial r} dr + \frac{\partial F_t}{\partial y} dy$$

$$= e^{-y(T-t)} dS_t + F_T e^{-r(T-t)}(T-t)dr - S_t e^{-y(T-t)}(T-t)dy$$

(25)

(ii) Option Contracts

In Section 2.3, and in Chapter 1, we discussed the pricing of European call options on an individual stock that does not pay any dividend, using the Black-Scholes formula (3):[29]

$$C = C(S, \sigma, r) = SN(d_1) - Ke^{-rT} N(d_2)$$

Then, according to the delta-normal approach to VaR, the change in value of the option can be approximated using the "Greeks" (Table 5.1), by:

$$dC = \frac{\partial C}{\partial S} dS + \frac{\partial C}{\partial \sigma} d\sigma + \frac{\partial C}{\partial r} dr$$

$$= \Delta \cdot dS + \text{vega} \cdot d\sigma + \text{rho} \cdot dr$$

(26)

4.3 Historical Simulation Approach

The historical simulation approach to VaR is conceptually simple. First, the changes that have been seen in relevant market prices and rates (the risk factors) are analyzed over a specified historical period, say, one to four years. The portfolio under examination is then revalued, using changes in the risk factors derived from the historical data, to create the distribution of the portfolio returns from which the VaR of the portfolio can be derived. Each daily simulated change in the value of the portfolio is considered as an observation in the distribution.

Three steps are involved:

- Select a sample of actual daily risk factor changes over a given period of time, say 250 days (i.e., one year's worth of trading days).
- Apply those daily changes to the current value of the risk factors and revalue the current portfolio as many times as the number of days in the historical sample.
- Construct the histogram of portfolio values and identify the VaR that isolates the first percentile of the distribution in the left-hand tail, assuming VaR is derived at the 99 percent confidence level.[30]

We now illustrate the approach using an example.[31] Assume that the current portfolio is composed of a three-month $US/DM call option. The market risk factors for this position are:

- $US/DM exchange rate
- $US three-month interest rate
- DM three-month interest rate
- Three-month implied volatility of the $US/DM exchange rate

In the following we neglect the impact of the interest rate risk factors and only consider the level of the exchange rate and its volatility. In this example we use daily observations over the past 100 days. They are reported in columns 2 and 3 of Table 5.5.

Historical simulation, like Monte Carlo simulation, requires the repricing of the position using the historical distribution of the risk factors.[32] In this example we use the Black-Scholes model adapted by Garman-Kholhagen (1983) to currency options (Table 5.6).

The last step consists of constructing the histogram of the portfolio returns based on the last 100 days of history, or equivalently sorting the changes in portfolio values to identify the first percentile of the distribution. Table 5.7 shows the ranking of the changes in value of the portfolio. Using this, we identify the first percentile as −$0.07.

Figure 5.8 shows the histogram of these values. VaR (1; 99) at

TABLE 5.5

Historical Market Values for the
Risk Factors Over the Last
100 Days

Day (t)	$US/DM (FX$_t$)	FX Volatility (σ_t)
−100	1.3970	0.149
−99	1.3960	0.149
−98	1.3973	0.151
. . .	. . .	. . .
−2	1.4015	0.163
−1	1.4024	0.164

the 99 percent confidence level is simply the distance to the mean ($0.01) of the first percentile, i.e., VaR (1; 99) = $0.08, while absolute VaR is the first percentile itself, i.e., VaR′ (1; 99) = $0.07.

This approach can easily be generalized to any portfolio of securities. The approach follows the same three-step procedure. Select the relevant risk factors and gather the historical data using the same historical period for all the factors. Calculate the changes in value for all the constituents of the portfolio, and sum up these changes across all positions, for each day, keeping the days synchronized. Construct the histogram of the portfolio returns, or

TABLE 5.6

Simulating Portfolio Values Using Historical Data
(Current Value of the Portfolio: $1.80)

	Change from Current Value ($1.80)
Alternate price 100 = C(FX$_{100}$; σ_{100}) = $1.75	−$0.05
Alternate price 99 = C(FX$_{99}$; σ_{99}) = $1.73	−$0.07
Alternate price 98 = C(FX$_{98}$; σ_{98}) = $1.69	−$0.11
. . . .	
Alternate price 2 = C(FX$_2$; σ_2) = $1.87	+$0.07
Alternate price 1 = C(FX$_1$; σ_1) = $1.88	+$0.08

TABLE 5.7

Identifying the First Percentile of the Historical Distribution of the Portfolio Return

Rank	Change from Current Value
100	−$0.11
99	−$0.07
98	−$0.05
. . .	. . .
2	+$0.07
1	+$0.08

equivalently sort the values to identify the first percentile of the distribution, assuming VaR is derived at the 99 percent confidence level.

Below, we illustrate these steps with regard to a portfolio composed of the $US/DM call option described above, and a German bond.[33]

- Step 1: Risk factors and historical market values (Table 5.8)
- Step 2: Change in the value of the portfolio (Table 5.9)

FIGURE 5.8

VaR from Historical Simulations

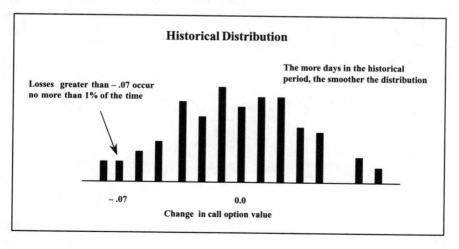

Historical Distribution

The more days in the historical period, the smoother the distribution

Losses greater than − .07 occur no more than 1% of the time

−.07   0.0

Change in call option value

TABLE 5.8

Risk Factors and Historical Market Values

Day (t)	$US/DM (FX_t)	FX Volatility (σ_t)	German Interest Rate (%) (DMYTM_t)
−100	1.3970	0.149	5.125
−99	1.3960	0.149	5.125
−98	1.3973	0.151	5.100
...	...	...	...
−2	1.4015	0.163	4.910
−1	1.4024	0.162	4.925

Note: The exchange rate and its volatility are reported in Table 5.5.

We have already discussed the pricing model for the foreign exchange call option. We use a simple discount valuation model for the German bond, employing the German bond's yield to maturity. This value in DM must then be translated into $US using the current exchange rate (Table 5.9).

Today's $US price of the German bond:
$P_0 = P_{DM}(DMYTM_0)/FX_0$
Alternate price $100_{\$US} = P_{DM}(DMYTM_{100})/FX_{100}$

. . . .

Alternate price $1_{\$US} = P_{DM}(DMYTM_1)/FX_1$

TABLE 5.9

Changes in Portfolio Value

Day	Change in $US/DM Call	Change in German Bond	Change in Portfolio Value
−100	−$0.05	−$0.03	−$0.08
−99	$0.07	$0.02	−$0.05
−98	−$0.11	$0.15	+$0.04
...	...	...	...
−2	$0.07	−$0.12	−$0.05
−1	$0.08	−$0.02	−$0.06

FIGURE 5.9

VaR from Historical Simulation for the Portfolio: USD/DM
Call and German Bond

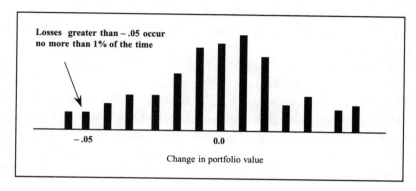

- Step 3: Identify the first percentile of the portfolio return
  distribution (Figure 5.9).

The major attraction of historical simulation is that the method
is completely nonparametric and does not depend on any assumption about the distribution of the risk factors. We do not need
to assume that the returns of the risk factors are normally distributed and independent over time.[34]

The nonparametric nature of historical simulation also obvi-
ates the need to estimate volatilities and correlations. Historical
volatilities and correlations are already reflected in the data set, and
all we need to calculate are the synchronous risk factor returns over
a given historical period. Historical simulation has also no problem accommodating fat tails, since the historical returns already reflect actual synchronous moves in the market across all risk factors. Another advantage of historical simulation over the
variance-covariance approach is that it allows the analyst to calculate confidence intervals for VaR.

The main drawback of historical simulation is its complete dependence on a particular set of historical data—and thus on the
idiosyncrasies of this data set. The underlying assumption is that
the past, as captured in the historical data set, is a reliable representation of the future. This implicitly presumes that the market
events embedded in the data set will be reproduced in the months
to come. However, the historical period may cover events such as

a market crash or, conversely, a period of exceptionally low price volatility, that are unlikely to be repeated in the future. Historical simulation may also lead to a distorted assessment of the risk if we employ the technique regardless of any structural changes anticipated in the market—such as the introduction of the Euro at the beginning of 1999.

Another practical limitation of historical simulation is data availability. One year of data corresponds to only 250 data points (trading days) on average, i.e., 250 scenarios. By contrast, Monte Carlo simulations usually involve at least 10,000 simulations (i.e., scenarios). Employing small samples of historical data inevitably leaves gaps in the distributions of the risk factors and tends to underrepresent the tails of the distributions, i.e., the occurrence of unlikely but extreme events.

4.4 Monte Carlo Approach[35]

Monte Carlo simulation consists of repeatedly simulating the random processes that govern market prices and rates. Each simulation (scenario) generates a possible value for the portfolio at the target horizon (e.g., 10 days). If we generate enough of these scenarios, the simulated distribution of the portfolio's values will converge towards the true, although unknown, distribution. The VaR can be easily inferred from the distribution, as we described above.

Monte Carlo simulation involves three steps.

• First, Specify All the Relevant Risk Factors
Like the other approaches, we need to select all the relevant risk factors. In addition, we have to specify the dynamics of these factors, i.e., their stochastic processes, and we need to estimate their parameters (volatilities, correlations, mean reversion factors for interest rate processes, and so on).

For example, a commonly used model for stock prices is the geometric Brownian motion, which is consistent with the Black-Scholes option-pricing model presented earlier in equation (3). It is described by the stochastic differential equation (SDE):

$$dS_t = \mu S_t dt + \sigma S_t dW_t \qquad (27)$$

where W_t is a standard Wiener process and the drift, μ, and volatility, σ, are constant parameters that need to be estimated using historical data.[36] The model assumes that the stock's rate of return is the sum of a known deterministic "drift" factor, μ, and an unknown factor, the "noise," which is drawn from a normal distribution. The "noise," or innovations, dW_t, in the stock price are assumed to be uncorrelated over time, or more generally independent and identically distributed (i.i.d.), with dW_t being a random variable normally distributed with mean zero and variance dt. The random shock, or innovation, at time t does not depend upon past information. This model is therefore consistent with the efficient market hypothesis.

Geometric Brownian motion describes adequately the behavior of financial assets such as equities and, to some extent, commodities, but it certainly does not describe the behavior of interest rates. Interest rates exhibit mean reversion, and the drift term cannot be assumed to be constant. Hull (2000) offers a detailed analysis of the stochastic processes followed by different classes of financial assets (in particular, fixed-income securities).[37]

• Second, Construct Price Paths

Geometric Brownian motion is one of the rare processes for which an explicit solution exists to SDE (27), i.e.:

$$S_t = S_0 \exp\left[\left(\mu - \frac{1}{2}\sigma^2\right)t + \sigma W_t\right] \tag{28}$$

with W_t denoting the cumulative innovations from 0 to t.

To generate a discrete path of the underlying stock price, we apply (28) between two time instants, t and $t-1$:

$$S_t = S_{t-1} \exp\left[\left(\mu - \frac{1}{2}\sigma^2\right)\Delta t + \sigma\Delta t Z\right] \tag{29}$$

where

Δt = time interval between t and $t-1$

Z = standard normal variable $N(0,1)$ such that $W_t = W_{t-1} + \sqrt{\Delta t} Z$

Price paths are constructed using random numbers produced by a random number generator.[38] For a simple portfolio without complex exotic options the forward distribution of portfolio returns at a 10-day horizon can be generated in one step with $\Delta t = 10$ days. Alternatively, if the simulation is performed on a daily basis (i.e., $\Delta t = 1$ day), a random distribution is drawn for each day to calculate the 10-day cumulative impact.

When several correlated risk factors are involved, we need to simulate multivariate distributions. Only in the case where the distributions are independent can the randomization be performed independently for each variable as in (29). Suppose now that we want to generate the paths of n multiple correlated assets, $S_t^1, \ldots, S_t^n$, each described by the process (27) with asset-specific drift and volatility, μ_i and σ_i, and Wiener process W_t^i ($i = 1, \ldots, n$).

If the instantaneous returns on securities i and j have correlation ρ_{ij}, which means that $E[W_t^i W_t^j] = \rho_{ij} t$, then we can write the multivariate process as:

$$S_t^i = S_0^i \exp\left[\left(\mu_i - \frac{1}{2}\sigma_i^2\right)t + \sqrt{t}\sigma_i X_i\right] \tag{30}$$

where $X = (X_1, \ldots, X_n)$ is a multivariate normal with mean zero and covariance matrix Σ, such that the i,j component is $\Sigma_{ij} = E(XX^T) = \rho_{ij}$, which is symmetric, positive definite.[39]

The process of generating a multivariate path starts with the generation of n independent standard normal random variables, $Y = (Y_t^1, \ldots, Y_t^n)$ with mean zero and variance unity so that, $E(YY^T) = I$, where I is the identity matrix of dimension n with 1 on the diagonal and zeros elsewhere.

Next, construct the variables $X = AY$ where A is a matrix such that $\Sigma = AA^T$.[40] We have thus generated the desired correlated innovations from uncorrelated processes that are easy to produce.

As an example, consider the two-variable case. The covariance matrix can be decomposed into:

$$\Sigma = \begin{pmatrix} 1 & \rho \\ \rho & 1 \end{pmatrix} = \begin{pmatrix} 1 & 0 \\ \rho & (1-\rho^2)^{1/2} \end{pmatrix}\begin{pmatrix} 1 & \rho \\ 0 & (1-\rho^2)^{1/2} \end{pmatrix}$$

Then, if $Y = (Y^1, Y^2)$ is a vector of independent unit-standard normal variables, the transformed variables:

$$\begin{pmatrix} X^1 \\ X^2 \end{pmatrix} = \begin{pmatrix} 1 & 0 \\ \rho & (1-\rho^2)^{1/2} \end{pmatrix}\begin{pmatrix} Y^1 \\ Y^2 \end{pmatrix}$$

that is,

$$X^1 = Y^1$$
$$X^2 = \rho Y^1 + (1 - \rho^2)^{1/2} Y^2$$

have a covariance matrix Σ.

• **Third, Value the Portfolio for Each Path (Scenario)**
Each path generates a set of values for the risk factors that are used as inputs into the pricing models, for each security composing the portfolio. The process is repeated a large number of times, say 10,000 times, to generate the distribution, at the risk horizon, of the portfolio return. This step is equivalent to the corresponding procedure for historical simulation, except that Monte Carlo simulation can generate many more scenarios than historical simulation.

Then, VaR at the 99 percent confidence level is simply derived as the distance to the mean of the first percentile of the distribution.

As is the case of historical simulation, a Monte Carlo simulation with full repricing requires the analyst to specify the pricing models for each security in the portfolio. It is also possible to implement a "hybrid" Monte Carlo simulation where the pricing model is replaced by the Taylor expansion (delta-normal or delta-gamma-vega-rho-theta method) that is used in the variance-covariance approach. This hybrid technique presents the advantage of being less computer intensive.

Monte Carlo simulation is a powerful and flexible approach to VaR. It can accommodate any distribution of risk factors to allow for "fat tail" distributions, where extreme events are expected to occur more commonly than in normal distributions, and "jumps" or discontinuities in price processes. For example, a process can be described as a mixture of two normal distributions, or as a jump-diffusion process (both processes are consistent with fat tails).

As we mentioned above, other distributions, such as the Student-t distribution, are also often suggested as ways to generate heavy tails. Also, as noted by Broadie and Glasserman (1998), the four-parameter family of Ramberg et al. (1979) provides enough flexibility to match a wide range of values of skew and kurtosis. It can also accommodate complex portfolios that contain exotic options. For example, the approach can cope with path-dependent options such as Asian options and barrier options, the value of which depends on the path followed by the underlying factors.

Monte Carlo, like historical simulation, allows the analyst to calculate the confidence interval of VaR, i.e., the range of likely values that VaR can take if we had to repeat many times the Monte Carlo simulation. The narrower this confidence interval, the more precise is the estimate of VaR. In the case of Monte Carlo simulation, however, it is easy to carry out sensitivity analyses by changing the market parameters used in the analysis—such as the term structure of interest rates.

The major limitation of Monte Carlo simulation is the amount of computer resources it usually requires. Variance reduction techniques can be used to reduce the computational time, such as the antithetic technique, the control variates approach, quasirandom sequences, and other methods of stratification.[41] Still, Monte Carlo simulation remains very computer intensive and cannot be used to calculate the VaRs of very large and complex portfolios. At most, it can be used for portfolios of a limited size.[42]

5. CONCLUSION: PROS AND CONS OF THE DIFFERENT APPROACHES

Each of the approaches we have described has advantages and limitations: no single technique dominates the others. Tables 5.10a–c summarize the pros and cons of the different approaches.

TABLE 5.10a

Pros and Cons of the Variance-Covariance Approach

Pros	Cons
Computationally efficient: it takes only a few minutes to run the position of the entire bank.	Assumes normality of the return portfolio.
Because of central limit theorem, the methodology can be applied even if the risk factors are not normal, provided the factors are numerous and relatively independent.	Assumes that the risk factors follow a multivariate log-normal distribution, and thus does not cope very well with "fat tail" distributions.

T A B L E 5.10a (continued)

Pros and Cons of the Variance-Covariance Approach

Pros	Cons
No pricing model is required: only the Greeks are necessary, and these can be provided directly by most of the systems that already exist within banks (i.e., the legacy systems).	Requires the estimation of the volatilities of the risk factors as well as the correlations of their returns.
It is easy to handle incremental VaR.	Security returns can be approximated by means of a Taylor expansion. In some instances, however, a second-order expansion may not be sufficient to capture option risk (especially in the case of exotic options).
	Cannot be used to conduct sensitivity analysis.
	Cannot be used to derive the confidence interval for VaR.

T A B L E 5.10b

Pros and Cons of the Historical Simulation Approach

Pros	Cons
No need to make any assumption about the distribution of the risk factors.	Complete dependence on a particular historical data set and its idiosyncrasies. That is, extreme events such as market crashes either lie outside the data set and are ignored, or lie within the data set and (for some purposes) act to distort it.
No need to estimate volatilities and correlations: they are implicitly captured by the actual (synchronous) daily realizations of the market factors.	Cannot accommodate changes in the market structure, such as the introduction of the Euro in January 1999.
Fat tails of distributions, and other extreme events, are captured so long as they are contained in the data set.	Short data set may lead to biased and imprecise estimation of VaR.
Aggregation across markets is straightforward.	Cannot be used to conduct sensitivity analyses.
Allows the calculation of confidence intervals for VaR.	Not always computationally efficient when the portfolio contains complex securities.

TABLE 5.10c

Pros and Cons of the Monte Carlo Simulation Approach

Pros	Cons
Can accommodate any distribution of risk factors.	Outliers are not incorporated into the distribution.
Can be used to model any complex portfolio.	Computer intensive.
Allows the calculation of confidence intervals for VaR.	
Allows the user to perform sensitivity analyses and stress testing.	

APPENDIX 1: DURATION AND CONVEXITY OF A BOND

Bonds typically promise their holders payments every six months during the life of the agreement. This stream of cash flows is fully characterized by the:

- Maturity of the bond, n, at which time the principal, or face value, of the bond, F, is paid and the bond is retired.
- Coupon rate, c, expressed as an annual rate of return; the annual cash flow is cF, and therefore, $cF/2$ is the semi-annual coupon paid every six months until maturity.

The entire income stream on a typical bond can then be represented by the $2n$ payments:

$$\frac{cF}{2}, \frac{cF}{2}, \frac{cF}{2}, \dots, \frac{cF}{2} + F \tag{A1}$$

For bonds paying an annual coupon, cF, there are n annual payments:

$$cF, cF, cF, \dots, cF + F \tag{A2}$$

For the sake of simplicity, we will limit the following analysis to annual coupon bonds, while the generalization to semi-annual coupon bonds is straightforward.[43]

A1. Valuation of a Bond and Yield to Maturity

The present value of a bond is determined by:

- Its stream of future cash flows, which consist of the n annual coupon payments, cF, during the life of the bond and the repayment of principal, F, at maturity, n
- Its discount curve, or zero-coupon curve, which specifies the spot rates, $R_1, R_2, \ldots, R_n$, at which each cash flow should be discounted to produce its present value.

The first coupon payable in one year has a present value of $cF/(1 + R_1)$. Similarly, the coupon payable in two years has a present value of $cF/(1 + R_2)^2$. The bond has a present value that is the sum of the present values of its future cash flows:

$$P = \frac{cF}{1 + R_1} + \frac{cF}{(1 + R_2)^2} + \cdots + \frac{cF}{(1 + R_{n-1})^{n-1}} + \frac{cF + F}{(1 + R_n)^n} \quad (A3)$$

To define the duration of the bond, we need first to derive its yield to maturity, y, which satisfies the relation:

$$P = \frac{cF}{1 + y} + \frac{cF}{(1 + y)^2} + \cdots + \frac{cF}{(1 + y)^{n-1}} + \frac{cF + F}{(1 + y)^n} \quad (A4)$$

In other words, y is the single rate of interest that makes the present value of the future cash flows equal to the price of the bond. This single rate is used to discount all the cash flows. It is only when the spot zero curve is flat (i.e., all the spot zero-coupon rates are the same across all maturities, and equal to R) that the yield to maturity, y, is equal to the level of interest rate, R.

Numerical Example

The following term structure of interest rates applies to a three-year bond that pays an annual coupon of 4 percent and has a nominal value of $100:

t	1	2	3
R_t (%)	3	3.75	4.25

Then, according to (A3), the price of the bond is:

$$P = \frac{4}{1.03} + \frac{4}{1.0375^2} + \frac{104}{1.0425^3} = 99.39 \quad (A5)$$

The yield to maturity, y, is the solution of (A4), i.e.:

$$P = \frac{4}{1 + y} + \frac{4}{(1 + y)^2} + \frac{104}{(1 + y)^3} = 99.39 \qquad \text{(A6)}$$

which gives $y = 4.22$ percent.

A2. Duration of a Bond

Given the pricing equation for a bond (A4), the duration is defined as the weighted average of the dates (expressed in years) of each cash flow, where the weights are the present value of the cash payment divided by the sum of the weights, i.e., the price of the bond itself:

$$D = \frac{\dfrac{1 \cdot cF}{1 + y} + \dfrac{2 \cdot cF}{(1 + y)^2} + \ldots + \dfrac{(n - 1) \cdot cF}{(1 + y)^{n-1}} + \dfrac{n \cdot (cF + F)}{(1 + y)^n}}{P} \qquad \text{(A7)}$$

Note that the sum of the weights in (A7) is equal to one, i.e.:

$$\frac{\dfrac{cF}{1 + y}}{P} + \frac{\dfrac{cF}{(1 + y)^2}}{P} + \ldots + \frac{\dfrac{cF}{(1 + y)^{n-1}}}{P} + \frac{\dfrac{cF + F}{(1 + y)^n}}{P} = 1 \quad \text{(A8)}$$

since the numerator of (A8) is, according to (A4), the price of the bond.

Numerical Example (Continuation)
Consider the three-year bond presented in (A5). Its duration is:

$$D = \frac{\dfrac{1 \cdot 4}{1.0422} + \dfrac{2 \cdot 4}{1.0422^2} + \dfrac{3 \cdot 104}{1.0422^3}}{99.39} = 2.89$$

Properties of the Duration[44]
From the definition of duration in (A6), it follows that its value depends on the maturity, the coupon, and the yield to maturity of the bond. More specifically:

- The duration of a bond is always less than its maturity, except for a zero-coupon bond where it is exactly equal to the maturity of the unique bullet payment of the bond at maturity. In general, increasing the maturity of a bond will also increase its duration. This is always true for bonds trading at a premium, i.e., when the coupon is higher than the yield to maturity. It is not always the case for long-term discount bonds with a coupon lower than the yield to maturity.

- Increasing the coupon of the bond, while keeping the maturity and the yield constant, reduces the duration of the bond. Indeed, bonds with higher coupons distribute relatively more of their cash flows sooner and, therefore, have a shorter average life.

- Increasing the yield to maturity of a bond, while keeping the maturity and the coupon rate constant, reduces the duration of the bond. Indeed, a higher discount rate implies a lower discount factor, and therefore a lower weight for remote cash flows, and consequently a shorter average life.

A3. Duration As a Measure of Interest Sensitivity

Simple differentiation of equation (A4), which relates the bond price to its yield to maturity, yields:

$$\Delta P = -P \, \frac{D}{1 + y} \, \Delta y = -PD^* \Delta y \qquad (A9)$$

where ΔP is the change in price corresponding to a change in yield Δy, and

$$D^* = \frac{D}{1 + y} \qquad (A10)$$

D is known as Macaulay duration after the name of the economist Frederick R. Macaulay who in 1938 first coined this term. D^* as defined in (A10) is called "modified duration."

According to (A9) there is a linear relationship between the change in price of a bond and the change in yield. The higher the duration, the higher the price volatility. However, as the price-yield relationship for a bond is nonlinear, duration is only a first-order approximation of the impact of a change in yield on the price of a

FIGURE A5.1

Duration As a Measure of Interest Rate Sensitivity

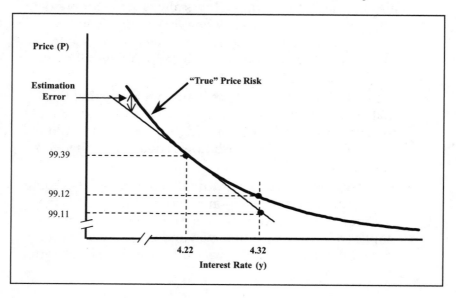

bond. This means that it only offers a good approximation for small variations in yield (Figure A5.1).

Numerical Example (Continuation)

Assume a change of 10 bp in the yield of the three-year bond defined by (A5) and (A6) with a price $P = 99.39$, a duration $D = 2.89$, and a yield $y = 4.22\%$. Then, according to (A9):

$$\Delta y = 0.0001$$

$$\Delta P = -99.39\,\frac{2.89}{1.0422}\,0.0001 = -0.28$$

A4. Duration and Risk

According to (A9), $\Delta P = -PD^*\Delta y$, so that :

$$\sigma(\Delta P) = PD^*\sigma(\Delta y)$$

The volatility of the change in bond prices is equal to the product of the modified duration and the bond price, times the volatility of the yield.

Numerical Example (Continuation)

Assume that the daily changes in yield for the three-year bond are normally distributed, with a daily volatility of 4 bp (0.04 percent). Then:

$$\sigma(\Delta P) = 99.39 \frac{2.89}{1.0422} 0.04\% = 0.11$$

So that VaR at the 99 percent confidence level is:

$$\text{VaR}(1; 99) = 2.33\sigma(\Delta P) = 0.26$$

A5. Convexity Adjustment to Interest Rate Sensitivity

The Taylor expansion at the second-order level of the bond price formula is:

$$P(y + \Delta y) = P(y) + \frac{\Delta P}{\Delta y} \Delta y + \frac{1}{2} \frac{\Delta^2 P}{\Delta y^2} \Delta y^2 + \text{error} \quad \text{(A11)}$$

If we neglect the third-order error term, (A11) can be rewritten as:

$$\frac{\Delta P}{P} = \frac{P(y + \Delta y) - P(y)}{P(y)} \equiv \underbrace{\frac{1}{P} \frac{\Delta P}{\Delta y}}_{D^*} \Delta y + \frac{1}{2} \underbrace{\frac{1}{P} \frac{\Delta^2 P}{\Delta y^2}}_{\text{CX}} \Delta y^2 \quad \text{(A12)}$$

so that:

$$\frac{\Delta P}{P} = -D^* \Delta y + \frac{1}{2} \text{CX} \Delta y^2$$

or, equivalently:

$$\Delta P = -PD^* \Delta y + \frac{1}{2} P \cdot \text{CX} \cdot \Delta y^2 \quad \text{(A13)}$$

The first term in (A13) is identical to (A9). The second term is the convexity adjustment where

$$\text{CX} = \frac{1}{P} \frac{\Delta^2 P}{\Delta y^2} = \frac{1}{P} \frac{\Delta}{\Delta y} \left[\frac{\Delta P}{\Delta y} \right]$$

denotes the convexity of the bond. A good numerical approximation of convexity is given by:

$$\text{CX} = 10^8 \left[\frac{P(y + 1\,\text{bp}) - P(y)}{P(y)} - \frac{P(y) - P(y - 1\,\text{bp})}{P(y)} \right] \quad \text{(A14)}$$

where the change in yield Δy is set to 1 bp, i.e., 10^{-4}.

FIGURE A5.2

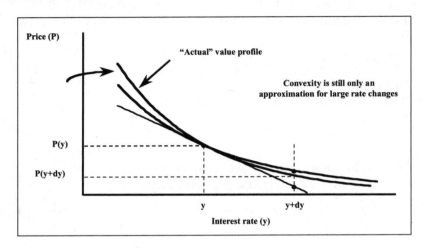

The convexity adjustment in (A13) compensates for the change in the slope of the price-yield curve, when the yield changes are substantial (see Figure A5.2).

Numerical Example

We can measure convexity as:

$$CX = 10^8 \left[\frac{P(y + 1\text{ bp}) - P(y)}{P(y)} + \frac{P(y - 1\text{ bp}) - P(y)}{P(y)} \right]$$

Example:

Six-year 8% (annual) coupon bond selling at par
   Duration = 4.99 years
   $P(8.01\%) = 99.953785$
   $P(7.99\%) = 100.046243$
   $CX = 10^8 \left[\dfrac{99.953785 - 100}{100} + \dfrac{100.046243 - 100}{100} \right]$
      $= 28$
Duration implied price change $= -\dfrac{4.99}{1.08} \cdot 0.02 \cdot 100 = -9.24$

Actual price change $= -8.71$

Duration and convexity $= -\dfrac{4.99}{1.08} \cdot 0.02 \cdot 100 + \frac{1}{2} \cdot 28 \cdot (0.02)^2 \cdot 100$
   implied price change $= -8.68$

A6. Limitations and Extensions of the Duration Model

The duration model assumes there is only one risk factor—the yield to maturity of the bond. It also implicitly assumes that the yield curve is flat, and that any interest rate shock will cause a parallel shift on the yield curve. The reality is different. The yield curve is not flat, and interest rates are imperfectly correlated. When there is a shock, interest rates along the yield curve are affected differently.

To capture this feature, we need a model with several risk factors, each factor being a key rate on the yield curve.[45]

NOTES

1. This claim is based on the famous interest rate parity condition (see, for example, Van Horne, 1994).
2. A famous example is Caterpillar, a U.S. heavy equipment firm, which began in 1987 a $2 billion capital investment program. A full cost reduction of 19 percent was eventually expected in 1993. During the same period the Japanese yen weakened against the U.S. dollar by 30 percent, which placed Caterpillar at a competitive disadvantage vis-à-vis its major competitor, Komatsu of Japan, even after adjusting for productivity gains.
3. The press is full of stunning examples of corporations that have incurred major foreign exchange transaction losses. See, e.g., Ahn and Falloon (1991).
4. Exceptional shocks means price and/or rate changes that are not consistent with the assumptions about the distributions of the risk factors as, for example, a price change 10 standard deviations away from its historical mean, when the distribution is assumed to be normal. Such a "jump" in price is inconsistent with the assumption of normality since its probability of occurrence under the normality assumption is very close to zero.
5. For example, it is common to make the assumption that stock prices are log-normally distributed in order to facilitate the modeling of risk in an equity portfolio.
6. DV01 is a trader's abbreviation for the change ("delta") in value consecutive to a change in yield of one basis point, i.e., 1 percent of a percentage point.
7. Macaulay (1938) first used the term "duration," and derived the first duration formula as a measure of the average life of a security.

8. See also Chapter 1, Section 4.

9. Many publications offer a good overall presentation of VaR, e.g., Dowd (1998), Fallon (1996), Jorion (1996a, 1996b), Linsmeier and Pearson (1996), and Phelan (1995).

10. A multiplier of 3 is applied to derive regulatory capital (Chapter 4, Section 3.1).

11. According to the statistics produced by KMV (see Chapter 9) the actual probability of default of an AA company is about 4 bp.

12. In statistics the standard deviation is a measure of the dispersion of a random variable. VaR is a generalization of this measure to any portfolio of securities whose individual prices may be influenced by many risk factors with correlated probability distributions.

13. Note that this definition is not satisfactory since it compares values at different time instants, the current time and the risk horizon, H. There is an element of inconsistency in this definition. Instead, VaR focuses on the forward distribution of the value of a position, or alternatively on the forward distribution of the portfolio returns, and then derives the forward maximum loss at the risk horizon at a given confidence level. Only expression (6) is consistent with this view.

14. CIBC's value-at-risk system is described in terms of "risk management units (RMUs). For example, a trading position that has 1 RMU of risk has a 1 percent chance of losing more than $1000 over a one-day period.

15. The use of derivatives on the portfolio components, or derivatives on broad indices, may also introduce significant deviation from the normal distribution.

16. See, e.g., Abramowitz and Stegum (1970) and Johnson et al. (1995).

17. See, e.g., Diebold et al. (1998), who illustrates the fallacy of the scaling the one-day VaR by the square root of time when volatility follows a GARCH process.

18. VaR should be reported not only for the aggregate portfolio, but also for each business unit in the tree hierarchy of the firm. In addition, VaR should also be reported by risk factor and/or combination of risk factors.

19. The generalized variance-covariance approach for nonlinear products such as derivative products is presented in Chapter 6.

20. A tractable alternative consistent with fat tails would be to assume that the portfolio return is distributed as Student-t (see Section 3.2.2).

21. The generalization to N assets, or N risk factors, is staightforward.

22. We assume that stock prices are adjusted for dividend in the return calculation; i.e., the stock price at time t is the price ex-dividend plus any dividend paid out in the period $t-1, t$.

23. A portfolio is said to be linear in risks when the change in the value of the portfolio is a linear expression of the risk factors. This is precisely the case for a stock portfolio where the risk factors are the rates of return on each individual stock. Then, according to (13), $\Delta V = V \sum_{i=1}^{N} \omega_i R_i$, where N denotes the number of stocks in the portfolio.

24. Note that $n_i S_i = \omega_i V$ for all stock i.

25. In the delta-normal approach we neglect the convexity adjustment term in dy^2 which is nonnormally distributed (see Chapter 6). The goodness of the delta-normal approximation depends on the length of the time period. The smaller the time period, the smaller the change in dy and, hence, the smaller the squared change dy^2. The delta-normal approximation is only legitimate for relatively short holding periods.

26. See, for example, Hull (2000, Chapter 3).

27. A storage cost can be viewed as a negative dividend yield. In some instances, the holder of some commodities benefits from holding physically the commodity because it can provide her/him with a competitive advantage if there is a shortage in supply in the future. The forward price incorporates this benefit in the form of a "convenience" yield which can be interpreted as an implicit dividend.

28. It is the well-known "cash and carry" equation (see Hull 2000, Chapter 3).

29. We have omitted the time subscript to simplify the notation.

30. Alternatively, order the resulting portfolio value changes from smallest to greatest and locate the change corresponding to the desired percentile. For example, if 500 days of historical data are used, the first percentile is given the fifth smallest change in the portfolio.

31. This example is taken from lecture notes at the CIBC School of Derivatives.

32. In fact, an alternative to historical simulation with full repricing is "hybrid" historical simulation where portfolio returns are derived from a Taylor expansion of the pricing models, as in the variance-covariance approach (delta-normal or delta-gamma-vega-rho-theta approach).

33. This example is taken from lecture notes at the CIBC School of Derivatives.

34. This statement is too strong in some instances, such as in our example, where we use Black-Scholes formulas to value the options.

35. An excellent reference to the Monte Carlo simulation approach and its application to the pricing of securities and risk management is Broadie and Glasserman (1998).

36. For the purpose of risk management we need to simulate the actual distribution of the risk factors, so that μ represent the actual instantaneous expected return. However, when pricing securities using Monte Carlo simulation, we need to use the risk neutral distribution for which the expected return $\mu = r$, where r is the instantaneous risk-free rate of interest.

37. It should be noted that over a short horizon, such as 10 days, we can omit mean reversion, even for bonds, in the modeling of the risk factors since mean reversion plays a role only over longer periods of time.

38. See Broadie and Glasserman (1998) for a detailed exposition of random number generation. In some cases these paths are generated using what is called "pseudo-random" numbers that do not mimic real random numbers as such, but instead attempt to fill the domain interval more uniformly and avoid the clusters that often occur with random numbers. This technique is very often used for high-dimensional problems.

39. We can then use the so-called Cholesky decomposition of the covariance matrix, i.e., express the covariance matrix as the product, $\sum = AA^T$, where A is a lower triangular matrix with zeros on the upper right part, and A^T denotes its transpose.

40. The covariance matrix of X is $E(AYY^T A^T) = AE(YY^T)A^T = AIA^T = AA^T = \sum$.

41. See, e.g., Broadie and Glasserman (1998).

42. Other approaches, such as Monte Carlo simulation with interpolation as proposed by Jamshidian and Zhu (1997), can be used.

43. See, e.g., Bierwag (1987), Tuckman (1995), and Fabozzi (1997).

44. For a detailed account of the properties of the duration of a bond, see Bierwag (1987) and Garbade (1996).

45. See, e.g., Schaefer (1986) and Ho (1992). An alternative to building a multifactor model is proposed by Litterman and Scheinkman (1988), who base their approach on factor analysis.

Measuring Market Risk: Extensions of the VaR Approach and Testing the Models

1. INTRODUCTION

Value at risk (VaR) is far from being a perfect measure of risk. One problem is that it aggregates the various components of risk into a single number. This is very useful when estimating the overall risk of an institution. But risk managers need to find out which of the component risks contribute most to the total risk. This is the purpose of the "Incremental-VaR" and "DeltaVaR" measures that are presented in the second section of this chapter.

To facilitate the implementation of a VaR model, it is common to assume that market conditions will remain normal, that is, that they will be characterized by risk factors that are lognormally distributed, with stationary expected returns and standard deviations. This does not reflect reality. In the third section of this chapter we therefore look at stress testing and scenario analysis. These methodologies can be used to analyze extreme events that lie outside normal market conditions.

Methodologies of this kind are important because we do not know how to construct a VaR model that would combine, in a meaningful way, periods of normal market conditions with periods of market crises characterized by large price changes, high volatility, and a breakdown in the correlations among the risk factors.

Another problem is that VaR is usually calculated within a static framework and is therefore not suitable for the incorporation of liquidity risk. It is only appropriate for relatively short time horizons. In the fourth section of the chapter we propose a dynamic VaR framework with which to assess the risk of portfolios over long time horizons.

As a statistical measure, VaR must be expressed in conjunction with an error term, or confidence interval. The fifth section of the chapter shows how to derive confidence intervals for VaR figures that have been calculated using historical and Monte Carlo simulations.

In order to produce timely risk reports, a VaR model must be both accurate and computationally efficient. To this end, the sixth section of the chapter introduces an extension of the DeltaVaR[1] model that we first presented in Chapter 5.

The VaR measure helps risk managers describe risk in terms of a loss level that might be breached on, say, one day in every 100 trading days. But it does not tell the manager anything about the magnitude of the potential loss in the tail of the distribution. In the final section of this chapter we propose an alternative risk measure: extreme value at risk or EVaR. This measure represents the expected loss in the tail of the portfolio distribution, provided that the loss is greater than VaR.

2. INCREMENTAL-VAR (IVAR), DELTAVAR (DVAR), AND MOST SIGNIFICANT RISKS

A key concern in risk management is the identification of the primary sources of risk in complex portfolios, and the hedging trades that will reduce those specific risks.[2] To achieve this, the portfolio VaR must be decomposed to determine the impact of individual instruments, or positions, on the overall VaR.

This is more complicated than it sounds since each position's contribution to the total risk of the portfolio depends on the composition of the portfolio. More specifically, it depends on how closely the position values are correlated with the values of other assets in the portfolio.

Two complementary measures can be used to investigate this: "Incremental-VaR" (IVaR) and "DeltaVaR" (DVaR).

2.1 Incremental-VaR (IVaR)

Incremental-VaR, or IVaR, measures the incremental impact on the overall VaR of the portfolio of adding or eliminating an asset, A, or a position:

$$\text{IVaR } (A) = \text{VaR (portfolio with asset } A) \\ - \text{VaR (portfolio without asset } A) \tag{1}$$

IVaR (A) can be positive if the asset is positively correlated with the rest of the portfolio and thus adds to the overall risk. Or it can be negative, if the asset is a hedge against existing risks in the portfolio, i.e., if it is negatively correlated with the rest of the portfolio.

The implementation of (1) is relatively straightforward and it can be calculated quite quickly when the methodology adopted for calculating VaR is based on the variance-covariance approach (Chapter 5).

2.2 DeltaVaR (DVaR)[3]

DeltaVaR, or DVaR, measures the risk contribution of an asset to the overall risk of the portfolio. The sum of the risk contributions is equal to the overall risk of the portfolio. DeltaVaR depends on the composition of the portfolio and the correlation structure of the assets. Consider a portfolio, P, composed of N assets, $i = 1, \ldots, N$; p_i and A_i are, respectively, the unit price and the number of units of asset i in the portfolio. The portfolio value is:

$$P(A_1, A_2, \ldots, A_N) = \sum_{i=1}^{N} p_i A_i \tag{2}$$

The DeltaVar property is:

$$\text{VaR}_P = \sum_i DVaR_i \quad \text{and} \quad DVaR_i = \frac{\partial \text{VaR}_P}{\partial A_i} A_i \tag{3}$$

The total VaR of the portfolio is the sum of the risk contributions, $DVaR_i$, of all the assets contained in the portfolio.[4] This is a useful decomposition since it highlights the "most significant risks," i.e., the positions to which the portfolio is most sensitive.[5]

$DVaR_i$ is the product of the marginal change in risk per unit change in asset i, and the position size itself. $DVaR_i$ represents the risk contribution of asset i to the portfolio.

Once the most significant risks have been recognized, the next step is to identify the hedge portfolios that can optimally reduce these risks, given hedging costs. These optimal hedge portfolios can be derived as the solution of an optimization problem.

3. STRESS TESTING AND SCENARIO ANALYSIS

The purpose of stress testing and scenario analysis is to determine the size—though not the frequency—of potential losses related to specific scenarios. A scenario may consist of extreme changes in the value of a risk factor (interest rate, credit spread, exchange rate, equity price, or commodity price) such as a shift of 100 bp in the level of interest rates over the period of a month. The calculation that tells us how much the portfolio might lose in such a scenario is known as a "stress test."

A scenario might also correspond to extreme historical events such as the stock market crash of October 1987. On October 19, 1987, stock prices fell by 23 percent in the United States, or approximately 22 times their daily standard deviation. Other historical scenarios might include the failure of the European exchange rate mechanism in September 1992, or the tightening of monetary policy by the Federal Reserve in the United States in May 1994 (and the subsequent fall in bond prices).

Regulators view stress testing and scenario analysis as a necessary complement to the use of internal VaR models. Indeed, as VaR is a statistical model, its implementation requires banks to make simplifying assumptions about risk factors, e.g.:

- Their number is most often dictated by the availability of data; for instance reliable data for implied volatilites can only be obtained for short maturities.

- The joint probability distribution of their rate of return: it is common practice to assume that the risk factors are log-normally, or normally, distributed, i.e., have a "smooth" behavior that excludes the possibility of jumps and other extreme events.

These simplifying assumptions are necessary to run computationally efficient models. They also reflect what are called "normal market conditions," i.e., those for which we have enough data to estimate volatilities and correlations. In the real world, however, we sometimes observe extreme events that correspond to price variations that are quite inconsistent with the normal distribution.

The Derivative Policy Group (1995) recommended specific guidelines for stress testing:

- Parallel yield curve shift of plus or minus 100 bp
- Yield curve twist of plus or minus 25 bp
- Equity index changes of plus or minus 10 percent
- Currency changes of plus or minus 6 percent
- Volatility changes of plus or minus 20 percent

These extreme price and rate variations may dramatically affect the value of a portfolio with strong nonlinearities and large negative gammas. Portfolios of this kind incur losses whether prices fall or rise, and the magnitude of the losses accelerates as the change in price increases. (Gamma is the nickname for the second derivative of the instrument's value with respect to the value of the underlying asset.)

The regulators also require that financial institutions run scenarios that capture the specific characteristics of their portfolios, i.e., scenarios that involve the risk factors to which their portfolios are most sensitive. Following the market crisis of the summer of 1998, when the disappearance of liquidity in some financial markets led to several well-publicized losses,[6] regulators require financial institutions to include "liquidity risk" in their scenario analyses.

3.1 Stress Testing

At CIBC, a new methodology named "stress envelopes" has been developed. Stress envelopes are produced by combining stress

TABLE 6.1

Stress Categories and the Number of
Stress Shocks

	Stress Category	Stress Shock
1	Interest rates	6
2	Foreign exchange	2
3	Equity	1
4	Commodity	2
5	Credit spreads	1
6	Swap spreads	2
7	Vega (volatility)	2

categories with worst possible "stress shocks," across all possible
markets for every business.

The methodology employs seven stress categories: interest
rates, foreign exchange rates, equity prices, commodity prices,
credit spreads, swap spreads, and vega (volatility). For each stress
category, the worst possible stress shocks that might realistically
occur in the market are defined. In the case of interest rates, for example, the methodology defines six stress shocks to accommodate
both changes in the level of rates and changes in the shape of the
yield curve. In the case of credit spreads and equities there is only
one stress shock, i.e., the widening of credit spreads and the fall of
equity prices, respectively. All other stress categories make use of
two stress shocks—spreads or prices increase or decrease as shown
in Table 6.1.

A stress envelope is the change in market value of a business
position in a particular currency or market, in response to a particular stress shock. A scenario is a combination of several stress
shocks (Figure 6.1).

The following example illustrates how the stress envelope
methodology works. Consider the following scenario:

1. 10 percent fall in the North American equity indices
2. 15 percent fall in European equity indices
3. a fall of 50 bp in North American short-term interest rates

FIGURE 6.1

The Seven Major Components of the Stress Envelope
Approach

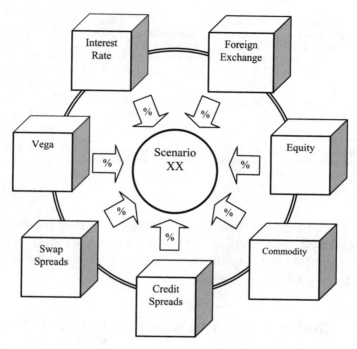

The components of the scenarios are first related to the corresponding extreme stress shocks and their stress envelope values:

1. 25 percent fall in the North American equity indices
2. 25 percent fall in European equity indices
3. a fall of 200 bp in North American short-term interest rates

The impact of the scenario on the position is then derived by summing the appropriate percentage (less than one) of the stress shock values, for each of the three stress shocks (Table 6.2).

The linear interpolation in the calculation of the scenario value, with the scenario value being the worst case stress envelope value times the scenario shock weight, is rather conservative. For nonlinear positions, the situation that concerns banks most is when gamma is negative, i.e., when the position experiences a loss whether the price of the underlying instrument moves up or down.

TABLE 6.2

Stress Scenario

	Stress Envelope Values	Stress Envelope Shocks	Scenario Shocks	Scenario Shock Weights	Scenario Values
1	($1,000)	25%	10%	10/25 = 40%	($400)
2	($500)	25%	15%	15/25 = 60%	($300)
3	$700	200 bp	50 bp	50/200 = 25%	$175
					Total = ($525)

Note: The scenario value is the product of the stress envelope value and scenario shock weight (less than one). The scenario shock weight is the ratio of the scenario shock to the stress envelope shock.
Numbers in parentheses are negative values.

For this situation, the scenario value derived using the methodology described above will overestimate the actual loss, since with negative gamma the magnitude of the loss accelerates with the size of the price change.

3.2 Summary of the Most Significant Risks

The stress testing methodology presented in the previous section can be combined with the VaR approach to produce a "summary of significant risks." This report ranks the risk exposure of the bank's positions. For each position, it shows the VaR, IVaR, and DVaR and the loss corresponding to the stress scenario that would affect the position the most. For example, the high-yield portfolio might well be most exposed to a widening of credit spreads. Therefore the relevant scenario corresponds to the stress envelope for a widening of credit spreads.

3.3 Scenario Analysis

At CIBC, two types of scenarios are run: replication scenarios that attempt to reproduce the effects of extreme historical events and hypothetical one-off events that depend on imagined future developments.

(i) Replication scenarios

Scenario 1: Stock market crash reminiscent of the October 1987 crash, characterized by a combination of the following events:

- Equity markets fall around the globe by 20 percent on average, with Asian markets, such as Hong Kong, declining by 30 percent, and an upward shift in implied volatilities from 20 to 50 percent.
- The U.S. dollar rallies against other currencies as a consequence of a flight to quality. Asian currencies lose up to 10 percent against the dollar.
- Interest rates fall in Western markets. Hong Kong interest rates rise by 40 bp at the long end of the term structure and by 100 bp at the short end.
- Commodity prices drop due to fears of a recession: copper and oil prices decline by 5 percent.

Scenario 2: U.S. inflation scare and a tightening of monetary policy by the Federal Reserve as in May 1994, characterized by:

- 100-bp increase in overnight interest rate and 50-bp upward shift in the long end of the curve.
- Interest rates also increase in other G-7 countries and Switzerland, but not as much as in the United States.
- G-7 currencies depreciate against the U.S. dollar as investors chase higher rates.
- Credit spreads widen.
- Equity markets decline from 3 to 6 percent with an upward shift in implied volatilities.

Scenario 3: Japanese earthquake:

- Japanese equity markets drop by 15 percent and other equity markets fall less sharply (Canada and the United States by 5 percent).
- Yen falls 3 percent against the U.S. dollar, and the U.S. dollar also appreciates slightly against other currencies.
- Interest rates rise in Europe and the United States through fear of the repatriation of Japanese funds.

(ii) Hypothetical one-off scenarios

- Canada crisis: "Yes" scenario at a referendum on the separation of Quebec from the rest of Canada.
- Credit spreads widen.
- Swap spreads widen or narrow.
- Chinese devalue their currency, which causes a crisis in Asia.

3.4 Worst Case Scenario Analysis

The kind of analysis we have just described complements the VaR approach. It determines the worst case losses for various extreme scenarios for which the underlying distribution of the risk factors deviates substantially from standard log-normality. An alternative approach to stress testing and scenario analysis is the "worst case scenario" analysis proposed by Boudoukh et al. (1995).

Like the VaR approach, such a worst case scenario analysis assumes that portfolio returns are normally distributed, with mean return μ_P and standard deviation σ_P. The fundamental difference between the two techniques is that while VaR expresses the price risk of a portfolio in terms of the frequency of a specific level of loss, worst case scenario analysis asks the question, "What is the worst that can happen to the value of the portfolio over a given period of time?"

Formally, to implement the worst case scenario we derive numerically the probability distribution of the maximum loss over a period of length H, say 250 days, i.e., $F[\min(Z_1, Z_2, \ldots, Z_H)]$, where $F[.]$ denotes the distribution function and Z_i is the normalized return of the portfolio in day i. The focus is on the worst daily scenarios.

Table 6.3 shows the values of the expected loss in the worst case scenario analysis (expected WCS) for different horizons $H = 5, 20, 100,$ and 250 days. The first percentile of the distribution of the minimum is also reported. Both the expected worst case loss and the first percentile of the worst case loss distribution are derived from a Monte Carlo simulation with 10,000 runs. For example, assuming a mean portfolio return of zero, VaR at the 99 percent confidence level is 2.33 σ_P. When the horizon is 250 days, i.e.,

TABLE 6.3

Worst Case Scenario Analysis

	Horizon (days)			
	5	20	100	250
E[number of $Z_i < -2.33$]	0.05	0.20	1.00	2.50
Expected WCS	-1.16	-1.86	-2.51	-2.82
First percentile of Z	-2.80	-3.26	-3.72	-3.92

The worst case scenario (WCS), i.e., $\min(Z_1, Z_2, \ldots, Z_H)$, denoted Z, is defined as the lowest observation in a vector $Z = (Z_1, Z_2, \ldots, Z_H)$ of length $H = 5, 20, 100,$ and 250 days of independent draws. These draws are normally distributed with mean 0 and volatility 1.

Source: Boudoukh et al. (1995), Risk 8(9).

one year, the expected worst case loss is 2.82 σ_P and the first percentile of the worst case loss is 3.92 σ_P.

In other words, while there is a 1 percent chance that actual losses in any trading day will exceed 2.33 σ_P, there is a probability of 1 percent that the size of the worst case loss will be greater than 3.92 σ_P in any given year. In other words, one year every 100 years, on average, the worst case daily loss will be greater than 3.92 σ_P. The same methodology can be applied to fixed-income products and derivatives.

Worst case scenario analysis is therefore more conservative than VaR. If an institution bases its economic capital on VaR, it will have enough capital to avoid loss on 99 percent of days. However, a more conservative approach might be to set aside capital that will absorb the worst case loss over a given period of time, say one year. In the context of the previous example, the worst case scenario approach would require the bank to hold 1.68 (= 3.92/2.33) times more capital than would the VaR approach.

3.5 Advantages of Stress Testing and Scenario Analysis

The major benefit of stress testing and scenario analysis is the identification of the vulnerability of a portfolio to a variety of extreme events. During a market crisis, historical correlations change as volatilities increase. Correlations may suddenly increase dramatically and become +1, as many markets collapse at the same time, and liquidity dries out. Alternatively, correlations may approach −1 as markets or instruments move in opposite directions. For example, a market event may trigger a flight to quality, while liquid and illiquid markets exhibit almost perfect negative correlation.

Each portfolio has specific characteristics that make it vulnerable to a particular scenario and/or stress test. Obviously, a high-yield bond portfolio is vulnerable to a widening of credit spreads. An equity portfolio diversified across many countries and sectors of activities is sensitive to a change in the correlation structure of the world equity markets. An equity derivative book that is short gamma is vulnerable to a sharp increase in volatility.

Stress testing and scenario analyses are very useful in highlighting these vulnerabilities to senior management.

3.6 Limitations of Stress Testing and Scenario Analysis

• Scenarios are based on an arbitrary combination of stress shocks (Section 3.1). Yet many such combinations are inconsistent with the basic laws of economics. They may violate, for example, no-arbitrage conditions such as interest rate parity. When constructing a scenario, it is important to examine the chain of events and make sure that it makes economic sense. The chain of events that may logically follow the major shock depends on the context, and may be quite different from one crisis to another. For example, the Asian crisis of the summer of 1997 was quite different from the Asian crisis of the summer of 1998 (triggered by the partial default of Russia).

• The potential number of combinations of basic stress shocks is overwhelming. In practice, only a relatively small number of scenarios can be routinely analyzed. This means that the scenarios have to be selected according to the vulnerabilities of the particular portfolio. In Section 3.2 we offered a list of the scenarios that are run daily at CIBC. Again, the choice is necessarily somewhat arbitrary. The usefulness and accuracy of the diagnosis that emerges out of the scenario analysis depends on the judgment and experience of the analysts who design and run these scenarios. Even the best analysts rely on the past as a guide to the future. Yet history is unlikely to repeat itself exactly.

• Market crises unfold over a period of time, during which liquidity may dry out. Yet most scenario analyses are static in nature, i.e., are one-period models and do not allow for the trading of positions in an environment where liquidity varies from one period to the next (Section 4). Stretching the period from one day to one week, or to six months, does not make the model more dynamic as it continues to assume that events occur simultaneously, and that the portfolio remains constant during the period. The modeling framework usually does not allow for dynamic hedging or the unwinding of positions.

• Scenario analysis produces worst case losses related to extreme events, but it does not specify their likelihood.

• Lastly, one major criticism of stress testing and scenario analysis is that it handles correlations very poorly. When stress testing correlations, the analyst has to make sure that the scenario is consistent. Any correlation matrix perturbed for the purpose of stress testing should be checked to ensure that it is "positive definite," i.e., that it has positive eigenvalues (Chapter 5).

4. DYNAMIC-VAR

Like scenario analyses, traditional VaR models are, by construction, static. Increasing the risk horizon from one day to ten days, one month, or one year, does not make the model more dynamic. They are one-period models, and the positions remain unchanged over the risk horizon. The model does not accommodate intraday decisions to change the portfolio's structure.

VaR models also assume that the market regime is stationary. As discussed in Chapter 5, it is supposed that risk factors are lognormally distributed. They are also supposed to exhibit constant volatilities and correlations, which are calibrated using data from normal market conditions with liquid markets.

Clearly, liquidity risk cannot be factored into this traditional static framework. To capture liquidity risk, we need a new framework, which we will call "dynamic-VaR" (Figure 6.2).

FIGURE 6.2

Dynamic VaR Framework

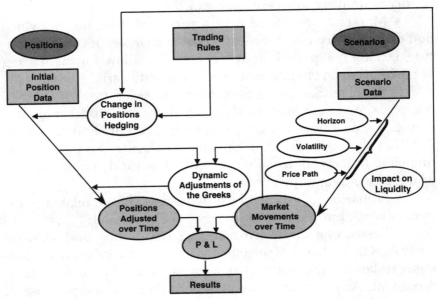

First, we need to define liquidity risk. When liquidity dries out during market turmoil, the bid-ask spread, i.e., the difference between the prices at which dealers are willing to buy and sell a security at any instant in time, increases dramatically. Furthermore, the quantities that can be traded at these prices become smaller and smaller. If large quantities need to be traded, then the bid-ask spread widens further. This means that positions can only be unwound at prices that are below the economic value of the securities. At some point, it may not make economic sense to continue trading: the opportunity cost of liquidity can be huge.

In addition, during market crises volatilities increase dramatically, and correlations break down. Either correlations move toward 1, as markets collapse at the same time, or they shift from positive to negative as a consequence of a flight to quality. This situation occurs when investors panic and follow a herd behavior—at the same time, they sell the same undesirable assets and buy alternative assets considered sheltered from market agitation.

To address these thorny issues, we propose a multiperiod framework that can be used to improve both VaR calculations and scenario analysis. In this framework, portfolio positions are allowed to evolve as the scenario unfolds. Prespecified trading rules are incorporated into the model to alter positions as the market environment changes. Hedge portfolios can be implemented or, alternatively, new exposures can be added to the portfolio. The prices at which trades can be executed, and the quantities that can be traded, depend on the liquidity of the markets.

Statistical scenarios are simulated over a period of time (the risk horizon), e.g., a quarter. The stochastic processes for the risk factors are no longer held stationary, and can allow for jumps or changes in regime. A liquidity crisis may be triggered by either a sharp drop in equity and/or commodity prices, and/or a significant move in exchange rates, and/or interest rates, and/or a large increase in volatilities. The simulation generates midprices, i.e., the average of the bid and asked prices. Different degrees of liquidity crises may be considered, and for each level a bid-ask spread ladder specified in percentage terms, coupled with the maximum quantity that can be traded at each price level.

Trading rules are preprogrammed. For example, risk limits may be imposed so that when they are breached a hedging program must be implemented to reduce the risk of the position. As the positions are adjusted, the daily profits and losses (P&L) are recorded for each simulation path. After a large number of simulations have been run, e.g., 10,000, the distribution of the daily P&L, for each day, over the risk horizon, can be produced.

The framework may also be used for scenario analyses. In this case, instead of simulating probabilistic scenarios, the analyst can run deterministic scenarios that follow a predetermined script for all the risk factors that affect the value of the positions in the portfolio.

5. MEASUREMENT ERRORS AND BACK-TESTING OF VAR MODELS

Whatever methodology is used to derive VaR—the variance-covariance, historical simulation, or Monte Carlo simulation approach—the result is simply a statistical estimate. The "exact" VaR cannot be known with certainty.

Instead, the accuracy of the VaR estimate depends on the precision of the measurement of the mean, the variance, and/or the quantiles of the distribution of the portfolio return. Obviously, such an estimate is only informative and useful for risk management purposes if is reasonably precise, i.e., if the "true" VaR is known to lie within a narrow confidence interval. In the next section we discuss the problem of estimating confidence intervals.

Once VaR and its confidence interval have been calculated, one should check the accuracy of the VaR model itself. Are the normality assumptions legitimate? Have any critical risk factors been omitted? Are the volatility and correlation estimates accurate? Back-testing, discussed in Section 5.2, provides one way of answering these questions.

5.1 Measurement Errors

Recall that, under normality, the "true" VaR is $\alpha \sigma_P P$, where α is the number of standard deviations consistent with the confidence level,[7] σ_P is the standard deviation (in percent) of the portfolio return, and $\sigma_P P$ is the standard deviation of the change in portfolio values. The problem is that σ_P is not known with certainty. It is a statistical estimate based on the estimates of the mean and variances of the various risk factors that enter into the pricing equations. It is only when VaR is calculated from historical or Monte Carlo simulation that it is possible to derive the confidence interval.

5.1.1 Variance-Covariance Approach
When VaR is derived using the variance-covariance approach, there is no natural method for computing a standard error or constructing a confidence interval.

5.1.2 Historical Simulation Approach
If VaR is derived using historical simulation, one of three techniques can be used to derive the confidence interval. The technique that is selected depends on whether the portfolio return is assumed to be normally distributed or not.

(i) Estimation error under normality
If a random sample of size n is drawn from a normal distribution, the variable $(n - 1)\hat{\sigma}^2/\sigma^2$ is distributed as a chi-squared with

$(n - 1)$ degrees of freedom, where $\hat{\sigma}^2$ is the known sample variance, and σ^2 is the unknown population variance.[8] Then, there is a 95 percent chance that the true variance will fall into the interval:

$$\frac{(n-1)\hat{\sigma}^2}{\chi^2_{0.975}} < \sigma^2 < \frac{(n-1)\hat{\sigma}^2}{\chi^2_{0.025}}$$

so that the 95 percent confidence interval for VaR is:

$$\alpha\hat{\sigma}_P P \sqrt{\frac{n-1}{\chi^2_{0.975}}} < VaR = \alpha\sigma_P P < \alpha\hat{\sigma}_P P \sqrt{\frac{(n-1)}{\chi^2_{0.025}}}$$

where $\chi^2_{0.975}$ ($\chi^2_{0.025}$) is the cumulative chi-square at the 97.5 percent (25 percent) probability level.

We can illustrate the calculation using data from Figure 5.6, which presented the daily net trading revenues for the CIBC trading book during 1998.

In our example, $\hat{\sigma}_P P$ is equal to C\$9.216 million, so the corresponding daily VaR, assuming normality at the 99 percent confidence level, is 2.33 $\hat{\sigma}_P P$ = C\$21.473 million. The number of trading days in 1998 was 256, so that $\chi^2_{0.975}$ = 300.64 and $\chi^2_{0.025}$ = 212.20.

This indicates that the confidence interval for the daily VaR is:

$$\left[21.473 \sqrt{\frac{255}{300.64}}, \; 21.473 \sqrt{\frac{255}{212.20}} \right] = C\$[19.8, 23.5] \text{ million}$$

Note that in Chapter 5, we computed VaR directly from the historical distribution and obtained VaR = C\$25.919 million. This number falls outside (i.e., to the right-hand side) of the confidence interval that we derived under the normality assumption. This demonstrates that the historical distribution, over a one-year period, exhibits a fatter tail than a normal distribution with the same mean and standard deviation. One explanation for this result is that the portfolio (trading book of the bank) keeps changing over time.

(ii) Estimation error under nonparametric distribution: kernel theory

Butler and Schachter (1996) propose using kernel theory to estimate the precision of any quantile of the portfolio return distribution and infer from it the confidence interval of VaR.[9]

(iii) *Estimation error for arbitrary distributions*

By using standard "theory of order" statistics we can estimate a confidence interval for any particular quantile of the portfolio return distribution.[10] The asymptotic standard error of the $(1-c)$ quantile, $\hat{q}(1-c)$, of the historical distribution is:

$$se(\hat{q}) = \sqrt{\frac{c(1-c)}{nf(q)^2}}$$

where n is the sample size and $f(.)$ is the probability distribution evaluated at the quantile q.[11] For example, with 250 days of data, which corresponds approximately to the number of trading days in a calendar year, and assuming that $f(.)$ is the normal distribution,[12] then the 95 percent confidence interval for the quantiles is:[13]

(1.38, 1.91) for the fifth percentile, while under normality the exact value is 1.65.

(1.85, 2.80) for the first percentile, while under normality the exact value is 2.33.

This test is less powerful than the chi-square test discussed in (i) under the normality assumption. For the first percentile, the chi-squared test indicates a confidence interval of [2.14, 2.55] instead of the [1.85,2.80] derived above. As Kupiec (1995) points out, the sample quantiles are increasingly unreliable as the analysis moves further into the tail of the distribution. Precision can only be improved by increasing the number of data points.

5.1.3 Monte Carlo Simulation Approach

Using Monte Carlo simulation to calculate VaR allows the analyst to derive explicit confidence intervals using standard "theory of order" statistics as discussed in Pritsker (1997).

To construct a 95 percent confidence interval for the pth percentile of a distribution generated by Monte Carlo simulation, it suffices to solve for L and H such that:

$$\text{Prob}(X_L \leq \text{VaR} \leq X_H) = 0.95$$

where X_i, for $i = 1, \ldots, N$, are the portfolio values generated by the simulation and ordered by increasing values. X_L and X_H according to "theory of order" statistics are such that:[14]

$$\sum_{i=L}^{H-1} \binom{N}{i} p^i (1-p)^{N-i} \geq 0.95$$

and such that:

$$\sum_{i=L+1}^{H-1} \binom{N}{i} p^i (1 - p)^{N-i} \leq 0.95$$

In addition L and H are chosen such that the confidence interval is as close to being symmetric as is possible, i.e.:

$$p - \frac{L}{N} \approx \frac{H}{N} - p$$

5.2 Back-testing VaR Models

There are many potential sources of error in a VaR system—random and systematic—besides estimation errors of the kind discussed above. For example, positions might not be correctly captured, volatility and correlations estimates might be wrong, risk factors might be omitted, and pricing models might be inaccurate.

Back-testing a VaR model simply means checking whether the realized daily returns are consistent with the corresponding daily VaR produced by the model, at the given confidence level. For example, if the confidence level is 99 percent, and the model is valid, the absolute value of the daily returns should not be greater than the predicted VaR number on more than one out of every 100 days, on average.

The regulators require banks to perform back-tests as "reality checks," and to report excess losses when they occur. If too many excess losses are recorded, then the regulator may impose additional capital charges in the form of a higher multiplier.[15]

(i) Which revenues should we compare to VaR?
VaR is usually computed at the close of the trading day, and is based on the market positions reported at that time. The VaR methodology does not take into account the next day's trading: it is derived under the assumption that the bank's position will stay the same until the next daily VaR is calculated. For any back-testing to be consistent, VaR should therefore be compared with what is called "static P&L" (static profit and loss), i.e., the revenue that would have been realized had the bank's positions remained the same throughout the next day.

(ii) Test of model adequacy

How many excess losses—i.e., losses in excess of the number indicated by the confidence level and time horizon—are necessary before an analyst should begin to question the validity of a model? At the 99 percent confidence level, we would expect, on average, two to three exceptions every trading year. But what if, in a given year, there are four exceptions? Is this statistically significant, and should it lead us to reject the validity of the model?

Kupiec (1995) proposes a test based on the proportion of failures. Assume we observe N excess returns over a T-day period. We want to know if this frequency is significantly different from the predicted value $1 - c$, say 0.01 if the confidence level is $c = 0.99$ percent. The probability of observing N excess returns over a T-day period is governed by a binomial process and is given by $p^N (1 - p)^{T-N}$ where p denotes the actual probability of an excess return in any day. The test of the null hypothesis that $p = 1 - c$ (say, 1 percent) is the likelihood ratio (LR) test:

$$ \text{LR} = -2 \ln[c^{T-N}(1 - c)^N] + 2 \ln\left[\left(1 - \frac{N}{T}\right)^{T-N} \left(\frac{N}{T}\right)^N\right] $$

which is distributed as a chi-squared distribution with one degree of freedom under the null hypothesis. Unfortunately, Kupiec finds that the power of this test is generally poor; i.e., often the test fails to indicate that the model is flawed even when the discrepancy between the actual and expected number of excess returns is large. The test becomes more powerful only when the number of observations (T) is very large. For example, according to Kupiec, it would require more than six excess losses during a one-year period to conclude that the model is flawed.

Kupiec also proposes a test that is based on the time that elapses before the first excess return is observed.

Let $\tilde{X}$ be a random variable that denotes the number of days until the first excess return occurs. The probability of observing the first excess return on day X is:

$$ \text{Prob}(\tilde{X} = X) = p(1 - p)^{X-1} $$

Given a realization X of $\tilde{X}$, the likelihood ratio (LR) test for the null hypothesis that $p = 1 - c$ (say, 1 percent) is:

$$LR(X, 1 - c) = -2 \ln[(1 - c)c^{X-1}] + 2 \ln[(1/X)(1 - 1/X)^{X-1}]$$

Under the null hypothesis, LR $(X, 1 - c)$ has a chi-squared distribution with one degree of freedom. Again, this test possesses little power. For $c = 99$ percent, the critical values for X are $X = 6$ and $X = 439$. That is, if the first excess return occurs before the seventh day, we can conclude that $p > 1$ percent. If the first excess return occurs after the 438th trading day, we can conclude that $p < 1$ percent.

Crnkovic and Drachman (1997) propose a test based on the distance between the probability distribution forecast (PDF) of the portfolio returns, on the one hand, and the actual distribution of the returns, on the other.

The test proceeds as follows. Each day we forecast the PDF of the portfolio return. On the next day, when the return is known, we determine in which percentile of the forecasted distribution the actual return falls. Over a period of N consecutive days, we simply keep track of the values of the percentiles that have occurred. Assuming that these percentiles are independent, and uniformly distributed, then a "goodness of fit" test can be constructed using Kuiper's statistics, which measure the distance between two cumulative functions.[16] According to Crnkovic and Drachman, at least four years of data are necessary for the test to be reliable.

In conclusion, the problem with all these procedures is that they are likely to classify a bad model as good. To be even somewhat reliable, they require several years of history: four years for Crnkovic and Drachman (1997), and 10 years for Kupiec (1995). This casts doubt on our ability to back-test any VaR model accurately.

6. IMPROVED VARIANCE-COVARIANCE VAR MODEL

In Chapter 5 we presented the "delta-normal" model, which constitutes the simplest implementation of the variance-covariance approach. But, it is only accurate for linear products such as stocks, forwards, futures, and to some extent, bonds with relatively low convexity.

For derivative products it is essential to incorporate, into the risk assessment of the position, the risk that is related to the convexity of prices (gamma risk), volatility risk (vega risk), and interest rate risk (rho risk). It is important to bear in mind that not only fixed-income derivatives, but also equity and other types of derivatives, are exposed to interest rate risk.

VaR calculations should also account for the drift in value due to the passage of time, also called "theta." This component is deterministic and does not itself constitute a risk factor. It plays, however, a determinant role in the calculation of the mean and the variance of the portfolio return.

The delta-gamma-vega-rho-theta (DGVRT) approach, which takes all these factors into account, offers a fairly accurate way of calculating the VaRs of portfolios with derivatives and hybrid instruments that incorporate embedded options. The approach is very attractive since it is computationally very fast, and takes just a few minutes even for very large portfolios. At CIBC we constantly compare DGVRT values to those derived from Monte Carlo simulations with full revaluations, for many different portfolios with options. For diversified portfolios, the difference in the result is always less than 5 percent. It is only in the calculation of VaR for certain kinds of exotic options, such as barrier options, that Monte Carlo simulation adds value.

The example below illustrates how one can apply the methodology, in this case to an option with only one underlying risk factor. As for the delta-normal approach, we begin by approximating the price change. In the delta-normal approach we limit ourselves to a first-order approximation; in the case of DGVRT we adopt a second-order approximation.

Consider an equity option, say a call, whose price, C, is given by the Black-Scholes formula (Chapter 5). The price C is a function of the price of the underlying stock, S_t, the stock return volatility, σ_t, the discount rate, r_t, the strike price, and the time to maturity; i.e., $C = f(S_t, \sigma_t, r_t, t)$ where t denotes the current time. The strike price and the maturity date, being constant, are omitted to avoid unnecessary notation. The change in the option price over the time interval $[t, t + \Delta t]$ can be expressed as:

$$\Delta C = f(S_{t+\Delta t}, \sigma_{t+\Delta t}, r_{t+\Delta t}, t + \Delta t) - f(S_t, \sigma_t, r_t, t) \qquad (4)$$

At time t, the quantity ΔC is stochastic, as it depends upon the risk factors, $S_{t+\Delta t}$, $\sigma_{t+\Delta t}$, and $r_{t+\Delta t}$. A second-order approximation of (4) is:

$$\Delta C \approx \delta(S_{t+\Delta t} - S_t) + \frac{1}{2}\gamma(S_{t+\Delta t} - S_t)^2$$
$$+ v(\sigma_{t+\Delta t} - \sigma_t) + \bar{\rho}(r_{t+\Delta t} - r_t) + \theta\Delta t \qquad (5)$$

where the Greeks, as defined in Chapter 5, represent the sensitivities of the option value to the change in the risk factors and time, i.e.,

$$\delta = \frac{\partial f}{\partial S} \qquad \gamma = \frac{\partial^2 f}{\partial S^2} \qquad v = \frac{\partial f}{\partial \sigma} \qquad \bar{\rho} = \frac{\partial f}{\partial r} \qquad \theta = \frac{\partial f}{\partial t}$$

where all the derivatives are evaluated at time t.

To derive the distribution of the change in the value of the portfolio, assumptions have to be made about the distribution of the risk factors, S_t, σ_t, and r_t. Usually, it is assumed that the risk factors are log-normally distributed, i.e.,

$$\frac{dx_t}{x_t} = \mu_x dt + v_x dz_{x,t} \qquad (6)$$

where x denotes any risk factor and μ_x and σ_x, the corresponding instantaneous expected return and volatility, are assumed to stay constant. The $z_{x,t}$ for $x = S$, σ, and r are standard Brownian motions that are assumed to be correlated with known and constant correlation coefficients.

From (6) it follows that:

$$\Delta x = x_{t+\Delta t} - x_t = x_t \left(\exp\left((\mu_x - \frac{v_x^2}{2})\Delta t + v_x Z_x \right) - 1 \right) \qquad (7)$$

with the random vector (Z_S, Z_σ, Z_r) being normally distributed with zero mean and covariance matrix $\Delta t U$, where U is the correlation matrix.

If we assume that the change in the portfolio value, ΔP, is normally distributed, then the VaR at the 99 percent confidence level is simply $VaR_P = 2.33 \, \sigma_P$, where σ_P denotes the standard deviation of the changes in portfolio value, ΔP. The derivation of σ_P is sketched out below.

Consider a set of risk factors $\{x_i, i = 1, \ldots, N\}$ and portfolio sensitivities $\{\delta_i, \gamma_{ij}, \theta\}$ where δ_i is the delta of the position with respect to the risk factor x_i, and γ_{ij} denotes the cross-gamma between the risk factors x_i and x_j, that is, $\gamma_{ij} = \partial^2 f / \partial x_i \partial x_j$. This representation is very generic and accommodates vega and rho risks. Vegas and rhos are simply represented by a sub-set of deltas, with the corresponding gammas being zero. Equation (5) can then be rewritten in a compact form:

$$\Delta P \approx \sum_i \delta_i \Delta x_i + \frac{1}{2} \sum_{i,j} \gamma_{ij} \Delta x_i \Delta x_j + \theta \tag{8}$$

Standard calculus shows that the variance of the changes in portfolio value can be expressed as:

$$\sigma_P^2 = \sum_{ij} \delta_i \delta_j (E_{ij} - E_i E_j) + \sum_{ijk} \delta_i \gamma_{jk} (E_{ijk} - E_i E_{jk})$$
$$+ \frac{1}{4} \sum_{ijkl} \gamma_{ij} \gamma_{kl} (E_{ijkl} - E_{ij} E_{kl}) \tag{9}$$

where $E_i \equiv E(\Delta x_i)$, $E_{ij} \equiv E(\Delta x_i, \Delta x_j)$, $E_{ijk} \equiv E(\Delta x_i, \Delta x_j, \Delta x_k)$, $E_{ijkl} \equiv E(\Delta x_i, \Delta x_j, \Delta x_k, \Delta x_l)$, and $E(.)$ is the expectation operator. Given the distributional assumptions (7) for the risk factors, (9) can be calculated.

7. LIMITATIONS OF VAR AS A RISK MEASURE

VaR does not provide any indication by how much any actual losses will exceed the VaR figure. To give an indication of the magnitude of the potential losses in the tail, we complement VaR by extreme value at risk, EVaR, i.e., the expected loss in the first quantile tail, provided that the loss exceeds VaR.

To illustrate how EVaR is calculated, consider a situation in which VaR is derived from a Monte Carlo simulation with 100,000 runs (scenarios). In this case EVaR at the 99 percent confidence level is simply the difference between the mean value of the portfolio and the average value of the 1000 worse case scenarios.

More formally, let v_c denote the cut-off value at the c, e.g., 99 percent, confidence level. It is defined by:

$$\text{Prob}(\omega : P(\omega) < v_c) = 1 - c \qquad (10)$$

where $P(\omega)$ is the portfolio value for scenario ω. According to the definition of VaR given in Chapter 5:

$$\text{VaR}_c = E(P) - v_c \qquad (11)$$

i.e., VaR_c is the distance from the mean $E(P)$ of the c-quantile of the distribution. EVaR_c at the c confidence level is defined as:

$$EVaR_c = E(P) - E(P(\omega)/P(\omega) < v_c) \qquad (12)$$

i.e., EVaR_c is the difference between the mean $E(P)$ of the portfolio, and the mean, conditional on the value of the portfolio being in the tail of the distribution beyond the cut-off point v_c.

It can be shown that EVaR is sub-additive, i.e., given two portfolios X and Y:

$$EVaR(X + Y) < EVaR(X) + EVaR(Y) \qquad (13)$$

This describes the EVaR of the combined portfolio as less than the sum of the EVaRs of the individual portfolios. By combining the two positions we benefit from a portfolio effect, in a way that is consistent with portfolio theory—the more diversified the portfolio, the less risky it is. Unfortunately VaR does not possess this desirable property.[17] One can imagine situations where it might be true that:

$$VaR(X + Y) > VaR(X) + VaR(Y) \qquad (14)$$

This is the case for distributions that cluster around the mean and present only a few outliers, far away in the tail of the distribution. Such a distribution is bimodal; i.e., it exhibits a "hole" between the tail and the mean (Figure 6.3). VaR may be very small at the 99 percent confidence level, but jump to a very high value for a higher confidence level, such as 99.5 percent.

This situation is never encountered in practical applications for market risk, where the distributions are very smooth, and where there is no discontinuity in the cut-off values that define the quantiles of the distribution.[18] However, the situation is common in credit risk when the portfolios are small and not well diversified.

FIGURE 6.3

Example of Portfolio Distributions for Which VaR Might Not Be Sub-additive

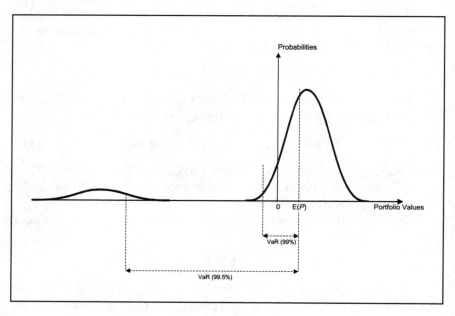

For such an instance, we propose adjusting VaR according to the following rule. Consider two portfolios X and Y for which the sub-additivity property is violated (Condition 14), and then the adjusted VaR for the two portfolios is:

$$\text{VaR}_{\text{adj}}(X) = \frac{\text{EVaR}(X)}{\text{EVaR}(X+Y)}\,\text{VaR}(X+Y) \tag{15}$$

$$\text{VaR}_{\text{adj}}(Y) = \frac{\text{EVaR}(Y)}{\text{EVaR}(X+Y)}\,\text{VaR}(X+Y)$$

We verify that the adjusted VaR satisfies the sub-additivity property, i.e.

$$\text{VaR}_{\text{adj}}(X) + \text{VaR}_{\text{adj}}(Y) > \text{VaR}(X+Y) \tag{16}$$

APPENDIX: PROOF OF THE DELTAVAR PROPERTY

The DeltaVar property is:

$$\text{VaR}_P = \sum_i \text{DVaR}_i \quad \text{with} \quad \text{DVaR}_i = \frac{\partial \text{VaR}_P}{\partial A_i} A_i \qquad \text{(A1)}$$

The total VaR of the portfolio is the sum of the risk contributions, $DVaR_i$, of each asset contained in the portfolio, P:

$$P(A_i, A_2, \ldots, A_N) = \sum_{i=1}^{N} p_i A_i \qquad \text{(A2)}$$

where p_i and A_i are, respectively, the unit price and the number of units of asset i in the portfolio.

When the return of the portfolio is normally distributed, VaR_P is simply $\alpha\sigma_P$, where σ_P denotes the standard deviation of the return on the portfolio P, and $\alpha = 2.33$ when VaR is derived at the 99 percent confidence level. Then, to show that (A1) is satisfied, it suffices to show that the following holds true:

$$\sigma_P = \sum_i \text{Delta}\sigma_i \quad \text{with} \quad \text{Delta}\sigma_i = \frac{\partial \sigma_P}{\partial A_i} A_i \qquad \text{(A3)}$$

(A3) follows directly from the first-order homogenity property in position sizes of the standard deviation operator. That is, given positions in N assets, $A_1, A_2, \ldots, A_N$, for any positive number k:[19]

$$\sigma_P(kA_1, kA_2, \ldots, kA_N) = k\sigma_P(A_1, A_2, \ldots, A_N) \qquad \text{(A4)}$$

From the homogeneity property (A4) it follows that:

$$\sigma_P(A_1, A_2, \ldots, A_N) = \frac{\partial \sigma_P(kA_1, kA_2, \ldots, kA_N)}{\partial k}$$

$$= \sum_{i=1}^{N} A_i \frac{\partial \sigma_P(kA_1, kA_2, \ldots, kA_N)}{\partial A_i} \qquad \text{(A5)}$$

Expression (A5) is true for any value of k. For $k = 1$ we obtain property (A3).

Property (A3) is a well-known property in portfolio theory.[20] If ω_i denotes the weight of asset i in the portfolio, i.e., $\omega_i = p_i A_i / P$, then:

$$\sigma_P = \sum_{i=1}^{N} \omega_i \frac{\text{cov}(R_i, R_P)}{\sigma_P} = \sum_{i=1}^{N} \omega_i \beta_i \sigma_P \tag{A6}$$

where R_i and R_P denote the rates of return on asset i and the portfolio P, respectively; β_i denotes the beta, or systematic risk of the asset i. The risk contribution of asset i to the overall portfolio is:

$$\omega_i \beta_i \sigma_P = \omega_i \frac{\text{cov}(R_i, R_P)}{\sigma_P} \tag{A7}$$

In fact the DeltaVaR property (A1) is quite general and holds true for any portfolio distribution since VaR satisfies the first-order homogeneity property, i.e.:

$$\text{VaR}_P(kA_1, kA_2, \ldots, kA_N) = k\text{VaR}_P(A_1, A_2, \ldots, A_N) \tag{A8}$$

In other words, VaR is linear in position sizes. (A8) can be derived directly from the definition of VaR. If α is the confidence level at which VaR is calculated, e.g., 99 percent, then VaR$_P$ is defined as the solution of the following equation:

$$\text{Prob}\{\Delta P(A_i, A_2, \ldots, A_N) < \text{VaR}_P(A_i, A_2, \ldots, A_N)\} = 1 - \alpha \tag{A9}$$

Then, from (A9) we have:

$$1 - \alpha = \text{Prob}\left\{\sum_{i=1}^{N} \Delta p_i A_i) < \text{VaR}_P(A_i, A_2, \ldots, A_N)\right\}$$

$$= \text{Prob}\left\{k \sum_{i=1}^{N} \Delta p_i A_i) < k\text{VaR}_P(A_i, A_2, \ldots, A_N)\right\}$$

$$= \text{Prob}\{\Delta P(kA_1, kA_2, \ldots, kA_N) < k\text{VaR}_P(A_1, A_2, \ldots, A_N)\}$$

which proves (A8).

NOTES

1. The DeltaVaR approach that we presented in Chapter 5, which is simply a first-order variance-covariance model where only the first-order sensitivities are accounted for (i.e., the deltas) and where convexity risk is ignored, should not be confused with DVaR (DVaR) that is discussed in the next section.

2. Litterman (1996) coined the expression "hot spots" for the positions in the portfolio that have the biggest impact on the overall risk of the portfolio.

3. The concept of DeltaVaR was introduced independently by Litterman (1996) and Garman (1996).

4. The proof of this property is supplied in the Appendix.

5. The "most significant risks" are equivalent to the "hot spots" proposed by Litterman (1996).

6. See, e.g., the story of the LTCM collapse as recounted in Chapter 15.

7. See Table 5.2.

8. See Kendall and Stuart (1973).

9. See also Sheather and Marron (1990). For a simple introduction to kernel theory see Silverman (1986) or Scott (1992).

10. See Kupiec (1995) and Pritsker (1996).

11. See Kendall and Stuart (1973). See also Kupiec (1995) and Jorion (1995).

12. Any distribution can be assumed for the tail.

13. According to Kupiec, the standard error of the estimate of the first (fifth) percentile from a sample of size n from a normal distribution with a variance of σ^2 is approximately $3.7689\,\sigma/\sqrt{n}$ ($2.1304\,\sigma/\sqrt{n}$).

14. See David (1981) and Pritsker (1996).

15. See Chapter 4.

16. See Press et al. (1992).

17. See Artzner et al. (1999)

18. Even small portfolios are sub-additive since the distribution results from the interaction of many risk factors.

19. The proof of (A4) is straightforward and follows from the statistical definition of the standard deviation:

$$\sigma_P(kA_1, kA_2, \ldots, kA_N) = [\sigma_P^2(\Delta P(kA_1, kA_2, \ldots, kA_N))]^{1/2}$$

$$= \left[\sum_{i=1}^{N} \sum_{j=1}^{N} k^2 A_i A_j \, \text{cov}(\Delta p_i, \Delta p_j)\right]^{1/2}$$

$$= k \left[\sum_{i=1}^{N} \sum_{j=1}^{N} A_i A_j \, \text{cov}(\Delta p_i, \Delta p_j)\right]^{1/2}$$

$$= k\sigma_P(A_1, A_2, \ldots, A_N)$$

where ΔP and Δp_i denote the change in portfolio value and in the unit price of asset i position, respectively, and A_i is the number of units of asset i in the portfolio.

20. See, e.g., Levy and Sarnat (1984).

CHAPTER 7

Credit Rating Systems

1. INTRODUCTION

In this chapter we explore the traditional and prevalent approach to credit risk assessment—the credit rating system. Most rating systems are based on both quantitative and qualitative evaluations. The final decision is based on many different attributes, but usually it is not calculated using a formal model that would show how to weight all these attributes in a normative way. In essence, the systems are based on general considerations and on experience, and not on mathematical modeling. They cannot therefore be regarded as precise, and they also clearly rely on the judgement of the ratings evaluators.

Ratings systems are usually applied to nonfinancial corporations, as special approaches are employed for banks and other financial institutions. First of all, we describe the rating systems of the two main credit rating agencies, Standard & Poor's and Moody's. Almost all of the public issues of debt instruments in the United States and Canada are rated by these agencies. Their ratings of public issues are made available to the public, as are the periodic revisions of these ratings. Companies and instruments are classified into discrete rating categories that correspond to the estimated likelihood of the company failing to pay its obligations.

In Section 3 we show how an internal rating system in a bank can be organized in order to rate creditors systematically. It should again be emphasized that while this system is based on the extensive experience of a commercial bank, it is not based on any normative model. Other banks may have somewhat different systems, but most are of a similar nature. In Sections 5 to 7 the details of the rating process and considerations are described.

The main problem faced by banks is obtaining information about companies that have not issued traded debt instruments. The data about these companies are of unproven quality and are therefore less reliable, and it can be a challenge to extract the minimum required information in order to improve the allocation of credit.

The credit analysts in a bank or a rating agency must take into consideration many attributes of a firm: financial as well as managerial, quantitative as well as qualitative. The analysts must ascertain the financial health of the firm, and determine if earnings and cash flows are sufficient to cover the debt obligations. The analysts would also want to analyze the quality of the assets of the firm and the liquidity position of the firm.

In addition, the analysts must take into account the features of the industry to which the potential client belongs, and the status of the client within its industry. The effects of macroeconomic events on the firm and its industry should also be considered, as well as the country risk of the borrower. Combined industry and country factors can be assessed to calculate the correlation between assets for the purpose of calculating portfolio effects. (Chapter 8 discusses portfolio effects with regard to credit risk.)

In a very schematic way, Figure 7.1 illustrates the environment of the borrower that the credit analyst must assess in order to determine the creditworthiness of the borrower and thus the interest spread that the bank should charge. A major consideration in providing a loan is the existence of a collateral, or otherwise of a loan guarantor, and the quality of the guarantee. This issue of guarantee is especially important for banks providing loans to small and medium-sized companies that cannot offer sufficient collateral.

In order to be reliable, the classification method must be consistent over time and be based on sound economic principles. The approach presented here to evaluate credit risk is consistent with the new directives of the BIS to implement a systematic procedure for credit risk assessment.

This is important because the output of the rating procedures is a key determinant when evaluating the probability of default

FIGURE 7.1

The Environment of the Borrower

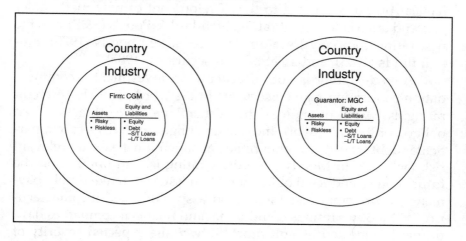

and the loss given default, which in turn are key inputs in credit VaR calculations. As we have discussed in earlier chapters, credit VaR calculations are used to determine the amount of capital that the bank should allocate against its exposure to credit risk.

For example, the loss distribution and capital assessment may be based on the RiskMetric's CreditMetrics model (originally developed by JP Morgan), which uses as inputs the probability that each obligor migrates from a certain rating to another rating over a one-year period, and the loss given default for each facility (see Chapter 8).

2. RATING AGENCIES

2.1 The External Agency Rating Process

The issuance of bonds by corporations is a twentieth-century phenomenon. It started at the beginning of the century, at approximately the same time that the first papers and articles were published on the analysis of accounting ratios, as a means of diagnosing the financial strength of a company.

By the 1920s, this approach had been commercialized and specialized firms were offering their services, and promoting the merits of ratio analysis. This was also the period when Moody's (1909),

Standard & Poor's (1916), and other agencies started to rate public debt issues. Over the last 30 years, the introduction of new financial products has led to the development of new methodologies and criteria for credit rating: Standard & Poor's (S&P) was the
first rating company to rate mortgage-backed bonds (1975), mutual funds (1983), and asset-backed securities (1985).

A credit rating is not, in general, an investment recommendation concerning a given security. In the words of S&P, "A credit
rating is S&P's opinion of the general creditworthiness of an
obligor, or the creditworthiness of an obligor with respect to a particular debt security or other financial obligation, based on relevant
risk factors."[1] In Moody's words, a rating is, "an opinion on the
future ability and legal obligation of an issuer to make timely payments of principal and interest on a specific fixed-income security."[2] "Moody's ratings of industrial and financial companies have
primarily reflected default probability, while expected severity of
loss in the event of default has played an important secondary role.
In the speculative-grade portion of the market, which has been developing into a distinct sector, Moody's ratings place more emphasis on expected loss than on relative default risk."[3]

Since S&P and Moody's are considered to have expertise in
credit rating and are regarded as unbiased evaluators, their ratings
are widely accepted by market participants and regulatory agencies. Financial institutions, when required to hold investment-
grade bonds by their regulators, use the ratings of credit agencies
such as S&P and Moody's to determine which bonds are of investment grade.

The subject of a credit rating might be a company issuing debt
obligations. In the case of such "issuer credit ratings," the rating is
an opinion on the obligor's overall capacity to meet its financial
obligations. The opinion is not specific to any particular liability of
the company, nor does it consider the merits of having guarantors
for some of the obligations. In the issuer credit rating category are
counterparty ratings, corporate credit ratings, and sovereign credit
ratings.

Another class of rating is "issue-specific credit ratings." In this
case, the rating agency makes a distinction, in its rating system and
symbols, between long-term and short-term credits. The short-term
ratings apply to commercial paper (CP), certificates of deposits

(CDs), and put bonds.[4] In rating a specific issue the attributes of the issuer, as well as the specific terms of the issue, the quality of the collateral, and the creditworthiness of the guarantors, are taken into account.

The rating process includes quantitative, qualitative, and legal analyses. The quantitative analysis is mainly financial analysis and is based on the firm's financial reports. The qualitative analysis is concerned with the quality of management, and includes a thorough review of the firm's competitiveness within its industry as well as the expected growth of the industry and its vulnerability to technological changes, regulatory changes, and labor relations.

Figure 7.2 illustrates the process of rating an industrial company. The process works through sovereign and macroeconomic issues, industry outlook and regulatory trends, to specific attributes (including quality of management, operating and financial positions), and eventually to the issue-specific structure of the financial instrument.

When rating a company, the nature of competition within its industry is a very important consideration. In trying to illustrate

FIGURE 7.2

Moody's Rating Analysis of an Industrial Company

its evaluation process, S&P uses an example of a firm from the airline industry. For such a firm, the analysis concentrates on issues such as market position in specific markets locally and internationally, including barriers to entry, revenue generation (including pricing, utilization of capacity, service reputation, and productivity), cost control (for labor, fuel, commissions), and the quality of the aircraft fleet.

The assessment of management, although subjective in nature, investigates how likely it is that it will achieve operational success, and its risk tolerance. The rating process includes meetings with the management of the issuer to review operating and financial plans, policies, and strategies. All the information is reviewed and discussed by a rating committee with appropriate expertise in the relevant industry, which then votes on the recommendation. The issuer can appeal against the rating before it is made public by supplying new information. The rating decision is usually issued four to six weeks after the agency is asked to rate a debt issue.

Usually the ratings are reviewed once a year, based on new financial reports, new business information, and review meetings with management. A "credit watch" or "rating review" notice is issued if there is reason to believe that the review may lead to a credit rating change. A change of rating has to be approved by the rating committee. The rating process of S&P is described in Figure 7.3. (An almost identical process is used by all rating agencies.)

2.2 Credit Ratings by S&P and Moody's

Standard & Poor's (S&P) is one of the major rating agencies in the world, operating in more than 50 countries. Moody's operates

FIGURE 7.3

Standard & Poor's Debt Rating Process

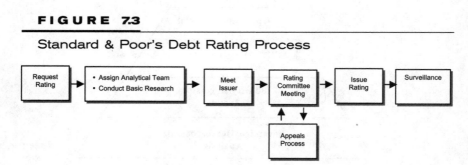

mainly in the United States but has many branches internationally. Moody's and S&P have a dominant position to such an extent that U.S. Justice Department inquiries have considered whether there may be "anticompetitive practices" in the bond rating industry.[5]

Table 7.1 and Table 7.2 provide the definitions of the ratings categories of S&P and Moody's for long-term credit. We also show in Table 7.3a and Table 7.3b the short-term ratings of S&P and Moody's, respectively. Moody's short-term debt ratings employ three designations only, all judged to be investment grade.

If we focus on S&P (Table 7.1), we can see that the symbols are identical for issue and issuer credit ratings, and also that the definitions closely correspond to one another. The categories are defined in terms of default risk and the likelihood of payment for the issuer. Issues rated in the four highest categories (i.e., AAA, AA, A, and BBB of S&P and Aaa, Aa, A, and Baa of Moody's) are generally considered as being of investment grade. Some financial institutions, for special or approved investment programs, are required to invest only in bonds or debt instruments that are of investment grade. Obligations rated BB, B, CCC, CC, and C (Ba, B, Caa, Ca, and C of Moody's), are regarded as having significant speculative characteristics. BB (Ba of Moody's) is the least risky and C is the most risky within the speculative grade category.

As can be seen in Tables 7.1 and 7.2, the rating categories used by S&P and Moody's are quite similar, though differences of opinion can lead in some case to different ratings of specific debt obligations. Moody's applies numerical modifiers 1, 2, and 3 in each generic rating classification from Aa through Caa. The modifier 1 indicates that the obligation ranks in the higher end of its generic rating category; the modifier 2 indicates a mid-range ranking; and the modifier 3 indicates a ranking at the lower end of that generic rating category. For example, B1 in Moody's rating system has an equivalent ranking to B+ in S&P's rating system.

2.3 The Differences in Ratings

While the rating agencies use similar methods and approaches to rate debt, they sometimes come up with different ratings of the same debt investment. In their studies of the credit rating

TABLE 7.1

S&P Ratings Category Definitions

AAA	An obligation rated AAA has the highest rating assigned by Standard & Poor's. The obligor's capacity to meet its financial commitment on the obligation is extremely strong.
AA	An obligation rated AA differs from the highest rated obligations only in small degree. The obligor's capacity to meet its financial commitment on the obligation is very strong.
A	An obligation rated A is somewhat more susceptible to the adverse effects of changes in circumstances and economic conditions than obligations in higher rated categories. However, the obligor's capacity to meet its financial commitment on the obligation is still strong.
BBB	An obligation rated BBB exhibits adequate protection parameters. However, adverse economic conditions or changing circumstances are more likely to lead to a weakened capacity of the obligor to meet its financial commitment on the obligation.
BB	An obligation rated BB is less vulnerable to nonpayment than other speculative issues. However, it faces major ongoing uncertainties or exposure to adverse business, financial, or economic conditions which could lead to the obligor's inadequate capacity to meet its financial commitment on the obligation.
B	An obligation rated B is more vulnerable to nonpayment than obligations rated BB but the obligor currently has the capacity to meet its financial commitment on the obligation. Adverse business, financial, or economic conditions will likely impair the obligor's capacity or willingness to meet its financial commitment on the obligation.
CCC	An obligation rated CCC is currently vulnerable to nonpayment, and is dependent upon favorable business, financial, and economic conditions for the obligor to meet its financial commitment on the obligation. In the event of adverse business, financial, or economic conditions, the obligor is not likely to have the capacity to meet its financial commitment on the obligation.
CC	An obligation rated CC is currently highly vulnerable to nonpayment.
C	The C rating may be used to cover a situation where a bankruptcy petition has been filed or similar action has been taken, but payments on this obligation are being continued.
D	The D rating, unlike other ratings, is not prospective; rather, it is used only where a default has actually occurred—and not where a default is only expected. Standard & Poor's changes ratings to D either: • On the day an interest and/or principal payment is due and is not paid. An exception is made if there is a grace period and S&P believes that a payment will be made, in which case the rating can be maintained; or • Upon voluntary bankruptcy filing or similar action. An exception is made if S&P expects that debt service payments will continue to be made on a specific issue. In the absence of a payment default or bankruptcy filing, a technical default (i.e., covenant violation) is not sufficient for assigning a D rating.
+ or −	The ratings from AA to CCC may be modified by the addition of a plus or minus sign to show relative standing within the major rating categories.
R	The symbol is attached to the ratings of instruments with significant noncredit risks. It highlights risks to principal or volatility of expected returns which are not addressed in the credit rating. Examples include: obligations linked or indexed to equities, currencies, or commodities; obligations exposed to severe prepayment risk—such as interest-only or principal-only mortgage securities; and obligations with unusually risky interest terms, such as inverse floaters.

Source: Reproduced from *Corporate Ratings Criteria* of S&P for 1998.

TABLE 7.2

Moody's Rating Category Definition

Aaa   Bonds which are rated Aaa are judged to be of the best quality. They carry the smallest degree of investment risk and are generally referred to as "gilt edged." Interest payments are protected by a large or by an exceptionally stable margin and principal is secure. While the various protective elements are likely to change, such changes as can be visualized are most unlikely to impair the fundamentally strong position of such issues.

Aa   Bonds which are rated Aa are judged to be of high quality by all standards. Together with the Aaa group they comprise what are generally known as high-grade bonds. They are rated lower than the best bonds because margins of protection may not be as large as in Aaa securities or fluctuation of protective elements may be of greater amplitude or there may be other elements present which make the long-term risk appear somewhat larger than the Aaa securities.

A   Bonds which are rated A possess many favorable investment attributes and are to be considered as upper medium-grade obligations. Factors giving security to principal and interest are considered adequate, but elements may be present which suggest a susceptibility to impairment some time in the future.

Baa   Bonds which are rated Baa are considered as medium-grade obligations (i.e., they are neither highly protected nor poorly secured). Interest payments and principal security appear adequate for the present but certain protective elements may be lacking or may be characteristically unreliable over any great length of time. Such bonds lack outstanding investment characteristics and in fact have speculative characteristics as well.

Ba   Bonds which are rated Ba are judged to have speculative elements; their future cannot be considered as well-assured. Often the protection of interest and principal payments may be very moderate, and thereby not well safeguarded during both good and bad times over the future. Uncertainty of position characterizes bonds in this class.

B   Bonds which are rated B generally lack characteristics of the desirable investment. Assurance of interest and principal payments or of maintenance of other terms of the contract over any long period of time may be small.

Caa   Bonds which are rated Caa are of poor standing. Such issues may be in default or there may be present elements of danger with respect to principal or interest.

Ca   Bonds which are rated Ca represent obligations which are speculative in a high degree. Such issues are often in default or have other marked shortcomings.

C   Bonds which are rated C are the lowest rated class of bonds, and issues so rated can be regarded as having extremely poor prospects of ever attaining any real investment standing.

Source: Moody's *Credit Ratings and Research*, 1995.

TABLE 7.3a

The Short-Term Credit Ratings of S&P

A-1	A short-term obligation rated A-1 is rated in the highest category by S&P. The obligor's capacity to meet its financial commitment on the obligation is strong. Within this category, certain obligations are designated with a plus sign (+). This indicates that the obligor's capacity to meet its financial commitment on these obligations *is extremely strong.*
A-2	A short-term obligation rated A-2 is somewhat more susceptible to the adverse effects of changes in circumstances and economic conditions than obligations in higher rating categories. However, the obligor's capacity to meet its financial commitment on the obligation *is satisfactory.*
A-3	A short-term obligation rated A-3 exhibits adequate protection parameters. However, adverse economic conditions or changing circumstances are more likely to lead to a *weakened capacity* of the obligor to meet its financial commitment on the obligation.
B	A short-term obligation rated B is regarded as having significant speculative characteristics. The obligor currently has the capacity to meet its financial commitment on the obligation; however, it faces major ongoing uncertainties which could lead to the obligor's *inadequate capacity* to meet its financial commitment on the obligation.
C	A short-term obligation rated C is *currently vulnerable to nonpayment* and is dependent upon favorable business, financial, and economic conditions for the obligor to meet its financial commitment on the obligation.
D	The rating 'D' is given where a short-term debt has actually defaulted.

Source: Reproduced from *Corporate Ratings Criteria* of S&P for 1998.

industry Cantor and Packer (1995) show that for 1168 firms rated by both Moody's and S&P at the end of 1993, only 53 percent of the firms rated AA or Aa and AAA or Aaa were rated the same by both agencies. For other investment-grade issues only 36 percent were rated in the same way, while 41 percent of those rated as below investment grade had been awarded the same ratings.

Table 7.4 is from Cantor and Packer (1995). It shows the differences between the ratings of the two largest rating agencies, S&P and Moody's, and those of the next two agencies in terms of size and reputation, namely Duff & Phelps and Fitch (which later joined forces with another rating agency, IBCA). The table compares 298 firms rated by Moody's, S&P, and Duff & Phelps and 161 firms rated jointly by Moody's, S&P, and Fitch at year-end 1993. The two smaller agencies, Duff & Phelps as well as Fitch, tend to rate debt issues higher or the same as S&P and Moody's. In only 10 percent or less of the cases did they give a lower rating.

TABLE 7.3b

Moody's Short-Term Debt Ratings

Prime–1	Issuers rated Prime–1 (or supporting institutions) have a superior ability for repayment of senior short-term debt obligations. Prime–1 repayment ability will often be evidenced by many of the following characteristics:

- Leading market positions in well-established industries.
- High rates of return on funds employed.
- Conservative capitalization structure with moderate reliance on debt and ample asset protection.
- Broad margins in earnings coverage of fixed financial charges and high internal cash generation.
- Well established access to a range of financial markets and assured sources of alternate liquidity.

Prime–2	Issuers rated Prime–2 (or supporting institutions) have a strong ability for repayment of senior short-term debt obligations. This will normally be evidenced by many of the characteristics cited above but to a lesser degree. Earnings trends and coverage ratios, while sound, may be more subject to variation. Capitalization characteristics, while still appropriate, may be more affected by external conditions. Ample alternate liquidity is maintained.
Prime–3	Issuers rated Prime–3 (or supporting institutions) have an acceptable ability for repayment of senior short-term obligations. The effect of industry characteristics and market compositions may be more pronounced. Variability in earnings and profitability may result in changes in the level of debt protection measurements and may require relatively high financial leverage. Adequate alternate liquidity is maintained.

Source: Moody's *Credit Ratings and Research*, 1995.

This issue of ratings differences is an important one. It raises two questions. First, to what extent is the rating quantitatively based and what is the role of judgment? (In Section 3.4 we discuss the measurement of default probabilities and recovery rates.) The second question concerns the independence of the rating agencies. Since the rated companies pay to be rated, there is a perceived danger that business pressures will affect the process.

3. INTRODUCTION TO INTERNAL RISK RATING

In this section we look at an internal risk rating system. A typical risk rating system (RRS) will assign both an obligor rating to each

TABLE 7.4

Credit Rating Differences Between Agencies

	Distribution of Duff & Phelps Ratings Relative to		Distribution of Fitch's Ratings Relative to	
	Moody's	S&P	Moody's	S&P
Rated higher (%)	47.6	39.9	55.3	46.6
Rated same (%)	42.3	46.5	37.9	43.5
Rated lower (%)	10.1	13.5	6.8	9.9
Average difference in matched rating	0.57	0.16	0.74	0.56

Source: Cantor and Packer (1995), Federal Revenue Bank of New York.

borrower (or group of borrowers), and a facility rating to each available facility. A risk rating (RR) is designed to depict the *risk of loss*[6] in a credit facility. A robust RRS should offer a carefully designed, structured, and documented series of steps for the assessment of each rating.

3.1 Objectivity and Methodology

The goal is to generate accurate and consistent risk ratings, yet also to allow professional judgment to significantly influence a rating where this is appropriate. The expected *loss* is the product of an exposure (say, $100) and the *probability of default* (say, 2 percent) of an obligor (or borrower) and the *loss rate given default* (say, 50 percent), in any specific credit facility. In this example, the expected loss is $100 \times .02 \times .50 = \$1$.

A typical risk rating methodology (RRM) initially assigns an obligor rating that identifies the expected *probability of default* by that borrower (or group) in repaying its obligations in the normal course of business. The RRS then identifies the *risk of loss* (principal or interest) by assigning an RR to each individual credit facility granted to an obligor.

Risk ratings quantify the quality of individual facilities, credits, and portfolios. If RRs are accurately and consistently applied, then they provide a common understanding of risk levels and allow for active portfolio management. An RRS also provides the initial basis for capital charges used in various pricing models. It can also assist in establishing loan reserves. The RRS can be used to rate credit risks in most of the major corporate and commercial sectors, but it is unlikely to cover all business sectors.[7]

The use of internal rating systems raises lots of issues. For example: what is the meaning of being in risk rating category X? Does it mean that the obligors in this category have an expected default probability (EDP) within a prespecified range? Or, is the rating associated with an expected loss given default? What is the horizon over which these estimations are derived? For instance, for the rating system to be consistent with the credit migration approach to modeling credit risk, each rating class should correspond to a range of default probabilities over a one-year period.

The internal ratings approach has practical implications for supervisors. Some key considerations will have to be addressed when assessing a bank's rating system: is the number of gradations appropriate to distinguish among the range of risks? How can the bank link the rating to a measurable credit loss? Are all the appropriate risk factors incorporated?

Notwithstanding these issues, the internal ratings approach is exciting because it would pave the way to the adoption of full credit risk modeling for the banking book in the future. The 1999 Basle consultative paper for a new capital adequacy framework (Basle, 1999) provides insight into the regulator's view of the role that an RRS can play in attributing regulatory capital.

A typical RRS, as shown in Table 7.5, includes a category 0 to capture government debt (say, Canadian or U.S. federal government debt). Category 1 is reserved for the highest credit quality of corporate debt. The risk grades below A (e.g., BBB) are often split (say, into 4 and 5) to obtain greater resolution.

The obligor rating represents the probability of default by a borrower in repaying its obligation in the normal course of business. The facility rating represents the expected loss of principal and/or interest on any business credit facility. It combines the likelihood of default by a borrower and the conditional severity of loss, should default occur, from the credit facilities available to that borrower.

TABLE 7.5

Risk Rating Continuum (Prototype Risk Rating System)

Risk	RR	Corresponding Probable S&P or Moody's Ratings	
Sovereign	0	Not applicable	
Low	1	AAA	
	2	AA	Investment Grade
	3	A	
Average	4	BBB+/BBB	
	5	BBB−	
	6	BB+/BB	
	7	BB−	Below Investment Grade
	8	B+/B	
	9	B−	
High	10	CCC+/CCC	
	11	CC−	
	12	In default	

The steps in the RRS (nine, in our prototype system) typically start with a financial assessment of the borrower (initial obligor rating) which sets a floor on the obligor rating (OR). A series of further steps (four) arrive at a final obligor rating. Each one of Steps 2 to 5 may result in a downgrade of the initial rating attributed at Step 1. These steps include analyzing the managerial capability of the borrower (Step 2), examining the borrower's absolute and relative position within the industry (Step 3), reviewing the quality of the financial information (Step 4) and the country risk (Step 5). The process ensures that all credits are objectively rated using a consistent process to arrive at accurate ratings.

Additional steps (four, in our example) are associated with arriving at a final facility rating, which may be above or below the final obligor rating. These steps include examining third-party support (Step 6), factoring in the maturity of the transaction (Step 7), reviewing how strongly the transaction is structured (Step 8), and assessing the amount of collateral (Step 9). The process, by steps, is described in detail in Sections 5 to 7 of this chapter.

One needs to determine which entity (or group of entities) one is rating. For example, the analysis of a group credit involves calculating the obligor rating for the entire group of entities, provided that all the important entities and borrowers are cross-guaranteed. If this is not the case, then one should rate any such borrower individually. If there are businesses or companies in different industries, or with different financial characteristics, then one often focuses on either the dominant entity (if there is one) or a balance of the important components, with specific recognition of any weak links.

A single entity might have a number of credit facilities with the bank that have different priority rules in case of bankruptcy. In this case, one must rate each facility with the credit. Conversely, if a number of facilities for a customer have similar characteristics (i.e., there are no distinguishing risk factors between the facilities), then one should apply the same facility rating to each facility.

3.2 Measuring Default Probabilities and Recovery Rates

"How accurate are ratings?" asks Moody's in its *Credit Ratings and Research* (1995, p.5). The answer is provided in Figure 7.4, which shows the average cumulative default rates for corporate bond issuers for each rating category over bond holding periods of one year up to 20 years after bond issuance. The data are for the period 1970 to 1994. It can be seen that the lower the rating, the higher the cumulative default rates. The Aaa and Aa bonds experienced very low default rates, and after 10 years less than 1 percent of the issues had defaulted. Approximately 40 percent of the B-rated issues, however, had defaulted after 10 years.

Figure 7.5 shows the average default rates within one year for different bond ratings during the period 1983 to 1993. In one year over 16 percent of the B-rated bonds defaulted, while the rate is 3 percent for the Ba3 bonds, and almost zero for the Aaa, Aa, and A bonds.

Credit rating systems can also be compared to multivariate credit scoring systems to evaluate their ability to predict bank-

FIGURE 7.4

Cumulative Default Rates for Corporate Bonds, 1970–1994

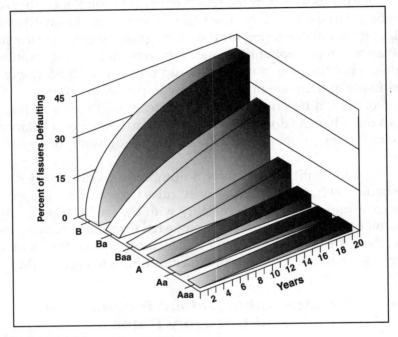

Source: Moody's *Credit Ratings and Research*, 1995.

ruptcy rates and also to provide estimates of the severity of losses. Altman and Saunders (1998) provide a detailed survey of credit risk measurement approaches. They compare four methodologies for credit scoring: (1) the linear probability model, (2) the logit model, (3) the probit model, and (4) the discriminant analysis model.

The logit model assumes that the default probability is logistically distributed, and applies a few accounting variables to predict the default probability. Martin (1977), West (1985), and Platt and Platt (1991) examine the logit model and find it useful in predicting bankruptcies. The linear probability model is based on a linear regression model, and makes use of a number of accounting variables to try to predict the probability of default. The multiple discriminant analysis (MDA), proposed and advocated by Altman

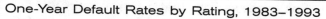

FIGURE 7.5

One-Year Default Rates by Rating, 1983–1993

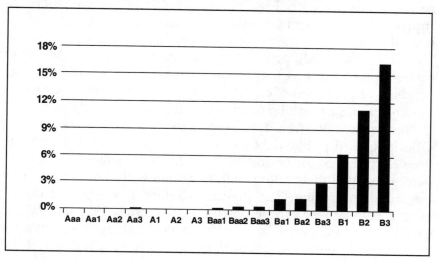

Source: Moody's *Credit Ratings and Research*, 1995.

(see, for example, Altman, 1997) is based on finding a linear function of both accounting and market-based variables that best discriminates between two groups: firms that actually defaulted, and firms that did not default.

The linear models are based on empirical procedures: they search out the variables that seem best at predicting bankruptcies. They are not founded on a theory of the firm or on any theoretical stochastic processes for leveraged firms. Another shortcoming is that most models are based on accounting data that are updated at discrete points and thus do not fully convey the dynamics of the firms and the continuous process leading to bankruptcy. In Chapter 9 the economic approach to the estimation of bankruptcy is described. It is based on the contingent claim model whereby the equity of the firm is regarded as a call option on the assets of the firm.

4. DEBT RATING AND MIGRATION

Bankruptcy, whether defined as a legal or economic event, usually marks the end of a corporation in its current form. It is a discrete event, yet it is also the final point of a continuous process—the moment when it is finally recognized that a firm cannot meet its financial obligations. Analysts that focus solely on the event of bankruptcy disregard a lot of useful information about the status of the firm, its total value, and the value of its liabilities.

Of course, credit agencies do not focus simply on default. At discrete points in time they revise their credit rating of corporate bonds. This evolution of credit quality is very important for an investor holding a portfolio of corporate bonds. In a study published in November 1993, Moody's summarized its experience of rating 4700 long-term public debt issuers in the period May 1, 1923, to June 23, 1993. For the period 1950 to 1979, 4.44 percent of the companies changed their ratings within a year, with the proportion of upgraded companies (2.26 percent) slightly above that of downgraded companies (2.18 percent). For the period 1980 to 1993 the change of rating intensified to 10 percent, but the proportion of downgraded companies more than tripled to 6.82 percent of the rated companies.

Table 7.6 provides data on upgrades and downgrades from 1983 through 1993, the period that followed the introduction of the numerical modifiers to the letter rating in 1982. This period is characterized by deteriorating credit quality. The percentage of downgrades is substantially higher than the percentage of upgrades. The last column summarizes the drift of credit quality by counting the total number of numerical notches changed for upgrades minus the total number changed for downgrades, divided by the number of rated companies. The "Rating Activity" column and the "Drift" column take into consideration the size of the change in rating and not only the event of rating change.[8]

Actually, 57 percent of all rating changes were of one notch only, 30 percent of two notches, and 7 percent of three notches. These changes are for the numerical modifiers to the letter ratings. One letter change, for example from Baa to Ba, occurred in 89 percent of the cases of letter change, and in 9 percent of the cases the change was two letters.

Using transition matrices, we can see how different rating categories have changed through time. Table 7.7 is based on Moody's experience from 1970 to 1993, and it contains the empirical results for the migration from one credit risk category to all other credit

TABLE 7.6

Long-Term, Modified Rating Changes by Year, 1983–1993

	Upgraded Issuers		Downgraded Issuers			
	Number	Percentage	Number	Percentage	Rating Activity %	Drift %
1983	122	8.91	148	10.81	32.85	−4.60
1984	191	12.46	173	11.29	42.80	−3.98
1985	169	9.37	237	13.14	47.17	−18.48
1986	171	8.02	345	16.19	50.40	−24.98
1987	159	6.22	274	10.72	35.87	−10.79
1988	178	6.00	324	11.04	38.97	−11.82
1989	168	5.12	337	10.37	32.97	−16.51
1990	138	3.82	489	13.52	33.88	−21.21
1991	153	3.99	485	12.65	29.26	−16.38
1992	178	4.33	451	10.98	25.27	−11.54
1993[1]	238	5.40	450	10.21	23.88	−8.53

[1]The numbers for 1993 are assimilated from data available from January 1, 1993, through June 22, 1993.

TABLE 7.7

Transition Matrices for Bond Ratings for 1, 2, 5, and 10 Years

Part A: One-year rating transition matrix

To	Aaa %	Aa %	A %	Baa %	Ba %	B %	Caa %	Default %	WR %
From									
Aaa	89.6	7.2	0.7	0.0	0.0	0.0	0.0	0.0	2.5
Aa	1.1	88.8	8.9	0.3	0.2	0.0	0.0	0.0	2.8
A	0.1	2.5	89.0	5.2	0.6	0.2	0.0	0.0	2.5
Baa	0.0	0.2	5.2	85.3	5.3	0.8	0.1	0.1	3.0
Ba	0.0	0.1	0.4	4.7	80.1	6.9	0.4	1.5	5.8
B	0.0	0.1	0.1	0.5	5.5	75.7	2.0	8.2	7.8
Caa	0.0	0.4	0.4	0.8	2.3	5.4	82.1	20.3	8.4

Part B: Two-year rating transition matrix

To	Aaa %	Aa %	A %	Baa %	Ba %	B %	Caa %	Default %	WR %
From									
Aaa	80.9	12.6	1.6	0.1	0.1	0.0	0.0	0.0	4.8
Aa	2.2	78.6	12.1	1.1	0.8	0.0	0.0	0.1	5.4
A	0.1	4.9	79.6	8.6	1.5	0.5	0.1	0.1	4.6
Baa	0.1	0.5	9.8	73.3	8.6	1.6	0.2	0.4	5.6
Ba	0.1	0.1	0.8	8.4	64.4	10.5	0.7	4.3	10.7
B	0.0	0.2	0.2	1.0	8.2	58.8	2.4	14.7	14.6
Caa	0.0	0.4	0.4	2.2	3.1	8.7	44.5	27.1	13.5

risk categories within one year, two years, five years, and 10 years. The values on the diagonals of the transition matrix show the percentage of bonds that remained in the same risk category at the end of the specified time period as they occupied at the beginning of the specified time period.

For example, from Part A of the table, we see that 89.6 percent of the bonds rated Aaa stayed in the same rating category a year

TABLE 7.7

Transition Matrices for Bond Ratings for 1, 2, 5, and 10 Years (*Continued*)

Part C: Five-year rating transition matrix

To	Aaa %	Aa %	A %	Baa %	Ba %	B %	Caa %	Default %	WR %
From									
Aaa	62.5	21.8	4.9	0.5	0.7	0.2	0.1	0.2	9.1
Aa	5.5	52.9	22.3	3.9	1.8	0.5	0.0	0.4	12.7
A	0.7	9.9	59.6	15.0	3.9	1.1	0.2	0.8	9.3
Baa	0.2	1.9	18.8	49.7	12.6	3.2	0.3	1.7	11.6
Ba	0.2	0.5	3.6	13.6	37.4	12.8	0.8	10.1	21.2
B	0.1	0.1	0.7	3.1	10.3	31.8	1.7	24.8	27.4
Caa	0.0	0.0	0.6	7.8	5.8	14.0	19.9	35.1	17.0

Part D: Ten-year rating transition matrix

To	Aaa %	Aa %	A %	Baa %	Ba %	B %	Caa %	Default %	WR %
From									
Aaa	47.1	31.5	8.8	3.6	1.7	0.2	0.1	1.0	6.0
Aa	8.4	33.6	30.6	9.6	3.3	0.8	0.2	1.3	12.1
A	0.8	14.8	43.0	17.9	5.9	2.5	0.4	1.1	13.9
Baa	0.3	4.7	28.4	29.9	13.2	4.2	0.4	4.0	17.0
Ba	0.4	1.7	10.0	18.6	19.8	10.4	0.6	13.9	24.6
B	0.8	0.0	4.9	6.1	11.6	16.5	1.4	30.2	28.5
Caa	0.0	0.7	4.3	14.6	6.8	8.5	8.5	48.7	8.5

Source: Carty and Fons (1993).

later. Observe that 7.2 percent were downgraded to Aa, 0.7 percent downgraded to A, etc. A firm rated Baa stayed in the same risk category after two years in 73.3 percent of the cases (see Part B), while there was a 9.8 percent chance of the firm being upgraded to a rating of A. Bonds rated Baa had a 0.4 percent chance of defaulting within two years. The last column, "WR," reports the percentage of issuers that had their ratings withdrawn at the end of the period.

It is interesting to note that bonds with an initial rating of Caa defaulted in 27.1 percent of the cases within two years, and that 35.1 percent of them defaulted after five years. For bonds rated Aaa the percentages were 0.0 percent and 0.2 percent for two years and five years, respectively. After five years, only 62.5 percent of the Aaa-rated bonds had maintained their initial rating, and about 28 percent of the Aaa bonds were downgraded, while over 9 percent had their ratings withdrawn.

Issuers rated Aaa can either maintain their rating or be downgraded. Caa-rated bonds can maintain their rating, be upgraded, or go into default. But what of Baa-rated bonds? Based on their history, they seem to have an equal chance of being upgraded or downgraded within a period of one and two years. However, over periods of five and 10 years they seem more likely to be upgraded than downgraded.

The transition matrices play a major role in the credit evaluation system of JP Morgan's CreditMetrics described in Chapter 8. Moody's also supplies transition matrices for the modified rating categories, i.e., categories with number modifiers (e.g., A2) added to the letter ratings. The number modifiers, as pointed out in Section 2.2, enable Moody's to further differentiate the letter rating from, say, the highest quality A-rated credit (i.e., A1) to the lowest A-rated credit quality (i.e., A3) with a mid-range allowance for credit quality (i.e., A2). Additional statistics are given for issuers of short-term instruments. Moody's also suggests that a Wiebull distribution most closely models the characteristics of bond ratings over their life spans. Figures 7.6 and 7.7 provide, respectively, the estimated average length of letter rating lives and the average length of modified rating lives.

Based on past transition experience, researchers suggest various methodologies to estimate transition probabilities. Altman and Kao (1992a, 1992b) use the Markovian stable and unstable models. Bennet (1987) analyzed the rating migration of bank's assets. In a recent article, Altman (1998) compares expected rating changes for Moody's and S&P over the period 1970 to 1996. The two agencies include in their statistics both newly issued bonds as well as seasoned bonds of all ages at a given date. They follow the migration for each pool of bonds for up to 15 years after the initial period. The major problem with this analysis is that while all the bonds in

FIGURE 7.6

Average Length of Letter Rating Lives

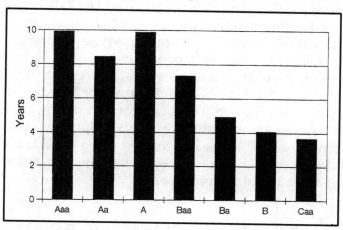

Source: Moody's *Credit Ratings and Research*, 1995.

the pool initially had the same credit rating, they had different maturities. Older bonds have a greater tendency to migrate than newly issued bonds. Hence the pools may contain biases. Altman and Kao (1992) investigate the migration of ratings from the initial bond rating until up to 10 years later.

FIGURE 7.7

Average Length of Modified Rating Lives

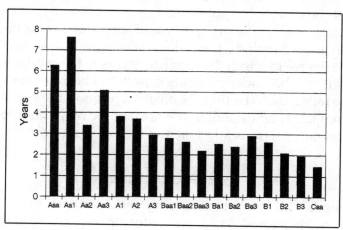

Source: Moody's *Credit Ratings and Research*, 1995.

Table 7.8 is reproduced from Altman (1998). It shows the one-year transition matrix for long-term senior bonds based on statistics of Moody's, S&P, and Altman and Kao (A/K).[9] The time period covered by the different studies is not identical; this explains some of the differences, since migration is time-dependent, and is probably affected by macroeconomic trends.

The aging problem affects the results, and consistently, the values on the diagonal for A/K are higher than for Moody's and S&P. In A/K the bonds in each initial category are newly issued and therefore have longer maturities. A/K also adjust for rating withdrawn (RW) since in many cases the fact that a bond is no longer rated is due to mergers and acquisitions of the issuer, and hence to early redemption of the principal.

5. FINANCIAL ASSESSMENT (STEP 1)

5.1 Introduction

This step formalizes the thinking process associated with a good credit analyst (or good equity analyst) whose goal is to ascertain the financial health of an institution. For example, the credit analyst would study the financial reports to determine if the earnings and cash flows are sufficient to cover the debt. The credit analyst will study the degree to which the trends associated with these "financials" are stable and positive. The credit analyst would also want to analyze the degree to which the assets are of high quality, and make sure that the obligor has substantial cash reserves (e.g., substantial working capital[10]). The analyst would also want to examine the firm's leverage. Similarly, the credit analyst would also want to analyze the degree to which the firm had access to the capital markets, and whether it has an appropriate capacity to borrow money.

The rating should reflect the financial position and performance of the company and its ability to withstand possibly unexpected financial setbacks. This is a key step in the credit assessment.

5.2 Procedure

The obligor will almost always be the borrower (or group of borrowers). Nevertheless, a guarantor, in certain circumstances

TABLE 7.8

Rating Transition Matrix—One-Year Horizon

	Aaa/AAA	Aa/AA	A/A	Baa/BBB	Ba/BB	B/B	Caa/CCC	Def C/D	RW
AAA (A/K)	94.3	5.5	0.1	0.0	0.0	0.0	0.0	0.0	—
Aaa (M)	88.3	6.2	1.0	0.2	0.0	0.0	0.0	0.0	4.3
AAA (S&P)	88.5	8.1	0.7	0.1	0.1	0.0	0.0	0.0	2.6
AA (A/K)	0.7	92.6	6.4	0.2	0.1	0.1	0.0	0.0	—
Aa (M)	1.2	86.8	5.8	0.7	0.2	0.0	0.0	0.0	5.4
AA (S&P)	0.6	88.5	7.6	0.6	0.1	0.1	0.0	0.0	2.4
A (A/K)	0.0	2.6	92.1	4.7	0.0	0.2	0.0	0.0	—
A (M)	0.7	2.3	86.1	4.7	0.6	0.1	0.0	0.0	6.0
A (S&P)	0.1	2.3	87.6	5.0	0.7	0.2	0.0	0.4	3.6
BBB (A/K)	0.0	0.0	5.5	90.0	2.8	1.0	0.1	0.3	—
Baa (M)	0.0	0.3	3.9	82.5	4.7	0.6	0.1	0.3	7.7
BBB (S&P)	0.0	0.3	5.5	82.5	4.7	1.0	0.1	0.2	5.7
BB (A/K)	0.0	0.0	0.0	6.8	86.1	6.3	0.9	0.0	—
Ba (M)	0.0	0.1	0.4	4.6	79.0	5.0	0.4	1.1	9.4
BB (S&P)	0.0	0.1	0.6	7.0	73.8	7.6	0.9	1.0	8.9
B (A/K)	0.0	0.0	0.2	1.6	1.7	93.7	1.7	1.1	—
B (M)	0.0	0.0	0.1	0.6	5.8	73.1	3.5	10.5	7.8
B (S&P)	0.0	0.1	0.2	0.4	6.0	72.8	3.4	4.9	12.2
CCC (A/K)	0.0	0.0	0.0	0.0	0.0	2.8	92.5	4.6	—
Caa (M)	0.0	0.0	0.0	0.3	1.3	5.3	71.9	12.4	8.8
CCC (S&P)	0.2	0.0	0.3	1.0	2.2	9.6	53.1	19.3	14.2

(All numbers are percent.)

Sources and Key:
A/K: Altman and Kao (1971–1989) from Altman and Kao (1992A,b)—Newly issued bonds.
M: Moody's (1920–1996) from Moody's (1997)—Cohorts of bonds.
S&P: Standard & Poor's (1981–1996) from Standard & Poor's (1997)—Static pools of bonds.
RW: rating withdrawn.
Source: Altman (1998).

(outlined below) may be substituted and regarded as the obligor. For example, one may substitute a guarantor for the borrower where the credit risk lies solely on the guarantor (i.e., the borrower's position is not a meaningful factor) and the guarantor is a large national (or international) entity warranting, say, an investment-grade rating (i.e., a risk rating (RR) of 4 or better).

Further, the debt needs to be structured so as to ensure that the bank will not be in an inferior position to other obligations of the guarantor, and the bank must make sure that a "clean 100 percent" guarantee is held.[11] One needs to monitor the guarantor's performance with the same care as if the guarantor were the direct borrower.

A prototype financial assessment table encompassing the risk ratings 4 is shown in Table 7.9. The three main assessment areas, as illustrated at the top of Table 7.9, are: (1) earnings (E) and cash flow (CF); (2) asset values (AV), liquidity (LIQ), and leverage (LEV); and (3) financial size (FS), flexibility (F), and debt capacity (DC).

A measure for earnings/cash flow in column 1 would include interest coverage such as EBIT/interest expense and EBITDA/interest expense.[12] A measure for leverage in column 2 would include the current ratio, which is defined as current assets divided by current liabilities. A measure for leverage in column 2 would also include debt-to-net-worth ratios such as total liability/equity or (total liabilities-short-term debt)/equity.

One would calculate an RR for each of the three assessment areas and then arrive at an assessment of the best overall risk rating.[13] This is the initial obligor rating (OR). The remaining portions of a prototype financial assessment table for RR 4 are shown in Table 7.9.

There will be cases and/or industries where one of the three main assessment areas should be more heavily (or lightly) weighted when arriving at the overall financial assessment. The use of judgment is essential. One should benchmark any assessment to those of other companies in the same industry grouping.

One needs to emphasize the current year's performance, with some recognition of the previous few years as appropriate when assessing the earnings and cash flow category. Cash flow is assessed using whatever methodology is most appropriate to the industry or individual situation (e.g., EBITDA). When assessing companies

TABLE 7.9

Step 1—Financial Assessment

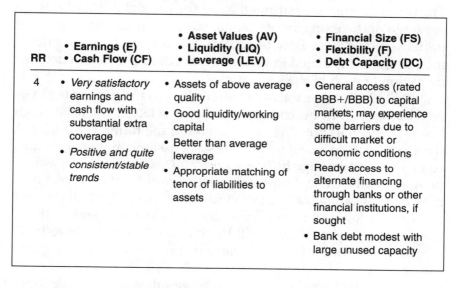

RR	• Earnings (E) • Cash Flow (CF)	• Asset Values (AV) • Liquidity (LIQ) • Leverage (LEV)	• Financial Size (FS) • Flexibility (F) • Debt Capacity (DC)
4	• *Very satisfactory earnings and cash flow with substantial extra coverage* • *Positive and quite consistent/stable trends*	• Assets of above average quality • Good liquidity/working capital • Better than average leverage • Appropriate matching of tenor of liabilities to assets	• General access (rated BBB+/BBB) to capital markets; may experience some barriers due to difficult market or economic conditions • Ready access to alternate financing through banks or other financial institutions, if sought • Bank debt modest with large unused capacity

in cyclical industries one should adjust the financial results and key ratios so that the cyclical effect is incorporated. This is reasonable so long as downturns are within the scope of a normal cycle (i.e., not a remote fundamental correction). This means that strong performance during a very positive economic period should be modified downward somewhat (and vice versa during a weak period).

When assessing the financial size, flexibility, and debt capacity category, the size of market capitalization will also be an important factor. "Access to capital markets" in this third assessment area refers to the demonstrated ability (or potential in the near-term) to issue public securities (equities or medium- to long-term debt instruments), which generally will have necessitated the assignment of a public rating. For private or smaller companies one should consider the ability to access these markets. If financial information/data are not available (such as for new ventures, projects, etc.) then "proforma" data are often acceptable.

5.3 Industry Benchmarks

The analysis of the competitive position and operating environment of a firm helps in assessing its general business risk profile.

This leads to the calibration of the quantitative information drawn from the financial ratios for the firm, using industry benchmarks. The ratios summarize information on the profitability and interest coverage of the issuer, on its capital structure (i.e., leverage), asset protection, and cash flow adequacy. The major ratios considered include those stipulated in Box 7.1. Appendix 1 provides a detailed definition of each of the key ratios.

Table 7.10 shows the interaction between the general business risk[14] assessment of a company and two selected financial ratios (ratios 3 and 8 in Box 7.1) in determining the rating categories. A company with an excellent business can assume more debt than a company with average business possibilities. For example, a company with an excellent business position will be able to take on a debt-to-total-capitalization ratio (ratio 8 in Box 7.1) of 50 percent, and qualify for rating category A. By contrast a company with average business possibilities will be able to take on a debt-to-total-capitalization ratio of only 30 percent if it is to qualify for rating category A.

Table 7.11 provides data on average ratios for risk categories for three overlapping periods (1992 to 1994, 1993 to 1995, 1994 to 1996). The table indicates that the ordinal nature of the categories corresponds well, on average, to the financial ratios. For example, if we examine the EBIT interest coverage ratio (i.e., EBIT divided by interest expense), then we would observe that the median for the AA credit class for the 1994 to 1996 period was 11.06, while the BB was 2.27. The ratio for the AA credit class ranged from a low

BOX 7.1

1.	EBIT interest coverage ($\times$)
2.	EBITDA interest coverage ($\times$)
3.	Funds from operations/total debt (%)
4.	Free operating cash flow/total debt (%)
5.	Pretax return on capital (%)
6.	Operating income/sales (%)
7.	Long-term debt/capital (%)
8.	Total debt/capitalization (%)

TABLE 7.10

Guidelines for Adjustments in Two Financial Ratios As a Function of the Business Risk Profile to Qualify to a Given Rating Category

Funds From Operations/ Total Debt Guidelines (%)	Rating Category				
Company Business Profile	AAA	AA	A	BBB	BB
Excellent business position	80	60	40	25	10
Above average	150	80	50	30	15
Average	—	105	60	35	20
Below average	—	—	85	40	25
Vulnerable	—	—	—	65	45

Total Debt/Capitalization Guidelines (%)	Rating Category				
Company Business Profile	AAA	AA	A	BBB	BB
Excellent business position	30	40	50	60	70
Above average	20	25	40	50	60
Average	—	15	30	40	55
Below average	—	—	25	35	45
Vulnerable	—	—	—	25	35

Source: S&P *Corporate Ratings Criteria*, 1998.

of 11.06 to a high of 9.67 over the three (1992 to 1994, 1993 to 1995, 1994 to 1996) three-year overlapping sample periods, while the ratio for the BB class ranged from 2.09 to 2.27.

5.4 Combining Balance Sheet, Income Statement, and Ratio Analyses

The analysis of loans for the purpose of arriving at a risk rating requires one to think through certain classic relationships between balance sheet, income statement, and ratio analysis. We will first examine a few of these relationships for purely illustrative purposes and then show how they might be useful in arriving at a risk rating.

TABLE 7.11

Key Industrial Financial Ratios for Rating Categories

U.S. Industrial Long-Term Debt Three-Year (1994 to 1996) Medians	AAA	AA	A	BBB	BB	B
1. EBIT interest coverage (×)	16.0	11.0	6.2	4.1	2.2	1.1
2. EBITDA interest coverage (×)	20.3	14.9	8.5	6.0	3.6	2.2
3. Funds from operations/total debt (%)	116.4	72.3	47.5	34.7	18.4	10.9
4. Free operating cash flow/ total debt (%)	76.8	30.5	18.8	8.4	2.4	1.2
5. Pretax return on capital (%)	31.5	23.6	19.5	15.1	11.9	9.1
6. Operating income/sales (%)	24.0	19.2	16.1	15.4	15.1	12.6
7. Long-term debt/capital (%)	13.4	21.9	32.7	43.4	53.9	65.9
8. Total debt/capitalization (%)	23.6	29.7	38.7	46.8	55.8	68.9
U.S. Industrial Long-Term Debt Three-Year (1993 to 1995) Medians	**AAA**	**AA**	**A**	**BBB**	**BB**	**B**
1. EBIT interest coverage (×)	13.5	9.6	5.7	3.9	2.1	1.1
2. EBITDA interest coverage (×)	17.0	12.8	8.1	6.0	3.4	2.1
3. Funds from operations/total debt (%)	98.2	69.1	45.5	33.3	17.7	12.8
4. Free operating cash flow/ total debt (%)	60.0	26.8	20.9	7.2	1.4	(0.9)
5. Pretax return on capital (%)	29.3	21.4	19.1	13.9	12.0	9.0
6. Operating income/sales (%)	22.6	17.8	15.7	13.5	13.5	12.3
7. Long-term debt/capital (%)	13.3	21.1	31.6	42.7	55.6	65.5
8. Total debt/capitalization (%)	25.9	33.6	39.7	47.8	59.4	69.5
U.S. Industrial Long-Term Debt Three-Year (1992 to 1994) Medians	**AAA**	**AA**	**A**	**BBB**	**BB**	**B**
1. EBIT interest coverage (×)	18.0	9.7	5.3	2.9	2.1	1.0
2. EBITDA interest coverage (×)	22.6	12.8	8.0	4.8	3.5	1.9
3. Funds from operations/total debt (%)	97.5	68.5	43.8	29.9	17.1	9.9
4. Free operating cash flow/ total debt (%)	51.0	29.7	20.2	6.2	3.4	1.1
5. Pretax return on capital (%)	28.2	20.6	16.7	12.7	11.6	8.3
6. Operating income/sales (%)	22.0	17.7	15.2	13.2	13.6	11.6
7. Long-term debt/capital (%)	13.2	19.7	33.2	44.8	54.7	65.9
8. Total debt/capitalization (%)	25.4	32.4	39.7	49.5	60.1	73.4

EBIT refers to earnings before interest and taxes.
EBITDA refers to earnings before interest, taxes, depreciation, and amortization.
Source: S&P *Corporate Ratings Criteria,* 1998.

BOX 7.2

BALANCE SHEET

Assets	Liabilities	Key Relationships
CA	CL	WC = CA − CL
FA	LTD	FW = FA − LTD
	NW	NW = WC + FW
TA = CA + FA	TL = CL + LTD	TA = TL + NW

Total assets (TA), as shown in Box 7.2, are identically equal to total liabilities (TL) and net worth (NW).

Current assets (CA) are identical to current liabilities (CL) and working capital (WC):

   1. TA = TL + NW

   2. WC = CA − CL

Total assets are also composed of current assets (CA) and fixed assets (FA), which is:

   3. TA = CA + FA

Total liabilities are composed of current liabilities (CL) plus long-term debt (LTD), as follows:

   4. TL = CL + LTD

If we refer to LTD + NW as permanent capital, then by rearranging our terms the "working capital" can be shown to equal the permanent capital minus the fixed assets:

   5. WC = LTD[15] + NW − FA[16]

Fixed worth (FW) is defined as fixed assets − long term debt:

   6. FW = FA − LTD

Net worth can be expressed as working capital plus fixed worth.

   7. NW = WC + FW

A working capital leverage ratio would express the riskiness of the current capital structure. One would also analyze certain key ratios. For example, a ratio of current liabilities to working capital (called the working capital leverage ratio) is analogous to the leverage ratio of total liabilities to net worth.

8. Working capital leverage ratio = CL/WC.

The leverage ratio expresses the riskiness of the overall capital structure, or how long-term debt is supported by equity:

9. Leverage ratio = TL/NW.

10. Current ratio = CA/CL.

A prototype high-level customer financial information (CFI) report is shown in Table 7.12 for General Motors Acceptance Corporation. Such a report is typically produced to facilitate credit analysis (at, say, the senior credit committee meeting of the bank). The CFI report is divided into a balance sheet, income statement, and ratio analysis section. The ratio analysis section is further subdivided into leverage ratio and solvency ratio. An experienced credit analyst can quickly analyze such a report and get a "feel" for the financial assessment portion of the risk rating process. For example, one may analyze the leverage ratio (say, total liabilities/equity), solvency ratio (say, interest coverage), or other key financial analysis measures (see Appendix 2) as part of arriving at the appropriate financial assessment.

6. FIRST GROUP OF ADJUSTMENT FACTORS FOR OBLIGOR CREDIT RATING

6.1 Management and Other Qualitative Factors (Step 2)

This second step considers the impact on an obligor rating of a variety of qualitative factors such as discovering unfavorable aspects of a borrower's management. We will assume for illustrative purposes that this Step 2 analysis has no effect on the RR if the obligor seems to reach an acceptable standard, but that it may bring about a downgrade if standards are not acceptable.

A typical Step 2 approach would require one to examine day-to-day account operations (AO) and assess management (AM), as well as perform an environmental assessment (EA) and examine contingent liabilities (CL), etc.

TABLE 7.12

Example Customer Financial Information Report: Balance Sheet, Income Statement, and Ratio Data

	Factors	General Motors Acceptance Corporation 12/31/1997	12/31/1996
Balance Sheet	Current assets (CA)	44,658	41,598
	Current liabilities (CL)	64,288	50,469
	Working capital (WC=CA−CL)	−19,630	−8,871
	Fixed assets (FA)	64,661	56,980
	Mortgages/other (LTD)	36,275	39,841
	Fixed worth (FW=FA−LTD)	28,386	17,139
	Net worth (NW=WC+FW)	8,756	8,268
Income Statement	Sales for year	16,595	15,974
	Operating profit (EBIT)	7,471	7,415
	Depreciation and amortization (DA)	4,735	4,668
	Bad debts	523	669
	Income taxes	913	837
	Net profit/loss	1,301	1,241
	Dividends/drawings	750	1,200
	Sundry adjustments	−63	−42
	Net capital expenses	0	0
	Interest expense (I)	5,256	4,938
Ratios	**Leverage Ratios:**		
	Total liabilities/equity	11.49[1]	10.92
	(Total liab − sub-debt)/equity	44.49	10.92[2]
	Working capital	0.69[3]	0.82
	Solvency Ratios:		
	Interest coverage (EBIT/I)	1.42[4]	1.42
	Cash interest coverage (EBITDA/I)	2.32[5]	2.37

1. TL = CL + LTD = 64,288 + 36,275 = 109,124; TL ÷ Equity (NW) = 109, 124/8, 756 = 11.49.
2. No subordinated debt in 1996.
3. Working capital current ratio = CA/CL = 44,658/64,288 = 0.69.
4. EBIT = operating profit. Note that EBIT/I = 7471/5256 = 1.42.
5. EBITDA = EBIT + DA = 7471 + 4735 ≈ 12,206. Note that EBITDA/I = 12,206/5256 = 2.32.

If one is examining the day-to-day AO, then one would ask a series of carefully structured questions. For example, if the financial and security reporting is on a timely basis, is it of good quality? Does it satisfactorily explain significant variations from projections? One would also ask if the credit limits and terms are respected and examine whether any past requests for temporary excesses, terms, etc., were made before rather than after the fact. One would also ask if the company honors its obligations with creditors (legitimate disputes aside), as evidenced by a lack of writs, lawsuits, judgments, etc.

One would ask, in terms of performing a management assessment, if management skills are sufficient for the size and scope of the business. This would include examining if management has a satisfactory record of success as well as appropriate industry experience. One should also examine if management has adequate "depth"; for example, are succession plans in place?

One would ask a series of practical questions. For example: is there an informed approach to identifying, accepting, and managing risks? Does management stay current on how to conduct business operations, introducing and updating methods and technology when warranted? Does management address problems promptly, exhibiting the will to take hard decisions as necessary and with an appropriate balance of short- to long-term concerns? Is a reasonable business and financial plan in place, which does not depend on unrealistic levels of business growth or profitability improvement? Is management remuneration (cost to firm) prudent and appropriate to the size and financial strength/progress of the company?

One should ask from an EA point of view if management is aware of, monitors and complies with all relevant environmental regulations and practices. One should also examine any contingent liabilities, e.g., litigation, or warranty claims.

6.2 Industry Ratings Summary (Step 3A)

This portion of the third step recognizes the very important effect of an industry rating based on the type of industry and the relative position of the borrower (i.e., their tier assessment) within their industry. Experience has shown that poorer-tier performers in weak, vulnerable industries are major contributors to credit losses.

To do this, the analyst needs to rate each industry type on, say, a scale of 1 to 5 (see Table 7.13). One should provide an industry assessment (IA) ratings scheme for each industry broken down into selective sub-industry groupings. For example, the forest products industry may be broken down into a sub-industry grouping such as wood products. Similarly, the mining industry may be broken down into sub-industry groupings such as gold mines, base metal mines, etc. A rating is assigned to each of the industry groupings.

To calculate the industry assessment, the analyst first assigns a score of, say, 1 (minimal risk) to 5 (very high risk) for each of a set of, say, eight criteria established by the bank. For example, one can describe the industry rating in terms of competitiveness (see Table 7.13 for detailed definitions), trade environment, regulatory framework, restructuring, technological change, financial performance, long-term trends affecting demand, and vulnerability to macroeconomic environment.

The sum of the scores, which will range from 8 (most favorable) to 40 (least favorable), can then be converted to an industry rating. For example, the asset would be rated 1 if it has a score ranging from 8 to 11. Similarly, a total score of between 9 and 19 yields an industry score of 2; between 20 and 27 a score of 3; between 27 and 35 a score of 4; and a score of 5 for a total score of between 36 to 40.

TABLE 7.13

Rating the Competitiveness of an Industry

Industry Risk				
Minimal **1**	**Low** **2**	**Medium** **3**	**High** **4**	**Very High** **5**
Competitiveness The potentital of the industry to sell in its domestic market and/or external markets based only on: cost structure (determined by factors such as economies of scale, capital intensity, input costs, location, infrastructure, and use of appropriate technology), international reputation, and effectiveness in targeting market niches.				
On balance, the combination of the relevant listed factors makes the industry very competitive.	On balance, the combination of the relevant listed factors makes the industry somewhat competitive.	The relevant listed factors have off-setting impacts on the competi-tiveness of the industry.	On balance, the combination of the relevant listed factors makes the industry somewhat uncompetitive.	On balance, the combination of the relevant listed factors makes the industry very uncompetitive.

Competitiveness (Table 7.13) can be defined as the potential of the industry to sell its products in its domestic market and/or external markets, given its cost structure (determined by factors such as economies of scale, capital intensity, input costs, location, infrastructure, and use of appropriate technology), international reputation, and effectiveness in targeting market niches.

The trade environment can be defined as all the institutional factors that affect interjurisdictional commerce in goods and services, including trade agreements that have an impact (or potential impact) on the industry.

The regulatory framework can be defined as the legal/institutional setting including laws and regulations of applicable levels of government direct and indirect taxation, grant programs, trade finance, and subsidies. One needs to take into account present policies and trends, the industry's ability to absorb and influence these policies and trends, and the impact of both supply and demand.

Restructuring can be defined as the impact of the process of adjusting (often through a reduction in capacity or employees) to a change in market conditions, such as demand patterns, technology, number and quality of competitors, or regulations.

Technological change can be defined as industry vulnerability to technological change that could result in changing costs, an alteration in the range of products or services of the industry, or an alteration in the range/price of competitive products/services. Knowledge of previous technological change and current relevant global research and development efforts must be taken into account.

Financial performance can be defined as an assessment based on the present level, trends, and sustainability of standard ratios such as return on equity, interest coverage, current ratio, debt/equity, and debt/cash flow.

Long-term trends that affect demand include demographics (i.e., age structure, gender distribution, composition, and wealth distribution of the relevant market), vintage of durables and infrastructure (age of fleet and age and condition of roads, bridges, etc.), and lifestyle changes and consumer attitudes.

Vulnerability to macroeconomic environment describes how sensitive the industry is to economic downturns, fiscal policy, movements in interest rates and exchange rates, and other macroeconomic variables.

Appendix 3 of this chapter offers a condensed example of an illustrative prototype assessment of the telecommunication industry (Appendix 3A) as well as the footwear and clothing industry (Appendix 3B).

6.3 Tier Assessment (Step 3B)

The second part of Step 3 involves establishing tier assessment (TA)—the relative position of each business within its own industry. This is an important survival factor, particularly during downturns. One can use the criteria and process used to assess industry risk to determine a company's relative position in one of relative tiers—say, on a scale of 1 to 4 within an industry.

A business should be ranked against its relative competition. For example, if the company supplies a product/service that is subject to global competition, then it should be ranked on a global basis. If the company's competitors are by nature local or regional, as are many retail businesses, then it should be ranked on that basis, while recognizing that competition may increase. If a business is local but has no local competitors, e.g., a local cable operator, then it should be ranked against such companies in other areas, with some recognition of the benefit of the exclusivity of its market (assuming that this is likely to continue).

Tier 1 players are major players with a dominant share of the relevant market (local, regional, domestic, international, or niche). They have a diversified and growing customer base with low production costs that are based on sustainable factors (such as a diversified supplier base, economies of scale, location and resource availability, continuous upgrading of technology, etc.). Such companies respond quickly and effectively to changes in the regulatory framework, trading environment, technology, demand patterns, and macroeconomic environment.

Tier 2 players are important or above-average industry players with a meaningful share of the relevant market (local, regional, domestic, international, or niche). Tier 3 players are average (or modestly below average) industry players, with a moderate share of the relevant market (local, regional, domestic, international, or niche). Tier 4 players are weak industry players and have a declining customer base. They have a high cost of production due to factors such as low leverage with suppliers, obsolete technologies, etc.

6.4 Industry/Tier Position (Step 3C)

This is the final part of the third step (Step 3C). If one can combine assessments of the health of the industry (i.e., industry rating) and the position of a business within its industry, then one can assess the vulnerability of any company (particularly during recessions). Low-quartile competitors within an industry class almost always have higher risk (modified by the relative health of the industry).

One needs to combine the industry rating and the tier assessment using the grid in Table 7.14 to determine the "best possible" OR. The rating is "best possible" in the sense that it acts as a cap on the OR. While the rating can be lowered if the industry/tier assessment is weak, it will not be raised if it is strong.

For example, if the industry rating assessment indicates that the industry rating is 2, and is considered to be tier 3, then the "best possible" obligor rating is 5. If Steps 1 and 2 had suggested a rating of 4, then Step 3 would require that this rating be lowered to 5.

6.5 Financial Statement Quality (Step 4)

This fourth step recognizes the importance of the quality of the financial information provided to the analyst. Again, this step is not used to improve the rating, but to define the best possible OR.

TABLE 7.14

Best Possible Obligor Rating (Given Initial Industry and Tier Ratings)

		Industry Rating (From Step 3A)				
		1	2	3	4	5
Tier	Tier 1	No effect	Specific adjustments are			
assessment	Tier 2	on rating	provided with each row column			
within	Tier 3		combination			
industry	Tier 4					9
(from Step 3B)						

The bank must always be fully satisfied as to the quality, adequacy, and reliability of the financial statement information irrespective of the RR. This includes consideration of the size and capabilities of the accounting firm, compared to the size and complexities of the borrower and its financial statements.

Exceptions may be made. For example, they may be appropriate in the case of subsidiaries of large international/national corporations where the obligor's financial statements are eventually consolidated into audited financial statements of the parent. One may also make exceptions for new entities (or certain specialized industries) as well as obligors in countries where accepted practices differ from North American standards.

6.6 Country Risk (Step 5)

This fifth step adjusts for the effect of any country risk. Country risk is the risk that a counterparty, or obligor, will not be able to pay its obligations because of cross-border restrictions on the convertibility or availability of a given currency. It is also an assessment of the political and economic risk of a country. The economics department of a bank is typically involved in analyzing the macro- and microeconomic factors that allow an analyst to calculate a country risk rating. (Naturally, if the counterparty has all or most of its cash flow and assets in the local market, then one may skip this step.)

A table should be developed to determine whether a country rating will affect the OR. Country risk exists when more than a prescribed percentage (say 25 percent) of the obligor's (gross) cash flow or assets is located outside of the local market. Country risk may be mitigated by hard dollar cash flow received/earned by the counterparty. Hard dollar cash flow refers to revenue in a major (readily exchangeable) international currency (primarily U.S. dollars, U.K. pounds, Euros, and Japanese yen, as well as Canadian dollars).

If the obligor is strong, then short-term country risks (primarily trade finance and trading products) may warrant a better rating than the country. One may also mitigate country risk or improve the rating in a later step in the process. Obtaining political risk insurance (or similar mitigants) may also (partially) mitigate country risk.

TABLE 7.15

Adjustment for Country Risk

Division Country Ratings	Adjustment to Obligor Rating
Excellent, very good, good, or satisfactory	None
Fair	Best possible obligor rating is 5
Selectively acceptable	Best possible obligor rating is 6
Marginal/deteriorating	Best possible obligor rating is 7

Again, Step 5 acts to limit the best possible rating. For example, if the client's operation has a country rating in the "fair" category, then the best possible OR is 5 (see Table 7.15). On the other hand, if the country is rated "selectively acceptable," then the best possible obligor rating is 6.

A condensed version of an illustrative prototype country analysis is provided in Appendix 4.

7. SECOND GROUP OF ADJUSTMENT FACTORS FOR FACILITY RATING

7.1 Third-Party Support (Step 6)

This sixth step adjusts a facility rating (FR) where important third-party support is held. (This step can therefore be skipped if the guarantor was substituted for the borrower at the outset.)

Considerable care and caution is necessary if ratings are to be improved because of the presence of a guarantor. In all cases, one must be convinced that the third party/owner is committed to ongoing support of the obligor. Typically, one establishes very specific rules for third-party support as described in Box 7.3. Based on the quality of the third-party support, the risk rating of the firm can be upgraded or downgraded. Personal guarantors and other undertakings from individuals, and guarantees for less than 100 percent of the indebtedness, do not qualify for consideration in this category.

THIRD-PARTY SUPPORT

Type of Support

Guarantee	A 100 percent clean guarantee is held.*
Completion guarantee	A 100 percent clean guarantee is held until completion of the project.
Keepwell agreement or operating agreement	A strong keepwell[17] or operating agreement is held and is considered legally enforceable.
Comfort letter or ownership	A comfort letter[18] is held or no written assurance is held.

*See Note 11 for a definition of "clean guarantee."

7.2 Term (Step 7)

This seventh step recognizes the increased risk associated with longer-term facilities and the lower risk of very short term facilities. A standard approach is to combine the adjusted facility rating (after any third-party support adjustment, in Step 6) with the remaining term to maturity in order to determine the adjustment to the facility rating, as shown in the matrix in Table 7.16. One would also need to apply judgement of the primary use of the facility, particularly with respect to financial products.

7.3 Structure (Step 8)

This eighth step considers the effect of how strongly a facility is structured, its covenants, its conditions, etc., in order to prompt appropriate adjustment(s) to the rating. The lending purposes and/or structure may influence (positively or negatively) the strength and quality of the credit. These may refer to the status of the borrower, the priority of the security, the covenants (or lack thereof) attached to a facility, etc. Take, for example, a facility that has been downgraded due to the term of a loan. If the structure contains very strong covenants which mitigate the effect of the term to maturity of the facility, it may be appropriate to make an adjustment to offset (often partially) the effect of the term to maturity of the facility.

TABLE 7.16

Adjustment to Facility Rating

	Term to Maturity of the Facility		
	Less Than x Days	x to 365 Days	1 to y Years
FACILITY RATING 0 1 2 3 4 5 6 7 8 9 10 11 12		Specific adjustments are provided by each row/column combination	

Some instances that might affect ratings are listed in Box 7.4. Other considerations may affect the facility rating. For example, facilities that are readily saleable into the market may merit an upgrade due to their liquidity.

7.4 Collateral (Step 9)

This last and ninth step recognizes that the presence of security should heavily affect the severity of loss, given default, in any facility. The quality and depth of security vary widely and will determine the extent of the benefit in reducing any loss.

Security should be valued as it would be in a liquidation scenario. In other words, if the business fails, what proceeds would be available? If the total security package includes components from various collateral categories, then one should generally use the worst category containing security on which any significant reliance is placed. The collateral category should reflect only the security held for the facility that is being rated. (Exceptions are where all security is held for all facilities, and where they are being rated as one total.) Documentation risk (the proper completion

BOX 7.4

STRUCTURE

STRUCTURE ADJUSTMENT

Covenants/term: Covenants are in place which effectively mitigate all (or part) of any increased risk due to term, by means of default clauses that provide a full opportunity to make demands, or by means of repayment arrangements that ensure rapid pay-down.

ACTION: Upgrade only to offset (possibly partially) any downgrade for term.

Poor covenants: Appropriate covenants are not in place, or are very loose, so that review/default may/will not be triggered, even though significant deterioration occurs.

ACTION: Downgrade.

Subordinated/loans security: The bank's loan is subordinated, putting one's position and/or security significantly behind other creditors.

ACTION: Downgrade.

Corporate organization: The borrower is highly cash flow dependent on related operating companies that have their own financing.

ACTION: Downgrade.

of security) is always a concern and should be considered when assessing the level of protection. A few examples of collateral categories are shown in Box 7.5. Collateral can have a major effect on the final facility rating. One should also observe that the value of the collateral is often a function of movements in market rates. Accordingly, the final facility rating is dependent on movement of rates and therefore may be adversely impacted by a significant change in rates.

8. CONCLUSION

The utilization and appropriate processing of a variety of factors (e.g., key financial analysis measures) can provide the credit ana-

COLLATERAL

COLLATERAL CATEGORIES

Pledged assets are of very high caliber (generally no reliance on inventory) and provide substantial overcoverage (using conservative valuations, with liquidation appraisals held where warranted).

A first charge is held over specific company assets or all company assets (depending on the type of credit facility).

Background support may also add strength (personal guarantees do not qualify unless strongly supported).

lyst with a tool to arrive at the obligor and facility ratings of a counterparty. The 1999 Basle Conceptual Paper has explicitly recognized that, in the future, an internal risk rating–based system could prove useful to banks in their calculation of the minimum required regulatory capital.[19] Basle has surveyed banks in terms of their methodology, mapping to losses, consistency, oversight, and control as well as internal applications. We would expect that over time more sophisticated banks would all adopt a system based on internal ratings in lieu of a standardized external rating system.

APPENDIX 1: DEFINITIONS OF KEY RATIOS

1. EBIT interest coverage =
    (times interest earned)

$$\frac{\text{Earnings from continuing operations before interest and taxes}}{\text{Gross interest incurred before subtracting (1) capitalized interest and (2) interest income}}$$

2. EBITDA interest coverage =
    (cash interest coverage)

$$\frac{\text{Earnings from continuing operations before interest, taxes, depreciation, and amortization}}{\text{Gross interest incurred before subtracting (1) capitalized interest and (2) interest income}}$$

3. Funds from operations/total debt =

$$\frac{\text{Net income from continuing operations plus depreciation, amortization, deferred income taxes, and other noncash items}}{\text{Long-term debt plus current maturities, commercial paper, and other short-term borrowings}}$$

4. Free operating cash flow/total debt =

Funds from operations minus capital expenditures, minus (plus) the increase (decrease) in working capital (excluding changes in cash, marketable securities, and short-term debt)
_____
Long-term debt plus current maturities, commercial paper, and other short-term borrowings

5. Pretax return on capital =

Pretax income from continuing operations plus interest expense
_____
Sum of (1) average of beginning-of-year and end-of-year current maturities, long-term debt, noncurrent deferred taxes, and equity and (2) average short-term borrowings during year as disclosed in footnotes

6. Operating income/sales =

Sales minus cost of goods manufactured (before depreciation and amortization), selling, general and administrative, and research and development costs
_____
Sales

7. Long-term debt/capitalization =

Long-term debt
_____
Long-term debt plus shareholders' equity (including preferred stock) plus minority interest

8. Total debt/capitalization =

Long-term debt plus current maturities, commercial paper, and other short-term borrowings
_____
Long-term debt plus current maturities, commercial paper, and other short-term borrowings plus shareholders' equity (including preferred stock) plus minority interest

Source: S&P's *Corporate Ratings Criteria,* 1998.

APPENDIX 2: KEY FINANCIAL ANALYSIS MEASURES

A. *Liquidity—ability to meet short-term obligations*

1.   Current ratio (CR) =   Current assets(CA)/current liabilities(CL)

2. Working capital leverage ratio (WCLR) =   Current liabilities (CL)/working capital (WC)

3.   QR = Quick ratio (acid test ratio) = $\dfrac{\text{Cash} + \text{MS*} + \text{A/R**}}{\text{Current liabilities}}$

$$QR = \dfrac{\text{CA} - \text{Inventories}}{\text{CL}}$$

*MS: marketable securities
**A/R: accounts receivable

B. *Solvency—ability to meet key term obligations (ability to service debts)*

1.   Interest coverage (times interest earned) = $\dfrac{\text{EBIT}^1}{\text{I}^2}$

2.   Cash Interest Coverage $=$ $\dfrac{\text{EBITDA}^3}{\text{I}}$
(times interest earned)

LEGEND:

1. EBIT = earnings before interest and taxes
2. I = Interest expense
3. EBITDA = Earnings before interest, taxes, depreciation, and amortization

C. *Leverage and capital measure*

1.   Debt to net worth $=$ TL/NW

2.   Senior debt to net worth $=$ $\dfrac{\text{TL-SD}}{\text{NW}}$
Note: SD = subordinated debt

3.   Debt to tangible net worth $=$ $\dfrac{\text{Total liabilities}}{\text{Total equity} - \text{Intangible assets}}$

4.   Debt to assets $=$ $\dfrac{\text{Total liabilities}}{\text{Total assets}}$

5.   Long-term debt $=$ $\dfrac{\text{Long-term debt}}{\text{Total assets}}$

6.   Total coverage ratio $=$ $\dfrac{\text{Current assets}}{\text{Total liabilities}}$

7. Fixed assets (a measure of illiquidity) $=$ $\dfrac{\text{Net fixed assets}}{\text{Total assets}}$

D. *Operating performance (profitability of a business)*

1.   Return on assets(ROA) $=$ $\dfrac{\text{Net income after tax}}{\text{Book value of assets}}$

2.   Return as equity (ROE) $=$ $\dfrac{\text{Net income after tax}}{\text{Book value of equity}}$

3. Gross product margin (GPM) $=$ $\dfrac{\text{Net sales} - \text{COGS}}{\text{Net sales}}$

4.   Net profit margin $=$ $\dfrac{\text{Net income after tax}}{\text{Net sales}}$

5.   Operating leverage (OL) $=$ $\dfrac{\text{Gross profit (=sales} - \text{COGS)}}{\text{PBT(=FP} - \text{FC)}}$

6.   Operating profit $=$ $\dfrac{\text{Operating profit}}{\text{Net sales}} =$

$\dfrac{\text{Earnings befoer interest and taxes (EBIT)}}{\text{Net sales}}$

7.   Return on investment (ROI) $=$ $\dfrac{\text{Net income}}{\text{Capital invested}}$

8. $$\text{Asset turnover ratio} = \frac{\text{Annual sales revenue}}{\text{Total assets}}$$

9. $$\text{Dividend yield} = \frac{\text{Annual cash dividend}}{\text{Price per share}}$$

Note: ROE = ROA × asset-to-debt ratio.

E. Securities analysis

1. $$\text{EPS} = \frac{\text{Net income available for common stockholder}}{\text{Total number of outstanding common stock shares}}$$

2. Earnings yield = EPS/P

3. Price-to-earnings ratio = P/EPS

Note: Market cap = Price of equity × total number of shares outstanding

F. Ratios for evaluating the expenses of a business

1. $$\text{Cost of sales} = \frac{Cost\ of\ goods\ sold}{Net\ sales}$$

2. $$\text{Overhead ratio (burden ratio)} = \frac{\text{Sales, general, and administrative expenses}}{\text{Net sales}}$$

3. $$\text{Sales per employee} = \frac{\text{Net sales}}{\text{Average number of full-time equivalent employees}}$$

4. $$\text{Gross profit per employee} = \frac{\text{Gross profit}}{\text{Average number of full-time equivalent employees}}$$

5. $$\text{Direct employee expense} = \frac{\text{Total salary and bonus expense}}{\text{Average number of full-time equivalent employees}}$$

G. Ratios for evaluating the sufficiency of a firm's cash flow

$$\text{Cash flow adequacy} = \frac{\text{Cash from operating activities}}{\text{Long-term debt paid} + \text{fixed assets purchased} + \text{dividends paid}}$$

H. Ratios for evaluating collateral

$$\text{Collateral coverage} = \frac{\text{Loan balance}}{\text{Appraised or approximated value of collateral}}$$

Note: If the borrower has more than one loan outstanding, and the loans are owed to the same bank, the balances on all such loans may be combined in the denominator, and the total value of all of the collateral may be combined in the numerator. However, such combinations should never be made if the loans are not explicitly cross-collateralized.

APPENDIX 3A: PROTOTYPE INDUSTRY ASSESSMENT: TELECOMMUNICATIONS IN CANADA

COMMENTARY ON RISK ASSESSMENT CRITERIA

COMPETITIVENESS

The Canadian industry's competitive position is favorable with regard to that of its trading partners due to its advanced and technologically up-to-date telecommunications infrastructure. Moreover, changes in the regulatory framework over the past three years have resulted in downward pressure on rates spurred on by the innovative service offerings and pricing plans of the new entrants and the competitive response of the incumbents (especially in the long-distance area). While the erosion of the incumbents' long-distance market share has recently stabilized, the entry of new players in the local market, which was opened to competition on January 1, 1998, will result in renewed losses in market share in local telephony. The move from rate-of-return regulation to a price cap regime will improve the competitiveness of the industry, as the primary means of improving profitability will shift from growing assets to cutting costs and adding new revenue generating services.

TRADE ENVIRONMENT

Telecommunications services were not included in the NAFTA. Canada agreed to eliminate the monopoly in overseas telephone and fixed domestic satellite services as part of the WTO agreement liberalizing trade in telecommunications. While Canada agreed to remove foreign ownership restrictions in very limited areas (global mobile satellites and submarine cable landings), the 46.7 percent ceiling for telecommunications and broadcast industries was maintained.

REGULATORY FRAMEWORK

Effective January 1995, the industry's competitive businesses, principally long-distance voice, data, and enhanced services such as ATM and frame relay, have been free of regulation. As of January 1998, the CRTC has opened the local telephone market to competition. By not forcing the incumbent telcos to offer cheap access rates to their local networks, the CRTC eliminates resale as a long-term strategy for the local market in the hope of attracting competitors who are willing to make long-term investments in their own facilities. The incumbent telcos, however, are expected to unbundle their services and provide new entrants with access to local network facilities which they cannot realistically duplicate themselves (e.g., local loops).

RESTRUCTURING

Driven by major regulatory, technological, and competitive forces, the telecommunications industry has undergone significant restructuring over the past 3 to 4 years. Further restructuring is expected as a result of new entrants in the provision of local telephony.

TECHNOLOGICAL CHANGE

Technology is what drives this industry and has resulted in the introduction of a host of new enhanced high-margin services. As change is a constant in this industry, substantial capital investments are required and ongoing R&D is imperative if the industry is to keep its competitive edge, and to upgrade its systems to provide the additional services that have been allowed by the CRTC. While the industry as a whole is cash rich and can undertake these expenditures, keeping up with technological change represents a major challenge to smaller telephone systems.

FINANCIAL PERFORMANCE

Ratios are satisfactory and sustainable.

LONG-TERM TRENDS AFFECTING DEMAND

Corporate cost-cutting has led to a greater reliance on electronic communications technology, boosting the demand for the industry's services. The increasing use of computers at home will keep demand for telecommunications services high even if some market share in the provision of these services is lost to alternate providers such as the cable companies.

VULNERABILITY TO MACROECONOMIC ENVIRONMENTS

The industry is mildly affected by the domestic cycle, as consumers may reduce the number of long-distance calls and discontinue some value-added services during a downturn.

Source: CIBC Economics Division.

APPENDIX 3B: PROTOTYPE INDUSTRY ASSESSMENT: FOOTWEAR AND CLOTHING IN CANADA

COMMENTARY ON RISK ASSESSMENT CRITERIA

COMPETITIVENESS

The apparel industry is dominated by a large number of small firms employing fewer than 50 persons, with very few of these operations benefiting from economies of scale. While some apparel companies are competitive in specific niche markets, such as men's suits and women's lingerie, labor costs in Canada relative to those in low-wage countries leave many apparel operations at a competitive disadvantage. Except in a few specialized areas, Canadian footwear companies are not competitive with the large U.S. operations or the offshore low-cost manufacturers.

TRADE ENVIRONMENT

All tariffs on Canada-U.S. apparel trade were eliminated on January 1, 1998. All apparel tariffs between Canada and Mexico under NAFTA will be eliminated by January 1, 2003. Under NAFTA, Canadian apparel manufacturers face stricter rules of origin, although in some product cases, duty refunds and tariff preference levels (TPLs) are available. TPLs will be reviewed in 1999. Under the WTO trade rules, Canada has reduced its tariff rates on both footwear and clothing while quantitative restrictions on apparel imports will be eliminated by December 31, 2004. As a result, the Canadian apparel and footwear industries will be facing significantly more import competition in the future.

REGULATORY FRAMEWORK

Currently, the apparel and footwear industries are not subject to any federal environmental legislation. Some labeling requirements are mandatory, especially if the product is to be exported to a NAFTA country. New simplified (symbols only) U.S. care-labeling rules, when harmonized under the NAFTA, should reduce costs to manufacturers who export within the region.

RESTRUCTURING

Increased competition from low-cost imports will necessitate further downsizing of the apparel industry. Apparel operations producing standard products that complete directly with low-cost imports will likely close. Further downsizing of leather footwear and skate manufacturing operations is anticipated.

TECHNOLOGICAL CHANGE

Highly flexible, fast, responsive manufacturing configurations and CAD/CAM design systems allow for more flexibility in terms of product design, layouts for cutting, and short runs. They reduce input waste, as well as labor and inventory costs. Investment in such equipment is difficult to absorb by many of the smaller players in the industry, as is the procurement/hiring of the skilled labor needed to operate this machinery.

FINANCIAL PERFORMANCE

Overall, ratios are weak and are expected to weaken. Equity levels continue to decline as do profitability ratios.

LONG-TERM TRENDS AFFECTING DEMAND

With more casual days and flexible working arrangements in business, casual apparel and footwear continues to gain in popularity at the expense of more formal attire (a major portion of Canadian output). This trend is reinforced by the increasing importance of fitness and leisure activities in Canadian lifestyles.

VULNERABILITY TO MACROECONOMIC ENVIRONMENTS

Both the footwear and apparel industries are highly vulnerable to changes in the Canadian economy. An economic downturn and/or rise in interest rates affects consumer spending. These two industries are also vulnerable to exchange rate movements as many of their inputs are sourced from the United States or offshore. Changes in exchange rates also affect the price of imports, of which most come from low-cost sources. Imports account for 75 percent of Canada's footwear market and 47 percent of Canada's apparel market.

Source: CIBC Economics Division.

APPENDIX 4: PROTOTYPE COUNTRY ANALYSIS REPORT (CONDENSED VERSION): BRAZIL

Country Report: Brazil

Date: July 1999

Performance Indicators		1996	1997	Forecasts 1998	1999	2000
Nominal GNI	US$bn	515	541	496	468	483
GNI per capita	US$	3,262	3,384	3,058	2,847	2,894
Real growth	(% ch)	2.8	3.2	0.2	(4.0)	(0.5)
Investment/GNI ratio	(%)	19.4	19.9	17.8	16.0	16.5
Domestic credit growth	(%)	25.3	16.0	27.0	11.0	12.0
Unemployment rate (urban centers)	(%)	5.4	5.7	7.1	11.0	10.8
Inflation rate	(% ch)	15.8	6.9	6.1	10.0	20.0
PSBR/GNP ratio (minus sign designates surplus)	(%)	6.1	5.9	7.9	11.0	10.0
Total exports	US$bn	60.6	67.3	65.1	68.2	71.3
Total exports/GNI ratio	(%)	11.8	12.4	13.1	14.6	14.8
Merchandise exports	US$bn	47.8	53.0	51.1	53.9	57.0
Trade balance	US$bn	(5.6)	(8.4)	(6.2)	0.4	(.4)
Current account balance	US$bn	(23.6)	(33.9)	(35.2)	(29.1)	(27.5)
Balance of payments	US$bn	8.6	(7.6)	(8.2)	1.2	1.0
Int'l reserves (gold @ 35 sdr/oz)	US$bn	58.6	51.0	42.8	44.0	45.0
Exchange rate (average)	Reais/US$	1.01	1.08	1.16	1.79	2.25
Est. gross financing required	US$bn	91.9	112.4	96.2	100.0	91.8
Total external debt	US$bn	179.1	182.9	206.4	226.8	256.3
Short-term external debt	US$bn	63.8	55.7	38.9	37.1	35.3
Current account/GNI ratio	(%)	4.6	6.3	7.1	6.2	5.7
External debt/GNI ratio	(%)	34.8	33.8	41.6	48.5	53.1
External debt/exports ratio	(%)	295.7	272.0	316.9	332.6	359.2
Debt service ratio	(%)	45.8	66.6	69.7	90.9	82.9

Positives

Privatization (utilities, ports, mining; telecoms)

Largest market in Latin America

IMF-led rescue package from the international community

Negatives

Economy is in recession

Large fast-growing public sector domestic debt (48% of GDP)

Still large current account and budget deficits

High reliance on foreign investments

Needs to Happen

Reduce internal debt

More structural reforms (i.e. privatization, tax system, social security system)

Rapid export growth so that the large external debt can be serviced

Comparative Data 1998

	Argentina	Chile	Mexico	Venezuela
Real growth %	3.9	3.1	4.6	1.0
Inflation %	0.7	5.0	15.6	36.5
PSBR/GNI % (minus sign denotes surplus)	1.8	(0.6)	7.5	3.3
Current account/GNI %	(4.8)	(6.4)	(3.5)	(2.2)
debt service ratio	49.1	24.4	39.9	29.1

Country Risk Rating Profile

Basics High real interest rates, fiscal austerity measures continue to limit the scope for business. Unsatisfactory repayment experience and poor data availability.

Shockability Pressured by excessive public sector spending and external factors, Brazil was forced to devalue (then float) the real. Foreign savings and IMF are financing budget and current account deficits.

Politics Due to the devaluation, the president's popularity is low and his leadership ability has evaporated. The political will to carry out commitments to fiscal adjustment will be tested in the months ahead.

Internal economics Fiscal austerity (to control the public debt and reduce dependence on external savings) and high interest rates amid unfavorable conditions in world markets have led to a deep recession.

External economics Due to devaluation of the real, asset prices are now cheaper and this has attracted FDI inflows. After devaluation the current account is adjusting slowly. High financing requirements.

Conclusion: The economy—and the political system—are far from healthy. President Cardoso's leadership ability has evaporated since the January 1999 real devaluation. The political will to carry out important commitments to fiscal adjustment (needed to control the public debt and reduce the economy's dependence on external savings) will be tested in the months ahead. While structural reforms have been approved, they are not being implemented swiftly. Conditions in the financial markets will soon be critical again. Other events or conditions could also trigger problems including rising unrest, as unemployment remains high, political corruption scandals, or domestic debt problems.

Source: CIBC Economics Division: Country And International Analysis Group.

NOTES

1. S&P *Corporate Ratings Criteria*, 1998, p.3.
2. Moody's *Credit Ratings and Research*, 1998, p.4.
3. Moody's Investors Service, *Rating Methodology: The Evolving Meaning of Moody's Bond Ratings*, 1999, p.4.
4. A put bond is a bond stipulation that allows the holder to redeem the bond at face value at a specific, predetermined time so that if interest rates go up the holder can avoid losing money as long as the stipulation is operative; or in other words, it is a bond giving the investor the right to liquidate the bond, or to sell it back to the issuing party.
5. See Nusbaum (1996).
6. The risk of loss is a very general notion since it can be described in several distinct dimensions. For example, one can describe it in relation to the expected loss dimension, the unexpected loss (economic capital) dimension, the 10-bp tail probability of loss dimension, etc. One would need to describe risk of loss in a precise fashion in order to appropriately back-test the degree to which one's RRS was predictive.
7. A typical RRS generally excludes real estate credits, banks, agriculture, public finance, and other identified groups.
8. If, for example, our universe contained 100 rated companies, of which 10 were upgraded during the year and 10 were downgraded, and if the upgraded companies moved on average by 1.5 notches (e.g., five were upgraded by one class and five companies by two risk classes) and if the downgraded firms were all downgraded by one single class, then the rating activity is 25% (= $10 \times 1.5 + 10 \times 1/100$), and the drift is 5% (= $10 \times 1.5 - 10 \times 1/100$).
9. The article also presents the five- and 10-year transition matrices.
10. Working capital is defined as the difference between current assets and current liabilities.
11. A clean 100 percent guarantee refers to a straightforward guarantee for 100 percent of the obligation without any conditionality as to the enforceability or collectibility; i.e., the bottom line is that the guarantor is "on the hook" just as firmly as the original obligor, and has no extra defense under law.
12. For definitions of key accounting ratios, see Appendix 1.
13. As an appropriate control, the average might first be compared to the worst of the three risk levels. The rating should not be more than 1.0 better than the worst rating. In other words, if it exceeds this

control, then it must be adjusted downwards. For example, if the three assessment areas were respectively rated 2, 2, and 5, then the average is 3, but the rating should be adjusted to 4 (being 1.0 better than the 5 risk level). If the worst of the three risk levels is not an integer (say 4.5), then reducing by 1 would leave a 3.5. One typically uses judgement to set the rating at either a 3 or 4.

14. Business risk is defined as the risk associated with the level and stability of operating cash flows over time. Further detail can be found in Chapter 17.

15. A company can create working capital by borrowing on a long-term basis and employing the proceeds of the loan for current assets. Working capital will increase by the amount of additional long-term debt less any addition to current liabilities.

16. Working capital is sometimes created by the sale of fixed assets and it increases by the exact amount of the reduction of fixed assets. As companies grow, however, it is more likely that the fixed assets in the formula will represent a competing use of the various working capital sources

17. A keepwell agreement is an agreement in which one party agrees to maintain a certain status or condition at another company; e.g., a parent company may agree to maintain the net worth of a subsidiary company at a certain level. This is a legally enforceable contract; however, only the party that the keepwell is in favor of may sue under such a contract.

18. A comfort letter is a letter generally requested by securities underwriters to give comfort on the financial information included in an SEC registration statement. It generally expresses the support of the parent company for the activities and commitments of subsidiaries. However, it does not constitute a guarantee.

19. See also Chapter 2.

The Credit Migration Approach to Measuring Credit Risk

1. INTRODUCTION

With the Bank for International Settlements (BIS) 1998 reform in place, internal models for both general and specific market risk have been implemented at the major G-10 banks and are used every day to report regulatory capital for the trading book.

The next step, as we discussed in Chapter 2, is to extend the VaR framework so that it can be used to allocate capital for credit risk in the banking book.

The current BIS requirements for the "specific risk" component of market risk are subject to broad interpretation (Chapter 4).[1] To qualify as an internal model for specific risk, the regulator should be convinced that "concentration risk," "spread risk," "downgrade risk," and "default risk" are appropriately captured. The exact meaning of "appropriately" is left to the appreciation of both the bank and the regulator. The capital charge for specific risk is then the product of a multiplier (the minimum value of which is currently set to 4) times the sum of the VaR at the 99 percent confidence level for spread risk, downgrade risk, and default risk over a 10-day horizon.

There are several problems with this piecemeal approach to credit risk. First, spread risk is related to both market risk and credit risk. Spreads fluctuate either because equilibrium conditions in capital markets change, which in turn affects credit spreads for all credit ratings, or because the credit quality of the obligor has improved or deteriorated, or because both conditions have occurred simultaneously. In addition, spreads depend on the liquidity of the market for corporate bonds.

Downgrade risk, on the other hand, is a pure credit spread risk. When the credit quality of an obligor deteriorates, then the spread relative to the Treasury curve widens, and vice versa when the credit quality improves.

Simply adding spread risk to downgrade risk may lead to double counting. In addition, the current regime incorporates the market risk component of spread risk into the calculation for credit risk. This means that the regulatory capital multiplier for this risk is 4 instead of 3.

Second, the problem of disentangling the market risk– and credit risk–driven components in spread changes is further obscured by the fact that often market participants anticipate forthcoming credit events before they actually happen. Therefore, spreads already reflect the new credit status by the time the rating agencies effectively downgrade an obligor, or put the obligor on "credit watch."

Third, default is simply a special case of downgrade: the credit quality has deteriorated to the point at which the obligor cannot service its debt obligations. An adequate credit VaR model should therefore address migration risk (i.e., credit spread risk) and default risk within a consistent and integrated framework.

Finally, changes in market and economic conditions, as reflected by changes in interest rates, stock market indexes, exchange rates, unemployment rates, etc., may affect the overall profitability of firms. As a result, the exposures of the various counterparties to each obligor, as well as the probabilities of default and of migrating from one credit rating to another, are linked to market risks. Thus, in an ideal world, the risk framework would fully integrate market risk and credit risk.

Over the last few years, a number of new approaches to credit modeling have been made public. CreditMetrics from JP Morgan, first published in 1997, is reviewed in the next section of this chapter. The CreditMetrics approach is based on the analysis of credit migration, i.e., the probability of moving from one credit quality to another, including default, within a given time horizon (often arbitrarily taken to be one year). CreditMetrics models the full forward distribution of the values of any bond or loan portfolio, say one year forward, where the changes in values are related to credit migration only; interest rates are assumed to evolve in a deterministic fashion.

The credit VaR of a portfolio is then derived in a similar fashion as for market risk. It is simply the distance from the mean of the percentile of the forward distribution, at the desired confidence level. (This definition applies to all credit risk models, and is independent of the underlying theoretical framework.)

Tom Wilson (1997a, 1997b) proposes an improvement to the credit migration approach by allowing default probabilities to vary with the credit cycle. In this approach, default probabilities are a function of macrovariables such as unemployment, the level of interest rates, the growth rate in the economy, government expenses, and foreign exchange rates. These macrovariables are the factors that, to a large extent, drive credit cycles. This methodology is reviewed in Section 3 of this chapter.

Over the last few years, KMV Corporation, a firm that specializes in credit risk analysis, has developed a credit risk methodology and extensive database to assess default probabilities and the loss distribution related to both default and migration risks. KMV's methodology differs somewhat from CreditMetrics, in that it relies upon the "expected default frequency," or EDF, for each issuer, rather than upon the average historical transition frequencies produced by the rating agencies for each credit class. The KMV approach is based on the asset value model originally proposed by Merton (1974), the main difference being the simplifying assumptions required to facilitate the model's implementation. It remains to be seen whether these compromises prevent the model from capturing the real complexity of credit. KMV's methodology, together with the contingent claim approach to measuring credit risk, is reviewed in Chapter 9.[2]

At the end of 1997, Credit Suisse Financial Products (CSFP) released an approach that is based on actuarial science. CreditRisk+, which focuses on default alone rather than credit migration, is examined briefly in Chapter 10. CreditRisk+ assumes that the dynamics of default for individual bonds, or loans, follow a Poisson process.

Finally, the "reduced form" approach—currently the foundation of credit derivative pricing models—is reviewed in Chapter 11. These models allow one to derive the term structure of default probabilities from credit spreads, while assuming an exogenous and somewhat arbitrary recovery rate.

In Chapter 12 we compare CreditMetrics, KMV, CreditRisk+, and the BIS 1988 standardized approach for a benchmark portfolio composed of more than 1800 bonds. The bonds we chose were diversified across 13 currencies covering North America, Europe, and Asia; across various maturities; and across the whole spectrum of credit qualities. It appears that credit VaR numbers generated by these three models fall within a narrow range, with a ratio of 1.5 between the highest and the lowest values, provided consistent inputs across models are used. Thus although default is modeled differently, and in some instances (e.g., CreditRisk+) downgrade risk is ignored, the models produce relatively close results for the same portfolio.

This is not that surprising, since the main risk factor is default. However, it is interesting to note that when the portfolio contains a large proportion of bonds from OECD banks, the standardized approach produces a lower capital charge than the credit models. This is because the standardized approach allots very low risk weights to those institutions that do not always reflect their actual credit risk. But if we assume that all bonds are investment-grade corporate bonds, the credit models generate a capital charge that is substantially lower than that based on the 1988 BIS Accord.

It seems that any of these three models can be considered as a reasonable internal model to assess regulatory capital related to credit risk for straightforward bonds and loans without option features. However, all the models assume deterministic interest rates. This means that the models are inappropriate for measuring the credit risk of swaps, credit derivatives, and other derivative-like products such as loan commitments.[3]

For these instruments we need an integrated framework that permits the derivation of the credit exposure and the loss distribution in a consistent manner. Currently, none of the proposed models offers such an integrated approach. In order to measure the credit risk of derivative securities, the next generation of credit models should allow for stochastic interest rates, and possibly for

Corporate Defaults Worldwide (Number of Firms and the Amount Defaulted)

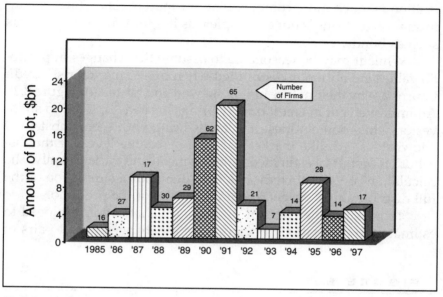

Source: Standard & Poor's.

default and migration probabilities that depend on the state of the economy.

In Figure 8.1 we present the record of defaults from 1985 to 1997. In 1990 and 1991, when the world economies were in recession, the frequency of defaults increased substantially. During the post-1991 period, which have been characterized by a "growth economy," the default rate has declined dramatically. Only recently the default rate has started to rise.

2. CREDITMETRICS FRAMEWORK[4]

CreditMetrics is a methodology that is based on the estimation of the forward distribution of changes in the value of a portfolio of loan- and bond-type products at a given time horizon, usually one year.[5] The changes in value are related to the migration, upwards and downwards, of the credit quality of the obligor, as well as to default.

In comparison to market VaR, credit VaR poses three challenges. First, the portfolio distribution is far from being a normal distribution. Second, measuring the portfolio effect due to diversification is much more complex than for market risk. Third, the information on loans is not as complete as it is for traded instruments such as bonds.

While it may be reasonable to assume that changes in portfolio values are normally distributed when due to market risk, credit returns are by their nature highly skewed and fat-tailed (Figure 8.2). An improvement in credit quality brings limited "upside" to an investor, while downgrades or defaults bring with them substantial "downsides." Unlike market VaR, the percentile levels of the distribution cannot be estimated from the mean and variance only. The calculation of VaR for credit risk thus demands a simulation of the full distribution of the changes in the value of the portfolio.

To measure the effect of portfolio diversification, we need to estimate the correlations in credit quality changes for all pairs of

FIGURE 8.2

Comparison of the Probability Distributions of Credit Returns and Market Returns

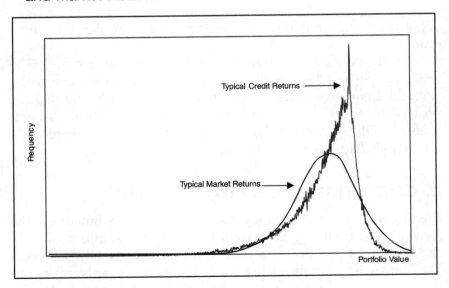

Source: CIBC.

obligors. However, these correlations are not directly observable. CreditMetrics bases its evaluation on the joint probability of equity returns. This entails making some strong simplifying assumptions about the capital structure of the obligor, and about the process that is generating equity returns. We will elaborate on this key feature of the model later on.

Finally, as we mentioned above, CreditMetrics, like KMV and CreditRisk+, makes no provision for market risk: forward values and exposures are derived from deterministic forward curves. The only uncertainty in CreditMetrics relates to credit migration, i.e., the process of moving up or down the credit spectrum.

The CreditMetrics risk measurement framework is summarized in Figure 8.3, which shows the two main building blocks:

1. "Value at Risk Due to Credit" for a single financial instrument.
2. Value at Risk at the portfolio level, which accounts for portfolio diversification effects ("Portfolio Value at Risk Due to Credit").

There are also two supporting functions. "Correlations" derives the equity return correlations used to generate the joint migration probabilities; "exposures" produces the future exposures of derivative securities, such as swaps.

3. CREDIT VAR FOR A BOND (BUILDING BLOCK 1)

The first step is to specify a rating system, with rating categories, together with the probabilities of migrating from one credit quality to another over the credit risk horizon.

This transition matrix is the key component of the credit VaR model proposed by JP Morgan. The matrix may take the form of the rating system of Moody's, or Standard & Poor's, or it might be based on the proprietary rating system internal to the bank. A strong assumption made by CreditMetrics is that all issuers within the same rating class are homogeneous credit risks. They have the same transition probabilities and the same default probability. (KMV departs from CreditMetrics in the sense that in KMV's framework each issuer is specific, and is characterized by its own asset returns distribution, its own capital structure, and its own default probability.)

Second, the risk horizon should be specified. This is usually taken to be one year. When one is concerned about the risk profile over a longer period of time, as for long-dated illiquid instruments, multiple horizons can be chosen, such as one to 10 years.

The third step consists of specifying the forward discount curve at the risk horizon(s) for each credit category. In the case of default, the value of the instrument should be estimated in terms of the "recovery rate," which is given as a percentage of face value or "par." In the final step, this information is translated into the forward distribution of the changes in the portfolio value consecutive to credit migration.

Figure 8.3, taken from the technical document of CreditMetrics, illustrates the steps of the credit VaR model. In their example we

FIGURE 8.3

CreditMetrics Framework: The Four Building Blocks

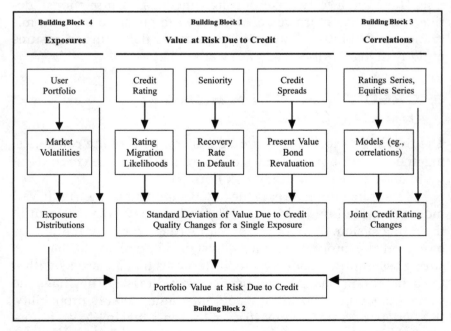

Source: CreditMetrics, JP Morgan.

calculate credit VaR for a senior unsecured BBB rated bond maturing in exactly five years, and paying an annual coupon of 6 percent.

Step 1: Specify the transition matrix

The rating categories, as well as the transition matrix, are chosen from an external or internal rating system (Table 8.1).

In the case of Standard & Poor's, there are seven rating categories. The highest credit is AAA; the lowest, CCC. Default is defined as a situation in which the obligor cannot make a payment related to a bond or a loan obligation, whether the payment is a coupon payment or the redemption of the principal. "Pari passu" clauses are such that when an obligor defaults on one payment related to a bond or a loan, the obligor is technically declared in default on all debt obligations.

The bond issuer in our example is currently a BBB rating. The BBB row in Table 8.1 shows the probability, as estimated by Standard & Poor's, that this BBB issuer will migrate over a period of one year to any one of the eight possible states, including default. Obviously, the most probable situation is that the obligor will remain in the same rating category, i.e., BBB; this has a probability of 86.93 percent. The probability of the issuer defaulting within one

TABLE 8.1

Transition Matrix: Probabilities of Credit Rating Migrating From One Rating Quality to Another, Within One Year

Initial Rating	Rating at Year-End (%)							
	AAA	AA	A	BBB	BB	B	CCC	Default
AAA	90.81	8.33	0.68	0.06	0.12	0	0	0
AA	0.70	90.65	7.79	0.64	0.06	0.14	0.02	0
A	0.09	2.27	91.05	5.52	0.74	0.26	0.01	0.06
BBB	0.02	0.33	5.95	86.93	5.30	1.17	1.12	0.18
BB	0.03	0.14	0.67	7.73	80.53	8.84	1.00	1.06
B	0	0.11	0.24	0.43	6.48	83.46	4.07	5.20
CCC	0.22	0	0.22	1.30	2.38	11.24	64.86	19.79

Source: Standard & Poor's CreditWeek (April 15, 1996).

year is only 0.18 percent, while the probability of it being upgraded to AAA is also very small, i.e., 0.02 percent. Such a transition matrix is produced by the rating agencies for all initial ratings, based on the history of credit events that have occurred to the firms rated by those agencies. (Default is taken to be an "absorbing state"; i.e., when an issuer is in default, it stays in default.)

Moody's publishes similar information. The probabilities published by the agencies are based on more than 20 years of data across all industries. Obviously, these data should be interpreted with care since they represent average statistics across a heterogeneous sample of firms, and over several business cycles. For this reason many banks prefer to rely on their own statistics, which relate more closely to the composition of their loan and bond portfolios.

Moody's and Standard & Poor's also produce long-term average cumulative default rates, as shown in Table 8.2 in a tabular form and in Figure 8.4 in graphical form. For example, a BBB issuer has a probability of 0.18 percent of defaulting within one year, 0.44 percent of defaulting in two years, 4.34 percent of defaulting in 10 years, and so on.

Tables 8.1 and 8.2 should, in fact, be consistent with one another. From Table 8.2 we can derive the transition matrix that best replicates the average cumulative default rates. Indeed, assuming

TABLE 8.2

Average Cumulative Default Rates (Percent)

Term	1	2	3	4	5	7	10	15
AAA	0.00	0.00	0.07	0.15	0.24	0.66	1.40	1.40
AA	0.00	0.02	0.12	0.25	0.43	0.89	1.29	1.48
A	0.06	0.16	0.27	0.44	0.67	1.12	2.17	3.00
BBB	0.18	0.44	0.72	1.27	1.78	2.99	4.34	4.70
BB	1.06	3.48	6.12	8.68	10.97	14.46	17.73	19.91
B	5.20	11.00	15.95	19.40	21.88	25.14	29.02	30.65
CCC	19.79	26.92	31.63	35.97	40.15	42.64	45.10	45.10

Source: Standard & Poor's *CreditWeek* (April 15, 1996).

FIGURE 8.4

Average Cumulative Default Rates (%) by Rating

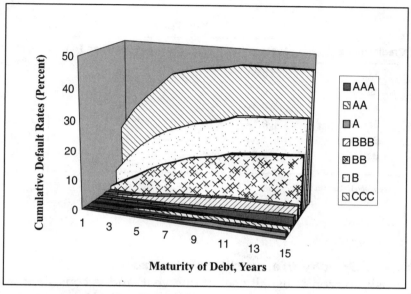

Source: Standard & Poor's *CreditWeek* (April 15, 1996).

that the process for default is Markovian and stationary, then multiplying the one-year transition matrix n times generates the n-year matrix. The n-year default probabilities are simply the values in the last default column of the transition matrix, and should match the column in year n of Table 8.2.[6]

The realized transition and default probabilities vary quite substantially over the years, depending upon whether the economy is in recession or is expanding (Figure 8.1). When implementing a model that relies on transition probabilities, one may have to adjust the average historical values, as shown in Table 8.1, to be consistent with one's assessment of the current economic environment. A study provided by Moody's (Carty and Lieberman, 1996) provides historical default statistics, both the mean and standard deviation, by rating category for the population of obligors that they rated during the period 1970 to 1995 (Table 8.3).

TABLE 8.3

One-Year Default Rates by Rating, 1970–1995

Credit Rating	One-Year Default Rate	
	Average (%)	Standard Deviation (%)
Aaa	0.00	0.0
Aa	0.03	0.1
A	0.01	0.0
Baa	0.13	0.3
Ba	1.42	1.3
B	7.62	5.1

Source: Carty and Lieberman (1996).

Step 2: Specify the credit risk horizon

The risk horizon is usually set at one year, and is consistent with the transition matrix shown in Table 8.1. But this horizon is arbitrary, and is mostly dictated by the availability of the accounting data and the financial reports processed by the rating agencies. In KMV's framework, which relies on market data as well as accounting data, any horizon can be chosen—from a few days to several years. Indeed, market data can be updated daily; it is assumed that the other characteristics of the borrowers remain constant (until new information for these, too, becomes available).

Step 3: Specify the forward pricing model

The valuation of a bond is derived from the zero curve corresponding to the rating of the issuer. Since there are seven possible credit qualities, seven "spread" curves are required to price the bond in all possible states. All obligors within the same rating class are then marked-to-market using the same curve. The spot zero curve is used to determine the current spot value of the bond. The forward price of the bond one year from the present is derived from the forward zero curve, one year ahead, which is then applied to the residual

TABLE 8.4

One-Year Forward Zero Curves for Each
Credit Rating (%)

Category	Year 1	Year 2	Year 3	Year 4
AAA	3.60	4.17	4.73	5.12
AA	3.65	4.22	4.78	5.17
A	3.72	4.32	4.93	5.32
BBB	4.10	4.67	5.25	5.63
BB	5.55	6.02	6.78	7.27
B	6.05	7.02	8.03	8.52
CCC	15.05	15.02	14.03	13.52

Source: CreditMetrics, JP Morgan.

cash flows from year 1 to the maturity of the bond. Table 8.4 gives
the one-year forward zero curves for each credit rating.

   Empirical evidence shows that for high-grade investment
bonds, the spreads tend to increase with time to maturity, while for
low-grade bonds (e.g., CCCs) the spread tends to be wider at the
short end of the curve than at the long end, as shown in Figure 8.5.

FIGURE 8.5

Spread Curves for Different Credit Qualities

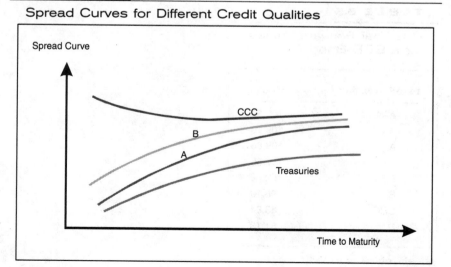

If the obligor remains rated BBB, the one-year forward price, V_{BBB}, of the five-year, 6 percent coupon bond (Box 8.1) is:

B O X   8.1

$$V_{BBB} = 6 + \frac{6}{1.041} + \frac{6}{(1.0467)^2} + \frac{6}{(1.0525)^3} + \frac{106}{(1.0563)^4} = 107.55$$

where the discount rates are taken from Table 8.4.

If we replicate the same calculations for each rating category, we obtain the values shown in Table 8.5.[7]

We do not assume that everything is lost if the issuer defaults at the end of the year. Depending on the seniority of the instrument, a recovery rate of par value is recuperated by the investor.

T A B L E   8.5

One-Year Forward Values
for a BBB Bond

Year-End Rating	Value ($)
AAA	109.37
AA	109.19
A	108.66
BBB	107.55
BB	102.02
B	98.10
CCC	83.64
Default	51.13

Source: CreditMetrics, JP Morgan.

TABLE 8.6

Recovery Rates by Seniority Class (Percent of Face Value, i.e., "Par")

Seniority Class	Mean (%)	Standard Deviation (%)
Senior Secured	53.80	26.86
Senior Unsecured	51.13	25.45
Senior Subordinated	38.52	23.81
Subordinated	32.74	20.18
Junior Subordinated	17.09	10.90

Source: Carty and Lieberman (1996).

These recovery rates are estimated from historical data by the rating agencies. Table 8.6 shows the expected recovery rates for bonds by different seniority classes as estimated by Moody's.[8] In our example the recovery rate for senior unsecured debt is estimated to be 51.13 percent, although the estimation error is quite large (s.d. = 25.45 percent) and the actual value lies in a fairly large confidence interval.

When the loss distribution is derived from a Monte Carlo simulation, it is generally assumed that the recovery rates are distributed according to a beta distribution with the same mean and standard deviation as shown in Table 8.6.

Step 4: Derive the forward distribution of the changes in portfolio value

The distribution of the changes in the bond value, at the one-year horizon, due to an eventual change in credit quality is shown Table 8.7 and Figure 8.6.

This distribution exhibits a long "downside tail." The first percentile of the distribution of ΔV, which corresponds to credit VaR at the 99 percent confidence level, is −23.91. It is a much lower value than if we computed the first percentile assuming a normal distribution for ΔV. In that case credit VaR at the 99 percent confidence level would be only −7.43.[9]

TABLE 8.7

Distribution of the Bond Values, and Changes in Value of a
BBB Bond, in One Year

Year-End Rating	Probability of State: p (%)	Forward Price: V ($)	Change in Value: ΔV ($)
AAA	0.02	109.37	1.82
AA	0.33	109.19	1.64
A	5.95	108.66	1.11
BBB	86.93	107.55	0
BB	5.30	102.02	−5.53
B	1.17	98.10	−9.45
CCC	0.12	83.64	−23.91
Default	0.18	51.13	−56.42

Source: CreditMetrics, JP Morgan.

4. CREDIT VAR FOR A LOAN OR BOND PORTFOLIO (BUILDING BLOCK 2)

First, consider a portfolio composed of two bonds with an initial rating of BB and A, respectively. Given the transition matrix shown in Table 8.1, and assuming no correlation between changes in credit quality, we can then derive easily the joint migration probabilities shown in Table 8.8. Each entry is simply the product of the transition probabilities for each obligor. For example, the joint probability that obligor 1 and obligor 2 will stay in the same rating class is the product of the probability of bond A remaining at its current rating at the end of the year, 91.05 percent, and the probability of bond BB remaining as BB, 80.53 percent:

$$73.32\% = 80.53\% \times 91.05\%$$

Unfortunately, when we need to assess the diversification effect on a large loan or bond portfolio, this table is not very useful in practice. In reality, the correlations between the changes in credit quality are not zero. And it will be shown in Section 5 that the overall credit VaR is quite sensitive to these correlations. Their accurate estimation is therefore one of the key determinants of portfolio optimization.

FIGURE 8.6

Histogram of the One-Year Forward Prices and Changes in Value of a BBB Bond

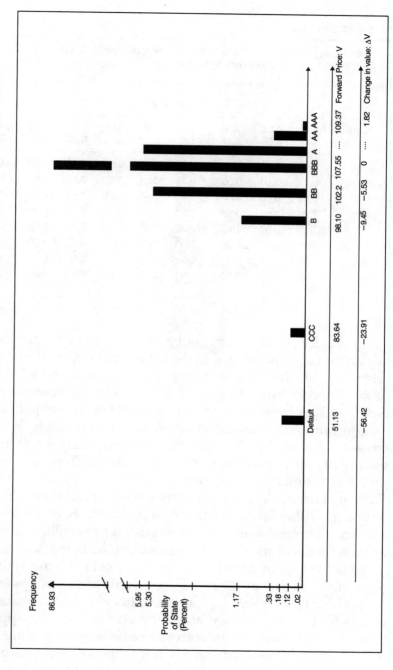

TABLE 8.8

Joint Migration Probabilities (Percent) with Zero Correlation for Two Issuers Rated BB and A

		Obligor 2							
Obligor 1 (BB)		AAA 0.09	AA 2.27	A 91.05	BBB 5.52	BB 0.74	B 0.26	CCC 0.01	Default 0.06
AAA	0.03	0.00	0.00	0.03	0.00	0.00	0.00	0.00	0.00
AA	0.14	0.00	0.00	0.13	0.01	0.00	0.00	0.00	0.00
A	0.67	0.00	0.02	0.61	0.40	0.00	0.00	0.00	0.00
BBB	7.73	0.01	0.18	7.04	0.43	0.06	0.02	0.00	0.00
BB	80.53	0.07	1.83	73.32	4.45	0.60	0.20	0.01	0.05
B	8.84	0.01	0.20	8.05	0.49	0.07	0.02	0.00	0.00
CCC	1.00	0.00	0.02	0.91	0.06	0.01	0.00	0.00	0.00
Default	1.06	0.00	0.02	0.97	0.06	0.01	0.00	0.00	0.00

Default correlations might be expected to be higher for firms within the same industry or in the same region than for firms in unrelated sectors. In addition, correlations vary with the relative state of the economy in the business cycle. If there is a slowdown in the economy, or a recession, most of the assets of the obligors will decline in value and quality, and the likelihood of multiple defaults increases substantially. The opposite happens when the economy is performing well: default correlations go down. Thus, we cannot expect default and migration probabilities to stay stationary over time. There is clearly a need for a structural model that relates changes in default probabilities to fundamental variables. Both CreditMetrics and KMV derive the default and migration probabilities from a correlation model of the firm's assets, as detailed in the next chapter.

For the sake of simplicity, CreditMetrics makes use of the stock price of a firm as a proxy for its asset value as the true asset value is not directly observable. (This is another simplifying assumption in CreditMetrics that may affect the accuracy of the approach.) CreditMetrics estimates the correlations between the equity returns of various obligors, and then it infers the correlations between changes in credit quality directly from the joint distribution of these equity returns.

TABLE 8.9

Balance Sheet of Merton's Firm

	Assets	Liabilities/ Equity	
	Risky Assets: V_t	Debt:	$B_t(F)$
		Equity:	S_t
Total:	V_t		V_t

The theoretical framework underlying all this is the option pricing approach to the valuation of corporate securities first developed by Merton (1974). The basic model is presented in Appendix 1 of this chapter, and it is described in detail in Chapter 9 as it forms the basis for the KMV approach. In Merton's model, the firm is assumed to have a very simple capital structure; it is financed by equity, S_t, and a single zero-coupon debt instrument maturing at time T, with face value F, and current market value B_t. The firm's balance sheet is represented in Table 8.9, where V_t is the value of all the assets, and $V_t = B_t(F) + S_t$.

In this framework, default occurs at the maturity of the debt obligation only when the value of assets is less than the promised payment, F, to the bondholders. Figure 8.7 shows the distribution of the assets' value at time T, the maturity of the zero-coupon debt, and the probability of default (i.e., the shaded area on the left-hand side of the default point, F).

Merton's model is extended by CreditMetrics to include changes in credit quality as illustrated in Figure 8.8. This generalization consists of slicing the distribution of asset returns into bands in such a way that, if we draw randomly from this distribution, we reproduce exactly the migration frequencies as shown in the transition matrices that we discussed earlier.

Figure 8.8 shows the distribution of the normalized assets' rates of return, one year ahead. The distribution is normal with a mean of zero and a variance of 1. The credit rating "thresholds" correspond to the transition probabilities in Table 8.10 for a BB-rated obligor. The right tail of the distribution, down to Z_{AAA}, corresponds to the probability that the obligor will be upgraded

FIGURE 8.7

Distribution of the Firm's Asset Value at Maturity of the Debt Obligation

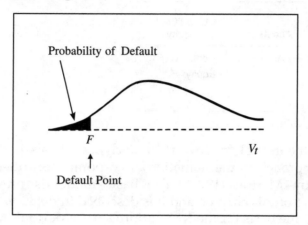

FIGURE 8.8

Generalization of the Merton Model to Include Rating Changes

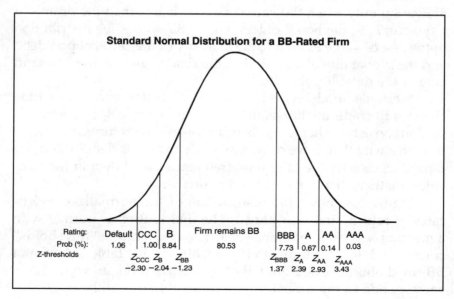

TABLE 8.10

Transition Probabilities and Credit Quality Thresholds for BB and A Rated Obligors

Rating in One Year	A Rated Obligor		BB Rated Obligor	
	Probabilities (%)	Thresholds: Z (σ)	Probabilities (%)	Thresholds: Z (σ)
AAA	0.09	3.12	0.03	3.43
AA	2.27	1.98	0.14	2.93
A	91.05	−1.51	0.67	2.39
BBB	5.52	−2.30	7.73	1.37
BB	0.74	−2.72	80.53	−1.23
B	0.26	−3.19	8.84	−2.04
CCC	0.01	−3.24	1.00	−2.30
Default	0.06		1.06	

from BB to AAA, i.e., 0.03 percent. Then, the area between Z_{AA} and Z_{AAA} corresponds to the probability of being upgraded from BB to AA, etc. The left tail of the distribution, on the left-hand side of Z_{CCC}, corresponds to the probability of default, i.e., 1.06 percent.

Table 8.10 shows the transition probabilities for two obligors rated BB and A, respectively, and the corresponding credit quality thresholds. The thresholds are given in terms of normalized standard deviations. For example, for a BB rated obligor the default threshold is −2.30 standard deviations from the mean rate of return.

This generalization of Merton's model is quite easy to implement. It assumes that the normalized log-returns over any period of time are normally distributed with a mean of 0 and a variance of 1, and that the distribution is the same for all obligors within the same rating category.

If Prob(Def) denotes the probability of the BB rated obligor defaulting, then the critical asset value V_{Def} is such that:

$$\text{Prob(Def)} = \text{Prob}[V_t \le V_{Def}]$$

which can be translated into a normalized threshold Z_{CCC}, such that the area in the left tail below Z_{CCC} is Prob(Def).[10] Z_{CCC} is simply the threshold point in the standard normal distribution, $N(0,1)$, corresponding to a cumulative probability of Prob(Def). Then, based on the option pricing model, the critical asset value V_{Def} which triggers default is such that $Z_{\text{CCC}} = -d_2$. This critical asset value is also called the "default point."[11]

Note that only the threshold levels are necessary to derive the joint migration probabilities, and these can be calculated without it being necessary to observe the asset value, and to estimate its mean and variance. To derive the critical asset value V_{Def} we only need to estimate the expected asset return μ and asset volatility σ. Accordingly, Z_B is the threshold point corresponding to a cumulative probability of being either in default or in rating CCC, i.e., Prob(Def) + Prob(CCC), etc.

We mentioned above that, as asset returns are not directly observable, CreditMetrics makes use of equity returns as their proxy. Yet using equity returns in this way is equivalent to assuming that all the firm's activities are financed by means of equity. This is a major drawback of the approach, especially when it is being applied to highly leveraged companies. For those companies, equity returns are substantially more volatile, and possibly less stationary, than the volatility of the firm's assets.

Now, assume that the correlation between the assets' rates of return is known, and is denoted by ρ, which is assumed to be equal to 0.20 in our example. The normalized log-returns on both assets follow a joint normal distribution, as described in Appendix 1. We can then compute the probability for both obligors of being in any particular combination of ratings. For example, we can compute the probability that they will remain in the same rating classes, i.e., BB and A, respectively:

$$\text{Prob}(-1.23 < r_{\text{BB}} < 1.37, -1.51 < r_A < 1.98) = 0.7365$$

where r_{BB} and r_A are the instantaneous rates of return on the assets of obligors BB and A, respectively. If we implement the same procedure for the other 63 combinations, we obtain Table 8.11. We can now compare Table 8.11 with Table 8.8, which was derived under the assumption that there was zero correlation between the companies. Notice that the joint probabilities are different.

Figure 8.9 illustrates the effect of asset return correlation on the joint default probability for the rated BB and A obligors. If the prob-

TABLE 8.11

Joint Rating Probabilities (Percent) for BB and A Rated Obligors When Correlation Between Asset Returns is 20 Percent

Rating of First Company (BB)	Rating of Second Company (A)								
	AAA	AA	A	BBB	BB	B	CCC	Def	Total
AAA	0.00	0.00	0.03	0.00	0.00	0.00	0.00	0.00	0.03
AA	0.00	0.01	0.13	0.00	0.00	0.00	0.00	0.00	0.14
A	0.00	0.04	0.61	0.01	0.00	0.00	0.00	0.00	0.67
BBB	0.02	0.35	7.10	0.20	0.02	0.01	0.00	0.00	7.69
BB	0.07	1.79	73.65	4.24	0.56	0.18	0.01	0.04	80.53
B	0.00	0.08	7.80	0.79	0.13	0.05	0.00	0.01	8.87
CCC	0.00	0.01	0.85	0.11	0.02	0.01	0.00	0.00	1.00
Def	0.00	0.01	0.90	0.13	0.02	0.01	0.00	0.00	1.07
Total	0.09	2.29	91.06	5.48	0.75	0.26	0.01	0.06	100

Source: CreditMetrics, JP Morgan.

abilities of default for obligors rated A and BB are Prob(DefA) = 0.06 percent and Prob(DefBB) = 1.06 percent, respectively, and the correlation coefficient between the rates of return on the two assets is ρ = 20 percent, it can be shown that the joint probability of default is:

$$Prob(DefA, DefBB) = 0.0054\%$$

The correlation coefficient between the two default events is:[12]

$$corr(DefA, DefBB) = 1.9\%$$

Asset returns correlations are approximatively 10 times larger than default correlations for asset correlations in the range of 20 to 60 percent. This shows that the joint probability of default is in fact quite sensitive to pair-wise asset return correlations, and it illustrates how important it is to estimate these data correctly if one is to assess the diversification effect within a portfolio. In Section 5 we show that, for the benchmark portfolio we selected for the comparison of credit models, the impact of correlations on credit VaR is quite large. It is larger for portfolios with relatively low-grade credit quality than it is for high-grade portfolios. Indeed, as the

FIGURE 8.9

Probability of Joint Defaults as a Function of Asset
Return Correlation

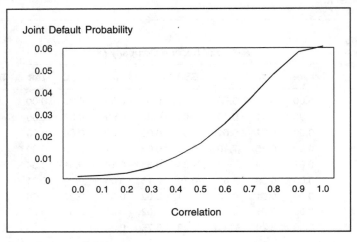

Source: CreditMetrics, JP Morgan.

credit quality of the portfolio deteriorates and the expected number of defaults increases, this number is magnified by an increase
in default correlations. (The statistical procedure employed to
estimate asset return correlations is discussed in the next chapter.[13])

5. ANALYSIS OF CREDIT DIVERSIFICATION (BUILDING BLOCK 2, CONTINUATION)

The analytic approach that we sketched out above for a portfolio
with bonds issued by two obligors is not practicable for large portfolios. Instead, CreditMetrics implements a Monte Carlo simulation to generate the full distribution of the portfolio values at the
credit horizon of one year. The following steps are necessary:

- Derivation of the asset return thresholds for each rating
  category.
- Estimation of the correlation between each pair of
  obligors' asset returns.

- Generation of asset return scenarios according to their joint normal distribution. A standard technique that is often used to generate correlated normal variables is the Cholesky decomposition.[14] Each scenario is characterized by n standardized asset returns, one for each of the n obligors in the portfolio.
- For each scenario, and for each obligor, the standardized asset return is mapped into the corresponding rating, according to the threshold levels derived in step 1.
- Given the spread curves, which apply for each rating, the portfolio is revalued.
- Repeat the procedure a large number of times, say 100,000 times, and plot the distribution of the portfolio values to obtain a graph (which will look like Figure 8.2).

Then, we can derive the percentiles of the distribution of the future values of the portfolio.

6. CREDIT VAR AND CALCULATION OF THE CAPITAL CHARGE

Economic capital is the financial cushion that a bank uses to absorb unexpected losses, e.g., those related to credit events such as credit migration and/or default. Figure 8.10 illustrates how the capital charge related to credit risk can be derived:

$P(c)$ = value of the portfolio in the worst case scenario at the $(I-c)\%$ confidence level

FV = forward value of the portfolio = $V_0 (1+ PR)$

V_0 = current mark-to-market value of the portfolio

PR = promised return on the portfolio[15]

EV = expected value of the portfolio = $V_0 (1+ ER)$

ER = expected return on the portfolio

EL = expected loss = FV − EV

The expected loss does not contribute to the capital allocation. Instead, funds equivalent to the expected loss are held in the bank's reserves and the expected loss figure is imputed as a cost into any risk-adjusted return on capital (RAROC) calculation that the bank

FIGURE 8.10

Credit VaR and Calculation of Economic Capital

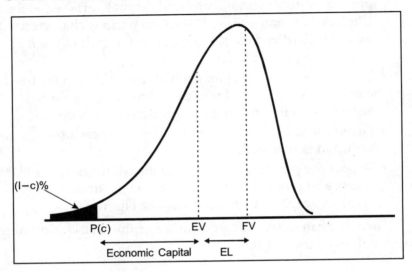

wishes to perform.[16] The capital charge is instead a function of the unexpected losses:

$$\text{Capital} = EV - P(c)$$

The bank should hold reserves against these unexpected losses at a given confidence level, say, 1 percent, so that there is only a probability of 1 percent that the bank will incur losses above the capital level over the period corresponding to the credit risk horizon, say, one year.

7. CREDITMETRICS AS A LOAN/BOND PORTFOLIO MANAGEMENT TOOL: MARGINAL RISK MEASURES (BUILDING BLOCK 2, CONTINUATION)

In addition to the overall credit VaR analysis for the portfolio, CreditMetrics offers the interesting feature of isolating the individual marginal risk contributions to the portfolio. For example, for each asset, CreditMetrics calculates the marginal standard deviation, i.e., the impact of each individual asset on the overall portfolio standard deviation. By comparing the marginal standard deviation to the stand-alone

FIGURE 8.11

Risk versus Size of Exposures within a Typical
Credit Portfolio

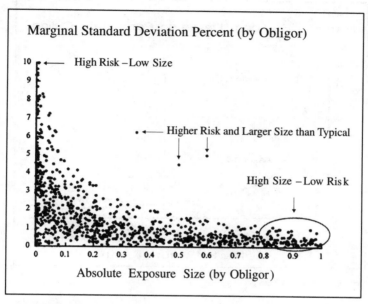

Source: CreditMetrics, JP Morgan.

standard deviation for each loan, one can assess the extent of the benefit derived from portfolio diversification when adding the instrument in the portfolio. Figure 8.11 shows the marginal standard deviation for each asset, expressed as a percentage of the overall standard deviation, plotted against the marked-to-market value of the instrument.

This is an important proactive risk management tool, as it allows one to identify trading opportunities in the loan/bond portfolio where concentration, and as a consequence overall risk, can be reduced without affecting expected profits. Obviously, for this framework to become fully operational it needs to be complemented by a RAROC model that provides information on the adjusted return on capital for each deal.[17]

The same framework can also be used to set up credit risk limits and monitor credit risk exposures in terms of the joint combination of market value and marginal standard deviation, as shown in Figure 8.12.

FIGURE 8.12

Possible Risk Limits for an Example Portfolio

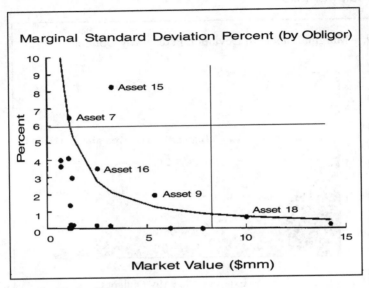

Source: CreditMetrics, JP Morgan.

8. ESTIMATION OF ASSET CORRELATIONS (BUILDING BLOCK 3)

As we discussed above, default correlations are derived from asset returns correlations, which in turn are proxied by equity returns correlations. For a large portfolio of bonds and loans, with thousands of obligors, this still requires the computation of a huge correlation matrix for each pair of obligors.

To reduce the dimensionality of this estimation problem, CreditMetrics uses multifactor analysis. This approach maps each obligor to the countries and industries that are most likely to determine its performance. Equity returns are correlated to the extent that firms are exposed to the same industries and countries. To implement CreditMetrics, the user specifies the industry and country weights for each obligor, as well as the "firm specific risk," which is idiosyncratic to each obligor and is not correlated to any other obligor or to any index.[18]

9. EXPOSURES (BUILDING BLOCK 4)

The term "exposures" in the CreditMetrics methodology is somewhat misleading since, in fact, the approach assumes that market risk factors are constant. So the "exposures" building block is, in fact, simply the term CreditMetrics gives to the use of the forward pricing model applied to each credit rating. For bond-type products such as bonds, loans, receivables, commitments to lend, and letters of credit, "exposure" simply relates to the future cash flows at risk beyond the one-year horizon. The forward pricing is derived from the present value model using the forward yield curve for the corresponding credit quality. The example presented in Section 2 illustrated how the exposure distribution is calculated for a bond.

For derivatives, such as swaps and forwards, the exposure is conditional on future interest rates. For these instruments, there is no simple way to derive the future cash flows at risk without making assumptions about the dynamics of interest rates.

The position is complicated because the risk exposure for a derivative is dynamic. For example, the credit risk exposure of a swap can be positive (if the swap is in-the-money for the bank) or negative (if it is out-of-the money). In the latter case, the swap is a liability to the bank and the swap counterparty is the only party to suffer credit risk. Figure 8.13 shows the average and maximum exposure profiles of an interest rate swap as a function of time, assuming no change in the credit ratings of the counterparty or the bank. The bank is at risk only when the exposure is positive.

CreditMetrics assumes as given the average exposure of a swap, which is supposed to have been derived from an external model. In CreditMetrics, as the interest rates are deterministic, the calculation of the forward price distribution relies on an ad hoc procedure:

Value of swap in one year, in rating R
    = Forward risk-free value in one year − $\qquad$ (1)

   expected loss in years one to maturity for the given rating R
where
    Expected loss in years 1 to maturity for the given rating R
        = average exposure from year 1 to maturity *
    Probability of default in years 1 through maturity for the
        given rating R * (1 − recovery rate) (2)

FIGURE 8.13

Risk Exposure of an Interest Rate Swap

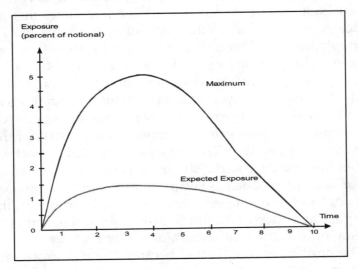

The forward risk-free value of the swap is calculated by discounting the future net cash flows of the swap, based on the forward curve, using the forward yield curve for government instruments. This value is the same for all credit ratings.

The probability of default from year 1 through until maturity can be either taken directly from Moody's or Standard & Poor's, or can be derived from the transition matrix (as we discussed earlier). The recovery rate is taken from statistical analyses provided by the rating agencies.

Obviously, this ad hoc calculation of the exposure of an interest rate swap is not satisfactory. Only a model that makes use of stochastic interest rates will allow a proper treatment of exposure calculations for swaps and other derivative securities.

10. CONDITIONAL TRANSITION PROBABILITIES: CREDITPORTFOLIOVIEW[19]

CreditPortfolioView is a multifactor model that is used to simulate the joint conditional distribution of default and migration probabilities for various rating groups in different industries, and for each country, conditional on the value of macroeconomic factors. CreditPortfolioView is based on the observation that default probabilities and credit migration probabilities are linked to the economy. When the economy worsens, both downgrades and defaults increase; when the economy becomes stronger, the contrary holds true. In other words, credit cycles follow business cycles closely.

Since the shape of the economy is, to a large extent, driven by macroeconomic factors, CreditPortfolioView proposes a methodology to link those macroeconomic factors to default and migration probabilities. It employs the values of macroeconomic factors such as the unemployment rate, the rate of growth in gross domestic product (GDP), the level of long-term interest rates, foreign exchange rates, government expenditures, and the aggregate savings rate.

Provided that data are available, this methodology can be applied in each country to various sectors and various classes of obligors that react differently during the business cycle—sectors such as construction, financial institutions, agriculture, services, etc. It applies better to speculative-grade obligors, whose default probabilities vary substantially with the credit cycle, than to investment-grade obligors, whose default probabilites are more stable.

Default probabilities are modeled as a logit function, whereby the independent variable is a country-specific index that depends upon current and lagged macroeconomic variables as described below:

$$\text{Prob}_{j,t} = \frac{1}{1 + e^{-Y_{j,t}}} \tag{3}$$

where $\text{Prob}_{j,t}$ is the conditional probability of default in period t, for speculative-grade obligors in country/industry j, and $Y_{j,t}$ is the country index value derived from a multifactor model described in Appendix 2. Note that the logit transformation (3) ensures that the probability takes a value between 0 and 1.

In order to derive the conditional transition matrix, we employ the (unconditional Markov) transition matrix based on Moody's or Standard & Poor's historical data, which we denote by ϕM. Transition probabilities are unconditional in the sense that they are historical averages based on more than 20 years of data covering several business cycles, across many different countries and industries.

As we discussed earlier, default probabilities for non-investment-grade obligors are higher than average during a period of recession. Also credit downgrades increase, while upward migrations decrease. It is the opposite during a period of economic expansion. We can express this in the following way:

$$\frac{SDP_t}{\phi SDP} > 1 \text{ in economic recession} \tag{4}$$

$$\frac{SDP_t}{\phi SDP} < 1 \text{ in economic expansion}$$

where SDP_t is the simulated default probability for a speculative-grade obligor, based on equation (3), and ϕSDP_t is the unconditional (historical average) probability of default for a speculative-grade obligor.

CreditPortfolioView proposes to use these ratios (4) to adjust the migration probabilities in ϕM in order to produce a transition matrix, M, conditional on the state of the economy:

$$M_t = M(Prob_{j,t}/\phi SDP)$$

where the adjustment consists in shifting the probability mass into downgraded and defaulted states when the ratio $Prob_{j,t}/\phi SDP$ is greater than 1, and vice versa if the ratio is less than 1. Since one can simulate $Prob_{j,t}$ over any time horizon $t=1, \ldots, T$, this approach can generate multiperiod transition matrices:

$$M_T = \prod_{t=1,\ldots,T} M(Prob_{j,t}/\phi SDP) \tag{5}$$

One can simulate the transition matrix (5) many times to generate the distribution of the cumulative conditional default probability for any rating, over any time period, as shown Figure 8.14. The same Monte Carlo methodology can be used to produce the conditional cumulative distributions of migration probabilities over any time horizon.

KMV, described in Chapter 9, and CreditPortfolioView base their approach on the same empirical observation that default and migration probabilities vary over time. KMV adopts a microeconomic approach that relates the probability of default of any obligor to the market value of its assets. CreditPortfolioView proposes a methodology that links macroeconomic factors to default and migration probabilities. The calibration of CreditPortfolioView thus requires reliable default data for each country, and possibly for each industry sector within each country.

FIGURE 8.14

Distribution of the Conditional Default Probability, for a Given Rating, over a Given Time Horizon, T

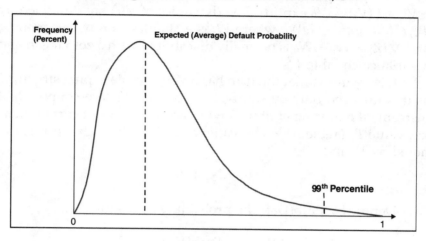

Another limitation of the model is the ad hoc procedure to adjust the migration matrix. It is not clear that the proposed methodology performs better than a simple Bayesian model, where the revision of the transition probabilities would be based on the internal expertise accumulated by the credit department of the bank and an internal appreciation of the current stage of the credit cycle (given the quality of the bank's credit portfolio). These two approaches are somewhat related since the market value of the firm's assets depends on the shape of the economy; an interesting avenue of future research would be to compare the transition matrices produced by both models.

APPENDIX 1: ELEMENTS OF MERTON'S MODEL

In this appendix we provide the basis of Merton's (1974) model of a firm's debt, as applied by CreditMetrics. Additional developments of the Merton model are presented in Chapter 9.

The firm's assets value, V_t, is assumed to follow a standard geometric Brownian motion, i.e:

$$V_t = V_0 \exp\left\{\left(\mu - \frac{\sigma^2}{2}\right)t + \sigma\sqrt{t}Z_t\right\} \qquad (1)$$

with $Z_t \sim N(0,1)$, μ and σ^2 being, respectively, the mean and variance of the instantaneous rate of return on the assets of the firm, dV_t/V_t. V_t is log-normally distributed with expected value at time t, $\overline{V}_t = E(V_t) = V_0 \exp\{\mu t\}$. The dynamics of $V(t)$ are described by $dV_t/V_t = \mu dt + \sigma dW_t$, where W_t is a standard Brownian motion, and $\sqrt{t}Z_t \equiv W_t - W_0$ is normally distributed with a zero mean and a variance equal to t.[20]

It is assumed that the firm has a very simple capital structure, as it is financed only by equity, S_t, and a single zero-coupon debt instrument maturing at time T, with face value F, and current market value B_t (Table 8.9). The value of the assets of the firm is denoted by V_t and:

$$V_t \equiv S_t + B_t$$

Denote by Prob(Def) the probability of default, i.e.:

$$\text{Prob(Def)} = \text{Prob}[V_t \leq V_{\text{Def}}]$$

where V_{Def} is the critical asset value below which default occurs. According to (1), default occurs when Z_t satisfies:

$$\text{Prob(Def)} = \text{Prob}\left[\frac{\ln\left(\frac{V_{\text{Def}}}{V_0}\right) - \left(\mu - \frac{\sigma^2}{2}\right)t}{\sigma\sqrt{t}} > Z_t \right] \tag{2}$$

$$= \text{Prob}\left[Z_t \leq - \frac{\ln\left[\frac{V_0}{V_{\text{Def}}}\right] + \left[\frac{\mu - \sigma^2}{2}\right]t}{\sigma\sqrt{t}} \right] = N(-d_2)$$

where the normalized return:

$$r = \frac{\ln\left(\frac{V_t}{V_0}\right) - \left(\mu - \frac{\sigma^2}{2}\right)t}{\sigma\sqrt{t}} \tag{3}$$

is $N[0,1]$. Z_{CCC} is simply the threshold point in the standard normal distribution, $N(0,1)$, corresponding to a cumulative probability of $Prob_{Def}$. Then, the critical asset value V_{Def} which triggers default is such that $Z_{CCC} = -d_2$ where:

$$
d_2 = \frac{\ln(\frac{V_0}{V_{Def}}) + (\mu - \frac{\sigma^2}{2})t}{\sigma\sqrt{t}}
\tag{4}
$$

and is also called "distance to default."[21]

If we denote by r_{BB} and r_A the instantaneous rates of return on the assets of obligors that are rated BB and A, respectively, and by ρ the instantaneous correlation coefficient between r_A and r_{BB}, then the normalized log-returns on both assets follow a joint normal distribution:

$$
f(r_{BB}, r_A; \rho) = \frac{1}{2\pi\sqrt{1 - \rho^2}} \exp\left\{\frac{-1}{2(1 - \rho^2)}[r_{BB}^2 - 2\rho r_{BB} r_A + r_A^2]\right\}
$$

This joint normal distribution is useful in calculating the joint-migration matrix for the two obligors initially rated A and BB. Consider two obligors whose probabilities of default are $Prob(Def_A)$ and $Prob(Def_{BB})$, respectively. Their asset return correlation is ρ. The events of default for obligors A and BB are denoted Def_A and Def_{BB}, respectively, and $Prob(Def_A, Def_{BB})$ is the joint probability of default. Then, it can be shown that the default correlation is:[22]

$$
corr(Def_A, Def_{BB}) =
\tag{5}
$$

$$
\frac{Prob(Def_A, Def_{BB}) - Prob(Def_A)\, Prob(Def_{BB})}{\sqrt{Prob(Def_A)[1 - Prob(Def_A)]Prob(Def_{BB})[1 - Prob(Def_{BB})]}}
$$

The joint probability of both obligors defaulting is, according to Merton's model:

$$
Prob(Def_A, Def_{BB}) = Prob[V_A \le V_{DefA}, V_{AB} \le V_{Def\,BB}]
\tag{6}
$$

where V_A and V_{BB} denote the asset values for both obligors at time t, and V_{DefA} and V_{DefBB} are the corresponding critical values that trigger default. Expression (6) is equivalent to:

$$
Prob(Def_A, Def_{BB}) = Prob[r_A \le d_2^A, r_2 \le d_2^{BB}] = N_2(-d_2^A, -d_2^{BB}, \rho)
\tag{7}
$$

where r_A and r_{BB} denote the normalized asset returns as defined in (3) for obligors A and BB, respectively, and d_2^A and d_2^{BB} are the corresponding distant to default as in (4). $N_2(x, y, \rho)$ denotes the cumulative standard bivariate normal distribution where ρ is the correlation coefficient between x and y.

APPENDIX 2: DEFAULT PREDICTION— THE ECONOMETRIC MODEL

Default probabilities are modeled as a logit function as follows:

$$Prob_{j,t} = \frac{1}{1 + e^{-Y_{j,t}}} \tag{1}$$

where $Prob_{j,t}$ is the conditional probability of default in period t, for speculative-grade obligors in country/industry j. $Y_{j,t}$ is the index value derived from a multifactor model described below. Note that the logit transformation ensures that the probability (1) takes a value between 0 and 1.

The macroeconomic index, which captures the state of the economy in each country, is determined by the following multifactor model:

$$Y_{j,t} = \beta_{j,0} + \beta_{j,1}X_{j,1,t} + \beta_{j,2}X_{j,2,t} + \ldots + \beta_{j,m}X_{j,m,t} + v_{j,t} \tag{2}$$

where $Y_{j,t}$ is the index value in period t for the jth country/industry/speculative grade; $\beta_{j,0}, \beta_{j,1}, \beta_{j,2}, \ldots, \beta_{j,m}$ are coefficients to be estimated for the jth country/industry/speculative grade; $X_{j,1,t}, X_{j,2,t}, \ldots, X_{j,m,t}$ are period t values of the macroeconomic variables for the jth country/industry; and $v_{j,t}$ is the error term assumed to be independent of $X_{j,t}$ and identically normally distributed.

The macroeconomic variables are specified for each country. When sufficient data are available, the model can be calibrated at the country/industry level. Both the probability of default, $P_{j,t}$, and the index, $Y_{j,t}$, are then defined at the country/industry level, and the coefficient, $\beta_{j,i}$ are calibrated accordingly.

In the proposed implementation, each macroeconomic variable is assumed to follow a univariate, autoregressive model of order 2 (AR2):

$$X_{j,i,t} = \gamma_{j,i,0} + \gamma_{j,i,1} X_{j,i,t-1} + \gamma_{j,i,2} X_{j,i,t-2} + e_{j,i,t} \tag{3}$$

where $X_{j,i,t-1}$, $X_{j,i,t-2}$ denote the lagged values of the macroeconomic variable $X_{j,i,t}$; $\gamma_j = (\gamma_{j,i,0}, \gamma_{j,i,1}, \gamma_{j,i,2})$ are coefficients to be estimated; $e_{j,i,t}$ is the error term assumed to be independent and identically distributed, i.e., $e_{j,i,t} \sim N(0, \sigma_{e_{j,i}})$ and $e_t \sim N(0, \Sigma_e)$, where e_t denotes the vector of stacked error terms $e_{j,i,t}$, of the $j \times i$ AR(2) equations and $\times \Sigma e$ is the $(j \times i)$ $(j \times i)$ covariance matrix of the error terms e_t.

To calibrate the default probability model defined by (1), (2), and (3), one has to solve the system:

$$\begin{cases} \text{Prob}_{j,t} = \dfrac{1}{1 + e^{-Y_{j,t}}} \\[2mm] Y_{j,t} = \beta_{j,0} + \beta_{j,i}X_{j,1,t} + \ldots + \beta_{j,m,t}X_{j,m,t} + v_{j,t} \\[2mm] X_{j,i,t} = \gamma_{j,i,0} + \gamma_{j,i,1}X_{j,i,t-1} + \gamma_{j,i,2}X_{j,i,t-2} + e_{j,i,t} \end{cases} \quad (4)$$

where the vector of innovations E_t is

$$E_t = \begin{bmatrix} v_t \\ e_t \end{bmatrix} \sim N(0, \Sigma)$$

with

$$\Sigma = \begin{bmatrix} \Sigma_v & \Sigma_{v,e} \\ \Sigma_{e,v} & \Sigma_e \end{bmatrix}$$

where $\Sigma_{v,e}$ and $\Sigma_{e,v}$ denote the cross-correlation matrices.

Once the system (4) has been calibrated, then one can use the Cholesky decomposition of Σ, i.e.:[23]

$$\Sigma = AA' \quad (5)$$

to simulate the distribution of speculative default probabilities. First, draw a vector of random variables Z_t, $\sim N(0,1)$ where each component is normally distributed $N(0,1)$. Then, calculate

$$E_t = A'Z_t$$

which is the stacked vector of error terms $v_{j,t}$ and $e_{j,i,t}$. Using these realizations of the error terms one can derive the corresponding values for $Y_{j,t}$ and $\text{Prob}_{j,t}$.

APPENDIX 3:TRANSITION MATRIX OVER A PERIOD OF LESS THAN ONE YEAR

Given a one-year transition matrix, for example, the matrix given in Table 8.1, how can we derive the corresponding transition matrix over a period of time that is shorter than one year? For example, a period of six months, a quarter, a month, or 10 days as is required for the reporting of regulatory capital supporting the trading account?

First, derive the eigen vectors $x_1, x_2, \ldots, x_n$ and the corresponding eigen values $\lambda_1, \lambda_2, \ldots, \lambda_n$ of the one-year transition matrix T, where N denotes the number of credit categories, e.g., eight in Moody's eight-state rating system. The eigen values and vectors satisfy the property:

$$Tx_i = \lambda_i x_i$$

Define X as the matrix of eigen vectors where the ith row is the transpose of x_i, and Λ is a diagonal matrix where the ith diagonal element is λ_i. A standard result in matrix algebra shows that:

$$T = X^{-1} \Lambda X$$

From this it is easy to see that the nth root of T, for example the 12th root for a monthly transition matrix, is:

$$T^{1/n} = X^{-1} \Lambda^{1/n} X$$

where $\Lambda^{1/n}$ is the diagonal matrix where the ith diagonal element is $\lambda_i^{1/n}$.

NOTES

1. Specific risk refers to idiosyncratic or credit risk. It is the risk of an adverse price movement due to idiosyncratic factors related to the individual issuer of a security.
2. See also Vasicek (1997).
3. In the case of a loan commitment, a corporate borrower has the option to draw down on its credit line. It is more likely to exercise this option when its credit standing is deteriorating.

4. CreditMetrics is a trademark of JP Morgan & Co., Inc. The technical document CreditMetrics (1997) provides a detailed exposition of the methodology, illustrated with numerical examples. CreditVaR is CIBC's proprietary credit value at risk model, which is part of CIBC's overall Credit Measurement Unit (CRMU) framework. The simple version implemented at CIBC, CreditVaR I, to capture specific risk for the trading book is based on the same principles as CreditMetrics. A more elaborate version, CreditVaR II, extends the CreditMetrics framework to allow for stochastic interest rates in order to address credit risk for derivatives including loan commitment and credit derivatives.

5. CreditMetrics' approach applies primarily to bonds and loans, which are both treated in the same manner. It can be easily extended to financial claims (such as receivables, financial letters of credit) for which we can derive the forward value at the risk horizon for all credit ratings. For derivatives such as swaps or forwards the model needs to be somewhat adjusted or "twisted," since there is no satisfactory way to derive the exposure, and the loss distribution, within the proposed framework (since it assumes deterministic interest rates).

6. In Appendix 3 we show how to derive from the one-year transition matrix a transition matrix over a period less than one year, e.g., one month.

7. CreditMetrics calculates the forward value of the bonds, or loans, including compounded coupons paid out during the year.

8. See Carty and Lieberman (1996). See also Altman and Kishore (1996, 1998) for similar statistics.

9. The mean, m, and the variance, σ^2, of the distribution for ΔV can be calculated from the data in Table 8.7 as follows:

$$m = \text{mean}(\Delta V) = \sum_i p_i \Delta V_i$$

$$=0.02\% \times 1.82 + 0.33\% \times 1.64 + \ldots + 0.18\% \times (-56.42)$$
$$= -0.46$$
$$\sigma^2 = var(\Delta V) = \sum_i p_i(\Delta V_i - m)^2$$

$$= 0.02\%(1.82 + 0.46)^2 + 0.33\%(1.64 + 0.46)^2 + \ldots + 0.18\%(-56.42 + 0.46)^2$$

$$= 8.95$$

and
$\sigma = 2.99$

The first percentile of a normal distribution $N(m, \sigma^2)$ is $m - 2.33\sigma$, i.e., -7.43.

10. See Appendix 1 for the derivation of the proof. In the next chapter we define the "distance to default" as the distance between the expected asset value and the default point.

11. Note that d_2 is different from its equivalent in the Black-Scholes formula since, here, we work with the "actual" instead of the "risk neutral" return distributions, so that the drift term in d_2 is the expected return on the firm's assets, instead of the risk-free interest rate as in Black-Scholes. See Chapter 1 for the definition of d_2 in Black-Scholes and Appendix 1 for d_2 in the above derivation.

12. The mathematical presentation of the joint probabilities and correlation of defaults is given in Appendix 1.

13. The correlation models for CreditMetrics and KMV are different. However, as the approaches are similar we detail only the more elaborate KMV model.

14. A good reference on Monte Carlo simulations and the Cholesky decomposition is Fishman (1997, p. 223).

15. If there were only one bond in the portfolio, PR would simply be the one-year spot rate on the corporate curve corresponding to the rating of the obligor.

16. See Chapter 14.

17. The RAROC concept will be presented and analyzed in Chapter 14.

18. See also KMV's correlation model, presented in the next chapter.

19. CreditPortfolioView is a risk measurement model developed by Tom Wilson (1997a, 1997b) and proposed by McKinsey & Company.

20. In fact the process for the market value of the firm should be written as

$$dV_t = (\mu V_t - C)dt + \sigma V_t dW_t$$

where C denotes the net dollar payout by the firm to shareholders and bondholders. Here, we assume that no dividend or coupon is paid out – debt is in the form of a zero coupon.

21. Note that d_2 is different from its equivalent in the Black-Scholes formula since, here, we work with the "actual" instead of the "risk neutral" return distributions, so that the drift term in d_2 is the expected return on the firm's assets, instead of the risk-free interest rate as in Black-Scholes.
22. See Lucas (1995).
23. See footnote 12.

The Contingent Claim Approach to Measuring Credit Risk

1. INTRODUCTION

The CreditMetrics approach to measuring credit risk, as described in Chapter 8, is rather appealing as a methodology. Unfortunately it has a major weakness: reliance on ratings transition probabilities that are based on average historical frequencies of defaults and credit migration.

As a result, the accuracy of CreditMetrics calculation depends upon two critical assumptions: first, that all firms within the same rating class have the same default rate and the same spread curve even when recovery rates differ among obligors; second, that the actual default rate is equal to the historical average default rate.

The same assumptions also apply to the other transition probabilities. In other words, credit rating changes and credit quality changes are taken to be identical, and credit rating and default rates are also synonymous, i.e., the rating changes when the default rate is adjusted, and vice versa.

This view has been strongly challenged (e.g., by researchers working for the consulting and software corporation KMV).[1] Indeed, these assumptions cannot be true since we know that default rates evolve continuously, while ratings are adjusted in a discrete fashion. (This lag is because rating agencies necessarily take time to upgrade or downgrade companies whose default risk has changed.)

KMV has shown through a simulation exercise that the historical average default rate and transition probabilities can deviate significantly from the actual rates. In addition, KMV has demonstrated that substantial differences in default rates may exist within the same bond rating class, and that the overlap in default probability ranges may be quite large; for instance, some bonds rated BBB and AA may in fact exhibit the same probability of default.

To illustrate this, KMV replicated 50,000 times, through a Monte Carlo simulation, Moody's study of default over a 25-year period.[2] For each rating they assumed a fixed number of obligors— approximately the same number as in the Moody's study. For each rating they assumed that the true probability of default was equal to the reported Moody's average default rate over the 25-year period. KMV also ran the simulation for several levels of correlation among the asset returns, ranging from 15 percent to 45 percent. A typical result is illustrated in Figure 9.1 for a BBB obligor. Given

FIGURE 9.1

Monte Carlo Simulated Distribution of Average Default Rate for a BBB Bond with a True Default Rate of 0.13 Percent

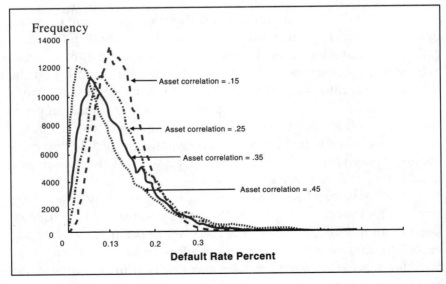

Source: KMV Corporation.

an exact default probability of 13 bp, the 25-year average historical default rate ranges between 4 bp and 27 bp at the 95 percent
confidence level, for an asset correlation of 15 percent.

The distribution is quite skewed, so that the mean or average
default rate usually exceeds the typical (median) default rate for
each credit class. Thus the average historical default probability
overstates the default rate for a typical obligor.[3]

What we will call the "structural" approach offers an alternative to the credit migration approach. Here, the economic value of
default is presented as a put option on the value of the firm's assets. The merit of this approach is that each case can be analyzed
individually based on its unique features. But this is also the principal drawback, since the information required for such an analysis is rarely available to the bank or the investor.

Various ways to implement the structural approach have
been proposed in the literature, all of which are consistent with
arbitrage-free pricing methodologies.[4] The option pricing model
approach, introduced by Merton (1974) in a seminal paper,[5] builds
on the limited liability rule which allows shareholders to default
on their obligations while they surrender the firm's assets to the
various stakeholders, according to prespecified priority rules. The
firm's liabilities are thus viewed as contingent claims issued against
the firm's assets, with the payoffs to the various debt holders completely specified by seniority and safety covenants. Default occurs
at debt maturity whenever the firm's asset value falls short of debt
value at that time. In this model, the loss rate is endogenously determined and depends on the firm's asset value, volatility, and the
default-free interest rate for the debt maturity.[6]

An alternative to this approach, proposed by Longstaff and
Schwartz (1995) and described in Appendix 3 of this chapter, allows bankruptcy to occur at a random default time. Bankruptcy is
triggered the first time the value of the firm's assets falls to some
prespecified default boundary; the approach also assumes that the
loss in the event of default is exogenous.

This approach simplifies the modeling of the bankruptcy
process by not relying explicitly on the priority structure of the debt
instruments. However, it loses its generality by assuming an exogenous recovery rate for each promised dollar in the case of a default. These models allow for stochastic interest rates.

The most recent reduced-form approach, developed independently by Duffie and Singleton (1994), Jarrow and Turnbull (1995), and Jarrow, Lando, and Turnbull (1997) and summarized in Chapter 10, characterizes bankruptcy as an exogenous process, e.g., as a Markov process in the firm's credit ratings. Thus the approach does not explicitly depend on the firm's asset value, and on the priority rules for the various debt instruments. However, the approach still assumes a given recovery rate in the event of default.

Contrary to the earlier approaches, the default event does not relate to the capital structure of the firm and occurs at a random time.[7] These models allow one to derive the term structure of default probabilities from credit spreads, while assuming exogenous and somewhat arbitrary the recovery rate.[8]

In this chapter we adopt the "traditional" option pricing framework to value corporate securities, and we show that it allows us to repeat results derived by Jarrow and Turnbull (1995). That is, the credit spread on a corporate bond is the product of the probability of default and the loss rate. In Section 2 we present the economic value of default as a put option. A numerical example is used to illustrate the application of option pricing theory to the assessment of credit risk. The probability of default and the conditional expected recovery rates are derived from the model described in Section 3.

2. A STRUCTURAL MODEL OF DEFAULT RISK: MERTON'S (1974) MODEL[9]

The model presented in this section assumes a simple capital structure with one type of (zero-coupon) debt. It can, however, be easily extended to the case where the firm has issued senior and junior debt. In this case, the loss rates for each type of debt are endogenously derived, together with the default probability.[10]

Consider the simple case of a firm with risky assets V, which are financed by equity S and by one debt obligation, maturing at time T with face value (including accrued interest) of F and market value B. The loan to the firm is subject to credit risk, namely the risk that at time T the value of the firm's assets, V_T, will fall below the obligation to the debt holders, F.

Credit risk exists as long as the probability of default, Prob $(V_T < F)$, is greater than zero. This implies that at time 0, $B_0 < Fe^{-rT}$; i.e., the yield to maturity on the debt, y_T, is higher than the risk-free rate r, where $\pi_T = y_T - r$ denotes the default spread that compensates the bond holders for the default risk that they bear. If we assume that markets are frictionless, with no taxes, and there is no bankruptcy cost, then the value of the firm's assets is simply the sum of the firm's equity and debt, i.e.:

$$V_0 \equiv S_0 + B_0 \qquad (1)$$

From the viewpoint of a bank that makes a loan to the firm, this gives rise to a series of questions. Can the bank eliminate/reduce credit risk, and at what price? What is the economic cost of reducing credit risk? And, what are the factors affecting this cost?

In this simple framework, credit risk is a function of the financial structure of the firm, i.e., its leverage ratio $LR \equiv Fe^{-rT}/V_0$ (where V_0 is the present value of the firm's assets, and Fe^{-rT} is the present value of the debt obligation at maturity, assuming debt is riskless), the volatility of the rate of return of the firm's assets, σ, and the time to maturity of the debt, T. The model was initially suggested by Merton (1974) and further analyzed by Galai and Masulis (1976).

To determine the value of the credit risk arising from this bank loan, we first make two assumptions: that the loan is the only debt instrument of the firm, and that the only other source of financing is equity. In this case, the credit value is equal to the value of a put option on the value of the assets of the firm, V, at a strike price of F, maturing at time T. If the bank purchased such a put option, it would completely eliminate the credit risk associated with the loan (see Table 9.1).

To phrase this another way, by purchasing the put on V for the term of the debt, with a strike price equal to the face value of

TABLE 9.1

Bank's Pay-Off Matrix At Times 0 and T For Making a Loan and Buying a Put Option

Time	0	$V_T \leq F$	$V_T > F$
Value of assets	V_0		
Bank's position:			
(a) Make a loan	$-B_0$	V_T	F
(b) Buy a put	$-P_0$	$F - V_T$	0
Total	$-B_0 - P_0$	F	F

the loan, the bank can completely eliminate all the credit risk and convert the risky corporate loan into a riskless loan with a face value of F. If the riskless interest rate is r, then in equilibrium it should be that $B_0 + P_0 = Fe^{-rT}$.

Thus, the value of the put option is the cost of eliminating the credit risk associated with providing a loan to the firm.* If we make the assumptions that are needed to apply the Black–Scholes (1973) (BS) model to equity and debt instruments (see Galai and Masulis 1976 for a detailed discussion of the assumptions), we can write the value of the put as:

$$P_0 = -N(-d_1)V_0 + Fe^{-rt}N(-d_2) \tag{2}$$

where P_0 is the current value of the put, $N(.)$ is the cumulative standard normal distribution, and

$$d_1 = \frac{\ln(V_0/F) + (r + \frac{1}{2}\sigma^2)T}{\sigma\sqrt{T}} = \frac{\ln(V_0/Fe^{-rT}) + \frac{1}{2}\sigma^2 T}{\sigma\sqrt{T}}$$

$$d_2 = d_1 - \sigma\sqrt{T}$$

and σ is the standard deviation of the rate of return of the firm's assets.

The model illustrates that the credit risk, and its costs, is a function of the riskiness of the assets of the firm, σ, and this risk is also a function of the time interval until debt is paid back, T. The cost is also affected by the risk-free interest rate r: the higher r is, the less costly it is to reduce credit risk. The cost is a homogeneous function of the leverage ratio, $LR = Fe^{-rT}/V_0$, which means that it stays constant for a scale expansion of Fe^{-rT}/V_0.

We can now derive the yield to maturity for the corporate discount debt, y_T, as follows:

$$y_T = -\frac{\ln\frac{B_0}{F}}{T} = -\frac{\ln\frac{Fe^{-rT} - P_0}{F}}{T}$$

so that the default spread, π_T, defined as $\pi_T = y_T - r$, can be derived from equation (2):

$$\pi_T = y_T - r = -\frac{1}{T}\ln\left(N(d_2) + \frac{V_0}{Fe^{-rT}}N(-d_1)\right) \tag{3}$$

---

* This put is an example of a credit derivative (see Chapter 12).

The default spread can be computed exactly as a function of the leverage ratio, $LR \equiv Fe^{-rT}/V_0$, the volatility of the underlying assets, σ, and the debt maturity, T. The numerical examples in Table 9.2 show the default spread for various levels of volatility and different leverage ratios.

Note that when the risk-free rate r increases, the credit spread π_T declines, i.e., $\partial \pi_T/\partial r < 0$. Indeed, the higher r is, the less risky is the bond (the lower is the value of the put protection). Therefore, the lower the risk premium π_T.

In Table 9.2, by using the BS model when $V_0 = 100$, $T = 1$, $r = 10$ percent, and also $\sigma = 40$ percent with the leverage ratio (LR) = 70 percent,[11] we obtain for the value of equity, $S_0 = 33.37$ and the value of the corporate risky debt, $B_0 = 66.63$. The yield on the loan is equal to $77/66.63 - 1 = 0.156$; i.e., there is a 5.6 percent risk premium on the loan to reflect the credit risk.

The model also shows that the put value is $P_0 = 3.37$. Hence the cost of eliminating the credit risk is $3.37 for $100 worth of the firm's assets, where the face value (i.e., the principal amount plus the promised interest rate) of the one-year debt is 77. This cost drops to 25 cents when volatility decreases to 20 percent, and to 0 for 10 percent volatility. The riskiness of the assets as measured by the volatility σ is a critical factor in determining credit risk.

TABLE 9.2

Default Spread For Corporate Debt (For $V_0 = 100$, $T = 1$, and $r = 10\%$[1])

Leverage ratio:	Volatility of underlying asset: σ			
LR	0.05	0.10	0.20	0.40
0.5	0	0	0	1.0%
0.6	0	0	0.1%	2.5%
0.7	0	0	0.4%	5.6%
0.8	0	0.1%	1.5%	8.4%
0.9	0.1%	0.8%	4.1%	12.5%
1.0	2.1%	3.1%	8.3%	17.3%

[1]10% is the annualized interest rate discretely compounded, which is equivalent to 9.5% continuously compounded.

To demonstrate that the bank eliminates all its credit risk by buying the put, we can compute the yield on the bank's position as:

$$F/(B_0 + P) = 77/(66.63 + 3.37) = 1.10$$

which translates to a riskless yield of 10 percent per annum.

In Appendix 1 we show how the conventional analysis, based on yield spreads, can be transformed into the options approach.

3. PROBABILITY OF DEFAULT, CONDITIONAL EXPECTED RECOVERY VALUE, AND DEFAULT SPREAD

From equation (2) one can extract the probability of default for the loan. In a risk-neutral world, $N(d_2)$ is the probability that the firm's value at time T will be higher than F, and $1 - N(d_2) = N(-d_2)$ is the probability of default.

By purchasing the put P_0, the bank buys an insurance policy whose premium is the discounted expected value of the expected shortfall in the event of default. Indeed, equation (2) can be rewritten as:

$$P_0 = \left[-\frac{N(-d_1)}{N(-d_2)} V_0 + Fe^{-rT} \right] N(-d_2) \qquad (4)$$

Equation (4) decomposes the premium on the put into three factors. The absolute value of the first term inside the bracket is the expected discounted recovery value of the loan, conditional on $V_T \leq F$. It represents the risk-neutral expected payment to the bank in the case where the firm is unable to pay the full obligation F at time T.

The second term in the bracket is the current value of a riskless bond promising a payment of F at time T. Hence, the sum of the two terms inside the brackets yields the expected shortfall in present-value terms, conditional on the firm being bankrupt at time T.

The final factor which determines P_0 is the probability of default, $N(-d_2)$. By multiplying the probability of default by the current value of the expected shortfall we derive the premium for insurance against default.

Using the same numerical example as in the previous section (i.e., $V_0 = 100$, $T = 1$, $r = 10$ percent, $\sigma = 40$ percent, $F = 77$, and $LR = 0.7$), we obtain:

Discounted expected recovery value $= \dfrac{0.137}{0.244} \times 100 = 56.1$

Value of riskless bond $= 77 \times e^{-0.0953} = 70$

Expected shortfall $= 70 - 56.1 = 13.9$

Probability of default $= 24.4\%$

Cost of default[12] $= 0.244 \times 13.9 = 3.39$

The above results are based on an assumption of risk neutrality. For the general case, when the assumption of a risk-neutral world is removed, the probability of default is given by $N(-d_2^1)$ where:

$$d_2^1 = \frac{\ln\left(\dfrac{V_0}{F}\right) + (\mu - \frac{1}{2}\,\sigma^2 T)}{\sigma\sqrt{T}}$$

and where μ is the expected rate of return on asset V, and V is assumed to be log-normally distributed. See Boness (1964) and Galai (1978) for an explanation of this result.

Referring to our numerical example, the risk-neutral probability of default is 24.4 percent. If we assume that the discrete time μ is 16 percent, then the probability of default is 20.5 percent. The expected recovery value is now:

$$\frac{N(-d_1^1)}{N(-d_2^1)}\, V_0 = \frac{0.110}{0.205} \cdot 100 = 53.7$$

From (4) we can compute the expected loss EL_T in the event of default, at maturity date T:

EL_T = probability of default x loss in case of default

$$= N(-d_2)F - N(-d_1)V_0 e^{rT} = F - N(d_2)F - N(-d_1)V_0 e^{rT}$$

$$= F\left(1 - N(d_2) - N(-d_1)\frac{1}{LR}\right) \tag{5}$$

Again, using our previous numerical example, we obtain:

$$EL_T = 0.244 \times 77 - 0.137 \times 100 e^{0.0953} = 3.718$$

This result is consistent with the definition of the default spread and its derivation in (3). Indeed, from (5) the expected payoff from the corporate debt at maturity is:

$$F - EL_T = F\left(N(d_2) + N(-d_1)\frac{1}{LR}\right)$$

so the expected cost of default, expressed in yield, is:

$$-\frac{1}{T}\ln\left(\frac{F}{F - EL_T}\right) = -\frac{1}{T}\ln\left(\frac{F\left(N(d_2) + N(-d_1)\dfrac{V_0}{Fe^{-rT}}\right)}{F}\right) = \pi_T$$

which is identical to (3).

The result in equation (5) is similar to the conclusion in Jarrow and Turnbull's (1995) model, which is used to price credit derivatives; i.e., the credit spread is the product of the probability of default and the loss in the event of default. However, in their model they assume that the term structure of credit spread is known and can be derived from market data. The forward spread can then be easily derived. By assuming that the recovery factor is given and exogenous to the model, they can imply the forward probability of default (see also Appendix 1 and Chapter 10).

In the contingent claim model we reach the same conclusion, but both the probability of default and the recovery rate are simultaneously derived from equilibrium conditions. From equations (3) and (4) it is clear that the recovery rate cannot be assumed to be constant: it varies as a function of time to maturity, and according to the value of the firm's assets.

4. ESTIMATING CREDIT RISK AS A FUNCTION OF EQUITY VALUE

In Section 2 we showed that the cost of eliminating credit risk can be derived from the value of the firm's assets. A practical problem arises over how easy it is to observe V. In some cases, if both equity and debt are traded, V can be reconstructed by adding the market values of both equity and debt. However, corporate loans are not often traded and so, to all intents and purposes, we can only observe equity. The question, then, is whether the risk of default can be hedged by trading shares and derivatives on the firm's stock.

In our simple framework, equity itself is a contingent claim on the firm's assets. Its value can be expressed as:

$$S = VN(d_1) - Fe^{-rT} N(d_2) \tag{6}$$

Equity value is a function of the same parameters as the put calculated in equation (2).

A put can be created synthetically by selling short $N(-d_1)$ units of the firm's assets, and buying $Fe^{rT}N(-d_2)$ units of government bonds maturing at T, with face value of F. If one sells short $N(-d_1)/N(d_1)$ units of the stock S, one effectively creates a short position in the firm's assets of $N(-d_1)$ units, since:

$$-\frac{N(-d_1)}{N(d_1)}S = -VN(-d_1) + Fe^{-rT}N(d_2)\frac{N(-d_1)}{N(d_1)}$$

Therefore, if V is not directly traded or observed, one can create a put option dynamically by selling short the appropriate number of shares. The equivalence between the put and the synthetic put is only valid over short time intervals, and must be readjusted frequently with changes in S and in time left to debt maturity.

Using the data from the previous numerical example, $-N(-d_1)/N(d_1) = -0.137/0.863 = -0.159$. This means that in order to insure against the default of a one-year loan with a maturity value of 77, for a firm with a current market value of assets of 100, the bank should sell short 0.159 of the outstanding equity. [Note that the outstanding equity is equivalent to a short-term holding of $N(d_1) = 0.863$ of the firm's assets. Shorting 0.159 of equity is equivalent to shorting 0.863 of the firm's assets.]

The question now is whether we can use a put option on equity in order to hedge the default risk. It should be remembered that equity itself reflects the default risk, and as a contingent claim its instantaneous volatility σ_s can be expressed as:

$$\sigma_s = \eta_{S,V}\sigma \tag{7}$$

where $\eta_{S,V} = N(d_1)V/S$ is the instantaneous elasticity of equity with respect to the firm's value $\eta_{S,V} = \frac{\partial S}{\partial V}\frac{V}{S}$, and $\eta_{S,V} \geq 1$.

Since σ_s is stochastic, changing with V, the conventional BS model cannot be applied to the valuation of puts and calls on S. The BS model requires σ to be constant, or to follow a deterministic path over the life of the option. However, it was shown by Bensoussan, Crouhy, and Galai (1994, 1995) that a good approximation can be achieved by employing equation (7) in the BS model.

In practice, for long-term options, the estimated σ_s from (7) is not expected to change widely from day to day. Therefore, equation

(7) can be used in the context of BS estimation of long-term options, even when the underlying instrument does not follow a stationary log-normal distribution.

5. KMV APPROACH

KMV derives the estimated default frequency or default probability, the EDF, for each obligor based on the Merton (1974) type of model. The probability of default is thus a function of the firm's capital structure, the volatility of the asset returns, and the current asset value.[13] The EDF is firm specific, and can be mapped onto any rating system to derive the equivalent rating of the obligor. EDFs can be viewed as a "cardinal ranking" of obligors relative to default risk, instead of the more conventional "ordinal ranking" proposed by rating agencies (which relies on letters such as AAA, AA, etc).

Contrary to CreditMetrics, KMV's model does not make any explicit reference to the transition probabilities which, in KMV's methodology, are already embedded in the EDFs. Indeed, each value of the EDF is associated with a spread curve and an implied credit rating.

Credit risk in the KMV approach is essentially driven by the dynamics of the asset value of the issuer. Given the capital structure of the firm,[14] and once the stochastic process for the asset value has been specified, then the actual probability of default for any time horizon, one year, two years, etc., can be derived. Figure 9.2 schematizes how the probability of default relates to the distribution of asset returns and the capital structure of the firm.

We assume that the firm has a very simple capital structure. It is financed by means of equity S_t and a single zero-coupon debt instrument maturing at time T, with face value F, and current market value B_t. The firm's balance sheet can be represented as follows: $V_t \equiv B_t(F) + S_t$, where V_t is the value of all the assets. The firm's assets value V_t is assumed to follow a standard geometric Brownian motion (see Chapter 8). In this framework, default only occurs at maturity of the debt obligation, when the value of assets is less than the promised payment F to the bond holders. Figure 9.2 shows the distribution of the assets' value at time T, the maturity of the zero-coupon debt, and the probability of default (i.e., the shaded area below F).

The KMV approach is best applied to publicly traded companies, where the value of the equity is determined by the stock market. The information contained in the firm's stock price and balance sheet can then be translated into an implied risk of default as shown in the next subsections.

The derivation of the actual probabilities of default proceeds in three stages:

- Estimation of the market value and volatility of the firm's assets
- Calculation of the distance to default, which is an index measure of default risk
- Scaling of the distance to default to actual probabilities of default using a default database

FIGURE 9.2

Distribution of the Firm's Asset Value at Maturity of the Debt Obligation

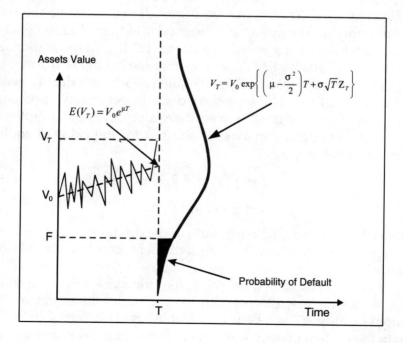

5.1 Estimation of the Asset Value, V, and the Volatility of Asset Return, σ

In the contingent claim approach to the pricing of corporate securities, the market value of the firm's assets is assumed to be lognormally distributed; i.e., the log-asset return follows a normal distribution.[15] This assumption is quite robust and, according to KMV's own empirical studies, actual data conform quite well to this hypothesis.[16] In addition the distribution of asset returns is stable over time; i.e., the volatility of asset returns remains relatively constant.

As we discussed earlier, if all the liabilities of the firm were traded, and marked-to-market every day, then the task of assessing the market value of the firm's assets and its volatility would be straightforward. The firm's asset value would be simply the sum of the market values of the firm's liabilities, and the volatility of the asset return could be simply derived from the historical time series of the reconstituted asset value.

In practice, however, only the price of equity for most public firms is directly observable, and in some cases only part of the debt is actively traded. The alternative approach to asset valuation consists of applying the option pricing model to the valuation of corporate liabilities as suggested in Merton (1974).[17] In order to make their model tractable, KMV assumes that the capital structure of a corporation is composed solely of equity, short-term debt (considered equivalent to cash), long-term debt (in perpetuity), and convertible preferred shares.[18] Given these simplifying assumptions, it is possible to derive analytical solutions for the value of equity, S, and its volatility, σ_S:

$$S = f\,(V, \sigma, LR, c, r) \qquad (8)$$

$$\sigma_S = g\,(V, \sigma, LR, c, r) \qquad (9)$$

where LR denotes the leverage ratio in the capital structure, c is the average coupon paid on the long-term debt, and r is the risk-free interest rate.

If σ_S were directly observable, like the stock price, we could solve simultaneously (8) and (9) for V and σ. But the instantaneous equity volatility, σ_S, is relatively unstable, and is in fact quite sensitive to the change in asset value; there is no simple way to measure precisely σ_S from market data.[19] Since only the value of equity, S, is directly observable, we can back out V from (8) so that it becomes a function of the observed equity value, or stock price, and the volatility of asset returns:

$$V = h (S, \sigma, LR, c, r) \qquad (10)$$

To calibrate the model for σ, KMV uses an iterative technique.

5.2 Calculation of the Distance to Default

In the option pricing framework default, or equivalently bankruptcy, occurs when the asset value falls below the value of the firm's liabilities. In practice, default is distinct from bankruptcy. Bankruptcy describes the situation in which the firm is liquidated, and the proceeds from the asset sale are distributed to the various claim holders according to prespecified priority rules. Default, on the other hand, is usually defined as the event when a firm misses a payment on a coupon and/or the reimbursement of principal at debt maturity. Cross-default clauses on debt contracts are such that when the firm misses a single payment on a debt, it is declared in default on all its obligations.

Since the early 1980s, Chapter 11 regulation in the United States has protected firms in default and helped to maintain them as going concerns during a period in which they attempt to restructure their activities and their financial structure. Figure 9.3 compares the number of bankruptcies to the number of defaults during the period 1973 to 1994.

Using a sample of several hundred companies, KMV observed that firms default when the asset value reaches a level that is somewhere between the value of total liabilities and the value of short-term debt. Therefore, the tail of the distribution of asset values below total debt value may not be an accurate measure of the actual probability of default. Loss of accuracy may also result from factors such as the non-normality of the asset return distribution, and the simplifying assumptions about the capital structure of the firm. This may be further aggravated if a company is able to draw on (otherwise unobservable) lines of credit. If the company is in distress, using these lines may (unexpectedly) increase its liabilities while providing the necessary cash to honor promised payments.

FIGURE 9.3

Bankruptcies and Defaults, Quarterly from 1973–1997

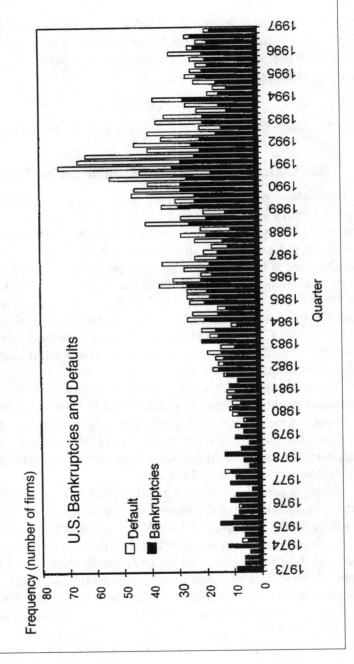

Source: KMV Corporation.

FIGURE 9.4

Distance to Default (DD)

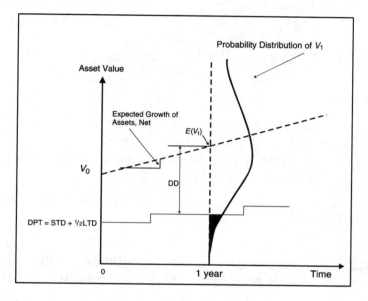

STD = short-term debt
LTD = long-term debt
DPT = default point = STD + ½ LTD
DD = distance to default, which is the distance between the expected asset
value in one year, $E(V_1)$, and the default point, DPT. It is often
expressed in terms of standard deviation of asset returns:

$$DD = \frac{E(V_1) - DPT}{\sigma}$$

For all these reasons, KMV implements an intermediate phase
before computing the probabilities of default. As shown in Figure
9.4, which is similar to Figure 9.2, KMV computes an index called
"distance to default" (DD). DD is the number of standard deviations between the mean of the distribution of the asset value, and
a critical threshold, the "default point," set at the par value of current liabilities including short-term debt to be serviced over the
time horizon, plus half the long-term debt.

Given the log-normality assumption of asset values, the distance to default, expressed in units of asset return standard deviation at time horizon T, is:[20]

$$DD = \frac{\ln\dfrac{V_0}{DPT_T} + (\mu - \frac{1}{2}\sigma^2)T}{\sigma\sqrt{T}} \qquad (11)$$

where

V_0 = current market value of assets
DPT_T = default point at time horizon T
μ = expected return on assets, net of cash outflows
σ = annualized asset volatility

It follows that the shaded area below the default point is equal to $N(-DD)$.

5.3 Derivation of the Probabilities of Default from the Distance to Default

This last phase consists of mapping the "distance-to-default" (DD) to the actual probabilities of default, for a given time horizon (see Figure 9.5). KMV calls these probabilities "expected default frequencies," or EDFs.

Using historical information about a large sample of firms, including firms that have defaulted, one can estimate, for each time horizon, the proportion of firms of a given ranking, say $DD = 4$, that actually defaulted after one year. This proportion, say 40 bp, or 0.4 percent, is the EDF as shown in Figure 9.5.

Example 1

Current market value of assets:	$V_0 = 1000$
Net expected growth of assets per annum:	20%
Expected asset value in one year:	$V_0 (1.20) = 1200$
Annualized asset volatility, σ:	100
Default point:	800

Then

$$DD = \frac{1200 - 800}{100} = 4$$

Assume that among the population of all the firms with a DD of 4 at one point in time, e.g., 5000, 20 defaulted one year later; then:

$$EDF_{1\ year} = \frac{20}{5000} = 0.004 = 0.4\% \text{ or } 40 \text{ bp}$$

The implied rating for this probability of default is BB$^+$.

The next example is provided by KMV and relates to Federal Express on two different dates: November 1997 and February 1998.

Example 2: Federal Express ($ figures are in billions of $US)

	November 1997	February 1998
Market capitalization (price × shares outstanding)	$ 7.7	$ 7.3
Book liabilities	$ 4.7	$ 4.9
Market value of assets	$12.6	$12.2
Asset volatility	15%	17%
Default point	$ 3.4	$ 3.5
Distance to default (DD)	$\frac{12.6 - 3.4}{0.15 \cdot 12.6} = 4.9$	$\frac{12.2 - 3.5}{0.17 \cdot 12.2} = 4.2$
EDF	0.06% (6 bp) $\equiv$ AA$^-$	0.11% (11 bp) $\equiv$ A$^-$

FIGURE 9.5

Mapping of the "Distance to Default" into the EDFs for a Given Time Horizon

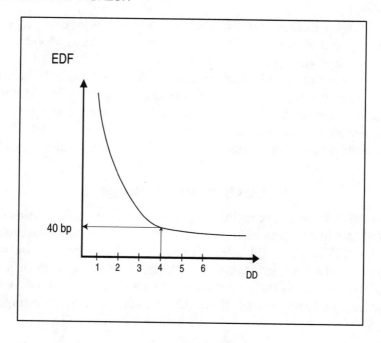

This last example illustrates the main causes of change for an EDF, i.e., variations in the stock price, the debt level (leverage ratio), and the asset volatility (i.e., the perceived degree of uncertainty concerning the value of the business).

5.4 EDF as a Predictor of Default

KMV has provided a "Credit Monitor" service for estimated EDFs since 1993. EDFs have proved to be a useful leading indicator of default, or at least of the degradation of the creditworthiness of issuers. When the financial situation of a company starts to deteriorate, EDFs tend to shoot up quickly until default occurs, as shown in Figure 9.6. Figure 9.7 shows the evolution of equity value and asset value, as well as the default point during the same period. On the vertical axis of both graphs the EDF is shown as a percentage, together with the corresponding Standard & Poor's rating.

KMV has analyzed more than 2000 U.S. companies that have defaulted or entered into bankruptcy over the last 20 years. These firms belonged to a large sample of more than 100,000 company-years with data, provided by Compustat. In all cases KMV has shown a sharp increase in the slope of the EDF a year or two prior to default.

Changes in EDFs tend to anticipate—by at least one year—the downgrading of the issuer by rating agencies such as Moody's and Standard & Poor's (Figure 9.8).

Contrary to Moody's and Standard & Poor's historical default statistics, EDFs are not biased by periods of high or low defaults. The distance to default can be observed to shorten during periods of recession, when default rates are high, and to increase during periods of prosperity characterized by low default rates.

5.5 EDFs and Ratings

Standard & Poor's risk ratings represent default probabilities only, while Moody's factors also include a measure of the probability of loss, i.e., EDF×LGD. Table 9.3 shows the correspondence between EDFs and the ratings systems used by Standard & Poor's and Moody's, as well as the internal risk ratings systems used by CIBC, Nationsbank, and Swiss Bank Corp. (The ratings systems of

FIGURE 9.6

EDF of a Firm That Defaulted versus EDFs of Firms in Various Quartiles and the Lower Decile.

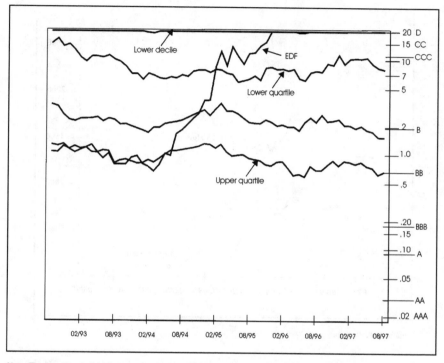

Note: The quartiles and decile represent a range of EDFs for a specific credit class (B rated firms).
Source: KMV Corporation.

Nationsbank and Swiss Bank were published during recent CLO transactions.)

Within any rating class the default probabilities of issuers are clustered around the median. However, as we discussed earlier, the average default rate for each class is considerably higher than the default rate of the typical firm. This is because each rating class contains a group of firms which have much higher probabilities of default, due to the (approximately) exponential change in default rates as default risk increases. These risky firms can be thought of as firms that should have been downgraded, though no downgrade has yet occurred. Conversely, there are also firms within each class

FIGURE 9.7

Asset Value, Equity Value, Short-Term Debt, and Long-Term Debt of a Firm That Defaulted

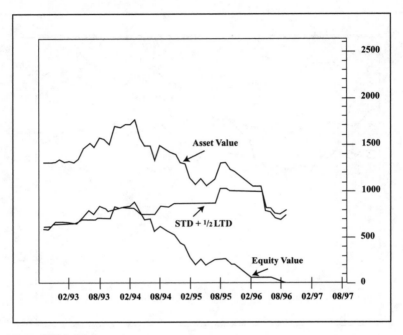

Source: KMV Corporation.

that should have been upgraded. Table 9.4 shows the variation of the EDFs within each rating class.

Three consequences follow from this analysis. First, since the rating agencies are slow to change their ratings, the historical frequency of remaining in a rating class should overstate the true probability of maintaining a particular credit quality. Second, the average historical probability of default overstates the true probability of default for typical firms within each rating class, due to the difference between the mean and the median default rates. Third, if both the probability of staying in a given rating class and the probability of default are too large, then the transition probabilities must be too small.

KMV has constructed a transition matrix based upon default rates rather than rating classes. They began by ranking firms into

FIGURE 9.8

EDF of a Firm That Defaulted versus Standard & Poor's Rating

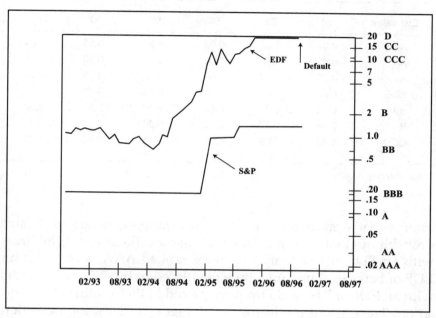

Source: KMV Corporation.

TABLE 9.3

EDFs and Risk Rating Comparisons

EDF	S&P	Moody's Factors	CIBC	Nationsbank	SBC
2 to 4 bp	>=AA	>=Aa2	1	AAA	C1
4 to 10 bp	AA/A	A1	2	AA	C2
10 to 19 bp	A/BBB+	Baa1	3	A	C3
19 to 40 bp	BBB+/BBB−	Baa3	4	A/BB	C4
40 to 72 bp	BBB−/BB	Ba1	5	BBB/BB	C5
72 to 101 bp	BB/BB−	Ba3	6	BB	C6
101 to 143 bp	BB−/B+	B1	7	BB	C7
143 to 202 bp	B+/B	B2	8	BB/B	C8
202 to 345 bp	B/B−	B2	9	B	C9

TABLE 9.4

Variation of EDFs Within Rating

Quantiles	10	25	50	75	90	Mean
AAA	0.02	0.02	0.02	0.02	0.10	0.04
AA	0.02	0.02	0.02	0.04	0.10	0.06
A	0.02	0.03	0.08	0.13	0.28	0.14
BBB	0.05	0.09	0.15	0.33	0.71	0.30
BB	0.12	0.22	0.62	1.30	2.53	1.09
B	0.44	0.87	2.15	3.80	7.11	3.30
CCC	1.43	2.09	4.07	12.24	18.82	7.21

Source: KMV Corporation.

groups that were based on the nonoverlapping ranges of default probabilities that are typical for a rating class. For instance, all firms with an EDF of less than 2 bp were ranked AAA; those with an EDF of between 3 bp and 6 bp were placed in the AA group; firms with an EDF of 7 bp to 15 bp were placed in the A rating class; and so on. Then, using the history of changes in EDFs, the transition

TABLE 9.5

KMV One-Year Transition Matrix Based on Nonoverlapping EDF Ranges

Initial Rating	Rating at Year-End (%)							
	AAA	AA	A	BBB	BB	B	CCC	Default
AAA	66.26	22.22	7.37	2.45	0.86	0.67	0.14	0.02
AA	21.66	43.04	25.83	6.56	1.99	0.68	0.20	0.04
A	2.76	20.34	44.19	22.94	7.42	1.97	0.28	0.10
BBB	0.30	2.80	22.63	42.54	23.52	6.95	1.00	0.26
BB	0.08	0.24	3.69	22.93	44.41	24.53	3.41	0.71
B	0.01	0.05	0.39	3.48	20.47	53.00	20.58	2.01
CCC	0.00	0.01	0.09	0.26	1.79	17.77	69.94	10.13

Source: KMV Corporation.

TABLE 9.6

Transition Matrix Based on Actual Rating Changes

Initial Rating	Rating at Year-End (%)							
	AAA	AA	A	BBB	BB	B	CCC	Default
AAA	90.81	8.33	0.68	0.06	0.12	0	0	0
AA	0.70	90.65	7.79	0.64	0.06	0.14	0.02	0
A	0.09	2.27	91.05	5.52	0.74	0.26	0.01	0.06
BBB	0.02	0.33	5.95	86.93	5.30	1.17	1.12	0.18
BB	0.03	0.14	0.67	7.73	80.53	8.84	1.00	1.06
B	0	0.11	0.24	0.43	6.48	83.46	4.07	5.20
CCC	0.22	0	0.22	1.30	2.38	11.24	64.86	19.79

Source: Standard & Poor's CreditWeek (April 15, 1996).

matrix shown in Table 9.5 was produced. It is similar in structure to the table produced in Table 8.1 of Chapter 8 and reproduced here as Table 9.6.

There are striking, if predictable, differences in the various probabilities between the two tables. According to KMV, except for the AAA rating class, the probability of staying in the same rating class is between half and one-third of historical rates produced by the rating agencies. KMV's probabilities of default are also lower, especially for the low-grade credits. Migration probabilities are also much higher as calculated by KMV, especially for the grade above and below the current rating class. These differences may have a considerable impact on credit VaR calculations.

6 KMV'S VALUATION MODEL FOR CASH FLOWS SUBJECT TO DEFAULT RISK

In the CreditMetrics approach, the valuation model is quite simplistic. As we described in Chapter 8, if the time horizon is one year, then the forward value of a bond is the discounted value of the future cash flows beyond one year, where the discount factors are derived from the forward yield curve. Each credit rating is associated with a specific spread curve, and the distribution of future values follows from the transition probabilities.

The KMV approach is quite different, and is consistent with the option pricing methodology used for the valuation of contingent cash flows. Given the term structure of EDFs for a given obligor, we can derive the net present value of any stream of contingent cash flows. More specifically, KMV's pricing model is based upon the "risk-neutral" valuation model, also known as the "martingale" approach to the pricing of securities. This derives prices as the discounted expected value of future cash flows using so-called "risk-neutral" probabilities (i.e., not the actual probabilities as they can be observed in the marketplace from historical data or from the EDFs).[21]

Assuming, for the time being, that we know how to derive the "risk-neutral probabilities" from the EDFs, then the valuation of risky cash flows proceeds in two steps: first, the valuation of the default-free component; and second, the valuation of the component that is exposed to credit risk. In Appendix 2 we illustrate how to use risk-neutral probabilities to value a bond or a loan subject to default risk, and how to use them to value a credit derivative.

6.1 Derivation of the "Risk-Neutral" EDFs

Equation (5) in Section 3 illustrates how the risk-neutral probability of default is used in order to estimate the expected loss in present-value terms from a risky zero-coupon bond. A similar procedure can be used for a multiperiod bond with a given coupon payment.

The practical problem faced by the analyst is that the empirical frequencies of default deviate from the risk-neutral probabilities. In theory, the difference for the simple case discussed in Section 3 is between $N(-d_2)$ for risk-neutral probability and $N(-d_2^1)$ for actual probability of default (24.4 percent and 20.5 percent, respectively, in our numerical example). While $N(-d_2)$ is a function of r, the risk-free interest rate, $N(-d_2^1)$ is a function of μ, the expected rate of return on the assets of the firm (and $\mu > r$).

Since $-d_2 + (\mu - r)\sqrt{T}/\sigma = -d_2^1$, it follows that the cumulative risk-neutral EDF, Q_T, at horizon T can be expressed as a function of the EDF:

$$Q_T = N\left[N^{-1}(\text{EDF}) + \frac{(\mu - r)}{\sigma}\sqrt{T}\right] \tag{12}$$

Since $\mu \geq r$, it follows that $Q_T \geq \text{EDF}_T$; i.e., the risk-neutral probability of default, after adjusting for the price of risk, is higher than the actual probability of default.

According to the continuous time CAPM:

$$\mu - r = \beta\pi \tag{13}$$

with

$$\beta = \text{beta of the asset with the market}$$
$$= \frac{\text{cov}(r_V, r_M)}{\text{var}(r_M)} = \rho_{V,M}\frac{\sigma}{\sigma_M} \tag{14}$$

where r_V and r_M denote the continuous time rate of return on the firm's asset and the market portfolio, respectively; σ and σ_M are the volatility of the assets return and the market return, respectively; $\rho_{V,M}$ is the correlation between the assets return and the market return; and

$$\pi = \text{market risk premium} = \mu_M - r \tag{15}$$

where μ_M denotes the expected return on the market portfolio, and r is the continuous time risk-free rate.

It follows that:

$$\frac{\mu - r}{\sigma} = \frac{\beta\pi}{\sigma} = \rho_{V,M}\frac{\pi}{\sigma_M} = \rho_{V,M}\,SR \tag{16}$$

where $SR = \pi/\sigma_M$ denotes the market Sharpe ratio, i.e., the excess return per unit of market volatility for the market portfolio.

Substituting (16) into (12) we obtain:

$$Q_T = N\left[N^{-1}(\text{EDF}_T) + \rho_{V,M}\frac{\pi}{\sigma_M}\sqrt{T}\right] \tag{17}$$

$\rho_{V,M}$ is estimated in terms of the linear regression of asset returns against market returns:

$$r_V = \alpha + r_M + \epsilon \tag{18}$$

where α is the intercept of the regression and ϵ is the error term. $\rho_{V,M}$ is simply the square root of the R-squared of this regression.

In practice, π, the market risk premium, is difficult to estimate statistically, and it varies over time. In addition, the EDF is not precisely the shaded area under the default point in Figure 9.2, and the asset return distribution is not exactly normal. For all these reasons, KMV estimates the risk-neutral EDF, Q_T, by calibrating the market Sharpe ratio, SR, and θ in the following relation, using bond data:

$$Q_T = N[N^{-1}(\text{EDF}_T) + \rho_{v,m}\, SR\, T^\theta] \qquad (19)$$

where θ is a time parameter which should, in theory, be equal to ½.

Assuming we have derived the zero-coupon curve for an obligor, then according to the pricing model (A3) presented in Appendix 2:

$$e^{-r_{v,i}t_i} = [(1 - \text{LGD}) + (1 - Q_i)\text{LGD}]e^{-r_i t_i} \qquad (20)$$

for $i = 1, \ldots, n$, where:

$r_{v,i}$ = continuously compounded zero-interest rate for the obligor, for maturity t_i,

r_i = continuously compounded zero-risk free rate, for maturity t_i

so that:

$$r_{v,i} - r_i = -\frac{1}{t_i}\ln[1 - Q_i\text{LGD}] \qquad (21)$$

Combining (15) and (17) we obtain:

$$r_{v,i} - r_i = -\frac{1}{t_i}\ln[1 - N(N^{-1}(\text{EDF}_{t_i}) + \rho_{v,m}\, SR\, T^\theta)\text{LGD}] \qquad (22)$$

where $r_{v,i} - r_i$ is the obligor's corporate spread for maturity t_i, which is directly extracted from corporate bond data.[22] SR and θ are calibrated to produce the best fit of (22) in the least-square sense.

7. ASSET RETURN CORRELATION MODEL

CreditMetrics and KMV derive asset return correlations from a structural model that links correlations to fundamental factors. By imposing a structure on the return correlations, sampling errors inherent in simple historical correlations are avoided, and a better accuracy in forecasting correlations is achieved.

In addition, there is a practical need to reduce dramatically the number of correlations that need to be calculated. Assume that a bank is dealing with $N = 1000$ different counterparties. Then, we have $N(N - 1)/2$ different correlations to estimate, i.e., 499,500. This is a staggering number. Multifactor models of asset returns reduce the number of correlations that have to be calculated to the limited number of correlations between the common factors that affect asset returns.

It is assumed that the firm's asset returns are generated by a set of common, or systematic, risk factors and idiosyncratic factors. The idiosyncratic factors are either firm specific, or country or industry specific, and do not contribute to asset return correlations (since they are not correlated with each other, and not correlated with the common factors). Asset return correlations between two firms can be explained only in terms of the factors common to all firms. Only the risks associated with the idiosyncratic risk factors can be diversified away through portfolio diversification, while the risk contribution of the common factors is, on the contrary, nondiversifiable.

For the sake of illustration, assume the asset return generating process for all firms is:

$$r_k = \alpha_k + \beta_{1k}I_1 + \beta_{2k}I_2 + \epsilon_k \text{ for } k = 1, \ldots, N \tag{23}$$

where:

N	= number of obligors (firms)
r_k	= asset return for firm k (r_{v_k} denoted r_k)
α_k	= component of asset return independent of common factors
I_1, I_2	= common factors
β_{1k}, β_{2k}	= expected changes in r_k, given a change in common factors I_1 and I_2, respectively
ϵ_k	= idiosyncratic risk factor with zero mean, and assumed to be uncorrelated with all the common factors, as well as with the idiosyncratic risk factors of the other firms

Then, using elementary statistical calculus, we can derive results that are well known in portfolio theory:[23]

$$\text{var}(r_k) = \sigma_k^2 = \beta_{1k}^2 \text{var}(I_1) + \beta_{2k}^2 \text{var}(I_2)$$
$$+ \text{var}(\epsilon_k^2) + 2\beta_{1k}\beta_{2k} \text{cov}(I_1, I_2) \tag{24}$$

$$\mathrm{cov}(r_i, r_j) = \sigma_{ij} = \beta_{1i}\beta_{2j}\,\mathrm{var}(I_1) + \beta_{2i}\beta_{2j}\,\mathrm{var}(I_2)$$
$$+ (\beta_{1i}\beta_{2j} + \beta_{2i}\beta_{1j})\,\mathrm{cov}(I_1, I_2) \qquad (25)$$

If we denote by ρ_{ij} the asset return correlation between firm i and firm j, then:

$$\rho_{ij} = \frac{\sigma_{ij}}{\sigma_i \sigma_j} \qquad (26)$$

To derive the asset return correlation between any number of firms, we only need, according to (24–26), to estimate the β_{ik}'s for $i = 1, 2$, and $K = 1, \ldots, N$, i.e., $2N$ parameters, and the covariance matrix for the common factors, i.e., three parameters. In the previous example, where we considered $N = 1000$ firms, the implementation of this two-factor model would require us to estimate only 2003 parameters (instead of 499,500 different historical asset return correlations). For K common factors, the number of parameters to be estimated is $KN + K(K - 1)/2$. If $K = 10$, then this number becomes 10,045. This result can be easily generalized to any number of common factors and idiosyncratic risk components.

The next problem is to specify the structure of the factors. CreditMetrics and KMV propose relatively similar models, so here we will present only the KMV model (which is more comprehensive and elaborate).[24]

KMV constructs a three-layer factor structure model as shown in Figure 9.9:

- First level: a composite company-specific factor, which is constructed individually for each firm based on the firm's exposure to each country and industry
- Second level: country and industry factors
- Third level: global, regional, and industrial sector factors

The first level of the structure divides between firm-specific, or idiosyncratic, risk and common, or systematic, risk. Systematic risk is captured by a single composite index, which is firm specific, and which is constructed as a weighted sum of the firm's exposure to country and industry factors defined at the second level of the structure:

$$r_k = \beta_k CF_k + \epsilon_k \text{ for all firms: } k = 1, \ldots, N$$

where

r_k = asset return for firm k

CF_k = composite factor for firm k

β_k = firm k's response to the composite factor, i.e., expected change in r_k given a change in the composite factor

ϵ_k = firm k's specific risk factor

The composite factor is constructed as the sum of the weighted country and industry factors specified at the second level of the structure:

FIGURE 9.9

Factor Model for Asset Return Correlations

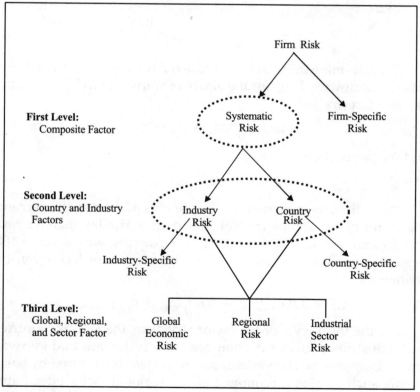

Source: KMV Corporation.

$$CF_k = \sum_m \alpha_{km} C_m + \sum_n \alpha_{km} I_n$$

where:

C_m = rate of return on country risk factor m

I_n = rate of return on industry risk factor n

α_{km} = weight of firm k in country m, with the constraint that $\Sigma_m \alpha_{km} = 1$

α_{kn} = weight of firm k in industry n, with the constraint that $\Sigma_n \alpha_{kn} = 1$

For example, consider a Canadian firm that has two lines of business, and assume that the data are extracted from Compustat:[25]

Business line	SIC[26]	Assets	Sales
Lumber and forestry	2431	35%	45%
Paper production	2611	65%	55%
Total		100%	100%

To determine the weight by industry, we average the asset and sales breakdowns. Thus for the above example the weight for lumber and forestry is:

$$40\% = (35\% + 45\%)/2$$

and for paper it is:

$$60\% = (65\% + 55\%)/2$$

Note that, by construction, the weights add up to 100 percent. The country exposures are calculated in a similar manner and should also sum to 100 percent. (In this example, we assume a 100 percent exposure to Canada.) Then the composite factor can be written as:

$$CF = 1.0\, C_{\text{Canada}} + 0.6\, I_{\text{paper}} + 0.4\, I_{\text{lumber}}$$

At the third level of the factor structure, the risk of countries and industries is further decomposed into systematic and idiosyncratic components. The systematic component is captured by basic factors such as global economic effect, regional factor effect, and sector factor effect. While the common factor is firm specific, the third-level factors are the same for all countries and all industries:

$$\begin{pmatrix} \text{Country} \\ \text{returns} \end{pmatrix} = \begin{pmatrix} \text{Global} \\ \text{economic} \\ \text{effect} \end{pmatrix} + \begin{pmatrix} \text{Regional} \\ \text{factor effect} \end{pmatrix}$$

$$+ \begin{pmatrix} \text{Sector} \\ \text{factor effect} \end{pmatrix} + \begin{pmatrix} \text{Country-} \\ \text{specific risk} \end{pmatrix}$$

$$\begin{pmatrix} \text{Industry} \\ \text{return} \end{pmatrix} = \begin{pmatrix} \text{Global} \\ \text{economic} \\ \text{effect} \end{pmatrix} + \begin{pmatrix} \text{Regional} \\ \text{factor effect} \end{pmatrix}$$

$$+ \begin{pmatrix} \text{Sector factor} \\ \text{effect} \end{pmatrix} + \begin{pmatrix} \text{Industry-} \\ \text{specific risk} \end{pmatrix}$$

We can now express this factor structure in a form similar to (23), from which it is easy to derive the asset return correlations (26).

APPENDIX 1: INTEGRATING YIELD SPREAD WITH OPTIONS APPROACH

In this Appendix we show how the option pricing framework can be combined with the conventional yield spread approach to extract from yield spreads the cost of credit risk and recovery values. Consider Table 9.7, which lists U.S. Treasury and corporate bond yields.

The above data can be transformed to derive the zero-coupon curves for the Treasury and the corporate bonds, as illustrated in Table 9.8. The zero-coupon table is used to derive the one-year forward rates N years forward (Table 9.9). This information is needed for CreditMetrics and other evaluation systems that are based on yield spreads.

We can use the data for the zero-coupon curves to evaluate the implied parameter for a firm with a T-year bond outstanding. Suppose that company X has a two-year bond outstanding. This bond should offer a yield consistent with 6.25 percent per annum for a zero-coupon bond. In other words, by converting the two-

TABLE 9.7

Prevailing Market Yields and Spreads

Maturity (years)	U.S. Treasury Par Yields	Company X Par Yields	Credit Spread
1	5.60%	5.85%	.25
2	5.99%	6.34%	.35
3	6.15%	6.60%	.45
4	6.27%	6.87%	.60
5	6.34%	7.04%	.70
6	6.42%	7.22%	.80
7	6.48%	7.38%	.90

Note: Semiannual 30/360 yields.

year corporate coupon bond into its two-year zero-coupon equivalent, its economic discrete time yield should be 6.25 percent. The risk-free yield on an equivalent two-year zero-coupon government bond is 5.91 percent.

If we also assume that the bond has a face value of $F = 100$ at $T = 2$, its present value, B_0, should be $B_0 = F/(1.0625)^2 = 88.58$.

TABLE 9.8

Zero-Coupon Curves

Maturity (years)	U.S. Treasury Par Yields	Company X Par Yield
1	5.52%	5.76%
2	5.91%	6.25%
3	6.07%	6.51%
4	6.19%	6.80%
5	6.27%	7.18%
6	6.36%	7.37%
7	6.42%	7.54%

Note: Continuously compounded 30/360 zero-coupon rates.

TABLE 9.9

One-Year Forward Rates N Years Forward

Maturity (years)	U.S. Treasury Forwards	Company X Forwards	One-Year Forward Credit Spreads N Years Forward
1	5.52%	5.76%	.24
2	6.30%	6.74%	.44
3	6.40%	7.05%	.65
4	6.56%	7.64%	1.08
5	6.56%	7.71%	1.15
6	6.81%	8.21%	1.40
7	6.81%	8.47%	1.65

Note: One-year continuously compounded 30/360.

If the standard deviation of the rate of return on the firm's assets, σ, is equal to 20 percent, we can calculate the equity value S_0 for any given firm's value, V_0. The problem is to find V_0 and hence S_0 such that $88.58 + S_0 = V_0$. This problem is equivalent to that of finding V_0 such that the put value is equal to:

$$P_0 = F/(1.0591)^2 - F/(1.0625)^2 = 0.57$$

By trial and error, given the above assumptions, we find that by introducing $V_0 = 144$ into the Black-Scholes model, the derived equity value is $S_0 = 55.44$ such that $88.58 + 55.44 = 144.02$ and also $P_0 = 0.58$.

The cost of credit risk for the two-year corporate bond can be derived from the value of a put option on V_0 given $F = 100$, which is 0.58 for the above parameters. The present value of the recovery value of the loan is given by:

$$\frac{N(-d_1)}{N(-d_2)} \cdot V_0 = -\frac{0.033}{0.060} \cdot 144 = 79.20$$

By following the same procedure for $\sigma = 15$ percent, we find that for $V_0 = 124$ the values of bond and equity are, respectively, 88.58 and 35.42. The cost of credit risk is $P_0 = 0.57$ and the present value of the recovery value is 81.5. For $\sigma = 25$ percent the yield spread is consistent with a market value of $V_0 = 170$, which implies a leverage ratio, LR, of only 0.524 and an equity value of 81.42.

APPENDIX 2: RISK-NEUTRAL VALUATION USING "RISK-NEUTRAL" EDFs

In Section 6 of this chapter we showed how to derive the "risk-neutral" EDFs from the actual EDFs. In this Appendix, we illustrate how to use these risk-neutral EDFs to value a bond or a loan that is subject to credit risk, and also how to value a credit derivative.

(i) Case of a single cash flow

Example 1

Valuation of a zero-coupon bond with a promised payment in one year of $100, with a recovery of $(1-\text{LGD})$ if the issuer defaults. LGD is the "loss given default," which in this example is assumed to be 40 percent (Figure 9.A2.1).

The default risk-free component, $100(1-\text{LGD})$ is valued using the default risk-free discount curve, i.e.:

$$PV_1 = PV \text{ (risk-free cash flow)} = \frac{100(1-\text{LGD})}{1 + R} = \$54.5$$

where R denotes the one-year risk-free rate discretely compounded, assumed to be 10 percent, and PV is the abbreviation for present value.

The risky cash flow is valued using the martingale approach, i.e.:

$$PV_2 \text{ (risky cash flow)} = E_Q \text{ (discounted risky cash flow)}$$

where the expectation is calculated using the risk-neutral probability. The risk-neutral probability that the issuer might default one year from now is denoted as Q, and it is assumed to be 20 percent. Then:

$$PV_2 = PV\text{(risky cash flow)} = \frac{100\text{LGD}(1 - Q) + 0 \cdot Q}{1 + R}$$

$$= \frac{100\text{LGD}(1 - Q)}{1 + R} = \$29.1$$

FIGURE 9.A2.1

Valuation of a Single Cash Flow Subject to Default Risk

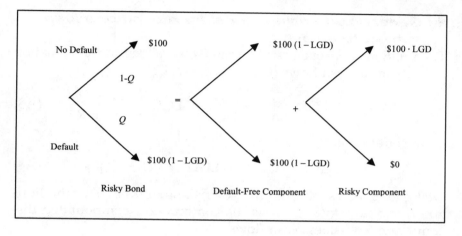

The present value of this zero-coupon bond subject to default risk is the sum of the default-free component and the risky component; i.e.:

$$PV = PV_1 + PV_2 = \$54.5 + \$29.1 = \$83.6$$

If the zero-coupon bond were default free, its present value would simply be its discounted value using the default-free interest rate; i.e.:

$$\$100/(1 + R) = \$90.9$$

We can then compute the implicit discount rate, Y, which accounts for default risk; i.e.:

$$Y = R + CS$$

where CS denotes the credit spread. It is a solution of:

$$\frac{100(1 - LGD)}{1 + R} + \frac{100LGD(1 - Q)}{1 + R} = \frac{100}{1 + R + CS} \qquad (A1)$$

Solving (5) for CS gives:

$$CS = \frac{LGD \cdot Q \cdot (1 + R)}{1 - LGD \cdot Q} \qquad (A2)$$

For this example, $Y = 19.6$ percent, so that the one-year credit spread for this issuer is 9.6 percent.

(ii) Generalized pricing model for a bond or a loan subject to default risk

The previous approach can be easily generalized to the valuation of a stream of cash flows $[C_1, \ldots, C_i, \ldots, C_n]$:

$$PV = (1 - LGD) \sum_{i=1}^{n} \frac{C_i}{(1 + R_i)^{t_i}} + LGD \sum_{i=1}^{n} \frac{(1 - Q_i)C_i}{(1 + R_i)^{t_i}} \quad (A3)$$

or, in continuous time notation:

$$PV = (1 - LGD) \sum_{i=1}^{n} C_i e^{-it_i} + LGD \sum_{i=1}^{n} (1 - Q_i)C_i e^{-it_i} \quad (A4)$$

where Q_i denotes the cumulative "risk-neutral" EDF at the horizon t_i and $r_i = \ln(1 + R_i)$, is the continuously compounded discount rate for riskless cash flows.

Example 2

What is the value of a 5-year bond with a face value of $100, which pays an annual coupon of 6.25 percent?

The risk-free interest rate is 5 percent, the loss given default (LGD) is 50 percent, and the cumulative risk-neutral probabilities are given in the table below:

Time	Q_i	Discount Factor $1/(1 + R_i)^{t_i}$	Cash Flow	PV_1 (Risk-Free Cash Flows)	PV_2 (Risky Cash Flows)
1	1.89%	0.9512	6.25	2.97	2.92
2	4.32%	0.9048	6.25	2.83	2.71
3	6.96%	0.8607	6.25	2.69	2.50
4	9.69%	0.8187	6.25	2.56	2.31
5	12.47%	0.7788	106.25	41.37	36.21
		Total	52.42	46.65	

$$PV = PV_1 + PV_2 = 99.07$$

This methodology also applies to simple credit derivatives such as default puts, as we describe below.

Example 3

What is the premium of a one-year default put that pays $1 if the underlying bond defaults?

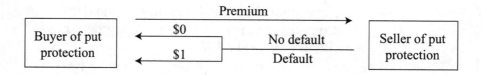

Assume a risk-neutral probability $Q = 0.39$ percent and an interest rate $R = 5.8$ percent; then:

$$\text{Premium} = \frac{Q}{1 + R} = \frac{0.0039}{1.058} = 0.37\%$$

APPENDIX 3: LIMITATIONS OF THE MERTON MODEL AND SOME EXTENSIONS

The Merton (1974) model is appealing from an economic standpoint since it relates default to both the asset value process and the capital structure of the firm, together with the various debt covenants. In this framework default is never a surprise. So long as the asset value remains greater than the firm's liabilities, default should never occur in the immediate future (at least, with a probability materially different from zero).[27]

The limitations of the Merton model are related to the practical difficulties in implementing it:

- The asset value and its volatility are not directly observable and are hard to estimate. KMV, however, proposes an elegant methodology with which to derive the implied asset values and asset volatility from equity prices (see Section 5).

- The risk-free interest rates are constant and therefore the relationship between interest rate risk and equity risk cannot be modeled. But this assumption has been relaxed by several authors. (See, e.g., Kim, Ramaswamy, and Sundaresan 1993; Shimko, Tejima, and van Deventer 1993; and Anderson and Sundaresan 1996.)

- Reliance on the absolute priority rule to describe the payoff to debt holders in default makes the valuation of coupon debt difficult, as a failure to pay a coupon may also trigger default. Thus, defaultable coupon debt can be viewed as a compound option. The value of the debt depends on whether the previous coupon payment passed without incident (see Geske 1977).

- For complex capital structures, the valuation of a risky bond depends on the value of the senior debt. Junior debt is a contingent claim on senior debt that substantially complicates valuation. In practice seniority rules are not fully enforced and in many bankruptcy cases we observe a transfer of value from senior claim holders to junior claim holders and equity holders.[28] Several recent contributions based on Merton's framework abandon this concept of interdependence in default in favor of simultaneous default or "cross-default" (see Section A3.2).

A3.1 Empirical Evidence

Jones, Mason, and Rosenfeld (1984) adopted a simple capital structure and compared Merton's model to the "naïve" method of discounting cash flows at the risk-free rate. They found that the model outperforms the naïve approach for non-investment-grade bonds, but not for investment-grade securities. According to this study, Merton's model consistently prices bonds higher than the traded price; i.e., implied credit spreads from Merton's model are too low.

These somewhat negative results may be due to several factors:

- The most serious is the violation of the seniority rules (see Footnote 27).
- The choice of a capital structure that is too simplistic, as a proxy for the actual capital structure.
- Deterministic interest rates. Kim, Ramaswamy and Sundaresan (1993) show that the introduction of stochastic interest rates in Merton's framework significantly improves the performance of the model.
- The poor quality of bond data and calculated yield, which do not correctly adjust for call features. Sarig and Warga (1989), using a new data set provided by Lehman Brothers, found that for corporate zero-coupon bonds, spreads seem to be qualitatively close to the Merton model predictions.

Delianedis and Geske (1998) use the option pricing model of Merton (1974) and Geske (1977) to estimate risk-neutral probabilities of default during the period 1987 to 1996. They show that these probabilities contain forward-looking information about rating migration and default. In addition, the short-term default probability from Geske's model is able to predict imminent cash flow problems.

A3.2 Extensions of Merton's Model

Geske (1977) extended Merton's model by showing that multiple default options for coupons, sinking funds, junior debt, safety covenants, or other payment obligations could be treated as compound options. In Geske's model default may occur before maturity, at a coupon payment date, even though the asset value is greater than the coupon payment that is due to be made. This happens when the value of equity is close to zero after the coupon payment is made and the shareholders are therefore better off not paying the coupon.

Black and Cox (1976) reinterpreted default as the event that occurs when the asset value V hits some boundary K at any time, and not just at maturity or at a coupon payment date. This assumption is consistent with a bond covenant that specifies some net-worth constraint. For example, if the value of the firm were to drop below a prespecified level K, then the bondholders can call the firm into paying the debt immediately, or alternatively force the firm to cross-default on all its debt at once if it is insolvent.[29] But, in this framework, financial distress is not explicitly modeled in the pricing of corporate debt.[30]

Kim, Ramaswamy, and Sundaresan (1993) propose a Merton-type model with stochastic interest rates where financial distress arises out of cash flow constraints, and bankruptcy is costly. Anderson and Sundaresan (1996) extend the previous model by allowing the firm to make a "take-it-or-leave-it" offer to the debtholders. The sharing of values by the debt holders and shareholders is obtained endogenously. The creditors have the choice of accepting or rejecting the debt service (which is bounded by the cash flows generated by the firm). If the debt service is rejected, the firm is liquidated and the stakeholders incur liquidation costs. This model generates spreads that are consistent with the observed spreads in the market, even at very low levels of debt and liquidation costs.

Longstaff and Schwartz (1995) allow deviations from the absolute priority rule, but the allocation of the value of the bankrupt firm amongst the various stakeholders is specified exogenously rather than being the outcome of an endogenous process of negotiation as in Anderson and Sundaresan (1993). Longstaff and Schwartz introduce three key assumptions:

- Default occurs when the asset value falls below a constant threshold K as in Black and Cox (1976). Default occurs simultaneously for all securities. Therefore, there is no need in their framework to model the bankruptcy process.
- The recovery rate is constant for each security and can be interpreted as the outcome of some complex post-bankruptcy bargaining process (exogenous to the model) among the various claimants.
- The risk-free interest rate is stochastic and follows a simple one-factor Vasicek process with mean reversion, which is correlated with the asset value process:

$$dr = \beta(m - r)dt + \eta dZ_r$$

$$dV = \mu V dt + \sigma V dZ_V$$

$$\text{corr}(dZ_r, dZ_V) = \rho dt$$

where β and m denote the mean reversion parameters of the interest rate process, ρ is the correlation between the processes for the default-free interest rate and asset value, and Z_r and Z_V are standard Brownian motions.

Longstaff and Schwartz make use of numerical approximation to compute the probability of default happening before the maturity of the debt. The Vasicek process for the default-free interest rate allows closed-form solutions for risky zero-coupon bonds. Coupon bonds can be valued as a portfolio of zero-coupon bonds because the event of default is not specific to a particular bond.

They find that the further away the asset value is from the default boundary, the lower is the credit spread. As time increases, the probability of default increases. Credit spreads can be monotone increasing, or hump-shaped, which is consistent with empirical evidence. Credit spreads increase with any increase in correlation between assets and interest rates.[31] The model produces a negative correlation between the level of Treasury yields and credit spreads, which is consistent with Merton's model.

While some aspects of the model are oversimplified, the model can be implemented in practice. Parameters can be estimated from term structure data and from historical firm data. Longstaff and Schwartz 's model has been extended by Saa-Requejo and Santa-Clara (1997). They suggest that the boundary value K should represent the present value of the liabilities rather than being a fixed number.[32]

Leland (1994) and Leland and Toft (1996) introduce costly bankruptcy and tax deductibility of interest rate charges. Shareholders then choose leverage to maximize the value of equity by selecting the best trade-off between tax benefits and bankruptcy costs. Bankruptcy is thus endogenized. It occurs when it ceases to be in the interest of shareholders to give up $1 to pay the next $1 of interest rate payment. This model provides useful insight but in its current form it is too restrictive to be of practical use.

NOTES

1. KMV is a trademark of KMV Corporation. The initials KMV stand for the first letter of the last names of Stephen Kealhofer, John McQuown, and Oldrich Vasicek, who founded KMV Corporation in 1989. S. Kealhofer and O. Vasicek are two former academics from U.C. Berkeley.

2. See Moody's (1995). See also Chapter 7 for a description of the Moody's data.

3. This can lead to adverse selection of corporate customers in banks. Indeed, if the pricing of loans is based on this average historical default rate, then a typical customer will be overcharged and may have an incentive to leave, while the worst obligors in the class will benefit from an advantageous pricing with regard to their actual credit risk.

4. See, for example, Duffie (1992).

5. This contribution has been followed by Galai and Masulis (1976); Black and Cox (1976); Merton (1977); Lee (1981); Ho and Singer

(1982); Pitts and Selby (1983); Johnson and Stulz (1987); Chance (1990); Cooper and Mello (1991); Shimko, Tejima, and van Deventer (1993); Leland (1994); and Kim, Ramaswamy, and Sundaresan (1996).

6. In the following "exogenous" refers to the assumptions specified outside the model and that constitute a given in the model derivation, while "endogenous" characterizes results derived from the model.

7. See also Litterman and Iben (1991) and Madan and Unal (1996). This approach is consistent with the CreditMetrics methodology suggested by JP Morgan (1997) to assess credit risk exposure for the banks' portfolio of fixed-income instruments.

8. This approach is difficult to implement in practice, and in some instances the model calibration yields negative default probabilities. This inconsistent result comes from the fact that liquidity risk is ignored (at least in early versions of this approach) and the recovery factors not only vary over time, but also should be endogenously determined in the model since the loss incurred by the debt holders should depend explicitly on the value of the firm's assets.

9. Sections 2 to 4 are drawn from our paper "Credit Risk Revisited," which appeared in *Risk*, March 1998.

10. The model builds on Black and Cox's (1976) extension of Merton's (1974) model.

11. A leverage factor equal to 0.7 is obtained by a face value $F = 77$.

12. The computed cost of default is slightly different from the put value due to rounding errors.

13. See Vasicek (1997) and Kealhofer (1995,1998). See also Appendix 1 of Chapter 8.

14. That is, the composition of its liabilities: equity, short-term and long-term debt, convertible bonds, and so on.

15. Financial models consider essentially market values of assets, and not accounting values, or book values, which only represent the historical cost of the physical assets, net of their depreciation. Only the market value is a good measure of the value of the firm's ongoing business, and it changes as market participants revise the firm's future prospects. KMV models the market value of assets. In fact, there might be huge differences between both the market and the book values of total assets. For example, as of February 1998 KMV has estimated the market value of Microsoft assets as $US228.6 billion versus $US16.8 billion for their book value, while for Trump Hotel and Casino the book value, which amounts to $US2.5 billion, is higher than the market value of $US1.8 billion.

16. The exception is when the firm's portfolio of businesses has changed substantially through mergers and acquisitions, or restructuring.

17. See also Crouhy and Galai (1994); Bensoussan, Crouhy, and Galai (1994,1995); and Vasicek (1997) for the valuation of equity for more complex capital structures which, for example, include equity warrants and convertible bonds.

18. In the general case, the resolution of this model may require the implementation of complex numerical techniques, with no analytical solution, due to the complexity of the boundary conditions attached to the various liabilities. See, for example, Vasicek (1997).

19. It can be shown that $\sigma_S = \eta_{S,A}\, \sigma$ where $\eta_{S,A}$ denotes the elasticity of equity to asset value; i.e., $\eta_{S,A} = (V/S)\,(\partial S/\partial V)$ (see Bensoussan, Crouhy, and Galai 1994). In the simple Merton framework, where the firm is financed only by equity and zero-coupon debt, equity is a call option on the assets of the firm with a striking price of the face value of the debt, and a maturity of the redemption date of the bond. Then, the partial derivative $\partial S/\partial V$ is simply the delta of the call with respect to the underlying asset of the firm.

20. See the Appendix for Chapter 8: the distance to default can be easily derived from expressions (1) and (4).

21. See, for example, Jarrow and Turnbull (1997b), Chapters 5 and 6.

22. An empirical issue is whether the corporate spread should be calculated over the Treasury curve, or instead over the LIBOR (swap) curve. It seems that the best fits are obtained when spreads are calculated over LIBOR.

23. See, for example, Elton and Gruber (1995, Chapter 8). While a multi-factor model can be implemented directly, the model gains very convenient mathematical properties if the factors are uncorrelated, i.e., orthogonal. There are simple techniques to convert any set of correlated factors into a set of orthogonal factors. In that case we would have $\text{cov}(I_1,I_2) = 0$.

24. For a review of multifactor models see Elton and Gruber (1995) and Rudd and Clasing (1988). The most widely used technique in portfolio management is the single-index model, or market model, which assumes that the comovement between stock returns is due to a single common index, the market portfolio. The return generating process for this model is described by $r_k = \alpha_k + \beta_k r_M + \epsilon_k$, where r_M denotes the rate of return on the market portfolio. This model can then be extended to capture industry effects beyond the general market effects. Rosenberg (1974) has developed a model for predicting extra market covariance which relates not only industry

factors, but also company-specific descriptors such as market variability, and which captures the risk of the firm as perceived by the market, earnings variability, index of low valuation and lack of success, immaturity and smallness, growth orientation, and financial risk (see Rudd and Clasing 1988). Finally, a number of multifactor models have been proposed which relate security returns to macroeconomic variables. Excess returns are explained by the unexpected changes, or innovations, in variables such as inflation, economic growth as measured by unexpected change in industrial production, business cycles as proxied by the corporate spread over Treasuries, long-term interest rates, short-term interest rates, and currency fluctuations (see Chen, Roll, and Ross 1986 and Berry, Burmeister, and McElroy 1988).

25. Compustat is a database of financial and economic information about firms.

26. SIC denotes the Standard Industrial Classification, which is a U.S.-based business classification system.

27. This is in contrast with the reduced-form approach presented in the next chapter, where default is modeled as an exogenous Poisson-type process independent of the capital structure of the firm and its asset value. In this framework default is always a "surprise" and does not relate to the financial health of the firm.

28. Frank and Torous (1989) found that substantial deviations from strict priority rules are common in the United States (Chapter 11). Essentially, all the observed deviations were in favor of equity holders and against the existing claims of debt holders. They estimate the impact of these deviations on the yield spread predicted by Merton's model as up to 120 to 150 bp for a 15-year bond. See also Kim, Ramaswamy, and Sundaresan (1993) and Anderson and Sundaresan (1996).

29. If we assume that shareholders do not have to put additional money into a firm to allow it to continue operating, then it is not in their interest to shut down the firm when the asset value falls below the threshold K. Indeed, when the assets value falls below K before debt maturity, there is still a positive probability that the firm will recover before the debt matures. Therefore, the value of equity (debt) is worth more (less) if the firm is not shut down.

30. See also Chance (1990).

31. In practice the correlation ρ is negative.

32. See also Hull and White (1995).

Other Approaches: The Actuarial and Reduced-Form Approaches to Measuring Credit Risk

1. INTRODUCTION

In the structural models of default that we discussed in Chapter 9, default time is jointly determined by the stochastic process of the firm's assets, and its capital structure. Default occurs when the asset value falls below a certain boundary such as a promised payment (e.g., the Merton 1974 framework).

By contrast, CreditRisk+ and the "reduced form" models that are analyzed in this chapter treat the firm's bankruptcy process, including recovery, as exogenous. CreditRisk+, released in late 1997 by Credit Suisse Financial Products (CSFP), is a purely actuarial model. This means that the probabilities of default that the model employs are based on historical statistical data of default experience by credit class.

CreditRisk+ assumes that the probability distribution for the number of defaults over any period of time follows a Poisson distribution. Under this assumption, CreditRisk+ produces the loss distribution of a bond or loan portfolio based on the individual default characteristics of each security and their pair-wise default correlations.

The reduced-form approaches also use a Poisson-like process to describe default. Contrary to the structural approach to modeling default, the timing of default is assumed to take the bondholders "by surprise." Default is treated as a stopping time with a hazard rate process.[1] The reduced-form approach is less intuitive than the structural model from an economic point of view, but it is calibrated using credit spreads that are "observable." We show in this chapter that, in this framework, the modeling of credit risky securities is similar to the modeling of ordinary term structures.

2. THE ACTUARIAL APPROACH: CREDITRISK+

2.1 The Probability of Default

CreditRisk+ applies an actuarial science framework to the derivation of the loss distribution of a bond/loan portfolio.[2] Only default risk is modeled; downgrade risk is ignored. Unlike the KMV approach to modeling default, there is no attempt to relate default risk to the capital structure of the firm. Also, no assumptions are made about the causes of default: an obligor A is either in default with probability P_A, or it is not in default with probability $1-P_A$.

It is assumed that:

- For a loan, the probability of default in a given period, say one month, is the same as in any other month.
- For a large number of obligors, the probability of default by any particular obligor is small, and the number of defaults that occur in any given period is independent of the number of defaults that occur in any other period.

Under these assumptions, the probability distribution for the number of defaults during a given period of time (say, one year) is well represented by a Poisson distribution:[3]

$$\text{Prob}(n \text{ defaults}) = \frac{\bar{n}^n e^{-\bar{n}}}{n!} \quad \text{for } n = 0,1,2,\ldots \quad (1)$$

where:

$$\bar{n} = \text{average number of defaults per year} \left(\bar{n} = \sum_A P_A\right)$$

The annual number of defaults, n, is a stochastic variable with mean $\bar{n}$, and standard deviation $\sqrt{\bar{n}}$. The Poisson distribution has

FIGURE 10.1

CreditRisk+ Risk Measurement Framework

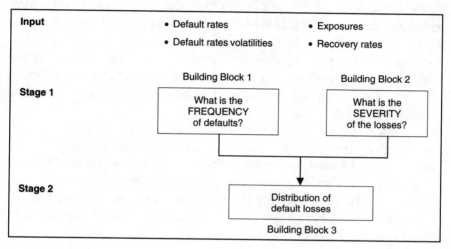

Source: CreditRisk+.

a useful property: it can be fully specified by means of a single parameter, $\bar{n}$.[4] For example, if we assume $\bar{n} = 3$, then the probability of "no default" in the next year is:

$$\text{Prob}(0 \text{ default}) = \frac{3^0 e^{-3}}{0!} = 0.05 = 5\%$$

while the probability of exactly three defaults is:

$$\text{Prob}(3 \text{ defaults}) = \frac{3^3 e^{-3}}{3!} = 0.224 = 22.4\%$$

The distribution of default losses for a portfolio is derived in two stages (Figure 10.1).

2.2 Frequency of Default Events (Building Block 1)

So far, we have assumed that a standard Poisson distribution approximates the distribution of the number of default events. If this were the case, we should expect the standard deviation of the default rate to be approximately equal to the square root of the mean, i.e., $\sqrt{\bar{n}}$, where $\bar{n}$ is the average default rate.

For example, turning to Table 8.3, we might expect the standard deviation of the default rate of obligors in rating category B to be close to $\sqrt{7.62}$, i.e., 2.76; in fact, the table reports an actual standard deviation of 5.1. We have derived similar observations for Baa and Ba obligors. In these circumstances, the Poisson distribution underestimates the probability of default. This is not surprising if we observe the variability of default rates over time.[5] (Intuitively, we expect the mean default rate to change over time depending on the business cycle.)

This suggests that the Poisson distribution can only be used to represent the default process if, as CreditRisk+ suggests, we make the additional assumption that the mean default rate is itself stochastic, with mean $\bar{n}$ and standard deviation $\sigma_{\bar{n}}$.[6]

Figure 10.2 shows what happens when we incorporate this assumption. The distribution of defaults becomes more skewed and exhibits a "fat tail" to the right-hand side of the figure.

FIGURE 10.2

Distribution of Default Events

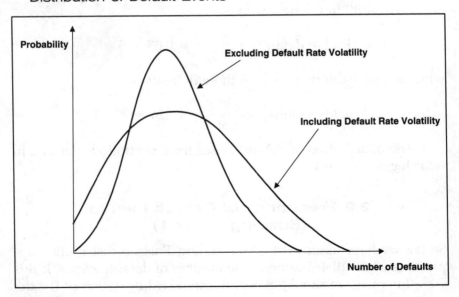

2.3 Severity of the Losses (Building Block 2)

In the event of default by an obligor, the counterparty incurs a loss that is equal to the amount owned by the obligor (i.e., its exposure, which is equal to the marked-to-market value, if positive—and zero otherwise) less a recovery amount.[7]

In CreditRisk+, the exposure for each obligor is adjusted by the anticipated recovery rate in order to calculate the "loss given default." These adjusted exposures are exogenous to the model, and are independent of market risk and downgrade risk.

2.4 Distribution of Default Losses for a Portfolio (Building Block 3)

In order to derive the loss distribution for a well-diversified portfolio, the losses (exposures, net of the recovery adjustments) are divided into bands. The level of exposure in each band is approximated by means of a single number.

Example

Suppose the bank holds a portfolio of loans and bonds from 500 different obligors, with exposures of between \$50,000 and \$1 million. We use the following notation:

	Notation
Obligor	A
Exposure	LGD_A
Probability of default	P_A
Expected loss	$EL_A = LGD_A \times P_A$

In Table 10.1, we show the exposures for the first six obligors. The unit of exposure is assumed to be $L = \$100,000$. Each band $j, j = 1, \ldots, m$, with $m = 10$, has an average common exposure $L_j = \$100,000 \times j$.

TABLE 10.1

Exposure per Obligor

Obligor A	Exposure ($) (Loss Given Default) LGD_A	Exposure (in $100,000)	Round-Off Exposure (in $100,000) L_j	Band j
1	150,000	1.5	2	2
2	460,000	4.6	5	5
3	435,000	4.35	4	4
4	370,000	3.7	4	4
5	190,000	1.9	2	2
6	480,000	4.8	5	5

In CreditRisk+, each band is viewed as an independent portfolio of loans/bonds, for which we introduce the following notation:

	Notation
Common exposure in band j in units of L	L_j
Expected loss in band j in units of L	EL_j
Expected number of defaults in band j	$\bar{n}_j$

Then, by definition we have:

$$EL_j = L_j \cdot \bar{n}_j$$

Hence:

$$\bar{n}_j = \frac{EL_j}{L_j} \tag{2}$$

Denote by E_A the expected loss for obligor A in units of L; i.e.:

$$E_A = \frac{EL_A}{L}$$

Then, the expected loss over a one-year period in band j, EL_j, expressed in units of L, is simply the sum of the expected losses E_A of all the obligors that belong to band j; i.e.:

$$EL_j = \sum_{A:L_A=L_j} E_A$$

TABLE 10.2

Expected Number of Defaults in Each Band

Band: j	Number of Obligors	EL_j	$\bar{n}_j$
1	30	1.5	1.5
2	40	8	4
3	50	6	2
4	70	25.2	6.3
5	100	35	7
6	60	14.4	2.4
7	50	38.5	5.5
8	40	19.2	2.4
9	40	25.2	2.8
10	20	4	0.4

From (2) it follows that the expected number of defaults per annum in band j is:

$$\bar{n}_j = \frac{EL_j}{L_j} = \sum_{A:L_A=L_j} \frac{E_A}{L_j} = \sum_{A:L_A=L_j} \frac{E_A}{L_A}$$

Table 10.2 provides an illustration of the results of these calculations. To derive the distribution of losses for the entire portfolio, we need to fulfil the three steps outlined below.

Step 1: Probability Generating Function for Each Band

Each band is viewed as a separate portfolio of exposures. The probability generating function for any band, say band j, is by definition:

$$G_j(z) = \sum_{n=0}^{\infty} \text{Prob}(\text{loss} = nL)z^n = \sum_{n=0}^{\infty} \text{Prob}(n \text{ defaults})z^{nL_j}$$

where the losses are expressed in the unit L of exposure.

To derive the distribution of losses for the entire portfolio, we proceed as follows. Since we have assumed that the number of defaults follows a Poisson distribution (1), then:

$$G_j(z) = \sum_{n=0}^{\infty} \frac{e^{-\bar{n}_j}\bar{n}_j^n}{n!} z^{nL_j} = e^{-\bar{n}_j + \bar{n}_j z^{L_j}} \tag{3}$$

Step 2: Probability Generating Function for the
Entire Portfolio

Since we have assumed that each band is a portfolio of exposures,
independent from the other bands, the probability generating function for the entire portfolio is simply the product of the probability generating function for each band:

$$G(z) = \prod_{j=1}^{m} e^{-\bar{n}_j + \bar{n}_j z^{L_j}} = e^{-\sum_{j=1}^{m} \bar{n}_j + \sum_{j=1}^{m} \bar{n}_j z^{L_j}} \tag{4}$$

where $\bar{n} = \Sigma_{j=1}^{m} \bar{n}_j$ denotes the expected number of defaults for the
entire portfolio.

Step 3: Loss Distribution for the Entire Portfolio

Given the probability generating function (4), it is straightforward
to derive the loss distribution, since:

$$Prob(\text{loss of } nL) = \frac{1}{n!} \frac{d^n G(z)}{dz^n} \Big|_{z=0} \qquad \text{for } n = 1, 2, \ldots$$

These probabilities can be expressed in closed form and depend on only two sets of parameters: EL_j and L_j.[8]

2.5 Extensions of the Basic Model

CreditRisk+ proposes several extensions of the basic one-period, one-
factor model. First, the model can be easily extended to a multiperiod framework, and second, the variability of default rates can be
assumed to result from a number of "background" factors, each
representing a sector of activity. Each factor k is represented by a random variable X_k, which is the number of defaults in sector k, and
which is assumed to be gamma distributed. The mean default rate for
each obligor is then supposed to be a linear function of the background
factors X_k. These factors are further assumed to be independent.

In all cases, CreditRisk+ derives a closed-form solution for
the loss distribution of a bond/loan portfolio.

2.6 Advantages and Limitations of CreditRisk+

CreditRisk+ has the advantage that it is relatively easy to implement.
First, as we mentioned above, closed-form expressions can be derived
for the probability of portfolio bond/loan losses, and this makes

CreditRisk+ very attractive from a computational point of view. In addition, marginal risk contributions by obligor can be easily computed. Second, CreditRisk+ focuses on default, and therefore it requires relatively few estimates and "inputs." For each instrument, only the probability of default and the exposure are required.

Its principal limitation is the same as for the CreditMetrics and KMV approaches: the methodology assumes that credit risk has no relationship with the level of market risk (interest rates are assumed to be deterministic). In addition, CreditRisk+ ignores what might be called "migration risk"; the exposure for each obligor is fixed and is not sensitive to possible future changes in the credit quality of the issuer, or to the variability of future interest rates. Even in its most general form, where the probability of default depends upon several stochastic background factors, the credit exposures are taken to be constant and are not related to changes in these factors.

Finally, like the CreditMetrics and KMV approaches, CreditRisk+ is not able to cope satisfactorily with nonlinear products such as options and foreign currency swaps.

3 THE REDUCED-FORM APPROACH OR INTENSITY-BASED MODELS

Like CreditRisk+, the reduced-form approach takes the firm's bankruptcy process, including recovery, as exogenous. In this section, we show that the modeling of defaultable securities in this framework is similar to the modeling of ordinary term structures.

3.1 The Basic Model

The following example illustrates the approach and provides a heuristic derivation of the main result. As is customary in the term structure literature, we assume that the securities are priced with regard to their discounted expected cash flows, where the expectation is based upon "risk-neutral" probabilities (see Chapter 9, Section 6 and Appendix 2).

Suppose that we are interested in pricing a two-year defaultable zero-coupon bond that pays 100, providing there is no default event. The annual (risk-neutral) risk-free rate process is shown in Figure 10.3 with:

FIGURE 10.3

Risk-Free Interest Rate Process

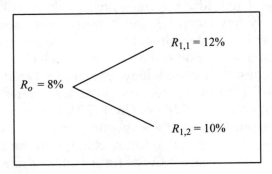

- Annual default (risk-neutral) probability, or hazard rate, $\lambda = 0.06$.[9]
- Loss given default, $LGD = 60$ percent, as a fraction of the security's price at the time of default.
- $1 - LGD = 40$ percent is the recovery rate.

The annual risk-free rate is taken to be 8 percent at the time of the calculation, and we assume that it might move up to 12 percent with probability $p = 0.5$, or move up to 10 percent with probability $1 - p = 0.5$.

If the riskless interest rate moves up to 12 percent, the value $V_{1,1}$, of the two-year bond at year 1 will be the survival probability, $1 - \lambda = 94$ percent, times the payoff given survival, i.e., 100, plus the default probability λ multiplied by the payoff given default, $(1 - LGD)100 = 40$, all discounted at 12 percent:

$$V_{1,1} = \frac{0.94 \times 100 + 0.06(1 - 0.6)100}{1.12} = 86.07$$

This means that the bond is discounted at an effective "default-adjusted" interest at that node in the interest rate tree of:

$$Y = \frac{100}{86.07} - 1 = 16.2\%$$

i.e., Y is solution of the following equation:

$$\frac{1}{1 + Y} = \frac{1}{1 + R}[(1 - \lambda) + \lambda(1 - LGD)] \tag{1}$$

so that:

$$Y = \frac{R + \lambda LGD}{1 - \lambda + \lambda(1 - LGD)} \tag{2}$$

Using (2) as a specification for the default risk-adjusted short-rate process, there is no loss of generality for the purpose of pricing a defaultable claim in treating the claim as default-free, but replacing the default-free discounting rate R by the default-adjusted short rate Y.

Figure 10.4 shows the full derivation of the two-year defaultable zero-coupon bond price. Figure 10.5 shows the tree of the default risk-adjusted short-rate process according to (2) and the corresponding pricing tree.

For time periods of length Δt we can follow the same reasoning as for (2) and obtain:

$$Y\Delta t = \frac{r\Delta t + \lambda\Delta t LGD}{1 - \lambda\Delta t + \lambda\Delta t(1 - LGD)} \tag{3}$$

where r, Y, and λ are in annualized form. Dividing by Δt, and taking the limits as Δt tends to zero, gives the "continuous time" continuously compounded default risk-adjusted short-rate process (Figure 10.6).

$$Y = r + \lambda LGD \tag{4}$$

where λLGD is the risk-neutral expected loss rate, which can be interpreted as the spread over the risk-free rate that is necessary to compensate the investor for the risk of default. Under this formulation, the credit spread is not easy to decompose into its default risk and loss risk components, unless additional assumptions are brought into the model. See Duffie and Singleton (1997) for a rigorous proof of this fundamental result.[10]

The price of an issuer's obligation to pay some random amount CF at time T has a market value at any time t before default happens of:

$$V(t,T) = E^*\left[\exp\left(-\int_t^T Y(s)ds\right)CF\right] \tag{5}$$

where E^* is the risk-neutral expectation operator and Y denotes the term structure of interest rates for the defaultable security (Figure 10.4).

FIGURE 10.4

Pricing of a Two-Year Defaultable Zero-Coupon Bond

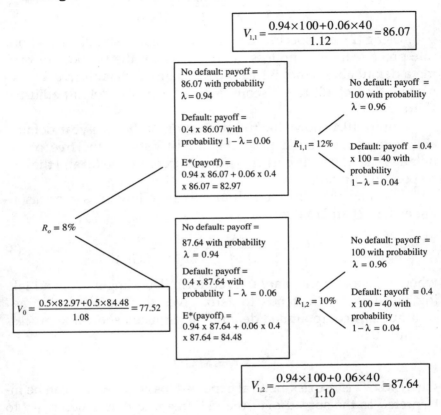

Note: E* (payoff) denotes the value of the bond at time 1-E, just before the investor discovers whether the bond is about to default.

By modeling the default-adjusted rate we can incorporate other factors that affect spreads such as liquidity:

$$Y = r + \lambda LGD + l \tag{6}$$

where l denotes the "liquidity" adjustment premium, which can be viewed as a convenience yield. It is positive (negative liquidity premium) when there is a shortage of bonds and one can benefit from holding the bond in inventory. The convenience yield is negative (positive liquidity premium) when it becomes difficult to sell the bond because of the lack of liquidity in the market. Note that the default time τ does not appear anywhere in (5) and (6). It has been replaced by the expected loss rate λLGD.

FIGURE 10.5

Default Risk-Adjusted Short-Rate Process

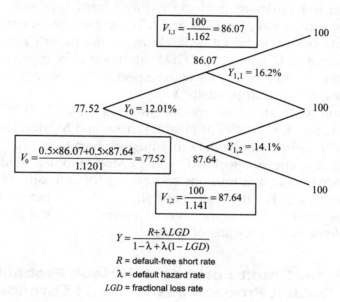

$$Y = \frac{R + \lambda LGD}{1 - \lambda + \lambda(1 - LGD)}$$

R = default-free short rate
λ = default hazard rate
LGD = fractional loss rate

FIGURE 10.6

Term Structure of Interest Rates

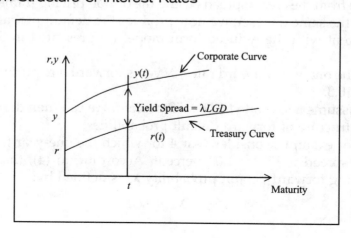

According to (6) the spread increases as the hazard rate λ, the loss rate LGD, and the liquidity premium l, rise.

The implementation of the reduced-form approach necessitates the estimation of λ, LGD and l. There are some identification problems since we cannot separate in (6) the hazard rate λ from the loss rate LGD. Generally, LGD is assumed to be given and constant. Implementations differ with respect to the assumptions made regarding the default intensity λ.

Any term structure model such as Vasicek (1977), Cox, Ingersoll, and Ross (1985) or Heath, Jarrow, and Morton (1992) can be applied directly to the default-adjusted short-term rate Y, or the forward rate curve associated with Y. More sophisticated implementations make assumptions concerning the intensity of the default process, λ. For the simple specification of λ where, for example, it depends solely on the level of interest rates, the model may be implemented by means of lattices.

3.2 From Credit Spreads to Default Probabilities and Default Probabilities to Credit Spreads: An Illustration of the Reduced-Form Approach

Example 1
How can we derive the term structure of implied default probabilities from the term structure of credit spread?

Consider the example of Appendix 1 in the previous chapter. We derived the cost of credit risk and the implied default probabilities from the credit spreads using the option pricing framework. Using the same data set, we now produce the default probabilities consistent with the reduced-form model (4) presented in Section 3.1.

The one-year forward rates, N years forward, are presented in Table 10.3.

Assume a loss rate $LGD = 50$ percent. We can then derive the term structure of forward default probabilities.

For example, consider year 4 for which the one-year forward credit spread is $FS_4 = 1.08$ percent. According to (4), the corresponding forward default probability λ_4 is defined by:

$$FS_4 = \lambda_4 \times LGD$$

TABLE 10.3

One-Year Forward Rates, N Years Forward

Maturity: t (Years)	U.S Treasury Forwards (%)	Company X Forwards (%)	One-Year Forward Credit Spreads t Years Forward: FS_t (%)
1	5.52	5.76	.24
2	6.30	6.74	.44
3	6.40	7.05	.65
4	6.56	7.64	1.08
5	6.56	7.71	1.15
6	6.81	8.21	1.40
7	6.81	8.47	1.65

from which it follows

$$\lambda_4 = \frac{FS_4}{LGD} = \frac{1.08}{0.5} = 2.16\%$$

From the term structure of forward default probabilities we can derive the cumulative default probabilities P_t (see Table 10.4):

$$P_t = P_{t-1} + (1 - P_{t-1})\lambda_t$$

TABLE 10.4

Term Structure of Default Probabilities

Maturity: t (Years)	Term Structure of Forward Default Probabilities: λ_t (%)	Cumulative Default Probabilities: P_t (%)	Conditional Default Probabilities: p_t (%)
1	.48	.48	.48
2	.88	1.36	.88
3	1.30	2.64	1.28
4	2.16	4.74	2.10
5	2.30	6.93	2.19
6	2.80	9.54	2.61
7	3.30	12.52	2.99

where P_t and λ_t denote the cumulative and the forward default probabilities for period t, respectively. The cumulative probability of default up to period t is equal to the cumulative default probability P_{t-1} up to period $t - 1$, plus the probability of survival up to period $t - 1$, $1 - P_{t-1}$, times the marginal probability of default during period t, λ_t. For the first period, $P_1 = \lambda_1 = 0.48\%$.

For example, the cumulative probability of default up to period 5 is:

$$
\begin{aligned}
P_5 &= P_4 + (1 - P_4)\lambda_5 \\
&= .0474 + (1 - .0474)\, 0.023 \\
&= 6.93\%
\end{aligned}
$$

Finally, we can compute the conditional probability of default, p_t, in period t. It is the probability of default in that period, conditional on no default in the previous years; i.e.:

$$p_t = (1 - P_{t-1})\lambda_t$$

For example, the conditional probability of default in period 5 is:

$$
\begin{aligned}
p_5 &= (1 - P_4)\lambda_5 \\
&= (1 - 0.0474)\, 0.0230 \\
&= 2.19\%
\end{aligned}
$$

The term structure of the conditional default probabilities is shown in Table 10.4.

Example 2

How can we derive the term structure of spreads from the term structure of default probabilities?

Consider a security that promises to pay \$1 each year for the next three years. Given the term structure of default probabilities in Table 10.4 and the zero-coupon curve (see Appendix 1 in Chapter 9), we can derive the cost of credit risk (Table 10.5).

In Table 10.5, the spread of 43 bp would be the annual fee for three years, for a default swap or a security paying \$1 each year for the next three years. (The calculation takes account only of issuer default risk, and assumes that there is no chance that the counterparty to the default swap itself will default.[11])

TABLE 10.5

Spread for a Defaultable Security

Maturity: t (Years)	Conditional Default Probability: p_t (%)	Loss Given Default: *LGD* (%)	Risk-Free Zero Rate (%)	Discounted Expected Loss (%)
1	.48	50	5.52	0.227
2	.88	50	5.91	0.392
3	1.28	50	6.07	0.536
			Total	1.155
	Annualized spread over the three-year period			0.43 (43 bp)

Notes: • The discounted expected loss is derived using the risk-neutral probability P_t

• The annualized spread S_3 satisfies the equation:

$$S_3\left(\frac{1}{1.0552} + \frac{1}{(1.0591)^2} + \frac{1}{(1.0607)^3}\right) = 1.155\%$$

3.3 Default Intensity Level Depends on the State of the Economy[12]

The Duffie-Singleton framework has been generalized by Lando (1997, 1998) and Jarrow and Turnbull (1998) to allow for the intensity of the default process, λ, to be random as it depends on X_t, the vector of state variables influencing credit risk, such as default-free interest rates, stock market indices, etc.

$$\lambda(t) = \lambda(X_t)$$

is modeled as a Cox process, which keeps the properties of a Poisson process, conditioned on X_t.[13]

The results of Duffie and Singleton (1997) obtain here; i.e.:

$$Y(t) = r(t) + \lambda(t)LGD + l \tag{7}$$

In order to facilitate the model's implementation, Jarrow and Turnbull propose the following assumptions:

• $r(t)$, the risk-free spot rate, follows a one-factor extended Vasicek (1977) model.

- $\lambda(t)$, the intensity process, is a function of two state variables, $r(t)$ and $W_M(t)$, the unexpected change in the market index:

$$\lambda(t) = \lambda_0 + \lambda_1 r(t) + \lambda_2 W_M(t)$$

where λ_0, λ_1, and λ_2 are constant.

$W_M(t)$ is the *innovation, i.e., random shock, of the level* of the market index, with the stock market index, $M(t)$, being assumed to follow a standard log-normal process:

$$dM(t) = [r(t)dt + \sigma_M dW_M(t)]M(t)$$

- *LGD*, the loss rate, is a constant.
- *l*, the liquidity premium, is assumed to depend on the risk-free rate $r(t)$, the stock market index $M(t)$, and a measure of intraday volatility:

$$l(t) = l_0 + l_1 r(t) + l_2 M(t) + l_3 [M_H(t) - M_L(t)]^2$$

where $M(t)$ is the closing price of the market index and $M_H(t)$ and $M_L(t)$ denote the high price and low price for the market index, respectively. This model applies to a portfolio of bonds and allows for the default correlations of various issuers. Default correlation is captured through the hazard functions of the various issuers i, $\lambda_i(r(t), M(t))$.[14]

3.4 Default Intensity Level Depends on the Credit Rating of the Issuer

Default events are modeled as a Markov process making use of the issuer's credit rating, in the spirit of the credit migration approach presented in Chapter 9; the approach was first proposed in Jarrow, Lando, and Turnbull (1997). It allows different recovery rates to be applied to debts of various levels of seniority.

The inputs for this model are:

- The term structure of default-free rates
- The term structure of credit spreads for each credit category
- The loss rate for each rating category
- The credit rating transition matrix

The model assumes:

- That there is no correlation between rating migrations and the dynamics of riskless interest rates (i.e., credit spreads are assumed to be uncorrelated with interest rates). This contradicts much of the empirical evidence.
- That credit spreads are deterministic as long as there are no rating changes.[15]
- That recovery rates are constant.[16]
- That when there is a default, recovery takes place at the maturity of the instrument.[17]

3.5 Spread-Based Models

An alternative approach is to make a direct assumption about the stochastic process that governs the dynamics of the credit spread. This is a parsimonious method, which may prove useful for valuing certain credit derivatives, such as options on credit spreads. These models are not derived from assumptions about the default process itself. Longstaff and Schwartz (1995a, 1995b) assume the following risk-adjusted processes for the default-free short rate r, and the logarithm of the credit spread U:[18]

$$dr = (\alpha - \beta r)dt + \sigma_r dZ_r$$
$$dU = (a - bX)dt + \sigma_u dZ_u$$
$$\text{corr}(dZ_r, dZ_u) = \rho$$

This specification implies that changes in U are mean reverting and homoskedastic, which is consistent with empirical data. It also implies that credit spreads remain positive and that they are conditionally log-normally distributed, i.e., log-normally distributed with parameters depending on the state of the economy at the time of the calculation. The riskless short-term interest rate is assumed to follow the single-factor Vasicek (1977) model. Z_r and Z_u are standard Brownian motion; ρ is the correlation coefficient between the interest rates and the logarithm of the spread; and α, β and a,b are the mean reversion coefficients for the interest rate and the spread processes, respectively.

NOTES

1. "Stopping time" is a probabilistic term for the time at which "death", i.e., default, occurs. "Hazard rate process" is an expression borrowed from the insurance literature that defines the frequency of rare events such as death or default. It is also the Poisson parameter μ in expression (1). In credit models of the family discussed in this chapter the default rate is not a constant, but depends on macro-economic factors such as interest rates and the level of equity markets.

2. CreditRisk+ is a trademark of Credit Suisse Financial Products (CSFP) now reorganized into CSFB. CreditRisk+ is described in a CSFP publication; see Credit Suisse (1997).

3. In any portfolio there is, naturally, a finite number of obligors, say n; therefore, the Poisson distribution, which specifies the probability of n defaults, for $n = 1, \ldots, \infty$ is only an approximation. However, if the number of obligors, n, is large enough, then the sum of the probabilites of $n + 1, n + 2, \ldots$ defaults become negligible.

4. Expression (1) can be derived from the probability generating function for a portfolio of independent obligors (see CreditRisk+ 1997, pp. 34–35).

5. See Figure 8.1 in Chapter 8.

6. CreditRisk+ assumes that the mean default rate is gamma distributed. Mean default rate volatility may also reflect the influence of default correlation and background factors, such as a change in the rate of growth in the economy, which may in turn affect the correlation of default events.

7. See Table 8.6 in Chapter 8.

8. See Credit Suisse (1997), p. 36.

9. If τ denotes the time to default, the survival probability at horizon t is:

$$\text{Prob}(\tau > t) = E\left[\exp\left(- \int_0^t \lambda(s)ds\right)\right]$$

When λ is a constant, then

$$\text{Prob}(\tau > t) = E[\exp(- \lambda t)]$$

The probability of default over the interval $(t, t + \Delta t)$, provided no default has happened until time t, is:

$$\text{Prob}[t < \tau \leq t + \Delta t] = \lambda(t)\Delta t$$

10. Lando (1994) derived the same result in his thesis, with no recovery, i.e., L = 1, but he employs a framework that uses a generalization of a Poisson process in which the default intensity λ is allowed to be random (Cox process). See also Hughston (1997).

11. See Duffie and Singleton (1995), Duffie and Huang (1996), and Jarrow and Turnbull (1995) for general pricing models that take into account the risk of bilateral default, based on the reduced-form approach. These approaches facilitate the pricing of credit derivatives where both the issuer of the underlying security and the counterparty to the credit derivative are default prone, and where default events are correlated.

12. Another stochastic intensity model is Madan and Unal (1995) where the intensity is modeled as a function of the excess return on the issuer's equity.

13. See Lando (1998).

14. Other generalizations involve the work of Duffie, Singleton, and Skiadas (1995) and Duffie and Huang (1995).

15. An extension of the model accounting for stochastic spreads can be found in Lando (1994).

16. Das and Tufano (1996) make a simple but useful extension by allowing the recovery rate to be stochastic and correlated to interest rates. This model remains computationally tractable and can be implemented in a two-variable binomial tree approach, with one tree for interest rates and one tree for the recovery rate.

17. This model is an extension of Jarrow and Turnbull (1995), who assume a constant hazard rate and constant recovery rate of par and maturity. See also Litterman and Iben (1991).

18. The credit spread is assumed to remain positive. See also Nielsen and Ronn (1995). Pedrosa and Roll (1998) show that the distribution of the changes in credit spreads exhibits a fat tail, and that a mixture of normal distributions provides a reasonably good representation of this distribution.

CHAPTER 11

Comparison of Industry-Sponsored Credit Models and Associated Back-Testing Issues

1. INTRODUCTION

In Chapters 8 to 10 we presented the four mainstream approaches to measuring credit risk in a portfolio context. These are the credit migration approach (CreditMetrics and CreditPortfolioView), the contingent-claim approach based on the Merton model (KMV), the actuarial approach (CreditRisk+), and the reduced-form approach based on models proposed by Duffie and Singleton (1997) and Jarrow and Turnbull (1995).[1]

Table 11.1 summarizes the key features of these models. The key input parameters common to all are credit exposures, recovery rates (or, equivalently, the "loss given default"), and default correlations.

Default correlations are captured in a variety of ways. KMV derives default correlations from asset returns correlations; CreditMetrics relies on a similar model but employs equity returns as a proxy for asset returns which are not directly observable. In the other models, the default probabilities are conditional on common systemic or macro factors. Any change in these factors affects all the probabilities of default, but to a different degree—depending on the sensitivity of each obligor to each risk factor.[2]

The current state of the art of risk modeling does not allow for the full integration of market and credit risk. Market risk models disregard credit risk, and credit risk models assume that

TABLE 11.1

Key Features of Credit Risk Models

Software	Credit Migration Approach		Contingent Claim Approach, KMV	Actuarial Approach, CreditRisk+	Reduced-Form Approach, Kamakura
	CreditMetrics	CreditPortfolio View			
Definition of risk	ΔMarket value	ΔMarket value	Default losses	Default losses	Default losses
Credit events	Downgrade/default	Downgrade/default	Continuous default probabilities	Default	Default
Risk drivers	Asset values	Macrofactors	Asset values	Expected default rates	Hazard rate
Transition probabilities	Constant	Driven by macrofactors	Driven by: –Individual term structure of EDF –Asset value process	N/A	N/A
Correlation of credit events	Standard multivariate normal distribution (equity factor model)	Conditional default probabilities function of macrofactors	Standard multivariate normal asset returns (asset factor model)	Conditional default probabilities function of common risk factors	Conditional default probabilities function of macrofactors
Recovery rates	Random (beta distribution)	Random (empirical distribution)	Random (beta distribution)	Loss given default deterministic	Loss given default deterministic
Numerical approach	Simulation/analytic	Simulation	Analytic/simulation	Analytic	Tree-based/simulation

credit exposures are determined exogenously. The next generation of credit models should remedy this.[3]

In this chapter we compare the various credit risk models by applying them to the same large diversified benchmark bond portfolio; the assumptions for each application are kept consistent. The results show that the models produce similar estimates of value at risk.[4]

The asset returns correlation model appears to be a critical factor in CreditMetrics, CreditVaR (CIBC's internal credit risk model), and KMV. When correlations are forced to 1, the values at risk are approximately 10 times greater than when correlations are assumed to be zero.

For models based on the principle of credit migration, the results are shown to be quite sensitive to the initial rating of the obligors. Value at risk for speculative portfolios is five or six times greater than for investment-grade portfolios. The results for CreditRisk+ are also very sensitive to default correlations as well as to the standard deviation of the default rate.

The study concludes that all these models are reasonable frameworks in which to capture credit risk for "vanilla" bonds and loans portfolios. For derivative instruments, such as swaps or loan commitments, which have contingent exposures, the models need to be extended to allow for stochastic interest rates. The incorporation of credit derivatives in those models creates another level of complexity, since the portfolio distribution is based on actual probabilities of default, while the pricing of the derivatives relies on risk-neutral probabilities. The next generation of credit risk models should address these thorny issues.

2. COMPARISON OF INDUSTRY-SPONSORED CREDIT RISK MODELS

For the test, we ran CreditMetrics, CIBC's internal CreditVaR model (based on the credit migration approach), KMV, and CreditRisk+ through a bond portfolio composed of 2000 exposures with maturities ranging from 1 to 30 years. The portfolio was diversified across 13 countries; the ratings of the issuers spanned the eight rating classes of Moody's rating system.

TABLE 11.2

Comparison of Industry-Sponsored Credit Risk Models: CreditMetrics, CreditVAR, and KMV

	CreditMetric Simulation (50,000 runs)	CreditVaR I Simulation (500,000 runs)	KMV Analytic
Current MTM value	911.1	911.1	890.0
Forward mean (one year from now)	928.5	861.4	
Standard deviation	27.3	25.4	20.5
10%—percentile loss	36.9	34.2	
5%—percentile loss	53.5	50.5	
1%—percentile loss	90.2	85.1	
0.1%—percentile loss	135.3	131.6	83.0

Notes: —MTM denotes the current mark-to-market value of the bond portfolio.
       —The forward mean value is computed cum reinvested coupons.
       —All values are reported in millions of U.S. dollars.

All values are reported in U.S. dollars. The one-year migration and default probabilites are 25-year averages taken from Moody's, while recovery rates for CreditMetrics, CreditVaR, and KMV are assumed to follow a beta distribution with a mean of 40 percent and a standard deviation of 25 percent. The yield curves were downloaded from the RiskMetrics web site. For CreditRisk+, we assumed a constant recovery rate of 40 percent, so that the aggregate exposure given default is simply 60 percent of the forward value. The horizon was taken to be one year.

Table 11.2 shows the results for CreditMetrics, CreditVaR, and KMV. The results for CreditMetrics and CreditVaR are very close. The difference in the forward values arises from the different bootstrapping techniques used in each model to produce the forward zero curves for interest rates.[5] We ran an early version of the KMV model, which derives the loss distribution analytically. The approximation is only accurate for confidence levels beyond 10 bp,[6] so we do not report the results for the one, five, and 10 percent confidence levels. (The current mark-to-market value differs from that in the other approaches because the KMV model relies on its

TABLE 11.3

Comparison of Industry-Sponsored Credit Risk Models: Credit Risk+

	Default Rate Standard Deviation			
	100%	50%	25%	0%
Current MTM value		911.1		
Forward mean (one year from now)		861.4		
Aggregate exposure given default		516.8		
Expected loss		30.4		
Standard deviation	20.4	13.0	10.3	9.2
5%—percentile loss	59.1	42.9	37.2	35.0
1%—percentile loss	92.2	58.3	47.7	43.8
0.1%—percentile loss	139.6	78.7	60.9	54.6

Notes: —Aggregate exposure given default = 60 percent of forward expected values.
　　　—All results are reported in millions of U.S. dollars.

own methodology to derive the spread curves from the government bond curves.)

Table 11.2 reveals that for a portfolio of loans with a current value of approximately $900 million, the one-year 1 percent VaR is $90.2 million for CreditMetrics and $85.1 million for CreditVaR. The 0.1 percent VaR shows a smaller discrepancy between CreditMetrics ($135.3 million) and CreditVaR ($131.6 million). For KMV, the 0.1 percent VaR is almost 40 percent lower, and is only $83 million.

Table 11.3 shows the results for CreditRisk+ for different levels of the standard deviation of the default rate. The Moody's statistics reproduced in Table 8.3 of Chapter 8 tell us that default rates are quite volatile from one year to the other, and a standard deviation of 100 percent seems to be a reasonable assumption. At the 10-bp confidence level, value at risk for CreditRisk+ is $139.6 million, which is very close to the results produced by CreditMetrics and CreditVaR I.

The results are thus contained within a relatively narrow range, i.e., $83 million (KMV) to $139 million (CreditRisk+). This empirical finding is consistent with the theoretical contributions of Koyluoglu and Hickman (1998) and Gordy (1998), who demonstrated that if the parameters are correctly harmonized in the various models, we can expect little difference in their results.

However, Tables 11.2 and 11.3 also illustrate that the differences between the models become more important, in relative terms, at higher (percentage) loss levels.

3. STRESS TESTING AND SCENARIO ANALYSIS

Each approach is sensitive to different key input parameters. For the credit migration approach, the key parameters are the asset return correlations that drive the default correlations, the credit quality of the obligors, the transition matrix, the recovery factors, and the spread curves.

The results from the contingent claim approach (KMV) are sensitive to asset return volatilities and correlations. The actuarial approach is sensitive to the standard deviation of the default rate and the rate of recovery (which determines the exposure for each facility).

Table 11.3 shows the sensitivity of value at risk for Credit-Risk+ when the standard deviation of the default rate is lowered from 100 percent to 0 percent. The portfolio becomes less risky and value at risk at the 10-bp level falls by a factor of 2.5 from $139.6 million to $54.6 million.

We have been able to carry out an extensive sensitivity analysis only in the case of our own internal model at CIBC, CreditVaR (Tables 11.4 to 11.6). The underlying portfolio is different from that used to compare CreditMetrics, CreditVaR, and KMV (Table 11.2). It represents 600 obligors, each with two facilities, a 10-year corporate bond, and a three-year loan. Table 11.4 illustrates the sensitivity of credit VaR to the credit quality of the portfolio. The first column reports the result for the initial portfolio.

We report not only value at risk at various confidence levels (i.e., 1 percent, 10 bp, and 3 bp[7]), but also EVaR at the same confidence levels. EVaR is the expected loss in the tail, i.e., the expected loss for all the possible losses beyond the threshold level corresponding to the confidence level.

TABLE 11.4

Sensitivity Analysis of Credit Migration Models to the Credit Quality of the Portfolio

	Initial Portfolio	Investment Grade	Speculative Grade	Downgraded By 2 Grade
Current MTM value	12,546	7,679	4,866	11,640
Forward mean (one year from now)	13,121	8,134	4,987	11,864
Standard deviation	151	22	139	351
1% VaR	3.6%	1.3%	8.1%	8.7%
1% EVaR	4.4%	1.7%	9.8%	10.5%
0.1% VaR	5.7%	2.3%	12.0%	12.8%
0.1% EVaR	6.5%	2.9%	13.5%	14.4%
0.03% VaR	6.6%	3.0%	13.9%	14.5%
0.03% EVaR	7.5%	3.8%	15.4%	16.1%

Note: Portfolio values and standard deviations are reported in millions of U.S. dollars. Credit VaR and EVaR are reported as a percentage of MTM value.

The second column shows the results for the sub-portfolio composed of investment-grade facilities, i.e., those rated AAA to BBB. Value at risk falls by a factor of 2 at the 3-bp level and by a factor of 3 at the 1 percent confidence level.

The third column shows the results for the complementary portfolio, i.e., the speculative portion of the portfolio rated BB, B, and CCC. Value at risk goes up by a factor of 2 relative to the portfolio's average. The last column shows the results for a portfolio where each issuer has been downgraded by two full grades and where there is a floor at the CCC rating. (That is, an obligor initially rated AA becomes BBB, but a B obligor is downgraded to CCC only.) This produces results similar to those of the speculative sub-portfolio.

In Table 11.5 we report the sensitivity of the analysis to the correlation of equity returns. In the first column we show the results when the correlations are forced to zero. Value at risk is reduced by a factor of 2. In the next column, the specific risk component of the correlation model is forced to zero, which increases the correlation with respect to the base case. Value at risk goes up

TABLE 11.5

Sensitivity Analysis of Credit Migration Models to Equity
Return Correlations

	Zero Correlation	Specific Risk = 0	Correlation = 1
Current MTM value	12,546	12,546	12,546
Forward mean (one year from now)	13,212	13,212	13,121
Standard deviation	99	305	618
1% VaR	2.1%	8.3%	21.9%
1% EVaR	2.4%	10.4%	25.6%
0.1% VaR	2.9%	13.2%	36.2%
0.1% EVaR	3.2%	15.2%	39.1%
0.03% VaR	3.2%	15.5%	39.2%
0.03% EVaR	3.4%	17.7%	43.4%

Note: Portfolio values and standard deviations are reported in millions of U.S. dollars. Credit VaR and EVaR are reported in percentage of MTM value.

by a factor of 2. In the last column, the correlation is forced to 1. Value at risk jumps up by a factor of 6! This shows that results are very sensitive to the correlation model and to its underlying multifactor structure (see Chapter 9, Section 7).

Table 11.6 reports what happened when we varied the default probabilities and the recovery rates. When the default probabilities are doubled, credit VaR increases by only 50 percent—a relatively low sensitivity. While increasing default probabilities increases default risk, it reduces migration risk—since migration probabilities (including default) must sum up to 1. In other words, default and migration risks partially compensate for one another.

In the base case we adopted a recovery rate of 40 percent for corporate (senior unsecured) bonds and 60 percent for the corresponding loans. When the recovery rates fall (increase) by 10 percentage points, value at risk increases (falls) by approximately 15 percent.

The base case, corresponding to the first column of Table 11.4, was computed using Moody's 25-year average transition matrix (Table 11.7). We take this matrix as a proxy for transition prob-

TABLE 11.6

Sensitivity Analysis of Credit Migration Models to Default Probability and Recovery Rates

	Default Probabiltiy ×2	Recovery Rate for Bonds 30% and for Loans 50%	Recovery Rate for Bonds 50% and for Loans 70%
Current MTM value	12,546	12,546	12,546
Forward mean (one year from now)	12,864	13,077	13,165
Standard deviation	198	173	130
1% VaR	4.5%	4.1%	3.1%
1% EVaR	5.5%	5.0%	3.8%
0.1% VaR	6.8%	6.5%	4.8%
0.1% EVaR	7.9%	7.3%	5.5%
0.03% VaR	7.9%	7.5%	5.7%
0.03% EVaR	9.5%	8.6%	6.4%

Note: Portfolio values and standard deviations are reported in millions of U.S. dollars. Credit VaR and EVaR are reported in percentage of MTM value.

abilities under normal market conditions. This gives rise to an interesting question: how sensitive are the results to this transition matrix? In particular, how sensitive are they to the transition matrix corresponding to the bottom of the credit cycle, when default rates are at a historical high?

Figure 8.1 of Chapter 8 shows the default rates for corporations world-wide during 1985 to 1997. The year 1990 is clearly the worst case historical scenario, both in terms of the number of firms that defaulted, and the amount that they defaulted on. The transition matrix derived from Moody's for 1990 is given in Table 11.8, while the value-at-risk figures for this transition matrix are reported in Table 11.9.

The 1 percent VaR is 20 percent higher than for the base case, while it is 10 percent higher at the 10-bp level, and 5 percent higher at the 3-bp level. Table 11.9 also shows what happens when credit spreads double: value at risk remains unchanged. The increase in the spreads reduces the mark-to-market value of the portfolio, but

TABLE 11.7

25-Year Average Transition Matrix From Moody's

Initial Rating	End-Period Rating							
	Aaa	Aa	A	Baa	Ba	B	Caa	D
Aaa	0.9338	0.0594	0.0064	0	0.0002	0	0	0.0002
Aa	0.0161	0.9055	0.0746	0.0026	0.0009	0.0001	0	0.0002
A	0.0007	0.0228	0.9242	0.0463	0.0045	0.0012	0.0001	0.0002
Baa	0.0005	0.0026	0.0551	0.8848	0.0476	0.0071	0.0008	0.0015
Ba	0.0002	0.0005	0.0042	0.0516	0.8691	0.0591	0.0024	0.0129
B	0	0.0004	0.0013	0.0054	0.0635	0.8422	0.0191	0.0681
Caa	0	0	0	0.0062	0.0205	0.0408	0.6919	0.2406
D	0	0	0	0	0	0	0	1

Note: The minimum default probabilities have been set to 2 bp.

TABLE 11.8

Worst Case Average Transition Matrix: 1990

Initial Rating	End-Period Rating Aaa	Aa	A	Baa	Ba	B	Caa	D
Aaa	0.8876	0.1123	0	0	0	0	0	0
Aa	0	0.9043	0.0928	0.0027	0	0	0	0
A	0	0.0273	0.8886	0.0684	0.0119	0.0034	0	0
Baa	0	0.0030	0.0340	0.9040	0.0495	0.0061	0.0030	0
Ba	0	0	0	0.0234	0.7837	0.1501	0.0093	0.0331
B	0	0.0057	0.0028	0.0057	0.0289	0.7486	0.0549	0.1530
Caa	0	0	0	0	0	0	0.4666	0.5333
D	0	0	0	0	0	0	0	1

TABLE 11.9

Scenario Analysis: Worst Case Transition Matrix and Credit
Spreads Doubled

	Initial Portfolio	Worst Case Transition Matrix: 1990	Credit Spread Doubled
Current MTM value	12,546	12,546	12,207
Forward mean (one year from now)	13,121	12,763	12,872
Standard deviation	151	238	168
1% VaR	3.6%	4.3%	3.5%
1% EVaR	4.4%	4.9%	4.3%
0.1% VaR	5.7%	6.2%	5.6%
0.1% EVaR	6.5%	6.9%	6.4%
0.03% VaR	6.6%	6.9%	6.6%
0.03% EVaR	7.5%	8.1%	7.4%

Note: Portfolio values and standard deviations are reported in millions of U.S. dollars. Credit VaR and EVaR are reported
in percentage of MTM value.

at the same time the whole loss distribution shifts so that the distance of each percentile from the forward mean value of the portfolio is unaffected.

From this series of results, it appears that the most sensitive
parameters are the credit quality of the portfolio and the correlation of the equity returns. It follows that special care should be
taken to make sure that issuers are correctly rated, and that the
multifactor structure underlying the correlation model is carefully
calibrated.

Stress testing and scenario analysis can be performed once a
week, given that the composition of the bank's corporate bond and
loan portfolio does not change dramatically from one week to the
next.

4. IMPLEMENTATION AND VALIDATION ISSUES

As we discussed in Chapter 2, some practitioners are concerned
about applying credit risk models to nontraded loans because of

the scarcity of data on their default frequencies and recovery rates, and the lack of good spread data. (Such data already exist for corporate bonds and loans, at least for the United States and Canada.) The major international banks are currently making real efforts to collect data and, at an industry level, projects are underway to pool data regarding default, losses, and recovery rates in terms of asset classes.

For their middle-market portfolios, banks should rely on their internal rating system rather than external ratings, since small nonpublic firms are hard to compare with large public firms. Middle-market loan portfolios are specific to each bank, and banks often have better information on their borrowers than do the rating agencies.

The use of credit models for allocating bank economic capital should be the first step in improving capital allocation for credit risk. Banks have to convince the regulators that they trust their models enough to use them to manage their loan portfolios before there is a real chance their internal models will be approved for regulatory capital calculations for the banking book.

Credit models are hard to validate because default is a rare event. The direct testing of any credit risk methodology imposes an impossible demand on the available data.[8] This does not mean, however, that models cannot be tested at all.

First, reduced-form models can be validated in the same way as market VaR models. That is, they should explain the term structure of the credit spreads that are directly observable from market data.

Secondly, models can be tested against cumulative credit profit and loss (P&L). This requires banks to record P&L separately for market and credit risks, which is a daunting task. A more realistic alternative is to use the "static P&L" methodology (Chapter 6) to disentangle the portion of the P&L that is related to market and credit risk. To this end, the DGVRT methodology presented in Chapter 6 can be applied to the position at the end of the previous day to determine the "theoretical" market risk P&L that applies to the end-of-previous-day portfolio, based on the observed changes in market factors. Assuming that the position remains constant over the next day, we can determine the change in the value of the position from the change in the value of the market risk factors. This gives a proxy for the P&L strictly related to market risk. Taking the difference between the observed P&L and the theoretical P&L related to market risk produces a proxy for the credit risk-related P&L. This proxy is only good when the portfolio remains stable from one day to the next.[9]

Thirdly, if direct testing is impossible, it is worth exploring indirect testing. That is, the model input, as opposed to the output, can be validated. For instance, the accuracy of the default rates fed into the model can be tested. Default prediction models have been around for at least 30 years. These models incorporate accounting and market data in order to predict default events. Professor E. Altman of the Stern School of Business at New York University is one of the pioneers in this area. His models have been tested using "out of sample" data.[10]

Internal credit rating methodologies developed for the middle market can be tested in the same way as default prediction models. A similar comment applies to credit card portfolios. It should also be noted that repeated sampling using replacement methodologies can help overcome the problem of insufficient data. Lopez and Saidenberg (1999) propose a back-testing methodology based on cross-sectional simulation. Specifically, models are evaluated not only for their forecasts over time, but also in terms of their forecasts at a given point in time for simulated portfolios. The problem with this approach is that the statistical test to assess the quality of the expected loss forecasts is not powerful.[11]

Finally, it might be argued that a more appropriate test of a credit risk model is a stress test, or sensitivity analysis, that identifies those areas where the model may be more apt to generate inappropriate results.

NOTES

1. Kamakura, a software product under development by Kamakura Corporation at the time of publication, will be based on the reduced-form approach. Professor Robert Jarrow is managing director of research at the firm.

2. Note that, conditional on the current realized value of the common risk factors, default events are independent across obligors. This greatly facilitates the derivation of the loss distribution.

3. The exception is the reduced-form approach, but this is not yet available as a software product (see Note 1). In the reduced-form models, rates are stochastic and default probabilities depend on systemic risk factors such as the level of interest rates and the stock market. At CIBC we are currently implementing a second-generation model, CreditVaR II, based on the credit migration paradigm, with stochastic interest rates and credit spreads. This framework can cope with derivatives and derivative-like products such as swaps and loan commitments, where the exposure is contingent on the term structure of interest rates. CreditVaR II also incorporates credit derivatives in a way that is consistent with the credit migration approach. Note that the pricing of credit derivatives means that it is necessary to derive the risk-neutral probabilities from the actual probabilities of default.

4. See also Crouhy et al (2000).

5. Bootstrapping is the technique that allows us to construct a theoretical spot-rate curve from the observed prices of zero-coupon and coupon securities. It is a recurrence that starts with the short-term zero rates directly derived from short-term zero-coupon instruments. It then proceeds forward in time to successively imply the rates for longer tenors from securities with increasing maturities (see, e.g., Fabozzi, 1997).

6. In the following we use a notation for the confidence level that is different from that adopted in Chapter 5. For market risk, it is common practice to report VaR at the 99 percent confidence level with a 10-day horizon. The horizon for credit risk is usually one year, and it is common practice to derive VaR at a higher confidence level such as 99.9 or 99.97 percent. In order to facilitate the notation we denote the confidence level by the percentile loss; i.e., VaR at the 99.97 percent confidence level becomes 3-bp VaR, and so on.

7. The 3-bp confidence level corresponds to a target rating of AA+.

8. Validation of portfolio loss probabilities over a one-year horizon at the 99 percent confidence level implies 100 years of data. This is clearly not feasible.

9. This is the back-testing methodology that we use at CIBC for the implementation of CIBC's value-at-risk model in the trading book.

10. See, e.g., Altman (1993).

11. See Chapter 5 and Crnkovic and Drachman (1996).

CHAPTER 12

Hedging Credit Risk

1. INTRODUCTION

Credit risk models of the kind discussed in earlier chapters provide an estimate of the credit risk in a portfolio. In doing so they not only measure risk but facilitate the segmentation and transfer of credit risk. For the first time, it is possible to measure, however imperfectly, the amount of credit risk in a portfolio that might be bought, sold, or repackaged. Credit risk is thus becoming an asset class in itself, and "credit investment management" businesses are likely to flourish in the years to come.

Over the years, banks have developed various "traditional" techniques to mitigate credit risk such as bond insurance, netting, marking-to-market, collateralization, termination, or reassignment. Selling a portion of the loans that the bank has originated is another possible tactic.[1] All these mechanisms reduce credit risk by mutual agreement between the transacting parties, but they lack flexibility. More importantly, they do not separate or "unbundle" the credit risk from underlying positions so that it can be redistributed among a broader class of financial institutions and investors.

This is why there has been so much interest in the financial world in the development of the credit derivative and wholesale securitization markets in recent years. Credit derivatives, the newest credit risk management tool, are specifically designed to allow financial institutions, and investors, to control their credit risk exposure by stripping credit risk out from market risk. They allow users to transfer credit risk independently of funding and relationship management concerns, much as the development of interest rate and foreign exchange derivatives in the 1980s allowed banks to manage market risk independently of liquidity risk.

In a related development, wholesale securitization gives institutions the chance to extract and segment a variety of potential risks from a pool of credit risk exposures and to repackage them to create notes, securities, or credit derivatives with a variety of credit risk features. These specially engineered securities can then be sold to a wide pool of investors—most of which would not have been interested in purchasing the bundled credit risk.

Taken together, credit derivatives, wholesale credit securitization, and credit risk models have the potential to change greatly the nature and the amount of credit risk borne by the banking system.

Credit derivatives also contribute to the "price discovery" of credit, as well as offering improved market efficiency for pricing credit-related instruments and for determining credit spreads. Credit risk, in this sense, is not simply the risk of potential default. It is the risk that credit premiums will change, affecting the relative market value of the underlying bonds, loans, and other derivative instruments. The premium can be thought of as a variable that fluctuates over time. For example, if one hedges a corporate bond with a Treasury bond, then the spread between the two bonds will vary as a function of the credit quality of the corporate bond.[2]

On the supply side, being able to trade credit risk at a fair price allows banks to "manufacture" yield-enhancing structures such as asset-backed credit-linked notes. The yield increment is simply the reward for assuming the credit exposure linked to the structured note.

Credit risk reduction through various arrangements is one of the 20 recommendations formulated by the Group of Thirty (G-30) derivatives project.[3] Sections 1 to 5 of this chapter discuss the many ways that banks have developed over the years to mitigate credit risk. In Section 2 we briefly review the traditional techniques used to reduce credit risk. Section 3 discusses how AAA-rated derivatives subsidiaries provide banks and derivatives dealing houses with the ability to deal in a market where counterparty risk has become a key determinant of any transaction. Section 4 introduces the use of credit derivatives to hedge credit risk. Section 5 reviews the most common forms of credit derivatives.

In Section 6 we discuss the securitization of loans and high-yield bonds via CLOs (collateralized loan obligations) and CBOs (collateralized bond obligations). Securitization is used by banks to free up capital through regulatory arbitrage, and/or to reduce credit risk exposures by moving loans and bonds out of the balance sheet. In the last section of the chapter we discuss some of the current regulatory issues related to the capital treatment of credit derivatives.

2. CREDIT RISK ENHANCEMENT

In this section we present the traditional mechanisms used by banks to mitigate part of their credit risk exposure.

2.1 Bond Insurance, Guarantees, and Letters of Credit

Insured municipal bonds constitute a substantial market in the United States. According to Das (1995), new insured issues in 1991 amounted to $51.6 billion, i.e., one-third of the market for new municipal bonds. This proportion of insured municipal bonds seems to have remained stable in recent years. Empirical evidence by Huesh and Chandy (1989) and Jaffe (1992) shows that municipalities have been able to lower their cost of financing by using bond insurance.

In the municipal bond ("muni") market, insurance is purchased by the issuer (in the corporate debt market, it is the lender who usually buys the protection against default). Fierce competition in the muni market has led bond insurers to guarantee ever riskier issues while being paid less and less for this service. In 1997 MBIA Insurance Corp. insured a $1.2 billion bond issue for a new Southern California toll road. In backing the bond, MBIA effectively lent the issue its AAA rating; without it, the bond barely qualified as investment grade.[4] So far, suppliers of municipal credit insurance have found the business quite profitable: default rates have stayed relatively low, at less than 0.5 percent of new issues each year.

Guarantees and letters of credit are really a type of insurance contract. A guarantee, or a letter of credit from a third party of a higher credit quality than the counterparty, reduces the credit risk exposure of a transaction. Even where the third party has the same credit quality, or even a lower credit quality, it still may improve the overall credit exposure of the insured party by reason of better diversification. Letters of credit have been known for many years and are extensively used in international trade. Local banks guarantee the payment obligations of domestic importers to foreign exporters.

2.2 Embedded Put Options

Put options embedded in corporate debt securities provide investors with default protection, in the sense that the investor holds the right to force early redemption at a prespecified price, e.g., par value. When the credit quality of the issuer starts to deteriorate, leading to a corresponding increase in the yield spread, the investor has the flexibility to liquidate his position at no loss, provided the issuer is not yet in default. Most floating-rate notes (FRNs) are puttable. Since an FRN coupon resets periodically to current market interest rates, fluctuations in market value due to interest rates are limited. The credit risk of the issuer is the primary driver of the spread between market value and par.

2.3 Netting

The current replacement value of a derivative is its marked-to-market or liquidation value, which in turn is the net present value of the future expected cash flows. This can be either positive or negative for contracts such as swaps, or forward-based derivatives, where both parties to the transaction have a firm commitment to deliver to each other. But it is only when the replacement value is positive that the position represents a credit risk exposure for the nondefaulting party. (Naturally, a position with a negative replacement value will not result in loss for the nondefaulting party if the other side of the transaction defaults.)

There are two aspects to replacement value: gross value and net value. Gross value represents a simple total of the value of outstanding positions, while net value represents the value after any positive and negative values have been set against each other. If a counterparty has only one swap outstanding with an institution, then there is no difference between the gross and net replacement value. But when the counterparty has entered into several transactions with the same institution, some with positive and others with negative replacement values, then the net replacement value represents the true credit risk exposure *provided* that the two parties have valid, legally enforceable netting agreements in place (and provided that legal actions cannot change the agreements in court).

The current standard contract of the International Swap and Derivatives Association (ISDA) calls for early termination with netting, and mandates that any default on a position covered under a master agreement is limited to the net market value of the total of all positions.[5] Netting not only reduces the overall replacement value, but also the BIS capital charge for credit risk.[6]

2.4 Marking-to-Market

Marking a derivatives position to market is equivalent to the margin call system applied by options and futures exchanges, whereby at the end of each trading day, each counterparty exchanges in cash the change in market value of their positions. It is a zero-sum transaction. That is, the counterparty whose position has declined in value compensates the other party for the gain it has made. If a party fails to meet its obligation to pay in cash for the daily losses, then the exchange immediately closes that party's position by substituting the clearing house for the defaulted party.

Marking-to-market the value of a transaction is one of the most efficient credit enhancement techniques. Indeed, it can practically eliminate credit risk. However, it requires the kind of sophisticated monitoring and back-office systems that only large institutions can afford.

2.5 Collateralization

In situations where there is an asymmetric exposure to credit risk, counterparties are commonly asked to pledge some form of collateral. This collateral, in the form of liquid assets, may be pledged in one of the following forms: (1) up-front and once and for all; (2) once an agreed marked-to-market threshold for all transactions has been crossed; (3) when the counterparty is downgraded; and (4) in real time, as a percentage of the marked-to-market value of the transaction. The latter tactic is equivalent to margin calls on an organized options and futures exchanges, as discussed in Section 2.4.

2.6 Termination or Reassignment

Another credit enhancement technique is early termination of the contract by means of a mid-market quote after an agreed event such as a credit downgrade has occurred. Ratings downgrade triggers can substantially reduce the risk of default. For example, a termination agreement when the counterparty is downgraded from AA to BB reduces the cumulative probability of default for horizons over a 10-year period by approximately 70 percent.[7]

Early termination can also be triggered by the exercise of a put option that allows the investor to force the early redemption of the bond, or loan, when the rating of the issuer has declined.

A reassignment clause conveys the right to assign one's position as a counterparty to a third party, in the event of a ratings downgrade.

3. DERIVATIVE PRODUCT COMPANIES

During the 1990s, a new type of investment vehicle was invented by financial institutions to improve the credit standing of their transactions. In effect, the derivative products company, or DPC (also known as an "AAA derivatives subsidiary"), is an over-collateralized AAA-rated subsidiary of a parent company that has a lower credit rating. DPCs allow banks and other derivatives dealing houses that have relatively low ratings (usually single A) to deal with end-users that can accept only highly rated counterparties.

When the first DPCs were set up, it was thought they might revolutionize the credit structure of the wholesale financial industry. In fact, only 13 DPCs have been launched since 1991.[8] This

FIGURE 12.1

Running a Matched Book Through a Derivatives Product Company (DPC)

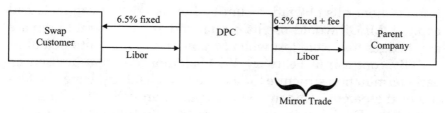

apparent lack of success is attributed by some bankers to the large amount of capital required by each DPC for the limited amount of extra business they generate. This may be an unfair criticism since most DPCs specialize in long-dated over-the-counter swaps, caps and floors, and swaptions, and other exotic deals. These inevitably represent only a small fraction of the global derivatives activity of a bank.[9]

The basic principle of a DPC is that it should run a matched book with the parent company using "mirror trades." Figure 12.1 illustrates the principle of setting up a mirror trade with the parent company. By means of the mirror trades, the DPC offsets the market risk related to the transaction with the original client. However, the DPC is left with the credit risk exposure of the parent, which also should be offset in order to obtain an AAA rating from the rating agencies. This credit offset is achieved by collateralizing all the mirror trades, and marking them to market.[10]

A DPC is "bankruptcy remote" from its parent, in the sense that the assets of the DPC would not be consolidated with those of the parent if the parent defaulted.[11] There are two basic ways to achieve this state, and these are known as the "continuation" and "termination" DPC structures. A continuation structure is one in which a well-capitalized institution is substituted for the original structure in case of default. A termination structure is one in which the failure of the parent company would lead to the immediate termination of the DPC and the unwinding of its portfolio.

Merrill Lynch was the first financial institution to launch a DPC in November 1991. Merrill Lynch Derivative Products (MLDP) adopted the continuation structure. If Merrill Lynch defaults, then two well-capitalized institutions, Sumitomo Bank and Mitsubishi Bank, would act as a contingent manager and would substitute for Merrill Lynch. MLDP would cease new originations, but would continue to honor its obligations until all of its existing contracts had expired. MLDP would use its capital and any collateral to replace any hedges that were lost when Merrill Lynch went into default.

By contrast, in February 1993 Salomon Brothers devised an early termination structure for its Swapco subsidiary. Here, the failure of the parent company would lead to an immediate termination of the DPC, but in such a manner as to fully protect the interests of Swapco clients. All outstanding contracts would then be settled on a marked-to-market basis at mid-price, i.e., half way between the bid and ask prices. The exact valuation of each Swapco contract would be derived by means of a proprietary model. (For other termination structures, the positions are closed at mid-prices, based on several dealers' quotes.[12])

DPCs are not considered by rating agencies to be free of default risk. However, the risk associated with them is taken to be consistent with that of conventional AAA ratings. Two AAA-rated DPCs were shut down in August 1996[13]—Fisher King Derivative Products (FISHCO) and the DPC of the Japanese Ninja Bank (NDP). In both cases, their counterparties experienced losses, although these were on a relatively small scale. In the case of FISHCO the closure was triggered by the downgrading of the parent to a rating of below BBB. The unwinding of all the positions created liquidity problems, and thus losses, for some counterparties, even though the capital of the DPC stayed well above the replacement value of the total book until liquidation.

NDP was a continuation structure, and its liquidation was triggered by the bankruptcy of the parent, Ninja Bank. The Bank of New Hampshire took over as the contingent manager. In this case, liquidity problems and a lack of confidence among market participants escalated the cost of replacing the hedges to the point at which the DPC itself failed just a few days after the parent.

4. CREDIT DERIVATIVES

4.1 Definition

Credit derivatives are over-the-counter financial contracts that have payoffs contingent on changes in the credit quality of a specified issuer. This specified issuer is typically not a party to the credit derivatives contract. As we describe below, credit derivatives can take various forms such as swaps, options, and credit-linked notes.

4.2 History

The market for credit derivatives was initiated in the early 1990s by large money-center commercial banks and investment banks. The market remains small but it is growing rapidly. According to a poll conducted by CIBC Wood Gundy in May 1996,[14] whose conclusions are shown in Table 12.1, the size of the credit derivatives market was around $40 billion.[15] By 1997, some market participants estimated that the credit derivatives market was in excess of $50 billion in notional value, and reckoned that it was likely to grow exponentially to reach $1 trillion by year 2000. In fact, by the third quarter of 1999 the OCC reported a notional amount of $234 billion.

4.3 Why a Market for Credit Derivatives?

Financial institutions and investors use credit derivatives in their portfolios for complementary reasons. Put simply, banks are looking for ways to shift aside part of their credit risk, while investors and other financial institutions are looking for ways to enhance their investment yield by accepting more credit exposure.

TABLE 12.1

Size of the Credit Derivatives Market in 1996

($ Million)	Corporate Bonds	Corporate Loans	Emerging Market Sovereign Bonds	Total
Forward agreements	100	0	250	350
Total return swaps	2,500	5,000	5,000	12,500
Price/spread options	250	50	7,500	7,800
Default puts	5,000	500	5,000	10,500
Correlation products	2,000	0	0	2,000
Notes	500	500	5,000	6,000
Total	10,350	6,050	22,750	39,150

Source: CIBC Wood Gundy.

FIGURE 12.2

Complementary Motives for the Use of Credit Derivatives

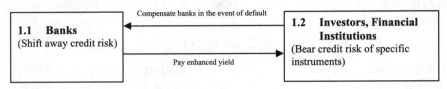

The complementarity motives, as illustrated in Figure 12.2, augurs well for the success of the credit derivatives market. It means that the potential market is not limited to a few large financial institutions trading credit risk among themselves.

Lending institutions, primarily commercial banks, no longer want simply to make loans and then hold them until they mature or the issuers default. Banks find it more profitable to concentrate on the origination and servicing of loans, because of their economies of scale in operations and the superior access that they enjoy to corporations.

They are also very aware that credit risk can concentrate in their portfolios. For example, if one bank has made $100 million worth of AA loans to airline companies, and another bank has made $100 million worth of AA loans to energy companies, then both banks would be better off after swapping $50 million of those loans because it is relatively unlikely that the airline and energy industries would run into difficulties at the same time. In other words, the bank portfolios would be better diversified. Having swapped the loans, both banks would be in a better position to exploit their proprietary information and economies of scale, and develop a good business relationship with corporate customers by extending more loans to their natural customer base.

Additionally, when managing their loan portfolio, banks often try to diversify away idiosyncratic credit risk and keep in their portfolio only "good risks." Credit derivatives constitute an efficient way of transacting synthetically part of the credit risk of a loan portfolio without the outright sale or purchase of loans.

The new BIS regulation on capital requirements[16] and RAROC capital attribution systems and internal objectives for return on capital[17] are other reasons why banks are increasingly willing to transact their assets.

Meanwhile, in an economic environment characterized by low interest rates, many investors are looking for ways to enhance their yields by switching to nontraditional markets. For example, they might consider high-yield instruments or emerging market debt and asset-backed vehicles. This implies that the investors are willing to accept lower credit quality and longer maturities. At the same time, however, most institutional investors are subject to regulatory or charter restrictions that limit their use of non-investment-grade instruments, or that limit the maturities they can deal in with regard to certain kinds of issuers. Credit derivatives provide investors with ready, if indirect, access to these high-yield markets by combining traditional investment products with credit derivatives. Structured products can be customized to the clients' individual specifications regarding maturity and the degree of leverage. For example, as will be discussed in the next section, a total return swap can be used to create a seven-year structure based on a portfolio of high-yield bonds with an average maturity of 15 years.

Even when institutional investors can directly access high-yield markets, credit derivatives may offer a cheaper way for them to invest. This is because, in effect, such instruments allow unsophisticated institutions to piggy-back on the massive investments made by banks in back-office and administrative operations.

Credit derivatives may also be used to exploit inconsistent pricing between the loan and the bond market for the same issuer, or to take advantage of any particular view that an investor has about the pricing (or mispricing) of corporate credit spreads.

Table 12.2 summarizes some of the applications of credit derivatives for end-users.

Three credit risk exposures influence the marked-to-market value of any type of credit derivative:

1. The credit risk of the underlying asset.
2. The risk of default of the counterparty to the credit derivative (e.g., the buyer of credit risk). This can be a substantial risk in the case of a leveraged transaction.
3. The risk of default of the seller of the credit derivative. This last risk is often neglected by the banks when they are pricing the deal.

TABLE 12.2

End-User Applications of Credit Derivatives

Investors
- Access to previously unavailable markets (e.g., loans, foreign credits, and emerging markets)
- Unbundling of credit and market risks
- Yield enhancement with or without leverage
- Reduction in sovereign risk of asset portfolios

Banks
- Reduce credit concentrations
- Manage the risk profile of the loan portfolio

Corporations
- Hedging trade receivables
- Reducing overexposure to customer/supplier's credit risk
- Hedging sovereign credit-related project risk

5. TYPES OF CREDIT DERIVATIVES

Credit derivatives are mostly structured or embedded in swap, option, or note forms. A common feature of existing credit derivatives is that their tenors are less than the maturity of the underlying instruments. For example, a credit default swap may specify that a payment is to be made if a 10-year corporate bond defaults at any time during the next two years.

5.1 Credit Default Swaps

Credit default swaps can be thought of as an insurance against the default of some underlying instrument, or as a put option on the underlying instrument. In a typical credit default swap, as shown in Figure 12.3, the party selling the credit risk (or the "protection buyer") makes periodic payments to the "protection seller" of a negotiated number of basis points, times the notional amount of the underlying bond or loan. The party buying the credit risk (or the "protection seller") makes no payment unless the issuer of the un-

FIGURE 12.3

Typical Credit Default Swap

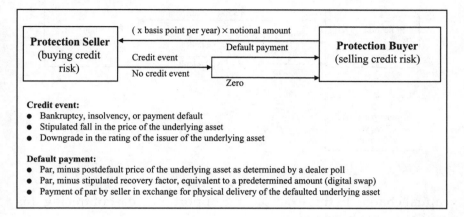

Credit event:
- Bankruptcy, insolvency, or payment default
- Stipulated fall in the price of the underlying asset
- Downgrade in the rating of the issuer of the underlying asset

Default payment:
- Par, minus postdefault price of the underlying asset as determined by a dealer poll
- Par, minus stipulated recovery factor, equivalent to a predetermined amount (digital swap)
- Payment of par by seller in exchange for physical delivery of the defaulted underlying asset

derlying bond or loan defaults. In the event of default, the "protection seller" pays to the "protection buyer" a default payment equal to the notional amount, minus a prespecified recovery factor.

Since a credit event, usually a default, triggers the payment, this event should be clearly defined in the contract to avoid any litigation when the contract is settled. Default swaps normally contain a "materiality clause" requiring that the change in credit status be validated by third-party evidence. The payment is sometimes fixed by agreement, but a more common practice is to set it at par, minus the recovery rate.[18]

Figure 12.4 illustrates why credit default swaps constitute such an efficient vehicle for banks seeking to free up capital. This example assumes that, in the case of a default by counterparty XYZ, the bank receives $25 million from the dealer. The $25 million compensation is equivalent to the amount of capital the bank would otherwise need to set aside in order to absorb credit risk-related losses. If we assume that the Bank is charged 5 percent of the notional amount in RAROC capital, the default put opens up new business opportunities of $500 million (i.e., $25 million is 5 percent of $500 million) with the same counterparty for no additional

FIGURE 12.4

The Use of a Default Swap to Free Up Credit Lines

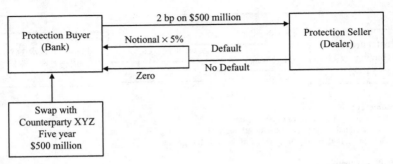

capital charge. In this example, the opportunity cost of freeing this capital is two basis points.

A variant of the credit default swap is the "first-to-default" put, as illustrated in Figure 12.5. The bank holds a portfolio of four high-yield loans rated B, each one with a nominal value of $100 million, a maturity of five years, and an annual coupon of Libor plus 200 bp. The loans are chosen such that default correlations are very small, i.e., such that there is a very low ex ante probability that more than one loan will default over the time until the expiration of the put, say two years. A first-to-default put gives the bank the

FIGURE 12.5

First-to-Default Put

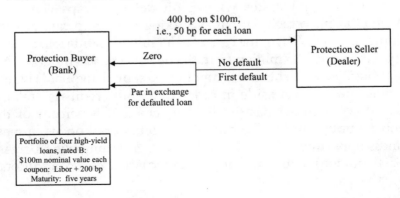

opportunity to reduce its credit risk exposure, by being compensated in case one of the loans in the pool of four loans defaults at any time during the two-year period. If more than one loan defaults during this period, the bank is only compensated for the first loan that defaulted.

The bank may have chosen to protect itself during a two-year period, while the loans might have a maturity of five years. Assume that the probability of default for each loan is 1 percent over a two-year period. Since default events are uncorrelated, the probability that the dealer (protection seller) will have to compensate the bank by paying it par, i.e., $100 million, against receiving the defaulted loan, is the sum of the default probabilities or 4 percent. This is approximately the probability of default on a loan rated B for which the default spread is 400 bp. The risk of default for the bank decreases geometrically with the number of loans:[19]

Probability of experiencing more than one default $\cong (1\%)^2 \frac{4 \times 3}{2}$
$$= 0.0006 = 0.06\%^{20}$$

Other customized structures have been proposed where payment is triggered by a downgrade in the rating of the counterparty, or by a significant movement in the credit spread.

5.2 Total Return Swaps

Total return swaps (TRSs) mirror the return on some underlying instrument such as a bond, a loan, or a portfolio of bonds and/or loans. In a typical total return swap, as shown in Figure 12.6, the party buying the credit risk makes periodic floating payments, typically tied to Libor. The party selling the credit risk makes periodic payments tied to the total return of some underlying asset including both coupon payments and the change in value of the instruments. TRSs can be applied to any type of security—for example, floating-rate notes, coupon bonds, stocks, or baskets of stocks. When the price of the underlying asset increases in value, the price appreciation is passed through to the buyer, while when the asset value deteriorates, the loss in value is passed through to the credit protection seller by the buyer.[21] For most TRSs the maturity of the swap is much shorter, e.g., three to five years, than the maturity of the underlying assets, e.g., 10 to 15 years.

FIGURE 12.6

Generic Total Return Swap (TRS)

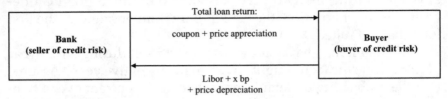

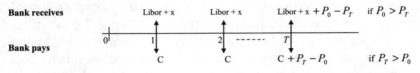

Cash flows for a TRS:

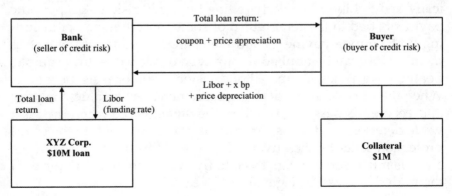

C = coupon
P_0 = market value of the asset (e.g., loan portfolio) at inception (time 0)
P_T = market value of the asset (e.g., loan portfolio) at the maturity of the TRS (time T)

Since in most cases it is difficult to mark-to-market the underlying loans, the change in value is passed through at the maturity of the TRS (Figure 12.6). Still, it may be difficult to estimate the economic value of the loan at that time, which may still be remote from the maturity of the loan. This is why in many deals the buyer is committed to take delivery of the underlying loans at a price P_0, which is the initial value.

FIGURE 12.7

Total Return Swap: Implementation

At time T, the buyer should receive $P_T - P_0$, if positive, and pay $P_0 - P_T$ otherwise. By taking delivery of the loans at their market value P_T, the net payment to the bank is P_0 in exchange for the loans.

For some levered TRSs, the buyer holds the explicit option to default on its obligation if the loss in value, $P_0 - P_T$, exceeds the collateral accumulated at the expiration of the TRS. In that case the buyer can simply walk away from the deal, abandon the collateral to the counterparty, and leave the counterparty to bear any loss beyond the value of the collateral.

A total return swap is equivalent to a synthetic long position in the underlying asset for the buyer. It allows for any degree of leverage, and therefore for unlimited upside and downside. There is no exchange of principal, no legal change of ownership, and no voting rights.

In order to hedge both the market and credit risk of the underlying assets of the TRS, a bank that sells a TRS typically buys the underlying assets. The bank is then only exposed to the risk of default of the buyer in the total return swap transaction. This risk will itself depend on the degree of leverage adopted in the transaction. If the buyer fully collateralizes the underlying instrument, then there is no risk of default and the floating payment should correspond to the funding cost of the bank. If, on the contrary, as shown in Figure 12.7, the buyer leverages its position, say 10 times, by putting aside 10 percent of the initial value of the underlying instrument as collateral, then the floating payment is the sum of the funding cost and a spread. This corresponds to the default premium, and compensates the bank for its credit exposure with regard to the TRS purchaser.

5.2.1 Economic Rationale for Buying (and/or Selling) a Total Return Swap

From the buyer of credit risk's perspective, a total return swap creates value if the buyer incurs a higher funding cost than the bank and/or the buyer wants to leverage its position. For example, the equity tranche of a credit-linked obligation (CLO)[22] is rarely sold outright, but is typically sold to a hedge fund via a leveraged total return swap transacted with a derivatives house. In the case illustrated in Figure 12.7, the hedge fund (buyer of credit risk) puts up only $1 million of collateral while the underlying assets are worth $10 million.

Total return swaps also provide buyers with an access to illiquid loan markets, either domestic or foreign, which otherwise would be inaccessible. Total return swaps offer a convenient alternative to outright investment for investors that do not have sophisticated back-office capability and who lack loan servicing capabilities (e.g., hedge funds).

On the sellers' side, TRSs facilitate the diversification and/or the reduction of credit risk exposures. The seller can sell synthetically a portfolio of loans without the need to deal in the open market, and thus maintain its relationship with its corporate customer (XYZ, in the figure).

5.3 Asset-Backed Credit-Linked Notes

An asset-backed credit-linked note (CLN) is a debt obligation with a coupon and redemption tied to the performance of a loan. Unlike a TRS, a CLN is a tangible asset. It may be leveraged by a multiple of 10. Since there are no margin calls, it offers investors limited downside and unlimited upside. Some CLNs can obtain a rating that is consistent with an investment-grade rating from agencies such as FitchIBCA, Moody's, or Standard & Poor's. A CLN is an on-balance-sheet instrument, with exchange of principal; there is no legal change of ownership of the underlying assets.

In Figure 12.8 a typical structure of a CLN is presented.[23] The bank buys the assets and locks them into a trust. In the example we assume that $105 million of non-investment-grade loans, with an average rating of B, yielding an aggregate Libor + 250 bp, are purchased at a cost of Libor, which is the funding rate for the bank. The trust issues an asset-backed note for $15 million, which is bought by the investor. The proceeds are invested in U.S. government securities, which are assumed to yield 6.5 percent, and which are used to collateralize the basket of loans. The collateral in our example is $15/105 = 14.3$ percent of the initial value of the loan portfolio. This represents a leverage multiple of 7 ($7 = 105/15$).

The net cash flow for the bank is 100 bp, that is, Libor + 250 bp (produced by the assets in the trust), minus the Libor cost of funding the assets, minus the 150 bp paid out by the bank to the

FIGURE 12.8

Asset-Backed Credit-Linked Note (CLN)

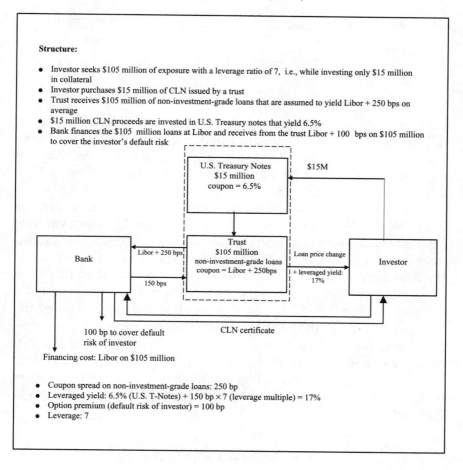

Structure:

- Investor seeks $105 million of exposure with a leverage ratio of 7, i.e., while investing only $15 million in collateral
- Investor purchases $15 million of CLN issued by a trust
- Trust receives $105 million of non-investment-grade loans that are assumed to yield Libor + 250 bps on average
- $15 million CLN proceeds are invested in U.S. Treasury notes that yield 6.5%
- Bank finances the $105 million loans at Libor and receives from the trust Libor + 100 bps on $105 million to cover the investor's default risk

U.S. Treasury Notes
$15 million
coupon = 6.5%

$15M

Bank

Libor + 250 bps

Trust
$105 million
non-investment-grade loans
coupon = Libor + 250bps

Loan price change

Investor

+ leveraged yield:
17%

150 bps

100 bp to cover default
risk of investor

CLN certificate

Financing cost: Libor on $105 million

- Coupon spread on non-investment-grade loans: 250 bp
- Leveraged yield: 6.5% (U.S. T-Notes) + 150 bp × 7 (leverage multiple) = 17%
- Option premium (default risk of investor) = 100 bp
- Leverage: 7

trust. This 100 bp applies to a notional amount of $105 million, and covers the bank for the risk of default of the issue beyond $15 million.

The investor receives a yield of 17 percent (i.e., 6.5 percent yield from the collateral of $15 million, plus 150 bp paid out by the bank on a notional amount of $105 million) on a notional amount of $15 million; this is in addition to any change in the value of the loan portfolio that is eventually passed through to the investor. In this structure there are no margin calls, and the maximum down-

FIGURE 12.9

Compound Credit-Linked Note

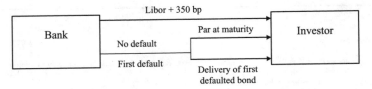

side for the investor is the initial investment of $15 million. If the fall in the value of the loan portfolio is greater than $15 million, then the investor defaults and the bank absorbs any additional loss beyond that limit. For the investor, this is equivalent of being long a credit default swap written by the bank.

A CLN may constitute a natural hedge to a TRS in which the bank receives the total return on a loan portfolio. Different variants can be proposed on the same theme, such as the compound credit-linked notes in Figure 12.9, where the investor is only exposed to the first default in the loan portfolio that was described in Figure 12.5. The investor invests $100 million in a CLN which pays a coupon of Libor + 350 bp. In the event of default of any of the loans in the basket, the bank terminates the note and puts, or transfers, the defaulted loan to the investor. The investor takes delivery of the loan and pays the bank the initial market value of the loan.

The example shown in Figure 12.9 constitutes a perfect hedge to the first-to-default put sold by the bank in the case presented in Figure 12.5.

5.4 Spread Options

Spread options are not pure credit derivatives, but have creditlike features. The underlying asset of the option is the yield spread between a specified corporate bond and a government bond of the same maturity. The striking price is the forward spread at the maturity of the option, and the pay-off is the greater of zero and the difference between the spread at maturity and the strike, times a multiplier which is usually the product of the duration of the underlying bond and the notional.

Payoff = Max (0, spread at maturity − strike)

$\qquad\qquad\qquad\qquad$ × modified duration × notional

FIGURE 12.10

Credit Intermediation Swap

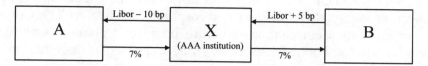

The pay-out of this option is related to the Macaulay dura-tion-based measure, i.e., $dP/P = -[D/(1 + y)] \, dy$, where P denotes the price of a bond and D its duration, $D/(1 + y)$ is the modified duration of the bond, and y is the yield to maturity.[24] The payout of the spread option compensates for the change in value of a bond consecutive to an increase in the bond spread.

5.5 Credit Intermediation Swaps

In a credit intermediation swap a third party, usually an AAA-rated DPC or other special-purpose vehicle, stands between two coun-terparties that might be otherwise unwilling to trade directly with one another.

Figure 12.10 illustrates the structure. Suppose A and B wish to transact a standard 10-year interest rate swap whereby B receives the fixed rate, say 7 percent, against Libor + 5 bp. A triple-A in-stitution, X, is asked to intermediate the swap. X executes the swap with B such that X pays the fixed rate of 7 percent to B. Institution X immediately backs this swap out to A, receiving the fixed rate of 7 percent from A and paying Libor − 10 bp. X therefore incurs no market risk from the transaction, but bears the counterparty risks of A and B (for which service it is paid 15 bp).

6. CREDIT RISK SECURITIZATION FOR LOANS AND HIGH YIELD BONDS

The U.S. domestic markets for loan sales, securitization of high-yield loans[25] via CLOs (collateralized loan obligations), and securitiza-tion of high-yield bonds via CBOs (collateralized bond obligations) have all grown dramatically over the past few years. The markets are used mainly as a way for banks to free regulatory capital, and thus leverage their intermediation business, and in some instances to reduce economic capital. (Note that CLOs and CBOs are also sometimes referred to as CDOs or collateralized debt obligations.[26])

CLOs and CBOs are simply securities that are collateralized by means of high-yield bank loans and corporate bonds.[27] A CLO (CBO) is an efficient securitization structure because it allows loans (or bonds) rated at below investment grade to be pooled together and the cash flows prioritized to achieve an investment-grade rating. This means that insurance companies and pension funds are able to invest in the "senior class" of notes. The main differences between CLOs and CBOs are the assumed recovery values for, and the average life of, the underlying assets. Recovery values on defaulted loans are assumed to be significantly higher than for corporate high-yield bonds. Rating agencies generally assume a recovery rate of 30 percent to 40 percent for unsecured corporate bonds, while the rate is around 70 percent for well-secured bank loans. Also, since loans amortize, they exhibit a shorter duration and thus present a lower risk than their high-yield bond counterparts. It is therefore easier to produce notes with investment-grade ratings from CLOs than it is from CBOs.

Figure 12.11 illustrates the basic structure of a CLO. A special-purpose vehicle (SPV) or trust is set up, which issues, say, three

FIGURE 12.11

Typical Collateralized Loan Obligation (CLO) Structure

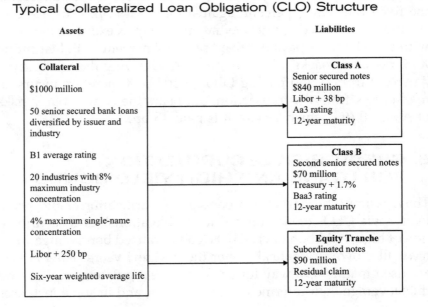

types of securities: senior secured class A notes, senior secured class B notes, and subordinated notes or "equity tranche."[28] The proceeds are used to buy high-yield notes that constitute the collateral. In practice, the asset pool for a CLO may also contain a small percentage of high-yield bonds (usually less than 10 percent). The reverse is true for CBOs: they may include up to 10 percent of high-yield loans.

A typical CLO would consist of a pool of assets of, say, 50 loans, with an average rating of, say, B1 (by reference to Moody's rating system). These might have exposure to, say, 20 industries, with no industry concentration exceeding, say, 8 percent.[29] The largest concentration by issuer might be kept, say, to under 4 percent. The weighted average life of the loans is assumed to be six years, while the issued notes have a stated maturity of 12 years. The average yield on these floating-rate loans is assumed to be Libor + 250 bp. The gap in maturities between the loans and the CLO structure requires an active management of the loan portfolio. A qualified high-yield loan portfolio manager is hired to actively manage the portfolio within constraints specified in the legal document. During the first six years, which is called the reinvestment or lock-out period, the cash flows from loan amortization and the proceeds from maturing or defaulting loans are reinvested in new loans.[30] Thereafter, the three classes of notes are progressively redeemed as cash flows materialize.

The issued notes consist of three tranches: two senior secured classes with an investment-grade rating and an unrated subordinated class or equity tranche. The equity tranche is in the first-loss position, and the idea is that it will absorb default losses before they reach the senior investors.[31] In our example, the senior class A note is rated Aa3 and pays a coupon of Libor + 38 bp, which is more attractive than the sub-Libor coupon on an equivalent corporate bond with the same rating. The second senior secured class note, or mezzanine tranche, is rated Baa3 and pays a fixed coupon of Treasury + 1.7 percent for 12 years. Since the original loans pay Libor + 250 bp, the equity tranche offers an attractive return— providing most of the loans underlying the notes are fully paid.[32]

The rating enhancement for the two senior classes is obtained by prioritizing the cash flows. Rating agencies such as FitchIBCA, Moody's, and Standard & Poor's have developed their own methodology to rate these senior class notes. They run a cash flow

TABLE 12.3

Stressed Default Rates for Bank Loan Portfolios

FitchIBCA Weighted Average Pool Rating	FitchIBCA Base Cumulative Default Rate*	Stress Default Rates		
		BBB	A	AA
BB+	12.7	16	22	28
BB	16.0	20	25	33
BB−	20.6	25	31	38
B+	25.2	30	35	43
B	29.9	34	39	45
B−	34.5	38	44	50

*For high-yield bonds.
Source: FitchIBCA.

model that employs default rates based on the weighted average credit quality of the underlying pool, and the desired rating category of the senior class notes that have been issued. Table 12.3 shows the assumptions made by FitchIBCA in stress testing the loan portfolio. These values vary depending on the quality of the loans, and the reputation and track record of the loan portfolio manager. FitchICBA distributes the default losses over five years; the agency assumes that 33 percent of the losses will occur in the first year, 25 percent in the second year, 16 percent in the third year, and 13 percent in each of the fourth and fifth years.

The average rating attributed by the rating agency to the loan portfolio depends on the credit quality of the underlying loans, the spread earned on the loans, industry and issuer diversification, overcollateralization, liquidity, interest rate and basis risk, and the experience of the loan portfolio manager. For example, let us assume that the average rating of the loans in the pool is BB−, that the five-year cumulative default rate adopted by FitchIBCA is 20.6 percent as shown in Table 12.3, and that the target rating for Class A is AA. In this case the pool should remain able to pay out the promised cash flows to Class A senior secured note holders even when the default rate is stressed to the 38 percent level.

There is no such thing as a "free lunch" in the financial markets. The credit enhancement of the senior secured class notes is obtained by simply shifting the default risk to the equity tranche. According to simulation results, the ex post return for the investor in this tranche can vary widely from −100 percent, when the investor loses everything, to more than 30 percent, depending on the actual rate of default on the loan portfolio. This tranche is often bought by investors such as "hedge funds,"[33] either outright or more often by means of a total return swap with a leverage multiple of 7 to 10.[34] But most of the time, the bank issuing a CLO retains the first-loss equity tranche.

The main motivation for issuing CLOs is thus to arbitrage regulatory capital: it is less costly to hold the equity tranche than it is to hold the underlying loans themselves.[35] In fact, the economic risk borne by the bank may not be reduced at all. Paradoxically, credit derivatives, which offer a more effective form of economic hedge, have so far secured little regulatory capital relief.[36]

With a piece of innovative financial engineering in 1998, JP Morgan bridged the gap between economic hedging and efficient regulatory capital management by combining securitization and credit derivative technology in a structure called "Bistro." In the Bistro transaction, a special-purpose vehicle (SPV) owned by JP Morgan entered into a credit default swap with JP Morgan itself. The swap was referenced to a portfolio of commercial loans and corporate and municipal bonds and to the counterparty credit exposure arising out of derivative contracts. The SPV then sold bonds to a broad base of investors, with the performance of the bonds referenced to the performance of the credit default swap. Through Bistro, JP Morgan successfully transferred credit risk from its banking book to the bondholders. Although economically efficient, the Bistro transaction was far less regulatory capital efficient than more straightforward CLO deals (Figure 12.12).

Financial intermediation via CLOs and CBOs is likely to expand rapidly in the future, since governments are under pressure to reduce their deficits. This will translate into a reduction in government financing needs and a drop in the issuance of Treasury securities. Corporations seem likely to fill the gap by issuing securities to finance their expansion projects. At the same time, institutional investors such as insurance companies and pension funds are competing for high-grade investments. With fewer Treasury issues and more non-investment-grade corporate bond

FIGURE 12.12

"Bistro" Structure

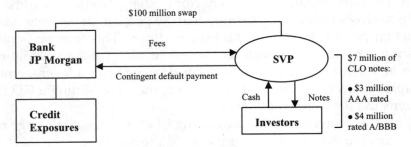

	Capital	Loss Exposure
Bistro	$7.44 million	Very low
Traditional CLO	$3 million	Very high

Explanations:
- For a traditional CLO, the capital is in the form of a first-loss exposure and it is typically 3 percent of the notional amount.
- In the Bistro structure, capital is 8 percent of ($100 − $7=) $93 million = $7.44 million. The first-loss risk is borne by the investors.

and loan issues,[37] there will soon be a need for financial institutions to step in and fill the gap by intermediating between credit qualities. This is precisely what is achieved by means of CLO and CBO structures.

7. REGULATORY ISSUES

The regulators have yet to make a major move with regard to the credit derivatives market. However, the Bank for International Settlements (BIS), the European Commission, the Federal Reserve Board, and the Office of the Comptroller of the Currency (OCC) are all watching the market and its development very closely.

Their main concern is the capital treatment for credit derivatives and their underlying assets. Under the European Union's Capital Adequacy Directive (CAD), there is an 8 percent capital charge for credit derivatives if they are held in the banking book. Yet there is a charge of only 1.6 percent if they are held in the trading book, as part of proprietary trading. Initially the Bank of England took the position that credit default puts should be treated differently from total return swaps.[38] According to the Bank of England, credit default puts share many of the characteristics of credit enhancement products such as guarantees and letters of credit, for which the pay-out is contingent on a credit event rather than a change in price. As such, credit default puts should not be included in the trading book, at least until credit risk models have been satisfactorily developed.

After some lobbying from ISDA and the British Bankers' Association, the Bank of England issued a new guideline for the capital adequacy treatment of credit derivatives which removes the distinction between default and total return swaps. It accepted the principle of marking-to-market credit derivatives, provided that appropriate pricing models are available. This position is consistent with the Federal Reserve's new guidelines, which state that capital treatment for credit derivatives will be the same as for other derivatives in the trading book. It allows banks to use internal models to price the derivative instrument in isolation from the counterparty risk, but with an extra add-on to compensate for the risk of default of the counterparty in the transaction. Although this amendment constitutes a first step in the right direction, the approach is still inconsistent with the current pricing methodology for credit derivatives (where market and credit risk exposure for the underlying, and for the counterparty risk, are modeled and priced simultaneously).

The inclusion of default swaps in the trading book may lead to greater capital charges under CAD, however. Indeed, the capital adequacy rule does not recognize offsets for credit derivatives unless the position is perfectly hedged. The hedge must be of the same maturity and must be referred to the same asset. Hence a 10-year loan exposure to a single-A corporation that is hedged with a five-year credit default put option receives no reduction in capital charge despite the mitigation of the credit risk. In fact, a regulatory capital penalty may result from the use of credit derivatives. A bank could find itself taking a counterparty risk charge of, say, 5 percent on a loan, and an additional 5 percent on the credit derivative that it has entered into to hedge that loan. This would create a total 10 percent capital charge compared with 8 percent under the old rule.

Currently, the regulatory capital treatment differs quite substantially depending upon whether the position takes the form of a long position in a corporate credit in the banking book, or whether the position has been created synthetically by means of a credit derivative. Suppose a bank buys outright a $100 million corporate bond. The charge is calculated in the following way:

Capital = notional amount * risk weight of issuer * 8%
$8 million = $ 100 * 100% * 8%

Alternatively, the bank can sell a credit swap or receive the returns of a total return swap that references the same $100 million corporate bond. This strategy lends itself to two different approaches:

- Credit product approach
  Capital = credit equivalent amount * risk weight of counterparty * 8%
  $ 1.6 million = ($ 100 million * 100%) * 20% (OECD bank) *8%
- Derivative product approach
  Capital = credit equivalent amount* risk weight of counterparty*8%
  $60,000 = (0 replacement cost + $ 100 million * 1.5% add-on for fixed income) * 50% maximum risk weight for derivatives counterparty * 8%

Figure 12.13 below summarizes the comparison of regulatory capital charges for the three different scenarios. Figure 12.14 illustrates how regulatory capital may affect the return on capital in different situations. Assume that two OECD banks with different

FIGURE 12.13

Credit Risk Capital Compensation

	Purchase Bond	Sell Credit Swap or Receive on Total Return Swap	
		Credit Product Approach	Derivative Product Approach
Regulatory Capital	$8 million	$1.6 million	$60,000

FIGURE 12.14

Capital Charge Against Credit Risk in Different Situations

1.   **Long a $100 million corporate loan issued by XYZ Corporation**

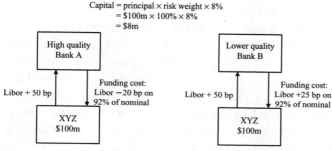

$$Capital = principal \times risk\ weight \times 8\%$$
$$= \$100m \times 100\% \times 8\%$$
$$= \$8m$$

High quality Bank A		Lower quality Bank B

Libor + 50 bp   Funding cost:
Libor −20 bp on
92% of nominal   Libor + 50 bp   Funding cost:
Libor +25 bp on
92% of nominal

XYZ
$100m   XYZ
$100m

Assume Libor = 5.2%
Risk weighting = 100%
Capital charge = 8% of risk weighted nominal value

Net revenue = $1.1m   Net revenue = $686,000
Return on capital = 13.75%   Return on capital = 8.6%

$$13.75\% = \frac{(L + 50\ bp) \times \$100 - (L - 20\ bp) \times \$92}{\$8}$$

2.   **Long a corporate loan and long a credit swap from an OECD Bank to hedge credit risk exposure**
      Capital treatment:
      ● Full offsetting of credit risk related to XYZ loan, no capital charge against credit swap plus
        loan package
      ● Capital add-on = Principal × risk weight (OECD Bank) × 8%
                       = $100m × 20% × 8%
                       = $1.6m

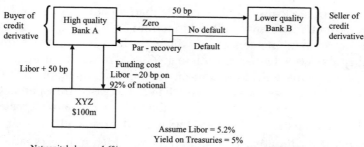

Buyer of
credit
derivative   High quality
Bank A   50 bp
Zero   No default   Lower quality
Bank B   Seller of
credit
derivative

Par - recovery   Default

Libor + 50 bp   Funding cost
Libor −20 bp on
92% of notional

XYZ
$100m

Assume Libor = 5.2%
Yield on Treasuries = 5%

Net capital charge =1.6%   Net capital charge = 8%
Net revenue = $280,000   Net revenue = $900,000
Return on capital = 17.5%   Return on capital = 11.25%

credit ratings invest in the same corporate loan XYZ. Their returns on capital differ not because of a different capital treatment, but simply because of their different financing costs. bank A, which can borrow at Libor -20 bp, generates a 13.7 percent return on capital, while bank B, with a higher funding cost of Libor $+25$ bp, exhibits a return of only 8.6 percent.[39] If bank A enters into a credit swap agreement with bank B with full offset of the credit risk related to XYZ loan, then its capital charge is only 1.6 percent and the return on its capital increases to 17.5 percent.[40] For bank B the situation is equivalent to a synthetic long position in the XYZ loan. A capital charge of eight percent is required for this credit derivative transaction, i.e., $8 million on a $100 million loan (which we assume to be invested in Treasury securities yielding five percent per annum). It follows that the return on capital for bank B is 11.25 percent, which is higher than if it had had to buy the XYZ loan outright.[41]

This example shows how credit derivatives can be used to arbitrage capital regulatory rules; the opportunity arises because the rules are not consistent with the real levels of risk exposure.[42]

NOTES

1. Selling loans is problematic because of what has become jokingly known as the "lemon" problem: banks have more information about the value of the loans they have made than do outsiders. Thus banks with high-quality loans will tend to refrain from selling that part of their portfolio if outsiders cannot distinguish such loans from low-quality loans (see Duffee and Zhou 1997). Asymmetric information is one of the primary determinants of whether risks are kept on the bank's balance sheet or are intermediated. Increased transparency implies greater potential liquidity in the loan market and a greater appetite on the part of end-investors to hold these loans.

2. There is also a liquidity risk premium embedded in the spread.

3. See Group of Thirty (1993), recommendation 14: credit enhancement (see also Chapter 2).

4. Spahr et al. (1991) estimate that corporate bond insurance could have been offered during the period 1970 to 1985 at a lower cost than the prevailing default risk spread. They propose an actuarial model that allows them to show that the present value of interest savings has been greater than the fair bond insurance premium.

5. See Litzenberber (1992). See also Hendricks (1994).

6. See Chapter 2.

7. See Wakeman (1996).

8. For more details, see Figlewski (1994), Bahar and Gold (1995), Curry et al. (1995), and Shirreff (1996).

9. See Paul-Choudhury (1996).

10. It should be noted that the same result could be achieved without the DPC, with the parent dealing directly with the client. The parent could simply collateralize and mark-to-market the transaction. While this might be perfectly acceptable for financial institutions, it would pose problems for end-users such as industrial corporations which, for accounting reasons and because they lack back-office capabilities, would find it quite inconvenient to mark-to-market the deals.

11. The function of such a bankruptcy remote structure, besides setting up an AAA entity, is to reduce the following risks for the counterparties dealing with a DPC instead of the parent company: (1) the risk that the parent company will file a voluntary bankruptcy petition, and (2) the risk that the parent company will be forced by its creditors into involuntary bankruptcy.

12. A variant is a collateralized "guarantee program." This is also a termination structure rated AAA, and makes use of a pool of transactions that are partially guaranteed by an AAA insurer. The counterparties deal directly with the bank, rather than with a DPC, but enjoy the protection of an AAA rating. Credit Lyonnais and Bankers Trust have opted for such structures, which are less expensive in capital than DPC entities.

13. See Shirreff (1996).

14. See Smithson (1996).

15. It was only $5 billion in 1993.

16. See Chapters 2 and 4.

17. See Chapter 14.

18. For a bond, the recovery rate is determined by the market price of the defaulted bond, after the actual default.

19. See Chapter 10 for the pricing of default swaps and first-to-default puts.

20. The probability that more than one loan will default is the sum of the probabilities that two, three, or four loans will default. The probability that three loans, or four loans, will default during the

same period is infinitesimal and has been neglected in the calculation. Moreover, there are six possible ways of pairing loans in a portfolio of four loans.

21. TRSs are in fact very similar to equity swaps in their structure, although the purpose is quite different. Equity swaps provide investors with synthetic investment in equity portfolios, which may be difficult for some investors to buy directly. Other trades are purely tax driven (see Reed 1994). A variant of both an equity swap and a standard TRS is a TRS whereby the underlying is an index of high-yielding corporate bonds, or an emerging bond market index as has been proposed by JP Morgan.

22. CLOs are presented in the next section, which discusses the securitization of loans.

23. In August 1996 JP Morgan structured the first big CLN, a $594 million note linked to the credit of Wal-Mart stores. Then, in September of that year, Chase arranged its first Chase Secured Loan Trust Note based on a $625 million managed portfolio of non-investment-grade bank loans.

24. See the Appendix in Chapter 5.

25. A high-yield loan is a non-investment-grade floating-rate instrument with the coupon rate tied up to Libor, with a rating of BB or lower. The pricing for a secured high-yield loan generally varies between Libor +150 and 350 bp depending on the credit quality of the issuer. They are callable at par with no penalty, and a typical up-front fee for call protection ranges from 25 to 75 bp. Senior secured loans have the following characteristics: they are the most senior debt in the capital structure, and they are secured by all the assets of the issuer including inventory, account receivables, and the common stock of subsidiaries.

26. The first CLO was offered by Bankers Trust back in 1991. What is happening in the late 1990s in the corporate loan market is similar to the development of CMOs (collateralized mortgage obligations). To begin with, savings and loan institutions originated, serviced, and held the credit risk of mortgages. The development of CMOs facilitated the transfer of the risks of mortgages to the most efficient holders. S&L institutions then became originators and servicers, but not investors.

27. A number of banks have also been exploring ways to securitize their project finance-related loan exposures, such as aircraft financing.

28. Some CLOs are two-tier structures: a rated senior note and an unrated subordinated note.

29. See Chapter 7 for a presentation of the two main competing rating systems, i.e., Moody's and Standard & Poor's. Fitch is also very active in the rating of CLO structures.

30. As the bank originating the loans typically remains responsible for servicing the loans, the investor in loan packages should be aware of the relevance of moral hazard and adverse selection for the performance of the underlying loans.

31. This equity tranche is also half-jokingly called "toxic waste."

32. The return on the equity tranche would fetch more than 20 percent if no default occurred.

33. Hedge fund is the term used in the markets for leveraged speculative funds.

34. Total return swaps are a form of credit derivatives, as we discussed earlier. They are often used to create leverage by providing the full return on the nominal value of the transaction, say 100, while making use of collateral on the other side of the transaction that represents only a fraction of the nominal value, say 10.

35. In its consultative paper issued in June 1999, the Basle committee proposes to eliminate this regulatory arbitrage (see Section 5 of Chapter 2).

36. BIS has failed so far to recognize the portfolio effects of credit hedging. Credit hedges only result in a reduction in aggregate regulatory capital charge when the synthetic position taken through the credit derivative exactly offsets that of the long cash position held on the bank's balance sheet.

37. It becomes more and more difficult to distinguish between corporate loans and bonds since both are now actively traded in the secondary markets. In fact, credit derivatives are used in some instances to arbitrage both markets when the yield spread becomes material.

38. Bank of England, "Developing a Supervisory Approach to Credit Derivatives" (see Risk 9(11), 1996).

39. The return for bank A is calculated as follows: ((Libor + 50 bp) 100 − (Libor − 20 bp) 92) / 8 = 13.75 percent, where Libor = 5.2 percent, Libor +50 bp is the return on the $100 million loan, Libor −20 bp is the funding cost which applies on the $92 million of borrowed money, while $8 million is provided in the form of equity capital. The same reasoning applies to Bank B, which yields a return of 8.6 percent on the $8 million capital required to enter the transaction.

40. Since the counterparty of bank A in the credit swap is an OECD bank, the capital charge is 8 percent of the risk-weighted underlying asset, where the weight factor is 20 percent, which yields a capital charge of 1.6 percent of the nominal value of the loan. The return on capital for bank A becomes: ((Libor +50 bp) 100 − (Libor − 20 bp) 98.4) / 1.6 = 17.5 percent.

41. For bank B the return on capital is equal to (5 percent 8 + 50 bp 100) / 8 = 11.25. Notice that bank B does not need to invest any cash in the transaction so the capital charge can be invested in Treasury securities.

42. This example is adapted from Wong and Song (1997).

Managing Operational Risk

1. INTRODUCTION[1]

Operational risk (OR) is not a well-defined concept. In the context of a trading or financial institution, it refers to a range of possible failures in the operation of the firm that are not related directly to market or credit risk. These failures include computer breakdown, a bug in a key piece of computer software, errors of judgement, deliberate fraud, and so on.

OR remains a fuzzy concept because it is hard to make a clearcut distinction between operational risk and the "normal" uncertainties faced by the organization in its daily operations. For example, if a client failed to pay back a loan, then one can reasonably inquire if the failure was due to either "normal" credit risk, or due to human error on the part of the loan officers. Usually all credit-related uncertainties are classified as part of business risk. Nevertheless, in certain situations one might say that the loan officer should have declined to approve the loan, given all the information concerning the client that was available to him or her at the time of the decision. For example, if the loan officer approved a loan against the bank's guidelines (maybe he or she was even given a bribe), then this should be classified as an operational failure, not a credit loss.

The management of an institution should define what is included in OR in order to minimize the degree of conceptual fuzziness within each firm. To do this, a typology of OR must first be established.

Another key problem is the quantification of operational risk. For example, how can one quantify the expected loss (EL) of a computer breakdown? EL is the product of the probability of the event occurring, which we will refer to as the "likelihood," and the cost of computer breakdown if it does indeed occur, which we will refer to as "severity." Both these numbers are difficult to calculate. By their nature, major operational risks of this kind occur infrequently and in the form of discrete events. How can we identify a historical event (or events) that can be used as part of a rational assessment? Unfortunately, a computer breakdown today is different in both probability and size of the damage than any similar event of 10 years ago.

Clearly, the difficulties in assessing OR do not imply that it should be ignored or neglected. On the contrary, management must pay attention to understanding OR and its potential sources in the organization precisely because it is so hard to identify and quantify.

In some cases OR can be insured against or hedged. For example, the bank can insure itself against losses arising from computer hardware problems, or it can hedge the risk by investing in a back-up system. The price of this insurance and the cost of such a hedge immediately raise the question of the economic rationale of removing the risks. Inevitably, the institution will need to assess the potential loss against the known insurance cost for each potential operational risk.

Failure to identify an operational risk, or to defuse it in a timely manner, can translate into a huge loss. Most notoriously, the actions of a single trader at Barings Bank, who was able to take extremely risky positions in a market without authority or detection, led to $1.5 billion in losses that brought about the liquidation of the bank in 1995.

The Bank of England report on Barings revealed some lessons about operational risk. Firstly, management teams have the duty to understand *fully* the businesses they manage. Secondly, responsibility for each business activity has to be *clearly* established and communicated. Thirdly, relevant internal controls, including an independent risk management function, *must* be established for all business activities. Fourthly, top management and the audit committee must ensure that significant weaknesses are resolved *quickly*.

Looking to the future, banks are becoming aware that technology is a double-edged sword. The increasing complexity of instruments and information systems increases the potential for operational risk. Unfamiliarity with instruments may lead to their misuse, and raises the chances of mispricing and wrong hedging; errors in data feeds may also distort the bank's assessment of its risks. At the same time, advanced analytical techniques combined with sophisticated computer technology create new ways to add value to operational risk management.

The British Bankers' Association (BBA) and Coopers & Lybrand conducted a survey among the BBA's members during February and March 1997. The results reflect the views of risk directors and managers and senior bank management in 45 of the BBA's members, covering a broad spectrum of the banking industry in the United Kingdom. The survey gave a good picture of how banks were managing operational risk, and how they were responding to the issue.

More than 67 percent of banks thought that operational risk was as (or more) significant as market risk or credit risk, and 24 percent of banks had experienced losses due to OR of more than £1 million in the three years before the survey was conducted.

The report indicated that many banks have some way to go to formalize their approach in terms of policies and generally accepted definitions; it is difficult for banks to manage operational risk on a consistent basis without an appropriate framework in place. As the report indicated, it is all too easy for different parts of a bank to inadvertently duplicate efforts when tackling operational risk or, conversely, for such risks to fall through gaps because no one has been made responsible for them.

According to the report, modeling and quantifying operational risk generates the most interest of all operational risk topic areas. However, the survey results suggest that banks have not managed to progress very far in terms of arriving at generally accepted models for operational risk. The report emphasized that this may well be because banks do not have the relevant data, and the survey revealed that data collection is an area that banks will be focusing on.

Banks that have not developed a sophisticated operational risk measurement approach sometimes use internal audit recommendations as the sole basis of their approach to operational risk, but the report authors suspected that this is only in relation to the kinds of operational risk identified by internal audit rather than all operational risks. Finally, almost half the banks were satisfied with their present approach to operational risk. However, the survey identified that, in general, there is no complacency among the banks. Further, a majority of them expected to make changes in their approach.

In this chapter we look at how Canadian Imperial Bank of Commerce (CIBC) has attempted to meet these present and future challenges by constructing a framework for operational risk control. After explaining what we think of as a key underlying rule—the control functions of a bank need to be carefully integrated—we examine the typology of operational risk. We then describe four key steps in implementing bank operational risk, and highlight some means of risk reduction. Finally, we look at how a bank can extract value from enhanced operational risk management by improving its capital attribution methodologies.

For reasons that we discuss towards the end of the chapter, it is important that the financial industry develops a consistent approach to operational risk. We believe that our approach is in line with the findings of a recent working group of the Basle committee in autumn 1998, as well as with the 20 best-practice recommendations on derivative risk management put forward in the seminal Group of Thirty (G-30) report in 1993 (Appendix 1).

2. TYPOLOGY OF OPERATIONAL RISKS

2.1 What Is Operational Risk?

Operational risk is the risk associated with operating a business. Operational risk covers such a wide area that it is useful to subdivide operational risk into two components, operational failure risk and operational strategic risk.

Operational failure risk arises from the potential for failure in the course of operating the business. A firm uses people, processes, and technology to achieve business plans, and any one of these factors may experience a failure of some kind. Accordingly, operational failure risk can be defined as the risk that there will be a failure of people, processes, or technology within the business unit. A proportion of the failures may be anticipated, and these risks should be built into the business plan. But it is the unanticipated, and therefore uncertain, failures that give rise to the key operational risks. These failures can be expected to occur periodically, although both their impact and their frequency may be uncertain.

The impact or *severity* of a financial loss can be divided into two categories: an expected amount, and an unexpected amount. The latter is itself subdivided into two classes: an amount classed as severe, and a catastrophic amount. The firm should provide for the losses that arise from the expected component of these failures by charging expected revenues with a sufficient amount of reserve. In addition, the firm should set aside sufficient economic capital to cover the unexpected component, or resort to insurance.

Operational strategic risk arises from environmental factors, such as a new competitor that changes the business paradigm, a major political and regulatory regime change, and earthquakes and other such factors that are outside the control of the firm. It also arises from major new strategic initiatives, such as developing a new line of business or re-engineering an existing business line. All businesses rely on people, processes, and technology outside their business unit, and the potential for failure exists there too; this type of risk will be referred to in this chapter as *external dependency risk*.

Figure 13.1 summarizes the relationship between operational failure risk and operational strategic risk. These two principal categories of risk are also sometimes defined (slightly differently) as "internal" and "external" operational risks.[2]

This chapter focuses on operational failure risk, i.e., on the internal factors enumerated in Figure 13.1 that can and should be controlled by management. However, one should observe that a failure to address a strategic risk issue can easily translate into an operational failure risk. For example, a change in the tax laws is a

FIGURE 13.1

Two Broad Categories of Operational Risk

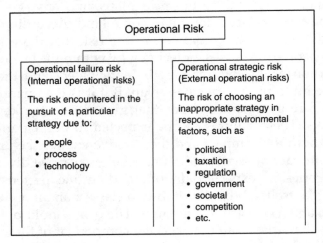

strategic risk.[3] The failure to comply with the tax laws is an operational failure risk. Furthermore, from a business unit perspective it might be argued that external dependencies include support groups within the bank, such as information technology. In other words, the two types of operational risk are interrelated and tend to overlap.

2.2 From Beginning to End

Operational risk is often thought to be limited to losses that can occur in operations or processing centers (i.e., where transaction processing errors can occur). This type of operational risk, sometimes referred to as operations risk, is an important component, but it by no means covers all of the operational risks facing the firm. Our definition of operational risk as the risk associated with operating the business means that significant amounts of operational risk are also generated outside of processing centers. If we take the example of a derivative sales desk, then one can see that operational risk can arise before, during, and after a transaction is processed (Figure 13.2).

FIGURE 13.2

Operational Risk in a Transaction Process

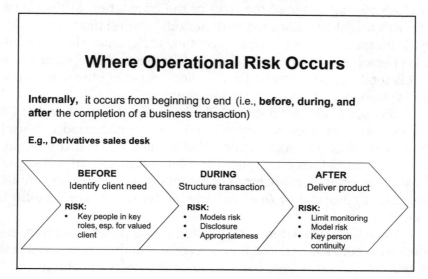

Risk begins to accumulate even before the design of the potential transaction gets underway. It is present during negotiations with the client (regardless of whether the negotiation is a lengthy structuring exercise, or a routine electronic negotiation) and continues after the negotiation as the transaction is serviced.

A complete picture of operational risk can only be obtained if the bank's activity is analyzed from beginning to end. Let us develop our example of a derivatives sales desk. Several things have to be in place before a transaction can be negotiated, and each exposes the firm to operational risk. First, sales may be highly dependent on a valued relationship between a particular sales person and the client. Second, sales are usually dependent on the highly specialized skills of the product designer who comes up with both a structure and a price that the client finds more attractive than competing offers. This means that the institution is exposed to "people risks." For example, there may be uncertainty as to whether these key people will continue to be available. In addition, do they have the capacity to deal with any increase in the sophistication of clients, or are they dealing with too many clients to be able to handle these demands?

During the processing of the transaction, the firm is exposed to several further risks. First, the sales person may knowingly not disclose the full range of the risks of the transaction to the client. This risk might be associated with periods when staff are under intense pressure to meet bonus targets for their desk. Similarly, the sales person might persuade the client to engage in a transaction that is totally inappropriate for the client, exposing the firm to potential lawsuits and regulatory sanctions.

"People risks" are not the only form of risk found early in a transaction. The sales person may rely on sophisticated financial models to price the transaction. This creates what is commonly called model risk (see Chapter 15). Model risk can arise because the wrong parameters are input to the model, or because the model is used inappropriately (e.g., outside its domain of applicability), and so on.

Once the transaction is negotiated and a ticket is written, errors can occur as the transaction is recorded in the various systems or reports. An error here may result in the delayed settlement of the transaction, which in turn can give rise to fines and other penalties. Further, an error in market risk and credit risk reports might lead to the exposures generated by the deal being understated. In turn, this can lead to the execution of additional transactions that would otherwise not have been executed. These are all examples of what is often called "process risk."

The list of what can go wrong before, during, and after the transaction is endless. The system that records the transaction may not be capable of handling the transaction or it may not have the capacity to handle such transactions. Or it may simply be unavailable (i.e., the computer system may be "down"). If any one of the steps is out-sourced, then external dependency risk also arises. However, each type of risk can be captured either as a people, processes, technology, or an external dependency risk, and each can be analyzed in terms of capacity, capability, or availability.

3. WHO SHOULD MANAGE OPERATIONAL RISK?

The responsibility for setting policies concerning operational risk remains with senior management, even though the development of those policies may be delegated, and submitted to the board of directors for approval. Appropriate policies must be put in place to limit the amount of operational risk that is assumed by an institution. Senior management needs to give authority to change the operational risk profile to those who are best able to take action. They must also ensure that a methodology for the timely and effective monitoring of the risks that are incurred is in place. To avoid any conflict of interest, no single group within the bank (Figure 13.3) should be responsible for simultaneously setting policies, taking action, and monitoring risk.

The authority to take action generally rests with business management, which is responsible for controlling the amount of operational risk taken within each business line. The infrastructure and governance groups share with business management the responsibility for managing operational risk.

The responsibility for the development of a methodology for measuring and monitoring operational risks resides most naturally with group risk management functions. Besides ensuring that the risks are transparent and well established, through measuring and reporting, this function can also attempt to manage the firm's operational risk on a portfolio basis. Portfolio management adds value

FIGURE 13.3

Policy Setting

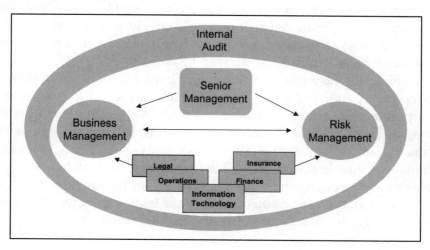

by ensuring that operational risk is adequately capitalized. Portfolio management also involves providing regular reviews of trends, as well as analyzing concentrations of operational risk. The risk management function also needs to ensure that proper operational risk/reward analysis is performed in the review of existing businesses and before the introduction of new initiatives and products. In this regard, the risk management function works very closely with, but independently from, business management, infrastructure, and the other governance groups.

Senior management needs to know whether the responsibilities it has delegated are actually being tended to, and whether the resulting processes are effective. The internal audit function within the bank is charged with this responsibility.

3.1 Managing Operational Risk as a Partnership

First of all, we ought to admit that at present many banks manage operational risk on an ad hoc basis. There is often a lack of coordination among functions such as risk management, internal audit, and business management. Most often there are no common bank-wide policies, methodologies, or infrastructure and thus no consistent reporting on the extent of operational risk within the bank as a whole. Bank-wide capital attribution models rarely incorporate meaningful measures of operational risk.

It follows from our earlier discussion that the key to success in managing operational risk more effectively is a *partnership* between business and its infrastructure, internal audit, and risk management. How can this partnership be constituted?

First, the necessary operational risk information has to travel from the operational environment, which includes infrastructure, corporate governance, and business units, to the operational risk management function. In return, the operational risk management function must provide operational risk analyses and policies to all units on a timely basis—as well as generating firm-wide and regulatory risk reports, and working with the audit function.

Second, the various businesses in the bank implement the policy, manage the risks, and generally run their business.

Third, at regular intervals the internal audit function needs to ensure that the operational risk, management process has integrity, and is indeed being implemented along with the appropriate controls. In other words, auditors analyze the degree to which businesses are in compliance with the designated operational risk management process. They also offer an independent assessment of the underlying design of the operational risk management process. This includes examining the process surrounding the building of operational risk measurement models, the adequacy and reliability of the operations risk management systems and compliance with external regulatory guidelines, and so on. Audit thus provides an overall assurance on the adequacy of operational risk management.

A key audit objective is to evaluate the design and conceptual soundness of the operational risk value-at-risk (operational risk VaR) measure, including any methodologies associated with stress testing, and the reliability of the reporting framework. Audit should also evaluate the operational risks that affect all types of risk management information systems—whether they are used to assess market, credit or operational risk itself—such as the processes used for coding and implementation of the internal models. This includes examining controls concerning the capture of data about market positions, the accuracy and completeness of these data, as well as controls over the parameter estimation processes. Audit would typically also review the adequacy and effectiveness of the processes for monitoring risk, and the documentation relating to compliance with the qualitative/quantitative criteria outlined in any regulatory guidelines.

Regulatory guidelines typically also call for auditors to address the approval process for vetting risk pricing models and valuation systems used by front- and back-office personnel, the validation of any significant change in the risk measurement process, and the scope of risks captured by the risk measurement model. Audit should verify the consistency, timeliness, and reliability of data sources used to run internal models, including the independence of such data sources. A key role is to examine the accuracy and appropriateness of volatility and correlation assumptions as well as the accuracy of the valuation and risk transformation calculations.

Finally, auditors should examine the verification of the model's accuracy through an examination of the back-testing process.

The bank's risk management team, to achieve all this, will need to develop policy, design the operational risk measurement methodology, and build the necessary infrastructure. The operational risk management group will then be able to monitor and analyze the risks, implement methodologies such as risk-adjusted return on capital (RAROC), and actively manage residual risk using tools such as insurance.

4. THE KEY TO IMPLEMENTING BANK-WIDE OPERATIONAL RISK MANAGEMENT

In our experience, eight key elements, as shown in Figure 13.4, are necessary to successfully implement a bank-wide operational risk management framework. They involve setting policy and identifying risk as an outgrowth of having designed a common language, constructing business process maps, building a best-practice measurement methodology, providing exposure management, installing a timely reporting capability, performing risk analysis inclusive of stress testing, and allocating economic capital as a function of operational risk. Let's look at these in more detail.

FIGURE 13.4

Eight Key Elements to Achieve Best-Practice Operational Risk Management

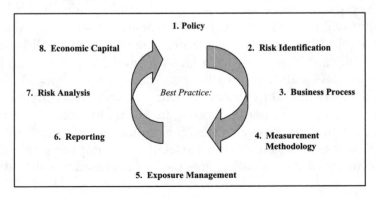

- Develop well-defined operational risk policies. This includes explicitly articulating the desired standards for risk measurement. One also needs to establish clear guidelines for practices that may contribute to a reduction of operational risk. For example, the bank needs to establish policies on model vetting, off-hour trading, off-premises trading, legal document vetting, and so on.
- Establish a common language of risk identification. For example, the term "people risk" would include a failure to deploy skilled staff. "Process risk" would include execution errors. "Technology risk" would include system failures, and so on.
- Develop business process maps of each business. For example, one should map the business process associated with the bank's dealings with a broker so that it becomes transparent to management and auditors. One should create an "operational risk catalogue," as illustrated in Table 13.1, which categorizes and de-

TABLE 13.1

Types of Operational Failure Risks

1. People risk:	• Incompetency
	• Fraud
2. Process risk:	
A. Model risk	• Model/methodology error
	• Mark-to-model error
B. Transaction risk	• Execution error
	• Product complexity
	• Booking error
	• Settlement error
	• Documentation/contract risk
C. Operational control risk	• Exceeding limits
	• Security risks
	• Volume risk
3. Technology risk	• System failure
	• Programming error
	• Information risk
	• Telecommunications failure

fines the various operational risks arising from each organizational unit in terms of people, process, and technology risks. This includes analyzing the products and services that each organizational unit offers, and the action one needs to take to manage operational risk. This catalogue should be a tool to help with operational risk identification and assessment. Again, the catalogue should be based on common definitions and language.[4]

• Develop a comprehensible set of operational risk metrics. Operational risk assessment is a complex process. It needs to be performed on a firm-wide basis at regular intervals using standard metrics. In the early days, as illustrated in Figure 13.5, business and infrastructure groups performed their own self-assessment of operational risk. Today, self-assessment has been discredited—the self-assessment of operational risk at Barings Bank contributed to the build-up of market risk at that institution—and is no longer acceptable. Sophisticated financial institutions are trying to develop objective measures of operational risk that build significantly more reliability into the quantification of operational risk. We mentioned earlier that operational risk assessment must include a review of the likelihood of a particular operational risk occurring, as well as the severity or magnitude of the impact that the operational risk

FIGURE 13.5

The Process of Implementing Operational Risk Management

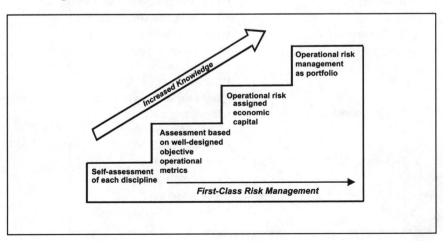

will have on business objectives. We examine this challenge in more detail in the next section.

• Decide how to manage operational risk exposure and take appropriate action to hedge the risks. The bank should address the economic question of the cost-benefit of insuring a given risk for those operational risks that can be insured.

• Decide how to report exposure. For example, an illustrative summary report for a bank's Tokyo equity arbitrage business is shown in Table 13.2.

• Develop tools for risk analysis, and procedures for when these tools should be deployed. For example, risk analysis is typically performed as part of a new product process, periodic business reviews, and so on. Stress testing should be a standard part of the risk analysis process. The frequency of risk assessment should be a function of the degree to which operational risks are expected to change over time as businesses undertake new initiatives, or as business circumstances evolve. This frequency might be reviewed as operational risk measurement is rolled out across the bank. A bank should update its risk assessments more frequently, say semi-annually, following the initial assessment of operational risk within a business unit. Further, one should reassess whenever the operational risk profile changes significantly, e.g., after the implementation of a new system, entering a new service, etc.

• Develop techniques to translate the calculation of operational risk into a required amount of economic capital. Tools and procedures should be developed to enable businesses to make decisions about operational risk based on risk/reward analyses, as we discuss in more detail later in the chapter.

5. A FOUR-STEP MEASUREMENT PROCESS FOR OPERATIONAL RISK

Clear guiding principles for the operational risk measurement process should be set to ensure that it provides an appropriate measure of operational risk across all business units throughout the bank. Figure 13.6 illustrates these principles. By "objectivity" we mean that operational risk should be measured using standard objective criteria. "Consistency" refers to ensuring that similar operational risk profiles in different business units result in similar re-

TABLE 13.2

Operational Risk Reporting Worksheet

The Overall Operational Risk of the Tokyo Equity Arbitrage Trading Desk is Low	
Category	**Risk Profile**
1. People Risk	
Incompetency	Low
Fraud	Low
2. Process Risk	
A. Model Risk	
Model/Methodology Error	Low
Mark-to-Market Error	Low
B. Transaction Risk:	
Execution Error	Low
Product Complexity	Medium
Booking Error	Low
Settlement Error	Low
Documentation/Contract Risk	Medium
C. Operational Control Risk	
Exceeding Limits	Low
Security Risk	Low
Volume Risk	Low/Medium
3. Technology Risk	
System Failure	Low
Programming Error	Low
Information Risk	Low
Telecommunication Failure	Low
Total Operational Failure Risk	**Low**
Strategic Risk	
Political Risk	Low
Taxation Risk	Low
Regulatory Risk	Low/Medium
Total Strategic Risk Measurement	**Low**

ported operational risks. "Relevance" refers to the idea that risk should be reported in a way that makes it easier to take action to address the operational risk. "Transparency" refers to ensuring that all material operational risks are reported and assessed in a way that makes the risk transparent to senior managers. By "bank-

FIGURE 13.6

Guiding Principles for Operational Risk Measurement

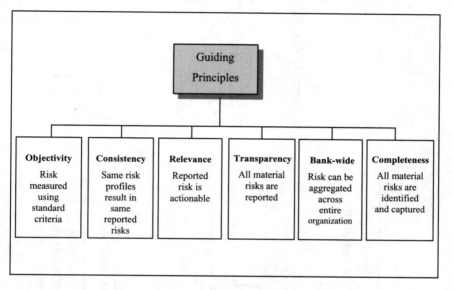

wide" we mean that operational risk measures should be designed so that the results can be aggregated across the entire organization. Finally, "completeness" refers to ensuring that *all* material operational risks are identified and captured.

Now let us turn to the problem of measuring operational risk in terms of the likelihood of operational failure, net of mitigating controls, and the severity of potential financial loss given that a failure occurs. This is best achieved by means of a four-step operational risk process, as illustrated in Figure 13.7 and discussed in detail below.

5.1 Input (Step 1)

The first step in the operational risk measurement process is to gather the information needed to perform a complete assessment of all significant operational risks. A key source of this information is often the finished products of other groups. For example, a unit that supports a business group often publishes reports or documents that may provide an excellent starting point for the operational risk assessment. Relevant and useful reports (e.g., Figure 13.8) include audit reports, regulatory reports, etc. The degree to

FIGURE 13.7

The Operational Risk Measurement Process

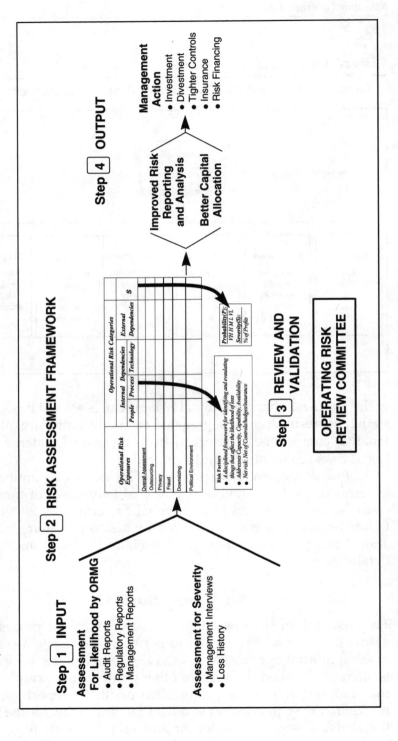

FIGURE 13.8

Sources of Information in the Measurement Process of
Operational Risk: The Input

Assessment For:	
Likelihood of Occurrence	**Severity**
• Audit reports • Regulatory reports • Management reports • Expert opinion • BRP (Business Recovery Plan) • Business plans • Budget plans • Operations plans	• Management interviews • Loss history

which one can rely on existing documents for control assessment
varies.

For example, if one is relying on audit documents as an indication of the degree of control, then one needs to ask if the audit
assessment is current and sufficient. Have there been any significant changes made since the last audit assessment? Did the audit
scope include the area of operational risk that is of concern to the
present risk assessment?

As one diligently works through the available information,
gaps often become apparent. These gaps in information often need
to be filled through discussion with the relevant managers.
Information from primary sources needs to be validated, and updated as necessary. Particular attention should be paid to any
changes in the business or operating environment since the information was first produced.

Typically, there are not sufficient reliable historical data available to confidently project the likelihood or severity of operational
losses. One often needs to rely on the expertise of business management, until reliable data are compiled to offer an assessment of
the severity of the operational failure for each of the key risks identified in Step 2. The centralized operational risk management group
(ORMG) will need to validate any such self-assessment by a business unit in a disciplined way.[5] Often this amounts to a "reason-

ableness" check that makes use of historical information on operational losses within the business and within the industry as a whole.

The time frame employed for all aspects of the assessment process is typically one year. The one-year time horizon is usually selected to align with the business planning cycle of the bank. Nevertheless, while some serious potential operational failures may not occur until after the one-year time horizon, they should be part of the current risk assessment.

For example, from the mid-1990s many banks had key employees under contract working on the year 2000 problem—the risk that systems might have failed on January 1, 2000. These personnel were employed under contracts that terminated more than 12 months into the future. However, while the risk event often lay beyond the end of the current one-year review period, it made sense to review any ongoing activity directed at mitigating the risk of that future potential failure as part of the risk assessment for 1996, 1997, and so on.

5.2 Risk Assessment Framework (Step 2)

The "input" information gathered in Step 1 needs to be analyzed and processed through the risk assessment framework sketched in Figure 13.9. The risk of unexpected operational failure, as well as the adequacy of management processes and controls to manage this risk, needs to be identified and assessed. This assessment leads to a measure of the net operational risk, in terms of likelihood and severity.

5.2.1 Risk Categories

We mentioned earlier that operational risk can be broken down into four headline risk categories, representing the risk of unexpected loss due to operational failures in people, process, and technology deployed within the business—collectively the "internal dependencies"—and "external dependencies."[6]

Internal dependencies should each be reviewed according to a common set of factors. Assume, for illustrative purposes, that we examine these internal dependencies according to the three key components of capacity, capability, and availability. For example, if we examine operational risk arising from the people risk category, then we might ask:

FIGURE 13.9

Second Step in the Measurement Process of Operational Risk: Risk Assessment Framework

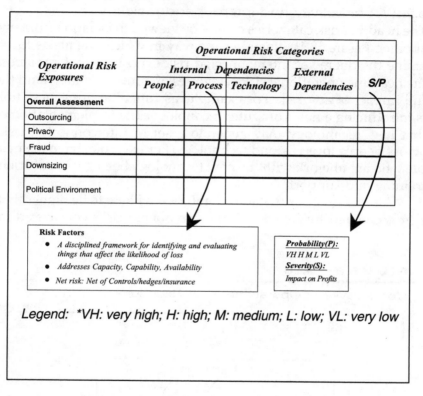

Operational Risk Exposures	Operational Risk Categories				
	Internal Dependencies			External Dependencies	S/P
	People	Process	Technology		
Overall Assessment					
Outsourcing					
Privacy					
Fraud					
Downsizing					
Political Environment					

Risk Factors
- A disciplined framework for identifying and evaluating things that affect the likelihood of loss
- Addresses Capacity, Capability, Availability
- Net risk: Net of Controls/hedges/insurance

Probability(P):
VH H M L VL
Severity(S):
Impact on Profits

Legend: *VH: very high; H: high; M: medium; L: low; VL: very low

- Does the business have enough people (capacity) to accomplish its business plan?
- Do the people have the right skills (capability)?
- Are the people going to be there when needed (availability)?

External dependencies are also analyzed in terms of the specific type of external interaction. For example, one would look at clients external to the bank, or an internal function that is external to the business unit under analysis, government regulatory agencies, suppliers (internal or external), contractors, out-sourced service providers (external or internal), investments, affiliations and competitors, etc.

5.2.2 Connectivity and Interdependencies

The headline risk categories cannot be viewed in isolation from one another. Figure 13.10 illustrates the way in which one needs to examine the degree of interconnected risk exposures that cut across the headline operational risk categories, in order to understand the full impact of any risk. For example, assume that a business unit is introducing a new computer technology. The implementation of that new technology may generate a set of interconnected risks across people, process, and technology. For example, have the people who are to work with the new technology been given sufficient training and support?

All this suggests that the overall risk is likely to be higher than that accounted for by each of the component risks considered in-

FIGURE 13.10

Connectivity of Operational Risk Exposure

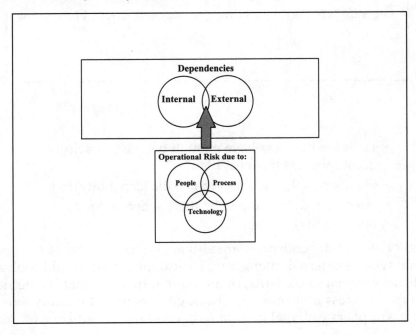

dividually. Similarly, the severity or financial impact assessment could be greater (or might be less) than the sum of the individual severity assessments.

5.2.3 Change, Complexity, Complacency

One should also examine the sources that drive the headline categories of operational risk. For example, one may view the drivers as falling broadly under the categories of change, complexity, and complacency.

Change refers to such items as introducing new technology or new products, a merger or acquisition, or moving from internal supply to outsourcing, etc. Complexity refers to such items as complexity in products, process, or technology. Complacency refers to ineffective management of the business, particularly in key operational risk areas such as fraud, unauthorized trading, privacy and confidentiality, payment and settlement, model use, etc.

Figure 13.11 illustrates how these underlying sources of a risk connect to the headline operational risk categories.

5.2.4 Net Likelihood Assessment

The likelihood that an operational failure might occur within the next year should be assessed, net of risk mitigants such as insurance, for each identified risk exposure and for each of the four headline risk categories (i.e., people, process, and technology, and external dependencies). Since it is often unclear how to quantify these risks, this assessment can be expressed as a rating along a five-point likelihood continuum from very low (VL) to very high (VH), as set out in Table 13.3.

5.2.5 Severity Assessment

Severity describes the potential loss to the bank given that an operational failure has occurred. Typically, this will be expressed as a range of dollars (e.g., $50 million to $100 million), as exact measurements will not usually be possible. Severity should be assessed for each identified risk exposure. As pointed out above, the severity of operational risks should be evaluated net of risk mitigants. For example, if one has insurance to cover a potential fraud, then one needs to adjust the degree of fraud risk by the amount of insurance.

FIGURE 13.11

Interconnection of Operational Risks

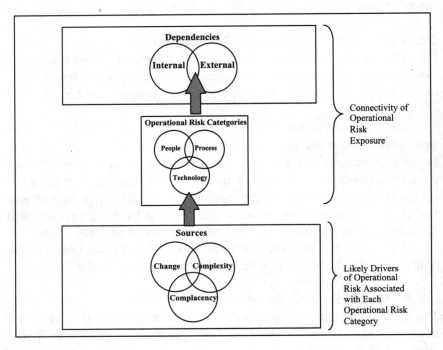

We expect over time that insurance products will play an increasingly larger role in the area of mitigating operational risk. We also expect over time that insurance products will help to provide additional price discovery for operational risk. In practice the operational risk management group, in the early stages of operational risk assessment, is likely to rely on the expertise of business management to recommend appropriate severity amounts.

5.2.6 Combining Likelihood and Severity into an Overall Operational Risk Assessment

Operational risk measures are constrained in that there is not usually a defensible way to combine the individual likelihood of loss and severity assessments into an overall measure of operational risk within a business unit. To do so, the likelihood of loss would need to be expressed in numerical terms—e.g., a medium risk rep-

TABLE 13.3

Five-Point Likelihood Continuum

Likelihood That an Operational Failure Will Occur Within the Next Year	
VL	Very low (very unlikely to happen: less than 2%)
L	Low (unlikely: 2–5%)
M	Medium (may happen: 5–10%)
H	High (likely to happen: 10–20%)
VH	Very high (very likely: greater than 20%)

resents a 5 to 10 percent probability of occurrence. This cannot be accomplished without statistically significant historical data on operational losses.

The fact is that for the moment the financial industry measures operational risk using a combination of both quantitative and qualitative points of view. One should strive to take a quantitative approach based on statistical data. However, where the data are unavailable or unreliable—and this is the case for many risk sources at the moment—a qualitative approach can be used to generate a risk rating. Neither approach on its own tells the whole story: the quantitative approach is often too rigid, while the qualitative approach is often too vague. The hybrid approach requires a numerical assignment of the amount at risk based on both quantitative and qualitative data.

Ideally, one would also calculate the correlation between the various risk exposures and incorporate this into the overall measure of business or firm-wide risk. Given the difficulty of doing this, for the time being risk managers are more likely to simply aggregate individual severities assessed for each operational risk exposure.[7]

5.2.7 Defining Cause and Effect

Loss data are easier to collect than data associated with the cause of loss. This complicates the measurement of operational risk because each loss is likely to have several causes. The relationship between these causes, and the relative importance of each, can be difficult to assess in an objective fashion. For example, according to best practice, a bank ought to have an independent analytical group within the risk management group vet all the mathematical models that its businesses are using. If losses occur as a result of model risk, any failure to have created such a group might be reckoned as the root cause of the loss—but there are many other possible causes such as human error or product complexity. Most banks start by collecting the losses and then try to fit the causes to them. The methodology is typically developed later, after the data have been collected.

Institutions need to develop a variety of empirical analyses to test the links between cause and effect. Consulting firms are currently providing services that may help institutions link cause and effect and source data (Table 13.4).

TABLE 13.4

Risk Categories: Example of Cause, Effect, and Source

Risk Category	The Cause	The Effect (The Loss)	Sources of Probability and Magnitude of Loss Data
People (human resource)	Loss of key staff, say, due to defection to a competitor	Variance in revenues/ profits (e.g., cost of recruiting replacements, costs of training, disruption to existing staff)	• Delphic[1] techniques based on business assessment
Process	Declining productivity as volume grows	Variance in process costs from predicted levels, excluding process malfunctions	• Historical variances • Supplier/vendor estimates • Industry benchmarking
Technology	Year 2000 upgrade expenditure	Variance in technology running costs from predicted levels	• Historical variances • Supplier/vendor estimates • Industry benchmarking

[1]An iterative technique for developing consensus and making group-based decisions in order to forecast future outcomes.

Source: Extracted from tables provided by Duncan Wilson, Head of Risk Management, EMEA, Global Financial Markets, IBM.

5.2.8 Sample Risk Assessment Report

What does this approach lead to when put into practice? Assume we have examined business unit A and have determined that the sources of operational risk are related to outsourcing, privacy, compliance, fraud, downsizing, and the political environment.

The sample report, as illustrated in Table 13.5, shows that overall the business has a "low" likelihood of operational loss within the next 12 months. Observe that an overall assessment has led to an overall exposure estimate of $150 to $300 million. Typically, one might display for each business unit a graph showing the relationship between severity and likelihood across each operational risk type (Appendix 4).

The summary report typically contains details of the factors considered when making a "likelihood" assessment for each operational risk exposure, broken down by people, process, technology, and external dependencies.

5.3 Review and Validation (Step 3)

What happens after such a report has been generated? First, the centralized operational risk management group (ORMG) reviews the assessment results with senior business unit management and key officers, in order to finalize the proposed operational risk rating. Key officers include those with responsibility for the management and control of operational activities, such as internal audit, compliance, information technology, human resources, and so on.

Second, one may want an operational risk rating committee to review the assessment—a validation process similar to that followed by credit rating agencies such as Standard & Poors when they validate credit ratings. This takes the form of a review of the individual risk assessments by knowledgeable senior committee personnel to ensure that the framework has been consistently applied across businesses, that there has been sufficient scrutiny to remove any imperfections, and so on. The committee should have representation from business management, audit, and functional areas, and be chaired by the risk management unit. A voting system can be used to determine the final risk rating, with risk management having the right to veto. ORMG may clarify or amend its original assessment based on feedback from the rating review committee before the assessments are published.

TABLE 13.5

Example of a Risk Assessment Report for Business Unit A

Operational Risk Scenarios	Internal Dependencies		Likelihood of Event (In 12 Months)	External Dependencies	Overall Assessment	Severity ($million)
	People	Process	Technology			
Outsourcing	L	VL	VL	M	M	50–100
Privacy	L	M	VL	L	L	50–100
Compliance	L	VH	VL	VL	L	35–70
Fraud	L	L	VL	VL	L	5–10
Downsizing	L	VL	VL	L	L	5–10
Political environment	VL	M	VL	VL	L	5–10
Overall assessment	**L**	**M**	**VL**	**L**	**L**	**150–300**

5.4 Output (Step 4)

The final assessment of operational risk will be formally reported to business management, the centralized risk-adjusted return on capital (RAROC) group, and the partners in corporate governance such as internal audit and compliance. As illustrated in Figure 13.12, the output of the assessment process has two main uses. First, the assessment provides better operational risk information to management for use in improving risk management decisions. Second, the assessment improves the allocation of economic capital to better reflect the extent of the operational risk that is being taken by a business unit, a topic we discuss in more detail below. Overall, operational risk assessment guides management action—for example, in deciding whether to purchase insurance to mitigate some of the risks.

The overall assessment of the likelihood of operational risk and severity of loss for a business unit can be plotted to provide relative information on operational risk exposures across the bank or a segment of the bank, as shown in Figure 13.13 (see also Appendix 4). Of course, Figure 13.13 is a very simplified way of representing risk; however, for many operational risks presenting a full probability distribution is too complex to be justified—and

FIGURE 13.12

Fourth Step in the Measurement Process of Operational Risk: Output

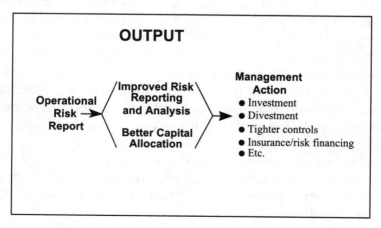

FIGURE   13.13

Summary Risk Reporting

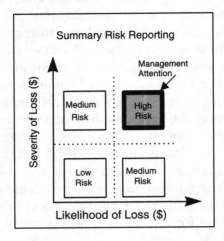

may even be misleading given the lack of historical evidence. In Figure 13.13, one can see very clearly that if a business unit falls in the upper right-hand quadrant, then the business unit has a high likelihood of operational risk and a high severity of loss, if failure occurs. These units should be the focus of management's attention.

A business unit may address its operational risks in several ways. First, one can invest (e.g., upgrade technology) in the business unit (investment). Second, one can avoid the risk by withdrawing from a business activity (divestment). Third, one can accept and manage the risk, say, through effective management, monitoring, and control (tighter controls). Fourth, one can transfer the risk to another party (e.g., through insurance or outsourcing). For example, after management identifies the sources of operational risks in its organization, it can ask several insurance companies to submit proposals for insuring those risks.

Of course, not all operational risks are insurable, and in the case of those that are insurable the required premium may be prohibitive. The strategy and the eventual decision should be based on a cost-benefit analysis.

6. CAPITAL ATTRIBUTION FOR OPERATIONAL RISKS

By attributing economic capital to operational risks we can make sure that businesses that take on more operational risk are assigned a greater allocation of capital, and incur a transparent capital charge. The idea is that this, in turn, will allow whole firms and individual businesses to use risk/reward analysis to improve their operational decisions.

In many banks, the methodology for translating operational risk into capital is developed by a RAROC group in partnership with the operational risk management group. One approach to allocating economic capital is really an extension of the risk measurement and ranking process that we described above. For example:

- First assign a risk rating to each business based on the likelihood of an operational risk occurring, e.g., on a scale of 1 for "very low" operational risk to 5 for "very high." This rating should be assigned to reflect the probability of a failure occurring, inclusive of mitigating factors introduced by management.
- Second, the degree of severity of the likely loss should be determined given that the operational failure occurs. As pointed out earlier, this risk severity is estimated utilizing a combination of internal loss history, losses at other banks, management judgment, etc.
- Third, a risk rating is assigned based on combining the likelihood and severity in the operational risk calculation. A review group ensures consistency and integrity of the operational risk rating process on a bank-wide basis, so that the result is a "relative" risk rating for each business that can then be used to attribute capital up to the desired "all-bank operational risk capital amount."

Note that for the purposes of capital allocation we need to take special account of the kind of worst case scenarios of operational losses illustrated in Figure 13.14. To understand this diagram, remember that operational risks can be divided into those losses that are expected and those that are unexpected. Management, in

FIGURE 13.14

Distribution of Operational Losses

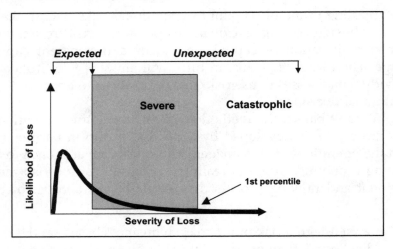

the ordinary course of business, knows that certain operational activities will fail. There will be a "normal" amount of operational loss that the business is willing to absorb as a cost of doing business, such as error correction, fraud, and so on. These failures are explicitly budgeted for in the annual business plan and are covered by the pricing of the product or service. We assume that a business unit's management is already assessing and pricing expected failures.

By contrast, the focus of this chapter, as illustrated in Figure 13.14,[8] is on unexpected failures, and the amount of economic capital that should be attributed to business units to absorb those losses. However, as the figure suggests, unexpected failures can themselves be further subdivided:

- Severe but not catastrophic losses. Unexpected severe operational failures, as illustrated in Table 13.6, should be covered by an appropriate allocation of operational risk capital. These kinds of losses will tend to be covered by the measurement processes described in the sections above.

TABLE 13.6

Distribution of Operational Losses

	Expected event (high probability, low losses)	Unexpected event (low probability, high losses)	
		Severe financial impact	Catastrophic financial impact
Operational Losses Covered by	Business plan	Operational risk capital	Insurable (risk transfer) or "risk financing"

- Catastrophic losses. These are the most extreme but also the rarest forms of operational risk events—the kind that might destroy the bank. Value-at-risk (VaR) and RAROC models are not meant to capture catastrophic risk, since potential losses are calculated only up to a certain confidence (probability) level and catastrophic risks are by their very nature extremely rare. Banks will attempt to find insurance coverage to hedge catastrophic risk since capital will not protect a bank from these risks.

Although VaR/RAROC models may not capture catastrophic loss, banks can use these approaches to assist their thinking about how insurance policies can be used to protect against operational risk. For example, it might be argued that one should retain the risk if the cost of capital to support the asset is less than the cost of insuring it. This sort of risk/reward approach can bring discipline to an insurance program that has evolved over time into a rather ad hoc set of policies—e.g., where one type of risk is insured while another is not, with very little underlying rationale.

Banks have now begun to develop databases of historical operational risk events in an effort to quantify unexpected risks of various sorts. They are hoping to use these databases to develop statistically defined "worst case" estimates that may be applicable to a select sub-set of a bank's businesses—in the same way that many banks already use historical loss data to drive credit risk measurement. Accounting firms such as PricewaterhouseCoopers are also building databases of operational risk.

It should he admitted that this is a new and evolving area of risk measurement. A bank's internal loss database will most likely be relatively small, and it is unlikely to reflect the major losses suffered occasionally by its peers. Hence, to be useful, the database should also reflect the experience of others. Blending internal and external data requires a heavy dose of management judgement.

Some banks are moving to an integrated or concentric approach to the "financing" of operational risks. This financing can be achieved via a combination of external insurance programs (e.g., with floors and caps), capital market tools, and self-insurance. Where risks are self-insured, the risk should be allocated economic capital.

How will the increasing emphasis on operational risk and changes in the financial sector affect the overall capital attributions in banking institutions? In the very broadest terms, we would guess that the typical capital attributions in banks now stand at around 20 percent for operational risk, 10 percent for market risk, and 70 percent for credit risk (Figure 13.15). We would expect that both operational risk and market risk exposures might evolve in the future to around 30 percent each—although, of course, much depends on the nature of the institution.

The likely growth in the weighting of operational risk can be attributed to the growing risks associated with people, process, technology, and external dependencies. For example, it seems inevitable that financial institutions will experience higher worker mobility, growing product sophistication, increases in business volume, rapid introduction of new technology, and increased merger/acquisitions activity—all of which generate operational risk.

Regulators require sufficient capital to be set against the market risk (i.e., BIS 98) and the credit risk (i.e., modified BIS 88) of a banking book, but there are no formal requirements to set capital against operational risk. At this stage, it remains an open issue but likely that BIS will ask banks to set capital aside to cover operational risk at, say, the 1 percent confidence level. If regulators move in this direction, the focus will quickly shift to determining the cri-

FIGURE 13.15

Capital Attribution: Present and Future

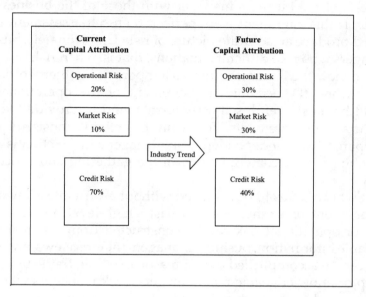

teria that will allow an appropriate allocation of capital to operational risk.

7. SELF-ASSESSMENT VERSUS RISK MANAGEMENT ASSESSMENT

It might be argued that the enormity of the task of assessing operational risk implies that the only way to accomplish it, without creating an army of risk managers, is to ask the management of the individual businesses to assess the operational risks they are running. However, this approach is not likely to provide the necessary information. At the extreme, one might point out that it is unlikely that Nick Leeson would have accurately self-assessed the operational risk of his business within Barings Bank. More generally, the issue is not only one of trust or competency, but also to do with the trade-off between seeking new opportunities and managing the associated risks.

In normal circumstances senior management tries to align, through the use of appropriate incentives, the short- and long-term interests of the business manager with those of the business as a whole. If this alignment were perfect, then self-assessment might indeed produce an accurate picture of risk. Unfortunately, business managers who face difficult situations, that is, when risks are high, tend to view the increase in risk as temporary. In other words, precisely when the accurate measurement of the operational risk would be most useful, self-assessments tend to provide the most inaccurate measurements. To ensure objectivity, consistency, and transparency, the independent risk management function is therefore obliged to become involved in the gathering and processing of data.

So how is this to be achieved without a veritable army of risk management personnel? First, a basic, high-level but reasonable view of operational risk can be constructed from the analysis of available information, business management interviews, and so on. This can be accomplished over a reasonable time frame by a small group of knowledgeable risk managers. Risk managers who have been trained to look for risk, and who have been made accountable for obtaining an accurate view of the risk at a reasonable cost, must manage the trade-off between accuracy, granularity of information (the level of focus of the data gathering exercise), and timeliness.

Second, risk managers must be placed "in the flow" of all relevant business management information. This can be accomplished by inviting risk managers to sit in on the various regular business management meetings, by involving them in new product approval processes, by making sure they receive regular management reports, and so on. (This is also how credit and market risk managers maintain a timely and a current view of their respective risk areas.)

Another argument often used in favor of self-assessment is that an operational risk manager cannot possibly know as much about the business as the business manager, and that a risk assessment performed by a risk manager will therefore be incomplete or inaccurate. This, however, confuses the respective roles and responsibilities of the risk and business managers. The business manager should indeed know more about the business than the operational risk manager. But the operational risk manager is trained in evaluating risk, much as a life insurance risk manager is trained to interpret the risk from a medical report and certain statistics. The life insurance risk manager is neither expected to be a medical expert nor even to be able to produce the medical report—only to interpret and extract risk information.

Again, an analogy can be drawn with the credit risk manager. A credit risk manager is expected to observe, analyze, and interpret information about a company so as to evaluate its credit risk. He or she is not expected to be able to *manage* that company. Operational risk can be mitigated by training personnel to use the tools associated with best-practice risk management (Appendix 5).

8. INTEGRATED OPERATIONAL RISK

At present, most financial institutions have one set of rules to measure market risk, a second set of rules to measure credit risk, and are just beginning to develop a third set of rules to measure operational risk. It seems likely that the leading banks will work to integrate these methodologies (Figure 13.16). For example they might attempt to integrate market risk VaR and credit risk VaR with a new operational risk VaR measure.

FIGURE 13.16

Integrated Risk Models

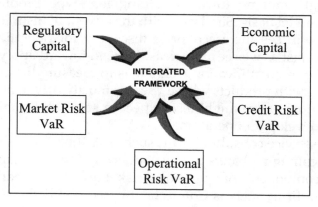

Developing an integrated risk measurement model will have important implications from both a risk transparency and a regulatory capital perspective. For example, if one simply added a market risk VaR plus an operational risk VaR plus a credit risk VaR to obtain a total VaR (rather than developing an integrated model), then one would overstate the amount of risk. The summing ignores the interaction or correlation between market risk, credit risk, and operational risk.

The Bank for International Settlement (1988) rules for capital adequacy are generally recognized to be flawed, as we discussed in earlier chapters of this book. We would expect that, in time, regulators will allow banks to use their own internal models (e.g., through utilizing the banks' internal rating system) to calculate a credit risk VaR to replace the outdated BIS 1988 rules, in the same way that the BIS 1998 Accord allowed banks to adopt an internal models approach for determining the minimum required regulatory capital for trading market risk.

The banking industry, rather than the regulators, sponsored the original market VaR methodology; in particular, JP Morgan's release of its RiskMetrics product pushed the industry forward. Industry has also sponsored the new wave of credit VaR methodologies such as CreditMetrics from JP Morgan, and CreditRisk+ from Credit Suisse Financial Products. All this suggests that in time the banking industry will sponsor some form of operational risk VaR methodology.

We can push the parallel a little further. The financial community, with the advent of products such as credit derivatives, is increasingly moving towards valuing loan-type products on a mark-to-model basis. Similarly, with the advent of insurance products, we will see increased price discovery for operational risk. Moreover, just as we see an increasing trend toward applying market risk–style quantification techniques to measure the credit VaR associated with products whose value is mostly driven by changes in credit quality, we might also expect to see such techniques applied to develop an operational risk VaR.

Full-service consulting firms such as Arthur Andersen[8] are already encouraging banks to develop a common risk map that details the components of operational risk. Further, risk management consulting firms such as Connecticut-based Net Risk are facilitating access to operational risk data (Appendix 6). The focus by both consultants and banking practitioners on operational risk is accelerating efforts to arrive at an operational risk VaR.

A major challenge for banks is to produce comprehensible and practical approaches to operational risk that will prove acceptable to the regulatory community. Ideally, the integrated risk model of the future will encompass market risk VaR, credit risk VaR, and operational risk VaR, and be able to calculate both regulatory capital and economic capital.

9. CONCLUSION

The developments discussed in this chapter are helping institutions manage their portfolios of risk more efficiently. Increasingly, institutions will be able to gain a competitive advantage by monitoring and managing all of their risks on a global basis—although to achieve this each firm is likely to have to confront some fundamental infrastructure issues.

A list of the sources that drive the headline categories of operational risk exposures should be developed to help identify a common taxonomy of the drivers of risks. The end product is a best-practice management of risk that is also consistent with business strategies. This is a "one firm, one view" approach that also recognizes the complexity of each business within the firm.

In this chapter we have stressed that operational risk should be managed as a partnership of business units, business infrastructure groups, and corporate governance units such as internal audit and risk management. We should also mention the importance of establishing a risk-aware business culture. Senior managers play a critical role in establishing a corporate environment in which best-practice operational risk management can flourish. Personnel ultimately behave in a manner that is dependent on how senior management rewards and trains them.

Indeed, arguably the key single challenge for senior management is to harmonize the behavior patterns of business units, infrastructure units, corporate governance units, internal audit, and risk management. Senior management must create an environment in which all sides "sink or swim" together in terms of managing operational risk.

APPENDIX 1: GROUP OF THIRTY RECOMMENDATIONS: DERIVATIVES AND OPERATIONAL RISK

In Chapter 2 we discussed the G-30 recommendations from an overall risk management perspective. These recommendations also lay out the desirable characteristics of an organizational structure designed to tightly control operational risk.

The G-30 emphasized that the successful implementation of systems operations and controls is important for the management of derivatives activities. The G-30 stressed that the complexity and diversity of derivatives activities make the measurement and control of those risks more difficult. This difficulty increases the importance of sophisticated risk management systems and sound management and operating practices These are vital to a firm's ability to execute, record, and monitor derivatives transactions, and to provide the information needed by management to manage the risks associated with these activities.

Likewise, the G-30 report stressed the importance of hiring skilled professionals: Recommendation 16 states that one should *"ensure that derivatives activities are undertaken by professionals in sufficient number and with the appropriate experience, skill levels, and degrees of specialization."*

The G-30 also stressed the importance of building best-practice systems. According to Recommendation 17, one should *"ensure that adequate systems for data capture, processing, settlement, and management reporting are in place so that derivatives transactions are conducted in an orderly and efficient manner in compliance with management policies."* Furthermore, *"One should have risk management systems that measure the risks incurred in their derivatives activities based on their nature, size, and complexity."*

Recommendation 19 emphasized that accounting practices should highlight the risks being taken. For example, the G-30 pointed out that one *"should account for derivatives transactions used to manage risks so as to achieve a consistency of income recognition treatment between those instruments and the risks being managed."*

People

The survey of industry practices examined the involvement in the derivatives activity of people at all levels of the organization. The survey indicated a need for further development of staff involved in back-office administration, accounts, and audit functions, etc. Respondents believed that a new breed of specialist, qualified operational staff, was required. The survey pointed out that dealers, large and small, and end-users face a common challenge of developing the right control culture for their derivatives activity.

The survey highlighted the importance of the ability of people to work in cross-functional teams. The survey pointed out that many issues require input from a number of disciplines (e.g., trading, legal, and accounting) and demand an integrated approach.

Systems

The survey confirmed the view that dealing in derivatives can demand integrated systems to ensure adequate information and operational control. The survey indicated that dealers were moving toward more integrated systems, between front and back office, across various types of transactions.

The industry has made a huge investment in systems, and almost all large dealers are extensive users of advanced technology. Many derivative groups have their own research and technology teams that develop the mathematical algorithms and systems necessary to price new transactions and to monitor their derivatives portfolios. Many dealers consider their ability to manage the development of systems capabilities an important source of competitive strength.

For large dealers there is a requirement that one develops systems that minimize manual intervention as well as enhance operating efficiency and reliability, the volume of activity, customization of transactions, number of calculations to be performed, and overall complexity.

Systems that integrate the various tasks to be performed for derivatives are complex. Because of the rapid development of the business, even the most sophisticated dealers and users often rely on a variety of systems, which may be difficult to integrate in a satisfactory manner. While this situation is inevitable in many organizations, it is not ideal and requires careful monitoring to ensure sufficient consistency to allow reconciliation of results and aggregation of risks where required.

The survey results indicated that the largest dealers, recognizing the control risks that separate systems pose and the expense of substantial daily reconciliations, are making extensive investments to integrate back-office systems for derivatives with front-office systems to derivatives as well as other management information.

Operations

The role of the back office is to perform a variety of functions in a timely fashion. This includes recording transactions, issuing and monitoring confirmations, ensuring legal documentation for transactions is completed, settling transactions, and producing information for management and control purposes. This information includes reports of positions against trading and counterparty limits, reports on profitability, and reports on exceptions, requiring action to be taken on outstanding confirmations, limit excesses, etc.

There has been significant evolution in the competence of staff and the adequacy of procedures and systems in the back office. Derivatives businesses, like other credit or securities businesses, give the back office the principal function of recording, documenting, and confirming the actions of the dealers. The wide range of volume and complexity that exists among dealers and end-users has led to a range of acceptable solutions.

The long time scales between the trade date and the settlement date, which is a feature of some products, mean that errors not detected by the confirmation process may not be discovered for some time.

While it is necessary to ensure that the systems are adequate for the organization's volume and the complexity of derivatives activities, there can be no single prescriptive solution to the management challenges that derivatives pose to the back office. This reflects the diversity in activity between different market participants.

Controls

Derivative activities, by their very nature, cross many boundaries of traditional financial activity. Therefore the control function must be necessarily broad, covering all aspects of activity. The primary element of control lies in the organization itself. Allocation of responsibilities for derivatives activities, with segregation of authority where appropriate, should be reflected in job descriptions and organization charts.

Authority to commit the institution to transactions is normally defined by level or position. It is the role of management to ensure that the conduct of activity is consistent with delegated authority. There is no substitute for internal controls; however, dealers and end-users should communicate information that clearly indicates which individuals within the organization have the authority to make commitments. At the same time, all participants should fully recognize that the legal doctrine of "apparent authority" may govern the transactions to which individuals within their organization commit.

Definition of authority within an organization should also address issues of suitability of use of derivatives. End-users of derivatives transactions are usually institutional borrowers and investors and as such should possess the capability to understand and quantify risks inherent in their business. Institutional investors may also be buyers of structured securities exhibiting features of derivatives. While the exposures to derivatives will normally be similar to those on institutional balance sheets, it is possible that in some cases the complexity of such derivatives used might exceed the ability of an entity to understand fully the associated risks. The recommendations provide guidelines for management practice and give any firm considering the appropriate use of derivatives a useful framework for assessing suitability and developing policy consistent with its overall risk management and capital policies. Organizational controls can then be established to ensure activities are consistent with a firm's needs and objectives.

Audit

The G-30 pointed out that internal audit plays an important role in the procedures and control framework by providing an independent, internal assessment of the effectiveness of this framework.

The principal challenge for management is to ensure that internal audit staff has sufficient expertise to carry out work in both the front and back offices. Able individuals with the appropriate financial and systems skills are required to carry out the specialist aspects of the work. Considerable investment in training is needed to ensure that staff understand the nature and characteristics of the instruments being transacted and the models that are used to price them.

Although not part of the formal control framework of the organization, external auditors and regulatory examiners provide a check on procedures and controls. They also face the challenge of developing and maintaining the appropriate degree of expertise in this area.

APPENDIX 2: TYPES OF OPERATIONAL RISK LOSSES

Operational risk is multifaceted, and the type of loss can take many different forms, including damage to physical assets, unauthorized activity, unexpected taxation, problems with customer satisfaction, and so on. It is critical that operational risk management groups are clear when they communicate with line management and senior managers. It follows that the various types of operational risk need to be tightly defined, and it can be helpful to publish a lexicon of key terms for the internal use of an institution. For example, an illustrative table of definitions such as those illustrated in

Table 13.A2.1 might be developed. (Note that this illustrative list is not intended to be exhaustive.)

APPENDIX 3: SEVERITY VERSUS LIKELIHOOD

The process of operational risk assessment should include a review of the likelihood, or frequency, of a particular operational risk, as well as a review of its possible magnitude or severity. For example, risk managers can publish graphs displaying the potential severity of a risk set against the frequency of certain operational failure risks, as shown in Figure 13.A3.1. This diagram allows managers to visualize the trade-off between severity and likelihood. All the risks along the curve exhibit the same expected loss, i.e., likelihood multiplied by severity. For example, A5 has a low likelihood and a medium level of severity. Given an acceptable level of expected loss, management should take appropriate actions to mitigate the risk located above the curve (A7 and A8). A7 has a medium likelihood and medium severity, while A8 has a medium severity but a high likelihood. For both of these risks, the expected level of loss is above the acceptable level.

APPENDIX 4: TRAINING AND RISK EDUCATION

One major source of operational risk is people—the so-called "human factor." Few managers doubt that operational risk due to people can be mitigated through better educating and training workers, especially in the case of critical activities. Of course, it is costly to select better people and to train them more thoroughly, and this added cost must be evaluated against the benefit of the reduced operational risk.

Training in the sense of risk education is also crucial: first-class risk education is a key component of any optimal firm-wide risk management program. Staff should be aware of why they may have to change the way they do things. Staff are more comfortable if

TABLE 13.A2.1

Lexicon of Key Terms

Key Terms	Definition
Asset loss or damage	• Risk of either an uninsured or irrecoverable loss or damage to bank assets caused by fire, flooding, power supply, weather, natural disaster, physical accident, etc. • Risk of having to use bank assets to compensate clients for uninsured or irrecoverable loss or damage to client assets under bank custody. Note: This term excludes loss or damage due to either theft, fraud, or malicious damage (separate category below).
Credit losses due to operational failures	• Risk of operational failure, e.g., failure of people, process, technology, or external dependencies resulting in credit losses. Note: This term defines an internal failure that is, in itself, unrelated to the creditworthiness of the borrower or guarantor. For example, such a loss might arise when an inexperienced credit adjudicator assigns a higher than appropriate risk rating to a loan, leading to the incorrect pricing of the facility.
Customer satisfaction	• Risk of losing current customers and being unable to attract new customers, with a consequent loss of revenue. Note: This definition includes reputational risk, as it applies to clients.
Disputes	• Risk of having to make payments to settle disputes either through lawsuits or negotiated settlement. Note: This definition includes disputes with clients, employees, suppliers, competitors, etc.
Market losses due to operational failures	• Risk of operational failure (failure of people, process, technology, external dependencies) resulting in market losses. Note: This term defines an internal failure that is, in itself, unrelated to market movements. For example, if a risk manager uses incomplete or inaccurate data when calculating VaR, then the true exposures might not be recorded, and decisions might be made that lead to greater losses than would otherwise have been the case.

Model risk	• Risk that the models used for limit monitoring and generating P&L, etc., are flawed (Chapter 15).
Project management	• Risk of projects failing to meet initial goals, e.g., costing more than budgeted.
Regulatory/ compliance	• Risk of regulatory fines, penalties, client restitution payments, or other financial cost to be paid. Example: risk of regulatory sanctions, such as restricting or removal of a bank's license, resulting in reduced ability to generate revenue or achieve targeted profitability.
Taxation	• Risk of incurring greater tax liabilities than anticipated.
Theft/fraud/malicious damage	• Risk of uninsured and irrecoverable loss of bank assets due to either theft, fraud, or malicious damage. The loss may be caused by people employed by the bank or acting externally to the bank. • Risk of having to use bank assets to compensate clients for either uninsured or irrecoverable loss of their assets under bank custody due to either theft, fraud, or malicious damage. Note: This risk excludes rogue trading (see separate category).
Transaction processing, errors and omissions	• Risk of loss due to error in processing transactions. This includes cost of correcting the problem that originally prevented the transactions from being processed.
Unauthorized activity (e.g., rogue trading)	• Risk of loss as a result of unauthorized activity.

FIGURE 13.A3.1

Operational Risk Severity versus Frequency

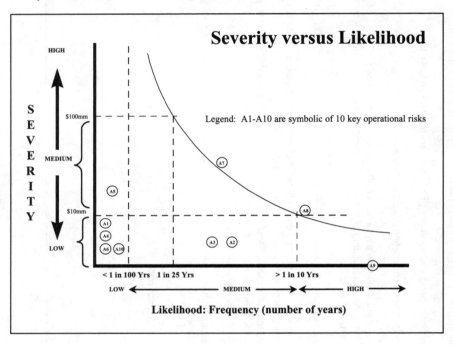

they know new risk control procedures exist for a good business reason. Staff also need to understand clearly risk management techniques that are more ambitious than the most basic limit monitoring techniques (i.e., the lowest level of knowledge illustrated in Figure 13.A4.1). Furthermore, managers may need to be educated on the mathematics behind risk analysis. In other words, managers need to be educated about the means by which risk is measured.

Business units, infrastructure units, corporate governance units, and internal audit should also be educated on how risk can be used as the basis for allocating economic capital. Business staff should learn how to use measures of risk as a basis for pricing transactions. Finally, as illustrated in the upper-right corner of the figure, one should educate business managers and risk managers on how to utilize the risk measurement tools to enhance their portfolio management skills.

FIGURE 13.A4.1

Increased Operational Risk Knowledge Required

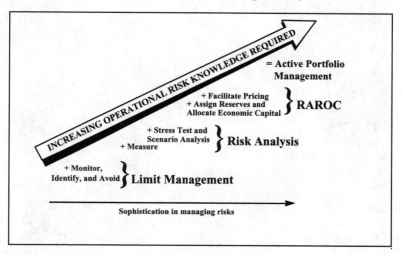

APPENDIX 5: IDENTIFYING AND QUANTIFYING OPERATIONAL RISK

NetRisk, a specialist consultancy firm in the field of risk management, has developed a risk management tool called RiskOps that is comprised of an operating losses database and a software application. The database stores loss event data made public by companies, and in the future it will also store private loss event data input by RiskOps sponsor companies.

The loss data include a full description of loss events and their causes and effects. The software application allows risk managers to analyze and report on operating loss data, and also allows the user to scale data by asset size and other measures. The application provides histogram and tabular views of the analyzed data at macro- and microlevels of detail. The software is web based, so that all the enhancements to the application and the updates to the data are executed at the server level and are immediately available to the user.

NetRisk has developed a tool that will allow the user to identify operational risk causes and quantify them (Figure 13.A5.1). For

FIGURE 13.A5.1

RiskOps™–Causes of Operational Risk

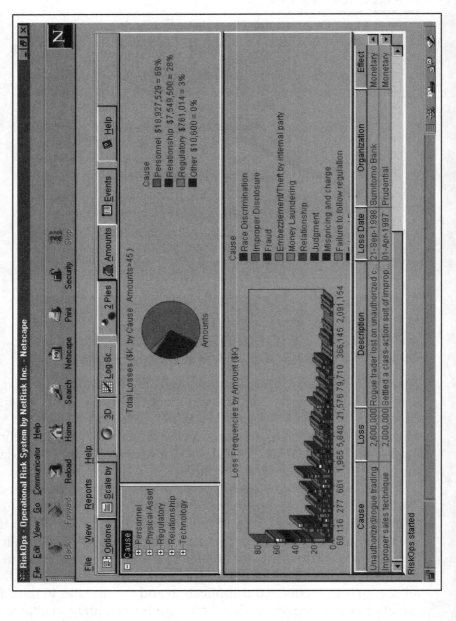

FIGURE 13.A5.2

RiskOps™—Operational Risks Related to Personnel

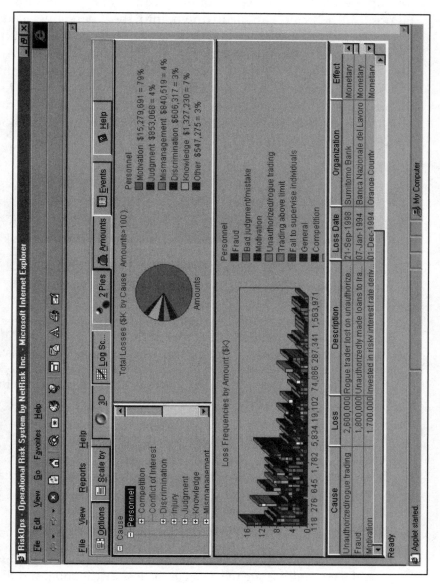

example, the RiskOps product enables the user to arrive at a history of operational risk loss amount by cause. Further, as shown in Figure 13.A5.2, one can drill down into the "personnel cause" screen for additional loss information. The RiskOps product also provides a description of specific losses. For example, as shown on the bottom of Figure 13.A5.1, RiskOps indicates that the Prudential has settled a class action suit arising from improper sales techniques. One can obtain details on each of the causes (personnel, physical asset, regulatory, relationship, and technology) as shown on the upper-left portion of Figure 13.A5.1.

NOTES

1. This chapter draws substantially on a previous work published by the authors as "Key Steps in Building Consistent Operational Risk Measurement and Management," *Operational Risk and Financial Institutions*, Chapter 3, Risk Books: London, 1998, pp. 45–62. The authors and publisher would like to thank Risk Books for their permission in this regard.
2. Operational risk, as pointed out in the introduction to this chapter, is not a well-defined concept. The academic literature dealing with the risks faced by financial institutions tends to ignore operational risk, or, more precisely, relates operational risk to operational leverage, i.e., to the shape of the production cost function, and in particular to the relationship between fixed and variable costs.
3. See also Chapter 15, section 4.5.
4. Lexicons such as those in Appendix 2 can help here.
5. See Step 3.
6. These categories are consistent with the typology introduced earlier in this chapter.
7. The corollary to severity in the credit risk model would be "exposure," i.e., the total loss given default of all loans in the portfolio.
8. The terminology "expected loss" and "unexpected loss" is used by practitioners to designate the mean of the loss distribution, and the distance to the mean of a given quantile of the loss distribution, e.g., the first percentile.
9. Arthur Andersen has developed a useful level taxonomy for cataloguing risk. Andersen divides risk into "environment risk,"

"process risk," and "information for decision making risk." These three broad categories of risk are then further divided. For example, process risk is divided into operations risk, empowerment risk, information processing/technology risk, and integrity risk. Each of these risks is further subdivided. For example, financial risk is further subdivided into price, liquidity, and credit risk.

CHAPTER 14

Capital Allocation and Performance Measurement

1. INTRODUCTION

In recent years, banks and consulting firms have sought to develop methodologies that will help financial institutions relate the return on capital provided by a transaction, or business, to the riskiness of the investment. The risk-adjusted return on capital (RAROC) methodology is one approach to this problem, and it is likely to prove a critical component of any integrated risk management framework. Indeed, one can think of RAROC analysis as the glue that binds a firm's risk management and business activities together.

As illustrated in Figure 14.1, RAROC analysis reveals how much economic capital is required by each business line, or product, or customer—and how these requirements create the total return on capital produced by the firm. Further, RAROC provides an economic basis from which to measure all the relevant risk types and risk positions consistently (including the authority to incur risk). Finally, because RAROC promotes consistent, fair, and reasonable risk-adjusted performance measures, it provides managers with the information that they need to make the trade-off between risk and reward more efficient.

RAROC thus generates appropriate risk/reward signals at all levels of business activity, and should form a critical part of the

FIGURE 14.1

RAROC Analysis

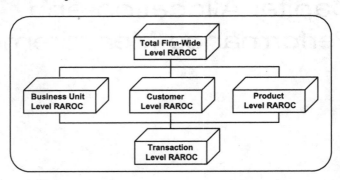

business "mindset." (Banks also need to take into account their regulator's capital adequacy requirements.)

Figure 14.2 shows how today's approach to measuring risk-adjusted returns has evolved out of relatively unsophisticated measures of appraisal, which used revenue as the primary criteria for judging business success.[1]

During the late 1990s, the RAROC approach began to be accepted as a best-practice standard by the financial industry and its regulators. This was made possible by the development of sophisticated risk measurement tools of the kind discussed in other chap-

FIGURE 14.2

Evolution of Performance Measurement

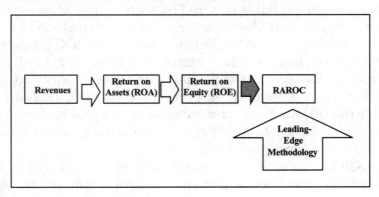

ters of this book. These tools offered banks the practical capability to assign economic capital and measure performance on a risk-adjusted basis.

These risk measurement tools also encouraged banks to manage their capital on an integrated, portfolio management basis. In particular, banks increasingly recognized that market risk and credit risk were interconnected and needed to be measured simultaneously.

The implementation of RAROC requires a well-judged blend of art and science. In Figure 14.3, we offer a rule-of-thumb guide to the current state of art in terms of how "scientific" each risk area in a bank really is. Methodologies tend to become more useful as they become more scientific. However, waiting for the science to be perfected before implementing a methodology can lead to damaging delays in implementation.

1.1 Definition of Capital

In a financial institution, economic capital is the cushion that provides protection against the various risks inherent in the institution's businesses—risks that would otherwise affect the security of funds that are deposited with, or loaned to, the institution. The purpose of economic capital is to provide confidence to claim holders such as depositors, creditors, and other stakeholders.

Economic capital is designed to absorb unexpected losses, up to a certain level of confidence. (By contrast, "reserves" are set aside to absorb any expected losses on a transaction, during the life of

FIGURE 14.3

Science and Art in Risk Management

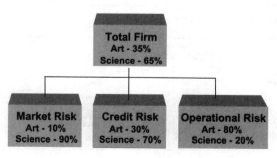

the transaction.) It would be too costly for a financial institution to operate at a 100 percent confidence level, i.e., the level that would ensure the institution would never default, whatever its future loss experience. Instead, economic capital is set at a confidence level that is less than 100 percent, say, 99 percent; this means that there remains a probability of, say, 1 percent, that actual losses will exceed the amount of economic capital.

Regulatory capital, on the other hand, is derived from a set of rules, such as the Bank for International Settlements (BIS) capital accords—BIS 88 and BIS 98. These are designed to ensure that there is enough capital in the banking system. In fact, most financial institutions hold more capital than the regulators require (see Chapter 1).

Economic capital is what really matters for financial institutions and their stakeholders. Economic capital may be derived from sophisticated internal models, but the choice of the confidence level and the risk horizon are key policy parameters that should be set by the senior management of the bank and endorsed by the board. The determination of economic capital, and its allocation to the various business units, is a strategic decision process that affects the risk/return performance of the business units and the bank as a whole. It influences dramatically the way that capital is allocated and reallocated among the various activities and projects.

Figure 14.4 offers an example that illustrates the RAROC calculation. On the loss distribution derived over a given horizon, say, one year, we show both the expected loss (EL), 15 bp, and the worst case loss (WCL), 165 bp, at the desired confidence level (set in this example to 99 percent).

FIGURE 14.4

The RAROC Equation

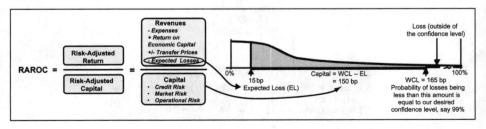

The unexpected loss is, therefore, the difference between the total loss and the expected loss, i.e., 150 bp at the 99 percent confidence level, over a one-year horizon. In Sections 3 and 4 we present the standard approach for determining economic capital.

The numerator of the RAROC calculation, as illustrated in Figure 14.4, is composed of revenues plus return on economic capital minus expenses for the given business activity, minus expected losses. A typical RAROC process also calls for specific business functions to be credited with revenue, or debited with relevant expenses, through a transfer-pricing mechanism. The denominator of the RAROC equation measures the capital required to absorb the unexpected loss. In Section 5 the procedure for extending expected loss is described.

To illustrate the RAROC calculation, let us assume the following: A loan portfolio with a principal of $1 billion is considered, paying an annual rate of 9 percent. The economic capital against such a loan is estimated to be $75 million (i.e., 7.5 percent of the loan) which is invested in Government securities returning 6.5 percent per annum. Therefore, $925 million should be raised by deposits with an interest charge of 6 percent.

The bank in our example has an operating cost of $15 million per annum, and the expected loss on this portfolio is assumed to be 1 percent per annum (i.e., $10 million). The RAROC for this loan is thus:

$$\text{RAROC} = \frac{90 + 4.9 - 55.5 - 15 - 10}{75} = 19.2\%$$

where 90 is the expected revenue, 4.9 is the annual return on the invested economic capital, 55.5 is the interest expense, 15 is the operating cost, and 10 is the expected loss. The RAROC for this loan portfolio is 19.2 percent. This number can be interpreted in terms of the annual expected rate of return on the equity that is required to support this loan portfolio.

We should emphasize at this point that RAROC was first suggested as a tool for capital allocation, on an ex ante basis. Hence, expected losses should be determined in the numerator of the RAROC equation. RAROC is sometimes also used for performance evaluation. In this case, it is calculated on an ex post basis, with realized losses rather than expected losses.

1.2 Three Broad Classes of Risk Capital: Market Risk, Credit Risk, and Operational Risk

Above, we talked about risk in a generic sense. In practice, banks manage risks according to three broad classifications: credit, market, and operational risk. Market risk, as described in Chapter 5, is the risk of losses arising from changes in market risk factors. Market risk can arise from changes in interest rates, foreign exchange, equity, and commodity price factors.

Credit risk, as described in Chapters 7 to 11, is the risk of loss following a change in the factors that drive the credit quality of an asset. These include adverse effects arising from credit grade migration (or credit default), and the dynamics of recovery rates. Credit risk includes potential losses arising from the trading book (e.g., contingent credit risk such as derivatives) as well as potential losses from the banking book. The possible impact of any credit concentration, or lack of liquidity in a portfolio, also needs to be incorporated into the level of credit risk capital attributed to the portfolio.

Operational risk, as described in Chapter 13, refers to financial loss due to a host of operational breakdowns (e.g., inadequate computer systems, a failure in controls, a mistake in operations, a guideline that has been circumvented, a natural disaster). The measurement of operational risk also needs to cover the risk of loss due to regulatory, legal, and fiduciary risks.

1.3 Integrated Goal-Congruent RAROC Process

The fact that banks classify, measure, and manage their risk in (at least) the three main categories just described poses a considerable challenge to risk-adjusted measurement and management. The huge number of business lines that need to be managed in any sizeable concern represent another major obstacle.

To be successful and consistent, an RAROC process must be integrated into the overall risk management process (Figure 14.5), as we discussed in more general terms in Chapter 3. An "integrated" RAROC approach is one that implements a set of RAROC risk management policies that flow directly from business strategies. A consistent RAROC process is one in which the policies and methodologies applied to various kinds of risk are consistent with one another.

FIGURE 14.5

Integrated Goal-Congruent Approach

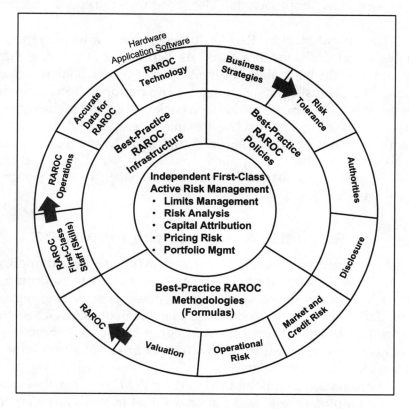

To achieve both integration and consistency, an institution requires a well-developed set of RAROC methodologies that are supported by an RAROC infrastructure that can function across all risk types and businesses. RAROC methodologies rely on analytical models to measure market, credit, and operational risk. A proper RAROC infrastructure implies that the bank should have sufficient data, processing ability, and skilled staff to implement RAROC throughout the entire firm.

One way of organizing this within a bank is to develop an RAROC policy and methodology unit, which has the task of synthesizing the bank's various risk methodologies. A key problem here is to ensure that the RAROC policy and methodology unit is not so removed from the complexities of the various bank businesses that it fails to add value to the process. The goal is a "one firm—one view" approach that also recognizes the specific risk dynamics of each business.

The output from an RAROC process affects a whole range of analyses and decisions in a bank. As Figure 14.6 illustrates, these include how the bank allocates limits, performs risk analyses, manages capital, adjusts pricing strategies, and performs portfolio management. RAROC analyses also feed back into capital management, financial planning, balance sheet management, and compensation practices. It should be emphasized that RAROC calculations may be adjusted for different applications. Again, all this implies that RAROC must be managed from an integrated firm-wide perspective (Figure 14.7).

1.4 Risk MIS: A Prerequisite for RAROC

A risk management information system (MIS) is a key component of the RAROC infrastructure. The risk management information for each business unit and customer should be credible, regular (e.g., daily), and useful to business management. RAROC performance reporting platforms must integrate risk-based capital and loan losses and ensure integrity with other financial information at various levels of aggregation.

When banks first attempt to build a risk MIS system, they often start with a prototype RAROC approach that tries to collect limited

FIGURE 14.6

Impact of Output from RAROC Process

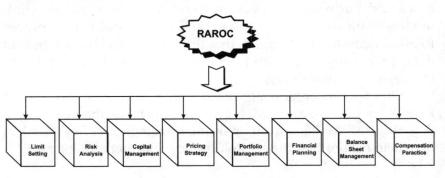

FIGURE 14.7

Integrated Bank-Wide Perspective

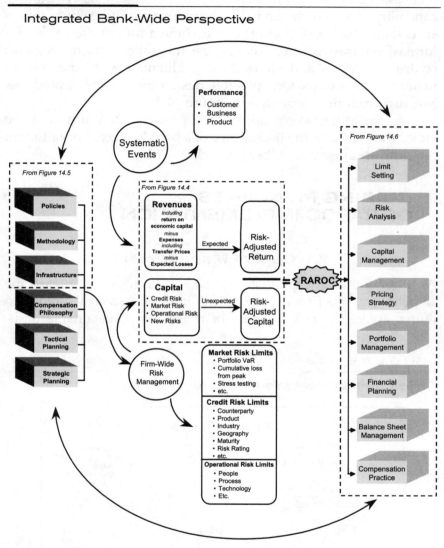

amounts of high-level data to help drive and develop the RAROC methodology. As a result of business pressure, the working prototype is often pressed into production prematurely. A short-term approach often also results in a system that is laborious and manually intensive.

Typically, banks then embark on a more comprehensive and integrated risk MIS system that requires sophisticated, detailed data collection, a powerful computation engine, massive storage capability, and information distribution capability. Where this is successful, the RAROC effort can become a hub of the bank's information infrastructure, fostering the integration of numerous risk control processes and strengthening alliances with and among many business units. One possible design for a sophisticated risk MIS architecture is provided in Figure 14.8.

As the MIS is so crucial, RAROC projects often turn out to be either the victim or the beneficiary of a bank's success or failure in building an integrated MIS approach.

2. GUIDING PRINCIPLES OF RAROC IMPLEMENTATION

2.1 Capital Management

As a general rule, capital should be employed so as to earn the shareholders of a firm at least the minimum risk-adjusted required return above the risk-free rate of return on a sustainable basis.

FIGURE 14.8

Risk Management Information Architecture

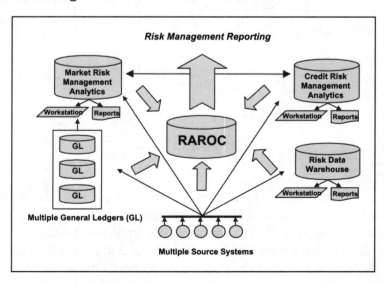

Otherwise the share price of a firm will underperform relative to top-performing competitors. In addition, within a firm capital is not an inexhaustible resource and should be used prudently.

For example, if one accepts the standard practitioner application of RAROC, in Figure 14.9 businesses A through D can be said to add value to the firm: they surpass the prespecified hurdle rate (say, 15 percent). On the other hand, business units F through H destroy shareholder value.

One should also examine the amount of risk-adjusted capital utilized by each line of business. For example, observe that business unit B has a higher adjusted return than business unit C, but business unit B utilizes more capital than business unit C.

An RAROC model, as we pointed out earlier, is not meant to capture catastrophic risk since potential losses are calculated only

FIGURE 14.9

Measure of Success—Building Shareholder Value

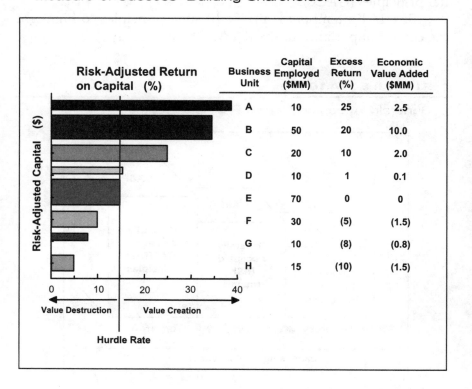

Business Unit	Capital Employed ($MM)	Excess Return (%)	Economic Value Added ($MM)
A	10	25	2.5
B	50	20	10.0
C	20	10	2.0
D	10	1	0.1
E	70	0	0
F	30	(5)	(1.5)
G	10	(8)	(0.8)
H	15	(10)	(1.5)

up to a certain confidence level. (Instead, since capital will not protect a bank against catastrophic risks, banks may choose to insure themselves.) However, banks can use the RAROC model to assist their insurance purchase decisions. For example, a bank may decide to retain (and set capital aside to cover) a risk if the cost of the capital to support the risk is less than the cost of insuring it.

2.2 Ten Commandments of RAROC

Generally Accepted Accounting Principles (GAAP) provide a level playing field in terms of providing a common set of rules to evaluate the health of a business entity. The banking industry has made significant advances in terms of the measurement of risk through what we will call here generally accepted risk principles (GARP). For example, a consensus has emerged on how to measure market risk in the trading book. The next evolution, beyond GARP (as shown in Figure 14.10), is toward a set of generally accepted capital principles (GACP).

Box 14.1 attempts to specify 10 such principles to highlight the central importance of the RAROC methodology.

FIGURE   14.10

Generally Accepted Capital Principles (GACP)

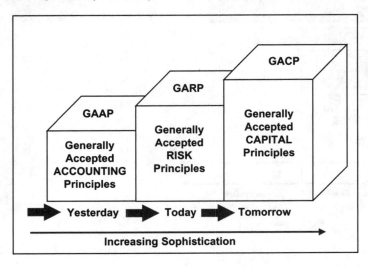

BOX 14.1

RAROC 10 COMMANDMENTS OF GENERALLY ACCEPTED CAPITAL PRINCIPLES

1. Include all business activities and the global operations of the bank.

2. Strive to implement an RAROC system impervious to arbitrage (including tax differentials).

3. Be explicit, consistent, and goal congruent with other policies (e.g., transfer pricing, price guidance, performance measurement, compensation, etc.).

4. Recognize different types of capital, but the primary emphasis will be on economic capital.

5. Use a single risk-adjusted hurdle rate charged as a cost of capital (which shall be broadly consistent with the bank's long-term target return on capital).

6. Develop and implement an economic risk framework comprising credit risks, market risk (trading and banking book), and operational risks (funding liquidity risk is captured in the transfer pricing system).

7. Recognize funding and time-to-close liquidity.

8. Attribute capital as a function of risk and the authority to take risk (e.g., market risk limit).

9. Economic capital should be based on a confidence level deemed appropriate to achieve target rating.

10. Promote matching of revenues and risk charges where risks are incurred.

2.3 Management as a Critical Success Factor

To implement RAROC on a bank-wide basis, the full cooperation of senior management is essential. This requires a clear understanding of the value of RAROC and a commitment to "stay on course." Strategic programs, such as RAROC, are apt to come under review for cancellation in difficult business environments.

RAROC must permeate the culture of an institution and be "second nature" to the business decision process. RAROC must be championed by the actions of senior management: risk-adjusted numbers should be used for performance measurement and compensation. Finally, successful implementation of a full RAROC program requires not only a sound conceptual framework but also careful planning and strong project management.

2.4 Implementation Stages

Like the implementation of a risk MIS system, the ambitious nature of the RAROC process typically requires a bank to implement RAROC in stages. The first stage is an initial product phase where one prototypes "top of the house" indicative numbers (Figure 14.11). This is, essentially, an educational phase.

The second stage involves producing reports that are used on a regular basis (say, monthly), through a repeated process across multiple business lines. The RAROC results in the second stage are used to add value to analyses as well as to provide input to the planning process.

FIGURE 14.11

RAROC Development Stages

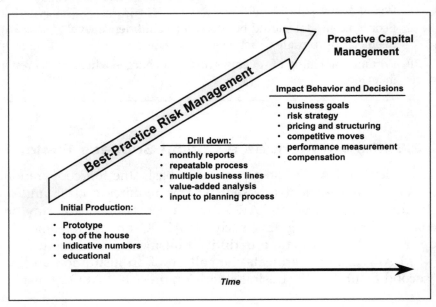

In the third stage, RAROC begins to have an impact on business decision making, including business goals and the associated risk strategy. RAROC is used as a critical input for pricing and structuring deals, and is applied to the measurement of a business unit's performance and the equitable compensation of staff.

3. RELATIONSHIP OF RAROC CAPITAL TO MARKET, CREDIT, AND OPERATIONAL RISKS

In this section we discuss how economic capital, or "RAROC capital," is set. We compare the approach to the procedure for setting regulatory capital (the subject of previous chapters). We divide the discussion into the problem of attributing capital to each risk element: market, credit, and operational risks.

3.1 Capital for Market Risk

The approach to allocating RAROC capital for market risk has evolved to attributing RAROC capital as a function of the amount of risk expressed in the value-at-risk calculation. Further, practitioners often charge RAROC capital as a function of both unused market risk limits and penalties for exceeding limits.

For example, let us assume that the formula for market risk capital is equal to $F_1 \times$ VaR (where VaR is set at, say, a 99 percent confidence interval) and F_1 is a preset constant based on adjusting the VaR measure to account for exceptional shocks (say, $F_1 = 2$). In other words, F_1 multiplies the VaR to account for a day-to-day event risk not captured by the VaR model. (One may also adjust VaR as a function of the time it would take to liquidate risky positions.)

The charge for the unused portion of a limit would equal F_2 $\times$ unused VaR, with F_2 equal, say, to 0.15 (i.e., 15 percent of the unused limit). So, if we assume that the VaR, at the 99 percent level of confidence, is \$200,000 and that the VaR limit equals \$500,000, then the RAROC capital is equal to 2*\$200,000 + 0.15*(\$500,000 − \$200,000) = \$445,000.

The penalty charge for exceeding a limit is $F3$*excess VaR (where, say, $F_3 = 3$). If, for example, the VaR had been \$600,000, then the RAROC capital charge would have been:

2*\$600,000 + 0.15*(0) + 3*(\$600,000 − \$500,000) = \$1,500,000

The interest rate risk in the "gap," i.e., the mismatch between the interest rate sensitivities of the liabilities and the assets, constitutes the major source of market risk in banks. Banks are also exposed to foreign exchange risk. All these risks, and others such as the risks originating from embedded options in mortgages, should be taken into consideration when estimating the loss distribution over the RAROC time horizon set by the bank. This horizon usually differs from the regulatory horizon used to derive regulatory capital. The RAROC horizon depends on whether the positions are structural and are core positions for the bank's franchise, the size of the positions, and how liquid they are.

RAROC, or equivalently economic capital, is set to provide a cushion against unexpected losses at a desired confidence level. Regulatory capital for market risk is derived at the 99 percent confidence level (see Chapter 4). The confidence level for economic capital is set at the level that corresponds to the targeted credit rating for the bank. As we discussed in Chapters 8 and 9, an AA rating, for example, corresponds to a confidence level of 99.96 percent (or, equivalently, 4 bp) for the bank as a whole. Given that the various businesses in the bank are not perfectly correlated, this confidence level at the top of the bank translates into a lower confidence level at each business level, say 99.865 percent, which accounts for the portfolio effect of the various bank's activities. In other words, attributing economic capital at, say, 99.865 percent confidence level for each business is such that the overall economic capital for the bank (i.e., the sum of the allocations to all the businesses) corresponds to an overall 99.96 percent confidence level at the top of the bank.

3.2 Capital for Credit Risk

Practitioners attribute credit risk capital as a function of exposure, the probability of default, and recovery rates. The probability of default is often determined as a function of a risk rating or directly from a carefully structured algorithm, as we described in Chapters 7 through 10. Clearly, as illustrated in Figure 14.12, the poorer the quality of the credit, the larger both the expected loss and the attributed capital.

A table of capital factors, such as those illustrated in Table 14.1, can be derived from a combination of sources. The capital factor is

FIGURE 14.12

The Poorer the Quality of the Credit, the Larger the Expected Loss and Attributed Capital

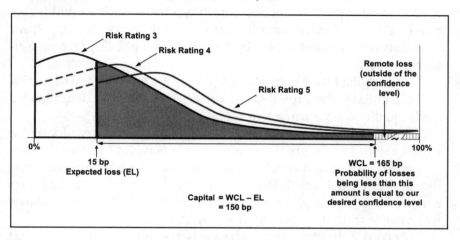

TABLE 14.1

General Capital Factors at a 99.865% Confidence Level
(Assuming 60% Recovery Rate or 40% Loss Given Default)

Risk Rating (RR)	Tenor									
	1	2	3	4	5	6	7	8	9	10
1										
2										
3				1.74%	1.89%	2.03%				
4				2.31%	2.47%	2.60%				
5				8.03%	8.32%	8.50%				
6										
7										
8										
9										
10										
11										
12										

Note: Only part of the table is shown.

typically expressed in terms of the percentage of the market value of the position. The capital factor expresses the amount of credit risk as a function of the risk rating and tenor. A risk rating can be mapped to each asset capital factor. For example, a five-year loan that is risk rated as 3 might have a capital factor of 1.89 percent. A five-year loan that is risk rated as 4 might be assigned a 2.47 percent capital factor, etc.

The capital factor rises as a function of the tenor for the same risk rating. Similarly, the capital factor rises as a function of deteriorating credit quality for the same tenor.

In other words, other things being equal, a five-year loan that is risk rated 4 has a greater capital factor (say, 2.47 percent), associated with a higher probability of loss, than does a four-year loan that is risk rated 4 (say, 2.31 percent). Similarly, a five-year loan that is risk rated 5 has a greater capital factor (say, 8.32 percent) than a five-year loan that is risk rated 4 (say, 2.47 percent).

Accordingly, the capital charge is the product of the capital factor and the market value of the position. The capital factors are obtained through publicly available sources (e.g., Moody's and S&P's corporate bond default data, as explained in Chapter 7), proprietary external models (e.g., KMV, explained in Chapter 9), and publicly available models (e.g., CreditMetrics, CreditRisk+, etc., explained in Chapters 8 and 10), as well as by means of proprietary internal models. A typical table of capital factors provides capital for a combination of risk rating and maturities.

The derivations of credit risk factors for these tables typically follow a four-step process. First, one needs to select a representative time period to study a portfolio (e.g., ideally over a full business cycle). Second, one needs to map risk ratings to the portfolio. Third, expected and unexpected losses need to be estimated. Fourth, one needs to exercise appropriate management judgment in terms of assigning capital factors to adjust for imperfections in the data.

RAROC factors should be examined to evaluate their ability to describe risk and to ascertain that a change in the inputs that drive these capital factors represents the appropriate sensitivity to risk. For example, we can evaluate the impact of risk rating and tenor on capital by comparing a risk rating of 4 with a maturity of five years (at 2.47 percent capital) to the capital required for a risk rating of 5 with

TABLE 14.2

Standardized Capital Factors

Credit Rating		Tenor		
Internal Rating	Moody's Rating	4	5	6
3	A	1.74%	1.89%	2.03%
4	Baa	2.31%	2.47%	2.60%
5	Ba	8.03%	8.32%	8.50%

the same maturity (at 8.32 percent capital). If the quality of the five-year loan rises to risk rating 3, then the capital factor declines to 1.89 percent. One could calibrate the risk rating (say, 4) assigned to these entities internally, to the ratings provided by an external agency (say, Moody's Baa rating), as shown on the left-hand side of Table 14.2.

The process flow for calculating credit risk capital typically involves utilizing loan equivalents as shown in Figure 14.13.

FIGURE 14.13

Credit Risk Methodology—Process Flow

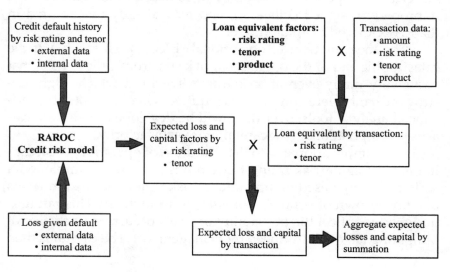

3.3 RAROC Capital for Operational Risk

Leading-edge banks have developed fairly good measurement methodologies for market and credit risk. However, as we reviewed in Chapter 13, operational risk is a comparatively difficult risk to quantify. Most banks admit to having poor measures of operational risk. An article in the December 1996 edition of *Euromoney* magazine pointed out that "Banks measure credit and market risk because they can, not because they are the biggest risks that they face. Operational risk is larger, more dangerous, and no one knows exactly what to do about it."

Operational risk measurement is very much a "work in progress." One approach is to define an operational value-at-risk as the loss that is likely to arise from an operational failure over a certain time period, with a particular probability of occurrence. A primary difficulty with estimating operational risk in this way is that there are very few internal data points available to build the loss distribution. Nevertheless, one can look to external information. Some of the information to build a loss database may be gathered from court records (e.g., extensive information is available on retail and wholesale money transfer operational losses). A database is relatively easy to develop for those losses that are incurred regularly, such as credit-card fraud.

One must be careful not to double-count operational failures. For example, operational risk may be reflected in loan losses (e.g., improperly assigned collateral), and may already be captured in the RAROC credit capital model.

The measurement of operational risks is least reliable at the catastrophic end of the operational risk spectrum—those risks that occur very rarely even at an industry level but which might destroy the bank. Here, judgment is required. One can expect that advanced analytic tools, over time, will be developed to analyze catastrophic operational risk capital more satisfactorily.

One simple approach to the allocation of operational risk capital is to assign a risk rating to each business (for example, on a scale of 1 to 5), based on operational risk factors defined in terms of a breakdown of people, processes, or technology. This rating is designed to reflect the probability of a risk occurring (inclusive of mitigating factors introduced by management). The capital is then assigned based on the operational risk rating of the transaction or business line. The expected loss and risk-based capital charge are attributed to a position on a sliding scale that is nonlinear. The bank needs to develop capital factors based on a combination of internal loss history, losses at other banks, management judgment, etc.

A central policy and procedure needs to be developed by banks to ensure the consistency and integrity of these ratings on a bankwide basis, as we described in Chapter 13. This will result in "relative" risk ratings for each business, which can then be attributed capital so that the desired "all-bank operational risk capital number" is achieved.

4. LOAN EQUIVALENT APPROACH

Modern banks offer many financial products in addition to straightforward loans. Capital must be allocated to these products, and it is helpful, as a first generation approximation, to think of the risks generated by them in terms of their "loan equivalence."

4.1 Loan Equivalence for Guarantees, Commitments, and Banker's Acceptances

Typically, the RAROC capital for each nonloan product is computed by multiplying the loan equivalent amount by a capital factor that is related to the risk rating and tenor. For example, if we examine typical RAROC factors for bankers acceptances, then we find that they typically have the same capital factors as for loans (Table 14.3).

Loan equivalents for bank guarantees and standby letters of credit vary from a high of 100 percent for financial related products to 50 percent for nonfinancial related products, and to a low of 20 percent for documentary products such as the Note Issuance Facility (NIF), the Revolving Underwriting Facility (RUF), and the Guaranteed Underwriting Note (GUN).

For NIFs, RUFs, and GUNs[2] the loan equivalents are, say, 50 percent for risk rating 1 to risk rating 9, and, say, 100 percent from risk rating 10 to risk rating 12.

TABLE 14.3

Loan Equivalent Factors (Illustrative Only)

	RR 1–9 (%)	RR 10–12 (%)
Loans and bankers' acceptances	100	100
Guarantees and standby L/C		
Financial	100	100
Nonfinancial	50	50
Documentary	20	20
NIFs, RUFs, and GUNs	50	100
Undrawn credit commitments		
>1 Year	50	100
<1 Year	10	100
General (demand)	5	100
Uncommitted/unadvised lines	0	0

To illustrate the way in which RAROC is calculated, suppose that a bank has made a $100 million credit commitment of a five-year tenor to a customer that has a risk rating of 3. Assume also that $60 million has been drawn down. The capital required to support this position equals the sum of the drawn amount plus the undrawn amount, multiplied by the capital factor. Accordingly, the required capital equals ($60,000,000 + ($100,000,000 − $60,000,000) * 50%) * 1.89% = $80,000,000 * 1.89% = $1,512,000.

In the case of bankers' acceptances, guarantees, and financial letters of credit, there is little a bank can do to reduce the risk within the time frame of the instrument and, therefore, these instruments are best treated as loans. For credit commitments, however, a number of factors may reduce the likelihood of a drawdown. In some instances, the customer is only allowed to draw sums at the discretion of the bank. In these cases, the "loan equivalent" figure would be only a fraction of the total commitment. Term commitments are more likely to suffer a drawdown in the event of a customer default. For term commitments, the remaining term and credit quality of the customer both affect the likelihood of drawdown. However, there may be covenants that allow the bank to withdraw these commitments if there is a deterioration in the credit quality of the customer.

4.2 Loan Equivalent for Derivatives

The RAROC methodology typically calculates loan equivalents for derivative products (e.g., swaps, forwards, forward rate agreements (FRAs), etc.), at both the deal and the counterparty level. The loan equivalent is an estimate of the average positive exposure, over the life of a deal. Accordingly, the loan equivalent value is equal to the mark-to-market value of the derivative instrument plus the expected exposure (as explained in Section 5.2). The counterparty loan equivalent, counterparty risk rating, and tenor are used to calculate capital in a manner that is similar to risk-rated lending.

For example, let us assume that a five-year, $100 million fixed/floating interest rate swap has a loan equivalent exposure of $2 million. If we assume that the swap has a counterparty risk rating of 4 (equivalent to Moody's BBB rating), then the capital attributed, at the inception of the deal, would be derived by multiplying $2 million by 2.47 percent, which equals $49,400.

5. MEASURING EXPOSURES AND LOSSES FOR DERIVATIVES[3]

5.1 Measuring Exposures

The crucial problem in developing an accurate loan equivalent measure of credit risk for derivatives for the purpose of an RAROC analysis is to quantify properly the future credit risk exposure. This is a complex problem because it is the outcome of multiple variables, including the structure of the financial instrument that is under scrutiny, and changes in the values of the underlying variables.

The amount of money that one can reasonably expect to lose as a result of default over a given period is normally called the "expected credit risk exposure." The expected credit exposure is an exposure at a particular point in time, while the "cumulative average expected credit exposure" is an average of the expected credit exposures over a given period of time. The average expected credit exposure is typically used as the loan equivalent exposure for the purpose of RAROC analysis.

The maximum amount of money that could be lost as a result of default within a given confidence interval is called the "worst case credit risk exposure" (sometimes called the "maximum potential credit risk exposure"). The worst case credit risk exposure is an exposure at a particular point in time, while a related measure, the average worst case credit risk exposure, is an average of the worst case exposures over a given period of time.

If one wishes to control the amount that could be at risk to a given counterparty, then the worst case exposure is particularly important in terms of allocating credit risk limits. One can use either the worst case or average worst case credit risk exposure as a measure when setting limits to credit risk exposure—one simply needs to be consistent. If one uses the worst case credit risk exposure to measure credit risk, then limits should obviously be set in terms of worst case credit risk exposures (in contrast to the average worst case credit risk exposures).

The bank needs to estimate how much economic and regulatory capital should be set aside for a transaction or portfolio. The amount and the cost of the capital set aside for a portfolio, and for incremental transactions added to that portfolio, are vital factors in determining the profitability of lines of business and of individual transactions. The cost of the capital set aside for a single transaction is also a vital factor in calculating a fair price for that transaction.

For a typical single cash flow product, for example an FRA, the worst case credit risk exposure at time t (W_t) grows as a function of time and peaks at the maturity of the transaction. Figure 14.14 illustrates the worst case credit risk exposure for such an instrument, and illustrates some typical relationships between this and the other measures mentioned above.

Let us look at the relationship between the worst case credit risk exposure and the average worst case credit risk exposure in more detail. The worst case credit risk exposure is defined as the maximum credit risk exposure likely to arise from a given position within the bounds of a predefined confidence interval.

For example, many dealers define the worst case credit risk exposure at a two-standard-deviation level, or a one-sided 97.5

FIGURE 14.14

Credit Exposure of an Instrument Expressed as Different Exposure Functions

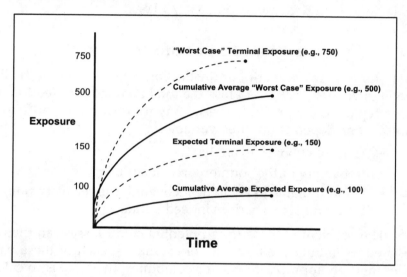

percent confidence level. Let us assume, for illustrative purposes, that the worst case credit risk exposure at time t is equal to $K \times \sigma \times \sqrt{t}$, where K is a function of the desired confidence interval, σ is the overnight volatility of the position's percentage change in price, and t varies from 0 to T.

Observe, for simplicity, that the standard deviation is assumed to come from a stable stochastic process where the risk grows as a function of the square root of time. For illustrative purposes, we will also assume that the probability of default is uniformly distributed over the time period. If we integrate the worst case function over the entire time period (and divide this result by the time period T), then we can see that the cumulative average worst case credit risk exposure is two-thirds of the worst case credit risk exposure, as indicated in Figure 14.14.[4]

Now let us look at how one can compute the expected terminal credit exposure—sometimes referred to as the expected terminal replacement cost. This computation, for time T ($E[RC_T]$), can be approached using an option pricing framework. Assume that the distribution of returns is normal, with a zero mean and a standard deviation that grows as a function of the square root of time. Then, ignoring present-value considerations, one needs only to perform the necessary integration to show that $E[RC_T] = FE/3.33$, where FE is defined in this application as $2/3 \; W_T$.

5.2 From Exposure to Loss

In a "nightmare" scenario, an institution might suddenly realize that it is virtually certain to lose the total amount exposed to loss. More typically, the probable loss on any transaction or portfolio of transactions depends on three variables:

- Amount exposed to credit risk
- Probability of the counterparty defaulting
- Amount that is likely to be recovered (the recovery rate) if the counterparty does indeed default

The problem of measuring potential credit losses can thus be restated as finding the best way of estimating each of these variables, and an appropriate way of combining them so as to calculate the loss given default.

With regard to default rates, an institution needs to develop techniques to calculate the default rate path and the distribution around the default rate path, estimated by examining those distributions at specific points in the future. The default rate distributions at specific points over the life of a transaction can be modeled through analyses of Standard & Poor's or Moody's data concerning the default rates of publicly rated institutions.

Most institutions combine information gathered from rating agency data with their own proprietary default rate data (e.g., loan default data). They also analyze the credit spreads of securities, e.g., yields of specific securities over duration-equivalent risk-free securities, to generate a default rate distribution.

These estimates of future default rate distributions are calculated for each credit grade. Just like the credit risk exposure measures described above, the distribution of future default rates can be usefully characterized in terms of an expected default rate (e.g., 1 percent) or a worst case default rate (e.g., 3 percent).

The difference between the worst case default rate and the expected default rate is often termed the "unexpected default rate" (i.e., 2 percent = 3 percent − 1 percent). Typically, as illustrated in Figure 14.15, the distribution is highly asymmetric. A worst case default rate (e.g., the aforementioned 3 percent) may be structured so that one can say that there is a prespecified probability (e.g., 2.5 percent) of exceeding the worst case default rate. The probability density function describes how the probability of default varies over time; clearly, the longer the maturity of the financial instrument, the greater the default rate.

The third factor needed to calculate counterparty credit loss is the recovery rate path. The distribution around the recovery rate path needs to be estimated at specific points in the future. Just like the other two variables, one can use the recovery rate distribution to determine an expected recovery rate, or a worst case recovery rate. The recovery rate distributions may be modeled by means of Standard and Poor's or Moody's recovery rate data.

Surveys on the recovery rate of senior corporate bonds that have defaulted indicate that they vary as a function of the "pecking order" (i.e., lien position) of the debt. For example, senior debt has a higher recovery rate than junior (subordinated) debt. As with default data, institutions normally combine information gathered

FIGURE 14.15

Distribution of Default Rates

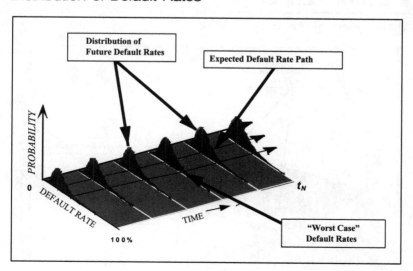

from rating agency recovery rate data with their own recovery rate data—some institutions also obtain input from specialized legal counsel or insolvency practitioners—in order to provide a recovery rate distribution for each credit grade.

These analyses, as illustrated in Figure 14.16, produce estimates of future recovery rate distributions that vary as a function of time. Just like default rate distributions, recovery rate distributions do not typically follow a normal probability density function.

Having analyzed the distributions of the three credit risk variables—credit risk exposure, default, and recovery data—these can be combined, as illustrated in Figure 14.17, to produce future credit loss distributions. One would perform the necessary integration in order to generate the expected credit loss. Theoretically, these three distributions can be combined by integrating across the combined function.[5]

Observe that the graph in Figure 14.17 does not pass through the origin, as there is a positive probability of a nonzero loss. Again, observe that the summary credit loss distribution can be characterized as an average expected credit loss (L_E) and an average worst case credit loss (L_W). Ideally, one needs to construct a cumulative probability density loss function by integrating the multivariate

FIGURE 14.16

Distribution of Recovery Rates

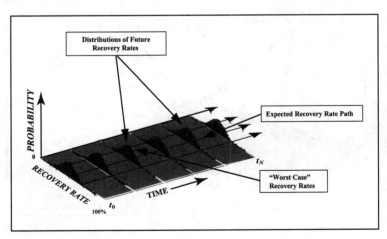

FIGURE 14.17

Creating a Credit Risk Loss Distribution Summary

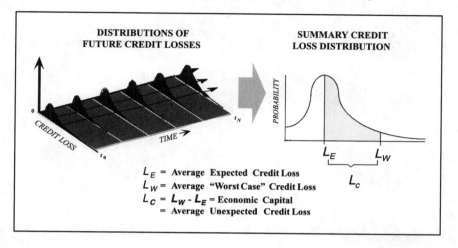

DISTRIBUTIONS OF
FUTURE CREDIT LOSSES

SUMMARY CREDIT
LOSS DISTRIBUTION

L_E = Average Expected Credit Loss
L_W = Average "Worst Case" Credit Loss
L_C = L_W - L_E = Economic Capital
    = Average Unexpected Credit Loss

probability density function, such that the worst case credit loss over the time period is set to the desired worst case probability of loss. The difference between L_W and L_E can be described as the average unexpected credit loss L_C (i.e., $L_C = L_W - L_E$).

If a Monte Carlo simulation approach is adopted, then one first simulates an exposure value from a credit risk exposure distribution given default, at a particular point in time. Second, one simulates a default distribution, typically a binomial probability function with a single probability of default. Finally, assuming negligible recovery rates, one then summarizes the credit losses that occur across all points in time. Future credit loss distributions at various points over the life of the instrument may be combined as illustrated in Figure 14.18 to produce a single summary credit loss distribution.

As pointed out earlier, combining credit risk exposure with the distribution of default rates, net of recovery, yields the distribution of credit risk losses. The distribution of credit loss needs to be translated into a provision (expected loss) and economic capital (unexpected loss). The loan equivalent approach estimates the loan equivalent as the average expected exposure.

For example, as illustrated in Figure 14.19, assume that the average expected credit risk exposure for our derivative is 480 and

FIGURE 14.18

Combining Variables to Produce Credit Loss Distributions

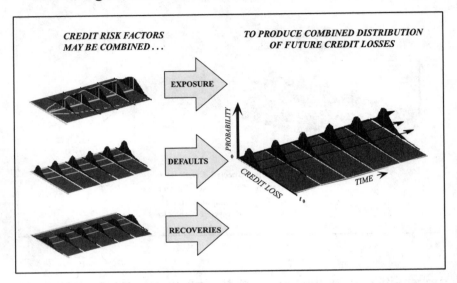

that the expected probability of default is 1 percent. In our example, the expected loss is calculated by multiplying the expected probability of default by the average expected credit risk exposure, to arrive at an expected loss of 4.8.

Further, since the worst case probability of default is 3 percent, then one can say that the worst case loss is 14.4 (=480 × .03); therefore, one would assign an unexpected loss (economic capital) of 9.6 derived from the difference between the worst case loss (14.4) and the expected loss (4.8). The loan equivalent approach utilizes the same default factors for contingent credit products as for loans.

The potential unexpected loss is clearly a function of the confidence level set by policy. For example, a confidence level of 97.5 percent would call for less economic capital than a confidence level of 99 percent.

This loan equivalent approach to calculating the average expected exposure is a proxy for more sophisticated approaches; it has the virtue of facilitating comparison to a more conventional loan product. Another approach would be to generate—using analytical, empirical, or simulation techniques—the full distribution

FIGURE 14.19

Calculating Risk-Adjusted Capital Requirements

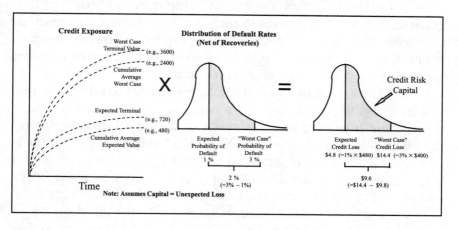

of losses, and then to select the appropriate confidence interval percentile. A third approach would be to multiply a binary probability of default by the difference between the average worst case credit risk exposure and the average expected credit risk exposure to compute L_C. This third approach may not provide the same answer as the earlier two approaches.

In any event, the amount of risk capital should be based on a preset confidence level (e.g., 97.5 percent). The amount of unexpected credit loss (L_C) should be used to establish the projected amount of risk capital. The dynamic economic capital assigned is typically the sum of the current replacement cost plus the projected L_C.

6. MEASURING RISK-ADJUSTED PERFORMANCE: SECOND GENERATION OF RAROC MODEL[6]

Many modern banks attempt to maximize their risk-adjusted return on economic capital (subject to regulatory constraints). The typical RAROC approach consists of calculating the risk-adjusted return on economic capital, and comparing this RAROC ratio to a fixed hurdle rate. According to the accepted paradigm, only activities for which the RAROC ratio exceeds the hurdle rate contribute to shareholder value.

Unfortunately, this commonly employed approach (first-generation RAROC), described earlier in this chapter, can result in decisions that adversely affect shareholder value. A second-generation methodology, "adjusted RAROC," corrects the inherent limitations of the first-generation method.

The key aim of this new RAROC measure is to adjust the risk of a business to that of the firm's equity. For example, if a firm is considering investing in a business (or closing a business down), then it might compute the RAROC for the business (e.g., 16.18 percent) and compare this figure to the firm's cost of equity capital (e.g., 16 percent). If the RAROC number is greater than the firm's cost of equity capital, then the business will add value to the firm.

To help clarify this, consider an all-equity firm undertaking a risky investment, with an economic capital reserve set up so that the probability of default remains constant at some prespecified level. It follows that risk-adjusted performance measures (such as RAROC) change as the risk of the business changes, even though the probability of default is kept constant. In other words, maintaining the probability of default constant is inconsistent with a constant expected rate of return on equity, and vice versa. The adjusted RAROC measure corrects this problem.

Crouhy, Turnbull, and Wakeman (1999) (CTW) designed an "adjusted RAROC" measure at CIBC. They consider a firm that undertakes a project and adjusts its capital structure so that the probability of default (p) is set at some prespecified level (say, 1 percent). They compute the expected rate of return on equity capital for two cases. First, they alter the volatility of the firm's risky assets (σ_A), adjust the firm's capital structure (say, the debt-to-equity ratio) so that the probability of default is kept constant, and compute the expected rate of return on equity capital ($\overline{R}_s$). Using the simple Merton model (see Chapter 9), they show that keeping the probability of default constant does not imply that the cost of equity capital is invariant to changes in the risk of the firm's assets (Table 14.4).

In Part A of Table 14.4, observe that in order to maintain the probability of default, p, constant (at 1 percent), the debt-to-equity ratio needs to be adjusted downward from 8.4 to 0.6, while the expected rate of return on equity increases from 10.46 to 12.48 percent as the standard deviation of the assets increases from 5 to 40 percent. In Part B, the correlation coefficient is set at 0.50.

Comparing Parts A and B, consider the case in which the standard deviation is 5 percent. Due to the higher correlation in Part B (ρ = .50), relative to Part A (ρ = .25), the expected rate of return on the risky asset is higher in Part B (i.e., 6.27 percent) than in Part A (5.70 percent). Consequently, the debt-to-equity ratio is also higher in Part B (i.e., 8.85) than in Part A (8.41), in order to keep the probability of default constant.

The expected rate of return on equity is 10.46 percent in Part A, compared to 16.28 percent in Part B. Table 14.4 illustrates the importance of the correlation coefficient.

The premise that underlies the first generation RAROC approach—keeping the probability of default constant—is inconsistent with a constant expected rate of return on equity for projects with different volatilities and correlations with the market portfolio.

In the second case considered in the CTW paper, the firm undertakes a pure financing decision to achieve a degree of leverage so that the expected rate of return on equity equals some prespecified level. CTW compute the probability of default. They alter the volatility of the firm's risky assets and adjust the firm's capital structure so that the expected rate of return on equity is kept constant.

It is shown that the probability of default is not invariant to changes in the risk of the firm's assets even if the expected rate of return on equity is kept constant. So the first generation RAROC approach is flawed in the sense that it is possible to pick a capital structure so as to achieve a required rate of return on equity, but the probability of default will change as the risk of the business changes (Table 14.5).

There is a striking difference between the results in the table. The probabilities of default are an order of magnitude higher in Part A than in Part B. An increase in the correlation coefficient, keeping volatility constant, increases the expected rate of return on the risky asset and reduces the degree of leverage necessary to reach the target return on equity.

For example, if we increase the correlation coefficient from ρ = 0.25 (Case A) to 0.50 (Case B) while keeping the volatility

TABLE 14.4

Altering the Capital Structure to Keep the Probability of Default Constant: $p = 1\%$

Part A: Correlation coefficient $\rho = 0.25$

Standard Deviation (percentage) σ_A	Expected Rate of Return on the Risky Assets (percentage) $\bar{R}_A$	Face Value of Debt F	Market Values		Ratio of D to E $D(0:T)/S(0)$	Expected Rate of Return on Equity (percentage) $\bar{R}_S$
			Debt $D(0:T)$	Equity $S(0)$		
5	5.70	939.8	893.7	106.3	8.41	10.46
10	6.27	838.0	796.8	203.2	3.92	10.71
20	7.42	661.2	628.4	371.6	1.69	11.25
40	9.71	399.4	379.3	620.7	0.61	12.48

562

Part B: Correlation coefficient ρ = 0.50

Standard Deviation (percentage) σ_A	Expected Rate of Return on the Risky Assets (percentage) $\overline{R}_A$	Face Value of Debt F	Market Values		Ratio of D to E $D(0;T)/S(0)$	Expected Rate of Return on Equity (percentage) $\overline{R}_S$
			Debt $D(0;T)$	Equity $S(0)$		
5	6.27	944.9	898.5	101.5	8.85	16.28
10	7.42	847.0	805.2	194.8	4.13	16.77
20	9.71	675.3	641.7	358.3	1.79	17.81
40	14.29	416.1	394.9	605.1	0.65	20.21

Probability of default: $p = N(-d_2^I)$ 1 percent
Default-free rate of interest: [1] R_F 5.13 percent
Expected rate of return on the market portfolio: [1] $\overline{R}_M$ 12.0 percent
Volatility of the return on the market portfolio: σ_M 15.0 percent
Market value of assets   1000
Maturity of debt   1 year
[1]Expressed as a discretely compounded rate of return.

TABLE 14.5

Altering the Capital Structure to Keep the Expected Rate of Return on Equity Constant: $\overline{R}_S = 17\%$

Part A: Correlation coefficient $\rho = 0.25$

Standard Deviation (percentage) σ_A	Expected Rate of Return on the Risky Assets (percentage) $\overline{R}_A$	Face Value of Debt F	Market Values		Probability of Default (percentage) $p = N(-d_2^l)$
			Debt $D(0:T)$	Equity $S(0)$	
5	5.70	1024.7	965.1	34.9	27.56
10	6.27	993.8	927.9	72.1	26.73
20	7.42	919.6	846.7	153.3	24.92
40	9.71	728.2	660.7	339.3	20.48

Part B: Correlation coefficient $\rho = 0.50$

Standard Deviation (percentage) σ_A	Expected Rate of Return on the Risky Assets (percentage) $\overline{R}_A$	Face Value of Debt F	Market Values		Probability of Default (percentage) $p = N(-d_2^1)$
			Debt $D(0:T)$	Equity $S(0)$	
5	6.27	952.1	905.2	94.8	1.48
10	7.42	851.4	809.3	190.7	1.15
20	9.71	647.7	615.8	384.2	0.56
40	14.29	239.8	228.1	771.9	0.01

Default-free rate of interest: [1] R_F — 5.13 percent

Expected rate of return on the market portfolio: [1] $\overline{R}_M$ — 12.0 percent

Volatility of the return on the market portfolio: σ_M — 15.0 percent

Market value of assets — 1000

Maturity of debt — 1 year

[1] Expressed as a discretely compounded rate of return.

constant (say, $\sigma_A = 5$ percent), then the degree of leverage in Case B declines from 27.6 (965.1/34.9) in Part A to 9.55 (905.2/94.8) in Part B, to reach the target return on equity of 17 percent. This reduces the probability of default, which is inversely related to the asset's expected rate of return and directly related to the face value of debt.

It is proposed by CTW to use adjusted RAROC to properly measure the contribution of a marginal project to the risk/return of the firm, where the adjusted RAROC (ARAROC) is defined as:

$$ARAROC \equiv \frac{RAROC - R_F}{\beta_E} \tag{1}$$

where β_E is the systematic risk of equity and R_F is the risk-free rate. They also show that a project will increase shareholder value when ARAROC is greater than the expected excess rate of return on the market, $\overline{R}_M - R_F$ (where $\overline{R}_M$ denotes the expected rate of return on the market).

Four points are worth noting. First, RAROC is sensitive to the level of the standard deviation of the risky asset (Table 14.6). So RAROC may indicate that a project achieves the required hurdle rate, given a high enough volatility (σ_A), even when the net present value of the project is negative. Second, RAROC is sensitive to the correlation of the return on the underlying asset and the market portfolio. Third, the ARAROC measure is insensitive to changes in volatility and correlation. Fourth, if a fixed hurdle rate is used in conjunction with RAROC, high-volatility and high-correlation projects will tend to be selected.

7. CONCLUDING REMARKS

Several trends in the banking industry seem likely to secure a growing role for RAROC analysis. These include a trend toward integrated risk, capital, and balance-sheet management as well as integration of credit risk and market risk. Meanwhile, the regulatory community is moving toward the use of internal models for the calculation of capital charges.

This transformation in capital and balance-sheet management is being driven largely by advances in risk management. Approaches to measuring and managing credit, market, and operational risk are merging together into one overall risk framework.

TABLE 14.6

Sensitivity of RAROC to Volatility for a Zero Net Present Value Investment

Part A: Correlation coefficient 0.25

| Standard Deviation[1] σ_A | Expected Rate of Return[1] | | Economic Capital E | RAROC[1] | ARAROC[1] |
	Risky Asset R_A	Equity R_E			
5	5.70	10.46	106.3	10.46	6.88
10	6.27	10.71	203.2	10.71	6.88
20	7.42	11.25	371.6	11.25	6.88
40	9.71	12.48	620.7	12.48	6.88

Part B: Correlation coefficient 0.50

| Standard Deviation[1] σ_A | Expected Rate of Return[1] | | Economic Capital E | RAROC[1] | ARAROC[1] |
	Risky Asset R_A	Equity R_E			
5	6.27	16.28	101.5	16.28	6.90
10	7.42	16.77	194.8	16.77	6.90
20	9.71	17.81	358.3	17.81	6.89
40	14.29	20.21	605.1	20.21	6.88

Default-free rate of interest: [2]R_f	5.13 percent
Expected rate of return on the market portfolio: [2]$\overline{R}_M$	12.0 percent
Volatility of the return on the market portfolio: σ_M	15.0 percent
Market value of the risky assets: $A(0)$ (= cost of investment)	1000
Maturity of debt: T	1 year
Probability of default: p	1 percent

[1]Expressed in percentage form.

[2]Expressed as a discretely compounded rate of return.

Figure 14.20 illustrates how tools developed to measure risk capital in the trading world are being applied to market risk capital in the banking book.

Over time, businesses within best-practice banks will find that they have to bid for scarce regulatory capital, balance-sheet limits, and risk limits. Managers will assess these bids by employing RAROC methodologies. The RAROC process will also integrate the entire risk process, as shown in Figure 14.21.

FIGURE 14.20

Integration of Credit and Market Risk

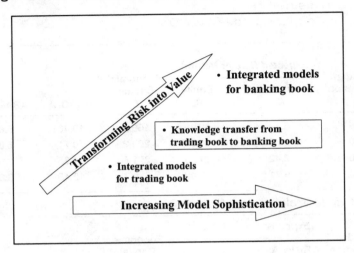

FIGURE 14.21

The RAROC Process Integrates a Number of Critical
Elements

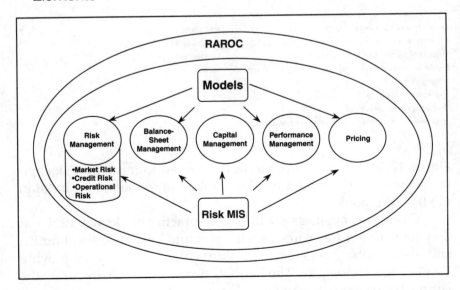

7.1 RAROC Link to Stakeholders

RAROC provides a link between the needs of bank management and a variety of external stakeholders (Figure 14.22). Some stakeholders, such as debt holders, regulators, and rating agencies, are interested in the bank's solvency in terms of the safety of its deposits. Others, such as shareholders, are interested in the bank's profitability. RAROC provides a "common language" for risk and measurement that supports each of these interests.

7.2 Regulatory Trends

Regulators are finding it increasingly difficult to keep pace with market developments such as credit derivatives. They are also becoming receptive to the use of internal models. Over time, an integrated RAROC framework that links regulatory capital and economic capital might well evolve (Figure 14.23).

The BIS 98 regulations, and the consultative paper on a new capital adequacy framework released in 1999 by the Basle Committee (BIS 1999), are important steps toward linking regulatory capital and economic capital.

FIGURE 14.22

How RAROC Balances the Desires of Various Stakeholders

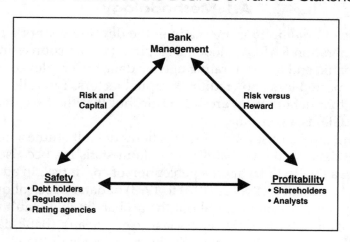

FIGURE 14.23

Integrated RAROC–Shareholder Value Creation

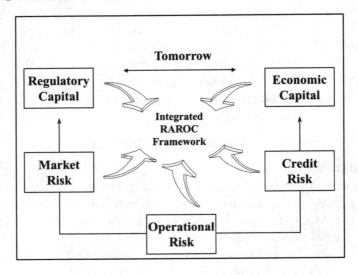

APPENDIX 1: FIRST GENERATION OF RAROC MODEL–ASSUMPTIONS IN CALCULATING EXPOSURES, EXPECTED DEFAULT, AND EXPECTED LOSSES

A.1 Methodology

A series of assumptions are made in the development of a typical first generation RAROC model. Default data from sources internal to the bank, and external rating agency data, are employed to generate expected loss and credit risk capital factors. Typically it is assumed that default rates are stochastic, but that the loss given default (LGD) is a constant.

The results of several Moody's bond default studies are often used to develop the probability of default statistics, because these provide a link to the market's perception of credit risk. In addition, Moody's provides 24 years (1970 to 1993) of data, which allows the analyst to make statements about the probability of default within the remaining term of the asset class (e.g., a loan). (Bank data are typically available only for much shorter periods of time.)

Loss given default (LGD) is defined as the expected severity of loss given that a default on a credit obligation has occurred. The LGD rate for a defaulted facility represents the ratio of the expected loss that will be incurred over the total gross loan outstanding. A typical analysis might suggest a 40 percent loss given default rate for a loan portfolio, on a portfolio-wide basis. Similarly, a typical analysis might suggest that a 60 percent loss given default for corporate bonds is reasonable, on a portfolio basis.

The analysis begins with an assumption of the distribution of the default rate. This assumption allows us to estimate the expected default rate, and the worst case default rates for a given confidence level, as well as the expected loss. From these estimates, and the assumptions concerning the LGD, and risk tolerance, we derive the capital factors to be used in RAROC calculations.

For first-generation RAROC models, it is typical to assume that the default rate for a portfolio of loans can be expressed as a simple distribution. Let p be a random variable representing the probability of default for a given risk rating and tenor. If we assume further that the probability of default p is such that $z = p/[1 - p]$ is log-normal distributed, then $y = \ln z = \ln(p/(1 - p))$ is normally distributed with mean μ_y and standard deviation σ_y (i.e., $y \sim N(\mu_y, \sigma_y)$).

We can express p in terms of the normally distributed variable y:

$$p = \exp(y)/(1 + \exp(y)) \tag{A1}$$

Figure 14.A.1 illustrates how the default distribution varies by tenor for loans that are risk rated 4.

A.2 Worst Case Default Rates and Expected Loss

Let us denote the mean and standard deviation of the default probability by α and β, respectively. Then the mean and standard deviation of $z = p/(1 - p)$ can be approximated,[7] respectively, by $\mu_z = \alpha/(1 - \alpha)$ and $\sigma_z = \beta/(1 - \alpha)^2$. The variance of $y = \ln z$ can be estimated by

$$\sigma_y^2 = \ln\left(1 + \frac{\sigma_z}{\mu_z^2}\right) \tag{A2}$$

FIGURE   14.A.1.1

Default Distribution of RR4 Loans

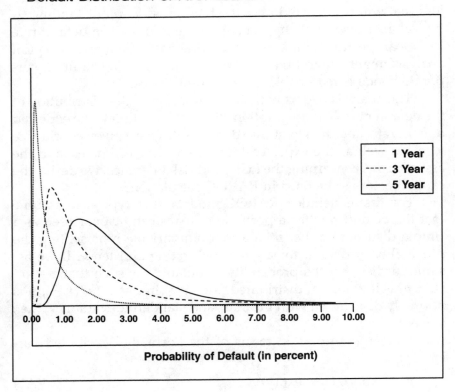

Accordingly, the worst case value of y at the 99.865 percent confidence level, which is three times the standard deviation away from the mean, is given by x:

$$x = E(z)\exp(3\sigma_y - 5\sigma_y^2) \qquad (A3)$$

The worst-case probability of default corresponding to x is

$$\kappa = \frac{x}{(1 + x)} \qquad (A4)$$

Under the assumption that the loss given default is a constant 40 percent, then:

- The expected loss rate is 40 percent of the expected default rate, α:

$$\text{Expected loss} = 40\% \times \alpha \qquad (A5)$$

- The capital factor is 40 percent of the difference between the worst case default rate κ and the expected default rate α:

$$\text{Capital factors} = 40\% \, (\kappa - \alpha) \qquad (A6)$$

A.3 Illustration of Capital and Expected Loss Model for Loans Accounted for on an Accrual Basis

Assume a loan is risk rated RR4 with a tenor of five years.

First, one needs to determine the expected default percentage over five years. The cumulative default rate, α, as shown in the cumulative default table (Table 14.A.1) is 1.97 percent. The source of the data used to derive the adjusted cumulative default table is Moody's default history of 1970 to 1993.[8] Observe that the expected default percentage in Table 14.A.1 declines from 1.97 percent to 1.46 percent as the tenor of loan declines from five years to four years.

Second, the expected loss would be estimated as the default rate times the loss given default. For example, if we assume a

TABLE 14.A.1

"Adjusted Cumulative" Expected Default Rates

Risk Rating	Tenor (years)									
	1	2	3	4	5	6	7	8	9	10
1										
2										
3					0.62%					
4				1.46%	1.97%	2.46%				
5					11.85%					
6										
7										
8										
9										
10										
11										
12										

Note: Only part of the table is shown.

constant 40 percent loss given default, then the expected loss for our five-year, risk rated 4 loan is simply:

$$1.97\% \times 40\% = 0.79\%$$

The expected loan losses for RR1 to RR6 are calculated by simply multiplying Table 14.A.1 by 40 percent. For convenience, a table of expected loan losses at a 40 percent loss rate is shown in Table 14.A.2. The expected loan loss rates for watch list ratings are mostly judgmental.

Next, we determine the worst case default and loss rates. For this we also require an estimate of the standard deviation, β, of the default rate. The estimate of the standard deviation of the default rate for a loan that is risk rated 4 and has a tenor of five years is 1.13 percent (Table 14.A.3).

Using these values, the equations developed above are:

$$\mu_z = \alpha/(1 - \alpha) = 1.97\%/(1 - 1.97\%) = 0.02010$$
$$\sigma_z = \beta/(1 - \alpha)^2 = 1.1347\%/(1 - 1.97\%)^2 = 0.01181$$

and plugging in numbers for μ_z and σ_z, we obtain:

TABLE 14.A.2

Adjusted Cumulative Expected Loan Losses
(@40% Loss Rate)

Risk Rating	Tenor (years)									
	1	2	3	4	5	6	7	8	9	10
1										
2										
3					0.25%					
4				0.58%	0.79%	0.98%				
5					4.74%					
6										
7										
8										
9										
10										
11										
12										

Note: Only part of the table is shown.

TABLE 14.A.3

Standard Deviation of Default

Risk Rating	Tenor (years)			
	1	3	5	10
1				
2				
3			0.64%	
4		0.78%	1.13%	1.77%
5			5.11%	
6				
7				
8				
9				
10				
11				
12				

Note: Only part of the table is shown.

$$\sigma_y^2 = \ln\left(1 + \frac{\sigma_z}{\mu_z^2}\right) = \ln\left(1 + \left(\frac{0.01181}{0.02010}\right)^2\right) = 0.29656$$

$$\sigma_y = 0.54456$$

The worst case value of y at the 99.865 percent confidence level (3σ) is then:

$$x = \mu_z \exp(3\sigma_y - 5\sigma_y^2) = 0.02010$$
$$\times \exp(3 \times 0.54456 - .5 \times 0.29656) = 0.08876$$

The worst case probability of default at 99.865 percent confidence level (for 3σ) is:

$$\kappa = x/(1 + x) = 0.08876/(1 + 0.08876) = 8.15\%$$

A table of the worst case probability of default is shown in Table 14.A.4.

The capital factor prior to adjusting for loss given default is the unexpected loss defined as the difference between the worst case probability of default and the expected default rate:

$$\kappa - \alpha = 8.15 - 1.97 = 6.18$$

TABLE 14.A.4

Worst Case Probability of Default

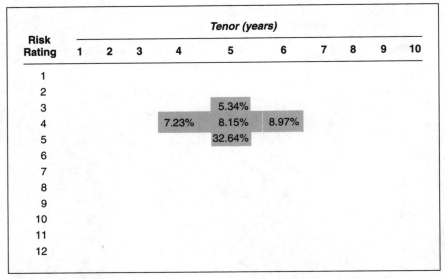

Risk Rating	Tenor (years)									
	1	2	3	4	5	6	7	8	9	10
1										
2										
3					5.34%					
4				7.23%	8.15%	8.97%				
5					32.64%					
6										
7										
8										
9										
10										
11										
12										

Note: Only part of the table is shown.

TABLE 14.A.5

Capital Factor at a 99.856 Percent Confidence Level
(Prior to Adjusting for Loss Given Default)

Risk Rating	Tenor (years)									
	1	2	3	4	5	6	7	8	9	10
1										
2										
3					4.72%					
4				5.77%	6.18%	6.51%				
5					20.79%					
6										
7										
8										
9										
10										
11										
12										

Note: Only part of the table is shown.

TABLE 14.A.6

Capital Factors at a 99.865 Percent Confidence Level (at 40 Percent Loss Given Default)

Risk Rating	Tenor									
	1	2	3	4	5	6	7	8	9	10
1										
2										
3					1.89%					
4				2.31%	2.47%	2.60%				
5					8.32%					
6										
7										
8										
9										
10										
11										
12										

The capital factors prior to adjusting for loss given default are presented in Table 14.A.5. Note that the capital factor represents the amount of capital that is required to cushion unexpected losses over the life of the transaction.

The capital factors adjusted for loss given default = 40 percent ($\kappa - \alpha$). For example, the capital factor for a RR4 five-year loan = 40 percent × (8.15 percent − 1.97 percent) = 40 percent × 6.18 percent = 2.47 percent.

For convenience, a table of capital factors adjusted for 40 percent loss given default is shown in Table 14.A.6.

NOTES

1. Figure 14.2 shows the evolution of performance measurement from a practitioner perspective. In Chapter 17 we examine the evolution of RAROC towards a more sophisticated theoretical paradigm.
2. NIFs, RUFs, and GUNs are term commitments by the bank to underwrite different types of public offerings.

3. This section is based on Mark (1999). See Appendix 1 for a detailed analysis of exposures and losses, including tables and assumptions made in quantifying exposures and losses.

4. The average worst case credit risk exposure, integrated from 0 to T, equals:

$$(\int_0^T K \times \sigma \times \sqrt{t}\, dt)/T = (K \times \sigma \times T^{3/2})/(3/2)$$
$$\times (1/T) = 2/3 \times [K \times \sigma \times \sqrt{T}] = 2/3 \times W_T$$

5. For example, the expected credit loss at a given point in time equals $\int\int\int CE \times DR \times (1 - RR) \times f(CE, DR, RR)dCEdDRdRR$, where CE denotes credit risk exposure, DR the default rate, RR the recovery rate, and $f(CE, DR, RR)$ the multivariate probability density function.

6. Portions of this section appeared in Crouhy, Turnbull, and Wakeman (1999).

7. The approximation is based on the Taylor series expansion, and by omitting higher-order terms in the series.

8. The Moody's data for short tenors are adjusted to reflect the bank's own experience for large corporate loans. See Chapter 7 for a description of Moody's and S&P's data.

CHAPTER 15

Model Risk

*At times we can lose sight of the ultimate purpose of the models when their
mathematics become too interesting. The mathematics of financial models can be
applied precisely, but the models are not at all precise in their application to the
complex real world. Their accuracy as a useful approximation to that world
varies significantly across time and place. The models should be applied in practice only tentatively, with careful assessment of their limitations in each application.*

Nobel Lecture by Robert Merton, December 9, 1997

1. INTRODUCTION

The special risk that arises when an institution uses mathematical models to value and hedge securities has come to be known as
"model risk." For simple instruments, such as stocks and straight
bonds, model risk is relatively insignificant. It becomes a com-
pelling issue, however, for institutions that trade over-the-counter
(OTC) derivative products and for institutions that execute complex arbitrage strategies.

In relatively efficient and liquid securities markets, the market price is, on average, the best indicator of the value of an
asset. In the absence of liquid markets and price discovery mechanisms, theoretical valuation models have to be used to mark-to-
model the bank's position, to assess the risk exposure in terms of
the various risk factors, and to derive the appropriate hedging
strategy.

In this situation, the trader and the risk manager are like the pilot and copilot of a plane that is dependent upon flying instruments to land safely. Any error in the electronics on board, and one heavy storm will be fatal to the plane. In the financial world, not a single market crisis passes, whether minor or more serious (e.g., the crisis in the Asian markets in the late 1990s), without several large trading losses appearing in the financial media. Some of these losses are so large they force institutions to restructure, to disappear, or to accept a takeover by a rival firm.[1]

In this chapter, we discuss some classic examples of "what can go wrong" when trading strategies are built on theoretical valuation models. These models are susceptible to many sources of error: from incorrect assumptions about price dynamics and market interactions, through estimation errors with regard to volatilities and correlations and other inputs that are not directly observable (and so must be forecasted), to the implementation of valuation models. Most models are derived under the assumption of perfect capital markets but, in practice, market imperfections lead to substantial and persistent differences between the way markets behave and the results generated by models.

Since 1973, with the publication of the Black-Scholes and Merton option pricing models, there has been a relentless increase in the complexity of valuation theories. The market for fixed-income instruments, and the derivatives markets more generally, provide the most striking examples. Throughout the 1970s, the market risk of bonds was assessed using a simple duration-based measure, with or without an adjustment for convexity. As securities increased in sophistication to include features such as embedded options, valuation came to be based on complex multifactor stochastic interest rate models. In some instances, these models are only properly understood by derivative "rocket scientists" (so-called because their expertise is in the kind of mathematical and quantitative techniques used in the space industry).

The pace of model development accelerated throughout the 1980s and 1990s to support the rapid growth of financial innovations such as caps, floors, swaptions, spread options, and other exotic derivatives. In fact, the growth in complexity was self-perpetuating. Product innovations, themselves made possible by developments in financial theory, allowed analysts to capture many new facets of financial risk. Technology was crucial, too. The models could not have been implemented in practice, or have come to be so well accepted on the trading floor, had the growth in computing power not accelerated dramatically.[2] Financial innovation, model development, and computing power are now engaged in a game of leapfrog: financial innovation calls for more model complexity, which in turn requires greater computing power. As they become familiar with the latest batch of complex models, and gain access to even more massive reserves of computing power, the level of comfort of traders increases—and soon they are keen to innovate again.

This dynamic process, however, can be treacherous if the risk management function in financial institutions does not have the authority to tame the beast.[3] In the next section we elaborate on what the financial industry means when it talks about "models," and look at the sources of model risk. Then, we present our typology of model risk, and show by means of a few famous examples what can go wrong when models are not applied with caution. In many instances, too much faith in models has led institutions unknowingly to take large bets on key parameters such as volatilities or correlations. The fact is that these parameters are difficult to predict and can be shown to be unstable over time. Finally, we present our views on how the market risk management function of a financial institution can attempt to mitigate model risk.

2. VALUATION MODELS AND SOURCES OF MODEL RISK

In financial markets two types of securities are traded: "fundamental" instruments such as stocks, bonds, and loans; and the more complicated "derivatives" securities.

Theoretical valuation models for fundamental assets are derived from general equilibrium considerations in the economy and the assumption that financial markets are perfect and efficient. The key principles for the valuation of fundamental securities are well known and are generally accepted: investors prefer high returns and dislike risk. Even so, the models are expected to produce guidelines rather than very precise valuations. For example, a risky security should offer a higher expected return than a risk-free security. But how much higher? Pricing theory cannot give a specific value unless it is fed with "perfect" information. The dependence of models on unobservable market factors—investor expectations and risk aversion—makes precise valuation difficult, therefore, even in the case of fundamental securities. It also means that market participants do not rely extensively on theoretical models when trading in these markets.

Pricing models for derivatives, on the other hand, value a derivative instrument relative to the price of its underlying asset. A swaption, for example, is an option on an underlying swap.[4] The values of the derivative and the underlying are perfectly correlated over short time intervals. It is not necessary that the underlying asset is priced correctly in the market in order to produce the equilibrium value of the derivative. This is because the pricing model for the derivative depends simply on considerations of no arbitrage between the derivative and its underlying asset. If the derivative's market price differs from the value predicted by the model, then an arbitrage strategy can be implemented that will earn a risk-adjusted return that is above normal. This is true whether or not the underlying is accurately priced vis-à-vis other securities in the market.

At the risk of oversimplifying, we can classify all the models that prevail in finance into three categories: structural models, statistical models, and models that are a mixture of structural and statistical models. It is worth reviewing these different types of models before looking in more detail at the kind of model risks that can occur.

(i) **Structural models** are based on a system of premises concerning how markets operate under the assumption of rational behavior. They employ assumptions about the underlying asset price process and market equilibrium conditions to allow the modeler to draw inferences about the equilibrium prices. The celebrated Black-Scholes (1973) formula is the best-known example of a structural model in the derivatives markets. It is derived from an arbitrage-based trading strategy that combines the option and its underlying to create a delta-neutral portfolio which is therefore unaffected by small changes in the underlying price over a short interval of time.

(ii) Statistical models rely on empirical observations that are formulated in terms of correlation rather than causation. A classic example is the market model, which specifies the return generating process for a stock as:

$$R_i = \alpha_i + \beta_i R_M + e_i \tag{1}$$

where R_i and R_M denote the rate of return on stock i and on a stock market index M, respectively, where α_i and β_i are the constant regression coefficients, and where e_i is the deviation of actual observed return from the straight linear relation $R_i = \alpha_i + \beta_i R_M$. The process generating the returns, as described by (1), is purely empirical, and should not be confused with the capital asset pricing model (CAPM), which is an equilibrium model.[5]

Another example of a statistical model is the generalized autoregressive conditional heteroscedasticity (GARCH) volatility model for equity returns. There are structural reasons why the equity volatility of an individual firm is likely to be nonstationary; for example, its financial leverage automatically changes whenever the asset value of the firm changes.[6] Instead of modeling the process for volatility through a structural model of the capital structure of the firm, one can capture most of the actual dynamics of equity volatility empirically from past returns, using a statistical model such as GARCH.[7]

(iii) Mixture of structural and statistical models. For example, the GARCH option pricing model combines features of both types of model.[8] In the case of the GARCH option pricing model, volatility is assumed to follow a GARCH process, calibrated on historical data, but the equilibrium price of the option is based on a no-arbitrage argument that is conditional on GARCH volatility.

In the next section of this chapter, we examine the typology of model risk more exactly. But at this stage it is helpful to divide the kind of mistakes that relate directly to the model itself into two main groups.

1. *The model is irrelevant.* There is no solid financial theory to support the model, or empirical evidence to verify its validity. This is the case, for example, with many of the "chartist" trading models that attempt to forecast stock prices or exchange rates. A basic premise in finance is that

financial markets are efficient, and therefore that price changes are purely random and cannot be predicted from past series of price changes. (Likewise, models that claim to relate stock prices to the occurrence of "sunspots" have not yet been proved to be valid or relevant.)

2. *The model is incorrect.*   Derivatives trading depends heavily on the use of mathematical models that make use of complex equations and advanced mathematics. In the simplest sense, a model is incorrect if there are mistakes in the set of equations, or in the solution of a system of equations. A model is also said to be incorrect if it is based on wrong assumptions about the underlying asset price process. For example, a model of bond pricing might be based on a flat and fixed-term structure, when the actual term structure of interest rates is steep and unstable.

Financial engineers are constantly struggling to find the optimal compromise between complexity (to better represent reality) and tractability. An example is the widespread use of the lognormal probability distributions with constant volatility to estimate security returns. The Black-Scholes model makes use of this assumption, even though it is well documented that volatility varies over time, and that actual returns in virtually every market exhibit what the statisticians call "fat tails"; i.e., the probability of a large price change, is, in reality, greater than the model allows for. What is less easy to discover, however, is the impact of this discrepancy on the risk exposure of a given position or trading strategy.[9]

The problem is compounded by the fact that derivatives models require the statistical estimation of a number of input parameters that are not directly observable, such as volatilities, correlations, and mean reversion. These parameters must be forecasted using statistical techniques but, necessarily, this introduces forecasting errors that increase any model risk.

Fischer Black was the first to admit that while the Black-Scholes model offers an excellent starting point, it is in no sense a "perfect" model. Indeed, in a 1992 note devoted to problems of estimating and applying the Black-Scholes model, he asserted that:

> Given the range of problems, it is remarkable that option formulae sometimes give values that are very close to the prices at which options trade in the market. As it stands, the Black-Scholes formula

gives at least a rough approximation to the formula we would use if we knew how to take all these factors into account. Further modifications of the Black-Scholes formula will presumably move it in the direction of that hypothetical perfect formula.

The difficulty of controlling model risk is further aggravated by errors in implementing the theoretical models, and differences between market prices and theoretical values that may persist over time due to apparently irrational behavior on the part of market participants, or some other misunderstood or forgotten factor. For example, there is still no satisfactory explanation as to why investors in convertible bonds do not exercise their conversion option in a way that is consistent with models of optimal exercise behavior.

Computers are now so powerful that there is a temptation to develop ever more complex models that are less and less understood by management. There is clearly a need for the risk management function to have a thorough understanding of the pros and limitations of all the models that are being used within a firm. As Alan Greenspan commented in March 1995, "The technology that is available has increased substantially the productivity for creating losses."[10]

3. TYPOLOGY OF MODEL RISKS

As our discussion so far has indicated, there are many aspects to model risk, both practical as well as philosophical. Figure 15.1 summarizes the stages of a transaction that are particularly vulnerable to model risk. In this section we discuss the practical issues that often lead to substantial trading losses, and which require considerable attention and monitoring from management. The risks are not described in order of importance, or frequency of occurrence; some model risks cross categories or belong to more than one category.

3.1 Erroneous Model and Model Misspecification

3.1.1 Errors in the Analytical Solution
Since most financial models rely on mathematical formulations, often using complex statistical tools, there is always the danger of

FIGURE 15.1

Various Levels of Model Risk

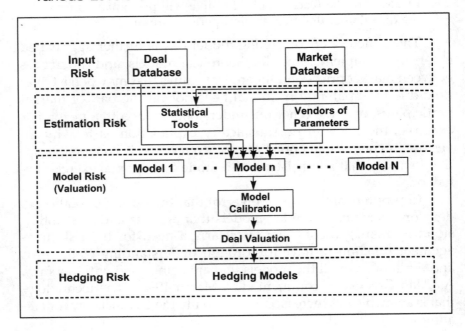

reaching the wrong solution. This problem is especially serious when pricing new complex derivatives with special features that make them path dependent, or dependent on more than one source of risk.

3.1.2 Misspecifying the Underlying Stochastic Process

The most frequent error in model building is to assume that the distribution of the underlying asset is stationary when, in fact, it is not. The case of volatility is striking.[11]

Derivatives practitioners know very well that volatility is not constant. They try to accommodate for this problem by using implied volatilities, which differ for each maturity and striking price; they use these implied volatilities to derive what is known as volatility term structure, volatility simile, or volatility surface. But such adjustments are simply rules of thumb and are not theoretically rigorous. An alternative is to assume that volatility is itself stochastic, and to develop a consistent option pricing model. Yet this means choosing between several possible assumptions:

- Assume that the price of the underlying instrument is generated by a mixture of processes, e.g., a log-normal distribution and a jump process such as that assumed for exchange rates; the existence of jumps is taken to be due to the arrival of new information in the market.
- Assume that volatility is driven by a GARCH-type process, and implement a pricing model in the spirit of Duan (1995) or Ritchken and Trevor (1997).
- Derive the implied distribution for the underlying asset from actual option prices of simple options, and price exotic derivatives accordingly, following the approach proposed by Derman and Kani (1994), Dupire (1994), and Rubinstein (1994).
- Adopt a corporate finance approach, whereby the variability of volatility is driven by the capital structure and the volatility of the assets of the firm as in Bensoussan, Crouhy, and Galai (1994).
- Derive a two-factor option pricing model as in Heston (1993), where volatility is itself a stochastic variable in addition to the asset price. This allows for jumps but creates an unhedgeable risk in the option price and eliminates preference-free pricing.

In any case, option valuation models become quite difficult computationally under any sort of stochastic volatility. Moreover, introducing new unobservable parameters associated with the volatility process into the valuation model makes the estimation problem even more severe. The same comments apply for the estimation of correlations, which become a critical risk factor for some instruments and portfolios when they are volatile. This is especially true for quanto options and credit derivatives.

The process may also have been misidentified, even in the case of a single stochastic factor model with a stationary distribution. Instead of equity returns being normally distributed and exhibiting a stochastic volatility, they may instead follow a stationary constant elasticity of variance (CEV) process.

Finally, where possible, empirical distributions should be used rather than theoretical distributions. This helps to alleviate the problem of the "fat tails" observed in the distribution of stocks' rates of return. For example, an analytic VaR model may yield unlikely results for highly volatile currencies in certain periods, e.g., the Indonesian rupiah during the Asian crisis. In such instances, the distribution of short-term interest rate changes is relatively clustered around the median, and only a few observations lie very far away in the tail of the distribution. Calibrating a log-normal distribution using such empirical observations leads to huge model errors. Historical simulation, based on the empirical distributions, produces a more reasonable risk measure.

Since it is so important to specify correctly the return distribution of risk factors, one can use Kuiper's statistic to measure how close the estimate and the actual probability density functions (PDFs) are to each other.[12] Crnkovic and Drachman (1996) suggest using this technique to assess if the VaR model can be back-tested using only 1000 data points, i.e., four years of profit and loss (P&L) history.[13]

3.1.3 Missing Risk Factors
For simple "vanilla" products, such as a callable bond, a one-factor term structure model might be enough to produce accurate prices and hedge ratios. For more complex products, such as spread options or exotic structures, a two- or three-factor model may be required to avoid presenting arbitrage opportunities to competitors.

3.1.4 Missing Considerations Such as Transaction Costs and Liquidity
Most financial models are derived under the assumption of the existence of perfect capital markets (see Chapter 1, Section 4 for a discussion of the academic background to theoretical models). In reality many markets, especially in less-developed countries, are far from being perfect. OTC products are not traded, and usually cannot be perfectly hedged.

Most derivative pricing models rely on the implementation of a delta-neutral hedging strategy. In practice a delta-neutral hedge of an option against its underlying is far from being completely risk free, and keeping such a position delta neutral over time requires what can be a very active rebalancing strategy. While the pricing of options depends heavily on theoretical models derived from dynamic hedging strategies, in reality banks rarely attempt the continuous rebalancing that these models assume. For one thing, the theoretical strategy implies an enormous number of transactions: Trading costs are too large for this to be feasible. Nor is continuous trading possible even disregarding transactions costs: markets close at night and on weekends. Potential arbitrageurs are also uncertain whether they know exactly the value of volatility and the other model parameters.

Liquidity, or rather the absence of liquidity, may also be a major source of model risk. Models assume that the underlying asset can be traded long or short at current market prices, and that prices will not change dramatically when the trade is executed.

An excellent example of this problem occurred during the 1994 bond market turmoil, after the Federal Reserve unexpectedly tightened interest rates. Askin Capital Management, which held a portfolio of the most complex mortgage-backed securities, was forced to liquidate these under stressed market conditions. The total loss realized on the portfolio was reported to be close to $600 million, or the entire equity base of the fund. This fiasco was the result of both liquidity and model risks. The portfolio of collateralized mortgage obligations (CMOs) was supposedly hedged (delta neutral), and therefore should have been relatively insensitive to the rise of interest rates during the period February to April 1994. The daily mark-to-market of the book and the hedge ratios were derived from proprietary pricing models, however, and these turned out to be flawed. The fund began to suffer increasing margin calls, which it was eventually unable to meet. As the fund was highly leveraged ($2 billion assets for $600 million equity), it was obliged to sell its assets under very unfavorable terms to meet calls for collateral as the value of the assets dropped.

Liquidity was also one of the causes of a $670 million loss at UBS. The problem arose from UBS's position in certain convertible preference shares that had been issued by Japanese banks. When the Japanese banking crisis worsened, in late November 1997, some of the banks' shares did not trade for days at a time. This meant that UBS was unable to adjust its hedge.[14]

3.1.5 Misclassifying or Misidentifying the Underlying Asset

Risk can arise from any misunderstandings about whether the underlying instrument is a primary asset, or is itself a contingent asset on another underlying asset (or assets). For example, if we look on equity as a call option on the firm's assets, then a call on the shares of the firm is a compound option (Galai and Masulis 1976).

3.2 Incorrect Implementation of the Model

3.2.1 Bugs in the Program and Approximation Errors

For complicated models that require extensive programming, there is always a chance that a programming "bug" may affect the model output.

Some implementations rely on numerical techniques that exhibit inherent approximation errors and limited ranges of validity. Many programs that seem error-free have only been tested under normal conditions, and so may be error-prone in extreme cases and conditions.

3.2.2 Insufficient Number of Simulation Runs

In models that require a Monte Carlo simulation, or models based on the tree approach, large inaccuracies in prices and hedge ratios can creep in if not enough simulation runs or time steps are implemented. In this case, the model might be right, and the data might be accurate, but the results might still be wrong if the computation process is not given the time it needs to converge.

3.2.3 Nonsimultaneous Data Feeds

For models evaluating complex derivatives, data are collected from different sources. The implicit assumption is that, for each time period, the data for all relevant assets and rates pertain exactly to the same time instant, and thus reflect "simultaneous" prices. Using nonsimultaneous price inputs can lead to a wrong pricing.

3.3 Incorrect Model Calibration

When implementing a pricing model, statistical tools are used to estimate model parameters such as volatilities and correlations, on the one hand, and to estimate the power of the estimation on the other hand. Problems inherent to all statistical procedures can thus affect the outputs of the model.

3.3.1 Competing Statistical Estimation Techniques

Usually more than one statistical procedure can be used to estimate parameters. For example, for estimating variance one might use the unbiased estimator (dividing by $n - 1$, where n is the number of observations), or the maximum likelihood estimate, which is the simple average of squared deviations from the mean (i.e., dividing by n only). Similarly, should a risk manager use ARCH or GARCH models to estimate nonstationary volatility?

3.3.2 Estimation Errors

All statistical estimators are subject to estimation errors of the inputs to the pricing model, which in turn may yield erroneous results. Statistical procedures may yield information on the nature of the estimation errors; however, this information does not help traders who must decide whether to buy or sell a given derivative, or who need to decide on a specific hedge ratio.

3.3.3 How to Deal with "Outliers"

A major problem in the estimation procedure is the treatment of "outliers," or extreme observations. Are the "outliers" really outliers, in the sense that they do not reflect the true distribution? Or are they important observations and relevant data that should not be dismissed? The results of the estimation procedure will be vastly different depending on how such observations are treated.

3.3.4 Estimation Intervals

Each bank, or even each trading desk within a bank, may use a different estimation procedure in order to estimate the model parameters. Some may use daily closing prices, while others may use transaction data. Whether one uses calendar time (i.e., the actual number of days elapsed), trading time (i.e., the number of days on which the underlying instrument is traded), or economic time (i.e., the number of days during which significant economic events take place) affects the calculation.[15]

3.3.5 Calibration and Revision of Estimated Parameters

Valuation models are used in a continuously changing environment. An important question, then, is how frequently should input parameters be refreshed? Should the adjustment be made on a periodic basis, or should it be triggered by an important economic event?

Similarly, should parameters be adjusted according to qualitative judgments, or should these adjustments be based purely on statistics? The statistical approach is bound to be in some sense "backward looking," while a human adjustment can be forward looking; i.e., it can take into account a personal assessment of likely future developments in the relevant markets.

For example, the instantaneous hedge ratios for an option must reflect expected changes in volatility, especially for short-term options. This is critical in periods during which announcements about important macroeconomic news or firm-specific news will be made. Volatility on "announcement days" can often be equivalent to several regular business days in its impact on the option value.[16]

3.4 Market Data Processing

The quality of a model depends heavily on the accuracy of the input parameter values that feed the model. The old adage "garbage in–garbage out" should never be forgotten when implementing models that require the estimation of several parameters. Volatilities and correlations are the hardest input parameters to judge accurately. Unlike the option's strike and maturity, which are fixed, or the asset price and interest rate, which can be easily observed directly in the market, volatilities and correlations must be forecasted.

The most frequent problems in estimating values, on the one hand, and assessing the potential errors in valuation, on the other hand, are listed below.

3.4.1 Length of the Sampling Period

This is a subtle question, since adding more observations improves the power of statistical tests and tends to reduce the estimation errors. But, the longer the sampling period, the more weight is given to potentially stale and obsolete information. Especially in dynamically changing financial markets, "old" data can become irrelevant and may introduce noise to the estimation process.

3.4.2 Inaccurate Data

Most financial institutions use internal data sources as well as external databases. The responsibility for data accuracy is often not clearly assigned. It is therefore very common to find data errors that can significantly affect the estimated parameters.

This problem is even more serious for volatility estimation, since variance is the average of *squared* deviations from the mean. Any error in the data weighs heavily on the accuracy of the calculations.

3.4.3 Problems with Bid/Ask Prices

Most liquid securities trade in markets that are led by market makers, or specialists, who quote buying and selling prices for given securities. For low-priced securities that are relatively illiquid, the bid-ask spread can be quite substantial. This trading procedure creates "noisy" prices, and hence biased estimations of volatilities and correlations. This problem can be more serious than the effect of direct commissions on the prices of securities.

3.4.4 Frequency of Trading and Market Depth

Like the previous issue, the frequency of trading and market-depth problem is related to the liquidity of the market. Observations of market prices are not equally spaced. Many securities are not frequently traded and, therefore, their time series of prices may contain stale or inaccurate information. For example, most corporate bonds are rarely traded. This is true also for many long-term government bonds. The prices of such instruments may constitute unreliable information with which to predict future price distributions.

3.5 Model Misapplication

A model can be found to be mathematically correct and consistent with finance theory, and to make use of accurate data, and yet be misapplied to a given situation.

3.5.1 Changing Market Conditions

As Derman (1997) observes, "the model you developed may be inappropriate under current market conditions, or some of its assumptions may have become invalid." For example, the Heath-Jarrow-Morton (HJM) model for the term structure of interest rates is widely accepted by practitioners. This multifactor model assumes log-normality of the forward rates and seems to fit relatively well when applied to most of the world's markets—except for Japan. In recent years, Japanese markets have been characterized by very low interest rates, for which Gaussian and square-root models for interest rates work much better than the HJM model.

3.5.2 Applying a Model to Value Derivatives with More Features Than in Its Original Design

Many OTC products have options embedded within them that are often ignored in the pricing model. For example, using a model to value warrants may yield biased results if the warrant is also extendable.

Other common errors are, for example, using the Black-Scholes option valuation model to price equity options, and adjusting for dividends by subtracting their present value from the stock price. This ignores the fact that the options can be exercised early.

4. WHAT CAN GO WRONG?[17]

The list of possible model risks that we have just discussed is so impressively long that it might seem unlikely that the same models, implemented by different institutions, would yield the same results. Indeed, a Bank of England survey conducted in 1997 illustrated the degree of variation that existed among 40 major derivative trading firms based in London. Vanilla foreign exchange instruments showed a relatively low level of variation in both value and sensitivities. However, some of the exotic derivatives displayed large variations not only in value but also in some of the sensitivity measures: 10 to 20 percent for swaptions and up to 60 percent for foreign exchange double barrier options, knock-out options, and digital options.[18] We suspect that even within the same financial institution, different groups might come up with different valuations for similar instruments.

In another study, Marshall and Siegel (1997) presented an identical asset portfolio to a number of commercial vendors of software for value-at-risk (VaR) calculations. Each was asked to use the same volatility inputs, obtained from JP Morgan's RiskMetrics, and to report the aggregate VaR for the entire portfolio and the VaR figure by type of instrument (such as swaps, caps and floors, and swaptions). The variation among vendors was striking, given that in this case they were supposed to be analyzing the same position (of relatively simple instruments), using the same methodology and the same market parameter values. For the whole portfolio, the estimates ranged from $3.8 million to $6.1 million, and for the portion containing options, the VaR estimates varied from $747,000 to $2,100,000.

It is therefore not surprising that trading firms experience substantial trading losses in stormy market environments. In the next section, we look at some real-life examples of how things have gone wrong. For the most part, the examples are provided in short form simply to demonstrate a point. However, at the end of the section we examine in more detail the most famous example of model risk to date: the Long-Term Capital Management crisis of 1998.

4.1 Volatility Input Risk

In 1997 it was discovered that certain traders at NatWest in London had been selling caps and swaptions in sterling and deutsche marks at the wrong price since late 1994, and had been hedging their short position by buying options priced at too high a volatility vis-à-vis the volatility implied by the swaption premiums. When these discontinuities, especially for long maturities, were removed from the volatility curves in 1997, the downward revisions of NatWest's portfolio value resulted in a loss of £90 million.

This sort of anomaly should be questioned immediately by a firm's risk management function. For risk managers around the world, verifying volatility estimates and, more generally, all the other principal inputs to a pricing model that are handed to them by a trader, is a critical issue. At CIBC, for example, risk managers are empowered to conduct independent checks on all the critical parameters that affect marking-to-market options positions.

4.2 Wrong Assumption About the Price Distribution: Fat Tails

A well-established hedge fund run by Victor Niedehoffer, a star trader on Wall Street, went bankrupt in November 1997.[19] The fund had been writing a large quantity of naked (i.e., uncovered), deeply out-of-the-money put options on the S&P 500 stock index, and collecting small amounts of option premium in return. His trading strategy was based on the premise that the market would never drop by more than 5 percent on a given day. The stock market fell by more than 7 percent on October 27, 1997, in reaction to the crisis brewing in the Asian markets. (Such a fall would be virtually impossible if market returns were indeed normally distributed.)

Liquidity, or rather the disappearance of liquidity after the market shock, brought the fund to its knees and it found itself unable to meet margin calls for more than $50 million. As a consequence, Niedehoffer's brokers liquidated the positions at fire-sale prices and the entire equity of the fund was lost.[20]

4.3 Yield Curve Valuation Risk

In the mid-1970s, the Wall Street bank of Merrill Lynch began to break down (or "strip") 30-year government bonds into their building-block components: coupon annuities and zero-coupon principal payments. They then offered these components to the market as "interest only" (IO) and "principal only" (PO) instruments.

Merrill used the 30-year par yield to price the IOs and the POs. As shown in Figure 15.2, the par yield curve was higher than the annuity yield, but lower than the zero curve. Therefore, by using the par rate rather than the annuity rate, the firm undervalued the IOs, and by using the par rate rather than the zero rate, it overvalued the POs, although the sum of the two valuations did add up to the bond's true value.

Merrill sold $600 million of the undervalued IOs, and none of the overvalued POs. In combination with a hedging mistake (discussed below), this resulted in the bank booking a $70 million loss.

Another example is that of the $1 billion interest rate cap, based on commercial paper, traded in 1989 by Chemical Bank and Manufacturers Hanover. Both banks used different models to create the yield curve for the commercial paper, which they then used as an input into (essentially similar) option pricing models. Ironically, both banks booked six-figure profits on the same deal. A further irony is that both banks subsequently merged with one another.

FIGURE 15.2

Yield Curve Valuation Risk

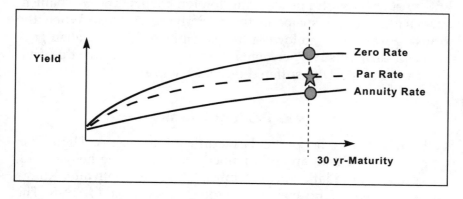

4.4 Choice of the Wrong Model

In 1994 Bank of Tokyo-Mitsubishi used a one-factor Black-Derman-Toy model to enter the swaption market. Although the model was initially calibrated to the market prices of at-the-money swaptions, it was structurally inadequate to price out-of-the-money swaptions and more complex swaptions such as Bermuda swaptions.

Traders have a tendency to shop around in the markets for bargains. Just as some traders learned to call NatWest Bank to obtain good prices for their sterling and deutsche mark caps at certain maturities, they also learned to call at Bank of Tokyo-Mitsubishi for certain swaptions. The mispricing was caught only in 1997 after the bank realized that it had lost $80 million. Subsequently the bank tested more sophisticated multifactor models.

4.5 The Forgotten Factor: Regulatory Risk Such as a Change in the Tax Law

Many structured deals are driven by tax law or by regulatory rules. Financial engineers devise structures and pricing models to take advantage of the existing environment, but they tend to forget about the risk of an unexpected change in the rules of the game. The rules tend to change precisely when large numbers of firms have begun to exploit the same loophole, and the government considers that they have crossed the line.

In one such case, the equity derivatives group of UBS decided to take advantage of British tax laws to capture dividend tax credit and to share it with participating foreign clients. The mechanism was a total return swap on the underlying equities. When the British government, following the example of the Australian government earlier in 1997, changed the tax code to remove this dividend tax benefit, UBS suffered quite hefty losses.

4.6 Political Risk

Political risk can be particularly difficult to assess. High Risk Opportunities Fund, an aptly named bond arbitrage hedge fund, was put into liquidation in September 1998, one month after Russia suspended bond and currency trading on August 14, 1998. The fund was attempting to take advantage of the 4 percent spread between the ruble-denominated Russian Treasury bills, known as the GKO, and the lower cost of borrowing rubles from banks. The fund was hit twice. First, the Russians unexpectedly halted trading in their domestic government debt market, an event that had never happened before in history. Second, several European banks that had sold currency hedges to the fund against the depreciation of the ruble abruptly suspended an estimated $400 million in payments to the fund, contending that their obligations were no longer tenable (since Russia had defaulted on hers).[21]

4.7 Liquidity Risk

In the fall of 1997, UBS bought $1.2 billion of convertible preferred shares issued by Japanese banks. UBS then sold off the debt component of these securities. What was left was essentially a put option, which gave investors the right to force UBS to buy the shares of the Japanese banks shares at a set strike price. That price was to be adjusted downwards to a floor if the price of the Japanese banks' shares edged down. Supposedly, this feature of the strategy protected UBS from large losses.

If bank shares had fallen moderately, this supposedly low-risk strategy would have succeeded. But when Japanese bank stock prices fell very sharply, UBS was unable to adjust its hedge by short-selling the banks' shares. As Japan's banking crisis worsened during November 1997, the shares of some banks were not traded on the market for days at a time. As a result, on these instruments alone, UBS lost more than $600 million.

4.8 Hedging Risk: The Wrong Hedge

In the case involving Merrill Lynch and the misvaluing of IOs and POs, described earlier, the Merrill Lynch trader hedged the 30-year bonds using a duration of approximately 13 years. This was the correct decision for the bonds while they remained intact and on the books of Merrill Lynch. However, even after he had sold all the IO components of the bonds, the trader maintained the hedge at 13 years, while the correct duration of a 30-year PO instrument is 30 years. When interest rates rose, the bank incurred severe losses.

4.9 Hedging Risk: Liquidity Squeeze

In 1993 MRGM (MG Refining and Marketing), the American subsidiary of Metallgesellschaft (MG), entered into contracts to supply end-user customers with 150 million barrels of oil products (gasoline and heating oil) over a period of 10 years, at fixed prices.

MGRM's fixed-price forward delivery contracts exposed it to the risk of rising energy prices. In the absence of a liquid market for long-term futures contracts, MGRM hedged this risk with both short-dated energy futures contracts on the New York Mercantile Exchange (NYMEX) and over-the-counter (OTC) swaps. The derivative positions were concentrated in short-dated futures and swaps, which had to be rolled forward monthly as they matured. Each month, the size of the derivatives position was reduced by the amount of product delivered that month, with the intention of preserving a one-to-one hedge. According to Culp and Miller (1994), "such a strategy is neither inherently unprofitable nor fatally flawed, provided top management understands the program and the long-term funding commitments necessary to make it work."

This rolling hedge strategy can be profitable when markets are in backwardation, but when markets are in contango it can result in losses. In a backwardated market, oil for immediate delivery commands a higher price than does oil for future delivery. When rolling the hedge position, the contract near expiration is therefore sold at a higher price than the replacement contract, which has a longer delivery date, resulting in a rollover profit. The contrary applies when the market is in contango.

This meant that MGRM was exposed to curve risk (backwardation versus contango), and to basis risk, which is the risk that short-term oil prices might temporarily deviate from long-term prices. Over 1993, cash prices fell from close to $20 a barrel in June to less than $15 a barrel in December, leading to $1.3 billion of margin calls that MGRM had to meet in cash. The problem was further compounded by the change in the shape of the price curve, which moved from backwardation to contango. MGRM's German parent reacted by liquidating the hedge, and thus turned paper losses into realized losses.

4.10 Breakdown of Patterns During a Liquidity Crisis and the Impact of High Leverage[22]

The failure of the hedge fund Long-Term Capital Management (LTCM) in September 1998 will remain as a classic example of the need for financial institutions to understand the limitations of models.[23] It was a shock to the financial community not only because of the reputation of its principals (they included two Nobel laureates, and seasoned and star traders from the legendary bond arbitrage desk at Salomon Brothers), but also because of the unprecedented amounts of capital represented by the firm's positions. LTCM employed $125 billion in total assets, nearly four times the assets of the next largest hedge fund. LTCM's balance-sheet leverage was also quite high, with an equity base (before the crisis) of $4.8 billion, i.e., a leverage ratio of more than 25. Such a ratio, however, is perfectly in line with the capital structure of major investment banks' proprietary trading desks.

Then, on August 17, 1998, Russia devalued the ruble and declared a debt moratorium. This led to dramatic movements in markets around the world that generated large losses for the fund.

LTCM' s portfolio value fell 44 percent, giving it a year-to-date decline of 52 percent, i.e., a loss of almost $2 billion.[24] LTCM's positions in the market were so great that the Federal Reserve Bank of New York took the unprecedented step of facilitating a bailout of the fund by a consortium of 14 leading banks and investment houses to avoid any risk of a meltdown in the world markets.[25] No public money was spent on the recapitalization.

How could a market event, however serious, have affected LTCM so badly? LTCM's arbitrage strategy was based on "market neutral" or "relative value" trading, which involves buying one instrument and simultaneously selling another. These trades are designed to make money whether prices rise or fall, as long as the spread between the two positions moves in the appropriate direction. According to Stulz (2000), LTCM told its investors that it was targeting the volatility of the fund to be roughly 20 percent per annum. Until August 1998 its volatility was consistently below its target.

LTCM, like other funds in early 1998, was betting that the spreads between corporate bonds and government Treasuries in different countries, such as the United States and the United Kingdom, were too large and would eventually return to their normal range (as they always had before). A trade to capture such "relative value" opportunities might consist of buying corporate bonds and selling short the relevant government bond. When the spread in yields narrows, the position makes money whether the price level goes up or down.[26]

Another relative value trade consisted of buying what are known as "off-the-run" Treasuries (30-year securities that have less than 30 years to their maturity date) and shorting "on-the-run" Treasuries (newly minted 30-year bonds). This strategy was designed to exploit the difference in liquidity, rather than any difference in credit quality.

Other relative value trades involved betting on convergence in the key European bond markets by selling German government bonds against the sovereign debt of other countries, such as Spain and Italy, which were due to sign up for European economic and monetary union (EMU).

The return of these apparently low-risk strategies is quite small, and it becomes smaller and smaller as more players enter the market to take advantage of the "opportunity." As a result, hedge funds are obliged to use leverage aggressively to boost their absolute performance.

Leverage can be achieved using different financing strategies. For relative value trades where you are long one asset, say the off-the-run bond, and short another one, say the on-the-run bond, financing with zero cash investment can be achieved either by pledging the long bond, or through the repo-reverse repo market.[27] Both strategies, however, have significantly different impacts on the size of the institution's balance sheet. In order to achieve the objective of shorting $100 of the on-the-run bond and buying the nearby off-the-run bond through the repo-reverse repo market, one would balloon the balance sheet by $200 worth of footings. One can achieve the same arbitrage objective by pledging $100 of the off-the-run bond against the borrowing of $100 of the on-the-run bond with half the footings of the repo-reverse repo trade.

This example illustrates how the traditional analysis of the riskiness of a financial institution in terms of "beauty contest" ratios such as a leverage ratio is flawed. The leverage ratio does not tell you anything about the risk of the position. What matters is the volatility of the residual equity. This was precisely the focus of LTCM. It is also the focus the VaR approach presented in Chapter 5.

Two categories of models are used to support market neutral strategies: (1) models based on statistical relationship, and (2) structure models (see Section 2). Statistical models are based on identifying historical relationships between the prices of kindred assets, be they bonds, stocks, or currencies. Data reflecting several years of market behavior are fed into computers to explore the precise relationships between the prices of the various assets and their correlation structure.

LTCM failed because both its trading models and its risk management models unanticipated the vicious circle of losses at a time of an extreme crisis when volatilities rise dramatically, correlations among markets and instruments become closer to one, and liquidity dried up. Clearly, risk management systems at LTCM and at other sophisticated institutions underestimated risks during that period. The rumor is that many banks incurred substantial losses, but not as dramatic as LTCM because the size of their positions was smaller and their leverage was lower. Let us take a closer look at both these aspects.

Trading Models

> *"The other author of the Black-Scholes model was Fischer Black, who worked with me at Goldman. I was always told how our model showed that one of our positions would be going up while another was going down. But when trouble came, all those positions went in one direction, which was down."*
>
> Treasury Secretary Robert Rubin, New York Post, October 4, 1998

Price relationships that hold during normal market conditions tend to collapse during market crises such as that of August 1998.[28] The crisis in Russia made many investors fear that other nations might follow Russia's lead and that there would be a general dislocation of the financial markets. Already Malaysia had applied rigid controls that prevented foreign investors from withdrawing their money. This triggered a "flight to quality," or "flight to safety," as investors exited the emerging markets, and any risky security, and fled to the liquid and safe haven of the U.S. and German government bond markets. Risk premium for bonds, worldwide, increased substantially during this crisis.

Once it started, this flight to quality propagated as a chain reaction, ultimately pushing the U.S. 30-year government bond's yield to as low as 5 percent and causing the price of riskier bonds, including those of emerging markets, U.S. mortgage-backed securities,[29] high-yield, and even investment-grade corporate bonds to sink. The same phenomena affected the relative yields of German and Italian bonds: Yields started to diverge because German bonds were regarded as safer than Italian bonds. Credit spreads widened as prices for Treasury bonds increased and prices for lower-quality bonds sank—in an unprecedented fashion.

When spreads widened, the gains a trader might make on short positions were not always enough to offset the losses on the long positions. In some instances, both sides of the relative trades ended up losing money. Lenders started to demand more collateral, forcing the funds either to abandon their arbitrage plays or to raise money for the margin calls by selling other holdings at fire-sale prices.

Most of the losses incurred by LTCM were the consequence of the breakdown of the correlation and volatility patterns that had been observed in the past. Several mechanisms came into play during this market turmoil as a consequence of the flight to quality and the disappearance of liquidity:[30]

1. Interest rates on Treasuries and stock prices fell in tandem, because investors deserted the stock market and purchased U.S. government bonds in a flight to quality.

2. When liquidity simultaneously dries out in many markets, it becomes impossible to unwind positions. Portfolios that seem to be well diversified across markets start to behave as if they are highly concentrated in a single market, and market-neutral positions become directionally exposed (usually to the wrong side of the market). LTCM was well diversified across markets, but diversification under normal conditions turned out to be very limited at time of crisis. Most of LTCM's trading positions were taken in the belief that spreads for liquidity risk, credit risk, and volatility risk were too high as compared to historical standards.

For all these reasons, LTCM found itself losing money on many of its trading positions and became insolvent. The fact that the fund was highly leveraged contributed to its problems. While LTCM never ran out of cash, the continuous decline in its net asset value (NAV) threatened at some point the solvency of the firm, as the value of the firm's liabilities could have exceeded the value of its assets. To keep the firm solvent, a number of major financial institutions were obliged to inject additional collateral.[31]

Risk Measurement Models and Stress Testing

"We recognize that stress testing is a developing discipline, but it is clear that adequate testing was not done with respect to the financial conditions that precipitated Long-Term Capital's problems. Effective risk management in a financial institution requires not only modeling, but models that can test the full range of financial transactions across all kinds of adverse market developments. Whether such models existed and, if so, whether they were not effective, are issues that we need to address."

William McDonough, President of the Federal Reserve Bank of New York before the Committee on Banking and Financial Services, U.S. House of Representatives, October 1, 1998.

Risk control at LTCM relied on a value-at-risk (VaR) model. As discussed in Chapter 5, VaR represents the worst case loss that can result from the portfolio of a firm under normal market conditions, at a given confidence level, and over a given period of time. By themselves, a \$1 trillion notional amount, or even a figure of \$125 billion in assets, do not say much about the level of risk that the LTCM positions involved. What matters is the overall volatility of the marked-to-market value of the fund, i.e., its VaR.

According to LTCM, the fund was structured so that the risk of investing in it should have been no greater than investing in the S&P 500. The average annual volatility of the S&P 500 over the last 10 years has been 15 percent, which translates for a fund with equity of \$4.7 billion to a daily volatility of:[32]

$$\$4700 * 0.15/\sqrt{252} = \$44 \text{ million}$$

While hedge funds are not under any obligation to satisfy minimum regulatory capital requirements, it is interesting to consider how this level of risk relates to the BIS 98 requirements.

At first sight, the situation seems consistent with the BIS 98 regulatory capital rules, where regulatory capital over a 10-day period would be for LTCM:[33]

$$\$44 * 2.33 * \sqrt{10} = \$993 \text{ million}$$

This number is calculated under the assumption that the portfolio returns are normally distributed and to confidence level of 99 percent, i.e., a daily VaR of 2.33 times the daily volatility. This result seems to be secured rather well by the initial capital figure of \$4.7 billion.

However, some assumptions that are usual in regulatory VaR calculations are not realistic for a hedge fund:

1. The horizon for economic capital should be the time it takes to raise new capital, or the period of time over which a crisis scenario will unfold. Based on the experience of LTCM, 10 days is clearly too short a horizon for the derivation of the VaR. When a crisis hits the global markets, liquidity dries up for a period that is longer than 10 days. Highly leveraged institutions cannot expect to gain access to fresh funds in such an environment.

2. Liquidity risk is not factored into traditional static VaR models. VaR models assume that normal market conditions prevail and that these exhibit perfect liquidity. During market turmoil, however, liquidity dries up and positions can only be unwound at fire-sale prices if a fund requires cash to meet its margin calls. All this implies that risk management models should be revised to include liquidity risk and bid-offer behavior.[34]

3. Correlation and volatility risks can only be captured through stress testing. For a hedge fund whose strategy is mainly based on relative value trading, correlation risk dominates any directional risks during a market crisis. LTCM also stress-tested its trading positions but no one had simulated an extreme "flight to quality" scenario, under which correlation patterns broke down and credit spreads widened.

Before the main crisis, but after LTCM had experienced a 16 percent drop in asset value during May and June 1998, the portfolio had been restructured to reduce its daily volatility from $45 million to $35 million. Unfortunately, as a result of the restructuring, the portfolio became much more illiquid. Instead of the envisaged $35 million daily volatility, the fund eventually experienced a $100 million and higher daily volatility. Something was clearly wrong in the way the firm was modeling risk.

LTCM partly recognized liquidity risk in its stress testing by using correlations that were greater than historical correlations (Stulz 2000). But it underestimated the impact of its imitators who, by their herd behavior, amplified price movements. As LTCM was moving out of its positions, its imitations would follow suit.

5. WHAT CAN MARKET RISK MANAGEMENT DO TO MITIGATE MODEL RISK?

Vetting the models that a trading firm uses has become a key corporate governance function. Vetting should be complemented by an independent oversight of the profit and loss (P&L) calculation.

5.1 Vetting

The role of vetting is to offer assurance to the firm's management that any model proposed by, say, a trading desk, for the valuation of a given security, is reasonable. In other words, that the model is likely to offer a good representation of how the market itself values the instrument. In addition, it should check that the implementation that is being proposed is a faithful representation of this model.

Vetting should consist of the following phases:

1. *Documentation.* Risk managers should ask for a full documentation of the model, including both the assumptions underlying the model and its mathematical expression. This should be independent of any particular implementation, such as a spreadsheet or a C++ computer code. The documentation must be stated in sufficient detail so that, in principle, the risk manager can implement the model so as to produce the same prices and hedge ratios as the model, using the same inputs.

Specifically, the documentation should include:

- The term sheet or, equivalently, a complete description of the transaction.
- A mathematical statement of the model, which should include:

  An explicit statement of all the components of the model: stochastic variables and their processes, parameters, equations, and so on.

  The pay-off function and/or any pricing algorithm for complex structured deals.

  The calibration procedure for the model parameters.

  The hedge ratios/sensitivities.

  Implementation features, i.e., inputs, outputs, and numerical methods employed (e.g., Levenberg-Marquardt, Crank-Nicholson, and so on).

  A working version of the implementation.

2. *Soundness of the model.* The risk manager needs to check that the mathematical model is a reasonable representation of the instrument. For example, the risk manager might accept the Black model for a short-term option on a long-maturity bond, but reject (without looking at the computer code) the use of this model to value a two-year option on a three-year bond. At this stage, the risk manager should concentrate on the finance aspects, and not become overly focused on the mathematics.

3. *Benchmark modeling.* The risk manager should develop a benchmark model based on the assumptions that are being made and on the specifications of the deal. Here, the risk manager may use a different implementation from the implementation that is being proposed. A proposed analytical model can be tested against a numerical approximation technique or against a simulation approach. For example, if the model to be vetted is based on a tree implementation, one may instead rely on the partial differential equation approach and use the finite element technique to derive the numerical results.

4. *Check results and stress test the model.* Compare the results of the benchmark test with those of the proposed model. Also make sure that the model possesses the basic properties that all derivatives models should possess, such as put-call parity and other nonarbitrage conditions. Finally, stress test the model, by looking at some limit scenarios, in order to identify the range of parameter values for which the model provides accurate pricing. This is especially important for implementations that rely on numerical techniques.

5.2 Models Database and Financial Rates Database

Each model should be well documented and the middle office should know precisely which model to associate with each deal for revaluation at the end of the day. In addition the middle office must have access to an independent risk management financial rates database to facilitate independent parameter estimation.

5.3 Position the Market Risk Management Function to Avoid the "Tinkerbell" Syndrome

Large trading profits, leading to large bonuses for senior managers, create an incentive for these managers to believe the traders that are reporting the profits, rather than the risk managers that are questioning the reported profits. This phenomenon tends to persist even when the circumstances develop in such a way as to strain the credulity of the senior managers. The psychology of this behavior is such that we are tempted to call it the "Tinkerbell" phenomenon, after the scene in *Peter Pan* in which the children in the audience shout, "I believe, I believe" in order to revive the poisoned fairy Tinkerbell.

Tinkerbell I: Orange County, 1994
At the beginning of 1994, Robert Citron, the treasurer of Orange County, managed a fund that had been rated as the top-performing local authority fund in the United States for four years in a row. His opponent in the reelection campaign immediately before disaster struck pointed out that Mr. Citron's strategy of investing in structured notes and using reverse repurchase agreements to provide additional leverage was likely to create serious losses if interest rates rose. Mr. Citron scoffed at this concern, and the Orange County board of supervisors, trusting Mr. Citron, chose to ignore the warning. After losing more than $1.5 billion when interest rates rose in 1994, Mr. Citron resigned, stating that he was relatively unskilled in finance and had been misled by his bankers. *The New York Times* summarized the situation in the following headline: "What Orange County Needed Was Oversight."

Tinkerbell II: Kidder Peabody, 1995
The Kidder Peabody saga described below is all based on newspapers' reports. This case has never been resolved in court and, hence, Mr. Jett has not been proven guilty of any crime. According to the reports, after Mr. Joseph Jett was promoted to head trader on the government desk, he reported over $300 million in profits, made by stripping and reassembling U.S. treasury bonds. This "arbitrage" profit was later claimed to be the artifact of a glitch in Kidder's accounting system. When Barry Finer, the risk manager for the government desk, pointed out the difficulty of making large arbitrage profits in the most efficiently traded bond market in the world, his concerns were dismissed out of hand, and he was reassigned. Because the accounting profits created were transitory, Jett was accused of continually increasing the size of his trades so as to ensure that his reported profits were not re-

versed. His trades are said to have become so large that, after a year, his positions exceeded 100 percent of the amount outstanding for each of three treasury bonds (with a high of 218 percent). This attracted the attention of the internal auditors. The discovery of the illusory profits played a part in the later demise of Kidder Peabody.

Tinkerbell III: Barings, 1995

After moving to Singapore in June 1993 as local head of operations, Nick Leeson started to execute trades for Barings' clients on Simex. He then received permission to implement an arbitrage strategy that was designed to exploit any differences between the prices for the Nikkei futures contract in Singapore and Osaka.

Since he still controlled the Singapore back office, he was able to use a reconciliation account, #88888 (which he arranged to be excluded from reports sent to London), to convert an actual loss of £200 million in 1994 into a sizeable reported profit. His reported profit was so large that it attracted the attention of Barings' London-based risk controllers in late 1994. However, their inquiries to his superiors were rebuffed with the comment that "Barings had a unique ability to exploit this arbitrage."

After he reported a £10 million profit for one week in January 1995, risk control concerns were summarily dismissed with the comment that, "Nick is a turbo-arbitrageur." Simple calculations show that, in order to make this profit, Leeson would have had to trade more than four times the total volume in the Nikkei futures contract in both Singapore and Osaka that week.

6. CONCLUSIONS

Trading in derivatives necessarily involves the heavy use of complex mathematical models to value positions and to understand price relationships and risk exposures. These models represent a compromise between realism and tractability.

In summary, our recommendations for managing model risk are:

- *Be aware of it.* Model risk is inherent in the use of models. Prudence dictates that firms avoid placing undue faith in model values, and that they make themselves aware of possible sources of inaccuracies in a model and think through situations in which the failure of a model might have a significant impact.

- *Estimate model risk quantitatively.* Model performance can be simulated using historical data. Managers should take care at each point that they are conducting an out-of-sample test, using only data that would have been available to a model user at the time. Stress testing should be used to examine possible inaccuracies in valuation models, both as to parameter values and model structure.
- *Reevaluate models periodically.* Also, reestimate parameters using best-practice statistical procedures.
- *Build a formal treatment of model risk into the overall risk management procedures.* Experience shows that simple but robust models tend to work better than more ambitious, but fragile, models. It is essential to monitor and control model performance over time.

NOTES

1. See *International Financing Review*, No. 1213, December 13, 1997, p. 6.
2. For example, IBM in June 2000 announced that they have developed a supercomputer, that processes 12,300 billion calculations per second. ASCI is three times more powerful than the fastest computer to date, and 1,000 times faster than the "Big Blue" chess-playing computer that defeated world chess master Gary Kasparov in 1999.
3. See *Global Investor*: "Can traders blow up banks?," February 1994.
4. A swap can also be viewed as an interest rate derivative.
5. See also Chapter 1, Section 4.
6. See Bensoussan, Crouhy, and Galai (1994)
7. See Bollerslev, Engle, and Nelson (1994) for a tutorial on GARCH-type models.
8. See, for example, Duan (1995).
9. See, for example, Figlewski (1998).
10. A simple arithmetic error, where a program tried to put a 64-bit number into a 16-bit space, caused an explosion in the Arianne 5

European Agency rocket shortly after takeoff. This destroyed a $7 billion investment and 10 years of work.

11. The same arguments also apply to correlations.
12. See Press et al. (1992).
13. See also Kupiec (1995).
14. See *The Economist,* January 24, 1998, p. 92.
15. See Leong (1992).
16. See Burghardt and Hanweck (1993) and Crouhy and Galai (1995).
17. We thank Lee Wakeman for his useful insights on this section.
18. See Walwyn and Byres (1997).
19. His acclaimed book, *The Education of a Speculator* (1997), became a national bestseller in the United States just before his hedge fund was liquidated. *Barron's* magazine even wrote ". . . this (book) is pure nectar for those who aim for consistently superior stock market performance."
20. See *Derivatives Strategy* 3(1), pp. 38–39.
21. The concomitant fall of LTCM is also somewhat related to the same political risk (see Section 4.10).
22. Many comments and articles have been published in the financial press which often provide a distorted and misleading story of LTCM. For an informative account of LTCM's trading strategies, its risk management, and the events in 1998 that led to the fall of LTCM, see Perold (1999), Mackenzie (2000), and Stulz (2000). See also Dunbar (2000).
23. Hedge fund is the denomination attributed to levered speculative funds. It is quite misleading since originally most of these investment funds were specialized in arbitrage trades to take advantage of mispricing opportunities between related markets. The return on each individual trade usually being modest, these funds are able to derive high returns only by leveraging their positions. According to the Securities and Exchange Commission (SEC), there were 140 funds operating in 1968. There are now approximately 3000 hedge funds (Report of the President's Working Group on Financial Markets [1999]). The investment philosophy of these funds has changed over the years. Today hedge funds are pools of aggressively managed money which actively speculate with high leverage in any market, or any security, which they think is not priced correctly, or for which they anticipate dramatic changes in the future (for structural and macroeconomic reasons). There are three main families of funds. "Global macrofunds" take positions based on their

forecasts of global macroeconomic developments. "Event-driven funds" invest in specific securities related to such events as bankruptcies, reorganizations, and mergers. Finally, "market-neutral hedge funds" implement relative value trading strategies and seek to profit by taking offsetting positions in two assets whose price relationship is expected to move in a favorable direction.

24. First, Russia suspended bond and currency trading on August 14 (see Section 4.6). Note that LTCM losses were not from holding ruble-bond positions (Stulz 2000).

25. Analysts say that this type of rescue falls under the "too big to fail" doctrine, or perhaps more appropriately, the "too big to fail immediately" doctrine (whereby enough time is allowed to arrange a nondisruptive burial or restructuring of the institution). As someone once said, "capitalism without failures and bankruptcies is like Christianity without hell."

26. Note that LTCM was hedging any credit risk exposure by shorting shares of the relevant stock.

27. Leverage is achieved by borrowing the bond that is shorted in the repo (or repurchase) market, and lending the bond that is long through a sale-repurchase agreement with banks and broker-dealers. (Under a "repo" agreement, an asset is sold for cash and a promise is made to buy it back at a prearranged price on some future date.) Normally, broker-dealers require collateral that is worth slightly more than the cash loaned, by an amount known as the "haircut." This is designed to provide a buffer against any fall in the value of the collateral. In the case of LTCM, however, the fund was able to obtain haircuts of almost zero, as it was widely viewed as safe by the institutions that were its lenders. The total haircut for LTCM's $110 billion in borrowing was reported to be around $500 million. When the collateral loses value the dealers call the borrower for additional cash collateral, or what are known as "margin calls." For these highly levered institutions, the only way to satisfy these margin calls is through the sale of securities. Lenders are particularly at risk when liquidity dries up and securities have to be sold at fire-sale prices, as this may precipitate the entire liquidation of the fund.

28. Although they tend to come back when markets return to normal. The best strategy, then, is to hold on to the positions—provided the fund has enough capital to meet its margin calls. As a matter of fact, the 14 banks participating in the bailout provided liquidity of 3.65 billion dollars, on which they earned 10 percent by the time the fund was dissolved in December 1999 (Stulz 2000).

29. The fall in the yield on U.S. Treasuries led to a fall in the interest rate for mortgages, leading to massive prepayments, and pushing down the prices of some mortgage-backed securities.

30. See the quotation above from Treasury Secretary Robert Rubin, *New York Post*, October 4, 1998.

31. See Chapter 2, Section 5.2.

32. See Jorion (1999).

33. See Chapter 2. According to Stulz (2000), the one-month VaR at the 5 percent confidence level, for an equity of 4.7 billion dollars, and annualized volatility of 20 percent, is 448 million dollars.

34. See Chapter 5, the discussion on the challenges in modeling liquidity risk, and Bangia et al. (1999).

CHAPTER 16

Risk Management in Nonbank Corporations

1. INTRODUCTION

While academics discuss whether nonfinancial corporations *should* manage financial risk, many corporations are already engaged in risk management activities. Nance, Smith, and Smithson (1993) surveyed 169 large firms to find out what determined their hedging policy. The study found a significant relationship between the use of derivatives and tax and dividend policies. Dolde (1993) also surveyed Fortune 500 companies, and found that 85 percent of the responding firms had used derivatives. Larger firms tended to use derivatives more than the smaller firms in the sample.

A survey conducted by the Wharton School and Chase Manhattan Bank (1995) found that more than a third of the responding companies used derivatives. This percentage of usage increased sharply among larger firms (those with a market value greater than $250 million), with 65 percent of this group responding positively. Most firms (75 percent) that made use of derivatives employed them for hedging specific transactions and contractual commitments, and 40 percent of firms used them to hedge positions on their balance sheets.

The striking difference in risk management between banks and nonbank corporations (NBCs) is that banks are regulated and are required by their regulators to manage their credit, market, and operational risks, and to hold sufficient capital against their risk positions. NBCs are not subject to similar regulation and are not required to hold minimal capital (insurance companies and investment banks are an exception to this rule in many countries).

While NBCs (or nonfinancial corporations, to be more accurate) are not required to hold minimum levels of capital, a recent initiative of the Securities and Exchange Commission (SEC) in the United States requires all publicly traded companies to disclose their risk management policies, and also to present a quantification of their exposure to market risk (see Section 5). The issue of risk management in NBCs is gaining momentum, and demanding the attention of corporate management, as well as that of participants in the investment industry. The process is feeding off the advances in risk management made by the banking industry, the expansion of financial markets, and the range of financial instruments now available to hedge risks. A contributing factor is the concern that boards of directors are beginning to show with regard to internal management procedures and controls; board members know that they may be held liable if the firm is exposed to undue risk through bad risk management practices.

In Section 2 we discuss in detail the pros and cons of modern risk management techniques as applied to NBCs. It should be remembered, however, that risk management in the widest sense is not new. All businesses are exposed to business risk. Earnings go up and down due to changes in the business environment, changes in the nature of the competition, changes in production functions due to new technologies, or changes in factors affecting suppliers. Firms do not sit idle when confronted with such business risks, but respond in various ways. For example, they may hold inventories of raw materials in case of unexpected interruptions in supply. They may also hold inventories of finished products to accommodate unexpected increases in demand. Another risk reduction strategy is to sign long-term supply contracts at a fixed price, or to negotiate long-term contracts with significant clients. Many horizontal and vertical mergers are intended to reduce uncertainties, and not necessarily to enhance value.

Another example of risk reduction is the purchase of property insurance, even at a price that is higher than the expected value of the potential damage that may occur if the risk materializes (as assessed in actuarial terms). Very few researchers have questioned the rationale of purchasing property insurance, which itself raises an interesting question: What is the difference between an insurance contract and a put option? Academic researchers have proposed various answers (e.g., Stulz 1996).

We believe that the relevant question is not whether corporations should engage in risk management but, rather, how they can manage risk in a rational way. Each firm has to consider which risks to accept, and which to hedge—as well as the price that it is willing to pay to manage those risks. In Section 3 we discuss in detail the procedure for risk management in a corporation. We emphasize the need to clarify objectives and to set goals to be achieved within a given time horizon and budget.

In Section 4 we discuss some new accounting standards that have been introduced to deal with the derivative and hedging activities of corporations. Section 5 summarizes the disclosure requirements now imposed by the SEC on all publicly traded companies, and looks at some of the results.

2. WHY MANAGE RISKS?

2.1 Why Firms Might Not Want to Manage Their Risks

Among economists and academic researchers, the starting point to this discussion is the perfect capital market (PCM) assumption. This states that, if markets are perfect, then financial risk management in the form of hedging activity cannot increase a firm's value. The assertion is based on a famous analysis by Modigliani and Miller (1958), which shows that the value of a firm under the PCM assumption cannot be changed merely by means of financial transactions. The economic reasoning is that whatever the firm can accomplish in the financial markets, the individual investor in the firm can also accomplish (or unwind) on the same terms and conditions. The markets are assumed to be "perfect" in the sense that they are taken to be highly competitive and that participants are not subject to transaction costs, commissions, contracting and information costs, or taxes.

This line of reasoning also lies behind the work of Sharpe (1964) and his capital asset pricing model (CAPM). In his work, Sharpe establishes that in a world with PCM, firms should not worry about their specific (or idiosyncratic) risk, and should base their investment decisions on their systematic (or beta) risk. All specific risks, according to this theory, are diversified away in the investors' portfolios, and the diversification is costless.[1]

The perfect capital market assumption, and all financial models that are based on this assumption, lead to the conclusion that firms should not engage in any risk reduction activity that individual investors can execute on their own (without any disadvantage due to economies of scale, for example). However, the models do not imply that risk reduction activity that has synergies with the operations of the firm should be avoided. For example, by hedging the price of a commodity that is an input to its production process, a firm can stabilize its costs and hence also its pricing policy. This may allow it to achieve a competitive advantage in the marketplace. Such an advantage cannot be replicated by the outside investor.

Another concern raised by those opposed to active risk management by NBCs is that "hedging is a zero-sum game and cannot increase earning or cash flows. Reducing volatility through hedging simply moves earnings and cash flows from one year to another" (Ralfe 1996). This line of argument is implicitly based on the perfect capital market assumption that the prices of derivatives fully reflect their risk characteristics; therefore, using such instruments cannot increase the value of the firm in any lasting way. It implies that self-insurance is a more efficient strategy. Ralfe emphasizes this point by arguing that trading in derivatives is a negative-sum game due to the transaction costs.

One additional argument against risk hedging is that it distracts management from their core business. Risk management requires certain skills and knowledge; it also requires infrastructure, data acquisition, and data processing. Especially in small and medium-sized corporations, management may lack the skills and time necessary to engage in such activity. Empirical evidence indicates that small firms are indeed less engaged in hedging than larger corporations. Nevertheless, one can argue that these small firms should outsource their risk management to professional firms that would act on their behalf with dealers.

As a final point, following the new SEC disclosure requirements (see Section 5 of this chapter) and the new accounting standards, such as FAS 133 and IAS 32 (see Section 4), it can be argued that firms may avoid trading in derivatives in order to reduce the cost of compliance, or to protect the confidential information that might be revealed by their forward transactions (e.g., the scale of sales they envisage in certain currencies). In some cases, given the new standards, economic hedging might act to increase the earnings variability as recorded in the firm's accounts, and therefore may reduce the demand for hedging.

2.2 The Reason for Managing Risks

The traditional approach to explaining why corporations manage financial risks is to claim that firms hedge in order to reduce the chance of default and to reduce the cost of financial distress (e.g., Smith and Stulz 1985). The argument arises out of a market "imperfection," in that there are fixed costs associated with financial distress. This suggests that smaller firms should have a greater incentive to hedge (Nance et al. 1993); as previously noted, however, smaller firms tend to avoid hedging activity.

A related argument is that managers act in their own self-interest. Since they may not otherwise be able to diversify the personal wealth that they have accumulated (directly and indirectly) in their company, they have an incentive to reduce volatility (Stulz 1984 and Santomero 1995). This approach is consistent with the "agency theory," and implicitly assumes that managers find it costly to diversify their risks in the marketplace. DeMarzo and Duffie (1992) support the self-interest argument, claiming that the observed results of a firm provide signals concerning the skills of its management.

An important argument in favor of hedging is that companies may be trying to reduce the cost of capital and enhance their ability to finance growth (e.g., Froot, Schafstein, and Stein 1993, 1994; Stulz 1990; and Santomezo 1995). Otherwise, in effect, a firm's volatile cash flows might lead it to reject investment opportunities. The debt capacity of the firm also may be adversely affected by high cash flow volatility.

Another line of argument in favor of hedging rests on the effect of a progressive tax rate (Santomero 1995, Smith and Stulz 1985, Stulz 1996). The idea is that volatile earnings induce higher taxation than stable earnings. Ralfe (1996) argues against this reasoning, pointing out that in many countries such an incentive does not exist. Berkman and Bradbury (1996) support this claim by pointing out that in New Zealand corporations are not subject to progressive taxation.

Stulz (1996) suggests a new line of reasoning. He proposes a model according to which the corporation hedges its downside risk, but preserves its ability to exploit profitable opportunities in relation to its comparative advantages and (possibly) its private information.

An empirical study by Géczy, Minton, and Schrand (1997) investigates why firms use currency derivatives. Rather than analyze questionnaires, the researchers looked at the characteristics of Fortune 500 nonfinancial corporations that in 1990 seemed potentially exposed to foreign currency risk (from foreign operations or from foreign-currency denominated debt). They found that approximately 41 percent of the firms in the sample (of 372 companies) had used currency swaps, forwards, futures, options, or combinations of these instruments. The major conclusion of the study was "that firms with greater growth opportunities and tighter financial constraints are more likely to use currency derivatives." They explain this as an attempt to reduce fluctuations in cash flow, so as to be able to raise capital for growth opportunities.

2.3 Hedging Operations versus Hedging Financial Positions

When discussing whether corporations should hedge, it is important to look at the components of risk. First, we should make a clear distinction between hedging activities related to the operations of the firm and hedging related to the balance sheet (Briys and Crouhy 1993).

If a company chooses to hedge activities related to its operations, such as hedging the cost of raw materials (e.g., gold for a jewelry manufacturer), this clearly has implications for its ability to compete in the marketplace. The hedge has both a size and a price effect; i.e., it might affect both the price and the amount of products sold. Obviously, such effects cannot be replicated by an outside investor using its investment account. Again, when an American manufacturing company buys components from a

French company, it can choose whether to fix the price in French francs or in U.S. dollars. If the French company insists on fixing the price in French francs, the American company can opt to avoid the foreign currency risk by hedging it. This is basically an operational consideration, outside the scope of the CAPM model, or the perfect capital market assumption.

In a similar way, if a company exports its products to foreign countries, then the pricing policy for each market is an operational issue. For example, suppose that an Israeli high-tech company in the telecommunication business is submitting a bid to supply equipment in Germany over a period of three years, at predetermined prices in deutsche marks. If most of the high-tech firm's costs are in dollars, then it is very natural for the company to hedge the future deutsche mark revenues against the dollar expenses. Why should the company retain a risky position in the currency markets?

It should be remembered that uncertainty takes up management attention. Moreover, uncertainty makes planning more difficult, and makes the optimization of operations and processes more complicated. It is generally accepted that companies should concentrate on business areas in which they have comparative advantages, and avoid areas where they cannot add value. It follows that reducing risk in the production process and in selling activities is usually advisable.

The story is quite different when we turn to the problem of the balance sheet of the firm. Why should a firm try to hedge the interest rate risk on its loan? Why should it swap a fixed rate for a variable rate, for example? In this case, the perfect capital market assumption suggests that the firm should not hedge. However, if we believe financial markets are perfect, we might argue that investors' interests are unlikely to be much harmed by any derivative trading. The trading, in such a case, is a "fair game." Nobody will lose from the activity, providing the firm's policy is fully transparent and is disclosed to all investors.

Conversely, if one argues that financial markets are not perfect, then the firm may have some advantage in hedging its balance sheet. It may have economies of scale, and sometimes it may have access to better information than investors.

Our conclusion is that firms should manage the risk of their operations. Firms might also engage in hedging their assets and liabilities so long as they disclose their hedging policy. In any case, whether or not it makes use of derivative instruments, the firm must make risk management decisions. The decision not to hedge is also, in effect, a decision.

3. PROCEDURE FOR RISK MANAGEMENT

As other chapters of this book have described, risk management in banks has developed over a long period of time and with the active involvement of the regulators.

In this section, we look at how an NBC might establish a clear policy for risk management.

3.1 Determining the Objective

A corporation should not engage in risk management before deciding clearly on its objectives in terms of risk and return. Without clear goals, fully reviewed and accepted by the board of directors, management is at risk of engaging in inconsistent, costly activities to hedge an arbitrary set of risks, with no obvious benefit to the firm and its owners.

First of all, it should be decided whether the firm is concerned with its economic or its accounting profits. The two measures of profit do not necessarily coincide and their risk exposure is, at times, vastly different. Imagine a U.S. firm, purchasing a plant in the United Kingdom that will serve U.K. clients, for a sum of £1 million. The investment is financed with a £1 million loan from a British bank. From an economic point of view, the sterling loan backed by a plant in the United Kingdom is fully hedged. However, if the plant is owned and managed by the U.S. company ("long-arm test")[2], its value is immediately translated into U.S. dollars, while the loan is kept in pounds. Hence, the company's accounting profits are exposed to foreign exchange risk. If the pound is more expensive, in terms of the dollar, at the end of the year, the accounts will be adjusted for these financial costs and will show a reduction in profits.

Should the U.S. company hedge this kind of accounting risk? If it buys a futures contract on the pound, its accounting exposure will be hedged, but the company will be exposed to economic risk! In this case, no strategy can protect both the accounting and economic risks simultaneously. It should be noted that while most managers claim that they are concerned with economic risk only, in practice many corporations, especially publicly traded corporations, hedge their accounting risks in order to avoid fluctuations in their reported earnings.

It should be the responsibility of the board to fully understand the impact of management policy to smooth accounting profits even at significant economic cost. Such a decision by senior management should be reviewed with the board, and conveyed to management as a guiding policy for management actions. If the board is concerned with economic risk instead, this policy should also be made clear, and a budget should be allocated.

Another important factor that should be made clear is the time horizon for any of the objectives set for management. Should hedging be planned to the end of the quarter, or the end of the accounting year? Should it be set three years into the future? It should be noted that hedging a future expected transaction with a long-term option or futures contract has both accounting and tax implications. For example, should the firm hedge a sales order from a French customer that will be delivered two years from now? Remember that the income will be allowed to enter the firm's books only upon delivery, while the futures contract will be marked-to-market at the end of each quarter.[3] (The derivatives contract may also incur a tax liability if, at the end of the tax year, it shows a profit.)

Any objectives that are set should not take the form of slogans, such as "maximum profit at minimal risk." Senior management should declare whether the aim is to hedge accounting profits or economic profits, short-term profits or long-term profits. Senior management should also consider which of the risks that the corporation is exposed to should be hedged, and which risks the company should assume as part of its business strategy. The objectives should be set in clear, executable directives. In addition, the criteria for examining whether the objectives are attained should be set in advance. A jewelry company may decide to fully hedge its gold inventory, or it may insure the price of gold below a certain level. By following such a policy, the company can remove the risk stemming from changes in raw material prices.

Usually, risk management analyzes risks individually, for example, interest rate risk or foreign exchange risk. An alternative approach is to look at the overall effect of risks on the profitability and the net worth of the corporation. As Meulbroek (2000) suggests, companies have three ways of implementing risk management objectives: modifying the firm's operations, adjusting its capital structure, or using targeted instruments. She knows how these three approaches can be considered on an integrated basis in order to better achieve the overall objective of the corporation. The integrated approach calls for strategic planning and not merely tactical planning.

It may make sense to make clear certain "risk limits," i.e., to allow management to operate within a given zone of prices and rates, and be exposed to the risk within the zone, but to disallow risk exposure beyond those limits. In such a case, the limits should be set clearly. For example, a British company might decide to avoid dollar exposures of above $5 million. It might also decide to tolerate fluctuations of the dollar rate within the exchange rate zone of $1.5 to $1.6 to the pound, but to hedge currency risks that fall outside these limits.

3.2 Mapping the Risks

After the objectives have been set, and the general nature of the risks to be managed is decided upon, it is essential to map the relevant risks and to estimate their current and future magnitudes.

For example, let us assume that senior management has decided not to hedge business risks due to its specific market situation and the nature of its competition, but to hedge currency risks arising from current positions and expected transactions in the next year. Now, the office of the chief financial officer (CFO) will have to map the specific risks likely to arise from exchange rate fluctuations. It should make a record of all assets and liabilities with values that are sensitive to exchange rate changes, and should classify all these positions in terms of the relevant currency. In addition, information from the sales or marketing division should be collected on firm orders from foreign clients for each currency that are due over the coming year, as well as expected orders from foreign clients that will need to be filled during this period. (A decision must be made about whether to hedge unconfirmed sales. It might be decided, for example, to base the hedge on expected revenues.)

FIGURE 16.1

Firm-Wide Approach to Risk Management

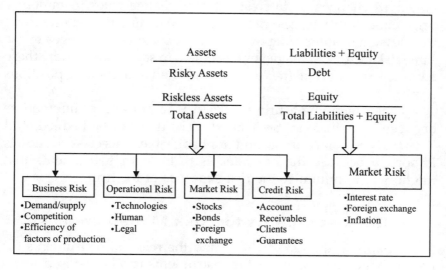

Then, all expected expenses over the coming year that are denominated in foreign currencies should be traced (with the help of the production division). Again, the firm will have to decide how it is going to distinguish between firm purchasing commitments and uncertain purchase orders. The timing of cash inflows and outflows can then be matched, for each foreign currency.

The same sort of mapping can be applied to other risk factors and risky positions, starting with the business risk of the firm, and moving to its market risks and credit risks. Operational risk elements should also be identified.

Figure 16.1 maps, in general terms, the risks of a firm, showing the risks stemming from the asset and operations side, and those due to the financial structure of the firm. Note that for banks, most of the risks on the asset side are credit risks and market risks, while general business and operational risks are of smaller importance. For NBCs, most of the risks on the assets side are business and operational risks, whereas credit and market risks are relatively less important.

In some firms the exposure to credit risk can be substantial, especially if the firm owns corporate bonds, offers loans or credit to other firms, or has entered into derivative transactions with counterparties of relatively low credit quality.

From 1998 the SEC has required publicly traded companies to assess and quantify their exposure to financial instruments that are linked to changes in interest rates, exchange rates, commodity prices, and equity prices. However, the SEC does not require firms to assess their underlying or "natural" exposure to changes in the same risk factors. Management, needless to say, cannot ignore these natural positions, whether they are matched to derivative positions or not.[4]

When mapping a firm's risks, it is important to differentiate between risks that can be insured, risks that can be hedged, and risks that are noninsurable and nonhedgeable. This classification is important because the next step is to look for instruments that might help to minimize the risk exposure of the firm.

3.3 Instruments for Risk Management

After mapping the risks we can find the relevant instruments for risk management. Some of the instruments can be devised internally. For example, a U.S. firm with many assets denominated in British pounds can borrow money in pounds and achieve a natural hedge (at least, an economic hedge, though not necessarily an accounting hedge, as discussed above). One division with a deutsche mark liability may be hedged internally against another division with deutsche mark denominated assets. Therefore, internal opportunities should be considered first.

Next, competing offers to insure any risks identified as insurable in the risk mapping process need to be collected. It should be remembered that, generally, trying to sell risks in order to avoid them is a costly activity. Therefore, management should evaluate each activity that can be insured and make a decision based on costs and benefits. The firm might decide to fully insure some risks, partially insure others, and refrain from insuring some insurable risks. Many well-diversified companies, operating in many different geographical areas, opt to self-insure their property (including cars, plants, and equipment).

There are plenty of financial instruments for hedging risks. A distinction should be made between exchange-traded instruments and over-the-counter (OTC) instruments. The exchange-traded instruments are based on a limited number of underlying assets and are standardized, meaning that their striking prices and maturities are well defined and are set in advance by the exchanges. OTC products are issued by commercial and investment banks and thus can be tailored to customers' needs. For example, an OTC option on the British pound can be customized to the size and maturity that fits the needs of the customer, and to a striking price that suits the client's strategy. However, exchange-traded instruments have some key advantages: their price is relatively transparent, and they are often highly liquid.

The active markets for exchange-traded instruments in the United States are mainly the Chicago Board Options Exchange (CBOE), which offers active markets in equity and index options; the Philadelphia Options Exchange, which is the leader in foreign exchange options; the Chicago Board of Trade (CBOT), which runs huge markets in futures on stock indexes, bonds, and major commodities; the Chicago Mercantile Exchange (CME), with major markets in currency futures; and the International Monetary Market (IMM), with options trading on futures on foreign currencies and on bonds and interest rates. There are also active markets for options and futures in London (LIFFE), Paris (MATIF), Frankfurt, and Zurich (EUREX), and in most major countries and financial centers.[5]

The variety of exchange and, especially, OTC instruments is huge. In fact, investment bankers are willing to price almost any possible derivative based on known, traded underlying financial instruments. This leaves the corporate hedger with the considerable problem of identifying the most suitable instruments to hedge the specific risky positions of his or her firm, taking into consideration cost and liquidity. Another concern in the OTC market is the credit risk associated with the counterparty to each contract.

3.4 Constructing and Implementing a Strategy

The office of the CFO must have access to all the relevant corporate information, market data, and statistical tools and models. The firm will need to select certain pricing and hedging models to help in the formation of the strategy. A firm can opt to purchase statistical estimates and/or models from external vendors. However, the officers in charge of risk management must have a deep understanding of the tools they are about to employ to reach rational decisions.

A key decision is whether to hedge risks by means of "static" strategies or whether to plan more dynamic strategies. In a static strategy, a hedging instrument is purchased against the risky position and is maintained for as long as the risky position exists. This kind of strategy is relatively easy to implement and monitor.

Dynamic strategies involve an ongoing series of trades that are used to calibrate the combined exposure and the derivative position. This strategy calls for much greater managerial efforts in implementing and monitoring the positions, and may incur higher transaction costs. For example, suppose that a U.S. company exporting to France is expecting to receive five million French francs three months from today, and wishes to hedge the downside risk, i.e., the risk that the dollar will devalue against the franc. It could simply follow the static strategy of buying a put option for the full quantity and term of the exposure.

To hedge dynamically, the firm might buy a long-term put option (if it is relatively underpriced compared to shorter-term puts) and adjust the quantity of the put so that it exhibits the same delta values as the put option in the static strategy. The dynamic strategy may require the hedger to adjust the put position on a daily or weekly basis and to increase or reduce the quantities of options, and possibly switch to other options with still lower relative risk premiums (maintaining the relevant hedge ratio through time). For example, long-maturity options often trade at a lower implied volatility, and thus cost. This approach means that the firm must have sophisticated and reliable models with which to trade in the markets and monitor its positions.

An important consideration in the hedging strategy is the planning horizon. The horizon can be fixed at the end of a quarter or the end of the tax year, or it might be a rolling horizon. Investment horizons should be made consistent with performance evaluations.

Other important considerations are accounting issues and potential tax effects. Accounting rules for derivatives are quite complex and are constantly being revised. Under the current rules, derivatives used for hedging must be perfectly matched to an underlying position (e.g., with regard to quantities and dates). They can then be reported together with the underlying risky positions. If the positions are not perfectly matched, the profit or loss for the derivative only will appear in the financial costs. Accounting rules affect how derivatives are presented in quarterly or end-of-year financial reports, and how they affect the profit and loss statement.

Tax considerations can be very important since they affect the cash flow of the firm. Different derivative instruments with different maturities may incur very different tax liabilities; tax treatment is also inconsistent from country to country. This means that a multinational corporation might find it advantageous to use derivatives in one country to hedge positions that are related to its business in another country. Professional advice on tax matters is a key factor when devising hedging strategies.

A strategy is only as good as its implementation. And however skillful the implementation, some deviation from the plan can be expected. Prices in the marketplace can change adversely and make some hedges unattractive. Since different people are often responsible within the firm for establishing risky positions and hedging positions, special care should be taken to monitor the positions. For example, if the French client in our earlier example in fact pays the firm after two, rather than three, months, then the three-month put must be liquidated before it matures.

3.5 Performance Evaluation

The corporate risk management system must be evaluated periodically. The evaluation should be based on the extent to which the overall goals were achieved, rather than on the basis of the profit or loss of specific derivative transactions. When a risky position is perfectly hedged, at the end of the hedging period one side of the hedged position inevitably shows a profit while the other side will show a loss. The problem is that the corporation can never know in advance which side will increase in value and which side will lose value. If the goal was to eliminate risk, and risk is eliminated, then the risk manager has done his job well.

It makes more sense to encourage the risk manager to save on the costs of hedging, and to reduce the tax payments due to derivatives. He should also act within a given budget; major deviations from the budget should be explored and explained.

When evaluating the performance of risk management, senior management should also decide whether or not to change its policy. There is nothing wrong with changing objectives, as long as the changes are based on thorough analysis and are consistent with the other activities of the firm. The new SEC requirements for the disclosure of risks (see Section 5) mean that policy changes in market risk management should be made public if the changes are material.

4. ACCOUNTING REPORTS

In Chapter 1 we discussed why accounting rules make it difficult to use accounting reports for risk assessment. The accountant's viewpoint is, in essence, retrospective; risk management is forward looking by nature.

Over the last few years, with the expansion in derivatives trading and hedging activities by corporations, accounting institutions have issued new rules and guidance about how corporations should report positions containing options and contingent positions, how to report on hedging activity, and when and how to recognize profits and losses. In this section we review some of the latest developments.

The adequacy of corporate disclosures about market risk became a major concern of the SEC during the 1990s. During 1994 and 1995 it studied approximately 500 firms and their annual financial reports. The review showed that the 1995 disclosures were more informative than the 1994 disclosures, due partly to the introduction of FAS 119, "Disclosure about Derivative Financial Instruments and Fair Value of Financial Instruments," in October 1994.

However, the SEC staff reviewing the annual reports also made the following observations:[6]

1. Footnote disclosures of accounting policies for derivatives were often too general to convey adequately the diversity in accounting that exists for derivatives. Thus, it often was difficult to determine the impact of derivatives on registrants' statements of financial positions, cash flows, and results of operations.

2. Disclosures about different types of market risk–sensitive instruments often were reported separately. Thus, it was difficult to assess the aggregate market risk exposures inherent in these instruments.

Disclosure about reported items in the footnotes to the financial statements, and selected financial data, may not have reflected adequately the effect of derivatives on such reported items. Thus, information about the reported items may have been incomplete and could be misleading.

4.1 IAS 32: "Financial Instruments: Disclosure and Presentation"

International Accounting Standard No. 32 ("IAS 32") of March 1995 deals with the presentation of financial instruments in the books of the company. First, it requires a company to clarify each instrument as an asset or a liability according to the terms of the instrument, and to maintain this classification over time. An instrument is classified as a liability if the firm is obligated to pay cash or kind (including in other financial instruments) to the counterparty. If the financial instrument is complex and contains, for example, liability and equity components (such as convertible bonds), the instrument should be broken down and the components should be classified separately. Netting of assets and liabilities is allowed only if offsetting can be legally enforced, or if the corporation will write off both asset and liability simultaneously.

IAS 32 also deals with disclosures. The corporation is required to disclose information for all financial instruments, both on- and off-balance-sheet, pertaining to the characteristics of the instruments and their size. In particular, the information should include material conditions that may impact timing, size, and uncertainties concerning future cash flows. The company should disclose the accounting policy and principles used in the reporting, including classification and measurement methods.

If financial instruments expose the firm, in a material way, to either market risk, credit risk, or liquidity risk, it should disclose information about these instruments, including their notional values, maturity dates, periodic payments (of dividends or interest), terms of options, etc. The disclosure should reveal relationships among various related instruments. The disclosure should also provide information on the assumptions made to determine the fair value of the instruments and how profits and losses are determined (either realized or unrealized). In some cases, the company should provide sensitivity analyses concerning the effect of changes in interest rates on its financial assets and liabilities.

It is recommended that corporations discuss their policy concerning the use of financial instruments, and the purpose of employing them. The discussion should include statements about the risk management policy of the firm, its hedging strategy, and how it copes with concentration risk. The standard recognizes the fact that some companies provide such information in their management review of the financial statement, rather than as footnotes to the financial statement.

IAS 32 requires firms to provide the fair value of financial instruments, both on- and off-balance-sheet. The fair value disclosure should be accompanied by an explanation of the methods and assumptions used in reaching the values. In some cases, for nontraded instruments, it may be advisable to provide a range of values rather than a single value. Where the fair value is below the book value, the company should explain why they have not adjusted the book value.

4.2 Financial Accounting Standard (FAS) 133

FAS 133, which deals with accounting procedures for derivatives and for hedging activities, was issued in June 1998. FAS 133 is a comprehensive treatment of the accounting rules concerning derivatives and hedging activities, and it will have profound impact on both financial and nonfinancial corporations.

The key principles underlying FAS 133 are:

- Derivative instruments represent rights and obligations, which characterize reported assets and liabilities.
- Fair value is the most appropriate measure for financial instruments in general, and for derivative instruments in particular.
- Only assets and liabilities should be reported as such in the financial reports.
- Special accounting rules can be applied to hedged items, but these are limited to "suitable" transactions. One criterion for judging whether a hedge is suitable is the assessment of the effectiveness of the offsetting changes in fair values or in cash flows due to the risk being hedged.

The Accounting Board demands that all derivatives should be reported on the balance sheet, based on their fair values. Recognition of losses or profits due to changes in fair values will depend on whether the derivative is approved for hedging. If it is not considered as a hedging tool, profits and losses of the derivative will be recognized on a quarterly basis, based on the change in value during the period without an offsetting profit or loss on the hedged item.

In the case of a derivative instrument that is used to hedge the fair value of an underlying position, only the net change in the fair value of the derivative and the underlying position is recognized in the profit and loss for the reporting period.

If cash flow is hedged, then the change in value of the hedging instrument is reported in a special capital account until the underlying position begins to affect the profit and loss statement. If the hedging is only partially effective, the ineffective part of the profit or loss from the derivative will be immediately assigned to the profit and loss account.

FAS 133 is applicable to the first-quarter report for the reporting year starting after June 15, 2000. Hence, annual reports submitted for 2000 must comply with FAS 133 in the first quarter of 2001. The new rules make a considerable difference to how hedging activities are reflected in accounting profits and losses. For example, it may be the case that static hedging positions will be adversely affected, in that such positions will introduce greater uncertainty to the accounting profit and loss statement.

FAS 133 contains extensive disclosure requirements, which replace those of FAS 80 and FAS 105 with respect to off-balance-sheet financial instruments, and instruments subject to credit risk, and replaces FAS 119 with regard to disclosures about derivatives and the fair values of financial instruments.

The new rules on disclosure encompass both qualitative and quantitative requirements. Companies are required to reveal their objectives in holding or issuing derivative instruments, as well as other instruments that can be used for hedging. Their reports should distinguish between tools to hedge fair values and cash flows, and highlight those used to hedge foreign currency exposures. The companies should describe their policies for the risk management of each type of risk, and their policy with regard to derivatives that are traded (i.e., not used for hedging purposes).

Each company should describe how it identifies, monitors, and manages risk. Also, it should provide information about the financial instruments that it uses to reduce risks and how these instruments are affecting the firm's risk exposure. It is expected that such disclosure will help the users of the financial reports to better understand the nature of the company's activities and be able to analyze the impact of such activity on the firm's value and on its future financial reports.

The quantitative information disclosed by the firm should help the analyst in determining whether the objectives of the management of the firm have been achieved. The nature of the quantitative disclosure is a function of the type of hedging activity. If derivatives are used to hedge fair value, then the information should include the profit or loss reported in the current period due to ineffective hedging or excess hedging. If the instruments are used to hedge cash flows, then, in addition, the report should include a description of transactions or events that may cause the firm to reclassify profits or losses within 12 months.

The company should also explain the time horizon it has adopted with regard to hedging the cash flows of upcoming transactions. The amount of profit and loss that is due to the termination of hedging activities in the current period should also be specified.

FAS 133 does not require companies to provide quantitative information about derivatives that are not used for hedging. Disclosure of such information is encouraged, but not required. More generally, companies are encouraged to provide any information that would help investors to better understand the policy and position of the company and its exposure to risks.

5. REPORTING REQUIREMENTS BY SECURITIES AUTHORITIES

5.1 The SEC Reporting Requirements

In January 1997 the SEC released its new disclosure requirements, both quantitative and qualitative, concerning the market risk exposure of companies listed for trading on a securities exchange. The disclosures pertain to market risk–sensitive instruments such as financial and commodity derivative instruments, as well as other financial instruments. Derivative financial instruments include futures, forwards, swaps, options, swaptions, forward rate and spread agreements, etc. Other financial instruments include loans, structured notes, mortgage-backed securities, indexed debt instruments, interest-only (IO) and principal-only (PO) obligations, deposits, and different types of debt obligations. The disclosure is relevant for all market risk–sensitive instruments to which the firm is committed, and which are affected by changes in exchange rates, interest rates, commodity prices, stock market indexes, and other broad market indexes.

The SEC disclosure requirements were precipitated by the expanded use of derivative instruments by corporations, as well as by the significant increase in the variety and magnitude of debt instruments used to raise capital. It was realized that traditional accounting procedures did not yield sufficient information about the exposure of a firm to abrupt changes in market prices. As we mentioned previously, a team of SEC analysts checked hundreds of annual reports of corporations for the years 1994 and 1995 and found that firms with similar objectives concerning risk management reported identical derivative positions very differently.

The risk reporting requirements for banks proposed by the Basle Committee at the Bank for International Settlements (BIS) gave a major boost to the SEC in its effort to impose new risk disclosure requirements on nonbank corporations. While the early efforts of the BIS focused on credit risk, the new SEC reporting requirements focused on the market risk exposure of market risk–sensitive instruments.

In forming its disclosure requirements, the SEC employed the following guiding principles:

- Disclosures should make transparent the impact of derivatives on a registrant's statements of financial positions, cash flows, and results of operations.
- Disclosures should provide information about a registrant's exposures to market risk.
- Disclosures should explain how market risk–sensitive instruments are used in the context of the registrant's business.

- Disclosures about market risk exposures should not focus on derivatives in isolation, but rather should reflect the risk of loss inherent in all market risk–sensitive instruments.
- Market risk disclosure requirements should be flexible enough to accommodate different types of registrants, different degrees of market risk exposure, and alternative ways of measuring market risk.
- Disclosures about market risk should address, where appropriate, special risks relating to leverage, option, or prepayment features.
- New disclosure requirements should build on existing requirements, where possible, to minimize compliance costs.

The disclosure requirements of the SEC are composed of two parts: qualitative and quantitative information. The qualitative disclosure requirements of the SEC include:

1. Description of the market risk exposure of the firm at the end of the fiscal year.
2. How these exposures are managed (including the objectives and general strategies and major instruments used to manage market risks).
3. Major changes in market risk exposure or changes in risk management strategies.

In particular, the SEC requires companies to explain which accounting methods are used to report on derivative positions. For example, is the fair value method, the deferral method, or the accrual method used?[7] If different accounting methods are used for different derivatives or market risk–sensitive positions, the company should note this and explain the criteria and the reasoning that lie behind the selection of the accounting methods.

The qualitative information should be presented separately for positions entered for trading purposes and those entered for other purposes. The objective of the quantitative disclosure is to allow the investor to assess the potential for future losses due to market risk exposure.

As we describe further below, the SEC allows firms to choose from among three quantitative methods for the presentation of their financial risks: tabulation, sensitivity analysis, or value at risk (VaR). In addition, the SEC allows the quantification of risks from three bases: earnings, cash flows, or fair values. Hence, each reporting company can choose one of nine permutations. Moreover, the SEC permits companies to report different financial risks by different methods as long as the report is consistent. As a consequence, it is almost impossible to compare the reported risks across companies in related industries. In effect, the SEC has opted for greater flexibility at the cost of comparability.

1. Tabular presentation

The company can present all or some of its market risk–sensitive instruments in tables. The information to be included in the tables should allow the analyst to determine the expected future cash flows from the instruments for each of the next five years. Cash flows expected beyond five years can be aggregated. The tables should also include the fair value of the instruments. This kind of reporting is quite similar to the gap analysis that banks employ for the purpose of asset/liability management.

The information is intended to allow the investor to analyze the impact of market risk on the firm's future cash flows, and thus should supply any basic data that are needed as input for the financial models. The instruments should be segregated in the tables according to common market risk characteristics. Therefore, reporting will distinguish:

1. Between instruments for trading and those held for other than trading purposes
2. By sensitivity to different market risk factors (foreign currencies, interest rates, etc.)
3. By specific risk factor exposures within each exposure category (e.g., specific currencies, specific commodities, etc.)

The reporting firm is responsible for aggregating and segregating the various instruments into tables following the materiality and relevance criteria.

2. Sensitivity analysis

The sensitivity analysis should provide information on the potential for losses due to market risk factors. The SEC allows three bases for sensitivity analysis:

1. Accounting earnings
2. Fair values
3. Cash flows

The reporting firm can opt to use any of the above bases for any group of financial instruments.

The reporting firm has to select hypothetical changes in risk factors, such as interest rates, foreign currency exchange rates, commodity prices, and other relevant rates or prices, and assess their impact on future earnings, fair values, or cash flows. The changes in risk factors should be "reasonably possible" changes within the "near term." "Near term" indicates a period of time going forward up to one year from the date of the financial statement. "Reasonably possible" is defined by FAS 5 ("Accounting for Contingencies") and means that the chance of a future transaction or event occurring is more than remote, but less than likely. If there is no economic justification for selecting any particular hypothetical changes, the reporting firm should use rate and price changes of at least 10 percent.

The sensitivity analysis must be accompanied by a description of the models and assumptions used in the analysis. In particular, the reporting should include the following information:

1. Definition of "loss" (i.e., in earnings, fair values, or cash flow)
2. Description of the economic model used in assessing the impact of change in the risk factors
3. The types of instruments covered by the model
4. All relevant assumptions underlying the model and pertaining to the model's parameters

3. Value at Risk (VaR)

VaR reporting allows the firm to summarize the potential loss from all market risk–sensitive instruments in one risk number. The VaR is the expected future loss, within a given time period, such that the probability of incurring any higher loss is set in advance at, say, 1 percent.[8] The report should include any assumptions about the probability distribution of changes in market factors (such as interest rates, commodity prices, stock market indexes, etc.) and the resulting probability distribution of losses from financial instruments.

The VaR can be based on accounting earnings, fair values, or cash flows. For each category of assets for which VaR is reported, one of the following reporting methods should be used:

1. Low, average, and high amounts, or the distributions, of VaR for the reporting period
2. Low, average, and high amounts, or the distribution, of actual changes in fair values, earnings, or cash flows occurring during the reporting period
3. Number of times that the actual changes in fair values, earnings, or cash flows exceeded the VaR during the reporting period (or an equivalent percentage figure)

The report must include all relevant assumptions concerning the models used, and the parameter estimation methods that were employed. In particular, the firm should specify how loss is defined, which instruments are included, and the method that has been used for estimating the VaR (e.g., variance/covariance method, historical simulation, or Monte Carlo simulation).

Since quantitative reporting can be partial, and not reveal the true exposure to market risk factors, the SEC requires the firm to supply qualitative information on the potential discrepancies between the quantitative assessment and the economic exposure. For example, holding physical commodities for hedging purposes is not formally included in the reporting requirements but can, nevertheless, leave the firm exposed to changes in commodity prices. The firm should clarify the limitations of its quantitative reporting.

The reports contain forward-looking information, and quantitative reporting can reveal, directly or indirectly, information about the future expected activities of the firm. Therefore, the SEC provides for the protection of the reporting firm under the Safe Harbor rules.

5.2 Survey Results of SEC Disclosure Requirements

In 1999 KPMG published its "Survey of Disclosure: SEC Market Risk." For the survey, KPMG selected 30 companies from the

TABLE 16.1

Nontrading Disclosure Alternative Used for Each Market Risk Exposure

Market Risk Factor	Reporting Method		
	Tabular	Sensitivity	VaR
Interest rate	10	17	4
Foreign currency	5	15	6
Commodity	4	6	1
Equity	1	6	1

Source: KPMG.

Standard & Poor's 500 list, representing the 24 industry categories. KPMG reviewed the market risk disclosures filed by these companies with their 1997 Annual Reports.

Five companies disclosed information for both trading and nontrading instruments. It is not clear whether the other 25 companies held instruments solely for nontrading purposes. Four of the five firms used VaR and one company used sensitivity analysis. Of the five companies, two were utilities and were exposed only to commodity risk.

Two-thirds of the companies in the survey used one method consistently for all risk exposure categories, i.e., tabular presentation, sensitivity analysis, or VaR. The distribution of the reporting companies for instruments kept for nontrading purposes was as illustrated in Table 16.1.

Two firms provided information on market risk exposure for segments of the business. For example, AIG Inc. gave quantitative information for its general insurance and life insurance segments (based on VaR) as well as for its financial services (based on sensitivity analysis) and the holding company.

Three-quarters of the firms disclosed, qualitatively, the material limitations in their quantitative reporting. Some companies stated that the sensitivity analysis does not reflect potential changes in sales levels or the effect on competitive risk. Other companies noted that the effects of cross-correlation among market risk factors were ignored. It was also stated that the models excluded items such as anticipated transactions, firm commitments, receivables, and account payables denominated in foreign currencies.

It was felt by the companies that quantitative information alone is not sufficient to convey the information on the extent of the true economic exposure to market risk.

Twenty companies used sensitivity analysis for at least one of their risk exposures. Almost all provided the year-end reporting amount; only one company provided the low, average, and high sensitivity analyses. Fifteen of the 20 companies used loss of earnings as a basis for the sensitivity analysis, 11 used loss in fair values, and only in four cases was the analysis based on cash flows. The most common technique was to model the change in net present value (NPV). Six companies used duration as the basic model.

Nine companies used VaR analysis for at least one of their risk exposures. All reported year-end amounts only. Chase Manhattan Corp. provided information on the number of days that its trading losses exceeded the VaR figure. (Note that VaR statistics for the reporting period were not required for 1997, as the first year of reporting.) The VaR analysis was applied to loss of earnings in four cases, to loss in fair value in six cases, and only in one case to a reduction in cash flows.

Historical simulation was used in four cases, and Monte Carlo simulation in three cases; the variance/covariance method was also used in three cases.

The SEC conducted its own survey of disclosures made by companies and made the following general observations:[9]

- Companies have not provided sufficient information about the relevant terms of the instruments in their tabular presentations. Also, the segregation of instruments was inadequate.

- In cases where instruments were sensitive to more than one risk factor, companies failed to include that instrument in each market risk category.

- There were instances where contract terms were not sufficient to derive future cash flows for each year.

- Companies failed to provide adequate information about the types of instruments included in the VaR and sensitivity analysis.

- Insufficient information was provided regarding the models and assumptions used in deriving the VaR and the sensitivity analysis.
- Many companies failed to supply qualitative information about how they manage their market risk exposure. General strategies and instruments used during the year were not sufficiently disclosed.

Appendix 1 offers excerpts from the annual reports for 1998 of three American companies: Merck, Nike, and Microsoft. Part of this information is drawn from the management review or management discussion and analysis, preceding the financial statement; part of the information is drawn from footnotes to the financial statements. It can be seen that the companies offered quite different amounts of information about their market exposures. As a result of the flexibility in reporting allowed by the SEC, it is almost impossible to compare exposures among firms. It can be expected that the SEC will change the reporting rules to allow for more comparability.

5.3 The Example of Israel: New Reporting Requirements

From August to October 1998, exchange rates around the world changed dramatically and volatilities more than doubled. Businesses in smaller countries were strongly affected, particularly if their borrowing facilities were denominated in foreign currencies. For example, in Israel many local construction firms had arranged loans denominated in U.S. dollars, Japanese yen, and Swiss francs. At the time, these arrangements offered the firms a "cheap" way of borrowing, compared to the local interest rate for similar loans. As a result of the sharp changes in international exchange rates and the rapid devaluation of the Israeli shekel, firms that had borrowed in foreign currencies suffered significant accounting losses.

In October 1998 a commission led by Professor Dan Galai (the "Galai Commission") was asked by the Israeli Securities Authority to provide recommendations on the reporting requirements that might be imposed on publicly traded nonfinancial companies, with respect to their risk exposure. The commission submitted its recommendations in August 1999.

The information that companies will be asked to provide will be limited to that required to assess market risk, and will form part of the board's report (which accompanies the financial statements). The key reasons for reporting exposure to market risks, according to the commission, can be summarized as follows:

1. It increases the awareness of the board of directors and management to the way risks are being managed by emphasizing the responsibility of board members with regard to the potential risk exposure of the firm. It is expected that the decision-making process will be improved, and that the monitoring of exposures will be enhanced.

2. The financial management of the corporation will have clearer instructions concerning the goals of the firm with respect to risk management, budgets will be defined, and limits will be set.

3. Investors will gain better information about the risk exposure of the firm and how this is being managed. Therefore, the investing public should be less surprised by fluctuations in profits that are due to changes in market risk factors.

Like the SEC, the Galai Commission recommended that reporting should be divided into qualitative and quantitative information. However, the commission felt that requiring companies to use models at this stage might delay implementation. Therefore, a two-stage approach is envisaged: to ask immediately for relatively simple forms of quantitative information, and to recommend that, after two years, more sophisticated tools should be used to quantify risks.

The commission envisaged requiring companies to provide qualitative information that is more detailed than that required by the SEC. They would be asked:

- To name the officer in charge of risk management in the corporation (and to state specifically whether such a role is being fulfilled).

- What is the policy of the board with respect to market risk exposure?
- What is the objective that the board wishes to achieve by means of its risk management activities (e.g., to hedge accounting earnings or economic values)?
- What are the risk limits (if any) set by the board?
- What basic tools are used to hedge risks?
- How are risks monitored? If there is a deviation from the strategy set by the board, is there a contingency plan to identify and cope with this?
- If strategy or goals change, an explanation of the change should be provided.
- Is there a budget for the firm's risk management activity?

To begin with, the quantitative information will be based on tabular presentations; emphasis will be placed on exposures to foreign currencies and the inflation rate. The quantitative information requirements are:

1. Balance-sheet statement decomposed according to foreign exchange sensitivities. For example, if 20 percent of fixed assets are located in the United States and 10 percent in France, and the rest are local, then fixed assets will appear in three columns, one for each of the functional currencies. By decomposing assets and liabilities, it is believed that investors will obtain a better understanding of the firm's static exposure to exchange rate fluctuations.

2. For the reporting period, the company should report on the maximal gap experienced (on a monthly basis) between assets and liabilities, with and without derivatives, for each functional currency.

3. A table describing all derivative instruments, and other financial instruments sensitive to market risk factors, should be included. The table will separate instruments held for trading and nontrading purposes. The instruments for nontrading purposes will be segregated into those recognized by the accounting rules as hedges and those that are not recognized by the accounting rules as hedges.

The table will be categorized according to each family of derivatives (i.e., options, futures, swaps, etc.), and according to each exposure factor (i.e., $/shekel exchange rate, £/shekel exchange rate, interest rate, inflation rate, etc.). For each group of instruments, these tables should distinguish between long and short positions, and between instruments that mature within one year and instruments that mature after one year. For each cell in the table, two values should be included: notional value and fair value.

APPENDIX 1: EXAMPLES OF REPORTS ON RISK EXPOSURE BY NIKE, MERCK, AND MICROSOFT, 1998

A. Report by Nike

Market Risk Measurement

Foreign exchange risk and related derivatives use is monitored using a variety of techniques including a review of market value, sensitivity analysis, and Value-at-Risk (VaR). The VaR determines the maximum potential one-day loss in the fair value of foreign exchange rate-sensitive financial instruments. The VaR model estimates were made assuming normal market conditions and a 95 percent confidence level. There are various modeling techniques that can be used in the VaR computation. The Company's computations are based on inter-relationships between currencies and interest rates (a "variance/co-variance" technique). These inter-relationships were determined by observing foreign currency market changes and interest rate changes over the preceding 90 days. The value of foreign currency options does not change on a one-to-one basis with changes in the underlying currency rate. The potential loss in option value was adjusted for the estimated sensitivity (the "delta" and "gamma") to changes in the underlying currency rate. The model includes all of the Company's forwards, options, cross-currency swaps and yen-denominated debt (i.e., the Company's market-sensitive derivative and other financial instruments as defined by the SEC). Anticipated transactions, firm commitments and accounts receivable and payable denominated in foreign currencies, which certain of these instruments are intended to hedge, were excluded from the model.

The VaR model is a risk analysis tool and does not purport to represent actual losses in fair value that will be incurred by the Company, nor does it consider the potential effect of favorable changes in market rates. It also does not represent the maximum possible loss that may occur. Actual future gains and losses will differ from those estimated because of changes or differences in market rates and interrelationships, hedging instruments and hedge percentages, timing and other factors.

The estimated maximum one-day loss in fair value on the Company's foreign currency sensitive financial instruments, derived using the VaR model, was $11.7 million at May 31, 1998. The Company believes that this amount is immaterial and that such a hypothetical loss in fair value of its derivatives would be offset by increases in the value of the underlying transactions being hedged.

The Company's interest rate risk is also monitored using a variety of techniques. Notes 5 and 14 to the Consolidated Financial Statements outline the principal amounts, weighted average interest rates, fair values and other terms required to evaluate the expected cashflows and sensitivity to interest rate changes.

Derivatives [*Financial Review*, p. 36]

The Company enters into foreign currency contracts in order to reduce the impact of certain foreign currency fluctuations. Firmly committed transactions and the related receivables and payables may be hedged with forward exchange contracts or purchased options. Anticipated, but not yet firmly committed, transactions may be hedged through the use of purchased options. Premiums paid on purchased options and any gains are included in prepaid expenses or accrued liabilities and are recognized in earnings when the transaction being hedged is recognized. Gains and losses arising from foreign currency forward and option contracts and cross-currency swap transactions are recognized in income or expense as offsets of gains and losses resulting from the underlying hedged transactions. Hedge effectiveness is determined by evaluating whether gains and losses on hedges will offset gains and losses on the underlying exposures. This evaluation is performed at inception of the hedge and periodically over the life of the hedge. Occasionally, hedges may cease to be effective or may be terminated prior to recognition of the underlying transaction. Gains and losses on these hedges are deferred and included in the basis of the underlying transaction. Hedges are terminated if the underlying transaction is no longer expected to occur and the related gains and losses are recognized in earnings. Cash flows from risk management activities are classified in the same category as the cash flows from the related investment, borrowing or foreign exchange activity. See Note 15 for further discussion.

NOTE 14: FAIR VALUE OF FINANCIAL INSTRUMENTS

The carrying amounts reflected in the consolidated balance sheet for cash and equivalents and notes payable approximate fair value as reported in the balance sheet. The fair value of long-term debt is estimated using discounted cash flow analyses, based on the Company's incremental borrowing rates for similar types of borrowing arrangements. The fair value of the Company's long-term debt, including current portion, is approximately $384.4 million, compared to a carrying value of $381.0 million at May 31, 1998, and $295.9 million, compared to a carrying value of $298.2 million at May 31, 1997. See Note 15 for fair value of derivatives.

NOTE 15: FINANCIAL RISK MANAGEMENT AND DERIVATIVES

The purpose of the Company's foreign currency hedging activities is to protect the Company from the risk that the eventual dollar cash flows resulting from the sale and purchase of products in foreign currencies will be adversely affected by changes in exchange rates. In addition, the Company seeks to manage the impact of foreign currency fluctuations related to the repayment of intercompany borrowings. The Company does not hold or issue financial instruments for trading purposes. It is the Company's policy to utilize derivative financial instruments to reduce foreign exchange risks where internal netting strategies cannot be effectively employed. Fluctuations in the value of hedging instruments are offset by fluctuations in the value of the underlying exposures being hedged.

The Company uses forward exchange contracts and purchased options to hedge certain firm purchases and sales commitments and the related receivables and payables including other third party or intercompany foreign currency transactions. Purchased currency options are used to hedge certain anticipated but not yet firmly committed transactions expected to be recognized within one year. Cross-currency swaps are used to hedge foreign currency denominated payments related to intercompany loan agreements. Hedged transactions are denominated primarily in European currencies, Japanese yen and Canadian dollars. Premiums paid on purchased options and any realized gains are included in prepaid expenses or accrued liabilities and recognized in earnings when the underlying transaction is recognized. Deferred option premiums paid, net of realized gains, were $21.7 million and $14.5 million at May 31, 1998 and 1997, respectively. Gains and losses related to hedges of firmly committed transactions and the related receivables and payables are deferred and are recognized in income or as adjustments of carrying amounts when the offsetting gains and losses are recognized on the underlying transaction. Unrealized gains on forward contracts deferred at May 31, 1998 and 1997 were $12.0 million and $28.0 million, respectively.

The estimated fair values of derivatives used to hedge the Company's risks will fluctuate over time. The fair value of the forward exchange contracts is estimated by obtaining quoted market prices. The fair value of option contracts is estimated using option pricing models widely used in the financial markets. These fair value amounts should not be viewed in isolation, but rather in relation to the fair values of the underlying hedged transactions and the overall reduction in the Company's exposure to adverse fluctuations in foreign exchange rates. The notional amounts of derivatives summarized below do not necessarily represent amounts exchanged by the parties and, therefore, are not a direct measure of the exposure to the Company through its use of derivatives. The amounts exchanged are calculated on the basis of the notional amounts and the other terms of the derivatives, which relate to interest rates, exchange rates or other financial indices.

The following table (Table 16.2) presents the aggregate notional principal amounts, carrying values and fair values of the Company's derivative financial instruments outstanding at May 31, 1998 and 1997 (in millions).

TABLE 16.2

Derivative Financial Instruments Outstanding at May 31, 1998 and 1997 (in Millions)

May 31	1998			1997		
	Notional Principal Amounts $	Carrying Values $	Fair Values $	Notional Principal Amounts $	Carrying Values $	Fair Values $
Currency swaps	300.0	30.8	30.3	200.0	19.4	13.7
Forward contracts	2,453.1	3.0	62.3	2,328.5	14.8	47.4
Purchased options	232.4	7.7	1.9	413.7	9.7	9.4
Total	2,985.5	41.5	94.5	2,914.2	43.9	70.5

At May 31, 1998, and May 31, 1997 the Company had no contracts outstanding with maturities beyond one year except the currency swaps which have maturity dates consistent with the maturity dates of the related debt. All realized gains/losses deferred at May 31, 1998 will be recognized within one year.

The counterparties to derivative transactions are major financial institutions with high investment grade credit ratings and, additionally, counterparties to derivatives three years or greater are all AAA rated. However, this does not eliminate the Company's exposure to credit risk with these institutions. This credit risk is generally limited to the unrealized gains in such contracts should any of these counterparties fail to perform as contracted and is immaterial to any one institution at May 31, 1998 and 1997. To manage this risk, the Company has established strict counterparty credit guidelines which are continually monitored and reported to Senior Management according to prescribed guidelines. The Company utilizes a portfolio of financial institutions either headquartered or operating in the same countries the Company conducts its business. As a result, the Company considers the risk of counterparty default to be minimal.

B. Report by Merck

A significant portion of the Company's cash flows are denominated in foreign currencies. The Company relies on sustained cash flows generated from foreign sources to support its long-term commitment to U.S. dollar-based research and development. To the extent the dollar value of cash flows is diminished as a result of a strengthening dollar, the Company's ability to fund research and other dollar-based strategic initiatives at a consistent level may be impaired. To protect against the reduction in value of foreign currency cash flows, the Company has instituted balance sheet and revenue hedging programs to partially hedge this risk.

The objective of the balance sheet hedging program is to protect the U.S. dollar value of foreign currency denominated net monetary assets from the effects of volatility in foreign exchange that might occur prior to their conversion to U.S. dollars. To achieve this objective, the Company will hedge foreign currency risk on monetary assets and liabilities where hedging is cost beneficial. The Company seeks to fully hedge exposure denominated in developed country currencies, such as those of Japan, Germany, France and Canada, and will either partially hedge or not hedge at all exposure in other currencies, particularly exposure in hyperinflationary countries where hedging instruments may not be available at any cost. The Company will minimize the effect of exchange rate risk on unhedged exposure, principally by managing operating activities and net asset positions at the local level. The Company manages its net asset exposure principally with forward exchange contracts. These contracts enable the Company to buy and sell foreign currencies in the future at fixed exchange rates. For net monetary assets hedged, forward contracts offset the consequences of changes in foreign exchange on the amount of U.S. dollar cash flows derived from the net assets. Contracts used to hedge net monetary asset exposure have average maturities at inception of less than one year. A sensitivity analysis to changes in the value of the U.S. dollar on foreign currency denominated derivatives and monetary assets and liabilities indicated that if the U.S. dollar uniformly weakened by 10 percent against all currency exposures of the Company at December 31, 1998 and 1997, income before taxes would have declined by $53.9 million and $10.9 million, respectively. The balance sheet hedging program has significantly reduced the volatility of U.S. dollar cash flows derived from foreign currency denominated net monetary assets. The cashflows from these contracts are reported as operating activities in the Consolidated Statement of Cash Flows.

The objective of the revenue hedging program is to reduce the potential for longer-term unfavorable changes in foreign exchange to decrease the U.S. dollar value of future cash flows derived from foreign currency denominated sales. To achieve this objective, the Company will partially hedge forecasted sales that are expected to occur over its planning cycle, typically no more than three years into the future. The Company will layer in hedges over time, increasing the portion of sales hedged as it gets closer to the expected date of the transaction. The portion of sales hedged is based on assessments of cost-benefit profiles that consider natural offsetting exposures, revenue and exchange rate volatilities and correlations, and the cost of hedging instruments. The Company manages its forecasted transaction exposure principally with purchased local currency put options. On the forecasted transactions hedged, these option contracts effectively reduce the potential for a strengthening U.S. dollar to decrease the future U.S. dollar cash flows derived from foreign currency denominated sales. Purchased local currency put options provide the Company with a right, but not an obligation, to sell foreign currencies in the future at a predetermined price. If the value of the U.S. dollar weakens relative to other major currencies when the options mature, the options would expire unexercised, enabling the Company to benefit from favorable movements in exchange, except to the extent of premiums paid for the contracts. While a weaker U.S. dollar would result in a net benefit, the market value of the Company's hedges would have declined by $86.3 million and $67.0 million, respectively, from a uniform 10 percent weakening of the U.S. dollar at December 31, 1998 and 1997. Over the last three years, the program has reduced the volatility of cashflows and mitigated the loss in value of cash flows during periods of relative strength in the U.S. dollar for the portion of revenues hedged. The cash flows from these contracts are reported as operating activities in the Consolidated Statement of Cash Flows.

In addition to the balance sheet and revenue hedging programs, the Company hedges interest rates on certain fixed and variable rate borrowing and investing transactions. Interest rates are hedged with swap contracts that exchange the cash flows from interest rates on the underlying financial instruments for those derived from interest rates inherent in the contracts. For foreign currency denominated borrowing and investing transactions, cross-currency interest rate swap contracts are used, which, in addition to exchanging cash flows derived from rates, exchange currencies at both inception and termination of the contracts. On investing transactions, swap contracts allow the Company to receive variable rate returns and limit foreign exchange risk, while on borrowing transactions, these contracts allow the Company to borrow at more favorable rates than otherwise attainable through direct issuance of variable rate U.S. dollar debt. The cash flows from these contracts are reported as operating activities in the Consolidated Statement of Cash Flows.

A sensitivity analysis to measure potential changes in the market value of the Company's investments, debt and related swaps from a change in interest rates indicated that a one percentage point increase in interest rates at December 31, 1998 and 1997 would have positively impacted the net aggregate market value of these instruments by $424.8 million and $60.0 million, respectively. A one percentage point decrease at December 31, 1998 and 1997 would have negatively impacted the net aggregate market value by $616.6 million and $71.0 million, respectively. The increased impact of a change in interest rates on the net aggregate market values at December 31, 1998 primarily results from increased levels of longer-term fixed rate debt.

Financial Instruments [*Financial Review*, pp. 38–39]

Foreign currency risk management

The Company has established revenue and balance sheet hedging programs to protect against reductions in value and volatility of future foreign currency cash flows caused by changes in foreign exchange rates. The objectives and strategies of these programs are described in the Analysis of Liquidity and Capital Resources section of the Financial Review.

The Company partially hedges forecasted revenues denominated in foreign currencies with purchased currency options. When the dollar strengthens against foreign currencies, the decline in the value of foreign currency cash flows is partially offset by the recognition of gains in the value of purchased currency options designated as hedges of the period. Conversely, when the dollar weakens, the increase in the value of foreign currency cash flows is reduced only by the recognition of the premium paid to acquire the options designated as hedges of the period. Market value gains and premiums on these contracts are recognized in Sales when the hedged transaction is recognized. The carrying value of purchased currency options is reported in Prepaid expenses and taxes or Other assets.

The Company continually reviews its portfolio of purchased options and will adjust its portfolio to accommodate changes in exposure to forecasted revenues. The most cost-effective means of decreasing coverage provided by purchased options is to write options with terms identical to purchased options that are no longer necessary. Deferred gains or losses that accumulate on purchased options prior to writing an offsetting position will remain deferred and are recognized when the hedged transaction occurs. Subsequent changes in the market value of the written options and related purchased options are recorded in earnings. Because the changes in market value of the purchased options equally offset the written options, there is no net impact on earnings. The carrying value of written currency options is reported in Accounts payable and accrued liabilities or Deferred income taxes and noncurrent liabilities.

Deferred gains and losses on currency options used to hedge forecasted revenues amounted to $12.6 million and $45.3 million at December 31, 1998 and $95.4 million and $5.9 million at December 31, 1997, respectively.

The Company also hedges certain exposures to fluctuations in foreign currency exchange rates that occur prior to conversion of foreign currency denominated monetary assets and liabilities into U.S. dollars. Prior to conversion to U.S. dollars, these assets and liabilities are translated at spot rates in effect on the balance sheet date. The effects of changes in spot rates are reported in earnings and included in Other (income) expense, net. The Company hedges its exposure to changes in foreign exchange principally with forward contracts. Because monetary assets and liabilities are marked to spot and recorded in earnings, forward contracts designated as hedges of the monetary assets and liabilities are also marked to spot with the resulting gains and losses similarly recognized in earnings. Gains and losses on forward contracts are included in Other (income) expense, net, and offset losses and gains

TABLE 16.3

Notional Amounts for $U.S. Contracts

	1998	1997
Purchased currency options	$4,583.5	$1,462.7
Forward sale contracts	1,973.3	1,500.9
Forward purchase contracts	542.8	412.1

on the net monetary assets and liabilities hedged. The carrying values of forward exchange contracts are reported in Accounts receivable, Other assets, Accounts payable and accrued liabilities or Deferred income taxes and noncurrent liabilities.

At December 31, 1998 and 1997, the Company had contracts to exchange foreign currencies, principally the Japanese yen, French franc and deutsche mark, for U.S. dollars in the following notional amounts (see Table 16.3).

Interest rate risk management

The Company uses interest rate swap contracts on certain borrowing and investing transactions. Interest rate swap contracts are intended to be an integral part of borrowing and investing transactions and, therefore, are not recognized at fair value. Interest differentials paid or received under these contracts are recognized as adjustments to the effective yield of the underlying financial instruments hedged. Interest rate swap contracts would only be recognized at fair value if the hedged relationship is terminated. Gains or losses accumulated prior to termination of the relationship would be amortized as a yield adjustment over the shorter of the remaining life of the contract or the remaining period to maturity of the underlying instrument hedged. If the contract remained outstanding after termination of the hedged relationship, subsequent changes in market value of the contract would be recognized in earnings. The Company does not use leveraged swaps and, in general, does not use leverage in any of its investment activities that would put principal capital at risk.

In 1995 the Company entered into a five-year combined interest rate and currency swap contract with a notional amount of

$231.3 million at December 31, 1998 and $313.6 million at December 31, 1997 and, in 1997, a seven-year interest rate and currency swap contract with a notional amount of $344.1 million at December 31, 1998 and $334.2 million at December 31, 1997. In 1998, a portion of the 1995 swap contract was terminated in conjunction with the sale of a portion of the related asset with an immaterial impact on net income. These swaps convert two different variable rate Dutch guilder investments to variable rate U.S. dollar investments. The market values of these contracts are reported in Other assets or Deferred income taxes and noncurrent liabilities with unrealized gains and losses recorded, net of tax, in Accumulated other comprehensive income.

At December 31, 1997, the Company had one variable maturity interest rate swap contract outstanding with a notional amount of $85.0 million to convert 7.25 percent U.S. dollar callable debt issued in 1997 to variable rate U.S. dollar debt. This swap contract was terminated in February 1998 in conjunction with the retirement of the callable debt.

Fair value of financial instruments

Summarized in Table 16.4 are the carrying values and fair values of the Company's financial instruments at December 31, 1998 and 1997. Fair values were estimated based on market prices, where available, or dealer quotes.

Table 16.5 is a summary of the carrying values and fair values of the Company's investments at December 31.

Table 16.6 is a summary of gross unrealized gains and losses on the Company's investments at December 31.

Gross unrealized gains and losses with respect to available-for-sale investments are recorded, net of tax and minority interests, in Accumulated other comprehensive (loss) income.

Available-for-sale debt securities and held-to-maturity securities maturing within one year totaled $535.5 million and $214.0 million, respectively, at December 31, 1998. Of the remaining debt securities, $1.8 billion mature within six years.

At December 31, 1998, $507.3 million of held-to-maturity securities maturing within five years set off $507.3 million of 5.0 percent nontransferable note obligations due by 2003 issued by the Company.

TABLE 16.4

Carrying Values and Fair Values of the Company's Financial Instruments at December 31, 1998, and 1997

	1998		1997	
	Carrying Value	Fair Value	Carrying Value	Fair Value
Assets				
Cash and cash equivalents	$2,606.0	$2,606.2	$1,125.1	$1,125.1
Short-term investments	749.5	749.5	1,184.2	1,184.2
Long-term investments	3,607.7	3,604.3	2,533.4	2,531.8
Purchased currency options	170.2	137.5	54.6	144.1
Forward exchange contracts and currency swaps	72.8	72.8	197.0	197.0
Interest rate swaps	—	—	.1	.3
Liabilities				
Loans payable and current portion of long-term debt	$ 624.2	$ 654.7	$ 902.5	$ 900.5
Long-term debt	3,220.8	3,336.5	1,346.5	1,387.0
Forward exchange contracts and currency swap	86.1	86.1	22.0	22.0

TABLE 16.5

Carrying Values and Fair Values of the Company's Investments at December 31

	1997		1998	
	Carrying Value	Fair Value	Carrying Value	Fair Value
Available-for-sale				
Debt securities	$2,639.0	$2,639.0	$1,947.2	$1,947.2
Equity securities	1,000.6	1,000.6	887.6	887.6
Held-to-maturity securities	717.6	714.2	882.8	881.2

TABLE 16.6

Gross Unrealized Gains and Losses

	1998		1997	
	Gross Unrealized		Gross Unrealized	
	Gains	Losses	Gains	Losses
Available-for-sale				
Debt securities	$ 22.1	$(12.5)	$11.1	$ (2.8)
Equity securities	124.1	(64.2)	11.3	(91.9)
Held-to-maturity securities	.6	(4.0)	2.9	(4.5)

Concentrations of credit risk

As part of its ongoing control procedures, the Company monitors concentrations of credit risk associated with financial institutions with which it conducts business. Credit risk is minimal as credit exposure limits are established to avoid a concentration with any single financial institution. The Company also monitors the creditworthiness of its customers to which it grants credit terms in the normal course of business. Concentrations of credit risk associated with these trade receivables are considered minimal due to the Company's diverse customer base. Bad debts have been minimal. The Company does not normally require collateral or other security to support credit sales.

C. Report by Microsoft

Foreign exchange

A large percentage of the Company's sales, costs of manufacturing, and marketing is transacted in local currencies. As a result, the Company's international results of operations are subject to foreign exchange rate fluctuations.

Investments value sensitivity

The Company's investment portfolio is subject to interest rate and market price risk. A 10 percent increase in treasury security yields would reduce the carrying value of interest-sensitive securities at June 30, 1998, by $128 million, and a 10 percent decrease in market values would reduce the carrying value of the Company's publicly traded equity by $300 million.

Financial instruments

The Company considers all liquid interest-earning investments with a maturity of three months or less at the date of purchase to be cash equivalents. Short-term investments generally mature between three months and five years from the purchase date. All cash and short-term investments are classified as available for sale and are recorded at market. Cost approximates market for all classifications of cash and short-term investments; realized and unrealized gains and losses were not material.

Publicly tradable equity securities are recorded at market; unrealized gains and losses are reflected in stockholders' equity. The pretax unrealized gain was $1.4 billion at June 30, 1998.

Financial risks

The Company's investment portfolio is diversified and consists primarily of short-term investment grade securities. Interest rate fluctuations impact the carrying value of the portfolio. While no hedge was in place on June 30, 1998, the Company routinely hedges the portfolio in case of a catastrophic increase in interest rates. At June 30, 1997 and 1998, approximately 31 percent and 40 percent of accounts receivable represented amounts due from ten customers. One customer accounted for approximately 13 percent, 12 percent, and 8 percent of revenue in 1996, 1997, and 1998.

Finished goods sales to international customers in Europe, Japan, and Australia are primarily billed in local currencies. Payment cycles are relatively short, generally less than 90 days. European manufacturing costs and international selling, distribution, and support costs are generally disbursed in local currencies. Local currency cash balances in excess of short-term operating needs are generally converted into U.S. dollar cash and short-term investments on receipt. Therefore, foreign exchange rate fluctuations generally do not create a risk of material balance sheet gains or losses. As a result, Microsoft's hedging activities for balance sheet exposures have been minimal.

Foreign exchange rates affect the translated results of operations of the Company's foreign subsidiaries. The Company hedges a percentage of planned international revenue with purchased options. The notional amount of the options outstanding at June 30, 1998, was $2.1 billion. At June 30, 1998, the fair value and premiums paid for the options were not material.

NOTES

1. See also Chapter 1.
2. "Long-arm test" relates to the accounting principles that determine whether a subsidiary should be considered as an integral part of the parent company, or as an independent unit.
3. See Metallgesellschaft, Chapter 5.
4. It is interesting to follow the reports of some publicly traded companies and read their comments on the limitations of their risk exposure report. Some of the information can be found in *the Survey of Disclosures: SEC Market Risk* compiled by KPMG in 1999. For example, from page 8 of the survey we find: "Dell Computer Corporation and Phillip Morris Companies Inc. provided VaR amounts for foreign currency risk and cautioned that the model excluded items such as anticipated transactions, firm commitments, receivables, and accounts payable denominated in foreign currencies. In addition, they commented that a loss in fair value of foreign currency instruments for hedging anticipated transactions is typically mitigated by increases in the value of the underlying exposure. Dell Computer Corporation also added 'firmly committed transactions' to their comment on loss of fair value of foreign currency instruments since their model excluded these types of transactions."
5. See Kolb (1991) for a description of exchanges for futures.
6. From Release No. 48 of the SEC (1997).
7. According to the fair value method, derivatives are included in the balance sheet at their economic values and changes in values are reported in the periodic profit and loss statement. The deferral method allows firms to postpone the reporting of profits and losses

and to match the positions in derivatives to the on-balance items that were hedged. The accrual method allows firms to account for cash flows from derivatives in the profit and loss accounts.

8. For a detailed analysis of VaR, see Chapter 5.
9. From remarks by J. Goodwin at the 1998 26th National Conference on Current SEC Developments (Dec. 9, 1998).

Risk Management in the Future

1. THE TOTAL RISK-ENABLED BANK

The bank of the future will be reorganized around a new vision. To succeed, it will have to be able to respond to opportunities as they present themselves. And it will have to strive to improve the portfolio management of its balance sheet and capital.

To manage conflicting objectives, it will need to determine a number of policy variables such as a target risk-adjusted rate of return (RAROC), target regulatory return, target tier 1 ratio, target liquidity, and so on (Figure 17.1).

In turn, this will mean transforming the risk management function. Risk management will need to encompass limit management, risk analysis, RAROC, and active portfolio management of risk (APMR) (Figure 17.2).

In the first part of this chapter, we look at how these changes in risk management will be induced—and facilitated—by advances in technology, the introduction of more sophisticated regulatory measures, rapidly accelerating market forces, and an increasingly complex legal environment.

1.1 Advances in Technology

Banking is moving into an era in which complex mathematical models programmed into risk engines will provide the foundation

FIGURE 17.1

Conflicting Objectives

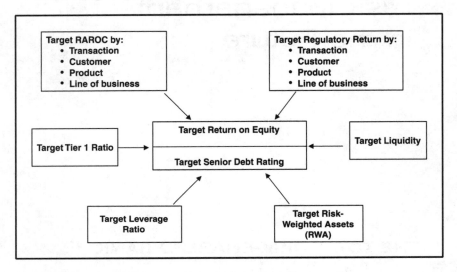

FIGURE 17.2

Implementation of Mandate

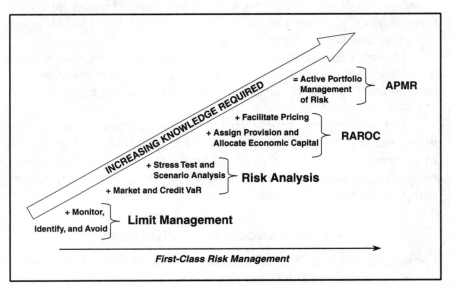

of portfolio management. Banks with a sophisticated risk engine will be able to measure the risk of sophisticated products, compute and implement hedging strategies, and understand the relative risk-adjusted return almost instantaneously.

Given the current trend toward consolidation, vast and complex organizations will demand the ability to quickly and consistently provide key decision-support tools for comparing profitability measures and risk tolerances for diverse businesses.

Technology will allow risk management information to be integrated into overall management reporting—including intraday risk reporting. The Internet and intranet will become the delivery vehicles of choice for the results of risk analyses.

Infrastructure investments will be required within many banks to improve performance in a variety of tasks. The tasks include information collection and normalization, storage and dimensioning, and analytics processing, as well as information sharing and distribution.

One method of deployment for information, as shown in Figure 17.3, will be via either the intranet or the Internet. There

FIGURE 17.3

Standard Components with Consistent Content

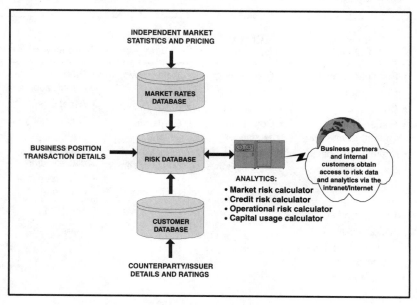

should only be one official risk measure from a fully integrated risk system infrastructure. Real-time access will be provided to the risk system via web-based technologies. Independent risk calculators may exist for offline use, but these will be able to use the same analytics as the official reporting process (via the intranet).

The benefits of this type of infrastructure are consistency—one source for one "answer"; efficiency—work is executed once to serve multiple purposes; and ease of use—one place, one view.

The risk database will include transaction details (e.g., cash flows); cross references to other internal systems which house critical data (e.g., credit ratings); external data (e.g., yield curves); and a variety of dimension indicators (e.g., product identification codes), as shown in Table 17.1. The risk management data will need to be harmonized with the broader data needs of the bank.

The infrastructure will include appropriate linkages within a robust environment for data collection and scrubbing, data warehousing, and risk analytics—as well as the appropriate data and

TABLE 17.1

A Diverse Set of Information Must Be Collected to Calculate Total Exposure

Transaction Details	Cross References	External Data	Dimensions
• Principal amount	• Credit ratings	• Yield curves	• Product identification
• Cash flows	• Counterparty	• Prices	
• Currencies	• Instrument	• Credit ratings	• Asset class
• Frequency of interest payments	• Contracts/ exchanges	• Corporate actions	• Counterparty or issuer
• Interest reset dates	• Internal organization ID	• Industry classifications	• Industry classification
• Date of maturity			• Branch/division/ department
• Holiday rule for interest			• Currency
• Current market value			
• Asset bucket			
• Commissions, fees, expenses			
• Profit or loss amount			

systems maintenance component as shown in Figure 17.4. (Vendors of risk management systems are already moving in this direction.)

Above all, the risk management information system (risk MIS) should be designed to provide full risk transparency from the bottom to the top of the house.

1.2 Regulatory Measures and Market Forces

In the future, the regulatory review process (e.g., review of bank internal models) will become more sophisticated. Regulators will hire staff with a greater risk management expertise. Regulators will increasingly serve as a catalyst for quantifying risk (market, credit, operational, liquidity, etc.) through their imposition of new capital regimes, as discussed in the 1999 Basle Accord Consultative Paper (Basle 1999).

Market forces will also bring change. External users of financial information will demand better information on which to make investment decisions. In the future there will be more detailed and more frequent reporting of risk positions to company shareholders,

FIGURE 17.4

Mechanism for Data Capture—Best Practice

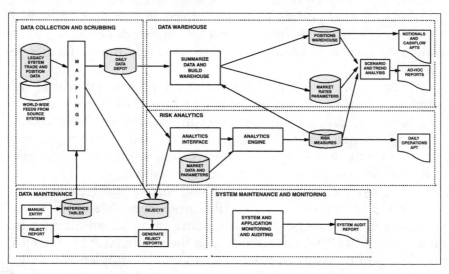

creditors, etc. This will lead to generally accepted reporting principles (GARP) for risk along the lines of the existing generally accepted accounting principles (GAAP) for financial statements.

There will be an increasing growth in consulting services such as data providers, risk advisory service bureaus, treasury transaction services, etc. Independent external reviewers may even be hooked up to a bank's systems to allow them to offer regular automated independent risk reviews. The reviews will be intended to provide comfort to senior managers and regulators, and to show that internal systems provide sound risk measures.

The risk management function will be fully independent from the business and centralized. Risk management processes will be fully and seamlessly integrated into the business process. Risk/return will be assessed for new business opportunities and incorporated into the design of new products. All risks—credit, market, operational, liquidity, and so on—will be combined, reported, and managed on an ever more integrated basis.

The total figures for credit risk by counterparty will use credit value-at-risk methodologies to combine the risk arising from credit derivative activities with that arising from more traditional lending. The problem of liquidating portfolios during turbulent markets will also become an important factor in the total risk numbers.

The demand for RAROC-based performance measures will increase. The Holy Grail in this area will be the ability to produce RAROC-adjusted pricing for dealers before deal capture. This development will maximize the potential for teamwork between traders, originators and risk managers—though oversight must remain independent.

The bank of the future will have a sophisticated central risk engine capable of measuring the risk and the price of anything that the bank trades and originates. Risk management will be a value added "nerve center" for trading, ideas and deal structuring as well as provide the impetus for new marketing initiatives, while pricing will become more complex and competitive.

The risk management function will become much more tightly integrated with profit and loss (P&L) reporting. Risk capital will be charged to a business unit according to its contribution to the total risk of the firm, not according to the volatility of the business line's revenues. And the balance sheet will be supplemented by a business unit value-at-risk (VaR) report. Information will pass back and forth between the risk management function and the business units, and they will work in partnership to balance risk and return.

1.3 Legal Environment

What happens in U.S. courts may help to shape the global financial industries of the future. For example, innovative financial products implemented on computer, are now regarded as patentable in the United States. This includes new trading system functionality, financial engineering innovations, new risk management software, user interfaces, and so on.

For some banks, this offers the potential for realizing commercial gains through licensing. Should financial institutions start investing in their own patent portfolios?[1] The losers in this new era of intellectual property are likely to be banks that ignore the dangers of patent litigation or that fail to devise defensive strategies.

The lessons from a recent case between Signature Financial Group and State Street have broad implications. Signature patented a computer system that was trademarked "Hub and Spoke." State Street Bank opted to seek to have the patent declared invalid. Judge Giles Rich, in the U.S. Court of Appeal for the Federal Court (July 23, 1998), ruled in favor of Signature. He stated that, "the transformation of data, representing discrete dollar amounts, by a machine through a series of mathematical calculations into a final share price, constitutes a practical application of a mathematical algorithm, formula, or calculation, because it produces a 'useful,' concrete, and tangible result."[2]

1.4 Building Blocks to Create Shareholder Value

To use a sporting analogy, first-class risk management is not only about outstanding goal keeping, but also about the ability to move upfield and help the team score. Advances in leading-edge risk and capital management tools suggest that banks are ready to move to this next stage of implementation. RAROC will be used to drive pricing, performance measurement, portfolio management, and capital management. The new paradigm of a total risk enabled enterprise (TREE) will increase shareholder value at tactical and strategic levels, as well as attracting new clients (Figure 17.5).

FIGURE 17.5

Increasing Shareholder Value through Total Risk-Enabled Enterprise (Project TREE)

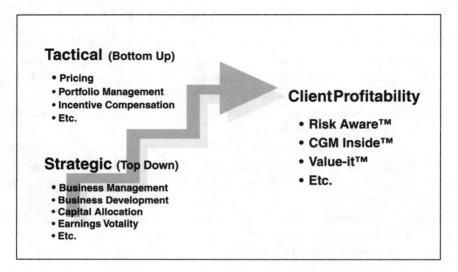

The transformations in capital and balance-sheet management will be driven by advances in risk management. We will see integration in the measurement and management of the various risks (market, credit, operational) and between the trading book and the banking book; we will also see risk measurement as a primary driver of capital and balance-sheet management.

Dynamic economic capital management has already emerged as a powerful competitive weapon. The challenge is to pull all these component parts together to create and sustain shareholder value (Figure 17.6). The evolution of risk management towards simultaneously serving both internal and client-related needs is natural. Risk management tools that have been developed to serve internal bank purposes also have significant external commercial value.

The structure of a total risk enabled enterprise (TREE) is therefore likely to evolve from attempts to leverage risk management skills in a whole variety of ways. The trunk of the TREE represents policy, methodology, and infrastructure elements that were built for internal risk management purposes. The branches of the TREE make use of elements of this framework to serve both tactical and strategic bank ambitions.

FIGURE 17.6

Create and Sustain Shareholder Value

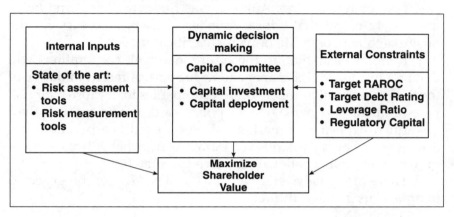

The tactical elements touch on pricing, portfolio management, and incentive compensation issues, and thus provide bottom-up shareholder value. The strategic elements shape business management, business development, capital allocation, and earnings volatility, while helping management to provide top-down shareholder value. The branches of TREE also reach out to connect with bank clients and to serve their objectives.

2. EXTERNAL CLIENT PROFITABILITY: A PARTNER PLUS™ APPROACH

In the future, a select subset of leading-edge tools developed by banks to serve their internal needs will be leveraged and redeployed to provide value-added services to bank clients.

To try to make clear what is meant by this, let us imagine a hypothetical bank called CGM that leverages its risk management policy, methodology, and infrastructure to offer a suite of services to clients. We can call those services, for illustrative purposes, Partner Plus (Partner+™). Our hypothetical CGM bank might create revenue through establishing a service bureau, in joint ownership with an external technology-enabled institution, to sell risk management services through an independent legal entity. The service bureau might offer to run VaR calculations and stress test certain risks for clients.

As with any step-change in how an industry is structured, banks may need to act quickly. "The easiest way is to be first: Yahoo was first, eBay was first, Amazon was first, etc. Being first helps immensely to get that critical number of users necessary for the business to take on a life of its own: critical mass."[3]

It seems clear that, in the future, nonbank corporations will demand extensive risk management support. A recent initiative of the SEC requires all publicly traded companies to disclose their risk measurement and management policy, and also to publish their quantified exposure to market risk. As a result, corporations are asking how they can establish an infrastructure that will allow them to manage risk in a rational way (see Chapter 16).

Therefore, a news story such as in Box 17.1 can be expected to appear in the near future.

2.1 Risk Aware™

One component of a suite of Partner Plus products offered by CGM might be called for illustrative purposes the "Risk Aware" product client set. The Risk Aware™ toolset would include an educational module. Providing first-class risk education is a key component of every successful integrated risk management program.

Clients should understand why they have to change the way they do things. Staff are more comfortable if they know that new risk procedures are being introduced for a good business reason. Risk education, moreover, can prevent human error by actively involving staff at all levels of the risk process.

Clients should also be shown how risk measures can be used as the basis for allocating economic capital, and how this is linked to the pricing of risk. One very useful educational tool is to provide clients with an economic capital calculator that shows the break-even price required to cover the cost of economic capital for each type of deal. Clients might also be taught how to utilize risk measurement tools to enhance their portfolio management skills.

2.2 CGM Inside™

It is quite possible that, in the future, bank clients will turn to their banks for a total off-the-shelf risk solution. In the rest of this section

BOX 17.1

HYPOTHETICAL NEWS STORY OF THE FUTURE:
PARTNER PLUS TAKES CGM TO THE TOP

The electronic interactive tools that have propelled Bank CGM to the top of the wholesale and retail banking pyramid look set to revolutionize financial services, say industry analysts. Bank CGM's product, Partner Plus, has elicited numerous copycat strategies among CGM's competitors over the last two months.

The catalyst for Bank CGM's expansion in retail securities activity can be traced in part to the decision to partner with suppliers to create a web-based, 24-hour, real-time risk management dealing system.

CGM enhanced its traditional trading services through the Internet by leveraging customer information and account representative services. The bank's account representatives, with the approval of clients, "push" the type of deals and portfolio offerings that their clients need through the Internet. The marketing is based on a uniquely detailed knowledge of the risk profiles and preferences of the client.

The account representative also makes use of predictive risk models based on proprietary credit algorithms to cross-sell other CGM services. The bank claims that client purchases of CGM services have tripled.

CGM seems to have successfully matched trading services with account representative support. Part of the reason for the success seems to be the inclusion in the software package of industry standard risk analysis and capital management tools for professional fund managers. These include a tool that calculates required economic capital as a function of the market and credit risk of the customer's portfolio.

The client can also place program trading execution orders and request "wake-ups" when target trade levels are reached.

In the past, to expand a retail client base a bank had to increase the number of account representatives. This was expensive, as it required physical space and training. CGM matched call center technology and e-commerce expertise to allow account representatives to expand significantly the number of clients served and to allow the clients a choice of service contact.

By means of the new product, CGM looks set to be the first bank to deliver on the promise and potential of electronic commerce—low-cost globalization. In contrast to 2000, when CGM had no significant retail business outside of North America, in 2002 CGM expects 30 percent of the fixed-income and equity products it retails to go to clients outside its home market.

we take a closer look at what such a product might look like, again using the imaginary example of CGM Bank. We will call the product "CGM Inside."

The entire set of methodological tools developed by CGM would be made available to the client via the CGM Inside product. In effect, the client would be certified by CGM as having the appropriate risk methodologies in place. For example, the client might use CGM tools to establish its own analytically driven capital management program.

2.3 Value-it™

Clients of Bank CGM are likely to be particularly interested in using the bank valuation capabilities for their own internal corporate valuation adjustment[4] and corporate governance purposes.

As we discussed in Chapter 6, banks are developing techniques to value products that are transacted in a highly illiquid market. Corporations will also discover that they need to differentiate between transactions that are easy to value and those where there is much more limited price discovery, e.g., long tenor and highly structured derivative transactions such as a 10-year option on a 20-year swap. Valuing transactions such as these involves assumption-driven valuation methodologies (e.g., constructing the term structure of interest rates beyond 10 years) and mark-to-model pricing techniques.

The need to make assumptions in the valuation of illiquid transactions typically leads to a wider range of valuations. In addition, the wider range of values drives the calculation of the average expected and average unexpected credit risk exposure levels (which in turn is utilized to establish the projected level of loss). This implies that corporations should set aside more capital for investments with wider valuation ranges, or they will make themselves vulnerable to the default of counterparties. But to do so effectively, they need access to Bank CGM's state-of-the-art techniques.

2.4 Hypothetical CGM Trading Products

A CGM client might also use a trading service provided by CGM, which we will call CGM Trader™. CGM Trader is one of the series

FIGURE 17.7

CGM Partner Plus (Partner+) Family

CGM Partner Plus (Partner +™) Family	
Trader	Retail investment clients with solid investment knowledge.
Pro	Professional fund managers.
Business	Small- to medium-sized businesses.
Banker	Retail clients looking for basic but customizable electronic banking services.
Wealth	Retail clients demanding comprehensive banking, investment, insurance, and wealth management services. A sophisticated, customizable virtual-realty product that answers investment, tax, and wealth-management questions.

of products shown in Figure 17.7. The product would give the client access to real-time prices and trading capability for nearly every security traded in the G-7 capital markets.

If a client decides to trade, then CGM Trader™ routes the trade to the designated trading institution. CGM acts as the clearing agent for all transactions, thus preserving the anonymity of the client.

With every transaction, CGM expands its competitive assembly of client information. This information database is fundamental to its success in the development of retail-structured products. Having exclusive access to client trading patterns would enable CGM to develop unique structured products that meet specific investor needs. These products could then be marketed through Trader™ and the other CGM Partner+™ products.

Also included in the Partner+™ suite is a real-time trading system called CGM Pro™. CGM Pro™ is a risk management toolkit that fund managers use to stress test their portfolios. CGM Pro™ is a service that links the fund manager to CGM's risk management service. This linkage provides the fund manager with real-time capital and risk monitoring, as well as historical data services through numerous data partners.

Once a fund has chosen to link with CGM, the fund is allowed to use the CGM Pro™ trademark as a part of its advertising program. Such a trademark might quickly come to represent excellence in independent risk and capital management oversight—an attribute that is increasingly demanded by fund investors.

With CGM Pro™ professional traders have real-time access to market prices and electronic trading. Other systems offer this capability; however, CGM Pro™ separates itself from the pack by means of its stress and scenario analysis tool and database management capability.

To use CGM Pro™, clients dynamically load their portfolios into the CGM database. Once the portfolio is loaded, the fund manager can choose from a number of preset stress scenarios to create an unlimited number of customized stresses and shocks. If these shocks reveal weaknesses in the portfolio, the manager can execute trades with CGM electronically.

If the manager wants to discuss a situation with a CGM relationship manager, he or she can contact the manager by simply pushing a button on the screen. The relationship manager is linked to the client via a video-conference call, and with the full client portfolio available the situation can be resolved in a virtual environment.

3. PROCESS FOR REVIEWING RISK IN EXTREME MARKETS WILL BECOME STANDARDIZED

The industry will develop a standardized set of tools to review the performance of a portfolio or business in extreme markets. The use of these tools will be encouraged by the regulators and will prove to be quite useful in terms of examining potential future losses caused by extreme market conditions.

For example, over the last year banks have asked how they can avoid significant losses in market conditions such as those of August–October 1998. Some market commentators have called market conditions during these three months a "Series of Firsts." There is no easy answer to this. Banks need to review continually their risk management performance, and ask themselves a series of tough questions in terms of each element of the risk management framework introduced earlier (see Figures 3.2 to 3.5 in Chapter 3).

They also need to ask how they can improve their risk management policies. It is not enough to measure risks; banks need to ensure continually that in the future the risks in extreme markets will be properly disclosed, made transparent, and—most difficult of all—understood.

Of course, the methodological perspective is vital too, and everchanging. Banks will need to ask themselves a series of questions. How well will the bank's risk measurement models serve the organization in the future? Will risk measurement models appropriately capture all the risk of future business lines? How advanced is the bank's measurement of risk in comparison to its competitors? Finally, a series of questions concerning infrastructure should be asked. Will the bank's risk management infrastructure—staff, as well as its systems—serve it well in extreme markets?

Let's first analyze the policy component of the risk management framework. The tolerance for risk should follow directly from the bank's business strategy. For example, the strategic plan at the beginning of the year may call for the daily value at risk for credit spread risk to be set at a certain level which is in excess of current trading limits in order to earn the income projected for credit-intensive business, e.g., a high-yield business.

Recall that the value-at-risk number tells the bank how much it could, and is willing to, lose in a single day. A best-practice policy calls for the active management of the risk limits set for individual businesses. For example, an analysis of market conditions that indicated that a reduction in risk authorities was appropriate should prompt the risk committee to "slow down" some of the bank's businesses as illustrated in Figure 17.8. It could do this by reducing the business's risk authorities (by, say, 33 percent).

Figure 17.9, for illustrative purposes, displays the value-at-risk authority in terms of risk measurement units. The overall (tier 1) risk authorities are shown as having been reduced in July prior to uncertain markets in August, September, and October.

Recall also that risk authorities are intended to limit overall trading risk exposure, as well limiting overall exposure by asset class (e.g., equity asset class). Recall from Chapter 2 that business unit risk authorities (called tier 2 limits) are intended to ensure that the bank maintains control of trading risk at the business unit level. The risk committee should therefore also reduce the business unit (tier 2) risk authorities.

The bank's policies should call for a full disclosure of risks through the publication of a variety of risk reports. These should be circulated from the bottom of the house (trading desk level) to the top of the house (management committee level). In the future the family of risk reports is likely to build on those in use today.

FIGURE 17.8

Changed Business Strategy to Reduce Risk

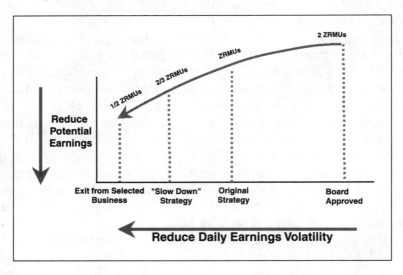

The bank should publish a daily value-at-risk report that corresponds to the risk associated with the mark-to-market values of the bank portfolio, and which compares the bank's actual performance to its daily value-at-risk limit (see Figure 17.10).

The bank should also publish a daily stress test report, which shows the results of a series of relatively extreme, although realistic, worst case stress tests over a time frame of 1 week, 1 month,

FIGURE 17.9

Reduced Tier 1 Risk Authorities Prior to Uncertain Markets

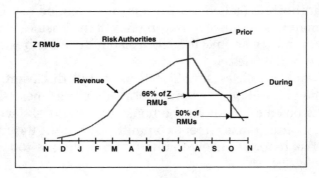

FIGURE 17.10

Daily Net Trading Revenue versus Value at Risk

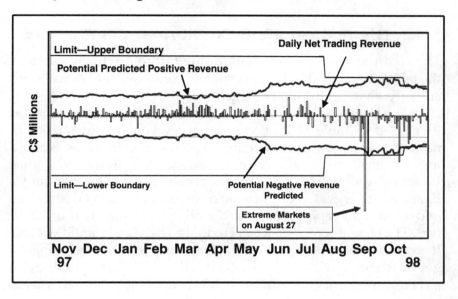

and 1 quarter. The report should reveal whether the bank is keeping within preset stress test loss limits.

Banks should also produce risk-adjusted return on capital (RAROC) reports on a monthly basis.

Reports should also include a weekly summary of significant risks that describes risk at the business unit level, and ranks risks from high to low. Typically, the top 10 risks on a summary of significant risks report would be associated with core businesses, i.e., the businesses that are integral to the bank's business strategy.

Written reports are not enough. To make sure that risks are made transparent, banks must also institute daily and weekly meetings. For example, risks can be reviewed and disclosed at, say, a daily trading room meeting that includes the most senior trading management. A weekly review of risk at a risk committee and the management committee should also be instituted. In times of difficult markets, the bank should hold weekly ALCO meetings.

In short, the frequency and quality of risk communication is crucial. It should involve the most senior management, and they should strive to make sure it is at least as intense as in comparable trading institutions.

4. THE CREDIT ANALYSIS PROCESS AND THE NEED FOR INTEGRATING RISKS

4.1 The Future of the Credit Analysis Process

The credit analysis process will, in the future, routinely combine the best features of the classic corporate credit decision process and advanced asset portfolio management.

The elements of the classic corporate credit decision model (as illustrated in Table 17.2) encompass analysis of business risks, financial risks, and credit structure. Business risk involves evaluating the level and stability of operating cash flows over time. Financial risk involves assessing the risk inherent in the company's financial strategy. Credit structures involve the capital structure and sources of repayment, and the adequate protection of creditors. The classic accept-or-reject credit decision (i.e., should we take the credit exposure?) on a transaction basis involves bringing together business risk analysis, financial risk analysis, and credit structure elements. The more modern approach embraces asset portfolio management (APM).

Asset portfolio management (APM) will seek to improve the risk/return characteristics of the portfolio by proactive portfolio management including (but not limited to) buying and selling credits in the secondary market, securitizing assets, and active hedging. Hedge instruments may include corporate bonds, equity derivatives and, of course, credit derivatives. APM will seek, like other portfolio management units, to improve the RAROC of the bank's aggregate credit portfolio by transacting proactively in the capital markets. It will employ well-developed analytics to assist in structuring the transactions as well as in dealing with intercreditor issues and documentation. Analytic credit models will dramatically upgrade the institution's ability to perform optimal portfolio management.

While a company's level of business risk is primarily affected by factors outside of its short-term control (i.e., the economy, industry competition, etc.), a company's level of financial risk generally reflects management decisions. Companies often try to balance these two risks. For example, companies in highly cyclical and/or competitive industries often assume a conservative financial strategy. This suggests that a firm should analyze financial risk only after it has completed its business risk analysis.

By combining assessments of business and financial risks, a judgment can be made as to the credit quality of a company: the company's ability to service its financial obligations as they come due. This is not a yes or no question, but rather an assessment of the company's likelihood of default. This assessment is often expressed as a company credit rating or credit score.

Most banks in the future will combine the strength of the classic corporate credit model with the strength of powerful analytic models. For example, if the size of the credit spread can be analytically predicted from a model, then it can be used as a complement to the classic corporate decision model in terms of arriving at an internal risk rating. We showed in Chapter 9 that if we follow Merton's contingent claim assumption, then we can also derive a formula to calculate the credit spread.

In the future, commercially available standardized models, as a natural evolution of a contingent claim approach, will be able to calculate the credit spread (say, over treasury rate) of a credit-risky asset as a function of a joint distribution of interest rates and default probabilities. For example, if we examine Merton's original contingent claim framework, then one can incorporate stochastic interest rates (in lieu of utilizing a constant risk-free rate of return).

Similarly, if we examine external models, such as the CreditMetrics model discussed in Chapter 8, then appropriate methods will be made commercially available to incorporate stochastic interest rates (in lieu of utilizing a constant forward spread curve) into these models.

4.2 The Need for Integrating Risks

The traditional approach to risk management has been to calculate the amount of trading market risk and trading credit risk separately without considering their interaction with one other, and to add the amount of trading market risk to the amount of trading credit risk. Adding these two types of risk tends to overstate significantly the overall risk. Further, from an organizational perspective, failing to integrate the trading market risk function and a trading credit risk function into one overall price risk function can lead to a significant organizational disfunctionality.

For example, traditionally, credit spread risk for a corporate bond has been managed solely by the trading market risk function.

TABLE 17.2

Corporate Credit Decision Model

Credit Quality		Credit Decision
The company's ability to service its financial obligations as they come due		*Should we assume credit exposure?*
Business Risk	**Financial Risk**	**Credit Structure**
Evaluate the level and stability of operating cash flows over time	*Assess the risk inherent in the company's financial strategy*	*Provide an appropriate credit structure for the client and adequate protection for creditors*

Business Risk

1) **Business Environment**
   a) Sales Patterns
      • Secular
      • Cyclical
      • Seasonal
   b) Drivers of Sales
      • Economy
      • Demographics
      • Lifestyle
      • Government
      • Technology
2) **Industry Characteristics**
   a) Competition and Profitability
      1. Rivalry
      2. Buyer power
      3. Supplier power

Financial Risk

1) **Financial Strategy**
   a) Dividend policy
   b) Investment in operating assets
   c) Capital structure: target leverage and credit rating
   d) Interest rate and currency mixes
2) **Financial Flexibility**
   a) Liquidity
   b) Debt maturity structure
   c) Capital markets access
3) **Financial Management**
   a) Clear and appropriate financial strategy
   b) Appropriate disclosure and accounting standards
   c) Integrity
4) **Financial Analysis**
   a) ratio analysis
      • Trends and comparables

Credit Decision

1) **Transaction Type**
   a) Use of funds
   b) Sources of repayment
      • Cashflow
      • Refinancing
      • Asset sales
   c) Facility type
   d) Maturity schedule
2) **Intercreditor Issues**
   a) Collateral
   b) Subordination
   c) Guarantees
3) **Documentation**
   a) Covenants
   b) Defaults

4. Substitutes
5. New entrants
   b) Cycle of Development
      • Start-up
      • Growth
      • Maturity
      • Decline

3) **Company Position**
   a) Market Share
   b) Operating Efficiency
   c) Business Strategy

—Profitability
—Coverage
—Leverage
   b) Cash flow analysis
   c) Financial forecast and sensitivity analysis

Portfolio Management
Optimize use of capital
1) **Underwriting Standards**
   a) Target risk profile
   b) Risk-adjusted return on capital
2) **Relative Value**
   a) Concentration
   b) Liquidity
   c) Relationship

Source: (1998) Financial Training Partner

1. **Rivalry** refers to a struggle for market share. Companies use pricing, advertising, promotions, new features, new products, quality, service, and other means to compete with one another. Price competition is the easiest type to match and the most destabilizing. Rivalry is often the most intense in industries with high operating leverage and barriers to exit.

2. **Buyer power** refers to bargaining for lower product prices. Buyers bargain for lower prices, higher quality, or more service. They encourage competition by pitting rivals against one another. The greater the buyer power, the higher the overall level of competition in the industry.

3. **Supplier power** refers to bargaining for higher input prices. Suppliers can raise prices or reduce quality. They affect profitability and competition in an industry by increasing its costs.

4. **Substitutes**. New products replace established ones. Substitutes are other products that perform the same functions as an industry's products. They affect competition by limiting the prices an industry can charge.

5. **New entrants**. New competitors come into the industry, reducing profitability for every company in the industry by bidding down prices and increasing costs. The likelihood of a new entry depends on the barriers to entry and the threat of retaliation.

Yet credit spread risk is a clear function of interest rate risk, default risk, and recovery rate risk. Similarly, contingent credit risk has often been managed solely by the trading credit risk function; yet credit exposure in traded instruments is driven primarily by a change in market rates.

In the future, models will integrate market risk and credit risk so as to capture in a consistent framework the market component, the credit component, and the liquidity component of bonds and loans.

The term "price risk" management might be a useful way of describing the trading risk that arises due to combinations of changes in credit quality of the issuer and changes in market rates that affect the value of the bank's trading position. In other words, price risk management sits at the intersection of trading credit risk management and trading market risk management.

The VaR analytics developed for the trading book will be readily adopted and applied to calculate VaR for the banking book. Further, the introduction of innovative products (such as credit derivatives) will blur the distinction between the banking book and the trading book. We believe that increasingly sophisticated regulation, which allows banks to use their own internal models to arrive at the minimum required regulatory capital (such as BIS 98), in lieu of a "one size fits all" standardized regulatory approach, will force practitioners to integrate their thinking across the banking book and the trading book.

Practitioners who fail to integrate their thinking will be arbitraged by those working for institutions that operate under a fully integrated risk framework.

To illustrate the notion of price risk, let us consider a traded corporate bond. Its price, B, will change as a result of one of three major reasons:

1. A change in interest rates. This is the market risk factor.
2. A specific change in the credit quality of the bond due, for example, to changes in the business environment of the firm.
3. A random change, due to random demand and supply fluctuations.

These three factors are not independent, as can be demonstrated by means of a simple model of the leveraged firm (see

Merton 1974, Galai and Masulis 1976, and Chapter 8 of the present volume). The firm, as a whole, with all its assets and current and future activities, is subject to business risk, which measures the dispersion of its market value (either in absolute or relative terms).

The business risk of the firm is related to the market risk, where the market risk is estimated as the risk of a broad index of risky assets such as the S&P 500. In the Appendix, based on Crouhy, Galai, and Mark (1997), we illustrate the relationships between market risk and business risk and how business risk is reflected in the financial risk of a firm, due to its capital structure; using basic financial models, we relate default risk to the business risk of the firm, as a function of its sensitivity to market risk.

Figure 17.11 summarizes the relationships between market risk, business risk, financial risk, and credit risk in a unified and consistent framework. Market risk, through all its components, i.e.,

FIGURE 17.11

Relationships Between Market Risk, Business Risk, Financial Risk, and Credit Risk

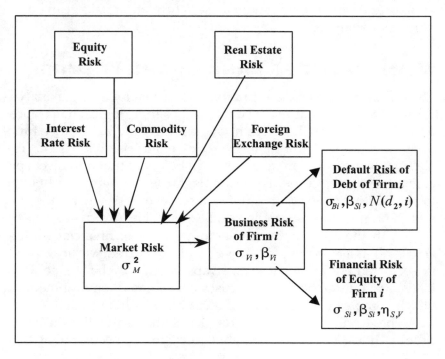

interest rate risk, equity risk, foreign exchange risk, commodity risk, etc., affects the business risk of the firm. The business risk of the firm is shared by the claim holders of the firm. If the firm is a pure equity firm, equity holders are the only stakeholders and are exposed to business risk. If the company is partially financed by debt, and where there is no risk of default, shareholders alone assume financial risk (which is an amplification of the business risk). Where there is a chance of the firm defaulting on its debt, bondholders are exposed to credit risk, and so are shareholders. In this case, debt holders assume part of the business risk of the firm and must be compensated accordingly.

This simple analysis suggests that all risks should be assessed within a unified framework in order to maintain consistency. Credit risk cannot be separated from the business risk of the firm and its claim structure. The business risk analysis cannot be separated from the analysis of market risk. The unified framework is especially important when assessing risk of various situations simultaneously. The above analysis can be easily expanded to the cases of several companies with different business risks and capital structures. Using the framework, the "correlation risks" can be derived and analyzed.

5. AN IDEALIZED BANK OF THE FUTURE

The efficient bank of the future will be driven by a single analytical risk engine that draws its data from a single logical data repository. This engine will power front-, middle-, and back-office functions, and supply information about enterprise-wide risk. The ability to control and manage risk will be finely tuned to meet specific business objectives. For example, far fewer significantly large losses, beyond a clearly articulate tolerance for loss, will be incurred and the return to risk profile will be vastly improved.

With the appropriate technology in place, financial trading across all asset classes will move from the current vertical, product-oriented environment (e.g., swaps, foreign exchange, equities, loans, etc.) to a horizontal, customer-oriented environment in which complex combinations of asset types will be traded.

There will be less need for desks that specialize in single product lines. The focus will shift to customer needs rather than instrument types. The management of limits will be based on capital, set in such a manner so as to maximize the risk-adjusted return on capital for the firm. Business managers will be remunerated on their risk-adjusted earnings rather than on earnings alone, orienting them much more consistently with the goals of the firm.

The firm's exposure will be known and disseminated in real time. Evaluating the risk of a specific deal will take into account its effect on the firm's total risk exposure, rather than simply the exposure of the individual deal.

Banks that dominate this technology will gain a tremendous competitive advantage. Their information technology and trading infrastructure will be cheaper than today's by orders of magnitude. Conversely, banks that attempt to build this infrastructure in-house will become trapped in a quagmire of large, expensive IT departments—and poorly supported software.

The successful banks will require far fewer risk systems. Most of which will be based on a combination of industry standard, reuseable, robust risk software and highly sophisticated proprietary analytics. More importantly, they will be free to focus on their core business and offer products more directly suited to their customers' desired return to risk profiles.

APPENDIX: THE RELATIONSHIP BETWEEN MARKET RISK, BUSINESS RISK AND CREDIT RISK

A1 Defining Market Risk and Business Risk

The business risk of the firm is affected by the "market risk," where the market risk is represented by the risk of a broad index of the stock market (e.g., the S&P 500 or the NYSE Index). The market risk is measured by the variance of the rate of return of the market portfolio, denoted by, σ_M^2.[5] The business risk of the firm can then be measured by the relative contribution of our firm to the market risk. This is the outcome of the capital asset pricing model (CAPM) of Sharpe (1964) and Lintner (1965) described in Chapter 1:

$$\beta_V = \frac{\text{cov}(R_V, R_M)}{\sigma_M^2}$$

and $\text{cov}(R_V, R_M)$ denotes the covariance between the rate of return on the assets of the firm, R_V, and the rate of return on the market portfolio of risky assets, R_M. It should be noted that the sum of all the covariances weighted by the proportion of the assets in the market portfolio is σ_M^2. Therefore, β_V of the firm measures its relative contribution to the total risk of the market. This beta risk is a measure of the systematic risk of the firm based on its comovements with the whole market. The specific risk of the firm is diversified away in the market portfolio.

The proponents of the beta approach for which β_V is the appropriate measure of the business risk of the firm, rather than σ_V^2, argue that σ_V^2 contains elements of uncertainty which can be diversified away at no significant cost. Indeed, the total variance of the rate of return on the assets of the firm can be partitioned[6] into "systematic risk", $\beta_V^2 \sigma_M^2$, and "unsystematic risk" or "idiosyncratic risk," σ_e^2, i.e. $\sigma_V^2 = \beta_V^2 \sigma_M^2 + \sigma_e^2$. Idiosyncratic risk, σ_e^2, is not correlated with the market portfolio and as such can be eliminated by simple diversification. Hence, investors should be compensated only for $\beta_V^2 \sigma_M^2$, which cannot be eliminated through diversification. The risk premium above the risk-free rate, R, which rewards investors for bearing systematic risk, is $\beta_V(\overline{R}_M - R)$ where $\overline{R}_M - R$, the excess of the expected return on the market portfolio, $\overline{R}_M$, over the risk-free rate, R, is the price of risk per unit of beta.[7]

According to the beta approach, market risk is the only explanatory variable of the business risk of the firm for which investors should be compensated. If σ_V^2 is used, then market risk still has an important impact on σ_V^2, but additional specific factors related to the firm's unique activities may also affect σ_V^2.

A2 Defining Financial and Credit Risk

The firm, as a whole, is not subject to "financial risk." "Financial risk" is a measure of the volatility of the stakeholders' claims on the firm's assets, i.e., the uncertainty faced by the shareholders, bond holders, warrant holders, etc. In terms of the simple model of the firm, business risk measures the volatility of V, and this business risk is shared by the debt holders and shareholders whose claims have market values of B and S, respectively. In short, the claim holders share the value of the firm, as well as its overall business risk. The "sharing rule" for business risk is what we call "financial risk."

In a firm financed solely by equity, shareholders are only exposed to business risk, and do not assume any financial risk. The latter originates from the capital structure of the firm and its financial leverage. Since debt holders have priority on the assets of the firm, they assume less risk than the shareholders who have a claim on the residual value of the firm. Assuming that the firm doesn't go bankrupt, bond holders are being compensated by a fixed payment and shareholders get the residual earnings above the interest payment. The compensation to the shareholders is thus subject to greater volatility than the volatility of the firm. Shareholders have a claim on part of the assets of the firm while they assume the totality of the business risk of the firm, shifting it away entirely from the bond holders. Therefore, shareholders should be compensated for the relative increase in risk. By how much? The answer is provided by M&M Proposition II.[8]

According to M&M Proposition II, the expected return on equity, $\overline{R}_s$, also called the cost of equity or the required return on equity, is a linear function of the firm's debt-to-equity ratio, or financial leverage, B/S:

$$\overline{R}_s = \overline{R}_V + (\overline{R}_V - R)\frac{B}{S} \tag{1}$$

where $\overline{R}_V$ is the expected rate of return of the firm's assets, and R is the risk-free interest rate. Shareholders are compensated, in terms of their expected rate of return, for financial leverage. Each additional unit of leverage as measured by B/S adds $(\overline{R}_V - R)$ to $\overline{R}_s$. The difference $\overline{R}_V - R$ measures the risk premium of the firm due to its business risk. $\overline{R}_s$ is an increasing linear function of B/S to reflect the greater volatility of net earnings per share as the leverage increases; this is the financial risk for which equity holders should be compensated.

Up to this point it is implicitly assumed that corporate debt is riskless, and debt holders expect to receive R with certainty. Shareholders, according to equation (1), are compensated for the potentially greater fluctuations in equity value due to their obligation to pay a fix amount to the debt holders, regardless of the firm's performance. In equation (1) there is no compensation for the risk of default, since so far we have assumed it away.

"Credit risk," or equivalently "default risk" in this simple model, is the risk of the firm going into insolvency, i.e., not being able to meet its obligations to the debt holders. Since the firm, when partially financing its activities with debt, enters into an agreement to pay a fixed amount of interest on set dates, regardless of its profitability, it may run into liquidity problems and default on its obligation to the debt holders. This happens when the market value of the firm's assets declines below the payment to be made to the debt holders. This kind of risk should be the concern of debt holders, and they should require a compensation for assuming default risk in terms of higher interest rate than R. In the previous framework, with no default risk, bond holders were not subject to any risk, and the financial risk was a concern of shareholders alone, as expressed in (1). By introducing a probability of default, business risk is now shared by both bond holders and shareholders. Introducing default risk does not affect the business risk of the firm, given its investment policy, and assuming its business activities are not affected by the way they are financed.[9]

In theory, the firm can only default at the maturity of the debt, when the firm's asset value V_T is less than the promised payment to debt holders F (assuming, for simplicity of exposition, that F includes the principal and the promised interest payments, and that there are no interest payments before the debt matures). In practice, default can be triggered by a liquidity squeeze, when the firm's asset value is above F but it has difficulties in raising sufficient cash on time to meet its obligations.[10] Also in practice, the option of asking for Chapter 11 protection may affect the probability and cost of default since it changes the "sharing rule" between bond holders and shareholders.

In what follows, for the sake of simplicity, we continue to analyze the case of a firm financed only by equity and a one-period bond, with default defined at maturity by $V_T < F$. This simple model has the merit to illustrate clearly the functional relationship between market risk, business risk, financial risk, and default risk.

A3 The Relationships Between Market, Business, Financial, and Default Risks

Merton (1974) and Galai and Masulis (1976) analyzed equity and debt values using the simple framework that we described in Chapter 9. It can be shown that equity may be priced as a call option on the firm's assets, and that the systematic risk of equity, defined by its beta, is given by:

$$\beta_s = \eta_{s,V}\beta_V \tag{2}$$

where $\eta_{s,V}$ denotes the elasticity of S with respect to V, i.e.:

$$\eta_{s,V} = \frac{\partial S}{\partial V}\frac{V}{S} = N(d_1)\frac{V}{S}$$

where:

$$d_1 = \frac{\ln(V/F) + (R + \frac{1}{2}\sigma_V^2)T}{\sigma_V\sqrt{T}}$$

$$d_2 = d_1 - \sigma_V\sqrt{T}$$

$N(\cdot)$ is the cumulative standard normal distribution, σ_V^2 is the continuous time variance of the rate of return on the assets of the firm, and T is the time to debt's maturity. $N(d_1)$ is the delta of equity, or its sensitivity to a \$1 change in the value of the firm's assets, and $1 - N(d_2) = N(-d_2)$ is the probability of default.[11]

Similarly, the beta of the risky debt is:

$$\beta_B = \eta_{B,V}\beta_V \tag{3}$$

where, $\eta_{B,V}$ is the elasticity of B with respect to V, i.e.:

$$\eta_{B,V} = N(-d_1)\frac{V}{B}$$

β_B is a measure of the price risk of a corporate bond which incorporates all the systematic effects on the value of the bond.

It should be noted that $\eta_{s,V} > 1(\eta_{B,V} < 1)$; hence the beta risk of equity (debt) is higher (lower) than the systematic risk of the firm:

$$\beta_B \leq \beta_V \leq \beta_s$$

At the same time it can be shown that the weighted betas of debt and equity sum up to the beta of the firm:

$$\beta_V = \frac{S}{V}\beta_s + \frac{B}{V}\beta_B$$

Thus the business risk of the firm is shared by equity and debt holders.[12]

The deltas of equity, $N(d_1)$, and of debt, $N(-d_1)$, reflect the potential for default of the debt. If the probability of default is zero, then $N(d_1) = N(d_2) = 1$ and $N(-d_1) = N(-d_2) = 0$ and the beta of debt is zero, while that of equity is equal to $\beta_V[V/S]$. Still, equity is exposed to financial risk as reflected in V/S due to the existence of the fixed obligation to the debt holders, i.e., the financial leverage.

From the continuous-time capital asset pricing model (CAPM), the cost of equity capital is given by:

$$\overline{R}_S = R + \beta_S(\overline{R}_M - R) \tag{4}$$

which is equivalent to M&M Proposition II stated in equation (1). In (4) the risk premium is the market excess return, or market risk premium, $(\overline{R}_M - R)$, when risk is measured by the beta of equity. By substituting β_S from (2) in (4), we obtain:

$$\overline{R}_S = R + N(d_1)\frac{V}{S}\beta_V(\overline{R}_M - R) \tag{5}$$

From (5) the risk of equity is clearly expressed as the product of a function of the nondefault risk, $N(d_1)$, the financial risk, V/S, the business risk of the firm, β_V, with the price of risk being the market risk premium $(\overline{R}_M - R)$.

Similar expressions can be derived for the expected return on the risky corporate debt:

$$\overline{R}_B = R + \beta_B(\overline{R}_M - R) \tag{6}$$

By substituting β_B from (3) in (6), $\overline{R}_B$ can be written as follows:

$$\overline{R}_B = R + N(-d_1)\frac{V}{B}\beta_V(\overline{R}_M - R) \tag{7}$$

where $N(-d_1) = 1 - N(d_1)$. The risk premium for the corporate bond is a product of the adjusted leverage $N(-d_1)[V/B]$, the beta risk of debt, β_V, and the price per unit of risk $(\overline{R}_M - R)$. The systematic risk of the firm β_V is related to market risk σ_M^2 by $\beta_V = \text{cov}(R_V, R_M)/\sigma_M^2$, which can be substituted in (7).

NOTES

1. A patent becomes an asset of the firm and is written off over a prescribed number of years. For a recent discussion of the patent

issue, see William Falloon's "Patent Power: Who Owns the Ideas That Drive Derivatives?", *Risk* (December 1999), pp. 22–27.

2. Intellectual Property Briefing Paper, August 1998, see Origin.co.uk, "Briefing Papers" website.

3. *Financial Post*, Thursday, January 28, 1999.

4. A valuation adjustment risk refers to the degree to which one fails to adjust properly the valuation of a position for risk. For example, the G-30 recommends that clients who deal in derivatives should take the mid-market price of the trade, less the sum of the expected credit loss and the forward administrative cost, when valuing a perfectly matched derivative transaction. Accordingly, an institution needs to analyze the reasonableness of its approach to estimating an expected credit loss. The G-30 also suggests additional adjustments for close-out costs (i.e., "eliminating" market risk), as well as investing and funding costs.

5. See Chapter 1, Section 4.

6. The partitioning is based on a single-factor model, the market model, to explain how rates of return are generated: $R_{V,t} = a + bR_{M,t} + \epsilon_t$.

7. See also Appendix for a discussion of the risk premium in the case of a leveraged firm. According to the capital asset pricing model (CAPM), the required rate of return on equity for an all-equity financed firm is $\overline{R}_s = R + \beta_V(\overline{R}_M - R)$.

8. See Modigliani and Miller (1958).

9. See Crouhy and Galai (1994) for a discussion of cases when the financing policy may affect the value of the firm. If, for example, the firm issues equity warrants, then cash is paid out to the firm twice, first when the warrants are issued, and later on when the warrants are exercised. Depending on the assumptions regarding the use of the proceeds from the exercise of the warrants, the value of the firm and its business risk may be affected.

10. See Chapter 9 for KMV's definition of the default trigger.

11. In a risk-neutral world, $N(d_2)$ is the probability that the firm's value at time T, V_T, will be higher than F.

12. Indeed, $\beta_S[S/V] + \beta_B[B/V] = N(d_1)[V/S]\beta_V[S/V] + N(-d_1)[V/B]\beta_V[B/V] = \beta_V$

REFERENCES

Abramowitz, M., and I. A. Stegum, *Handbook of Mathematical Functions*. New York: Dover Publications, 1970.

Ahn, D., J. Boudoukh, M. Richardson, and R. F. Whitelow, "Optimal Risk Management Using Options." NBER Working Paper 6158. Cambridge, MA: National Bureau of Economic Research, 1997.

Ahn, M. J., and W. D. Falloon, *Strategic Risk Management*. Chicago: Probus, 1991.

Allen, S. L., and A. D. Kleinstein, *Valuing Fixed Income Investments and Derivative Securities: Cash Flow Analysis and Calculations*. New York: Simon and Schuster, 1991.

Altman, E. I., *Corporate Financial Distress and Bankruptcy*. New York: John Wiley and Sons, 1993.

Altman, E. I., "The Importance and Subtlety of Credit Rating Migration." *Journal of Banking and Finance* 22 (1998), pp. 1231-1247.

Altman, E. I., and D. L. Kao, "Rating Drift in High-Yield Bonds." *The Journal of Fixed Income* 1 (1992a), pp. 15-20.

Altman, E. I., and D. L. Kao, "The Implications of Corporate Bond Ratings Drift." *Financial Analysts Journal* 48 (1992b), pp. 64-75.

Altman, E. I., and V. Kishore, "Almost Everything You Wanted to Know about Recoveries on Defaulted Bonds." *Financial Analysts Journal* 52(6), (November/December 1996), pp.57-64.

Altman, E. I., and V. Kishore, "Defaults and Returns on High Yield Bonds: Analysis through 1997." New York University Salomon Center: Working Paper S-98-1, 1998.

Altman, E. I., and A. Saunders, "Credit Risk Measurement: Developments over the Last 20 Years." *Journal of Banking and Finance* 21 (1997), pp. 1721-1742.

Anderson, R. W., and S. M. Sundaresan, "Design and Valuation of Debt Contracts." *Review of Financial Studies* 9 (1) (1996), pp. 37-68.

Apostol, T. M., *Calculus*, volume 1, second edition. Waltham, MA: Blaisdell Publishing Company, 1967.

Artzner P., F. Delbaen, J. M. Eber, and D. Heath, "Coherent Measures of Risk." *Mathematical Finance* 9(3) (1999), pp. 203-228.

Bahar, R. and M. Gold, "Structuring Derivative Product Companies: Risks and Safeguards." In *Derivative Credit Risk: Advances in Measurement and Management*. London: Risk Books, 1995.

Bangia, A., F. X. Diebold, T. Schuermann, and J. D. Stroughair, "Modeling Liquidity Risk, with Implications for Traditional Market Risk Measurement and Management." The Wharton School: Working Paper 99-06, 1999.

Bank of England, "Developing a Supervisory Approach to Credit Derivatives." *Risk* 9(11) (1996), p. 7.

Bansal, A., R. J. Kauffman, R. M. Mark, and E. Peters, "Financial Risk and Financial

Risk Management Technology." *Information and Management*, 24 (1993), pp. 267-281.

Basle Committee on Banking Supervision, 1988, *International Convergence of Capital Measurement and Capital Standards*. Basle, Switzerland: Basle Committee on Banking Supervision, 1988.

Basle Committee on Banking Supervision, *An Internal Model-Based Approach to Market Risk Capital Requirements*. Basle, Switzerland: Basle Committee on Banking Supervision, 1995.

Basle Committee on Banking Supervision, *Amendment to the Capital Accord to Incorporate Market Risks*. Basle, Switzerland: Basle Committee on Banking Supervision, 1996.

Basle Committee on Banking Supervision, *Framework For International Control Systems In Banking Organizations*. Basle, Switzerland: Basle Committee on Banking Supervision, 1998a.

Basle Committee on Banking Supervision, *Operational Risk Management*. Basle, Switzerland: Basle Committee on Banking Supervision, 1998b.

Basle Committee on Banking Supervision, *A New Capital Adequacy Framework*. Basle, Switzerland: Basle Committee on Banking Supervision, 1999a.

Basle Committee on Banking Supervision, *Banks' Interactions with Highly Leveraged Institutions*. Basle, Switzerland: Basle Committee on Banking Supervision, 1999b.

Basle Committee on Banking Supervision, *Credit Risk Modelling: Current Practices and Applications*. Basle, Switzerland: Basle Committee on Banking Supervision, 1999c.

Bauer, W., "Implementing and Managing Risk-Adjusted Return on Risk-Adjusted Capital." *Bank Treasurer Manual. Sheshunoff Information Services*, 1998.

Beaver, W.H., and G. Parker, *Risk Management, Problems, and Solutions*. New York: McGraw-Hill, 1995.

Bennet, P., "Applying Portfolio Theory to Global Bank Lending." *Journal of Banking and Finance* 8(2) (1984), pp. 153-169.

Bensoussan A., M. Crouhy, and D. Galai, "Stochastic Equity Volatility Related to the Leverage Effect I: Equity Volatility Behaviour." *Applied Mathematical Finance* 1 (1994), pp. 63-85.

Bensoussan A., M. Crouhy, and D. Galai, "Stochastic Equity Volatility Related to the Leverage Effect II: Valuation of European Equity Options and Warrants." *Applied Mathematical Finance* 2 (1995), pp. 43-59.

Bensoussan, A., M. Crouhy, and D. Galai, "Black-Scholes Approximation of Complex Option Values: The Cases of European Compound Call Options and Equity Warrants." In *Option Embedded Bonds*, ed. I. Nelken. Chicago, IL: Irwin Professional Publishing, 1997.

Berger, A. N., R. J. Herring, and G. P. Szego, "The Role of Capital in Financial Institutions." *Journal of Banking and Finance* 19 (1995), pp. 393-430.

Berger, A.N., and G. F. Udell, "Relationship Lending and Lines of Credit in Small Firm Finance." *Journal of Business* 68 (1995), pp. 351-381.

Berkman, H., and M. Bradbury, "Empirical Evidence on the Corporate Use of Derivatives." *Financial Management* 25(2), (Summer 1996), pp. 5-13.

Berry, M., E. Burmeister, and M. McElroy, "Sorting Our Risks Using Known APT Factors." *Financial Analysts Journal* 44(2) (March/April 1988), pp. 29-42.

Bessembinder, H., "Forward Contracts and Firm Value: Investment Incentive and Contracting Effects." *Journal of Financial and Quantitative Analysis* 26(4), (December 1991), pp. 519-532.

Bester, H., "Screening vs. Rationing in Credit Markets with Imperfect Information." *American Economic Review* 75 (1985), pp. 850-855.

Bierwag, G. O., *Duration Analysis: Managing Interest Rate Risk.* Cambridge, MA: Ballinger, 1987.

Binder, B., and R. Mark, "Technical ALCO in the New Marketplace." In *Bankers Treasury Handbook,* 1988.

Black, F., 1992, "The Holes in Black-Scholes." In *From Black-Scholes to Black Holes.* London: Risk Books, 1992.

Black, F., and J. C. Cox, "Valuing Corporate Securities: Some Effects of Bond Indenture Provisions." *Journal of Finance* 31 (1976), pp. 351-68.

Black, F., and M. Scholes, "The Pricing of Options and Corporate Liabilities." *Journal of Political Economy* 81 (1973), pp. 637-654.

Block, S. B., and T. J. Gallagher, "The Use of Interest Rate Futures and Options by Corporate Financial Managers." *Financial Management,* (Autumn 1986), pp. 73-78.

Bollerslev, T., "Generalized Autoregressive Conditional Heteroskedasticity." *Journal of Econometrics* 31 (1986), pp. 307-327.

Bollerslev, T., R. F. Engle and D. B. Nelson, *ARCH Models,* in Engle, R. and McFadden, D., (eds.), *The Handbook of Econometrics* 4, pp. 2959-3038, Amsterdam: North Holland, 1994.

Bondar, G.M., G. S. Hayt, R. C. Marston, and C. W. Smithson, "Wharton Survey of Derivatives Usage by U.S. Non-Financial Firms." *Financial Management* 24(2), (Summer 1995), pp. 104-114.

Boness, J., "Elements of a Theory of Stock-Option Value." *Journal of Political Economy* 12 (1964), pp. 163-175.

Boudoukh, J., M. Richardson, and R. Whitelaw, 1995, "Expect the Worst." *Risk* 8(9) (1995), pp. 100-101.

Brealey, R., and S. Myers, *Principles of Corporate Finance,* sixth edition. New York: McGraw-Hill, 2000.

Brickley, J., C. Smith, and J. Zimmermon, *The Economics of Organizational Architecture.* Bradley Policy Research Centre, 1995.

Briys, E., and M. Crouhy, "Playing Against the Devil: Managing Financial Risks for Better Corporate Return." *European Management Journal* 11(3) (1993), pp. 304-312.

Broadie, M., and P. Glasserman, "Simulation for Option Pricing and Risk Management." In *Risk Management and Analysis, Vol. 1: Measuring and Modelling Financial Risk,* ed. C. Alexander. New York: John Wiley and Sons, 1998.

Burghardt, G., and G. A. Hanweck, "Calendar-Adjusted Volatilities." *Journal of Derivatives* 1(2), (Winter 1993), pp. 23-32.

Butler, J.S., and B. Schachter, "Improving Value-at-Risk Estimates by Combining

Kernel Estimation with Historical Simulation." Vanderbilt University: mimeo, 1996.

Campbell, J. Y., A. W. Lo, and A. C. MacKinlay, *The Econometrics of Financial Markets*. Princeton, NJ: Princeton University Press, 1997.

Cantor, R., and F. Packer, "The Credit Rating Industry." *Federal Reserve Bank of New York Quarterly Review* 19 (2) (1994), pp.1-26.

Cantor, R., and F. Packer, "Sovereign Credit Ratings." Federal Reserve Bank of New York: *Current Issues in Economics and Finance* 1 (3) (1995).

Cantor, R., and F. Packer, "Differences of Opinion in the Credit Rating Industry." *Journal of Banking and Finance* 21 (10) (1997), pp. 1395-1417.

Caouette, J. B., E. I. Altman, and P. Narayanan, *Managing Credit Risk*. New York: John Wiley and Sons, 1998.

Carty, L. V., and D. Lieberman, *Defaulted Bank Loan Recoveries*. Moody's Investors Service, Global Credit Research, Special Report, 1996.

Carty, L., and J. S. Fons, *Measuring Changes in Credit Quality*. Moody's Investors Service, Special Report, November 1993; also in *Journal of Fixed Income* (June 1996), pp. 27-41.

Chance, D., "Default Risk and the Duration of Zero Coupon Bonds." *Journal of Finance* 45(1) (1990), pp. 265-274.

Chen, N., R. Roll, and S. Ross, "Economic Forces and the Stock Market." *Journal of Business* 59 (1986), pp. 368-403.

Chew, L., *Managing Derivative Risks: The Use and Abuse of Leverage*. New York: John Wiley and Sons, 1996.

Cooper, I., and A. Mello, "The Default Risk of Swaps." *Journal of Finance* 46(2) (1991), pp. 597-620.

Coopers & Lybrand, and The British Bankers' Association, *1997 Operational Risk Management Survey*, 1997.

Cox, J., J. Ingersoll, Jr., and S. Ross, "A Theory of the Term Structure of Interest Rates." *Econometrica* 53 (1985), pp. 385-407.

Credit Suisse, *CreditRisk+: A Credit Risk Management Framework*. Credit Suisse Financial Products, 1997.

Crnkovic, C., and J. Drachman, "Quality Control." Risk 9(9) (1996), pp. 138-143; also in *VaR: Understanding and Applying Value-at-Risk*. London: Risk Books, 1997.

Crouhy, M., and D. Galai, "An Economic Assessment of Capital Requirements in the Banking Industry." *Journal of Banking and Finance* 10 (1986), pp. 231-241.

Crouhy, M., and D. Galai, "A Contingent Claim Analysis of a Regulated Depository Institution." *Journal of Banking and Finance* 15 (1991), pp. 73-90.

Crouhy, M., and D. Galai, "The Interaction between the Financial and Investment Decisions of the Firm: The Case of Issuing Warrants in a Levered Firm." *Journal of Banking and Finance* 18 (1994), pp. 861-880.

Crouhy, M., and D. Galai, "Hedging with a Volatility Term Structure." *Journal of Derivatives* 2(3) (Spring 1995), pp. 45-52.

Crouhy, M., D. Galai, and R. Mark, "What's in a Name?" *Risk*, Enterprise-wide Risk Management Supplement (November 1997), pp. 36-40.

Crouhy, M., D. Galai, and R. Mark, "Credit Risk Revisited." *Risk,* Credit Risk Supplement (March 1998), pp. 40-44.

Crouhy, M., D. Galai, and R. Mark, "Key Steps in Building Consistent Operational Risk Measurement and Management." In *Operational Risk and Financial Institutions,* ed. R. Jameson. London: Risk Books, 1998.

Crouhy, M., D. Galai, and R. Mark, " A Comparative Analysis of Current Credit Risk Models." *Journal of Banking and Finance* 24(1/2) (January 2000), pp. 59-117.

Crouhy, M., S. Turnbull, and L. Wakeman, "Measuring Risk Adjusted Performance." *Journal of Risk* 2(1) (1999), pp. 1-31.

Culp, C. L., and M. H. Miller, "Risk Management Lessons from Metallgesellschaft." *Journal of Applied Corporate Finance* 7 (4) (1994), pp. 62-76.

Culp, C. L., and M. H. Miller, "Hedging in the Theory of Corporate Finance: A Reply to our Critics." *Journal of Applied Corporate Finance* 8 (1995), pp. 121-127.

Curry, D. A., J. A. Gluck, W. L. May, and A.C. Backman, "Evaluating Derivative Product Companies." In *Derivative Credit Risk: Advances in Measurement and Management.* London: Risk Books, 1995.

Das, S., and P. Tufano, "Pricing Credit Sensitive Debt when Interest Rates, Credit Ratings and Credit Spreads are Stochastic." *Journal of Financial Engineering* 5(2) (1995), pp. 161-198.

Das, S. R., "Credit Risk Derivatives." *Journal of Derivatives* 2(3) (Spring 1995), pp. 7-23.

David, H. A., *Order Statistics,* second edition. New York: John Wiley and Sons, 1981

Davidson, C., "Testing the Testers." *Risk* 10(6) (1997), pp. 58-63.

Delianedis, G., and R. Geske, 1998, "Credit Risk and Risk Neutral Default Probabilities: Information about Rating Migrations and Default." UCLA: Working Paper 19-98, 1998.

DeMarzo, P., and D. Duffie, "Corporate Incentives for Hedging and Hedge Accounting." *Review of Financial Studies* 8 (1995), pp. 743-772.

Derivatives Policy Group, *A Framework for Voluntary Oversight,* 1995.

Derman, E., "Model Risk." In VAR — *Understanding and Applying Value-at-Risk.* London: Risk Books, 1997.

Derman, E., and I. Kani, "Riding on a Smile." *Risk* 7 (2) (1994), pp. 32-39.

Diebold, F., A. Hickman, A. Inoue, and T. Schuermann, 1998, "Scale Models." *Risk* 11(1) (January 1998), pp. 104-107.

Dolde, W., "The Trajectory of Corporate Financial Risk Management." *Journal of Applied Corporate Finance* 6 (1993), pp. 33-41.

Dowd, K., *Beyond Value at Risk.* New York: John Wiley and Sons, 1998.

Duan, J. C., "The GARCH Option Pricing Model." *Mathematical Finance* 5 (1995), pp. 13-32.

Duffee, G. R., and C. Zhou, " Credit Derivatives in Banking: Useful Tools for Loan Risk Management." Federal Reserve Board, Washington: Working Paper, 1997.

Duffie, D., *Dynamic Asset Pricing Theory.* Princeton, NJ: Princeton University Press, 1992.

Duffie, D., and M. Huang, "Swap Rates and Credit Quality." Stanford University: Working Paper, 1995.

Duffie, D., M. Schroder, and C. Skiadas, "Recursive Valuation of Defaultable Securities and the Timing of Resolution of Uncertainty." Stanford University: Working Paper, 1995.

Duffie, D., and K. Singleton, "Econometric Modeling of the Term Structure of Defaultable Bonds." Stanford University, Graduate School of Business: Working Paper, 1994.

Duffie, D. and K. Singleton, "Modelling Term Structures of Defaultable Bonds," *Review of Financial Studies* 12(4) (1999), pp. 687-720.

Dunbar, N., *Inventing Money*. New York: John Wiley and Sons, 2000.

Dupire, B., "Pricing with a Smile." *Risk* 7 (1) (1994), pp. 18-20.

Elderfield, M., "Capital Countdown." *Risk* 8(2) (1995), pp. 18-21.

Elton, E.J., and M.J. Gruber, *Modern Portfolio Theory and Investment Analysis*. New York: John Wiley and Sons, 1995.

Engle, R. F., "Autoregressive Conditional Heteroskedasticity with Estimates of the Variance of United Kingdom Inflation." *Econometrica* 50 (1982), pp. 987-1007.

Ernst & Young, *Survey of Investment Concerns*, 1995.

Fabozzi, F. J., *Fixed Income Mathematics*, Chicago, IL: Probus Publishing Company, 1993.

Fabozzi, F. J., *The Handbook of Fixed Income Securities*, fifth edition. New York: McGraw-Hill, 1997.

Falkenstein, E., "Value-at-Risk and Derivatives Risk." *Derivatives Quarterly* 4(1) (Fall 1997), pp. 42-50.

Fallon, W., "Calculating Value-at-Risk." Columbia University: mimeo, 1996.

Fama, E. F., 1968, "Risk, Return and Equilibrium: Some Clarifying Comment." *Journal of Finance* 23(1) (March 1968), pp. 29-40.

Fama, E., and M. Miller, *The Theory of Finance*. New York: Holt, Rinehart and Winston, 1974.

Figlewski, S., "Derivatives Risks, Old and New." New York University: mimeo, 1998.

Figlewski, S., "The Birth of the AAA Derivatives Subsidiary." *Journal of Derivatives* 1(4) (1994), pp. 80-84.

Fishman, G., *Monte Carlo: Concepts, Algorithms, and Applications*. New York: Springer Series in Operations Research, Springer, 1997.

Fite, D., and P. Pfleiderer, "Should Firms Use Derivatives to Manage Risk?" In *Risk Management, Problems and Solutions*, ed. W. H. Beaver and G. Parker. New York: McGraw-Hill, 1995.

Fons, J.S., and L.V. Carty, "Probability of Default: A Derivatives Perspective." In *Derivative Credit Risk — Advances in Measurements and Management*. London: Risk Books, 1995.

Frank, J., and W. Torous, "An Empirical Investigation of Firms in Reorganization." *Journal of Finance* 44 (1989), pp. 747-779.

Friedman, M., "The Methodology of Positive Economics." In *Essays in Positive Economics*. Chicago: University of Chicago Press, 1953.

Froot, K. D., D. Scharfstein, and J. Stein, "Risk Management: Coordinating Investment and Financing Policies." *Journal of Finance* 48 (1993), pp. 1629-1658.

Froot, K. D., D. Scharfstein, and J. Stein, "A Framework for Risk Management." *Harvard Business Review* (November/December 1994).

Galai, D., "Characterization of Options." *Journal of Banking and Finance* 11 (1977), pp. 373-385.

Galai, D., "On the Boness and Black-Scholes Models for Valuation of Call Options." *Journal of Financial and Quantitative Analysis* 13 (1978), pp. 15-27.

Galai, D., and R. W. Masulis, "The Option Pricing Model and the Risk Factor of Stocks." *Journal of Financial Economics* 3 (January-March 1976), pp. 53-82.

Garbade, K. D., *Fixed Income Analytics*. Cambridge, MA: The MIT Press, 1996.

Garman, M. B., "Improving on VaR." *Risk* 9(5) (1996), pp. 61-63.

Garman, M. B., and S. Kolhagen, "Foreign Currency Option Values." *Journal of International Money and Finance* 2 (1983), pp. 231-237.

Géczy, C., B. A. Minton, and C. Schrand, "Why Firms Use Currency Derivatives." *Journal of Finance* 82 (4) (1997), pp. 1323-1354.

Geske, R., "The Valuation of Corporate Liabilities as Compound Options." *Journal of Financial and Quantitative Analysis* 12 (1977), pp. 541-552.

Gibson, R., "Rethinking the Quality of Risk Management Disclosure Practices." HEC Lausanne: Working Paper, 1999.

Gordy, M. B., "A Comparative Anatomy of Credit Risk Models." Finance and Economics Discussion Series, Federal Reserve Board, Washington DC: Working Paper 1998-47, 1998.

Government Accounting Office of the United States, *Risk-Based Capital: Regulatory and Industry Approaches to Capital and Risk*. Report to the Chairman, Committee on Banking, Housing, and Urban Affairs, US Senate, and the Chairman, Committee on Banking and Financial Services, House of Representatives, July 1998.

Group of Thirty, Global Derivatives Study Group, *Derivatives: Practices and Principles*. Washington, DC: Group of Thirty, 1993.

Group of Twelve, *Improving Counterparty Risk Management Practices*. Counterparty Risk Management Policy Group, June 1999.

Guldiman, T., P. Zangari, J. Longerstaey, J. Mateo, and J. Howard, *RiskMetrics, Technical Document*, third edition. New York: Morgan Guaranty Trust Company, 1995.

Gumerlock, R., "Lacking Commitment." *Risk* 9 (6) (June 1996), pp. 36-39.

Hayt, G., and S. Song, "Handle with Sensitivity." *Risk* 8 (9) (September 1995), pp. 94-99.

Heath, D., R. Jarrow, and A. Morton, "Bond Pricing and the Term Structure of Interest Rates: A New Methodology for Contingent Claims Valuation." *Econometrica* 60 (1992), 77-106.

Helfat, C., and D. Teece, (1987) "Vertical Integration and Risk Reduction." *Journal of Law Economics and Organizations* 3(1) (Spring 1987), pp. 47-67.

Hendricks, D., "Netting Agreements and the Credit Exposures of OTC Derivatives Portfolios." *FRBNY Quarterly Review* 19(1) (Spring 1994), pp. 7-18.

Hentschel, L., and C. Smith, "Control Risk Derivatives Market." *The Journal of Financial Engineering* 4(2) (1995), pp. 101-125.

Heston, S., "A Closed-Form Solution for Options with Stochastic Volatility." *Review of Financial Studies* 6 (1993), pp. 327-344.

Ho, T., "Key Rate Durations: Measures of Interest Rate Risks." *Journal of Fixed Income* 2(2) (1992), pp. 29-44.

Ho, T., and R. F. Singer, "Bond Indenture Provisions and the Risk of Corporate Debt." *Journal of Financial Economics* 10 (1982), pp. 375-406.

Hoffman, D., and M. Johnson, 1996, "Operating Procedures." *Risk* 9(10) (October 1996), pp. 60-63.

Hsueh, L.P., and P.R. Chandy, "An Examination of the Yield Spread between Insured and Uninsured Debt." *Journal of Financial Research* 12 (Fall 1989), pp. 235-244.

Hughston, L.R., "Pricing Models for Credit Derivatives." AIC Conference on Credit Derivatives, London: mimeo, April 1997.

Hull, J. C., *Options, Futures, and Other Derivatives*, fourth edition. Upper Saddle River, NJ: Prentice Hall, 2000.

Hull, J., and A. White, "The Impact of Default Risk on the Prices of Options and Other Derivative Securities." *Journal of Banking and Finance* 19(2) (1995), pp. 299-322.

International Institute of Finance, *Report of the Working Group on Quantitative Issues: Capital Adequacy of Specific Risk,* Washington DC: International Institute of Finance, September 1996.

International Swaps and Derivatives Association, *Amendment to the Capital Accord to Incorporate Market Risks: The Use of Internal Models for Supervisory Purposes,* Comments of the ISDA/LIBA Joint Models Task Force. New York: International Swaps and Derivatives Assocation, October 1996.

Jaffe, A., "Bond Insurance: A Financing Tool for I.O.Us." *Public Utilities Fortnightly* 129 (1992), pp. 21-22.

James, C., "RAROC Based Capital Budgeting and Performance Evaluation: A Case Study of Bank Capital Allocation." School of Business Administration, University of Florida: Working Paper, 1996.

Jameson, R. (ed.), *Operational Risk and Financial Institutions.* London: Risk Books, 1998.

Jamshidian, F., and Y. Zhu, "Scenario Simulation: Theory and Methodology." *Finance and Stochastics* 1 (1997), 43-67.

Jarrow, R., D. Lando, and S. Turnbull, "A Markov Model for the Term Structure of Credit Spreads." *Review of Financial Studies* 10 (1997), pp. 481-523.

Jarrow, R. and S. Turnbull, "Pricing Derivatives on Financial Securities Subject to Credit Risk." *Journal of Finance* 50 (1) (1995), pp. 53-85.

Jarrow, R., and S. Turnbull, *Derivatives Securities,* second edition. Cincinnati, Ohio: South-Western College Publishing, 2000.

Jarrow, R., and S. Turnbull, "The Intersection of Market and Credit Risks." Canadian Imperial Bank of Commerce: Working Paper, 1998.

Jilling, M., *Foreign Exchange Risk Management in US Multinational Corporations.* Ann Arbor, MI.: UMI Research Press, 1978.

Johnson, H., and R. Stulz, "The Pricing of Options with Default Risk." *Journal of Finance* 42(2) (1987), pp. 267-280.

Johnson, N., S. Kotz, and N. Balakrishan, *Continuous Univariate Distributions*, volume 2, second edition. New York: John Wiley and Sons, 1995.

Jones, D., and K. K. King, "The Implementation of Prompt Corrective Action: An Assessment." *Journal of Banking and Finance* 19 (1995), pp. 491-510.

Jones, E. P., S. P. Mason, and E. Rosenfeld, "Contingent Claims Analysis of Corporate Capital Structures: An Empirical Analysis." *Journal of Finance* 39 (1984), pp. 611-625.

Jorion, P., "Risk2: Measuring the Risk in Value-at-Risk." *Financial Analysts Journal* 52 (November/December 1996a), pp. 47-56.

Jorion, P., *Value-at-Risk: The New Benchmark for Controlling Market Risk*. Chicago: Irwin, 1996b.

Jorion, P., "Risk Management Lessons from Long-Term Capital Management." University of California at Irvine: Working Paper, 1999.

J.P. Morgan, *CreditMetrics*, Technical Document, 1997.

Kealhofer, S., "Managing Default Risk in Portfolios of Derivatives." In *Derivative Credit Risk*. London: Risk Books, 1995.

Kealhofer, S., "Portfolio Management of Default Risk." *Net Exposure* 1(2) (1998).

Kendall, M. G., and A. Stuart, *The Advanced Theory of Statistics, Volume 2: Inference and Relationship*, third edition. London: Griffin, 1973.

Kim, I. J., K. Ramaswamy, and S.M. Sundaresan, "Valuation of Corporate Fixed-Income Securities." *Financial Management* 22(3) (1993), pp. 60-78.

Kolb, R., *Understanding Futures Markets*, third edition. Miami: Kolb Publishing Co., 1991.

Koyluoglu, H. U., and A. Hickman, "A Generalized Framework for Credit Risk Portfolio Models." Oliver Wyman and CSFP Capital: Working Paper, 1998.

KPMG, "Survey of Disclosures: SEC Market Risk." Mimeo, 1999.

Kupiec, P., "Techniques for Verifying the Accuracy of Risk Measurement Models." *Journal of Derivatives* 3 (1995), pp. 73-84.

Kupiec, P., and J.O'Brien, "The Use of Bank Trading Risk Measurement Models for Regulatory Capital Purposes." Washington DC: Federal Reserve Board, FEDS Working Paper 95-11, 1995a.

Kupiec, P., and J.O'Brien, "A Pre-commitment Approach to Capital Requirements for Market Risk." Washington DC: Federal Reserve Board, FEDS Working Paper 95-34, 1995b.

Kupiec, P., and J. O'Brien, "Internal Affairs." *Risk* 8(5) (1995c), pp. 43-47.

Kupiec, P., and J. O'Brien, "Model Alternative." *Risk* 8(6) (1995d), pp. 37-40.

Kupiec, P., and J. O'Brien, "Commitment Is the Key." *Risk* 9(9) (1996), pp. 60-63.

Kupiec, P., and J. O'Brien, "The Pre-Commitment Approach: Using Incentives to Set Market Risk Capital Requirements." Washington DC: Board of Governors of the Federal System, 1997-14, 1997.

Lando, D., "Three Essays on Contingent Claims Pricing." Cornell University: Ph.D. Dissertation, 1994.

Lando, D., "Modelling Bonds and Derivatives with Default Risk." In *Mathematics of Derivatives Securities*, eds. M. Dempster and S. Pliska. Cambridge: Cambridge University Press, 1997.

Lando, D., "On Cox Process and Credit Risky Securities." *Review of Derivatives Research* 2(2-3) (1998), pp. 99-120.

Lee, C. J., "The Pricing of Corporate Debt: A Note." *Journal of Finance* 36 (1981), pp. 1187-1189.

Leeson, N., *Rogue Trader.* New York: Little, Brown and Company, 1996.

Leland, H., "Corporate Debt Value, Bond Covenants and Optimal Capital Structure." *Journal of Finance* 49 (1994), pp. 1213-1252.

Leland H., and K. Toft, "Optimal Capital Structure, Endogenous Bankruptcy, and the Term Structure of Credit Spreads." *Journal of Finance* 51 (1996), pp. 987-1019.

Leong, K., "Exorcising the Demon." In *From Black-Scholes to Black Holes.* London: Risk Books, 1992.

Levy, H., and M. Sarnat, *Portfolio and Investment Selection: Theory and Practice.* Englewood Cliffs, NJ: Prentice Hall, 1984.

Linsmeier, T. J., and N. D. Pearson, "Risk Measurement: An Introduction to Value-at-Risk." University of Illinois at Urbana Champaign: mimeo, 1996.

Lintner, J., "Security Prices, Risk and Maximal Gains from Diversification." *Journal of Finance* 20 (December 1965), pp. 587-615.

Litterman, R., "Hot Spots™ and Hedges." *Journal of Portfolio Management* Special Issue (December 1996), pp. 52-75.

Litterman, R., and T. Iben, "Corporate Bond Valuation and the Term Structure of Credit Spreads." *Financial Analysts Journal* 47 (Spring 1991), pp. 52-64.

Litterman, R., and J. Scheinkman, "Common Factors Affecting Bond Returns." *Journal of Fixed Income* 1(1) (1988), pp. 54-61.

Litzenberger, R. H., "Swaps: Plain and Fanciful." *Journal of Finance* 47(3) (1992), pp. 831-850.

Longstaff, F., and E. Schwartz, "A Simple Approach to Valuing Risky Fixed and Floating Rate Debt." *Journal of Finance* 50 (1995), pp. 789-819.

Longstaff, F., and E. Schwartz, "Valuing Credit Derivatives." *Journal of Fixed Income* 5(1) (June 1995), pp. 6-12.

Lopez, J. A., and M. R. Saidenberg, "Evaluating Credit Risk Models." Federal Reserve Banks of New York and San Francisco: Working Paper, 1999.

Lucas, D. J., "Default Correlation and Credit Analysis." *Journal of Fixed Income* 4(4) (March 1995), 76-87.

Macauley, F.R., "Some Theoretical Problems Suggested by Movements of Interest Rates, Bond Yields, and Stock Prices in the U.S. since 1856." New York: National Bureau of Economic Research, 1938.

Machauer, A., and M. Weber, "Bank Behavior Based on Internal Credit Ratings of Borrowers." *Journal of Banking and Finance* 22 (1998), pp. 1355-1383.

MacKenzie, Donald, *Fear in the Markets.* London Review of Books, April 13, 2000.

Madan, D., and H. Unal, "Pricing the Risks of Default." University of Maryland: Working Paper, 1995.

Mark, R., "Risk Management." *International Derivative Review* (March 1991a), pp. 12-14.

Mark, R., "Units of Management." *Risk* 4(6) (June 1991b), pp. 3-7.

Mark, R., "Risk According to Garp." *Wall Street Computer Review* (December 1991c).

Mark, R., "Integrated Credit Risk Measurement." *Risk* 8 (1995).

Mark, R., "Risk Oversight for the Senior Manager: Controlling Risk in Dealers." In *Derivatives Handbook.* London: Wiley Financial Engineering Series, 1997.

Mark, R., "Integrated Credit Risk Management." In *Derivative Credit Risk,* second edition. London: Risk Books, 1999.

Markowitz, H. M., "Portfolio Selection." *Journal of Finance* 7 (1952), pp. 77-91.

Markowitz, H. M., *Portfolio Selection: Efficient Diversification of Investments.* New York: John Wiley and Sons, 1959.

Marshall C., and M. Siegel, "Value at Risk: Implementing a Risk Measurement Standard." *Journal of Derivatives* 4(3) (1997), pp. 91-111.

Marshall, J. F., and K. R. Kapner, *Understanding Swaps.* New York: John Wiley and Sons, 1993.

Martin, D., "Early Warning of Bank Failure: A Logit Regression Approach." *Journal of Banking and Finance* 1 (1977), pp. 249-276.

Marvin, S., "Capital Allocation: A Study of Current and Evolving Practices in Selected Banks." Office of the Comptroller of the Currency, 1995.

Matten, C., *Managing Bank Capital.* New York: John Wiley and Sons, 1996.

May, D. O., "Do Managerial Motives Influence Firm Risk Reduction Strategies?" *Journal of Finance* 50 (1995), pp. 1275-1290.

McDonough, W. J., "Issues for the Basle Accord." Speech delivered before the Conference on Credit Risk Modeling and Regulatory Implications, Bank of England, September 1998, reproduced in the 1998 Annual Report of the Federal Reserve Bank of New York.

McNew, L., "So Near, So VAR." *Risk* 9(10) (1996), pp. 54-56.

Merton, R. C., "An Inter-temporal Capital Asset Pricing Model." *Econometrica* 41(5) (1972), pp. 867-888.

Merton, R. C., "Theory of Rational Option Pricing." *Bell Journal of Economics and Management Science* 4(1) (1973), pp. 141-183.

Merton, R.C., "On the Pricing of Corporate Debt: The Risk Structure of Interest Rates." *Journal of Finance* 28 (1974), pp. 449-470.

Merton, R. C., "An Analytic Derivation of the Cost of Deposit Insurance and Loan Guarantees." *Journal of Banking and Finance* 1 (1977a), pp. 9-13.

Merton, R. C., "On the Pricing of Contingent Claims and the Modigliani-Miller Theorem." *Journal of Financial Economics* 5 (1977b), pp. 241-249.

Merton, R. C., and A. Perold, "Theory of Risk Capital for Financial Firms." *Journal of Applied Corporate Finance* 6(3), (1993), pp.16-32.

Meulbroek, L. "Total Strategies for Company-Wide Risk Control." *Financial Times,* Mastering Risk Series, May 9, 2000.

Mian, S., "Evidence on Corporate Hedging Policy." *Journal of Financial and Quantitative Analysis* 31 (1996), pp. 419-439.

Miller, M. H., "Debt and Taxes." *Journal of Finance* 32 (1977), pp. 261-275.

Miller, M. H., *Financial Innovation and Market Volatility,* Cambridge, MA: Blackwell, 1991.

Modigliani, F., and M. H. Miller, "The Cost of Capital, Corporation Finance, and the Theory of Investment." *American Economic Review* 48 (1958), pp. 261-297.

Moody's Investors Service, *Corporate Bond Defaults and Default Rates:* 1970-1994. New York: Moody's Investors Service, 1995a.

Moody's Investors Service, *Moody's Credit Ratings and Research.* New York: Moody's Investors Service, 1995b.

Moody's Investors Service, *Ratings in Regulation: A Petition to the Gorillas.* New York: Moody's Investors Service, 1995c.

Moody's Investors Service, *Global Credit Analysis.* London: IFR Publications, 1995d.

Moody's Investors Service, *Corporation Default Rates,* 1970-1995. New York: Moody's Investors Service, 1996.

Moody's Investors Service, *Corporate Bond Defaults and Default Ratios,* 1920-1996. New York: Moody's Investors Service, 1997.

Mussman, M., "In Praise of RAROC." *Balance Sheet* (Winter 1995/96).

Nance, D. R., C. W. Smith, and C. W. Smithson, "On the Determinants of Corporate Hedging." *Journal of Finance* 48(1) (1993), pp. 267-284.

Niederhoffer, V., *The Education of a Speculator.* New York: John Wiley and Sons, 1997.

Nielsen, L.T., J. Saa-Requejo, and P. Santa Clara, "Default Risk and Interest Rate Risk: The Term Structure of Default Spreads." INSEAD: Working Paper, 1993.

Nielsen, S. S., and E. I. Ronn, "The Valuation of Default Risk in Corporate Bonds and Interest Rate Swaps." *Advances in Futures and Options Research* 9 (1997), pp. 175-196.

Nusbaum, D., "Moody's Blue." *Risk* 9(10) (1996), pp. 57-59.

Parsley, M., "Risk Management's Final Frontier." *Euromoney* (December 1996).

Paul-Choudhury, S., "DPCs in the Dock," *Risk* 9(7) (1996), pp. 28-29.

Pedrosa M., and R. Roll, 1998, "Systematic Risk in Corporate Bond Credit Spreads." *Journal of Fixed Income* 8(3) (December 1998), pp. 7-26.

Perold, André F. (1999), *Long-Term Capital Management, L.P.,* case study. Harvard Business School, N9-200-007.

Phelan, M. J., "Probability and Statistics Applied to the Practice of Financial Risk Management: The Case of J.P. Morgan RiskMetrics." The Wharton Financial Institutions Center: Working Paper 95-19, 1995.

Pitts, C. G. C., and M. J. P. Selby, "The Pricing of Corporate Debt: A Further Note." *Journal of Finance* 38 (1983), pp. 1311-1313.

Platt, H. D., and M. B. Platt, "A Note on the Use of Industry-Relative Ratios in Bankruptcy Prediction." *Journal of Banking and Finance* 15(6) (1991), pp. 1183-1194.

President's Working Group on Financial Markets, "Hedge Funds, Leverage, and the Lessons of Long -Term Capital Management." Washington, D.C.: April 1999.

Press, W., S. Teukolski, W. Vetterling, and B. Flannery, *Numerical Recipes in C,* second edition. Cambridge University Press, 1992.

Pritsker, M., "Evaluating Value-at-Risk Methodologies: Accuracy versus Computational Time." *Journal of Financial Services Research* 12(2-3) (1997), pp. 201-242.

Rafle, J., "Reasons to Be Hedging - 1, 2, 3." *Risk,* 9(7) (1996), pp. 20-21.

Ramberg, J. S., E. J. Dudewicz, P. Tadikamalla, and E. F. Mytkytka, "A Probability Distribution and Its Uses in Fitting Data." *Technometrics* 21 (1979), pp. 201-214.

Rawnsley, J., *Going for Broke, Nick Leeson and the Collapse of Barings Bank.* London: HarperCollins, 1995.

Ray C., *The Bond Market: Trading and Risk Management.* Homewood, IL: Business One Irwin, 1993.

Reed, N., "Explosive Consolidation." *Risk* 7(4) (1994), pp. 26-32.

Ritchken, P., and R. Trevor, "Pricing Options under Generalized GARCH and Stochastic Volatility Processes." Case Western Reserve University: mimeo, 1997.

Rodriguez, R.M., "Corporate Exchange Risk Management: Theme and Aberrations." *Journal of Finance* 36(2) (May 1981), pp. 427-438.

Rosenberg, B., "Extra Market Components of Covariances in Security Returns." *Journal of Financial and Quantitative Analysis* 9(2) (1974), pp. 263-74.

Rubinstein, M., "Implied Binomial Trees." *Journal of Finance* 69 (1994), pp. 771-818.

Rubinstein, M., and J. C. Cox, *Options Markets.* Englewood Cliffs, NJ: Prentice Hall, 1985.

Rudd, A., and H.K. Clasing Jr., *Modern Portfolio Theory: the Principles of Investment Management.* Orinda, CA: Andrew Rudd, 1988.

Saa-Requejo, J., and P. Santa-Clara, "Bond Pricing with Default Risk." UCLA: Working Paper, 1997.

Santomero, A. M., "Financial Risk Management: The Why and Hows." *Financial Markets, Institutions and Instruments* 4(5) (1995), pp. 1-14.

Sarig, O., and A. Warga, "Some Empirical Estimates of the Risk Structure of Interest Rates." *Journal of Finance* 44(5) (1989), pp. 1351-1360.

Schaefer, S., "Immunisation and Duration: A Review of Theory, Performance and Applications." In *The Revolution in Corporate Finance*, eds. J.M. Stern and D.H. Chew, Jr. Oxford, UK: Blackwell, 1986.

Schiller, R.J., *Market Volatility.* Cambridge, MA: MIT Press, 1990.

Schmerken, I., "Middle Office Closes Gap in Trading Support." *Wall Street & Technology*, 9(12) (1992), pp.18-27.

Schwartz, R. J., and C. W. Smith Jr., *The Handbook of Currency and Interest Rate Risk Management.* Englewood Cliffs, NJ: New York Institute of Finance, 1990.

Schwartz, R. J. and C. W. Smith Jr., *Advanced Strategies in Financial Risk Management.* Englewood Cliffs, NJ: New York Institute of Finance, 1993.

Scott, D., *Multivariate Density Estimation: Theory, Practice and Visualization.* New York: John Wiley and Sons, 1992.

Securities and Exchange Commission, *Disclosure of Accounting Policies for Derivative Financial Instruments and Derivative Commodity Instruments and Disclosure of Quantitative and Qualitative Information About Market Risk Inherent in Derivative Financial Instruments, Other Financial Instruments, and Derivative Commodity Instruments.* Washington DC: Securities and Exchange Commission, Release No. 48, 1997.

Sharpe, W. F., "Capital Asset Prices: A Theory of Market Equilibrium under Conditions of Risk." *Journal of Finance* 19 (1964), pp. 425-442.

Sharpe, W., and G. J. Alexander, *Investments.* Englewood Cliffs, NJ: Prentice-Hall, 1990.

Sheather, S. J. and J.S. Marron, "Kernel Quantile Estimators." *Journal of the American Statistical Association* 85(4) (1990), pp. 410-416.

Shimko, D., "VAR for Corporates." *Risk* 9(6) (1996), pp. 28-29.

Shimko, D., "Accentuate the Positive." *Risk* (VAR for End-Users Supplement), March 1997, pp. 10-15.

Shimko, D., N. Tejima, and D. van Deventer, "The Pricing of Risky Debt when Interest Rates are Stochastic." *Journal of Fixed Income* 3 (1993), pp. 58-65.

Shirreff, D., "Let's Rip Apart Those Triple-A Subs." *Euromoney* (June 1996), pp. 120-126.

Shirreff, D., "Company-at-Risk." *Euromoney* (June 1997), pp. 64-67.

Silverman, B. W., *Density Estimation for Statistics and Data Analysis.* London: Chapman and Hall, 1986.

Smith, C. W., C. Smithson, and D. Wilford, *Strategic Risk Management.* New York: Harper and Row (Institutional Investor Series in Finance), 1990.

Smith, C.W., and C.W. Smithson, *The Handbook of Financial Engineering.* New York: Harper and Row, 1990.

Smith, C. W., and R. Stulz, "The Determinants of Firms' Hedging Policies." *Journal of Financial and Quantitative Analysis* 18 (1985), pp. 391-405.

Smithson, C. W., "A Financial Risk-Management Framework for Non-Financial Corporations." *Financial Derivatives and Risk Management* 4 (1995), pp. 3-11.

Smithson, C. W., "Credit Derivatives (2)." *Risk* 9(6) (1996), pp. 47-48.

Smithson, C. W., "Firm-Wide Risk." *Risk* 10 (3) (1997), pp. 25-26.

Smithson, C. W., C. W. Smith, and D. S. Wilford, *Managing Financial Risk: A Guide to Derivative Products, Financial Engineering, and Value Maximization.* Chicago: Irwin, 1995.

Spahr, R.W., M.A. Sunderman, and C. Amalu, "Corporate Bond Insurance: Feasibility and Insurer Risk Assessment." *Journal of Risk and Insurance* 58(3) (1991), pp. 418-437.

Standard & Poor's, *Ratings Performance 1996: Stability and Transition.* New York: Standard & Poor's, 1997.

Steinherr, A., Derivatives: *The Wild Beast of Finance.* New York: John Wiley and Sons, 1998.

Stoll, H., "The Relationship Between Put and Call Option Prices." *Journal of Finance* 24(5) (1969), pp. 801-824.

Stulz, R. M., "Optimal Hedging Policies." *Journal of Financial and Quantitative Analysis* 19(2) (1984), pp. 127-140.

Stulz, R. M., "Rethinking Risk Management." *Journal of Applied Corporate Finance* 9(2) (1996), pp. 8-24.

Stulz, R. M., "Why Risk Management Is Not Rocket Science." *Financial Times,* Mastering Risk Series, June 27, 2000.

Tuckman, B., *Fixed Income Securities: Tools for Today's Markets.* New York: John Wiley and Sons, 1995.

Van Horne, J. C., *Financial Market Rates & Flows,* fourth edition. Englewood Cliffs, NJ: Prentice-Hall, 1994.

Vasicek, O., "An Equilibrium Characterization of the Term Structure." *Journal of Financial Economics 5* (1977), pp. 177-88.

Vasicek, O., "Credit Valuation." *Net Exposure* 1(1) (1997).

Wakeman, L., "Credit Enhancement." In *The Handbook of Risk Management and Analysis*, ed. C. Alexander. New York: John Wiley and Sons, 1996.

Walwyn, H., and W. Byres, "Price Check." *Risk* 10(11) (1997), pp. 18-24.

Warner, J., "Bankruptcy Costs: Some Evidence." *Journal of Finance* 52 (May 1997).

Watt, R.C., "A Factor-Analytic Approach to Bank Conditions." *Journal of Banking and Finance* 9(2) (1985), pp. 253-266.

Weiss, L., "Bankruptcy Resolution: Direct Costs and Violation of Priority Claims." *Journal of Finance and Economics* 27(2) (1990), pp. 285-314.

Weston, J.F., and T.E. Copeland, *Managerial Finance*. Orlando, FL: The Dryden Press, 1989.

Wilson, D., 1995, "VAR in Operation." *Risk* 8(12) (1995), pp. 24-25.

Wilson, T., "Portfolio Credit Risk I." *Risk* 10 (9) (1997a), pp. 111-117.

Wilson, T., "Portfolio Credit Risk II." *Risk* 10 (10) (1997b), pp. 56-61.

Wong, M., and S. Song, "A Loan in Isolation." *Risk* (June 1997, Asia supplement), pp. 21-23.

Wunnicke, D., D. Wilson, and B. Wunnicke, *Corporate Financial Risk Management: Practical Techniques of Financial Engineering*. New York: John Wiley and Sons, 1992.

Zachman, J.A., and J.F. Sowa, "Extending and Formalizing the Framework for Information Systems Architecture." *IBM Systems Journal* 31(3) (1992), pp. 590-616.

Zaik, E.T., J. Walter, G. Kelling, and C. James, "RAROC at Bank of America: From Theory to Practice." *Journal of Applied Corporate Finance* 9(2) (1996), pp. 83-92.

INDEX

MICHEL CROUHY, Ph.D., is Senior Vice President, Global Analytics, Risk Management Division at Canadian Imperial Bank of Commerce (CIBC), where he is in charge of market and credit risk analytics. He has published extensively in academic journals, is currently associate editor of both *Journal of Derivatives* and *Journal of Banking and Finance,* and is on the editorial board of *Journal of Risk.*

DAN GALAI, Ph.D., is the Abe Gray Professor of Finance and Business Administration at the Hebrew University and a principal of Sigma P.C.M. Dr. Galai has consulted for the Chicago Board Options Exchange and the American Stock Exchange and published numerous articles in leading journals. He was the winner of the First Annual Pomeranze Prize for excellence in options research presented by the CBOE.

ROBERT MARK, Ph.D., is Senior Executive Vice President and Chief Risk Officer at CIBC reporting to the Chairman and CEO of the bank. Dr. Mark is a member of the Senior Executive Team (SET) of CIBC. In 1998 he was named Financial Risk Manager of the Year by the Global Association of Risk Professionals (GARP).